ANIMAL DISCRIMINATION LEARNING

Edited by

R. M. GILBERT
Alcoholism and Drug Addiction Research Foundation, Toronto, Canada

N. S. SUTHERLAND
University of Sussex, Sussex, England

1969

Academic Press
London and New York

ACADEMIC PRESS INC. (LONDON) LTD.
Berkeley Square House
Berkeley Square
London, W1X 6BA

U.S. Edition published by
ACADEMIC PRESS INC.
111 Fifth Avenue
New York, New York 10003

Library of Congress Catalog Card Number: 69–16497

258984

PRINTED IN GREAT BRITAIN BY
THE WHITEFRIARS PRESS LTD., LONDON & TONBRIDGE

"The meaning doesn't matter if it's only idle chatter of a transcendental kind"—*Patience*

Contributors

R. A. BOAKES University of Sussex, Brighton, Sussex, England

M. E. BITTERMAN Bryn Mawr College, Bryn Mawr, Pennsylvania, U.S.A.

T. M. BLOOMFIELD University of Sussex, Brighton, Sussex, England

P. V. DILLOW University of Tennessee, Knoxville, Tennessee, U.S.A.

R. M. GILBERT Alcoholism and Drug Addiction Research Foundation, Toronto, Ontario, Canada

J. A. GRAY Institute of Experimental Psychology, Oxford, England

P. HARZEM University College of North Wales, Bangor, North Wales

H. S. HOFFMAN The Pennsylvania State University, University Park, Pennsylvania, U.S.A.

W. K. HONIG Dalhousie University, Halifax, Nova Scotia, Canada

H. M. B. HURWITZ University of Tennessee, Knoxville, Tennessee, U.S.A.

J. D. KEEHN Alcoholism and Drug Addiction Research Foundation, Toronto, Ontario, Canada

N. J. MACKINTOSH Dalhousie University, Halifax, Nova Scotia, Canada

B. McGONIGLE The Pennsylvania State University, University Park, Pennsylvania, U.S.A.

†S. SIEGEL University of Missouri, Columbia, U.S.A.

P. T. SMITH Institute of Experimental Psychology, Oxford, England

L. STEELE RUSSELL Medical Research Council, Unit for Research on Neural Mechanisms of Behaviour, University College, London, England

N. S. SUTHERLAND University of Sussex, Brighton, Sussex, England

D. R. THOMAS University of Colorado, Boulder, Colorado, U.S.A.

A. R. WAGNER Yale University, New Haven, Connecticut, U.S.A.

J. M. WARREN The Pennsylvania State University, University Park, Pennsylvania, U.S.A.

† Present Address: McMaster University, Hamilton, Ontario, Canada.

Preface

This book grew out of the proceedings of a symposium held by the Experimental Analysis of Behaviour Group at the University of Sussex in April, 1967. Not all the papers delivered at the conference are included in this volume: some speakers thought it was premature to publish, others were already publishing the same material elsewhere. In order to round out the discussion of certain topics, several of the papers in the present volume were specially solicited from authors not present at the conference.

Each paper presents original material whether it be in the form of an integrative review of an area or in the presentation of detailed new results. The first eight chapters deal in various ways—some favourably, some not so favourably—with the role of selective attention. Of these the first four are concerned mainly with generalization and with the way in which learning is influenced by different ways of correlating stimuli with reinforcement. The chapters by Warren and McGonigle, and by Mackintosh and Bitterman review some important but still neglected issues on the comparative psychology of discrimination learning. Bloomfield, and Gray and Smith propose some new ways of thinking about frustration and emotional effects, and Hurwitz reviews work on aversive schedules. The problem of temporal discrimination is treated by Harzem and by Boakes. Sutherland sketches a new theory of pattern recognition, and Russell describes some experiments that throw new light on the old problem of mass action. Finally, two chapters (by Keehn and Gilbert) consider some rather broader issues affecting the methodology and interpretation of work on discrimination learning.

It would today be impossible within a single volume to cover in depth all issues in animal discrimination learning. We have therefore not been able to give adequate coverage to some research topics. In particular, frustration theory receives less attention than its importance merits, and there is little mention of stimulus after-effects on which there is a growing volume of work. We have also had to exclude any detailed discussion of motivational variables and of the application of mathematical models to discrimination learning. We apologise for what is left out, but make no apologies for what is included.

Our thanks must go mainly to the contributors for their cooperation, but also to the various members of the Psychology Department of the

1*

University of Aberdeen and of the Laboratory of Experimental Psychology at the University of Sussex, to the Royal Society and to the Society for the Experimental Analysis of Behaviour: the assistance of these bodies made it possible to hold the original symposium and hence provided the impetus for this book.

OCTOBER 1968   R. M. GILBERT
                                                      N. S. SUTHERLAND

Contents

10   An Arousal-decision Model for Partial Reinforcement and Discrimination Learning

JEFFREY A. GRAY   PHILIP T. SMITH

11   Consciousness, Discrimination and the Stimulus Control of Behaviour

J. D. KEEHN

12   Temporal Discrimination

PETER HARZEM

17   Discrimination Learning?
R. M. GILBERT

The Use of Operant Conditioning Techniques to Investigate Perceptual Processes in Animals

DAVID R. THOMAS

University of Colorado, Boulder, Colorado, U.S.A.

I. Introduction

In this paper two entirely different programs of research will be reported, each using similar subjects, apparatus and basic aspects of procedure, but differing greatly in the nature of the problems under attack. The first line of research is concerned with the investigation of certain complex perceptual phenomena (i.e. illusions) in pigeons. The second line, which might also be called perceptual, is concerned (loosely) with the concept of "attention" and more specifically with the investigation of the effects of various training procedures on the slopes of stimulus generalization gradients. The thread which ties these two lines of research together is the use of a generalization gradient as the basic datum in both cases. In each case, the nature of that gradient, its slope, its symmetry or asymmetry, and the location of its peak, is presumed to reflect certain intervening perceptual processes.

Because of the central significance of the generalization test procedure in all that is to follow, it is appropriate to review that procedure in substantial detail. In 1956 Guttman and Kalish reported a new method for obtaining reliable wavelength generalization gradients from individual organisms (pigeons) in a single test session, and that procedure, with

1

certain modifications, is the one used in all of the studies to be described. The birds are trained in a Skinner box to peck a key illuminated by a monochromatic light (say 555 mμ) for variable interval reinforcement. After perhaps 10 days of training (in half hour daily sessions) a steady stream of key pecking behavior with great resistance to extinction is generated. This makes it possible to test each S for generalization in extinction by presenting, in random sequence, many short (e.g. 30 sec) exposures of a wide range of wavelengths, and measuring the rate of responding emitted in the presence of each. During the test the birds typically yield a gradient of response strength with the highest rate made to the training stimulus and a progressively decreasing rate to stimuli increasingly dissimilar (along the wavelength scale) from this value. This test procedure may readily be seen as an adaptation of the psychophysical method of constant stimuli. Typically in human studies the S is presented a stimulus and asked to remember it; then the stimulus is removed, and subsequently a random sequence of stimuli is presented with the S instructed to respond when he "recognizes" the original. Clearly, Guttman and Kalish substituted variable interval training in the presence of the standard stimulus for simple exposure of that stimulus, and the pigeon substitutes responding at its highest rate for the verbal statement "That one is the original stimulus value". The psychophysical heritage of the Guttman-Kalish test procedure is made particularly explicit in a recent paper by Blough (1967) in which he applies a signal detection analysis to the pigeon's performance in the generalization test setting. In this context, a reduction in response rate is said to reflect increasing "uncertainty" that the test stimulus is the same as the training stimulus.

II. The Experimental Investigation of "Illusions"

A. SENSORY-TONIC INTERACTION

The Guttman-Kalish procedure for studying generalization has been successfully applied to a wide range of stimulus dimensions including brightness, loudness, pitch, click rate and floor inclination. It has been used with rats and monkeys as well as with pigeons. It was work on the visual dimension of "angularity", i.e. the angular orientation of a line on the pecking key, which led directly to the research to be reported here.

A number of studies (e.g. Hearst, *et al.*, 1964; Newman and Baron, 1965) have reported that when pigeons are trained to peck a key on which a vertical line is projected, and are subsequently tested for stimulus generalization in extinction with lines of differing orientation, they yield an approximately symmetrical gradient with a peak of responding

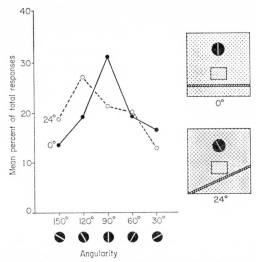

Fɪɢ. 1. Training and testing conditions for the study of sensory-tonic interaction, and some representative results.

at the vertical stimulus value. Such a gradient obtained in one of our studies is presented as part of Fig. 1.

It occurred to us that perception of the visual vertical has been a task in the context of which various perceptual distortions (i.e. illusions) have been investigated with humans, and with appropriate adaptations the Guttman-Kalish procedure might make it possible to do comparable studies with lower animals.

For example, Werner, *et al.* (1951) reported that, when tilted in a sidewise direction and required to set a luminescent rod in a vertical position, human Ss tend to set the rod so that it is tilted a number of degrees opposite to the direction of bodily tilt. The extent of the over-compensation varies positively with the amount of muscular involvement and the degree of body tilt. To account for this phenomenon, Werner and Wapner (1952) and their associates have formulated a sensory-tonic field theory of perception which postulates that any "percept" is determined by an interaction between sensory activity (i.e. that occurring in the sense organs) and tonic activity (i.e. proprioceptive feedback from muscles). We reasoned that a study comparable to that reported by Werner, *et al.* (1951) might be carried out with pigeons by training them in a darkened Skinner box to peck at a vertical line and then testing them for "recognition" (i.e. generalization) under conditions of tonic manipulation. The result should be a change in the location of the peak and/or an asymmetry of the response gradient.

1. *The Lyons and Thomas (1968) Experiment*

The procedure and the results of such an experiment are both represented in Fig. 1. In part of this study, ten pigeons were trained to peck
a key illuminated by a white vertical line in an otherwise dark experimental
chamber. The floor was in a flat (horizontal) position. After ten days of
variable interval training, the Ss were tested for generalization to other
visual angles with the floor tilted 24° laterally in a counter-clockwise
direction. The generalization test series consisted of lines of five different
angular orientations, 30° (30° counter-clockwise rotation from horizontal),
60°, 90° (CS), 120° and 150°, randomly presented for 1 min periods
during extinction.

The pigeons showed enhanced responding to angles inclined in the
same direction as the floor was inclined (counter-clockwise). The mode
of the generalization gradient was displaced to an angle 30° from true
vertical, and since the floor was inclined 24° in the same direction we concluded that quite probably no compensation for floor tilt had taken place.

In the human literature on sensory-tonic interaction, it has been
shown that the influence of body tilt on perception of vertical is eliminated
by making veridical visual cues to verticality available to the S during
the test (cf. Witkin and Asch, 1948). To determine whether the same
rule held true with pigeons and with the present experimental procedure,
one group of pigeons ($n = 10$) was trained with the "house light" on
in the Skinner box so that the visual cues to vertical were available during
training. In testing, the floor was tilted 24° counter-clockwise for this
group and the house light was left on. As a result, this group showed
no perceptual distortion. Their gradient of response strength was indistinguishable from that of a control group ($n = 10$) trained and tested
in the darkened Skinner box with the floor kept in the horizontal (0°)
condition (See Fig. 2).

The data already presented was part of a larger study reported by
Lyons and Thomas (1968). The major purpose of this study was to
demonstrate a systematic relationship between the degree to which
the response gradient is distorted and the extent of floor tilt used in
testing. Four groups of Ss ($n = 10$ in each) were used in this part of the
study. All Ss were first trained in the darkened Skinner box to peck at
the vertical line for variable interval reinforcement. The groups were
then tested for generalization in extinction with the floor tilted 0°, 12°,
24° and 36° counter-clockwise. In generalization testing, the five test
stimuli (30°, 60°, 90° (CS), 120° and 150°) were randomized within a
series and nine different series were presented to each S. As Fig. 3 shows,
the greater the degree of floor tilt, the greater the extent of distortion
obtained in the resulting gradient. The gradient of the 0° group was

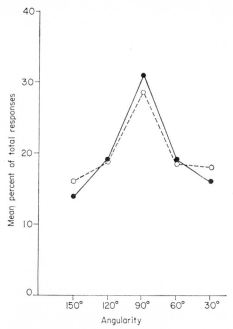

FIG. 2. Mean generalization gradients of the *S*s in the 24° "lights on" and control (0° tilt) conditions. ●—● 0° tilt: ○---○ 24° "light on".

From Lyons J. and Thomas D. R., *J. exp. Psychol.*, 1968. **76,** 120–124.

quite symmetrical, the 12° floor tilt group showed asymmetry with enhanced responding to 120°, the 24° group showed a peak displaced to the 120° value, and the 36° group showed even a stronger peak at this value. The gradient of the 36° group shows a secondary peak at 60°, the mirror image of 120°. Actually, 6 of the 10 *S*s showed this bimodal gradient; four of the 10 *S*s in the 24° group did the same. This mirror image reversal phenomenon has been reported in a paper by Thomas, *et al.* (1966) and cannot be discussed in detail here. Why it occurs in some *S*s but not in all is still unknown at this time.

The major result of the preceding study seems clear, i.e. the greater the degree of floor tilt, the greater the degree of distortion of the perception of the vertical. The *S*s respond to a line tilted in the same way that the floor is tilted as if it were the original (vertical) CS.

2. *Relationship to the Human Literature*

At this point it should be made clear that the finding that pigeons perceive as vertical a line tilted the same way that the floor is tilted appears

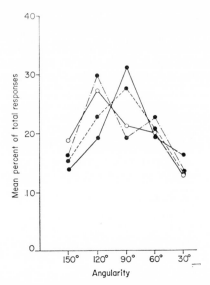

FIG. 3. Mean generalization gradients obtained under four different floor tilt conditions.
●—● 0° Tilt: ●---● 12° Tilt: ○—○ 24° Tilt: ●—·● 36° Tilt.

opposite to the results reported for humans. It should be remembered,
however, that in the human studies the *S*'s body was tilted so that he
viewed the luminescent rod from an angle. With pigeons, when the
floor is tilted, the bird maintains an upright stance, and thus the effect
is probably attributable to the muscular involvement required to maintain
that stance. In order to make a more legitimate inter-species comparison,
LaMonica and Thomas (1966) performed a study in which humans
were tested for perception of the vertical while standing on a sidewise
inclined plane. In part of their study, they tested twenty male college
students standing on a 24° inclined plane for their ability to adjust an
illuminated bar to a vertical position. Many trials were given with the
plane inclined in each direction. The human *S*s reliably perceived as
vertical an inclination of the bar in the direction toward which the plane
was tilted. Though the magnitude of error was far less than in the pigeon
studies, the direction of error was the same.

3. *Further Demonstrations of Sensory-Tonic Interaction*

The basic phenomenon of sensory-tonic interaction in pigeons has
been further explored in two studies which will now be described. The
first of these was the simpler of the two. In the work previously described,
we trained *S*s with the floor flat and then tested with the floor tilted.

What would have happened if we had reversed the procedure, and trained with the floor tilted and tested with the floor flat? If our interpretation of the earlier work has merit, a clear prediction can be made. When the floor was tilted 24° counter-clockwise in the test, the Ss responded maximally to a value tilted approximately the same amount also counter-clockwise. Thus, the true (gravitational) vertical is displaced by *that* amount from the value at which maximal responding occurs, in the direction opposite that of the floor tilt. Therefore, if Ss were trained to peck at a true vertical line with the floor tilted laterally and then were tested for generalization (recognition) with the floor now flat, they should pick out ("recognize") a value tilted opposite to the direction toward which the floor was tilted in training. Such an experiment was performed by Thomas, *et al.* (1966) and the results were as predicted, as indicated in Fig. 4.

The second study referred to above is much more complex and perhaps more intriguing. It was based upon the peak-shift phenomenon—the finding by Hanson (1959), Honig, *et al.* (1959), Thomas (1962), etc. that, following successive discrimination training with one wavelength as $S+$ (say 550 mμ) and another wavelength as $S-$ (say 570 mμ), the peak (mode) of the resulting generalization gradient falls on a value displaced from $S+$ so as to be farther removed from $S-$ (e.g. at 540 mμ). If the peak shift were also obtainable with the angularity dimension, then the following experiment would be feasible. Discrimination training between two "different" visual angles might be accomplished by manipulating the floor tilt during $S+$ and $S-$ conditions while the actual

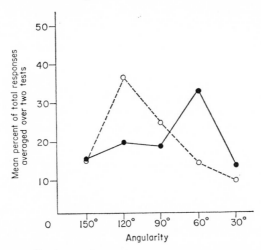

FIG. 4. Mean generalization gradients of groups of Ss trained with the floor tilted and tested with the floor flat. ●—● trained 24° left: ○---○ trained 24° right.
From Thomas, Lyons and Freeman (1966).

angle on the key remained unchanged. Evidence that the floor tilt manipulation was equivalent to an actual manipulation of the visual angle
itself would come from a generalization gradient with a peak of responding
displaced from the $S+$ value along the dimension of visual angle. Such
a study has recently been performed in our laboratory (c.f. Thomas and
Lyons, 1968).

Our first task was to demonstrate a post-discrimination peak shift
along the angularity dimension. An angle of 49° was chosen as $S+$
and 33° was chosen as $S-$; these values were presented for 1 min periods,
randomly alternated. Responding to $S+$ was reinforced on a 1 min
variable interval schedule; responding to $S-$ was extinguished. The
discrimination was a difficult one, requiring well over a hundred daily
sessions for mastery. Several birds seemed incapable of learning it
altogether and were discarded. Eventually 5 Ss which achieved a criterion
ratio of ten responses to one in favor of $S+$ were tested for generalization
and all showed the predicted peak shift.

Next, a group of Ss was trained in the following manner. The 49°
angle was again used and the floor was flat (horizontal) during $S+$ periods.
During $S-$ periods the floor was tilted 16° counter-clockwise; the angle
on the key, however, remained the same. On the basis of the earlier
work, it was presumed that this manipulation of the floor in the $S-$
condition would make the 49° line on the key equivalent to one of 33°.

After achieving the same ten to one $S+/S-$ criterion, four Ss were
tested for generalization along the angularity dimension with the floor in the
flat (positive) condition and all showed the predicted peak shift. In fact,
as Fig. 5 reveals, the mean gradient of these Ss was quite comparable

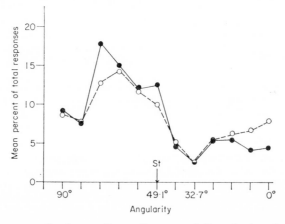

FIG. 5. Mean generalization gradients of groups of Ss trained under the ($\bullet$—$\bullet$)
key $S-$ and ($\circ$---$\circ$) floor $S-$ conditions.

— to that of the *S*s for whom the visual angle on the key had been directly manipulated! Clearly visual cues, rather than postural ones, dominated these *S*s' behavior. This study is in striking agreement with prediction and thus supports the conclusions based on all of the earlier findings.

Certainly there can be no doubt that postural manipulation via tilting the floor on which the pigeon *S* stands alters its perception of vertical in a highly predictable manner. One direction of future research is toward more exact specification of the magnitude of the obtained distortion. More precise methods are already available. The pigeon may be trained to respond more selectively to a given angle (say, vertical) by discrimination training involving *S*— values on both sides of *S*+ . To facilitate the mastery of such a discrimination, the *S*— values may initially differ greatly from *S*+, perhaps along more than one dimension, with these differences gradually reduced as training progresses. Such training would make an animal a skilled psychophysical observer which would respond only to vertical (with a narrow margin of error) or to a value which is equivalent to vertical as a consequence of some experimental manipulation. Suppose that once trained in this manner the bird were placed in the box with the floor tilted a given amount, say 15°. Then the angle of the line on the key could be progressively manipulated, in a method of limits procedure, which would then pinpoint the exact extent of the distortion produced by the 15° floor tilt. The same bird could be tested again with different floor tilts, thus providing a complete and detailed function relating floor tilt to visual distortion. With this degree of specification of the magnitude of the sensory-tonic interaction, it becomes feasible to ask such questions as "Does the animal adapt to the floor tilt as a function of continued exposure?" The procedures heretofore employed would not be sufficiently sensitive to detect an adaptation of a few degrees should one occur in this situation.

B. The Investigation of "Visual Field Dependency" in Pigeons

Another direction which this program of research is taking is toward the application of these techniques and concepts to the investigation of other complex perceptual phenomena. One such study has already been completed and may now be described. One of our earlier experiments demonstrated that in the presence of veridical visual cues to verticality, the tilting of the floor of the experimental chamber had no effect on the birds' performance. If the pigeon relies on such visual cues to the exclusion of postural ones, we wondered what would happen to the bird's perception of vertical if it were supplied with erroneous visual information. In effect, we were asking whether the pigeon is "visually field dependent". To find out, we performed an experiment, the logic and procedure of which are clearly an outgrowth of our earlier work on sensory-tonic interaction. This study has recently been reported by Thomas and Lyons (1968).

Thirty-eight adult homing pigeons were conditioned to peck a key illuminated by a vertical (90°) line and then were given ten daily half-hour sessions of variable interval training. During all training and subsequent generalization testing the chamber was illuminated by a 10 W house light which made the walls, ceiling, and floor clearly visible. Immediately following the tenth variable interval training session, the birds were removed from the chambers and subsequently replaced for generalization testing in extinction. For the control group ($n = 10$) the apparatus was undisturbed for the test. For the three experimental groups ($n = 9$, $n = 10$, $n = 9$, respectively), the entire apparatus was propped up on a specially constructed ramp so that it leaned sidewise 8°, 16°, or 24°, respectively, in a clockwise direction. In each case the floor of the experimental chamber on which the S stood was propped up an equal number of degrees in the opposite direction so that it remained horizontal.

In generalization testing three different angular orientations of the line were employed; these three stimuli were randomized in a series and nine different random series were presented. Each stimulus exposure was for 60 sec with no intervening time-out or no-stimulus periods. No food reinforcement was presented during the test.

On the basis of earlier work, it was presumed that the birds would respond in a totally field dependent manner, and a test was employed which is sensitive to deviations from this expectation. For each group the three test stimuli held the same relationship to the visual field (excepting the floor); the values employed were: (1) the visual vertical, i.e. parallel to the walls and the sides of the feeder opening; (2) 30° clockwise rotation from visual vertical; and (3) 30° counter-clockwise rotation from visual vertical. Note that for the control group the actual (gravitational values were thus: (1) 90°, (2) 60°, and (3) 120°. For the 8° tilt group, each of these values was actually 8° less; for the 16° tilt group, 16° less, etc. The training and test conditions are schematically represented in Fig. 6.

In generalization testing the control group would be expected to respond most to 90°, less but equally to 60° and 120°, producing a symmetrical gradient. If the Ss were totally visually field dependent, symmetrical gradients should be obtained from each of the experimental groups, since the relationship of the three test stimuli to the visual field was the same for each (c.f. Fig. 6 c,d,e, and f). On the other hand, if the birds were not visually field dependent, the gradients of the experimental groups should be asymmetrical with increased responding to the value 30° counter-clockwise from visual vertical as the (clockwise) tilt of the chamber increases. In the four different groups this angle was in reality

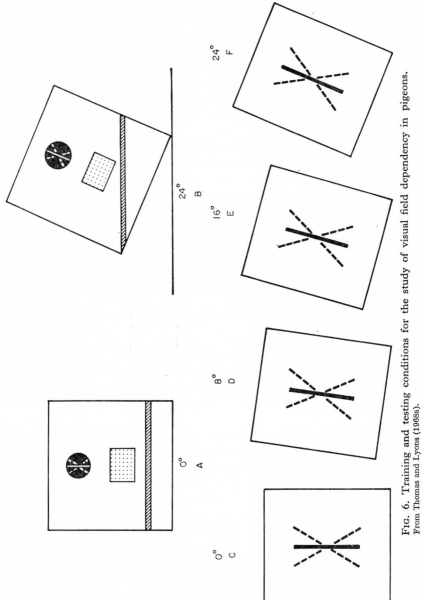

FIG. 6. Training and testing conditions for the study of visual field dependency in pigeons. From Thomas and Lyons (1968a).

120°, 112°, 104°, and 96°. If the birds were responding on the basis of true (gravitational) angle, they should respond more and more to this stimulus as it more closely approximates the 90° training stimulus value.

The test procedure employed here provides still another test of visual field dependency, this one based on a between-groups comparison. Field dependency presumes that the training stimulus is perceived by the S as visual vertical, rather than true or gravitational vertical. If so, the number of responses emitted to the visual vertical stimulus should be the same for all groups despite the fact that the true angle changes systematically from group to group.

The primary results of this experiment are presented in Fig. 7. For each S the percent of total responses given to each of the three test stimuli was computed and the group means of these percent values are plotted in the figures. It is evident that there is no trend toward increasing asymmetry as the degree of tilt of the apparatus is increased. In fact, the only gradient which tends (non-significantly) toward asymmetry is asymmetrical in a direction opposite that required to reject the hypothesis of visual field dependency.

The gradient of the 24° group is (significantly) flatter than that of the others. This difference in steepness was not predicted, and its meaning

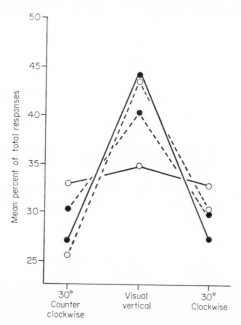

Fig. 7. Mean generalization gradients obtained under four different box tilt conditions. ●—● 0°: ●---● 8°: ○---○ 16°: ○—○ 24°.

is not immediately obvious. It may simply reflect a breakdown in stimulus control, i.e. a "confusion" resulting from the extreme distortion of the pigeon's visual world. Witkin and Asch (1948) also reported greater variablility of judgment under conditions of extreme visual field distortion.

Additional evidence for visual field dependency is provided by a comparison of the number of responses made to the visual vertical stimulus by the birds in the four different groups. Though the actual gravitational angles were 90°, 82°, 74°, and 66°, there was no gradient of response strength; the corresponding median numbers of responses were 228, 211, 226, and 233. Thus, as far as response strength is concerned, the visual vertical stimulus is functionally equivalent in all four groups.

Clearly visual contextual cues dramatically influenced the generalization gradients of the Ss in this experiment, despite the fact that kinesthetic (postural) cues to verticality were readily available. Having been trained to respond to a line which was both gravitationally and visually vertical, the Ss, when tested with distorted visual cues, continued to respond maximally to the "visual vertical" stimulus, seemingly ignoring its gravitational orientation. There is of course an alternative interpretation to "visual field dependency" which would account for these findings. Perhaps the Ss conceptualized of the CS as a line parallel to the walls of the chamber and the sides of the feeder opening, i.e. as "visual vertical". If so, responding maximally to "visual vertical" in testing would be expected and must therefore be considered veridical rather than reflective of an illusion. A convincing basis for the rejection of the "relational learning" interpretation of the present findings in favor of field dependency would require that Ss be trained in a situation which does not allow "relational learning", i.e. in darkness with only the vertical line CS available. In subsequent generalization testing with distorted visual cues introduced, if the Ss then responded maximally to "visual vertical", genuine field dependency would seem to be uniquely indicated.

To perform this test, ten additional pigeons were trained as in the original experiment except that the chamber was dark. During reinforcement presentations the key light was turned off so that even on those rare occasions when the birds did not immediately enter the food hopper the reflected light from the hopper bulb could not provide contextual cues for the CS line on the key. Testing was carried out under the 16° chamber-tilt condition, and the resulting mean gradient was almost perfectly symmetrical. The Ss gave 36·6% of their total responses to the "visual vertical" (actually 74°), and 31·2 and 31·9% to values rotated 30° clockwise and counter-clockwise, respectively. Again, as was true for the four original groups of Ss, the symmetrical group average gradient was representative of individual performance. Thus, without being trained to do so, the pigeons employed the main lines of the visual field to establish gravitational vertical, just as humans do, and the birds made comparable errors in perception as a consequence thereof.

The use of contextual visual cues by these birds raises the important question of whether or not field dependent behavior requires a history of past experience with gravitationally vertical lines, e.g. the walls of the home cage, of the room in which the cage is kept, of the buildings outside, etc. Quite possibly birds reared in a restricted visual environment would show no such tendency. Future research will be designed to determine the nature and amount of visual experience necessary to generate subsequent field dependent behavior.

C. RELATED WORK IN OTHER LABORATORIES

The use of operant conditioning and generalization testing procedures for the investigation of illusions in animals has proved fruitful in a number of laboratories in addition to our own. One example is seen in a study by Mello (1965) who trained pigeons, with one eye covered, to peck at a key illuminated by a 45° line. In a subsequent generalization test with a wide range of angular orientations, if the eye used in training was used in the test the birds responded veritically, i.e. with maximal rate to the 45° stimulus. When tested with the trained eye covered and the untrained eye in use the birds showed peak responding to an angle of 135°, the mirror image of the training stimulus. Mello interpreted this effect as evidence of inter-hemispheric transfer across the two optic tecta. In a study performed in our laboratory we (i.e. Thomas, *et al.* 1966) extended Mello's finding by showing that pigeons binocularly trained to respond to an oblique line showed bimodal generalization gradients, with peaks both at the training stimulus value and at its mirror-image.

The use of generalization testing to study the Müeller-Lyer illusion in pigeons has recently been demonstrated by Malott and his colleagues (Malott and Malott, 1967; Malott, *et al.* 1967a; and Malott, *et al.* 1967b). The basic procedure used in these studies is first to train the birds to respond to a given length of line with flat "arrowheads" (short 90° lines at right angles to the principal line). In subsequent generalization testing different lengths of line are used, with arrowheads pointing inward or outward. If pigeons are subject to the illusion, when the arrowheads point outward, peak responding should occur to a line longer than the CS, whereas when the arrowheads point inward the opposite should be true. The former effect has been repeatedly observed, although for some reason yet to be determined, the latter has not.

The use of operant conditioning and generalization testing procedures for the study of illusions in animals is of very recent origin and seems to hold great promise. Research along these lines currently underway in our laboratories is attempting to demonstrate in pigeons several illusions heretofore unexplored in any infrahuman species. Like the better known stimulus tracking procedure developed by Blough (1955, 1956) the generalization method effectively provides a language through which the perceptual processes of non-verbal organisms can be objectively studied.

III. The Effects of Discrimination Training on Stimulus Generalization

For a number of years now in our laboratory we have been concerned with the effects of different kinds of discrimination training on various properties of the post-discrimination generalization gradient. Switalski, *et al.* (1966) have differentiated three types of discrimination training on the basis of their relationship to the subsequent test of stimulus generalization. The first type, called "intra-dimensional", involves positive and negative stimuli selected from the same dimension, which, in turn, is the dimension along which generalization is tested. In the second type, "inter-dimensional training", one of the training stimuli (either the positive or the negative) is on the generalization test dimension, while the other stimulus is not. In the third type, called "extra-dimensional", neither the positive nor the negative stimulus is on the dimension tested for generalization.

A. INTRA-DIMENSIONAL DISCRIMINATION TRAINING

The initial investigation of the effects on generalization of intra-dimensional discrimination training was carried out by Hanson (1959). This investigator trained pigeons to respond to one wavelength stimulus (for variable-interval reinforcement), randomly alternated with another wavelength stimulus, (to which responding was extinguished). Following the mastery of the discrimination, a Guttman-Kalish (1956) type generalization test revealed gradients different, in several respects, from those typically obtained following single stimulus training. The most striking difference was the displacement of the peak (mode) of response strength from the $S+$ to a value farther removed from $S-$. A steady stream of subsequent experiments appeared designed to investigate the variables which affect this "peak shift". One early study (Honig, *et al.* 1959) found that the peak shift required the alternation of positive and negative stimuli in training; pigeons trained to respond to one wavelength and subsequently given massed extinction with another failed to show the shift in subsequent generalization testing. Thomas (1962) inserted short generalization tests during the formation of the discrimination and found that the peak shifts (and asymmetry in the gradient increases) gradually during the acquisition, starting sometimes before there is any noticeable change in relative rate of responding to $S+$ and $S-$. Honig (1962) found that the peak shift occurs with successive discrimination training but not with simultaneous, and Terrace (1964) found that it occurs only when "errors" (i.e. responses to $S-$) are made during discrimination training but not when the discrimination is learned errorlessly.

It has further been shown by Guttman (1959) that the peak shift occurs when responding to the $S-$ is reinforced but at a lower frequency than is responding to $S+$. This study has been elaborated on by two recent experiments from our laboratory. In one of these (Mariner, 1967) a peak-shift was obtained with an $S-$ reinforced equally often but with lesser magnitude (shorter duration) than the $S+$. In another study (Frieman and Thomas, 1968) a shift was obtained on the basis of a differ- ence in delay of reward, by placing two wavelength stimuli at different positions in a "chained schedule" of reinforcement. Some other very recent work has demonstrated that the peak-shift phenomenon is not restricted to the wavelength stimulus dimension. Riccio, *et al.* (1966) reported a peak-shift along the floor tilt dimension; Bloomfield (1967) found a peak-shift along the angularity dimension, and Thomas and Lyons (1968) not only observed a peak-shift away from a line angle $S-$, but also away from the angle which they inferred that the pigeons saw when the angle of the floor on which they stood was altered. This latter study was described in some detail in an earlier section of this paper. In a study paralleling the earlier work with pigeons, Doll and Thomas (1967) have obtained a peak-shift following wavelength discrimination training in human subjects.

In all of the work just described, the major focus was, in each case, the peak-shift. It is to be noted, however, that another typical effect of intra-dimensional discrimination is the steepening of the post-discrimina- tion generalization gradient, which is reflected in an elevation of response strength to the modal stimulus and a narrowing of the range of stimuli to which responding occurs. Where stimulus control is slight or absent on the basis of single stimulus training, e.g. as in Peterson's (1962) study with ducklings reared monochromatically and the Riccio *et al.* (1966) study with floor tilt, intra-dimensional discrimination training steepens the gradient strikingly, perhaps by calling "attention" to the relevant dimension of the positive stimulus. It is hardly surprising that training within a dimension would have such an effect, and thus with regard to the steepness of generalization gradients it is more interesting to consider the effects of discrimination training in which the positive and negative stimuli are not both on the generalization test dimension.

B. INTER-DIMENSIONAL DISCRIMINATION TRAINING

The best known study demonstrating the effects of interdimensional discrimination training on generalization along the dimension of the positive stimulus is that by Jenkins and Harrison (1960). These investigators trained pigeons to peck a key for food reinforcement in the presence of a 1000 c.p.s. tone and then tested for generalization along the dimension of tonal frequency, obtaining an extremely flat gradient: When they trained the Ss that the presence of the tone was $S+$ (reinforced) and its absence (silence) was $S-$ (extinguished), a steep gradient along the frequency dimension was then obtained. Since the tones were equated in loudness, silence was no closer to one frequency than to another, and thus the $S-$ could be considered orthogonal to the dimension of $S+$. Nevertheless, training was adequate to produce stimulus control by the frequency of the tone.

One question which has concerned researchers in the area of stimulus control is why Jenkins and Harrison's (1960) pigeons needed interdimensional discrimination training to yield steep generalization gradients along the auditory frequency dimension whereas other dimensions (like wavelength) require no such preliminary training. One reason which Terrace (1966a) suggests is that there are additional sources of differential reinforcement with regard to wavelength which may contribute to the development of stimulus control along this dimension. One of these is the necessary discrimination which occurs between the small localized illuminated key and the surrounding dark wall of the experimental chamber. Heinemann and Rudolph (1963) have shown, in a brightness generalization study, that the smaller the area of a stimulus display, the sharper the generalization gradient when the brightness of that display is varied.

Terrace (1966a) also suggests that pigeons reared in the normal manner may have learned to utilize wavelength cues in their feeding, nesting, and other natural behaviors. Peterson (1962) reared ducklings in a monochromatic light of 589mμ (from a sodium vapor lamp), then trained them in a Skinner box to peck a key illuminated by this value, and thereafter obtained completely flat response curves. Control ducklings, reared in white light, gave "normal" decremental generalization gradients.

Unlike the situation in which visual stimuli are employed, the tone in Jenkins and Harrison's (1960) experiment was not localized at the site of the response. On the other hand, the fact that explicit discrimination training with tone as $S+$ and silence as $S-$ resulted in sharp gradients indicates that neither the localization of the training stimulus nor the spatial contiguity between stimulus and response is essential for the establishment of stimulus control. In contrast to what probably occurs with wavelength, however, there is no reason to suspect that pigeons reared normally would have any pre-experimental differential reinforcement history with regard to pure tones. For this reason, Thomas *et al.* (1968) performed a study which replicated that of Jenkins and Harrison (1960) except that two of the three groups were provided a past history of tone experience.

1. *The Thomas* et al. *Experiment*

In this experiment there were three groups of ten pigeons each. One of these groups ("No-tone") was simply maintained at 75% weight for 100 days and had no exposure to the 1000 c.p.s. tone until key-peck training was initiated. For a second group ("Tone-relevant") on each day the 1000 c.p.s. tone was presented in the *S*s' living area for 15 min. During this time, each *S* was presented with a food cup with grit and a premeasured amount of food in it; the cup was removed before the tone was shut off. A third group ("Tone-irrelevant") was visually (but not accoustically) isolated from the second. For this group, feedings were irregularly correlated with the tone. These *S*s were fed one-third of the time in the presence of the tone, one-third of the time 15 min earlier, and one-third of the time 15 min later.

At the end of the 100 day period all *S*s were magazine and key-peck trained and then given 25 daily half-hour sessions of V1-1 min training. During the training, which was the same for the three groups, the 1000

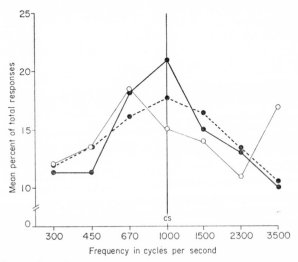

Fig. 8. Mean auditory frequency generalization gradients as a function of pre-experimental experience with tone. ●—● Tone relevant: ●---● Tone irrelevant: ○—○ No tone.

c.p.s. tone was always on in the experimental chambers. Masking noise was supplied to the home cage area, which was removed some distance from the room in which training was done. Thus after the initiation of training the Ss only experienced the 1000 c.p.s. tone in the experimental chambers, where they received their full daily ration of food.

Following 25 days of variable interval training the Ss were given the first of three generalization tests in extinction. The same test values were used as in the Jenkins and Harrison study, and, as in that study, there were three generalization tests separated by one training day between them.

The results of this experiment are presented in Fig. 8 in terms of the group mean percent of total responses to each test stimulus, averaged over the three tests for each S. Both the Tone-relevant and the Tone-irrelevant conditions yielded clear decremental generalization gradients which peaked at the CS value. Both gradients were statistically significant $(p < \cdot 01)$; and analysis of the gradients of the individual Ss in each of these two groups indicated that 8 of the 10 Tone-relevant gradients peaked at the 1000 c.p.s. tone, and 5 of the Tone-irrelevant gradients peaked at this point. In the No-tone group no gradient was obtained, and only one of the ten response curves peaked at the CS value.

In the Jenkins and Harrison (1960) experiment, upon which the Thomas, Mariner and Sherry study was based, *some evidence* was presented for a very shallow gradient of response strength following single stimulus training. That evidence was a ·05 significance level for stimuli, based on the gradients of three Ss, two of which did not peak at the 1000 cps CS value. In view of the tenuous nature of this evidence, reviewers such as Kimble (1961) and Terrace (1966a) have more conservatively concluded that single stimulus training fails to produce reliable control over response rate by tonal frequency. Certainly the results of the No-tone group in this experiment confirm the wisdom of the more cautious evaluation of the Jenkins and Harrison finding.

On the other hand there can be no doubt of the reliability of the gradients in the Tone-relevant and the Tone-irrelevant groups. In the Tone-relevant group, it seems reasonable to conclude that experience with the tone as a reliable feeding signal was adequate to insure that the Ss "noticed" the tone, i.e. associated the tone with reinforced key-pecking in subsequent training. It is quite possible that pairing the tone with food one-third of the time accomplished the same thing, though to a lesser extent, in the Tone-irrelevant group. On the other hand, the mere exposure to periods of tone and no tone, independent of feeding experience, might have sufficed to obtain the same result. It is difficult to evaluate this possibility since if the tone and food were never paired, the tone might gain significance as a cue that food was not forthcoming. The problems of determining how many pairings of tone and food with what consistency were required to assure the subsequent development of stimulus control were beyond the scope of the Thomas *et al.* (1968) study. Furthermore the difference between the Tone-relevant and Tone-irrelevant gradients indicates that the effect of prior exposure to tone is not all-or-none, thus it would be expected that different kinds and amounts of pre-experimental experience with the test dimension would probably result in different degrees of stimulus control subsequently being developed.

The Peterson (1962) study demonstrated that wave length generalization gradients appear in normally reared ducklings but not in those which have been deprived of differential experience with wave length prior to single stimulus training. The Thomas *et al.* study indicates that following a history of differential experience with tone, single stimulus training produces reliable gradients of tonal frequency; without such a history it does not. Terrace (1966a) has concluded that differential reinforcement with regard to the stimulus dimension in question is a necessary condition for the development of stimulus control. This differential reinforcement may be between two or more values on a dimension (e.g. different wave lengths) or between one value on a dimension and another value off of it (e.g. tone versus silence). We would agree with Terrace's position, though admitting that on empirical grounds it would be difficult to distinguish between the requirements of differential reinforcement and merely differential exposure, since the former is so readily inferrable from the latter.

2. Further Investigation of the Effect of Inter-dimensional Training on Generalization Along the Dimension of the Positive Stimulus

In the Jenkins and Harrison (1960) experiment the negative stimulus was silence, which is indeed orthogonal to the dimension of tonal frequency. A disadvantage of silence as $S-$, however, is that it cannot be manipulated along a dimension, so that it is impossible to evaluate the degree to which the negative stimulus (as opposed to simply the absence of the positive) controls behavior following such training. For this reason we have adopted the procedure in our laboratory of using a monochromatic light as $S+$ and a white vertical line on a black surround as $S-$ (or vice versa). The wavelength of the light and the angle of the line can be independently and orthogonally manipulated, and furthermore the two stimuli can be combined, producing a white line (at a variety of angles) on a monochromatic field (of a variety of colors).

3. *The Switalski, et al. Experiment*

Using these stimuli, Switalski, et al. (1966) recently reported a study indicating that the degree of control exercised by the wavelength dimension (reflected in the steepness of a generalization gradient along this dimension) is a function of the consequences of responding to a non-wavelength stimulus (a white vertical line on a black surround) which was programmed to alternate randomly with the reinforced wavelength stimulus. In their study a wavelength generalization gradient was first obtained from each of two groups of Ss following single stimulus training. After this, Group 1 was given additional training in which responding to the line and the color were equally reinforced ("interdimensional non-differential training") and a second generalization test revealed a gradient significantly flattened relative to the single stimulus control condition. For Group 2, following their first generalization test, only responding to the color, was reinforced ("interdimensional discrimination training") and relative to their control condition the wavelength generalization gradient of this group was significantly steepened.

The fact that the consequences of responding to the line influence generalization around an orthogonal dimension (wavelength) suggests a mediational interpretation of these findings. It may be that inter-dimensional discrimination training establishes "attention" or a "set-to-discriminate" whereas non-differential training encourages its opposite. These tendencies, when applied in the generalization test setting result in gradients of greater or lesser slope. Unfortunately, however, a great deal of research summarized by Mackintosh (1965) suggests that the effect of attention is generally quite specific, such that training Ss to discriminate along one stimulus dimension reduces stimulus control (as reflected in generalization slope or discrimination performance) along other dimensions.

The reason for the discrepancy between the Switalski, *et al.* (1966) findings and the results of a number of studies reviewed by Mackintosh (1965) remains obscure. We were sufficiently concerned by this discrepancy, however, to judge it desirable to replicate our findings a number of times.

4. *The Lyons and Thomas Extension of the Switalski et al. Experiment*

We did this most convincingly, I think, in a single experiment reported by Lyons and Thomas (1967). This study attempted to determine whether the effects of interdimensional non-differential and discrimination training on generalization are demonstrable in individual organisms, and also to ascertain whether these effects are recoverable following repeated alternations of these training conditions.

A group of nine pigeons was first trained to respond to a 555 mμ stimulus for variable interval reinforcement and then was tested for wavelength generalization. Next the Ss were given 16 days of discrimination training with one-minute periods of 555 mμ (VI-reinforced) alternated with one-minute periods of the white vertical line (extinguished), and this treatment was followed by a second generalization test. Then the birds were given 12 successive days in which both the 555 mμ and the vertical line stimuli were equally reinforced, followed by another generalization test.

On the day following the third test, the nine S were returned to the discrimination training condition for 16 more days, the last followed immediately by a fourth generalization test like the preceding three. On the next day the conditions were alternated again and the Ss underwent the first of 12 consecutive days of nondifferential training, the last followed by another generalization test, etc. Aside from the original single stimulus condition and the discrimination training condition which followed it,

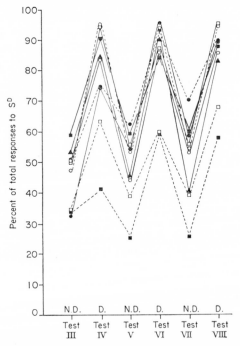

FIG. 9. Generalization slope following differential (discrimination) and non-differential training. ●—● F7: ●---● F2: ○—○ F3: ○---○ F4: ◼—◼ F5: ◼---◼ F6: □—□ F7: □---□ F8: ▲—▲ F9.

From Lyons, J., and Thomas, D. R., *J. exp. Psychol.*, 1967. **75,** 572–574.

each S was exposed to six alternations from discrimination to nondifferential training or vice versa. On each test the measure of gradient steepness used was the percent of total responses given to the 555 mμ ($S+$) value, the higher this percent the steeper the gradient. Since the primary interest was in the reversability of the two types of training, in the figure are presented data, i.e. the percentage of total responses given to $S+$ for each S, on all tests which followed a reversal of conditions, i.e. from the third test on.

As Fig. 9. shows, although individual differences in gradient steepness abound, every S shows a steepened gradient following discrimination training and a flattened gradient following non-differential training, with not a single deviation from this pattern.

As part of doctoral dissertation, Lyons (1968) has provided still another replication of the finding that interdimensional discrimination training steepens the generalization gradient along the dimension of the positive stimulus. Lyons ran three groups of ten pigeons each in this experiment. One group responded to 555 mμ for VI reinforcement but were extinguished for responding to the vertical line. A second group learned the same discrimination, but with a modification of Terrace's (1963) procedure allowing no responses to the line by blacking it out when it appeared that an S was about to peck at it. A third (control) group, was

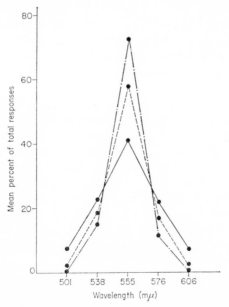

FIG. 10. Mean generalization gradient's following inter-dimensional discrimination training with and without errors. ●—·—● Error: ●----● Errorless: ●—● Control.

yoked to the second, such that everytime a member of Group 2 was reinforced or blacked out (for attempting to respond to the line) its yoked (control) partner was also. The stimulus on the key was always 555 mμ for this control group.

All three of these groups were tested for wavelength generalization, and the results are indicated in Fig. 10. Clearly inter-dimensional discrimination training (with errors) steepens the gradient around $S+$, and it does so in the absence of any prior generalization testing experience. The Ss in the Switalski *et al.* (1966) and Lyons and Thomas (1967) experiments had been tested for generalization prior to the administration of the discrimination training procedure and it was conceivable (though unlikely) that this somehow accounted for the steepening effect. Of additional interest is the fact that errorless inter-dimensional discrimination training also significantly steepens the gradient along the positive dimension, although not as much as does training with errors. Terrace (1966b) had claimed that the errorless stimulus in such training was neutral rather than negative, however Lyons' finding questions Terrace's definition of neutrality.

C. Extra-dimensional Discrimination Training

1. *The Work of Perkins* et al.

Of particular significance for "attentional" interpretations of generalization slope are those studies in which neither the positive nor the negative training stimulus is on the dimension along which generalization is subsequently measured. One such experiment was carried out by Reinhold and Perkins (1955) who reported that rats trained to discriminate between two floor textures showed a steepened generalization gradient along the dimension of the brightness of a background stimulus. A subsequent experiment by Perkins, *et al.* (1959) replicated this finding and extended it.

The steepening effect of extra-dimensional discrimination training seems so obviously to challenge the selective notion of "attention" expressed by Mackintosh (1965) and Sutherland (1964) that we have undertaken a series of investigations attempting to determine the reliability and the generality of this effect. In these studies we have borrowed heavily from work of an old friend, Werner K. Honig of Dalhousie University, and the kinship of the work now to be reported and that described in his chapter of this book will be obvious to all.

2. *Honig's Contributions*

In the work of Perkins and his colleagues the stimulus manipulated in the generalization test was present, but irrelevant, during discrimination training. Honig developed a procedure whereby the phase of discrimination training is separated from the acquisition of a response on the dimension tested for generalization. This is accomplished by first training pigeons on a discrimination along a given dimension, say, color, then training them to respond to black vertical lines on a white surround, and finally testing for generalization along the angularity dimension.

Another important innovation which Honig contributed was a new type of non-differential training condition, called pseudodiscrimination, in which the Ss are exposed to two different (wavelength) stimuli and to randomly alternating periods of VI reinforcement and extinction, but the two are not in phase. In this manner the patterning of reinforcements earned by the pseudodiscrimination birds matches that obtained under the true discrimination condition, however reinforcement is uncorrelated with the stimuli, and this is thus the only difference between the two training conditions.

With the procedures outlined, Honig has found that the angularity generalization gradients of true discrimination (TD) birds are steeper than those of pseudodiscrimination (PD) birds, with a control group without previous exposure to wavelength yielding an intermediate gradient. The use of angularity as the test dimension in Honig's work seems very reasonable since this is a dimension along which generalization gradients tend to be relatively flat and there is therefore much room to observe possible steepening by appropriate training conditions. We have replicated Honig's findings using angularity as the test dimension, but individual variability was so great that a very large number of subjects would have been required to achieve statistical significance. For this reason we reversed Honig's procedure, using angularity as the training dimension and wavelength as the test dimension. As we anticipated the effects we observed were smaller but the consequent reduction in variability was adequate to produce the confidence levels we required.

3. The Freeman Experiment

The following experiment was performed by Frederick Freeman as part of an M.A. thesis at Kent State University. In Stage 1, the TD group ($n = 15$) was trained to discriminate between a white vertical line on a black surround and a line angled 30° counter-clockwise from horizontal. A second (PD) group ($n = 13$) received pseudodiscrimination training with the same stimuli. When each of the TD birds reached a criterion of 10 responses to $S+$ to each response to $S-$ it progressed to the second stage of the experiment along with a PD bird. Originally there were 15 PD Ss, but two failed to respond in generalization testing. In Stage 2, a third group of control birds ($n = 10$) was added, and the treatment for all three groups was the same. It was single stimulus

2*

training to respond to a white vertical line superimposed on a 555 mμ surround for variable interval reinforcement. After five daily one-hour sessions of this training, a generalization test with five different wavelengths was performed in extinction; during the test the vertical line was not present.

On the basis of "Selective Attention Theory", Freeman predicted that TD *S*s which had been trained to discriminate on the basis of line angle in Stage 1 would therefore be less likely to attend to the wavelength of the surround in Stage 2 and would therefore yield a flattened generalization gradient relative to controls. On the other hand PD *S*s, trained that line angle was irrelevant, might be more likely to attend to the wavelength (rather than to the line) and thus yield gradients steeper than the controls.

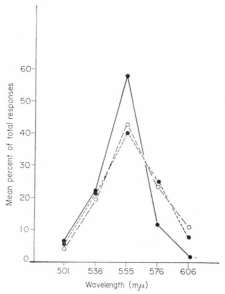

Fig. 11. Mean generalization gradients following extra dimensional true discrimination and pseudodiscrimination training. ●——● Discrimination: ○———○ Pseudodiscrimination: ●----● Control.

As Fig. 11 reveals the results obtained by Freeman were inconsistent with his predictions. The TD *S*s gradient was significantly steeper ($p + \cdot 01$) than those of the other two groups. The gradients of the PD and Control groups were virtually identical. With regard to the (highly significant) difference between TD and PD gradients these results further confirm those originally reported by Honig and indicate that training *S*s to attend to (or more operationally, to discriminate between) two stimuli on Dimension One steepens generalization gradients (presumably reflecting heightened attention to) an irrelevant dimension subsequently presented. It is important to note that this occurs when the dimension to which Ss were trained to attend in Stage 1 is present for them to continue to attend to in Stage 2. These results are clearly in contradiction to the position that attention to one attribute or dimension of a stimulus tends to be negatively correlated with attention to other dimensions.

4. *Cross Modal Transfer of Attention*

It has been suggested (c.f. Sutherland and Andelman, 1967) that attention may transfer positively within a modality but negatively across modalities. To test this hypothesis we have performed two experiments which are somewhat similar in methodology to the extra-dimensional studies reported earlier, except that the two training stages were compressed into one. In the first study, performed by William Klipec, 11 TD and 11 PD birds were trained with two values of white noise (on or off) and the 555 mμ light always on the key. After the 10/1 $S+/S-$ ratio was achieved by a member of the TD group, it was tested for wavelength generalization along with a member of the PD group. One PD bird died during training and another failed to respond during testing thus there were ultimately 9 Ss in this group. During this testing the sound value (on or off) which had been $S+$ continued to be present. The resulting generalization gradients are shown in Fig. 12 and they suggest that the TD condition produced the steeper gradient, just as it did in all of the previous studies which were restricted to the visual modality. Unfortunately, however, in the present case the differences in gradient slope were not adequate to achieve statistical significance.

In a final experiment, performed by Joseph Lyons, the modality of proprioception was employed. Five pigeons were given TD training with the floor in the horizontal ($S+$) position or rotated 10° laterally ($S-$); each of these birds had a yoked control partner which experienced only the horizontal floor condition but received the same pattern of reinforcements. Five other birds were given PD training with the same two floor tilts, and these also had yoked controls. For all Ss the 555 mμ stimulus was always on the key.

When a TD S achieved the 10/1 $S+/S-$ criterion, two pairs of birds were tested for wavelength generalization, the TD bird and its yoked partner, and also a PD bird with the same number of training days and its yoked partner.

The results of this experiment are presented in Fig. 13. As the left panel indicates, TD training produced a steeper gradient than its yoked control, and this time the difference was significant ($p < \cdot025$). Indeed,

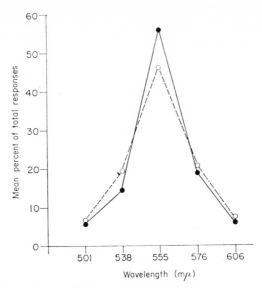

FIG. 12. Mean wavelength generalization gradients following extra-dimensional true discrimination and pseudodiscrimination training involving an auditory stimulus. ●—● Discrimination: ○---○ Pseudodiscrimination.

for each of the five pairs of Ss, the TD gradient was steeper than the control gradient. As the right panel indicates, the gradients of the PD group and its control are quite indistinguishable. It should be remembered that this was also the result obtained in the study by Freeman in which two different visual dimensions were employed.

5. *Summary of Extra-Dimensional Discrimination Training*

On the basis of all of the studies presented it cannot be doubted that extra-dimensional discrimination training steepens gradients of generalization along irrelevant dimensions including those from other modalities than that involved in such training. On the other hand, extra-dimensional pseudodiscrimination training seems to have absolutely no effect. This is in contrast to the flattening effect of inter-dimensional non-differential training demonstrated by Switalski *et al.* (1966) and replicated in our laboratory a number of times. This discrepancy may indicate a difference in the range of situations to which attention and "non-attention" generalize. A fact that these results emphasize is that we know a lot more about the conditions which make a stimulus "relevant" than about those which make a stimulus "irrelevant". There are dozens of studies designed to investigate the former, but only very recently have we even been concerned with the latter. It is quite clear from our most recent efforts that a stimulus

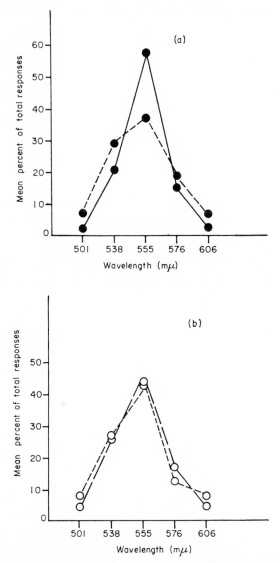

FIG. 13. Mean wavelength generalization gradients following extra-dimensional (a) true discrimination and (b) pseudodiscrimination training, each with an appropriate yoked control. ●—● discrimination: ●——● Control: ○——○ Pseudodiscrimination: ○---○ Control.

which remains constant while others are being varied may be irrelevant as far as the mastery of the discrimination is concerned, and yet may exercise a great deal of control over behavior. In other words, whereas the experimenter defines irrelevance in terms of logic, the pigeon clearly does not!

All of the research reported has indicated that discrimination training (of all types) steepens generalization along the dimension of the positive stimulus. Following Terrace (1966a) we have inferred from the steepened gradient a heightened attention to the dimension in question. Sutherland (1964) and Mackintosh (1965) have stressed the selective nature of attention and have argued that attention to one aspect or dimension of a stimulus tends to be negatively correlated with attention to other dimensions. On the other hand we (c.f. Switalski *et al.*) have thought of attention more generally as a tendency to attribute significance to stimulus differences, which transfers positively to new situations and to new stimulus dimensions. Both narrow and broad views of attention would lead to the expectation that intra-dimensional discrimination training would steepen gradients of generalization. A narrow view of attention has difficulty with the results of inter-dimensional training studies, and can accommodate these only at some cost; i.e. by stretching the theory such that training involving the mere presence of a stimulus as positive can be said to call attention (simultaneously) to several attributes of that stimulus. Such an extension of Selective Attention Theory was made by Sutherland and Andelman (1967) who presented evidence for a positive transfer of attention within a (visual) modality and a negative transfer across modalities. It should be noted that this finding is in direct contradiction to a number of studies Mackintosh (1965) reported as indicating a negative correlation between attention to different visual dimensions. Furthermore, even this modified view which argues that attention transfers positively within modalities, but negatively across modalities, is contradicted by the evidence of cross-modal positive transfer of attention obtained in our laboratories.

There can be no doubt that the bulk of the literature summarized in this paper is inconsistent with the view that attention is selective at any level. On the other hand a great deal of evidence for the selectivity of attention at the human level has recently been summarized by Egeth (1967) and the bulk of the work with rats as summarized by Mackintosh (1965) certainly supports such a view. In the face of this evidence, it seems clear that attention can be either specific or general, and that rather than arguing about which condition is typical, it would be more fruitful to attempt to determine the circumstances under which the two types or levels of attention attain. In this regard a number of needed steps seem obvious. In most of the animal literature which supports a narrow view of attention, attention is inferred from performance by rats on a new learning or transfer task, typically along a visual dimension. The generality of this evidence could be fruitfully assessed by studies with other species, other stimulus modalities, and a generalization test rather than a learning one. Because our studies employ such different subjects and procedures than those reported by Mackintosh (1965) the basis for the obtained discrepancies cannot be pinpointed at this time. We do intend, however, to systematically investigate the generality of the findings we have obtained. Wherever this research may lead us, it is clear that Selective Attention Theory, as currently constituted, cannot account for the findings already in our possession. The theory has received a great deal of "attention", and has stimulated a great deal of research which, we trust, will ultimately lead to a more complete understanding of the role of mediational processes in animal discrimination learning. If so, it will have played a valuable role in the advancement of our knowledge in this important area of inquiry.

Acknowledgements

The research reported and the preparation of the manuscript were supported by Research Grants N.I.H.—HD–00903, N.I.H.—HD–03486, N.S.F.—GE–5159, and Training Grant MH–10427.

References

Bloomfield, T. M. (1967). A peak shift on a line-tilt continuum. *J. exp. Anal. Behav.* **10**, 361–366.

Blough, D. S. (1955). Method for tracing dark adaptation in the pigeon. *Science, N.Y.* **121**, 703–704.

Blough, D. S. (1956). Tracing dark adaptation in the pigeon. *J. comp. physiol. Psychol.* **49**, 425–430.

Blough, D. S. (1967). Stimulus generalization as signal detection. *Science, N.Y.* **158**, 940–941.

Doll, T. J. and Thomas, D. R. (1967). Effects of discrimination training on stimulus generalization for human subjects. *J. exp. Psychol.* **75**, 508–512.

Egeth, H. (1967). Selective attention. *Psychol. Bull.* **67**, 41–57.

Freeman, F. (1967). The effect of extra-dimensional discrimination training on the slope of the generalization gradient. Masters Thesis, Kent State University.

Frieman, J. and Thomas, D. R. (1968). A peak shift within a chained reinforcement schedule. *J. exp. Anal. Behav.* (in press).

Guttman, N. (1959). Generalization gradients around stimuli associated with different reinforcement schedules. *J. esp. Psychol.* **58**, 335–340.

Guttman, N. and Kalish, H. I. (1956). Discriminability and stimulus generalization. *J. exp. Psychol.* **51**, 79–88.

Hanson, H. M. (1959). Effects of discrimination training on stimulus generalization. J. *exp. Psychol.* **58**, 321–334.

Hearst, E., Koresko, M. B. and Poppen, R. (1964). Stimulus generalization and the response reinforcement contingency. *J. exp. Anal. Behav.* **7,** 369–380.

Heinemann, E. G. and Rudolph, R. L. (1963). The effect of discriminative training on the gradient of stimulus-generalization. *Am. J. Psychol.* **76,** 653–658.

Honig, W. K. (1962). Prediction of preference, transposition, and transposition-reversal from the generalization gradient. *J. exp. Psychol.* **64,** 239–248.

Honig, W. K., Thomas, D. R. and Guttman, N. (1959). Differential effects of continuous extinction and discrimination training on the generalization gradient *J. exp. Psychol.* **58,** 145–152.

Jenkins, H. M. and Harrison, R. H. (1960). Effect of discrimination training on auditory generalization. *J. exp. Psychol.* **59,** 246–253.

Kimble, G. A. (1961). "Conditioning and Learning". Appleton-Century-Crofts, Inc., New York, U.S.A.

LaMonica, G. L. and Thomas, D. R. (1966). "Accuracy of perception of the visual vertical as a function of floor inclination." Paper delivered at Midwestern Psychological Association Meetings, Chicago.

Lyons, J. (1968). "Stimulus generalization as a function of interdimensional discrimination training with and without errors." Doctoral Dissertation, Kent State University.

Lyons, J. and Thomas, D. R. (1967). Effects of interdimensional training on stimulus generalization: II. Within-subjects design. *J. exp. Psychol.* **75,** 572–574.

Lyons, J. and Thomas, D. R. (1968). The influence of postural distortion on the perception of visual vertical in pigeons. *J. exp. Psychol.* **76,** 120-124.

Mackintosh, N. J. (1965). Selective attention in animal discrimination learning. *Psychol. Bull.* **64,** 124-150.

Malott, R. W., and Malott, M. K. (1967). An analysis of the Mueller-Lyer illusion in terms of stimulus generalization. *J. exp. Anal. Behav.* (in press).

Malott, R. W., Malott, M. K. and Pokrzywinski, J. (1967a). The effects of outward-pointing arrowheads on the Mueller-Lyer illusion in pigeons. *Psychon. Sci.* **9,** 55–56.

Malott, R. W., Malott, M. K. and Svinicki, J. G. (1967b). Generalization along the dimension of a length of a line without explicit discrimination training: A replication. *Psychon. Sci.* **9,** 17–18.

Mariner, R. W. (1967). "Reward duration, behavioral contrast and post-discrimination generalization gradients." Masters Thesis, Kent State University.

Mello, N. K. (1965). Interhemispheric reversal of mirror-image oblique lines after monocular training in pigeons. *Science, N.Y.* **148,** 252–254.

Newman, F. L. and Baron, M. R. (1965). Stimulus generalization along the dimension of angularity: A comparison of training procedures. *J. comp. physiol. Psychol.* **60,** 59–63.

Perkins, C. C. Jr., Hershberger, W. A. and Weyant, R. G. (1959). Difficulty of a discrimination as a determiner of subsequent generalization along another dimension. *J. exp. Psychol.* **57,** 181–186.

Peterson, N. (1962). Effect of monochromatic rearing on the control of responding by wavelength. *Science, N. Y.* **126,** 774–775.

Reinhold, D. B. and Perkins, C. C. Jr. (1955). Stimulus generalization following different methods of training. *J. exp. Psychol.* **49,** 423–427.

Riccio, D. C., Urda, M. and Thomas, D. R. (1966). Stimulus control in pigeons based on proprioceptive stimuli from floor inclination. *Science,* **153,** 434–436.

Sutherland, N. S. (1964). The learning of discriminations by animals, *Endeavour*, **23**, 140–152.

Sutherland, N. S. and Andelman, L. (1967). Learning with one and two cues. *Psychon. Sci.* **7**, 107–108.

Switalski, R. W., Lyons, J. and Thomas, D. R. (1966). Effects of interdimensional training on stimulus generalization. *J. exp. Psychol.* **72**, 661–666.

Terrace, H. S. (1963). Discrimination training with and without errors. *J. exp. Anal. Behav.* **6**, 1–17.

Terrace, H. S. (1964). Wavelength generalization after discrimination learning with and without errors. *Science, N. Y.* **144**, 78–80.

Terrace, H. S. (1966a). Stimulus control. *In* "Operant Behavior: Areas of Research and Application" (Honig, W. K. ed.) Appleton-Century-Crofts, Inc., New York, U.S.A.

Terrace, H. S. (1966b). "Discrimination learning and inhibition." *Science, N. Y.* **154**, 1677–1680.

Thomas, D. R. (1962). The effects of drive and discrimination training on stimulus generalization. *J. exp. Psychol.* **64**, 24–28.

Thomas, D. R., Klipec, W. and Lyons, J. (1966). Investigations of a mirror-image reversal effect in pigeons. *J. exp. Anal. Behav.* **9**, 567–571.

Thomas, D. R. and Lyons, J. (1968a). Further evidence of a sensory-tonic interaction in pigeons. *J. exp. Anal. Behav.* (in press).

Thomas, D. R. and Lyons, J. (1968b). Visual field dependency in pigeons. *Anim. Behav.* (in press).

Thomas, D. R., Lyons, J. and Freeman, F. (1966). The interaction between sensory and tonic factors in the perception of the vertical in pigeons: II. A replication via an alternative procedure. *Psychon. Sci.* **4**, 395–396.

Thomas, D. R., Mariner, R. R. and Sherry, G. (1968). The role of pre-experimental experience in the development of stimulus control. *J. exp. Psychol.* (in press).

Werner, H. and Wapner, S. (1952). Toward a general theory of perception. *Psychol. Rev.* **59**, 324–338.

Werner, H., Wapner, S. and Chandler, K. A. (1951). Experiments on sensory-tonic field theory of perception: II. Effect of supported and unsupported tilt of the body on the visual perception of verticality. *J. exp. Psychol.* **42**, 346–350.

Witkin, H. A. and Asch, S. E. (1948). Studies in space orientation: IV. Further experiments on perception of the upright with displaced visual fields. *J. exp. Psychol.* **38**, 762–782.

2

Attentional Factors Governing the Slope of the Generalization Gradient

WERNER K. HONIG

Dalhousie University, Halifax, Nova Scotia, Canada

I. Introduction

The primary effect of discrimination training is the development of differential stimulus control over behavior by those stimuli involved in the training procedure. In addition, discrimination training can have a number of more general secondary effects. In particular, it will affect the slope of generalization gradients obtained when stimuli other than the training values are presented. Terrace (1966) cites a number of relevant experiments, and points out that the term *attention* is often used to describe the differences in stimulus control obtained on a given stimulus dimension after various training conditions. He says that "Attention is typically used in those situations in which a stimulus or some element of a stimulus does *not* reliably control a response". (p. 287f). Thus, the increase in slope of a generalization gradient following some kinds of discrimination training reflects an increase in attention to the test dimension. Likewise, a flattening of the gradient after other kinds of training reflects a decrease in attention. But Terrace warns us that "Describing an unreliable relationship between the controlling properties of a stimulus and a response as attention is a different matter from *explain-*

ing the complete or partial absence of stimulus control. The use of attention as an explanatory principle in these instances . . . seems to be nothing more than a mask for our ignorance concerning the establishment of stimulus control". (p. 289).

This admonition suggests that if the variability of the slope of the generalization gradient can itself be brought under experimental control as an indirect result of discrimination procedures, the concept of attention can provide a useful category for the description of such effects, rather than serving as a "mask for our ignorance." Indeed, if the demonstration of such effects is combined with the considerable evidence on selective sensitization to, and selective utilization of, particular cues in discrimination learning (Mackintosh, 1965b), it may well be necessary to invoke the process of attention as an explanatory construct rather than a descriptive category. It is my view that the more indirect are the secondary effects of discrimination training, the more compelling is the argument in favor of an active attentional process. The current research, therefore, was designed to provide a demonstration of a truly "indirect" effect. We investigated effects of discrimination training on the slope of the generalization gradient when the training stimuli were on one visual dimension and the generalization gradient was obtained on another.

Any experiment concerned with this problem is necessarily composed of three phases: *discrimination training* between two stimulus values, *acquisition* of responding to a stimulus value lying on the *dimension of generalization*, and the *generalization test* on that dimension. One or both of the discrimination training stimuli may lie on the dimension of generalization: if the positive stimulus lies on this dimension, discrimination training automatically involves dimensional acquisition with the same value, and the mode of the generalization gradient is at the positive stimulus used in discrimination training.

The relationships between the stimuli used in discrimination training and the dimension of generalization are conveniently described with the terminology suggested by Switalski *et al.* (1966). In *intradimensional* training, the discrimination stimuli both lie on the dimension of generalization. Hanson (1959) and Honig (1962) examined spectral generalization after discrimination training between two monochromatic values, while Jenkins and Harrison (1962) carried out a corresponding study with auditory frequencies. In addition to the specific primary effects of discrimination training, all of these experiments demonstrated a general "tuning effect" in the form of enhanced slope of the generalization gradient following discrimination training, not only between $S+$ and $S-$, but also on the "other side" of the mode of the gradient which is requently displaced after discrimination training.

In *interdimensional training*, one of the stimuli—usually the positive, or $S+$—lies on the dimension of generalization, while the other lies on another dimension, at a value which is presumed to be equidistant from the various values on the dimension of generalization. Jenkins and Harrison (1960) obtained marked enhancement of the gradient on the dimension of auditory frequency after discrimination training between the presence of one tone as $S+$ and no tone as $S-$. Newman and Baron (1965) obtained a similar effect on the dimension of line orientation after a discrimination in which line presence was positive and line absence was negative. Switalski, *et al.* (1966) gave discrimination training in which responding to a round green key (555 mμ) was reinforced and responding to a white vertical line was extinguished. This sharpened the spectral generalization gradient. Equal reinforcement between the same training stimuli had the effect of flattening the same gradient. Thus, the secondary effects of interdimensional training on generalization slope are well established; indeed, the interdimensional studies are usually cited as the best evidence for "attentional" effects in the area of generalization (Mackintosh, 1965; Terrace, 1966).

A third procedure is *extradimensional* training, in which both $S+$ and $S-$ lie outside the dimension of generalization. This has been rather little explored with pigeons, and the present chapter provides a report on a number of studies on the effects of such training procedures. While intra- and interdimensional training experiments demonstrate general as well as specific effects of discrimination training, they cannot answer the question whether such effects may also be obtained if the positive training stimulus does not also lie on the dimension of generalization. The reason for this is that the differential training between $S+$ and $S-$, and the acquisition of responding to a stimulus on the dimension of generalization, are concurrent aspects of the discrimination procedure. The extradimensional design permits the complete separation of these two phases of training preceding the generalization test, and can answer the question whether the $S+$ must lie on the dimension of generalization to produce enhancement of the slope of the generalization gradient.

The separation of discrimination training and dimensional acquisition also provides an opportunity to vary the sequence in which these procedures are carried out. Discrimination training may precede, follow, or accompany dimensional acquisition. In the current research, two of these relationships are examined. Discrimination training on two colors precedes dimensional acquisition with a set of vertical lines in one group of experiments, and follows dimensional acquisition in another. In both groups of studies, the generalization test was carried out on the dimension of angular orientation, or "tilt" of the line. When discrimination training precedes dimensional acquisition, we are able to examine the proactive effects of such training on the acquisition of stimulus control; these are well described as attentional effects since such training may sensitize or desensitize the organism to subsequent stimulus inputs. The corresponding experiments are called "attention studies." When discrimination training follows dimensional acquisition, we are testing its retroactive effects on the stimulus control acquired from previous stimulus inputs. Such effects may be described as memory effects, and the studies are correspondingly called "memory studies."

II. General Procedures

All of the experiments to be reported in the next two sections have certain procedures in common. While there were minor deviations in certain experiments, these were held constant between all groups in a given experiment. Domestic pigeons were trained in standard Grason-Stadler pigeon boxes, in which one response key was trans-illuminated by an in-line digital display projector (pattern no. 165). Four plain colors were available for projection on the key: red, blue, green and white. If one of these colors is turned on together with white, a desaturated tint is obtained; we have in this manner trained discriminations between pink (red + white) and white alone. In addition, we could present patterns of three parallel dark lines, each of about $\frac{1}{8}$in diameter, on a white background, available in eight different orientations. The white background is very similar to the plain white; a line pattern and the plain white provided the stimuli for line-present versus line-absent discriminations. The lighted key and occasional presentations of the lighted food magazine provided the only illumination in the box.

A. Preliminary Training

All animals were trained to peck at the key with continuous reinforcement, were then switched to a VI 37·5 sec schedule for two sessions, and to a VI 62·5 sec schedule for two or three further sessions. A session consisted of 30 or 36 min of working time, presented either as 24 periods of 90 sec each, or as 30 periods of 60 sec each. Periods were separated by 5 sec blackouts, during which the reinforcement program was interrupted and responses (if any) had no programmed effect. Grain reinforcement was presented with 5 sec cycles of the food magazine.

B. Training and Testing

In discrimination training, two stimuli of different colors were alternated in a randomized order for 24 trials of 90 sec each. $S+$ and $S-$ were presented equally often, with six of each in the first and in the second sets of twelve trials. In *true discrimination* (TD) training, the reinforcement programmer ran on all $S+$ trials and on none of the $S-$ trials; thus the VI program was in effect on $S+$ trials only. Reinforcement during $S-$ trials was prevented, so that a reinforcement "set up" on a previous $S+$ trial could not be collected in the $S-$ condition.

In *pseudo-discrimination* (PD) training, the same sequence of $S+$ and $S-$ trials were presented as in TD, but the programmer ran during half of the $S+$ and half of the $S-$ trials. There were, again, six reinforced and six non-reinforced trials in each half of the 24-trial session. Thus, the total number of reinforced periods was the same in TD and PD, but reinforcement was randomly and equally associated with $S+$ and $S-$ in the PD procedure.

In a third procedure, called $S+$ *only control*, blackout periods were presented in the place of $S-$ periods within the randomized order of trials in a discrimination session. Reinforcement was available during the $S+$ periods, as in the true discrimination, but negative "trials" were merely extensions of the inter-trial blackouts. Thus, the number and temporal spacing of reinforcements was identical in TD and in the $S+$ only control procedure, but only one stimulus was presented, and discrimination learning thereby prevented. (Since pigeons do not respond in the dark, no errors occurred in the $S+$ only control procedure).

In most of the studies to be described, animals were grouped into squads during discrimination training in order to equalize the amount of training across treatment groups. All animals in a squad were run in the discrimination phase until the animal receiving TD training met criterion. This consisted of two consecutive sessions, or three out of four consecutive sessions (depending on the specific experiment) in which less than 10% of the total responses in a training session were emitted to $S-$. Thus, while different animals within each group were trained for different numbers of sessions, the number of training sessions was equated between groups.

Four VI training sessions were presented in dimensional acquisition. In most experiments, the three parallel lines were displayed in a vertical orientation. Generalization testing was carried out in extinction. Eight orientations of the three parallel lines were presented, at $0°$ (i.e. horizontal), $22\frac{1}{2}°$, $45°$, and so forth; in addition, one or both of the training stimuli could be presented during testing. Stimulus exposures lasted for 30 sec each, and were arranged in randomized blocks. Eight blocks of trials were presented in a testing session, and two sessions on successive days comprised a complete test. Responding was mostly extinguished by the end of the second session. This phase of the experiment will be called the $A + T$ (for acquisition and test) sequence.

III. Attention Studies

Experiment 1A

Method

The first group of studies was designed to examine the effects of extra-dimensional training upon generalization when dimensional acquisition followed discrimination training. After initial training to the white key for all groups, true discrimination was programmed with white positive and pink negative for the TD group. Pseudo-discrimination and $S+$ only (or "white-only") control groups were run in the manner described above. After the TD bird in each squad reached criterion, all animals in the squad received dimensional acquisition training with the three vertical lines. This was followed by a generalization test, with the eight line orientations, as well as white and pink. (In the white-only control, blank trials were substituted for pink.) There were six animals in each of the TD and PD groups, but the death of one white-only control subject reduced that group to five.

Results

Fig. 1 shows the total numbers of responses emitted during the generalization test. The TD group yielded the steepest overall gradient, the

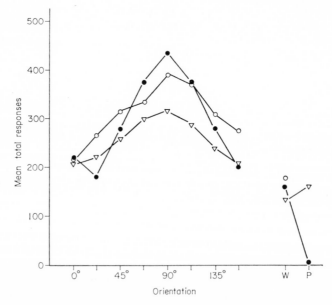

FIG. 1. Generalization gradients obtained in Experiment 1A in terms of mean total responses for the entire test. ○ TD; ● $S+$ only; ▽ PD.

PD group the flattest, with the $S+$ only group falling in between. Responding to white and pink reflected the training conditions: for the TD group, total responses to white far exceeded responses to pink, while these values were about equal for the PD birds.

Since slope differences may in part be due to different levels of response output in different groups, the generalization gradient of each subject was recalculated in terms of percentages. The response total to each of the orientations was divided by the total response output to all the orientation values. (Responses to white and pink were omitted from the calculations.) The resulting gradients, averaged across subjects, are presented in Fig. 2. It is evident that the patterns observed in Fig. 1 are maintained.

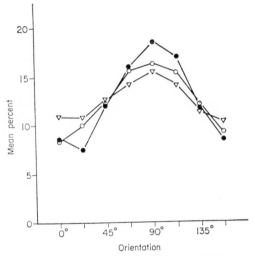

FIG. 2. Generalization gradients obtained in Experiment 1A in terms of mean percentages. ● TD; ○ $S+$ only; ▽ PD.

A mixed-design analysis of variance carried out on the percentage gradients revealed that the effect of orientation was highly significant, as might be expected. The interaction between orientation and training condition (i.e. the test for slope differences) was significant only at the 10% level of confidence. A Mann-Whitney U test carried out on the total percentage of responses to the central values of the gradient ($65\frac{1}{2}°$, 90°, and 112°) for the true- and pseudo-discrimination groups indicates a difference between these groups which is significant at about the 7% level of confidence. These statistics provide only limited support for the between-group differences observed in the obtained gradients. My confidence in the validity of the finding is based largely upon the fact that we have been able to obtain similar results under somewhat different conditions in a number of subsequent experiments, to be described below.

Discussion

These results indicate that extra-dimensional discrimination training procedures will affect generalization gradients. The flattening effect of PD training, compared to the $S+$ only control procedure, seems just as interesting and perhaps more remarkable than the sharpening effect of the TD procedure. Originally, the PD procedure was designed as a kind of control condition providing a stimulus sequence identical to that presented to the TD group. But non-differential positive training with more than one distinguishable value appears to have the effect of decreasing attention to subsequently presented stimuli, just as differential training appears to enhance it.

These results were obtained from comparable but independent groups. The next phase of the study was designed to determine whether the attentional states generated by the TD and PD procedures could each be modified by training the same subjects with the opposite procedure.

EXPERIMENT 1B

Design and Procedure

Three of the six PD birds were switched to TD training following the first $A + T$ sequence. Their "squad partners", which initially had received TD training, were switched to the PD training procedure. The remaining three squads were paired with these, with one bird from each squad continuing on TD and the other on PD training. The animals were thus run in squads of four, with the number of training sessions in each squad determined by the bird that was switched from PD to TD training. Since these animals now had to extinguish responding to pink, which had previously been reinforced, the new training procedure took many more sessions than initial training. Following completion of training, all animals again received a second $A + T$ sequence identical to the first.

Results

The results for this test are presented in Fig. 3 in terms of percentage gradients. The gradients have been "folded over" by averaging the percentage values for corresponding angular deviations from the vertical training stimulus. Since each group contained only three subjects, the data are not quite as regular as in Experiment 1A. The "second test" refers to the results obtained in Experiment 1B. The continuation of previous training as carried out with the true-true and pseudo-pseudo

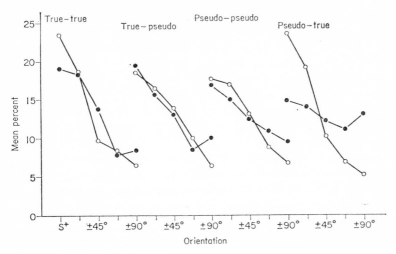

FIG. 3. Folded percentage gradients obtained in Experiment 1B (Second Test ○—○) compared to those from Experiment 1A (First Test ●—●).

groups appears to have little effect on the gradients. There is some steepening obtained with both groups, which, as we shall see, is probably due to the repetition of the $A + T$ sequence. The true-pseudo group also shows little change, except for an absence of the mild steepening of the gradients obtained with the two groups whose training procedures were not switched. The only marked change is observed with the pseudo-true group. Their gradient is greatly enhanced, and ends up with a slope quite similar to that obtained from the true-true group.

Discussion

These results suggest that the switch from PD to TD training enhances the attentional state of the subject, as reflected in the steepened generalization gradients; but that this state, once established by the TD procedure, is not markedly reduced by subsequent PD training. There are, however, some problems of interpretation associated with the two phases of Experiment 1, which led to extensions of this line of research in Experiments 2 and 3. First, we should note that while pink and white are extradimensional to various line orientations, the latter stimuli themselves were imposed on a white background. It is possible that during discrimination training, the birds were learning specifically to attend to the white key, and the enhancement of the slope of the generalization gradient may have been due to the stimulus elements common to $S+$ and the line stimuli on the orientation dimension. While it is never possible to eliminate all features common to two visual stimuli of this sort, some advantage could be gained by carrying out the initial discrimination with blue and green rather than white and pink. A second improvement consisted in the omission of $S+$ and $S-$ from the generalization test. It is possible that the presentation of these stimuli during testing may have temporarily aroused or reduced an attentional process, resulting in differential slopes of the gradients. This would certainly complicate the theoretical interpretation of these studies. Experiment 2 was designed to incorporate these improvements.

The interpretation of Experiment 1B is clouded by the fact that two sequences of dimensional acquisition and testing were administered to the same subjects. We do not know to what extent the slopes of the gradients obtained in the second test were affected by the previous procedures involving the line stimuli. It is reasonable to suppose that such repeated training and testing would sharpen the gradients (cf. Guttman and Kalish, 1956), but the degree of sharpening, and the possible interactions of such an enhancement with the intervening training procedures, could not be assessed. Experiment 3 was designed to overcome these problems, both by providing a switch from TD to PD procedures without intervening $A + T$, and by assessing the effects of repeated $A + T$ with and without intervening extra-dimensional training procedures.

EXPERIMENT 2

Procedure

Six birds were trained to respond to the white stimulus and adapted to the VI schedule as in Experiment 1. They were then divided into two groups, with three Ss receiving TD and three receiving PD training with blue as $S+$ and green as $S-$. Dimensional acquisition and generalization testing were carried out as in Experiment 1, but neither blue nor green was presented during the test.

Results

The percentage gradients are presented in Fig. 4. The gradient following PD training is almost flat, while the other has a marked slope, generally similar to that obtained after TD training in Experiment 1A. The mean percentage values are 17·6% at 90° and 8·4% at 0° in Experiment 3, corresponding to 18·5% and 8·8% in Experiment 1. It appears, then, that the extradimensional training effect in these studies does not depend on the similarity of $S+$ to the white background of the line stimuli, nor on the presentation of $S+$ and $S-$ in the generalization test. While the results of this experiment are based on a small number of subjects,

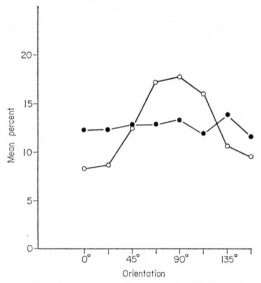

Fig. 4. Mean percentage gradients obtained in Experiment 2.

the confirmation of the findings of Experiment 1 under somewhat different circumstances encourages confidence in the reliability of extradimensional training effects.

EXPERIMENT 3A†

Design and Procedure

Five groups of pigeons were initially trained with the usual VI acquisition procedure to the white key. One group of 6 Ss was given S+ only training on blue for six sessions, followed by four sessions of dimensional acquisition with the three vertical lines, and a generalization test. A second group was given six sessions of TD training with blue as S+ and green as S— followed by the same A + T sequence. These groups are called BOC-IAT and TD-IAT respectively (where IAT stands for Immediate Acquisition and Test). Their purpose was to demonstrate again that TD training leads to an increase in the slope of the generalization gradient when dimensional acquisition and testing follow immediately; it seemed pointless to assess the effects of other procedures following TD training unless evidence for an initial attentional enhancement could be obtained.

Three further groups were also trained for six sessions with blue-green

†This experiment was carried out by Donald C. Moors as a portion of the research contributing to his M. A. Thesis.

TD, and then received eight treatment sessions before line acquisition and testing. One group received blue-green PD training, and is called the TD-PD group. A second group received eight further sessions of TD training (TD-TD group), while a third was weighed daily but not run in a "hold-only control" procedure (TD-HOC group). If PD training has the effect of decreasing the state of attention established initially by TD training, the TD-PD group should provide flatter gradients than the others. The HOC procedure was introduced to ascertain whether any such flattening of the gradient could be ascribed to the passage of time elapsing after the completion of TD training, rather than to the PD procedure.

Results

In this experiment, the amount of initial TD training was equated for all groups before they were shifted to other procedures. While the birds were not run to a criterion, the error rates at the end of six sessions were comparable to the 10% error criterion established in other experiments: the mean error rate on the sixth training session ranged from 0·7% for the TD-IAT group to 4·3% for the TD-TD group. The training procedures following initial TD training had their intended effects. The TD-TD group maintained discrimination performance, going from a mean of 4·3% errors at the end of initial training to 9·0% errors at the end of extended training. The TD-PD group went from 4·2% errors to 46·0% responses to the (now "pseudo-negative") green key in the same period.

The results of generalization testing can be seen in the left half of Fig. 5 in terms of folded percentage gradients.† Between-group differences are not marked and statistical analysis failed to reveal significant slope differences. Nevertheless it is apparent that the gradient from the BOC group is flatter than all the rest. The other gradients are all rather similar, although it could be argued on close inspection that the one obtained from the TD-PD group is somewhat flatter than those from the TD-TD and TD-IAT groups. But it is not any flatter than the TD-HOC group; any flattening of the gradient can therefore not be ascribed to the effects of the PD procedure *per se*.

---

†The "folded" gradients in this case were obtained by first calculating the mean responses for each subject to stimuli representing equal deviations from the vertical, and then obtaining the per cent of total responses for each of the resulting values. In these percentage gradients, the expected value for each test stimulus is 20%, rather than 12·5%, as in previous experiments. The overall gradient values are therefore higher than those obtained in the other experiments.

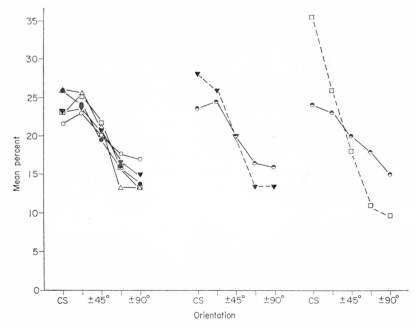

Fig. 5. Mean folded percentage gradients from Experiments 3A (left), and 3B (centre and right.) The half-filled circles represent the mean gradients obtained from the sub-divided TD and BOC groups on the first test. ○ BOC, ● TD, △ TD − TD, ▼ TD − PD, □ TD − HOC, ———— first test, ––– 2nd test.

Experiment 3B

Design and Procedure

The TD-IAT group and the BOC-IAT groups from Experiment 3A were divided into subgroups of three subjects each. Two subgroups were given eight sessions of PD training after the first $A + T$ sequence, followed by a repetition of the $A + T$ procedures. The members of the other subgroups were weighed daily during a comparable interval between the two acquisition and test series. In this way, we could assess the affects of repeated acquisition and testing, with and without the presentation of PD training in between.

Results

The centre and right portions of Fig. 5 provide a comparison of the gradients obtained from the first and second generalization tests, carried out without (centre) and with intervening PD training. (Since the effects of these conditions did not interact with the initial training conditions, the data from the appropriate subgroups have been combined.) Again,

PD training does not produce a flattening of the gradient, confirming the results of Experiment 1B. A mild increase in slope is seen instead. But a second series of acquisition and testing without any intervening treatment has a very marked steepening effect. This suggests that the repeated dimensional acquisition and testing with the line stimuli is sufficient to account for the kind of steepening observed in the group that was switched from PD to TD training in Experiment 1B. The effect of TD training in that experiment may well have been negligible. On the other hand, the present results suggest that the introduction of PD training between the first and second acquisition and test series inhibits the steepening effect obtained when no intervening treatment is administered. The reasons for this are suggested by the memory experiments to be described in the next section.

IV. Memory Studies

The experiments described this far deal with a proactive effect. Preliminary training on one dimension affects the stimulus control exerted by stimuli which are subsequently presented on another. This finding led to the question whether a similar effect may also occur retroactively; that is, whether extradimensional discrimination training can affect the control developed by stimuli presented *before* such training takes place. As indicated in the introduction to this paper, such experiments may be called "memory" studies, since their design is similar to standard memory experiments on retroactive interference. The general procedures were very similar to those described previously; the critical difference between the attention and the memory studies is the order of discrimination training and dimensional acquisition.

EXPERIMENT 4

Procedure

Eight pigeons were initially trained to peck with the vertical lines, and were then shifted to a VI 37·5 sec schedule for two sessions and to a VI 62·5 sec schedule for four sessions. This phase constituted dimensional acquisition with the vertical lines. Following this, all pigeons received two days of VI training with blue. Half of them then received blue-green TD training, and half received blue-green PD training. They were grouped into four squads of two each. After the TD animals reached criterion, both members of each squad received a two-session generalization test with eight orientations of the lines. Blue and green were not presented during the test.

Since the results from this test provided no evidence for any "memory effect" due to the discrimination training, the experiment was continued in order to confirm the reliability of the attentional effect obtained in similar circumstances. All animals were retrained on the TD and PD procedures until the TD birds met criterion a second time (in three of the four cases, this consisted only of the three criterion sessions), and were then given four sessions of dimensional acquisition with the three vertical lines. This was followed by a second generalization test.

Results

The results of the first test are shown in terms of mean percentage gradients at the left of Fig. 6. The gradients are rather flat and very similar for the two groups; thus there was no evidence of any differential effect of the training procedures which occurred between dimensional

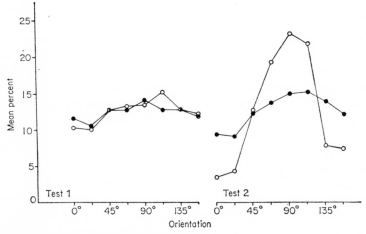

FIG. 6. Mean percentage gradients obtained in Experiment 4, from the first test (memory phase) and the second test (attention phase). O—O True discrimination; ●—● Pseudo discrimination.

acquisition and testing. The results from the second test, however, show a very marked difference between the two gradients, corresponding to the findings of the attentional studies described previously. Both gradients are steeper on the second test, but the enhancement of the slope following TD training is much more marked. The data from repeated acquisition and testing obtained in Experiment 3 suggest that some or all of this steepening is due to the fact that the subjects experienced a second $A + T$ sequence with the line stimuli. Nevertheless, there is a clear interaction between the training procedures following the first test and any such steepening effect; either the PD training inhibited the steepening effect, or the TD training enhanced it, or both. Unfortunately, we do not have a hold-only control group which did not receive any intervening training to provide a basis for comparison. It is in any case clear that TD and PD training on blue and green exert differential effects prior to the second acquisition and test sequence, and this finding again strengthens the conclusions based on the attention studies reported in the previous section.

EXPERIMENT 5

While there was no demonstration of any memory effect in Experiment 4, I was encouraged to undertake a further exploration by the following considerations. The gradients obtained from the first test were very flat, indicating that little stimulus control may have resulted from initial acquisition. Other studies not reported here had also provided rather flat gradients on the orientation dimension following initial acquisition with three vertical lines. Now if the level of attention to the stimulus in acquisition is low, it could well be that intervening training would have no effect on stimulus control by line orientation simply because there was no control to be affected. A more sensitive experiment, therefore, would be to build in some stimulus control initially, and then to study the effects of intervening training.

Procedure

Eight pigeons were trained to peck at the three vertical lines, and shifted to VI 37·5 sec and VI 62·5 sec for two sessions each. A small amount of discrimination training was then administered in the form of three TD sessions between vertical lines positive and line absent (white) negative. All birds received this training, which ended after three sessions irrespective of the level of discrimination attained. The animals were then divided into two groups, with four receiving TD training between blue and green, and four receiving PD training in the usual manner. The TD animals were trained to criterion. Generalization tests followed the blue-green discriminations and consisted of eight line orientations and the white line-absent stimulus.

Results

Gradients representing the mean total responses and mean percentages are presented in Fig. 7. The initial discrimination procedure appears to affect the results in two ways. First, both gradients are steeper than when no such procedure is administered as in Experiment 4, and second, a differential effect of TD and PD training now appears. Another finding is worth noting: responding to the white key, the negative stimulus in the initial discrimination, is maintained by the TD group at a very low

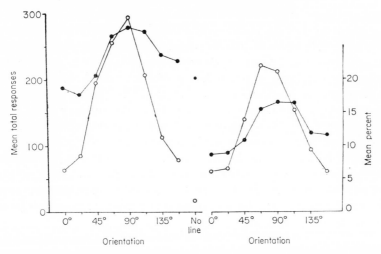

Fig. 7. Mean total response gradients and mean percentage gradients obtained in Experiment 5. ○—○ True discrimination; ●—● Pseduo discrimination.

level during the test, with a mean of about 16 responses, or a ratio between $S+$ and $S-$ of about 20 to 1. But the corresponding performance is much poorer for the PD group. The mean value is about 200 responses, and the $S+$ to $S-$ ratio is no higher than 1·4 to 1. It should be noted that during the last of the three training days on the line-present versus line-absent discrimination, the discrimination ratios were very good (less than 3% to $S-$) and about equal for both groups. It is rather remarkable that in terms of discrimination ratios, the test performance of the PD group was worse during the generalization test than during even the first day of the line-present versus line-absent discrimination training. This indicates that the PD training may actually interfere with previously established stimulus control.

Discussion

This experiment indicates that, once stimulus control is established on one dimension, it may be modified by subsequent training on another. The nature of the action of the secondary training is, however, not yet clear. We do not know whether TD training enhanced the previously established level of stimulus control, whether PD training reduced it, whether both processes occurred concurrently, or whether these procedures merely had differential effects on the loss of stimulus control over time, hastening or retarding the "forgetting" of the original discrimination. Experiment 6 was therefore designed to include an $S+$ only control, and to investigate the effects of the passage of time on the generalization gradient without the occurrence of intervening discrimination training.

The large differences in gradient slopes between corresponding groups in Experiments 4 and 5 have been attributed to the effects of preliminary discrimination training between line presence and line absence. There was, however, a confounding factor: the blue-green discriminations took on average only half as long to acquire in Experiment 5 as in Experiment 4 (presumably demonstrating the beneficial effects of the preliminary discrimination in yet another way), and the time between dimensional acquisition and testing was therefore a good deal shorter in Experiment 5. If the gradient flattens over time, as at least one previous study indicates (Thomas and Lopez, 1962), the over-all slope differences between Experiments 4 and 5 may in part be accounted for by this confounded difference.

EXPERIMENT 6

Procedure

Six birds were run in each of five groups. Three birds in each group were trained with horizontal, and three with vertical lines, to control for the possibility that some specific feature of the stimulus other than line orientation might be responsible for the generalization decrement between the training value and the other orientations. All birds received initial acquisition with three lines, and three sessions of discrimination training between lines present and lines absent, as described in Experiment 5. The immediate test (IT) group then received two days of generalization testing, with eight orientations and the white key. The other four groups were divided into squads. One group received TD training with the blue and green stimuli, while a second received PD training. A third, the blue-only control (BOC) group, had presentation of the green omitted during training sessions. The birds in the fourth group, called hold-only control (HOC), did not receive any discrimination training whatsoever, but were weighed daily while the other members of their squads received the TD, PD and BOC procedures. Each squad was tested after the TD bird completed training.

Results

The results are presented in Fig. 8 in terms of folded gradients, since two different line orientations were used in original training. The steepest gradient, both in terms of total responses and of percentages, is obtained immediately after completion of discrimination training between line present and line absent. There is again a sizable slope difference between the TD and the PD groups, confirming the results of Experiment 4. The slopes of the gradients following the BOC and HOC procedures are on

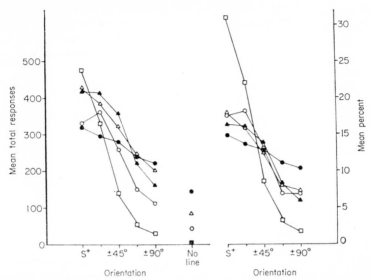

FIG. 8. Mean folded response gradients and mean folded percentage gradients obtained in Experiment 6. □ Immediate test; ○ True discrimination; ● Pseudo discrimination; △ Blue only control; ▲ Hold only control.

the whole similar to those of the TD groups. A mixed-design analysis of variance on the gradients of all but the IT group (which obviously differed from the rest) indicates that slope differences were significant, presumably due primarily to the flat gradient obtained from the PD group.

The IT and HOC groups gave almost no responses to the white, no-line key. The other three groups were ordered as one might expect. The TD group gave the fewest, the BOC birds an intermediate value, and the PD animals the most responses to the white key. At first glance it might appear surprising that the TD animals made more "errors" to white than the HOC group, but we should remember that the TD procedure actually involved reinforcement to a blue no-line stimulus, which might have generalized to some extent to white. The HOC groups and IT groups received no reinforcement to any no-line display following their discrimination training.

Discussion

We succeeded in Experiment 6 in answering a number of questions. First, we replicated the memory effect obtained in Experiment 5, which is always comforting when one is dealing with a rather elusive phenomenon. Secondly, we established with the IT and HOC groups that there is a definite loss of stimulus control on the dimension of generalization over time, although not between $S+$ and $S-$ *per se.* Third, we found in comparing the TD, BOC and HOC groups that the TD procedure does not enhance stimulus control over the loss due to the passage of time alone; that is, it does not retard the waning of stimulus control. The "active" effect in this study appears to be a *reduction* in stimulus control due to the PD procedure, which is added to the loss due to the passage of time alone.

V. General Discussion

A. A Summary of Findings

Let us at the outset summarize the principal findings of the research that has been described in this chapter. There is considerable evidence for a reliable attentional effect when extradimensional training precedes dimensional acquisition. This was obtained in Experiment 1A, in Experiment 2, and in Experiment 3A. Pseudo-discrimination training appears to flatten the gradient in relation to an $S+$ only control group, while true discrimination training enhances stimulus control. These comparisons are provided by Experiment 1, in which the extradimensional stimuli were white and pink. Unfortunately, the studies for which the extradimensional stimuli were blue and green do not provide a complete set of comparisons: Experiment 2 lacks the $S+$ only control, while Experiment 3 lacks a pseudo-discrimination group. Nevertheless, the extremely flat gradient obtained from the PD group in Experiment 2 suggests (in comparison to the $S+$ only control group in Experiment 3) that the PD treatment does produce a flattening effect when the training stimuli are blue and green, rather than white and pink.

There is also good evidence for a memory effect (Experiments 5 and 6). This effect was obtained only when the slope of the orientation gradient was made quite steep initially by discrimination training between line present and line absent; witness the failure to obtain memory effect when such discrimination training was not carried out (Experiment 4). It should be noted that other preliminary studies of the same nature, but not reported here, also failed to obtain a reliable memory effect. The available evidence (Experiment 6) suggests that the only "active" process is the reduction in slope due to PD training; TD training does not appear to enhance slope when compared to the $S+$ only control or the hold-only control procedures.

In this respect, the results of the memory studies are not symmetrical with those of the attention experiments, in which TD training did have the effect of steepening the slope of the generalization gradient. It may be, of course, that a more extensive experimental analysis will reveal an enhancing effect even in memory studies; a close look at Fig. 8 shows that the true discrimination gradient is in fact slightly steeper than the blue only control and hold-only control gradients. At this time, however, the simplest interpretation of the data from Experiment 6 is that the passage of time results in a loss of stimulus control (compare the immediate test and the hold-only control gradients), and that this loss sets an upper limit to the amount of stimulus control exercized by the orientation dimension at the time of the test. Extradimensional true discrimination between dimensional acquisition and testing does not enhance this "available" stimulus control, but pseudo-discrimination interferes with the stimulus control remaining after a given amount of time has elapsed.

The studies involving repeated acquisition and testing *all* demonstrate steeper slopes after the second $A + T$ sequence than after the first. The groups involved were the four subgroups of Experiment 1B, the two groups of Experiment 3B, and the two groups in Experiment 4, following the "memory" phase of that particular study. Only one of these groups (in Experiment 3B) received no intervening training between the $A + T$ sequences, and this group showed a marked steepening of the gradient. These findings show that repeated acquisition and testing does sharpen stimulus control, which makes it difficult to interpret the sequential effects of different kinds of extradimensional training on the generalization gradient in any design where repeated $A + T$ is used. But the nature of the intervening training does affect this sharpening process. In all cases where PD training intervened between the $A + T$ sequences, there was less sharpening than when TD training or no training intervened. Since the appropriate hold-only control groups were generally not run between the $A + T$ sequences, it is not clear to what extent this difference is due to an inhibition of steepening by the PD procedure, to an enhancement of sharpening by the TD procedure, or to both. But the marked steepening observed in the one case where no training intervened (Experiment 3B) suggests that most or all of the effect was due to the inhibiting effects of PD training.

This conclusion is supported by the following interpretation of differential training effects in these experiments. The sharpening effect of repeated $A + T$ procedures must be due to an interaction between these phases, implying that the subject retains some of the stimulus control acquired in the first $A + T$ sequence as he enters the second sequence. Experiments 5 and 6 suggest very strongly that PD training reduces the retention of stimulus control; thus it is quite likely that the PD training also interferes with the stimulus control gained in the first $A + T$ sequence before it can interact with the stimulus control produced by the second. It is of course possible that the effect of PD training is proactive rather than retroactive, reducing the animal's attention to the stimuli presented in the second $A + T$ sequence. But the results of Experiment 3 suggest that PD training does not reduce an attentional state once it is established, and in some of the groups we are discussing, such a state was presumably established by initial TD training.

The question whether an attentional state established by initial training can be modified by a switch to subsequent training with a different procedure has not completely been answered. As we have seen, our first attempt to make this determination in Experiment 1B was contaminated by the effects of repeating the $A + T$ sequence. The second attempt was carried out in Experiment 3A, where TD training was immediately followed by continued TD training, PD training, or no training (hold-only control) before $A + T$ were administered. Certainly the switch to PD had no marked effect; the subsequent gradient was somewhat flatter than that obtained from animals which received $A + T$ right after initial TD training, but this slight effect could be ascribed to the passage of time. The gradient of the TD-PD group was somewhat steeper than that obtained from the BOC group. Even if some flattening occurred as a result of the switch to the PD procedure, the level of attention was not reduced to that which would be expected from a group receiving only PD training before the $A + T$ sequence.

B.   FURTHER EMPIRICAL QUESTIONS

Further research is certainly necessary to answer the question whether an attentional state, once generated by a given training procedure, can be modified by the subsequent introduction of other procedures. At this time, it appears that pseudo-discrimination following true discrimination does not have a marked flattening effect. When pseudo-discrimination intervenes between two $A + T$ sequences, it seems to inhibit steepening of the gradient, but this may well be due to a memory effect rather than an attention effect, as discussed above. The question remains whether true discrimination can enhance an attentional state following pseudo-discrimination. The only evidence, from Experiment 1B, is unsatisfactory because it involved a repetition of the $A + T$ sequence. We need to carry out a study in which TD follows PD training without any intervening acquisition and test.

A second question of interest is as follows: none of the attention studies to date have used an "untreated" control group, i.e. a group which receives *no* preliminary extradimensional training of any sort. Such a group is desirable in order to determine whether the various training procedures *generally* enhance or reduce the slope of the generalization gradient, but do so to different degrees. An untreated control group was very valuable in the major memory study (Experiment 6), since it demonstrated that the differential effect of the various treatments administered after dimensional acquisition acted upon a loss of stimulus control which took place as a function of time. The gradient from that untreated control cannot, unfortunately, give us any indication of the gradient to be expected from an untreated control in the attention studies, since it followed discrimination training between line present and line absent, a procedure which greatly enhances the slope of the orientation gradient.

The relationships between the dimensions or modalities involved in discrimination training and dimensional acquisition have not been explored in any systematic way. The concept of attentional enhancement would receive support from a study showing that similar results can be obtained when the dimensions of color and line orientation are interchanged—initial discrimination is carried out with two line orientations, and subsequent acquisition and testing is carried out with color. Actually, some of the research on inter-dimensional training effects has been carried out with color as the test dimension (Switalski *et al.* 1966; Lyons and Thomas, 1967), with results quite parallel to those reported here. It is therefore reasonable to suppose that experiments involving such an interchange would be successful in demonstrating attentional effects. On the other hand, some stimulus dimensions are more "natural" than others for certain organisms.

It is also of interest to ask whether *extramodal* attentional effects could be demonstrated, with auditory discriminations perhaps affecting subsequent stimulus control on a visual dimension. Experiments carried out by Reinhold and Perkins (1955) and by Perkins *et al.* (1959) suggest that such effects can be obtained between auditory and visual stimuli, and between tactile and visual stimuli in rats. Furthermore, the effect of initial discrimination difficulty has not been explored. Boneau and Honig (1964) have suggested in a different context that very difficult or complex discriminations will restrict the "available" attention to the relevant stimulus aspects in a training situation and reduce the attention to irrelevant aspects. Their experiment involved interdimensional relationships among stimulus dimensions, but again, these considerations may apply to the extra-dimensional research paradigms†.

†Dr. D. R. Thomas kindly permitted me to see a draft of chapter 1 after this chapter was completed. He describes several valuable studies from his laboratory which are relevant to the empirical questions raised here. One study demonstrates an extradimensional training effect with different line orientations used in discrimination training, and spectral values used in acquisition and testing. This study also included an "untreated" control group. True discrimination enhanced stimulus control in relation to this group, but pseudo-discrimination did not reduce it. Furthermore, Thomas reports two extramodal experiments which confirm and extend the earlier work of Perkins and his students.

Suggestions of this nature may be multiplied almost indefinitely, but they do not provide a true analytical attack on the processes underlying the steepening of the generalization gradient which we have observed in this research. While we may describe the effect as an attentional one on the basis of an appropriate definition of attention, this description does not indicate whether extradimensional training increases the sensitivity to stimulus input, or whether it produces response patterns or strategies that facilitate differential performance on a generalization test. In the TD procedure, for example, the animal is trained to withold responses in the presence of $S-$. A steep generalization gradient can only be obtained if response rates are low at certain times during the test. Perhaps, then, the steepening of the gradient reflects a "readiness to inhibit" rather than a "readiness to look." Similarly, the flattening effect of pseudo-discrimination could be due to some kind of superstitious response patterning adopted by the subject when faced with an unsolvable discrimination.

An attack on this problem would be provided by experiments following the strategy of Lawrence (1949), in which two different kinds of response differentiation are required in training and testing. Ideally, the response dimensions, as well as the stimulus dimensions, should be orthogonal. Since any response differentiation requires a reduction in responding to some stimulus, this ideal cannot be achieved, but a good approximation would be provided by an initial discrimination involving a choice between simultaneously presented stimuli, rather than a successive differentiation between $S+$ and $S-$. Similarly, one could maintain the successive preliminary discrimination procedure and change the method of testing so that sensitivity to stimuli could be assessed in terms of the degree of preference between stimuli, rather than the response rates which they control on successive presentation.

C. SOME THEORETICAL CONSIDERATIONS

This paper has described some empirical phenomena in the area of stimulus generalization, which can conveniently be described as "attentional" since they reflect relatively non-specific effects of discrimination procedures. A general consideration of the theoretical status of attention in the area of stimulus control would be out of place here; nevertheless, it may be worthwhile to consider the implications of our findings for one theory of discrimination learning which suggests that attention plays an integral part in the learning process.

Stimulus analyzer theory, as presented in the writings of Sutherland (1964), Mackintosh (1965), and Lovejoy (1966), makes a clear separation between the attention to a stimulus dimension, and the attachment of responses to specific values on that dimension. Similarly, our research has distinguished attentional effects from the stimulus-response relationships specifically examined on a generalization test. These authors have taken the position that the development of attention is fundamentally selective; that is, relevant stimulus analyzers are strengthened in discrimination training or "switched in," while irrelevant ones are weakened or "switched out." This assumption is useful in accounting for certain interactions among discrimination problems observed in their research. Furthermore, it provides their theory with a desirable degree of specificity, and is in accord with modern notions regarding the processing of information: channel capacity presumably is limited, and attention is likely to be selective.

This kind of model can account for many of the generalization studies involving intra- and interdimensional training procedures. Intradimensional training will switch in the analyzer which governs the slope of the generalization gradient. Analyzer theory can also account for interdimensional effects, with the assumption that discrimination training may switch in more than one analyzer at a time. Since the contours presented in a line-present versus line-absent discrimination must have some orientation, it is not hard to see how such a discrimination steepens the slope of the orientation gradients even though orientation is not "relevant" in the formal sense. But it is much more difficult for analyzer theory to provide an explanation for the enhancement of generalization slopes following extra-dimensional training. If anything, this procedure should have the opposite effect. The color discriminations described in this paper should switch out the orientation analyzer, since the form and pattern of the training stimuli were identical, and the vertical lines were not presented at all. Pseudo-discrimination training should switch out the analyzer for color, and permit greater subsequent control by the analyzer for orientation. The data, of course, are contrary to this prediction.

Some experiments (Sutherland and Holgate, 1966) support the predictions based on analyzer theory that the strengths of different analyzers are negatively correlated. Our results indicate that a positive correlation may also be observed. While it is certainly premature to make any definitive statement, I would suggest that the following limitation on analyzer theory can reconcile this discrepancy. A negative correlation between different dimensional analyzers will develop only when stimuli representing the dimensions are presented concurrently in training, or when the elements of which the stimuli are composed have significant features in common. It is quite reasonable to suppose that stimuli from one dimension will be switched out if they are present while stimuli from another are switched in. Such a process is adaptive in the learning situation and would reflect some limitation on the organism's channel capacity. But this does not imply that the analyzer for one dimension needs to be switched out "in vacuo," as it were, in the absence of stimulus differences relevant to that analyzer.

This argument suggests a distinction between the effects of simultaneous and successive processing of stimulus inputs; simultaneous processing implies the *selection* of the input from one stimulus dimension among those available, while successive processing can involve the *sensitization* to stimuli lying on different dimensions. This distinction is supported by a comparison between the experiment of Newman and Baron (1965) and the current research. In their study, pigeons were trained to discriminate between red and green backgrounds of a white vertical line while the line was on the key. This procedure failed to enhance gradients obtained on the dimension of orientation. (It didn't flatten them either, as they were almost flat in a no-discrimination control condition.) Thus, extradimensional training had no effect when given the simultaneous presentation of stimuli lying on both dimensions. In our studies, of course, the successive presentation of stimuli from different dimensions has produced quite opposite results. It would be interesting to carry out an extradimensional training experiment of the kind reported here, but with the vertical lines present during the blue-green discrimination phase. In such a design, TD training might desensitize the subject to line orientation, and produce effects opposite to those obtained here.

A number of studies by Mackintosh (1962, 1964, 1965a) appear to contradict the principle suggested above. These have shown that preliminary training (and particularly overtraining) on one dimension reduces discriminative performance when non-reversal shifts are subsequently introduced. In general, *differences* on the dimension involved in secondary training (usually orientation) were not present in initial training (usually between brightnesses); the second dimension was not, therefore made explicitly irrelevant during initial training. But in all of these studies, the stimulus objects were rectangular, and the horizontal and vertical contours provided the stimulus elements on the basis of which the stimulus objects could be distinguished both in terms of brightness (contrast with the background) and shape (relative length of contours). Thus, while differences in orientation were not provided by the squares used in brightness discriminations, many of the stimulus elements necessary for the perception of orientation were certainly presented during this phase.

Even if these suggestions regarding the conditions necessary for a negative correlation between various analyzers should explain the discrepancies between such studies and the results reported in this paper, I feel that we still need an extension of analyzer theory to account for the attentional and memory effects. It is one thing to explain why true discriminations on color need not *reduce* subsequent control on the basis of orientation; it is another to suggest why it should *enhance* such control. In my view, attentional mechanisms must operate extradimensionally and thus somewhat more generally than Sutherland *et al.* have up to this point supposed (but see Sutherland and Andelman, 1967.) Although such a general action would detract somewhat from the specificity and thus from the elegance of their assumptions, it would by no means imply that the limits of attentional enhancement could not be empirically determined. The demonstration of experimental control over differences in the slopes of generalization gradients supports the empirical validity of the concept of attention, and provides some of the substantive background necessary for a valid incorporation of this concept into theories of learning.

Acknowledgements

I want to acknowledge the assistance of Mary Evelyn Porter, Paul Campbell, Donald Moors, and Cecily Honig, all of whom contributed to the research reported here. I am grateful to Dr. P. H. R. James for his careful reading of an earlier version of this chapter.

The research reported in this paper was supported by Grant APT-102 from the National Research Council of Canada.

References

Boneau, C. A. and Honig, W. K. (1964). Opposed generalization gradients based upon conditional discrimination training. *J. exp. Psychol.* **66**, 89–93.

Hanson, H. M. (1959). Effects of discrimination training on stimulus generalization *J. exp. Psychol.* **58**, 321–334.

Honig, W. K. (1962). Prediction of preference, transposition, and transposition-reversal from the generalization gradient. *J. exp. Psychol.* **64**, 239–248.

Jenkins, H. M. and Harrison, R. H. (1960). Effect of discrimination training on auditory generalization. *J. exp. Psychol.* **59**, 246–253.

Jenkins, H. M. and Harrison, R. H. (1962). Generalization gradients of inhibition following auditory discrimination learning. *J. exp. Anal. Behav.* **5**, 435–441.

Lawrence, D. H. (1949). Acquired distinctiveness of cues: 1. Transfer between discriminations on the basis of familiarity with the stimulus. *J. exp. Psychol.* **93**, 770–784.

Lovejoy, E. P. (1966). An analysis of the overlearning reversal effect. *Psychol. Rev.* **73**, 87–103.

Lyons, J. and Thomas, D. R. (1967). Effects of interdimensional training on stimulus generalization: II. Within-subjects design. *J. exp. Psychol.* **75**, 572–574.

Mackintosh, N. J. (1962). The effects of overtraining on a reversal and a non-reversal shift. *J. comp. physiol. Psychol.* **55**, 555–559.

Mackintosh, N. J. (1964). Overtraining and transfer within and between dimensions in the rat. *Quart. J. exp. Psychol.* **16**, 250–256.

Mackintosh, N. J. (1965a). The effect of attention on the slope of generalization gradients. *Brit. J. Psychol.* **56,** 87–93.

Mackintosh, N. J. (1965b). Selective attention in animal discrimination learning. *Psychol. Bull.* **64,** 124–150.

Newman, F. L. and Baron, M. R. (1965). Stimulus generalization along the dimension of angularity: A comparison of training procedures. *J. comp. Psychol.* **60,** 59–63.

Perkins, C. C. Jr., Hershberger, W. A. and Weyant, R. G. (1959). Difficulty of a discrimination as a determiner of subsequent generalization along another dimension. *J. exp. Psychol.* **57,** 181–186.

Reinhold, D. B. and Perkins, C. C. (1955). Stimulus generalization following different methods of training. *J. exp. Psychol.* **49,** 423–427.

Sutherland, N. S. (1964). The learning of discrimination by animals. *Endeavour,* **23,** 148–152.

Sutherland, N. S. and Andelman, L. (1967). Learning with one and two cues. *Psychon. Sci.* **7,** 107–108.

Sutherland, N. S. and Holgate, V. (1966). Two-cue discrimination learning in rats. *J. comp. physiol. Psychol.* **61,** 198–207.

Switalski, R. W., Lyons, J., and Thomas, D. R. (1966). Effects of interdimensional training on stimulus generalization. *J. exp. Psychol.* **72,** 661–666.

Terrace, H. S. (1966). *In* "Operant behavior", (W. K. Honig ed.), pp. 271–344, Appleton-Century-Crofts, New York, U.S.A.

Thomas, D. R. and Lopez, L. J. (1962). The effects of delayed testing on generalization slope. *J. comp. physiol. Psychol.* **55,** 541–544.

Stimulus Generalization versus Discrimination Failure in Conditioned Suppression

3

HOWARD S. HOFFMAN

The Pennsylvania State University, University Park, Pennyslvania, U.S.A.

I. The Theoretical Controversy

When a given response has come under the control of a particular stimulus, other stimuli which are similar will often exhibit the capacity to control that response. This phenomenon was initially investigated by Pavlov (1927), and in describing it he employed the label "stimulus generalization". During the four decades that have elapsed since Pavlov's original work, stimulus generalization has been the subject of numerous experiments (see Mostofsky, 1965), and it has also been the focus of a continuing theoretical controversy. The issue in question is whether or not the term "stimulus generalization" describes anything more than the observation that a subject has failed to discriminate among the stimuli in question (Lashley and Wade, 1946; Prokasy and Hall, 1963).

In part, the argument arises out of certain logical constraints imposed by the language. Stimulus generalization is mainfested when a subject makes the same response to different stimuli, but these are the identical observations that lead one to conclude that the subject is failing to discriminate.

After examining the historical background and the empirical data available at the time, Prokasy and Hall (1963) concluded that evidence for stimulus generalization as a construct distinct from discrimination failure was largely lacking. Accordingly, they suggested that use of the term "stimulus generalization" be avoided so that attention could focus on the factors responsible for discrimination (and/or the lack of it).

In spite of this suggestion, few, if any, investigators in the area have elected to abandon the terminology of stimulus generalization. There are two quite obvious reasons. First, the concept of stimulus generalization has great utility as an explanatory tool. Thus, by postulating stimulus generalization of both excitatory and inhibitory tendencies it has been possible to account for the results of numerous features of discrimination behavior under both appetitive controls (Spence, 1960; Hull, 1943) and aversive controls (Hoffman, in press). Second, for most investigators in the area, the language and concepts of stimulus generalization are so ubiquitous that their abandonment would require a radical revision in one's way of thinking.

Still, the issues raised by Lashley and Wade and by Prokasy and Hall are not merely academic, nor are they pedestrian, because despite the apparent utility of the concepts of stimulus generalization, we have not yet devised techniques for externalizing a subject's perceptions. Until we do so, we can never be sure that our subject is perceiving stimuli in the way we assume he is.

Over the past several years, however, data collected in the author's laboratory have consistently confirmed our impression that during tests for stimulus generalization the subject *is*, in fact, perceiving the differences among the several test stimuli. My purpose here is to examine those data for the light they can cast on the issue of whether or not stimulus generalization represents anything more than failure to discriminate.

II. The Phenomenon of Conditioned Suppression

In general, this research has focussed on an experimental analysis of the stimulus factors in conditioned suppression. The phrase "conditioned suppression" was initially used by Estes and Skinner (1941) in referring to the behavioral effects of a training history in which a neutral stimulus is consistently followed by an unavoidable noxious event. Given this history, it was observed that subsequent presentations of that stimulus will disrupt or otherwise interfere with ongoing positively reinforced behavior.

The bulk of the work in the author's laboratory has concerned itself with the manner in which conditioned suppression is mediated by stimuli which are like but not identical to the stimulus that was involved in the original training. This phenomenon, the "stimulus generalization of conditioned suppression", commanded special attention because it represents one of the mechanisms by which a history of aversive controls can affect large segments of an organism's behavior (Mednick, 1958).

Our approach has been to employ pigeons as subjects and key pecking on a variable interval schedule of food reinforcements as the baseline behavior. The choices were initially based upon practical considerations. Under properly arranged circumstances the key peck in pigeons can be a remarkably stable behavior. Moreover, substantial response rates can be readily generated. Both factors are obviously important when one seeks to establish a baseline for the assessment of suppression.

The decision as to the nature of the warning signal was also derived from practical considerations. We wanted a signal that did not require specific orienting behavior for its perception. Auditory stimuli seemed especially appropriate for this function. In addition, at the time, Jenkins and Harrison (1960) had just reported a study of auditory stimulus generalization in the pigeon using positive reinforcement only, and they had obtained very clean gradients. For these reasons we decided to use auditory signals as a warning of impending electrical shock, and like Jenkins and Harrison, we chose to measure stimulus generalization along the dimension of tonal frequency.

As a preliminary step, birds were trained to peck a standard Gerbrand's pigeon key on a variable interval schedule of food reinforcement, and they were concurrently adapted to the wing bands and swivel connector through which shocks would subsequently be delivered. (See Hoffman, 1960, for a description of the wing band technique for administering shock to pigeons, and see Fleshler and Hoffman, 1962, for a discussion of the type of schedule used to maintain key pecking.) Once the baseline rate of pecking was stable, subjects were periodically presented with the tone which, during conditioning, would be paired with shock. They also heard the several tones which subsequently would be employed in the tests for stimulus generalization. During this "adaptation" phase the tones were presented in random order (without shock) while the pigeon pecked the key for food. Since during adaptation the schedule of food reinforcement was independent of the schedule of tone presentation, reinforcement might occur at any time during either tone or silence. The purpose of the adaptation procedures was to mitigate any suppression which might be produced by the presentation of novel stimuli (i.e. the several different tones) during the subsequent tests for stimulus generalization. When the baseline rate was unaffected by the presence or absence of tone regardless of tone frequency, conditioned suppression procedures were initiated. In a given session, the subject ordinarily received two to four 1000 c.p.s. tones that ended with unavoidable electrical shock. Each tone had a duration of 125 seconds, with pulsing shock presented during the final five seconds. As during tone adaptation procedures, the schedule of food reinforcement was independent of other experimental events. Thus, food reinforcement might occur at any time during tone, during shock, and during the intervals between tones. In developing conditioned suppression, the typical session lasted approximately 70 minutes with tone presentations separated by at least 10 minutes. In most of the experiments discussed here subjects were exposed to 32 sessions of conditioning procedures with the sessions occuring every other day.

III. The Development of Conditioned Suppression

Figure 1 shows sample cumulative recordings from a single subject (Bird 15) during the acquisition of conditioned suppression to a 1000 c.p.s. tone. It illustrates the changes in performance that are observed during the several stages of conditioning. For a given stimulus the index of suppression is quantified as a ratio:

$$\text{Suppression Ratio} = \frac{\text{Pre-tone } R\text{'s minus Tone } R\text{'s}}{\text{Pre-tone } R\text{'s}}$$

where Pre-tone R's are equal to the number of responses in the 120 seconds of silence that ends with tone onset and Tone R's are equal to the number of responses during the 120 seconds of pre-shock tone.

As illustrated in Fig. 1, at the end of tone adaptation the peck rate is unaffected by tone presentation. Thus, the suppression ratio is typically very close to zero. In Session 8 the tone tends to disrupt the ongoing rate, and in the cumulative record shown, the suppression ratio equals ·47. By Session 20 the suppression ratio has increased to ·65, and by Session 32 the suppression ratio is ·80. As illustrated in Fig. 1 and documented in several papers (Hoffman and Fleshler, 1961; Hoffman, et al. 1966), the major effect of presenting a tone ending with electrical shock is that the rate during the warning period undergoes a decrease. Although there may be some disruption in the baseline during the initial stages of acquisition, after several sessions the baseline usually returns to its pre-acquisition level and thereafter stays relatively stable.

The stability of the baseline rate was illustrated in an experiment in which a sequence of tests for stimulus generalization of conditioned suppression was interrupted for 1·5 years (Hoffman et al. 1966). Both before and after the interruption the several birds exhibited wide individual differences in baseline rate, but for a given bird the rate after the rest

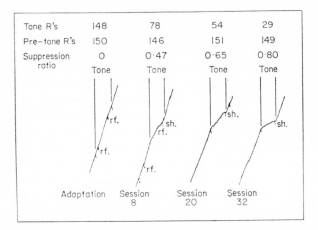

Tone R's	148	78	54	29
Pre-tone R's	150	146	151	149
Suppression ratio	0	0·47	0·65	0·80

FIG. 1. Sample cumulative recordings during the acquisition of conditioned suppression to a 1000 c.p.s. tone. Tone R refers to the number of responses during the 2-minute tone period. Pre-tone R refers to the number of responses in the 2-minute period that ended with tone onset. Adaptation refers to the final pre-acquisition session during which tone was presented without shock. The narrow, diagonal markings on the cumulative records indicate the beginning and end of the pre-shock warning interval; the broader markings reflect food reinforcements. *Sh.* refers to the point at which a 5-second sequence of shock pulses was delivered.

was within a few responses per minute of what it had been just prior to the initiation of the rest period (Hoffman and Selekman, 1967). The stability of the baseline rate and its insensitivity to the operations employed in generating and assessing conditioned suppression suggests that changes in rate during tone could readily be employed as an index of the effects of a given conditioning procedure. The use of a ratio for this index, however, provides a convenient control for the persistent individual differences in baseline rate among birds.

There are several details in Fig. 1 that deserve attention. Although the overall effect of repeated pairings of tone and shock is a reduction in the rate of pecking during tone, there is very little evidence of temporal discrimination. Tone onset is typically accompanied by an immediate reduction in rate, but thereafter the rate during tone tends to be relatively constant. In the early stages of conditioning, however, when reinforcement is delivered during tone (i.e. as occurred in Session 8), the rate following the reinforcement may return to the pre-tone level. Later on in the conditioning sequence, this effect is seldom seen.

Finally, as seen in Fig. 1, it is especially noteworthy that the development of conditioned suppression is a slow but nonetheless systematic process. On an intuitive basis one might expect that subjects would rapidly form the connection between tone presentation and the occurrence of electrical shock. Thus, they might be expected to exhibit suppression in an all or nothing fashion. Clearly, this is not the case. The tone slowly acquires the capacity to suppress behavior, and it does so in a fashion that suggests the gradual development of some form of S-R bond. When Estes and Skinner first developed the conditioned suppression paradigm, they described it as a technique for obtaining a quantitative measurement of anxiety. Subsequent investigators (for example, Brady and Hunt, 1955) have tended to agree with this proposition, but they have preferred to identify the learned reaction as a conditioned emotional response (CER). We too are inclined to interpret conditioned suppression as a reflection of a CER. Thus, through its repeated pairing with shock the warning signal acquires the capacity to evoke an anxiety-like CER, and the magnitude of the suppression effect on a given trial is conceived to be a reflection of the strength of the S-R bond between the warning signal and the CER.

A certain degree of caution must, however, be exercised in seeking to equate CER level with the magnitude of the suppression ratio. In general, the suppression ratio is a direct, simple measure of a relative performance decrement. However, measurement by relative suppression presupposes that under constant experimental conditions the warning signal will produce the same relative decrement independent of the rate of the responding at the moment of the warning signal presentation. The validity of this assumption has not been assessed.

A second factor of importance is that at some constant level of ongoing behavior, the suppression ratio is sensitive to only a particular range of variation in the emotional reaction controlled by the stimulus. While the ratio can assume negative values, it has a maximum of 1·00 and beyond this it does not vary with the strength of the CER. Moreover, within its range, the scale that best characterizes variation in the suppressing power of a stimulus is at present unknown; and the same scale might not be adequate for different levels of ongoing behavior or for behaviors that are maintained by different schedules and kinds of positive reinforcement. Although further research is needed if these scales are to be identified, it is convenient if not altogether correct to conceptualize the suppression ratio as a reflection of an underlying CER. In this sense suppression ratios with values near 1 are here conceived to reflect a strong CER, whereas ratios with values near zero are conceived to reflect weak CER's.

IV. Stimulus Generalization of Conditioned Suppression

Tests for stimulus generalization are typically begun at the completion of suppression training. In a given test session, tones with frequencies above, at, and below the frequency of the tone used in conditioning are presented *without shock* while the subject pecks the key on the previously established schedule of food reinforcement. In a given test session, the entire series of generalization test tones is presented with the order of tones randomized and the interval between tones approximately 10 minutes. The test tones ordinarily have the same duration as the pre-shock warning interval of the tones employed in conditioning, and their intensities are equated with each other and with the intensity of the tone used in conditioning (in most studies 88 dB re. ·0002 dynes per cm²).

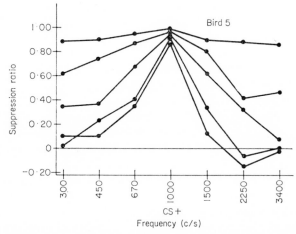

Fig. 2. Conditioned suppression as a function of tone frequency after conditioning procedures in which a 1000 c.p.s. tone served as a warning of impending electrical shock. Each gradient represents the data from five successive test sessions, and the sequence of gradients (from top to bottom) represent successive blocks of sessions. During these tests, no shocks occurred with any tones.

Figure 2 shows the gradients of stimulus generalization produced by a single subject (Bird 5) from one of our first experiments (Hoffman and Fleshler, 1961). For this bird, the conditioning procedures were essentially as described above, except that the warning period (i.e. the interval from the onset of the 1000 c.p.s. tone to the onset of the unavoidable shock) was 40 seconds. This subject received approximately 70 sessions of tone-shock pairings before shock was disconnected and tests for stimulus generalization were begun. Each gradient in Fig. 2 is averaged across five successive test sessions. At the beginning of testing, generalization of suppression was broad. As testing proceeded, however, the gradient gradually became steeper despite the fact that no shock occurred once testing began.

These findings seem to have several implications for the theoretical interpretation of stimulus generalization. First, and perhaps most importantly, we have in these functions a most dramatic example of a change in discrimination behavior with no prior or concurrent discrimination training. As seen in Fig. 2, initially the bird suppressed to all of the test stimuli, and it did so to an almost equal extent. Thus, an examination of the gradient from Sessions 1—5 would lead to the conclusion that although the bird was under the control of the tones (since suppression represents a change in performance in the presence of the tone), the dimension of tone frequency played little if any role in this control. In short, one could "explain" the gradient by assuming that the subject was attending to the tone but failing to attend to (and in this sense, discriminate along) the dimension of frequency. The data from test Sessions 21—25 suggest a different interpretation. Here suppression is again under the control of the stimulus used in the original conditioning, but stimuli on the wings of the generalization gradient do not exhibit any substantial degree of control over suppression. In essence, the subject now exhibits a fine degree of discrimination among the several stimuli. Finally, the gradients obtained during the sessions that intervened between the first and last sessions, reveal that the subject was also able to exhibit intermediate degrees of discrimination among the tones.

If stimulus generalization represents only failures in discrimination, we have in this experiment a subject which, after failing to discriminate, gradually and systematically acquires the capacity to perform a very nearly perfect discrimination. But how could subjects *acquire* discrimination behavior under the procedures used here? During testing, each of the tones was presented once in each session and none of the tones ended with electrical shock. Moreover, the several tones were always presented in random order. Thus, in the course of testing there was no specific set of experimental operations which could indicate which of the tones had previously been paired with shock. The events during adaptation to the several tones and those during the conditioning of suppression to the 1000 c.p.s. tone were equally antithetical to the formation of a discrimination among tones. The effect cannot be attributed to an artifact of averaging across subjects because all of the data were obtained from a single subject; nor can it be attributed to an artifact of averaging across stimuli in different sequences since there were sufficient sequences (25) so that any position effects that might exist would average out. Finally, it is noteworthy that the effect cannot be explained as the by-product of a generalized emotional reaction to the apparatus. An explanation of this sort would assume that during the initial test sequences the entire situation is aversive. Later, however, as sessions without shock accrue, the situation becomes less aversive and the subject is then able to attend to the dimension of frequency. The major difficulty with this account is that conditioned suppression consists of a departure from a baseline performance, and the stimuli that control the baseline performance are (with the exception of the tone itself) identical to situational stimuli during tone presentation. Since the baseline does not change appreciably during testing, it must be concluded that in the course of testing the situational stimuli underwent little, if any, change in aversiveness.

It would appear, therefore, that while the term "failure to discriminate" provides an adequate description of the broad generalization gradient obtained during the initial test sequence, use of that terminology leads to the conclusion that the bird subsequently *learned* to discriminate even though conditions were such as to prohibit that kind of learning.

V. A Theoretical Interpretation of Stimulus Generalization

One alternative to a "discrimination failure" explanation of these data involves the reasonable assumption that conditioning procedures produce lasting changes in the central nervous system. According to this view, the gradient of stimulus generalization is assumed to be a reflection of the nature of these changes. Indeed, Hull was suggesting this sort of thing when he assigned stimulus generalization the status of a postulate in his behavior system. The mathematical statement of this postulate is given by the equation:

$$s\overline{H}r = sHr\ e^{-j'd}$$

where sHr is the quantitative expression for the level of "habit strength" controlled by the stimulus that was employed in the original conditioning, and $s\overline{H}r$ is the level of habit strength controlled by a stimulus on the wing of the generalization gradient. Since in this equation d is expressed in multiples of the *jnd*, and since e and j are constants with values of 10 and approximately ·01 respectively, the expression asserts that the level of habit controlled by a stimulus on the wing of the generalization gradient is a negatively accelerated, decreasing function of the number of *jnd*'s separating that stimulus and the one used in conditioning the reaction.

VI. Neurophysiological Considerations in the Interpretation of Stimulus Generalization

In describing the construct for habit strength (sHr), Hull sought to convey the idea that the effect of reinforcing a given response in the presence of a given stimulus was to set up a connection in the nervous system whereby the afferent receptor discharge involved in conditioning is able to initiate the efferent discharge that controls the response system. Thus, the H in sHr refers to some form of physiological process whereby the afferent neural consequences of a stimulus are capable of initiating the efferent neural events that are responsible for the response. Stimulus generalization, according to this interpretation, represents a property of the nervous system such that the afferent neural consequences of stimuli which are similar, but not identical to the one employed in conditioning, are also able to initiate these effector discharges, but to a degree that is proportional to the similarity between the new stimuli and the one involved in conditioning.

Although Hull's conceptualization of sHr snd $s\overline{H}r$ was based on physiological considerations, the logic of his theorizing required only that the terms serve as intervening variables. Thus, the utility of his theory was in a sense independent of whether or not the constructs could, in fact, be identified in terms of known physiological processes; and indeed, at the time Hull developed his theory, direct evidence for such processes was unavailable. Recently, however, support for a neurophysiological interpretation of stimulus generalization has begun to appear in the literature.

Thompson (1962) reported that although normal cats exhibit a sharp gradient of stimulus generalization along the dimension of acoustic frequency, ablation of the auditory cortex results in a generalization gradient with zero slope. Since, as noted by Thompson, animals with this same kind of lesion can (given suitable procedures) be trained to discriminate frequency, the broad gradient produced by cortical ablation cannot be attributed to a breakdown of the discrimination process as such. Apparently, discrimination and stimulus generalization involve activity in different parts of the nervous system. In a later theoretical paper, Thompson (1965) employed an analysis of the response properties of the auditory neurons to derive remarkably accurate predictions of the generalization gradients exhibited by normal animals. Thus, the basic facts of stimulus generalization were derived from knowledge of the properties of the nervous system.

VII. Extinction Processes During Stimulus Generalization

These recent findings make it clear that the concept of stimulus generalization as something other than a failure of discrimination does no violence to current information about the properties of the central nervous system. Still, it remains to be shown that the concept of stimulus generalization can explain the progressive increases in the slope of the gradients shown in Fig. 2. One relatively direct way to account for this sharpening involves the assumption that the extinction curve for conditioned suppression is roughly ogival in shape. The data in Fig. 3 provide evidence for this proposition.

This figure shows the extinction of suppression for a bird (No. 22) who received the same training as Bird 5 but was then extinguished on the 1000 c.p.s. tone without either prior or concurrent tests for stimulus generalization. During each session, seven 1000 c.p.s. tones were presented without shock. Each point in the figure represents the mean

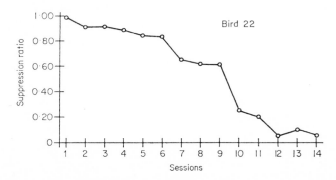

Fig. 3. Extinction of suppression to a 1000 c.p.s. tone only. In each session the 1000 c.p.s. tone was presented seven times without shock.

ratio per session. The tone lost its capacity to suppress very slowly, and the curve representing the extinction of suppression was roughly ogival.

Figure 4 illustrates how the progressive sharpening of the stimulus generalization gradient can be derived from the ogival shape of the extinction function for conditioned suppression. The upper half of Fig. 4 shows a hypothetical extinction function for conditioned suppression, and the top (relatively flat) gradient in the lower half of this figure shows a hypothetical gradient like those often obtained during the initial tests for stimulus generalization. The four other (progressively steeper) gradients in the lower half of Fig. 4 were derived by combining the information in the initial (relatively flat) gradient with the information provided by the hypothetical extinction function. If conditioned suppression extinguishes according to the function shown, and if (as in the present experiments) testing occurs during extinction, then for a given stimulus, the levels of suppression at a given stage in testing will depend upon

a) the level of suppression controlled by that stimulus at the start of testing, and,

b) the number of prior test (extinction) sessions.

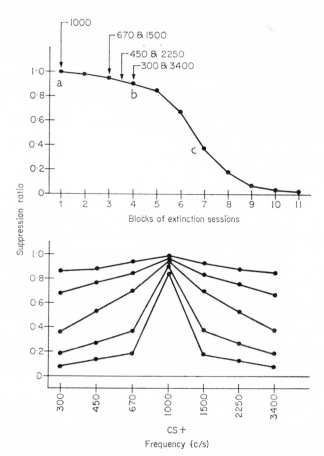

Fig. 4. Theoretical interpretation of the slope increases during tests for stimulus generalization. The top half of this figure shows a hypothetical extinction function for suppression. The arrows indicate the starting points for the extinction of the several test stimuli during a hypothetical series of test sessions. Their location is based on the assumption that an initial test for stimulus generalization yielded the levels (and hence starting points) seen in the relatively flat gradient shown in the botton half of this figure. The other functions in the bottom half of this figure were derived by assuming that during each block of test sessions, the level of suppression to a given stimulus declined by an amount indicated in the top theoretical extinction function. Thus, at the start of testing, the level of suppression to the 1000 c.p.s. tone is indicated by the ordinate at (a). After three blocks of tests, however, the level of suppression to this tone is given by the ordinate at (b). The 300 and 3400 c.p.s. tones, on the other hand, initially control the levels of suppression given by the ordinate at (b). After three blocks of tests, however, the levels of suppression controlled by these tones is given by the ordinate at (c).

The arrows in the top half of Fig. 4 indicate hypothetical starting points for the several test stimuli, based on the levels of suppression presumably controlled by the several stimuli during the initial test sequence. If, in the course of tests used to obtain a given gradient, all stimuli move one full step to the right along the extinction function, then if a given stimulus starts extinction rather close to the point where the function begins its accelerated drop, that stimulus will begin to lose its control over suppression much more rapidly than will a stimulus that begins extinction with only a slightly higher level of control over suppression.

The four lower gradients in the bottom half of Fig. 4 represent the theoretically expected levels of suppression to each of the several test stimuli after one, two, three, and four blocks of extinction sessions. As can be seen in Fig. 3, the slopes of these theoretical generalization gradients gradually increase and the effect is almost identical to the slope changes in the data produced by Bird 5.

On the basis of this rather straightforward derivation it would seem reasonable to suppose that the progressive sharpening of the generalization gradient during extinction tests may have little, if anything, to do with the subject's capacity to discriminate among the tones. As has been seen, what appears to be the acquisition of a discrimination can be readily explained as a product of the nature of the extinction process for conditioned suppression. If, however, the sharpening does not represent the *acquisition* of a discrimination, it follows that during the initial test sequence when the subject exhibited almost equal suppression to the several test tones, it did so despite the capacity to discriminate among them.

VIII. Long Term Effects in Stimulus Generalization

Additional evidence for the proposition that stimulus generalization represents more than a failure to discriminate is seen in the performance of a second pigeon (Bird 9) that was exposed to the same key peck training, tone adaptation, and conditioned suppression procedures as Bird 5.

Figure 5 provides a 3-dimensional representation of the course of extinction of conditioned suppression for Bird 9 during an extended and somewhat complex sequence of tests for stimulus generalization. As with other birds in our laboratory, once testing was initiated, the use of shock at the end of the tone was discontinued   In each test session the tone used in conditioning (1000 c.p.s.) along with tones with frequencies above and below 1000 c.p.s. were presented in random order while the bird continued to peck the key on the previously established variable interval schedule of food reinforcement.

Like Bird 5, Bird 9 exhibited a broad gradient during the initial block of test sessions, and as with Bird 5, the slope of Bird 9's gradient gradually

increased as testing proceeded. Moreover, as seen in Fig. 5, throughout
this and subsequent test procedures, the baseline peck rate (as measured
by the number of responses in the several 40 second pre-tone periods)
remained quite stable. Thus, as suggested earlier, the major effect of
the procedures used here was visible in the subject's rate during tone
but not in his rate during silence. At the completion of the first sequence

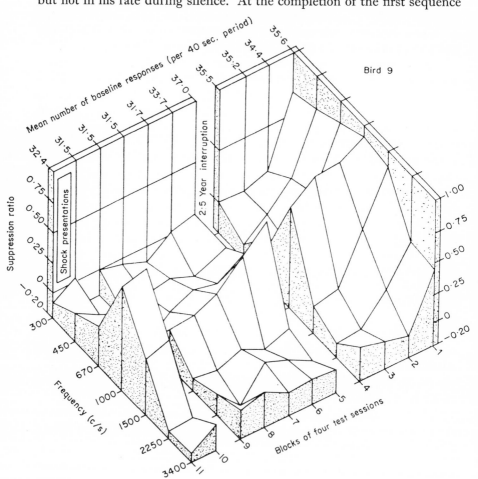

FIG. 5. Extinction of suppression after conditioning procedures in which a 1000 c.p.s.
tone ending with shock was repeatedly presented while the bird pecked a key for food.
In each test session, all seven tone frequencies were presented (without shock) while
the bird pecked the key. The figures along the upper border indicate the average number
of key pecks during the 28 pre-tone periods in each block of four test sessions. Shock
presentations refers to a sequence of test sessions during which a brief shock was administered in the middle of a sequence of 2-minute periods of total darkness that occurred
between the several tones.

of test sessions, Bird 9 was returned to its loft where it remained for 2·5 years. During this period the bird had continuous access to food and water, and was not exposed to any experimental procedures. At the conclusion of this lengthy interruption, the bird was again subjected to restricted feeding until body weight dropped to 80% of its average level. Next, the bird was run on the previously established variable interval schedule for 10 sessions, each of which lasted approximately 2 hours. This was done in order to reestablish a stable baseline of pecking. No tones were presented during these sessions, and during these as well as during the test sessions which followed, the shock connector was in place, but no shocks were presented.

When the baseline was stable, testing was resumed. As before, during each session the entire series of seven tones was presented in random order. As can be seen in Fig. 5, the effects of the 2·5 year interruption are virtually identical to the effects of the 48 hours that ordinarily intervened between test sessions. Clearly time, in and of itself, had no appreciable influence on the gradient of generalization. As testing was continued however, and the tones were repeatedly presented without any aversive consequences, extinction of suppression proceeded until it reached the point where only the 1000 c.p.s. tone produced any suppression at all, and the degree of suppression it controlled was slight.

At that time it had been almost 3 years since Bird 9 had experienced electrical shock. For this reason it seemed possible, that if the bird was again exposed to shock it might again exhibit suppression to the several tones. The two final gradients in Fig. 5 were obtained in a series of eight additional test sessions in which brief unsignalled electrical shocks were administered during a sequence of two minute time-outs (periods of total darkness) that occurred in the middle of the 10 minute intervals of silence that intervened between tones. Since pecking always ceased during darkness, the administration of a shock in the midst of each of the time-outs minimized the tendency for Bird 9 to form a direct association between shock and either the tones or the behavior of pecking. Moreover, since the time-outs with shock were distributed evenly throughout the test sessions, the relationship of tone to shock was uniform across tones.

Inspection of Fig. 5 reveals that the shock presentations resulted in an immediate recovery of the tendency for the tones to suppress key pecking. Thus, during the sessions involving shock presentations both the 1000 c.p.s. tone and the two tones adjacent to it controlled suppression, whereas in the final sessions prior to shock presentation only the 1000 c.p.s. tone yielded any suppression at all. This enhancement effect is especially relevant to interpretations of the processes responsible for stimulus generalization because it represents an instance in which the subject gives evidence of the capacity to discriminate *prior* to exhibiting a performance in which the discrimination is less well defined. Data such as these provide strong presumptive evidence for the proposition that subjects may fail to discriminate despite the fact that the stimuli are perceived as different.

Although there are probably numerous potential explanations of the effects of shocks during time-outs, the one most compatible with a theoretical analysis of stimulus generalization is that the shocks partially reinstated the overall motivational conditions that were contributing to suppression.

In the suppression paradigm, however, there is a second motivational condition that can presumably play a role in determining the magnitude of suppression: namely, the motivation for the ongoing behavior. In the present circumstances, this second motivational state can be controlled by manipulating the subject's body weight through restricted feeding. Fig. 6 shows the effects of manipulating a pigeon's body weight in the course of a series of tests for generalization of conditioned suppression. It represents data from the initial six test sessions for a bird (Bird 11) that was exposed to the same conditioning procedures as Birds 5 and 9. Like Birds 5 and 9, during conditioning this subject was maintained at

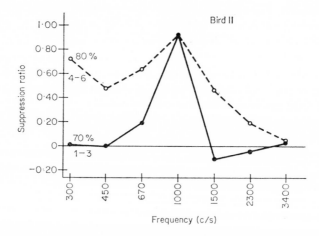

Fig. 6. Conditioned suppression as a function of tone frequency after conditioning procedures in which a 1000 c.p.s. tone served as a warning of impending electrical shock. Each gradient is based on the data from three test sessions where, in each session, the entire series of seven tones was presented in random order without shock. The solid gradient was obtained during Sessions 1–3 when the bird was maintained at 70% of its *ad libitum* body weight. The dashed gradient was obtained later (during Sessions 4–6) when the bird's body weight had been raised to 80% of its *ad libitum* level.

80% of its previously established *ad libitum* body weight. However, following conditioning but prior to testing, the bird's weight was gradually reduced to 70% of its *ad libitum* level. Next, the bird was exposed to three sessions of generalization testing (without shock). Finally, the bird's weight was increased back to 80% of its *ad libitum* level, and when the weight was stable, testing was resumed.

Figure 6 shows the gradients at the two different levels of body weight. The initial gradient (obtained when the bird was highly motivated for the ongoing behavior, i.e. when the bird was maintained at 70% *ad libitum* body weight) is quite sharp and indeed, the bird exhibits an almost perfect discrimination between the tone used in training (1000 c.p.s.) and the other generalization test tones. Later, however, when the bird's weight was increased to 80% of its *ad libitum* level, the gradient was much broader.

Apparently, like the presentation of shock during time-outs, manipulation of the bird's body weight can lead to a performance in which the subject gives clear behavioral evidence of the capacity to discriminate *prior* to exhibiting an apparent inability to make the same discrimination. Descriptions of stimulus generalization which postulate discrimination failure as the central explanatory concept hardly seem appropriate in view of data such as these.

IX. A Test of the Discrimination Failure Hypothesis

Finally, it can be noted that if "discrimination failure" is indeed basic to the kinds of data obtained in generalization experiments, one ought to be able to develop experimental procedures for manipulating the subject's tendencies to discriminate in much the same way that researchers have sought to manipulate the subject's tendencies to generalize.

For example, one way to explain a subject's failure to discriminate between a test stimulus and the stimulus employed in a prior acquisition sequence involves the assumption that the subject has not learned to attend to the appropriate dimensions of the stimulus. Thus, it is possible to explain a performance in which a subject exhibits suppression to a 450 c.p.s. tone after conditioning to a 1000 c.p.s. tone by hypothesizing that during conditioning, the subject attended to the presence of tone but failed to attend to the dimension of tone frequency. Fortunately, this explanation can be directly investigated by examining the effects of conditioning procedures that are specifically designed to eliminate the relevance of tone frequency as a cue for impending shock. An experiment of this sort provides a specific test for the "discrimination failure" hypothesis because it sets the occasion for discrimination failure to occur in its most exaggerated form.

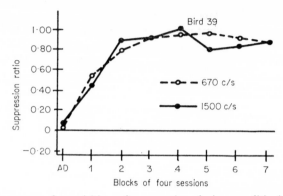

Fig. 7. The course of acquisition of suppression during conditioning procedures in which both a 670 and a 1500 c.p.s. tone served as a warning of impending electrical shock. AD refers to a sequence of tone adaptation sessions prior to conditioning in which the entire series of seven test tones was presented (without shock) while the bird pecked the key for food.

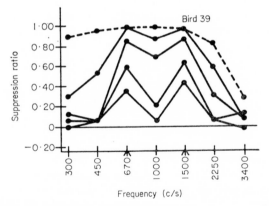

Fig. 8. Conditioned suppression as a function of tone frequency after conditioning procedures in which both a 670 and a 1500 c.p.s. tone served as a warning of impending shock. Each gradient is based on data from four test sessions, where in each session, the entire series of seven tones was presented in random order without shock. The dashed gradient was obtained in Sessions 1–4, and the other (descending) gradients were obtained in successive blocks of four sessions.

Figures 7 and 8 show the results of one such experiment. Figure 7 shows the levels of suppression during acquisition when a subject (Bird 39) received six 2-minute tones ending with shock on each conditioning session; three of the tones had a frequency of 670 c.p.s. and three had a frequency of 1500 c.p.s. The order of the tones was randomly varied from session to session, and the tones were equated for intensity.

As seen in Fig. 7, the effect of these procedures was to develop a performance in which both tones produced the same level of suppression. Figure 8 shows Bird 39's gradients of generalization throughout a sequence of 20 test sessions in which each of the seven test tones were presented in random order without shock. As in previous experiments, the gradient of stimulus generalization gradually steepened during the extinction tests, but in the present instance the gradients tended to exhibit two peaks (at the frequencies of the tones that previously were paired with shock).

The implications of these findings for the "discrimination failure" hypothesis becomes apparent when one considers that the gradients were a product of procedures that should, in principle, eliminate tone frequency as a relevant cue for the occurrence of impending shock. During conditioning, shock was paired with both the 1500 and 670 c.p.s. tones. The expected effect of this procedure (according to a "discrimination failure" explanation of stimulus generalization) would be to establish a condition whereby either tone onset, or tone presence, might acquire control over suppression, but tone frequency would be irrelevant to that control. The performance of Bird 39 throughout acquisition (Fig. 7) is consistent with this interpretation, as is his relatively flat gradient during the initial test sessions. If, however, these procedures had eliminated tone frequency as a relevant dimension, it would be predicted that the flat gradient would gradually move downward in the course of extinction. Figure 7 shows that this does not happen. On the contrary, the gradients gradually sharpen in a fashion similar to the sharpening obtained when subjects have been conditioned to suppress to a single tone.

As was seen earlier, the concept of stimulus generalization is able to provide a reasonable account of such sharpening. Since the discrimination failure hypothesis cannot do so, it must be concluded that the concept of stimulus generalization provides the better explanatory structure.

X. Conclusions

I have tried to relate some of the findings on conditioned suppression to the broad issues involved in the theoretical interpretation of stimulus generalization. An analysis of the performance of individual subjects in several kinds of experiments has led to the conclusion that generalization gradients are not merely the result of a "failure of discrimination".

Since the concept of stimulus generalization can satisfactorily account for the same data, it is apparent that stimulus generalization is both a viable and useful construct. Obviously, like other theoretical approaches, the concept of stimulus generalization can only provide approximations to the empirical world, and certainly, as more data are collected these approximations may prove less than adequate. Still, the value of any theoretical approach lies in its capacity to provide an organized structure within which a myriad of complex data can be systematically and thoughtfully viewed. At present, it appears that the concept of stimulus generalization does this quite efficiently.

Acknowledgement

This research was supported by National Institute of Mental Health grant numbers MH 02433–08 and MH 23824.

References

Brady, J. V. and Hunt, H. F. (1955). An experimental approach to the analysis of emotional behaviour. *J. Psychol.* **40**, 313–324.

Estes, W. K. and Skinner, B. F. (1941). Some quantitative properties of anxiety. *J. exp. Psychol.* **29**, 390–400.

Fleshler, M. and Hoffman, H. S. (1962). A progression for generating variable-interval schedules. *J. exp. Anal. Behav.* **5**, 529–530.

Hoffman, H. S. (1960). A flexible connector for delivering shock to pigeons. *J. exp. Anal. Behav.* **3**, 330.

Hoffman, H. S. (1968). *In* "Punishment" (Campbell, B. and Church R. eds.). Appleton-Century-Crofts, Inc. New York.

Hoffman, H. S. and Fleshler, M. (1961). Stimulus factors in aversive control: the generalization of conditioned suppression. *J. exp. Anal. Behav.* **4**, 371–378.

Hoffman, H. S., Selekman, W. and Fleshler, M. (1966). Stimulus aspects of aversive controls: long term effects of suppression procedures. *J. exp. Anal. Behav.* **9**, 659–662.

Hoffman, H. S. and Selekman, W. (1967). Stability of response rates maintained by positive reinforcement. *Perceptual and Motor Skills*, **24**, 91–93.

Hull, C. L. (1943). "Principles of Behavior, An Introduction to Behavior Theory". Appleton-Century-Crofts, Inc. New York.

Jenkins, H. M. and Harrison, R. H. (1960). Effect of discrimination training on auditory generalization. *J. exp. Psychol.* **59**, 246–253.

Lashley, K. S. and Wade, M. (1946). The Pavlovian theory of generalization. *Psychol. Rev.* **53**, 72–87.

Mednick, S. A. (1958). A learning theory approach to research in schizophrenia. *Psychol. Bull.* **55**, 316.

Mostofsky, D. I. Ed. (1965). "Stimulus Generalization". Stanford University Press. Stanford, California. U.S.A.

Pavlov, I. P. (1927). "Conditioned Reflexes". (G. V. Anrep translator) Oxford University Press. London.

Prokasy, W. F. and Hall, J. F. (1963). Primary stimulus generalization. *Psychol. Rev.* **70**, 310–322.

Spence, K. W. (1960). "Behavior Theory and Learning". Prentice-Hall, Inc. Englewood Cliffs, New Jersey. U.S.A.

Thompson, R. F. (1962). Role of the cerebral cortex in stimulus generalization. *J. comp. physiol. Psychol.* **55**, 279–287.

Thompson, R. F. (1965). The neural basis of stimulus generalization *In* "Stimulus Generalization" (Mostofsky, D. I. ed.). Stanford University Press, Stanford, California. U.S.A.

4 | Incidental Stimuli and Discrimination Learning

ALLAN R. WAGNER

Yale University, New Haven, Connecticut, U.S.A.

I. Introduction

Any discrimination learning situation contains many separate descriptive features to which a subject potentially can learn to respond, and which hence may be referred to as "cues" or "stimulus elements". Discrimination learning can then be viewed as a process by which a subject's behavior comes under the control of those stimulus elements in the discriminanda which are correlated with the presence versus absence of reinforcement, as compared to those which are relatively uncorrelated with reinforcement.

The present chapter will be devoted primarily to discussing the properties of those stimulus elements which, in a discrimination learning situation are relatively uncorrelated with the receipt of reinforcement, and hence are frequently referred to as "irrelevant" or "incidental". Although the systematic issues involved have general implications for discrimination theory, a number of points may be made rather succinctly, by concentrating on the characteristics of such "incidental" stimuli. The organization of the chapter will entail first a brief discussion of two contrasting theoretical treatments of incidental stimuli. Attention will then be directed to several experimental investigations from our laboratory which offer new evidence concerning the role of incidental stimuli in discrimination

learning. Finally, the significance of these and other recent findings for
theories of discrimination learning will be discussed.

II. Two Contrasting Treatments of Incidental Stimuli

For present purposes, it is important to distinguish between two classes
of discrimination theories, i.e. between so-called *conditioning-extinction*
theory and *stimulus-selection* theory.

A.   CONDITIONING-EXTINCTION THEORY

Conditioning-extinction theory is perhaps best known in the form
proposed by Spence (e.g. 1936) and adopted by Hull (e.g. 1950). According to such theory, the behavior eliciting property of any stimulus element
may be understood in terms of the reinforcement schedule associated
with that element, or at least (to acknowledge the role of stimulus generalization) with that and similar elements.

Each reinforcement is assumed to add to the excitatory strength of an
element (conditioning) and each non-reinforcement to subtract from
that strength (extinction) according to specified functions, such that an
element consistently associated with reinforcement will eventually tend
to elicit the learned response, whereas an element consistently associated
with non-reinforcement will eventually tend not to elicit the response.
These processes are assumed to apply equally to all stimulus elements
in a discrimination situation including those which are not specifically
arranged to be correlated with reinforcement. Thus, for example, in a
two-choice, black-white discrimination problem in which each brightness
element is scheduled to occur equally often to the right and to the left of
the other, the behavior eliciting characteristics of each spatial cue should
be determined by the additive effects of the number of reinforcements
and non-reinforcements actually experienced in its presence.

In his earliest articles (e.g. 1936, 1937) describing this theoretical
approach, Spence attempted to show that irrelevant cues, such as those
of position in the above example, may become equalized in excitatory
strength, may become more separated in strength, or may remain unchanged during training. But, in any event, he considered the separate
terminal strengths to be derivable on the basis of their initial, pretraining
value and the specific schedule of reinforcement with which they were
associated during training. Spence, in fact, was able to account for a
sizeable number of phenomena in the area of *selective learning* on the
basis of such a theory, by assuming that a subject will respond consistently
to the discriminanda in terms of the relevant stimulus elements, only
when the difference in excitatory strength between the relevant elements

is large enough to offset differences in the excitatory strength of "irrelevant" elements.

In 1950 Hull presented what he termed "[his own] interpretation of Spence's extension and formalization of Pavlov's analysis of discrimination learning", (1950, p. 303). In addition to establishing the genealogy of the theoretical approach involved, the article is presently noteworthy for several reasons. First, while Spence was primary concerned with selective discrimination learning, Hull attempted to deal with certain phenomena from differential conditioning or, as it is also termed, GO, NO-GO discrimination learning. Since the data to be discussed in the present chapter are drawn from such situations, Hull's theoretical observations are particularly relevant. Secondly, among the writings of conditioning-extinction theorists, Hull's article provides a uniquely detailed treatment of incidental stimuli, and clearly reveals the significant role which such stimuli are presumed to play, in determining the observed behavioral control of relevant, discriminative cues.

In simple differential conditioning the subject is typically presented with two discriminanda on separate occasions, and is reinforced for responding in the presence of one and nonreinforced in the presence of the other. Hull pointed out that although each discriminandum is typically arranged so as to include a different member from some specified (relevant) stimulus continuum, e.g. black versus white, each also will invariably contain many stimulus elements which are common to the two discriminanda, such as size, spatial location, etc. Designating the relevant elements which are consistently reinforced or nonreinforced as S_1 and S_2, respectively, and the common or incidental stimuli as S_c, the subject must then learn to respond to S_1S_c, but not to respond to S_2S_c.

If the measure of discrimination performance is the degree to which the subject responds to S_1S_c but does not respond to S_2S_c, it is clear that the response tendencies to S_c may appreciably determine the degree of discrimination observed. In an obvious case, suppose that S_c were capable, itself, of always eliciting a response, whenever presented. Then even if S_1 had appreciable response strength, and S_2 none, the differential tendencies would go undetected as the subject would consistently respond to both S_1S_c and S_2S_c.

The exact influence that is to be expected upon discrimination performance as a result of variations in S_c strength depends in many instances upon other characteristics of the theory. But, if it is assumed (e.g. Hull, 1943) that response strength must be above some threshold value before a response will occur, it can also be seen that some value of response strength to S_c greater than zero may under some circumstaces *favor* the detection of differential tendencies to S_1 and S_2. This would occur, for example, if S_1 and S_2 were associated with differential, but sub-threshold strengths so that no responding would occur to either S_1 or S_2 in isolation. The addition of response strength associated with S_c might then raise the excitatory strengths of $S_1 S_c$ and $S_2 S_c$ above the threshold so as to reveal the differential tendencies, in a greater likelihood of respond-ing to the former than to the latter complex.

Consistent with a conditioning-extinction theory approach, Hull assumed that the response strength to stimulus elements occupying the place of S_c in a discrimination situation would eventually come to reflect the additive and cancelling effects of the number of reinforcements and nonreinforcements with which they were associated, as a result of the reinforcement of $S_1 S_c$ and the nonreinforcement of $S_2 S_c$. While the response strength accruing to S_c in any situation might thus best be left as an empirical matter, depending upon the relative magnitudes of the conditioning and extinction effects involved, Hull suggested that, given an equal number of reinforcements and nonreinforcements, the excitatory strength of S_c would generally approach zero, so that, "the effective reaction potential under the control of the incidental stimuli will for most purposes gradually become relatively neutral and unimportant in the determination of overt action". (1950, p. 307.)

On the basis of knowledge available to Hull concerning the effects of partial reinforcement schedules—a 50% reinforcement schedule may produce an appreciable response tendency (Humphreys, 1939)—Hull's "neutralization" assumption appears rather gratuitous. Nonetheless, on the basis of this assumption, Hull proposed that one could account for certain cases of transfer of training in discrimination learning, and for instances of the steepening of generalization gradients with discrimina-tion training—two general phenomena to which attention will later be directed.

B. STIMULUS-SELECTION THEORY

The distinguishing characteristic of stimulus-selection theories is that a potential cue, or stimulus element, is viewed as competing with other available elements for the behavioral effects resulting from reinforcement and nonreinforcement.

One such theory has been proposed by Sutherland (1964) and Mackin-tosh (1965a), and is based upon the following tenets: (a) behavior con-trolled by an environmental cue is assumed to be mediated by a stimulus-selection mechanism (stimulus-analyzer), such that if an appropriate analyzer is not "switched-in" the cue will be ineffective either in eliciting a previously learned response or in acquiring new response tendencies as a result of reinforcement or nonreinforcement; (b) the likelihood that a given analyzer will be switched-in is assumed to depend, first, upon the *validity* of its outputs ("on differences in its outputs being consistently associated with the subsequent occurrence of events of importance to the animal", (Sutherland, 1964, p. 57); (c) the likelihood that a given analyzer will be switched-in is assumed also to depend inversely on the validity of the outputs of other analyzers, since the subject is assumed to be capable of attending simultaneously to only a limited number of cues, i.e. of having only a limited number of analyzers switched-in.

The general treatment of discrimination learning proposed by Restle (1955) incorporates a similar stimulus-selection mechanism, in the assumption that *adaptation* (or *neutralization*, Restle, 1959) occurs as a special process, separate from the incremental and decremental (conditioning) effects of reinforcement and non-reinforcement. Specifically, a cue is assumed to be "neutralized", i.e. lose its ability to control behavior, in proportion to the number and validity of cues more highly correlated with reinforcement.

In the present context, such proposals are alike in suggesting that the response eliciting properties of an incidental element in a discriminandum depends not only on the reinforcement schedule associated with the presence versus absence of that element, but also on the validity of the other available elements. Considering the case in which a subject is consistently reinforced in the presence of S_1S_c and consistently non-reinforced in the presence of S_2S_c, regardless of the response tendencies that would otherwise accrue to S_c as a result of a similar number of reinforcements and nonreinforcements, the presence of S_1 and S_2 which are more highly correlated with the reinforcement schedule, should serve to neutralize, or reduce the behavioral influence of S_c.

Recent stimulus-selection theories, no less than conditioning-extinction theories, have acknowledged the importance of irrelevant or incidental stimuli in determining discrimination performance. Restle, for example, in a series of theoretical papers (e.g. 1955, 1958, 1959) has attempted to show how a variety of discrimination phenomena, including so-called transfer-along-a-continuum, and the acquisition of learning-sets may be accounted for in terms of the differential neutralization of incidental cues.

The important issue between conditioning-extinction theory and stimulus-selection theory accounts of incidental stimuli is then, whether the behavioral tendencies commanded by such stimuli can be accounted for solely in terms of the reinforcement schedule with which they have been associated, or whether it is necessary also to take into account the number and validity of elements more highly correlated with reinforcement.

III. Experimental Evidence

A series of recent studies from our laboratory has been concerned with the role of incidental stimuli in differential conditioning. The initial studies were designed to evaluate conflicting expectations based upon conditioning-extinction theory, as compared to stimulus-selection theory. The later studies may perhaps best be viewed as demonstrations of the important role played by incidental stimuli in relationship to two discrimination phenomena which have been of some theoretical interest.

A. EVALUATIONS OF THE CONTRASTING THEORIES

Suppose that subjects are presented with each of two stimulus compounds, $S_1 S_c$ and $S_2 S_c$, on an equal number of separate occasions, and it is arranged that the number of reinforcements and nonreinforcements in the presence of S_c is the same for all subjects. According to conditioning-extinction theory the response strength accruing to S_c should not depend upon how the reinforcements are distributed between presentations of the two discriminanda, whereas according to stimulus-selection theory the distribution of reinforcements should be of major importance, as it would determine the validities of S_1 and S_2, and hence the degree of neutralization of S_c.

Wagner, *et al.* (1968) reported three variations of an experimental design based on the above reasoning. In each experiment, two stimulus compounds ($A_1 L$ and $A_2 L$) were formed from a constant visual element (L) and either of two auditory elements (A_1 or A_2). The two compounds were equally often presented, with half of the total presentations scheduled to be followed by reinforcement, and reinforcement was withheld in the absence of the compounds. The L component thus always had the same number of reinforcements and nonreinforcements in its presence and the same correlation with reinforcement (validity); its presence being associated with a 50% reinforcement schedule, its absence with no reinforcement. Two treatments within each experiment differed with respect to the validity of the auditory components of the compounds. In the *Correlated* condition, the compound containing A_1 always signaled reinforcement, whereas the compound containing A_2 was always nonreinforced. In the *Uncorrelated* condition, the compounds containing A_1 and A_2 were each equally as often associated with reinforcement and nonreinforcement. Thus, in the Uncorrelated treatment the occurrence of A_1 or A_2 provided no better basis than the occurrence of L for predicting reinforcement, whereas in the Correlated treatment the occurrence of A_1 was a more reliable predictor of reinforcement.

Following training all subjects were administered test trials on which L was presented alone, and the frequency of response to this element was evaluated as a function of the two treatment conditions. Simply on the basis of its correlation with reinforcement L alone should have been similarly responded to under the two conditions. However, if the effectiveness of L were inversely related to the validity of the auditory elements, as suggested by stimulus-selection theories, it should have produced less responding in the Correlated than in the Uncorrelated condition.

Experiment I employed rats in a discrete-trial bar-pressing situation, the compounds signaling the availability of food reward. Training and testing were conducted in an operant conditioning chamber, with two ceiling lamps serving as the light cue (L), and moderately intense tones of 1000 and 2500 Hz serving as the auditory cues (A_1 and A_2).

For all subjects a compound was scheduled to occur approximately once per minute, with A_1L and A_2L each presented on 50% of the trials according to an irregular sequence. A compound was terminated by a bar-press, or in the absence of a response, after 5 seconds. A reward pellet was scheduled to be delivered for a response on 50% of the compound presentations while bar-pressing in the absence of an AL compound was never reinforced; in fact, stimulus onset was delayed until the subject failed to bar-press during a 15-sec pre-onset interval.

Data were collected from 8 subjects assigned initially to the Correlated training condition in which a bar press was rewarded in the presence of A_1L but not A_2L, and from 8 subjects assigned initially to the Uncorrelated condition in which reinforcement was obtainable in the presence of both A_1L and A_2L according to a random 50% schedule. For half of the subjects in each group the 2500 Hz tone was designated as A_1 and the 1000 Hz tone as A_2. For the remaining subjects the two frequencies were reversed.

After 40 minutes of the fifth or sixth two-hour training session, the regular sequence of trials was interrupted every 6 trials for test presentations of either A_1, A_2, or L alone in balanced orders, until 8 trials with each were run. As in the case of the compounds, the element was terminated at the end of 5 seconds, or by a response, but all test trials were nonreinforced.

Following the testing described, half of the subjects in each group were continued on the same program they experienced during Stage I, while half were switched to the opposite program. After eight 1·5-hr daily training sessions in Stage II, a second test sequence was administered similar to that given after Stage I.

Figure 1 depicts the mean percentage responses on L alone trials during Stage I and Stage II test sessions for only those subjects in Experiment I which received both Correlated and Uncorrelated training in the two orders. Also presented for comparison are the similar percentages on A_1 and A_2 alone trials, as well as on compound training trials, within the same sessions for the two groups.

During Stage I, Correlated training resulted in appreciably less L responding than did Uncorrelated training. Not only was the size of this difference substantial, but it was strikingly stable across subjects. There

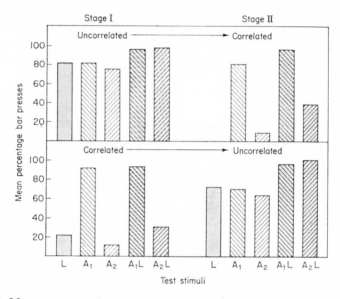

FIG. 1. Mean percentage bar presses to elements and compounds in two separate test sessions for groups of rats receiving first Uncorrelated and then Correlated training, or first Correlated and then Uncorrelated training. (Wagner, *et al.* 1968, Experiment I.)

was no overlap in the distribution of number of L responses in the two groups of 8 subjects receiving the different treatments, an observation which is associated with a chance probability of less than ·005 (Fisher's exact test.)

During Stage II, those subjects in the two groups which were continued under their original training schedule (and whose data are not included in Figure 1) continued to respond to L in a manner similar to that in Stage I. In contrast, the subjects in the two shifted groups evidenced a dramatic change in L responding in accordance with the schedule change. As may be seen in Figure 1, those subjects shifted from Correlated to Uncorrelated training greatly inccreased their number of responses to L, while subjects shifted from Uncorrelated to Correlated training sizeably decreased their number of responses to L.

Of the 8 shifted subjects whose L scores were available, following both Correlated and Uncorrelated training, all 8 gave fewer L responses following Correlated training than following Uncorrelated training ($p = \cdot008$, sign test) regardless of the order of experience with the two schedules.

Experiment II made use of a conditioned emotional response (CER) procedure, in which the compounds signaled the occurrence of unavoidable electric shock. Training and testing were conducted in an operant conditioning chamber, with 1/sec flashes, generated by an overhead strobe lamp, serving as the light cue (L) and moderately intense 4000 and 400 Hz tones serving as the auditory cues (A_1 and A_2).

Rats were first trained to bar press on a variable interval food reinforcement schedule (VI-1 min) and then subjected to CER training, during daily 1·5 hr bar-pressing sessions in which the food schedule remained in effect. At first four, then eight conditioning trials were included in each of the CER training sessions.

A CER training trial consisted of a 3-minute presentation of an AL compound which on 50% of the occasions terminated with a ·5-sec 1-mA foot shock. In each block of four trials two A_1L and two A_2L compounds were irregularly presented in the various possible orders: under Correlated training the two A_1L trials were followed by shock and the two A_2L trials were not, whereas under Uncorrelated training one A_1L and one A_2L trial were followed by shock.

Each of four subjects was sequentially subjected to both Correlated and Uncorrelated training with the length of any phase varying between 12 and 44 days in the several subjects. Two subjects received Correlated experience, and two Uncorrelated experience, first, and for one subject receiving each order the 4000 Hz tone was designated A_1 while for the other subject the 400 Hz tone was so designated.

During the last two training days in each phase three test trials were included in which L was presented alone for 3-minute periods as well as one similar trial with each of A_1 and A_2. All such test trials followed a reinforced trial, but were themselves nonreinforced.

To evaluate the effectiveness of the compounds and elements, the mean number of bar presses during 3-min stimulus periods was compared with the mean number of presses during the immediately preceding 3-min no-stimulus periods. The degree to which bar-pressing rate in the presence of the stimulus was less than the no-stimulus rate was expressed as a percentage of the no-stimulus rate. Thus, zero suppression indicates that the stimulus was ineffective in producing a diminution in bar pressing, whereas 100% suppression indicates a complete cessation of bar pressing in the presence of the stimulus.

Figure 2 depicts the mean percentage suppression on L alone trials during each of the two test sessions for those subjects which received Correlated and Uncorrelated training in each of the two orders. Also presented for comparison, are the similar mean percentages suppression on A_1 and A_2 alone trials, as well as on compound trials within the same sessions for the two groups.

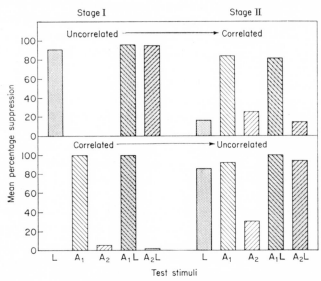

FIG. 2. Mean percentage suppression to elements and compounds in two separate test sessions, for groups of rats receiving first Uncorrelated and then Correlated CER training, or first Correlated and then Uncorrelated training. (Wagner, *et al.* 1967, Experiment II.)

In Stage I, it may be seen that Uncorrelated training was followed by nearly complete suppression to L alone. In comparison, following Correlated training, there was no suppression observed to L alone. An interesting feature of Stage I behavior is that under Uncorrelated training when the visual and auditory cues were equally valid, the auditory cues alone produced no suppression, and, in view of the sizeable suppression to L, apparently contributed little, if at all, to the suppression observed on compound trials. The visual cue employed would, in this event, generally be described as considerably more "salient" than the available auditory cues. It still may be observed however, that Correlated training during this stage, with A_1L reinforced and A_2L nonreinforced, eliminated any tendency for L alone to produce suppression.

Stage II training in which the treatments were reversed for all subjects was not continued for a sufficient duration either to equalize A_1 and A_2 suppression in the Uncorrelated condition, or to produce as marked a discrimination in the Correlated condition as had been obtained during Stage I. Nonetheless, both subjects shifted from Uncorrelated to Correlated training showed a concomitant decrease in suppression to L while both subjects shifted from Correlated to Uncorrelated training showed an increase in suppression to L. Considering the paired observations from all 4 subjects, the greater mean suppression to L following Uncorrelated as compared to Correlated training was highly significant ($t = 60{\cdot}65$, $df = 3$, $p < {\cdot}001$).

Experiment III involved classical conditioning of eyelid closure in the rabbit, with the compounds serving as CSs, signaling a 4-mA electric-shock US delivered to the subject's cheek. The light CS (L) consisted of 20/sec flashes generated by a strobe lamp directed so as to reflect relatively homogeneously from the surfaces of the experimental chamber surrounding the restrained subject, while the two auditory CSs (A_1 and A_2) consisted of a train of 12/sec clicks and a 2400 Hz tone.

A conditioning-trial involved a 600-msec presentation of an AL compound CS, which on 50% of the occasions overlapped and terminated with a 100-msec US. Sixty-four conditioning trials, half with A_1L and half with A_2L in an irregular order, were administered in each session with a mean intertrial-interval of 60 seconds. Under Uncorrelated training 50% of both the A_1L and A_2L trials were reinforced while under Correlated training all A_1L but no A_2L trials were reinforced.

Eight subjects were sequentially subjected to both Correlated and Uncorrelated training, the first stage consisting of 19 daily sessions and the second of 18 such sessions. Four subjects began with Correlated and 4 subjects with Uncorrelated training. For 2 subjects receiving each order the 12/sec clicks were designated A_1 while for the remaining subjects the 2400 Hz tone was so designated.

During the last session under each condition, 8 nonreinforced test trials were included with each of L, A_1 and A_2 alone. The order of the L, A_1 and A_2 trials was balanced over the session with the further provision that each of the three kinds of test trials equally often followed A_1L and A_2L conditioning trials, as well as reinforced and nonreinforced trials.

Movements of the subject's eyelid affected a micro-potentiometer and were graphically recorded so that a conditioned blink response (CR) could be scored as a deflection of the graphic record, during the first 500 msec of a training or test trial.

Figure 3 presents, in a manner similar to Figs. 1 and 2, the mean percentage CRs on L alone trials during Stage I and Stage II test sessions under the two treatment conditions as well as the similar percentages on

A_1 and A_2 alone trials and on compound training trials within the same session.

As may be seen in Fig. 3, there was less responding to L in Stage I following Correlated than following Uncorrelated training. There was no overlap in the distributions of number of L responses under the two treatments and the lower mean responding associated with Correlated

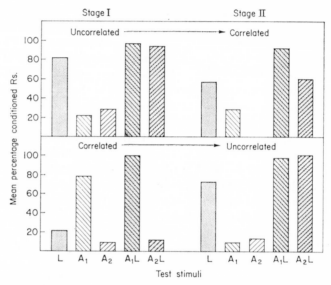

Fig. 3. Mean percentage conditioned eye-blink responses to elements and compounds in two separate test sessions, for groups of rabbits receiving first Uncorrelated and then Correlated conditioning, or first Correlated and then Uncorrelated conditioning. (Wagner, *et al.* 1968, Experiment III.)

training was statistically significant ($t = 3{\cdot}719$, $df = 6$, $p < {\cdot}01$). As in Experiment II, A_1 and A_2 responding was less than L responding in the Uncorrelated condition in Stage I. Yet, the absolute level of L responding was diminished in the Correlated condition, in which the auditory cues allowed a better prediction of US occurrence than did L.

By the end of Stage II it may be seen that the subjects shifted from Correlated to Uncorrelated training were responding at a high level to both compounds. Concomitant with this shift was an increase in responding to L but a decrease to A_1. Although the subjects shifted from Uncorrelated to Correlated training had not, by the end of the 18 postshift sessions, attained either a strong discrimination between the compounds, or an appreciable elevation in A_1 responding, there was, nevertheless, a relatively small but consistent decrease in number of CRs to L

alone. Ignoring the order of testing, each of the 8 subjects gave a larger number of CRs to L following Uncorrelated than following Correlated training ($p = \cdot008$, sign test).

The results of the above studies clearly indicate that a partially reinforced cue is much less likely to be an effective stimulus in isolation when it has been experienced in compounds containing elements more highly correlated with reinforcement, than when it has been experienced in similar compounds which do not contain more valid elements. The potency of the reported effect may be judged from the fact that, in all three studies, every subject which was tested following both training conditions responded less to L when the auditory cues were more highly correlated with reinforcement, than when L and the auditory cues were equally valid. These findings would appear to pose severe difficulties for a simple conditioning-extinction theory, but would find ready interpretation in the stimulus-selection theories described.

B. DIFFERENTIAL NEUTRALIZATION OF INCIDENTAL STIMULI: DEMONSTRATIONS

In describing the results of the prior studies it is convenient to say that the light element was "neutralized" because it occurred as an incidental stimulus during discrimination training.

As noted earlier, theorists have frequently appealed to the neutralization of incidental stimuli as the process responsible for a variety of phenomena associated with discrimination learning. Nonetheless, the involvement of such neutralization has remained in most instances only a *post-hoc* possibility, or has been evaluated only in very indirect ways. If the neutralization of incidental stimuli is an important ingredient in the production of a particular pnenomenon, it should be possible to demonstrate such neutralization with tactics similar to those employed by Wagner, *et al.* in the previous studies.

The final two investigations to be described were designed to provide such demonstrations in the case of two theoretically interesting discrimination phenomena.

A frequently obtained effect of discrimination training is a steepening of the generalization gradient along some dimension of a reinforced stimulus. This occurs when the reinforced and non-reinforced cues during discrimination training occupy different positions on the dimension explored in generalization testing (Hanson, 1959). However, the generalization gradient can also become steeper, when the discrimination training is carried out with stimuli that do *not* differ above the dimension varied in generalization testing. (See Ch. 2, Honig—and the references cited therein.)

A most informative example of the latter effect is reported by Honig. Pigeons were trained to peck a white key containing three vertical dark lines, and were given generalization tests, with different orientations of the lines, defining the generalization continuum. For all subjects, training with the white, lined discriminandum involved consistent reinforcement, according to a variable-interval schedule. Subjects differed however, in the training they received on two other discriminanda, which were unlined, and hence could be viewed as not occupying positions on the generalization test (i.e. line-orientation) dimension. One group received successive discrimination training, with key pecking reinforced, on a VI schedule, in the presence of a green key and non-reinforced in the presence of a blue key. The other group received "pseudo-discrimination" training in which the reinforcement schedule was in effect on 50% of both the green and blue key presentations.

The essential finding was that when both groups of subjects were given generalization tests, with different orientations of the black lines on a white key, a steeper generalization gradient was obtained in the group which had received discrimination training, as compared to the pseudo-discrimination group. Thus, the apparent stimulus-control exerted by line orientation was enhanced by discrimination, as compared to pseudo-discrimination training, even though presumably neither the discrimination nor pseudo-discrimination experience involved the orientation dimension.

In other instances in which discrimination training has led to a steepening of generalization gradients, appeal has often been made to the neutralization of incidental cues. Thus Hull (1950) indicated that the slope of an empirical generalization gradient should depend not only on the response eliciting tendencies of the various members of the stimulus continuum employed, but also on the response eliciting tendencies of other, invariant, stimuli, which occur on test trials together with each member of the generalization continuum. If discrimination training were to neutralize such invariant stimuli as a result of their occurrence as incidental cues, generalization gradients would be left to reflect more singularly the differences in strength associated with the generalization dimension. Jenkins and Harrison (1960, 1962) have also suggested the operation of such a neutralization process in instances in which discrimination training has not been specifically among members of the generalization dimension.

In the case of the Honig experiment this reasoning is especially compelling when it is seen that the Discrimination and Pseudo-discrimination treatments employed were conceptually identical to the Correlated and Uncorrelated treatments in the Wagner, Logan, Haberlandt and Price (1968) studies. On the basis of the latter studies it would be expected that any incidental cues common to the blue and green key occasions should have been more neutralized in Honig's Discrimination (Correlated) group, than in his Pseudo-discrimination (Uncorrelated) group. If some of these cues were also present during training and generalization testing with the lined-keys, it is reasonable to expect that the group for which they were least potent would also have the steeper generalization gradient along the orientation dimension.

A previously unpublished study, conducted in our laboratory with the collaboration of Gerd Lehmann, sought to reproduce the Honig findings, in the context of an experimental design that would also allow an evaluation of the degree of responding to a specifiable incidental stimulus.

The investigation involved eyelid conditioning in the rabbit, and followed many of the procedures employed by Wagner, Logan, Haberlandt and Price (1968), in their Experiment III. During training all subjects received experience, however, with *three* separate compounds, AV, L_1V and L_2V, formed from a vibratory element, V, an auditory element, A, and either of two light elements, L_1 and L_2. The AV compound was always reinforced during training, and may be identified with Honig's white lined key, as the ultimate stage in the experiment included an evaluation of generalization gradients produced by varying the frequency of the auditory element. All subjects also received an equal number of exposures to L_1V and L_2V during training, but for half the subjects L_1V was always reinforced and L_2V was always nonreinforced, while for the remaining subjects L_1V and L_2V were both reinforced on 50% of their occurrences. Thus the two treatment groups may be seen to have received identical, reinforced training with AV, but Correlated and Uncorrelated training, respectively on L_1V and L_2V, or in Honig's terminology, to have involved Discrimination versus Pseudo-discrimination training on the latter compounds.

An important feature of the present design was that all training compounds contained a specifiable, common element, V, which could be independently manipulated. Thus beginning with two groups of subjects, both of which, following training, responded at similar high levels to the AV compound, it was possible to evaluate the contribution of each of the elements to such responding. Responding to the auditory element was evaluated in terms of the generalization decrement produced by modifying its frequency, and responding to the vibratory element was similarly evaluated in terms of the decrement produced by its modification, which in this case was accomplished by its complete removal. The expectations, based both upon empirical and theoretical grounds, were that, if the AV compound were modified by changing the frequency of A, there would be *more* of a decrement in the Correlated as compared to the Uncorrelated group, whereas if it were modified by withdrawing the common, V, element, there would be *less* of a decrement in the Correlated group.

Stimulus-selection theory suggests that discrimination training as compared to pseudo-discrimination training should better neutralize an incidental element such as V, and *therefore* should insure a greater effectiveness of A, as a result of the reinforcement of the AV compound. The present design, in fact, can at best comment on the degree and kind of concomitant variation in the behavioral control exercised by V and A following the two training procedures. Such information, however, allows the evaluation of a possible alternative interpretation of the Honig findings, namely, that discrimination training creates a "set to discriminate" (Reinhold and Perkins, 1955). If discrimination training simply makes subjects more sensitive to *any* change in the discriminandum, which is what seems to be implied by such a "set" notion, it would be expected that the degree of response decrement produced by withdrawing V, as well as that produced by modifying A, should be greater in the Correlated than in the Uncorrelated group.

The experimental procedures involved several differences from those of Wagner, Logan, Haberlandt, and Price, and were calculated to increase the general efficiency of conditioning and testing. These included: a longer CS-UCS interval (1000 msec); a shorter mean intertrial-interval (30 sec); different shock-electrode placement (directly above and below the eye), and a larger number of trials per session. It was possible thereby to complete training and testing within 2 sessions as compared to the 19 daily sessions in the first stage of the earlier study. All subjects received 2 blocks of 72 training trials on Day 1 and 9 blocks of 72 training trials on Day 2, immediately followed by 72 test trials. The experiment was run in two replications which differed only in the distribution of compound trials in the first session. In Replication 1 all Day 1 trials were with the AV compound, whereas in Replication 2, each block of 72 trials on Day 1 included 24 trials with each of AV, L_1V, and L_2V. In both replications the Day 2 training blocks included an equal number of AV, L_1V and L_2V trials according to an irregular sequence.

There were 32 subjects in Replication 1 and 24 in Replication 2, half of each receiving Correlated and half Uncorrelated training on the L_1V and L_2V compounds. The auditory element during training was a 3100 Hz tone, and the vibratory stimulus was provided by a commercial massager held in contact with the rabbit's chest. For half the subjects in each experimental treatment, L_1 consisted of 20/sec flashes of a strobe-lamp while L_2 consisted of the illumination from a steady incandescent lamp of approximately equal intensity. For the remaining subjects in each treatment, the nature of L_1 and L_2 was reversed.

Immediately following the completion of training all subjects received 36 test trials with AV compounds in which A was either 1700 Hz, 3100 Hz, or 5600 Hz, given in such an order that 2 trials with each frequency occurred in each successive block of 6 test trials. Thirty-six additional trials were then administered in which the frequency of A was similarly varied, *but with the vibratory element removed.* All 72 test trials were reinforced.

Figure 4 presents the acqustion curves for conditioned responding to each of the compound stimuli within each experimental group in the two replications. It is most important to note that in both replications the Correlated and Uncorrelated groups attained similar high levels of

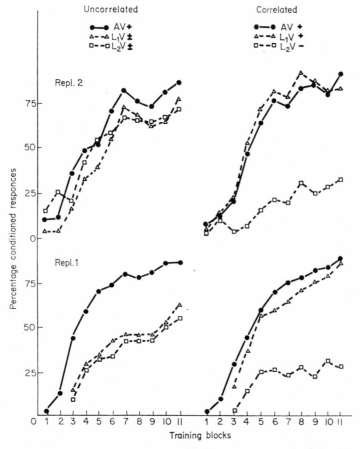

FIG. 4. Mean percentage conditioned eye-blink responses to each of three compound CSs during blocks of 72 total trials. Data are presented separately for two replications during which all subjects were consistently reinforced on AV, but either received Correlated or Uncorrelated training with L_1V and L_2V.

responding to the AV compound. It may also be seen that the Correlated groups acquired a consistent discrimination between L_1V and L_2V whereas the Uncorrelated group responded similarly to the latter compounds. The replications differed only in that the responding of the Uncorrelated group was appreciably higher to L_1V and L_2V in Replication 2 than in Replication 1, in which training to these cues was delayed until Session 2.

Figure 5 shows the percentage conditioned responses to each of the stimuli presented during the test session, for the two groups in each replication. The pattern of results from the two replications was identical: the generalization decrement produced by modifying the frequency of the A element was greater in the Correlated than in the Uncorrelated condition, whereas the decrement produced by withdrawing the vibratory element was greater in the Uncorrelated condition.

As may be seen, in the Correlated groups there was a greater difference between the percentage conditioned responses on those trials involving the training A frequency and those involving the generalization-test frequencies, than in the Uncorrelated groups. In contrast, in the Uncorrelated groups there was a greater difference between the percentage conditioned responses on those trials involving AV compounds and those involving only A compound, than in the Correlated groups. Separate analyses of variance computed for each of the two replications confirmed the reliability of these observations in both replications ($p < \cdot 05$ in each case). Although there was some tendency for the differences in the frequency generalization decrement between the two groups to be greater in the absence of the vibratory element than in its presence, and some tendency for the differences in the vibratory withdrawal decrement to be greater at the training frequency than at the other frequencies, the interaction term associated with these observations was not statistically reliable in either replication.

These results are of interest in several respects. First, the frequency generalization data reproduce the Honig findings in a quite different behavioral situation, and thereby reflect on the generality of that phenomenon. Secondly, they indicate that the Correlated versus Uncorrelated manipulation employed by Wagner, et al. (1968) is strong enough to produce differences in the behavioral control by an incidental cue, even when that cue is concomitantly a member of another compound which is consistently reinforced. Most important, of course, was the resultant observation that the decrements associated with modification of the unique (A) and incidental (V) elements of the AV compound were inversely related in the two training conditions.

All these findings are easy to account for in terms of a stimulus-selection

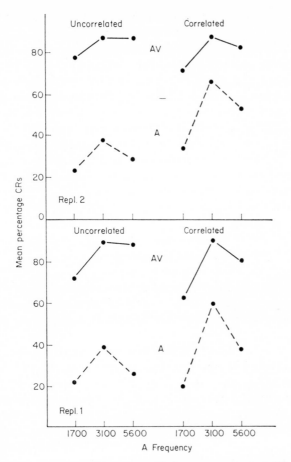

FIG. 5. Mean percentage conditioned eye-blink responses to test CSs involving an AV compound or A alone, at the training A frequency, as well as at a higher and lower frequency. Separate functions are presented for groups receiving prior Correlated or Uncorrelated training on L_1V and L_2V compounds, in each of two Replications.

theory, which acknowledges the differential neutralization of an incidental cue as a result of discrimination training, and which views the several stimuli in a compound as competing for the incremental effects of reinforcement. In comparison neither simple conditioning-extinction theory nor the proposal that discrimination training produces a "set to discriminate" would appear to be sufficient to account for the several results.

Among other data which have given encouragement to stimulus-selection theories, some of the most persuasive have been those reported by Pavlov (1927), Lawrence (1952), Restle (1955), and others on so-called "transfer of discrimination along a continuum." This "transfer" refers to instances in which training on an easy discrimination facilitates the acquisition of a difficult discrimination along the same dimension, more than does equal training on the difficult discrimination itself. In fact, Pavlov observed that pre-training on an easy discrimination was sometimes essential for acquiring a particularly difficult discrimination.

A common stimulus-selection interpretation of this effect (e.g. Lawrence, 1952; Sutherland *et al.* 1963) is that the easy discrimination better teaches the subject to switch in the relevant stimulus analyzer. Due to the subject's presumably limited analyzer capacity, this also implies that the easy discrimination also better causes the subject to abandon less relevant stimulus analyzers, i.e. "neutralize" less valid, incidental cues. Restle (1955) has made particular use of the latter notion, that incidental cues are better neutralized the greater the relevant discrepancy between the discriminanda, and has shown how various quantitative features of the choice data from transfer studies involving selective learning can be accounted for by a stochastic model incorporating such an assumption.

Haberlandt (1968), in a Doctoral dissertation conducted in our laboratory, attempted to produce this transfer phenomenon in a situation that would also allow a concomitant evaluation of the degree of neutralization of specifiable incidental cues.

This study again made use of differential eyelid conditioning in the rabbit, and followed in some detail the general procedures of the preceding investigation.

All subjects were eventually tested on compound CSs that may be represented as A_3VL and A_4VL, to indicate that they contained both a vibratory element and a light element, as common incidental cues, and different, but similar auditory frequencies. Sixteen subjects which will be referred to as the Difficult Group, received their prior discrimination training with the test compounds, A_3VL being consistently reinforced and A_4VL consistently nonreinforced. An additional sixteen subjects which will be referred to as the Easy Group, received an identical amount of pre-test discrimination training, but first with A_1VL reinforced and A_6VL nonreinforced, and then with A_2VL reinforced and A_5VL nonreinforced, that is with compounds in which the auditory frequencies were more separated than in the test pair, but less so in the last than in the first stage of training.

Discrimination training was accomplished in two sessions, 256 trials on Day 1 and 512 trials on Day 2. Half of the daily trials involved a reinforced compound and half a non-reinforced compound, according to irregular orders. The auditory frequencies employed were selected from among 3160, 4220, 4890, 6480, 7500, and 10,000 Hz with A_3 and A_4

referring to the two middle frequencies, A_2 and A_5 to the relatively similar adjacent frequencies and A_1 and A_6 to the most separated frequencies. Half of the subjects in each group had the lower of the middle two frequencies designated as A_3 and were correspondingly trained with the compound(s) containing the lower frequency(s) reinforced. For the remaining subjects this assignment was reversed.

The test sequence, which immediately followed, was designed to allow an evaluation of both the differential responding to A_3VL and A_4VL, in the two groups, and the degree of responding to incidental stimuli within the compounds. The procedure differed from that of the earlier studies in that an A_3VL or A_4VL compound CS was presented on every test trial, but the intensity of A_3 and A_4 was systematically varied. On one-third of the presentations of each of A_3VL and A_4VL, the intensity of the auditory cue was identical to its training value; on one third it was moderately reduced in intensity, and on one third it was very weak.

One rationale for this procedure of degrading the auditory stimulus, rather than completely removing it, in testing the responding to incidental cues, is that the compound containing the degraded stimulus retains a number of additional incidental cues which like V and L occur on all training trials, but which are within the auditory modality. For example, in the present experimental situation, as well as those previously described, a low level of white noise was always present during the intertrial intervals, but was removed during the occurrence of an auditory CS. Thus the cessation of noise and its replacement by a tonal stimulus was an incidental cue, occurring on all trials regardless of the quality of the tone presented. It is also important, of course, that the auditory stimulus be sufficiently degraded that the relevant cues can be considered absent. This was judged to be the case for the lowest intensity employed in Haberlandt's test sequence, in that at this level the subjects in neither group were observed to respond discriminatively to A_3VL and A_4VL. To human observers, who could consistently discriminate A_3 and A_4 under the training conditions, the two auditory events were tonal but not discriminable, at the lowest test intensity.

Specifically, the test sequence consisted of 16 trials of each of A_3VL and A_4VL at each of the intensity levels, the various combinations occurring in a balanced order. At the lowest test value, A_3 and A_4 were equal in intensity to the masking noise they replaced, whereas they were 5 dB and 10 dB more intense than the noise in the remaining conditions (the latter value also being the training intensity). During testing all A_3VL trials were reinforced and all A_4VL trials non-reinforced.

Figure 6 presents the percentage conditioned responses to the reinforced and nonreinforced compounds in the two groups, during pre-test

discrimination training. As would be expected the Easy Group, which
received more separated auditory frequencies during these trials, responded
more differentially to the reinforced and nonreinforced compounds.
This was true over the first 4 blocks of 128 trials during which the Easy
Group received A_1VL and A_6VL, and also over the last 2 blocks, when
the Easy Group had been shifted to A_2VL and A_5VL.

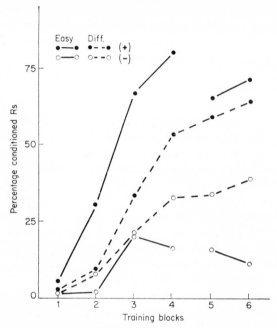

FIG. 6. Mean percentage conditioned eye-blink responses to reinforced ($+$) and
nonreinforced ($-$) compound CSs over blocks of 128 acquisition trials for Easy and
Difficult discrimination groups. The break in the curves for the Easy Group indicates
the point at which the CSs were increased in similarity for that group. (Haberlandt, 1968.)

Of major interest is the test trial performance of the two groups, which
is summarized in Fig. 7. The percentage conditioned responses to A_3VL
and A_4VL are presented separately for the two groups at each of the A
intensities. The results may be summarized rather simply. First, the
transfer phenomenon was obtained—the Easy Group which had been
trained with more separated frequencies evidenced a greater overall
discrimination between A_3VL and A_4VL, than did the Difficult Group
which had been trained with the test frequencies. Secondly, there was
evidence for more responding to incidental cues in the Difficult Group
than in the Easy Group—at the lowest A intensity, at which neither

group responded differentially to A_3VL and A_4VL, there were more total CRs by the Difficult than by the Easy Group. Analysis of variance confirmed the statistical reliability of both of these observations.

As in the case of the previous investigation, the Haberlandt study appears to provide reasonably direct evidence that the differential neutralization of incidental cues may be intimately involved in the discrimination phenomenon in question.

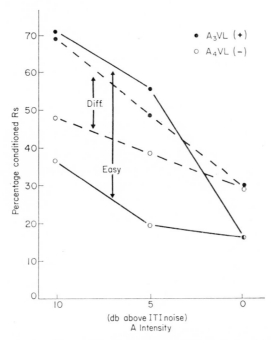

FIG. 7. Mean percentage conditioned eye-blink responses on blocks of test trials involving the compound CSs, A_3VL and A_4VL, for each of two groups which received prior discrimination training with the test compounds (Difficult Group) or with compounds containing more discriminable A cues (Easy Group). Separate points are represented for those test trials on which A was 10, 5 or 0 dB above the intertrial-interval noise level. (Haberlandt, 1968).

IV. Discussion

The important difference between stimulus-selection and conditioning-extinction theories concerns whether or not the behavior eliciting characteristics of a cue are sufficiently accounted for by knowledge of the schedule of reinforcements and nonreinforcements with which it has been associated. According to stimulus-selection theory they are not, since a cue is assumed to compete with other available cues for the behavioral effects resulting from each reinforcement and nonreinforcement. It should therefore be necessary also to take into account those variables which influence how favourably the cue is able to compete with others available. The data on incidental cues presented in the present chapter appear to support this contention.

A. CONDITIONING-EXTINCTION ALTERNATIVES

Mackintosh (1965a) has recently provided an excellent review of a sizeable literature which has also been viewed as supporting stimulus-selection theory. Unfortunately, a considerable portion of that literature is in fact silent on the major issue separating stimulus-selection and conditioning-extinction theory, or is at least, not necessarily inconsistent with the latter theory. It is appropriate to acknowledge this fact here, not only because of the general question involved, but also because it must be asked whether the present data are also conspicuously amenable to a conditioning-extinction theory interpretation.

The first possibility that need be mentioned involves the importance of receptor-orienting acts. Spence (e.g. 1945) and other conditioning-extinction theorists have consistently pointed out that the acquisition of gross receptor-orienting acts, which maximize the receipt of one cue on a sensory surface, can in some instances account for a concomitant decrease in the receipt of (and hence behavioral control accruing to) other potential cues in the environment. This approximates a stimulus-selection notion in that orienting to one cue may decrease the effects which reinforcement and nonreinforcement may have upon some other potential cue. It can be viewed however, as a special case, peculiar to only certain behavioral situations and best handled by treating the depreciated cue as simply not received.

Since this argument is a familiar one, it should not be necessary to develop it further. Yet, it may be noted that much of the recent data presumably favoring stimulus-selection theory (see, Mackintosh, 1965) has been collected in experimental situations such as the jumping-stand where gross receptor-orienting acts are likely to play an important role.

More pertinent is whether receptor-orienting acts are likely to be responsible for the present findings. Is it possible for example, that Correlated subjects, in the Wagner, Logan, Haberlandt, and Price (1968) studies, in learning to respond to the auditory cues, were less likely than Uncorrelated subjects to receive the incidental light cue on the retinal surface at the time of reinforcement and nonreinforcement? In each of the studies reported precautions were taken to minimize the importance of gross receptor-orienting acts, by ensuring that the light cue was reflected in a relatively homogeneous fashion from all surfaces of the subject's chamber, and in the case of the vibratory cue, that it was held in contact with the subject. While such precautions do not rule out all possibilities of peripheral receptor-adjustments, they do at least suggest that the findings should be generalizable to those simple and conventional learning situations in which "it is practically impossible for the animal... not [to] receive the relevant stimulation". (Spence, 1945).

The second possibility appears to have been less often appreciated and therefore deserves more detailed consideration. In effect, the question is simply whether variability in the behavior eliciting characteristics of an investigated cue, that might be attributed to a stimulus-selection process, cannot be attributed to experimentally allowed variability in the actual schedule of reinforcements and nonreinforcements experienced in the presence of that cue.

Consider for example, an experiment reported by Lovejoy and Russell (1967). Two groups of subjects were trained on a jumping-stand with vertical (V) rectangles reinforced and horizontal (H) rectangles non-reinforced. For one group, which may be referred to as a Two Cue Group, the vertical stimulus was always black (B) and the horizontal stimulus was always white (W), so that the subjects learned a discrimination (VB versus HW) in which both orientation and brightness cues were valid. For the other group, which may be referred to as a Single Cue Group, brightness cues were irrelevant, half the trials involving VB versus HW and half VW versus HB. Following training both groups were tested on the vertical-horizontal discrimination in the absence of differential brightness cues, that is on VB versus HB, VW versus HW, or with both orientation cues grey. The results clearly showed that the Single Cue Group, that had been trained with only the orientation cues relevant, responded more discriminatively to the latter cues than did the Two Cue Group that had also had the brightness cues relevant during training.

One interpretation of this finding is that the subjects in the Two Cue Group were likely to attend to the valid brightness cues, and that attending to brightness cues decreased their attention to, and hence learning about, the available orientation cues. Such a stimulus-selection interpretation would be necessitated in preference to a conditioning-extinction interpretation, however, only if the two groups during training received an equal number of reinforcements in the presence of the vertical cue, and an equal number of nonreinforcements in the presence of the horizontal cue. In this case they did not.

Lovejoy and Russell, prior to testing, gave all subjects 360 discrimination training "trials". However, the definition of a trial which they employed, and which is relatively common in the use of the jumping-stand, created a smaller number of exposures to the orientation cues in the Two Cue Group than in the Single Cue Group. That is, if a subject made an error, it was replaced with the same spatial arrangement of the discriminanda and allowed to jump again. As many as three such errors were allowed to occur within a single "trial". Since the Single Cue Group, without benefit of the added brightness cues, made more errors, it consequently also received a greater number of exposures to the orientation cues prior to test.

However, even if both groups of animals had received an identical number of stimulus exposure opportunities prior to test, it still could not be said that they had received an equal number of reinforcements in the presence of the vertical cue and an equal number of nonreinforcements in the presence of the horizontal cue. The Two Cue Group quickly attained nearly 100% choice of the reinforced compound, while the Single Cue Group only very slowly acquired the discrimination, never surpassing 80% choice of the reinforced compounds. Thus, the Two Cue Group received a large number of trials with V reinforced, but very few with H nonreinforced, whereas, in comparison, the Single Cue Group had fewer trials with V reinforced but many more trials with H nonreinforced. The subsequent finding, that the Single Cue Group responded more discriminatively to the different orientation cues than did the Two Cue Group, may consequently reveal no more than that nonreinforcing responses to H was overall more effective in producing discriminative behaviour between V and H than was reinforcing responses to V.

Unless it can be assumed that an equal amount of discrimination learning occurs as a result of reinforced responses to the positive stimulus and as a result of nonreinforced responses to the negative stimulus, it is clearly not sufficient simply to control in a selective learning situation the number of opportunities for one or the other in evaluation of conditioning-extinction versus stimulus-selection theory. The presence of an additional valid cue, or of a more valid cue or of an equally valid cue which is individually more "salient" for a subject may decrease the subject's discriminative behavior with respect to other available cues, but it may do so in a way which is perfectly compatible with conditioning-extinction theory, i.e. only by influencing the schedule of reinforcements and nonreinforcements which the subject receives in the presence of the latter cues.

The Lovejoy and Russell experiment was chosen for discussion only as a convenient example, in that it made use of a research design conceptually not too dissimilar from those that have otherwise been discussed. The same problems of interpretation are, however, unfortunately common to a large number of selective-learning studies which have been taken to support stimulus-selection theory. Space precludes full detailing of this point but arguments analogous to those raised with respect to the Lovejoy and Russell experiment can easily be constructed for those selective-learning experiments (e.g. Sutherland and Mackintosh, 1964; Sutherland and Holgate, 1966) which show that following two-cue discrimination training (such as VB versus HW in the Lovejoy and Russell experiment) there exists a negative correlation between the degree of discrimination subsequently exhibited to the separate dimensions, as well as for those studies (e.g. Sutherland *et al.* 1965; Mackintosh, 1965b) which have shown that pretraining in discrimination between one set of cues such as B versus W, may diminish the discriminative behavior observed to V versus H following selective-learning with the compounds VB versus HW.

In an instrumental learning situation, it is also extremely difficult to determine whether the effectiveness of an incidental cue is a function of the validity of other available cues, independent of the manner in which the differential validities may bring the subject into contact with different reinforcement experiences in the presence of the incidental cue. By design, the subjects' behavior will determine in most instrumental situations the number of reinforcements and nonreinforcements experienced. Even if a forcing procedure is incorporated in an instrumental situation, the subject may still influence such parameters as the delay between the receipt of the stimulus and the receipt of reward.

It was in view of the necessity, in this theoretical context, carefully to control stimulus exposures and reinforcement schedules, that Experiments II and III, in the Wagner, *et al.* (1968) study, as well as the later studies reported, employed classical conditioning procedures. Under Correlated and Uncorrelated training in this situation there is no doubt that the groups received an equal number of exposures to the incidental cue. To the degree that "reinforcement" is specified by the occurrence of a UCS and "nonreinforcement" by the absence of a UCS, it was also assured that the groups received an equal number and sequence of reinforcements and nonreinforcements in the presence of the incidental cue.

That the presence or absence of a more valid cue in the two conditions still produced marked differences in responding to the incidental cue would appear to offer unique and strong support for a basic stimulus-selection process.

B. Concluding Comments

The present chapter has concentrated on the properties of incidental stimuli in discrimination learning. In part this has been a choice of convenience, with the primary purpose being an evaluation of conditioning-extinction versus stimulus-selection theory. The behavioral characteristics of incidental stimuli as investigated in the several experiments reported clearly add support to stimulus-selection theory.

It is also the case that the neutralization of incidental stimuli has been given heavy theoretical responsibilities in conditioning-extinction and stimulus-selection theories alike. The Lehmann and Haberlandt studies suggest that this theoretical responsibility may be well placed, at least in the instances of the two discrimination phenomena investigated. (Although, again, the neutralization that does occur appears to be accountable for only in terms of a stimulus-selection process.) There is thus, added reason to appreciate the potential significance of incidental cues in the variety of discrimination learning situations that currently occupy research interest. Clearly, the terms "incidental" or "irrelevant" are by no means indicative of the degree of importance that the cues so-designated may have in determining discrimination performance.

Acknowledgement

Preparation of this chapter and the research reported were supported in part by National Science Foundation Grants GB-3623, and GB-6534.

References

Haberlandt, K. F. (1968). "Transfer along a Continuum in Classical Conditioning". Unpublished Ph.D. Thesis, Yale University.

Hanson, H. M. (1959). Effects of discrimination training on stimulus generalization. *J. Exp. Psychol.* **58**, 321–334.

Hull, C. L. (1943). "Principles of Behaviour". Appleton-Century-Crofts., Inc. New York. U.S.A.

Hull, C. L. (1950). Simple qualitative discrimination learning. *Psychol. Rev.* **57**, 303–313.

Humphreys, L. G. (1939). The effect of random alternation of reinforcement on the acquisition and extinction of conditioned eyelid reactions. *J. exp. Psychol.* **25**, 141–158.

Jenkins, H. M. and Harrison, R. H. (1960). Effect of discrimination training on auditory generalization. *J. exp. Psychol.* **59**, 246–253.

Jenkins, H. M. and Harrison, R. H. (1962). Generalization gradients of inhibition following auditory discrimination learning. *J. exp. Anal. Behav.* **5**, 435–441.

Lawrence, D. H. (1952). The transfer of a discrimination along a continuum. *J. comp. physiol. Psychol.* **45**, 511–516.

Lovejoy, E. P. and Russell, D. G. (1967). Suppression of learning about a hard cue by the presence of an easy cue. *Psychon. Sci.* **8**, 365–366.

Mackintosh, N. J. (1965a). Selective attention in animal discrimination learning. *Psychol. Bull.* **64**, 124–150.

Mackintosh, N. J. (1965b). Incidental cue learning in rats. *Quart. J. exp. Psychol.* **17**, 292–300.

Pavlov, I. P. (1927). "Conditioned Reflexes". (G. V. Anrep translator) Oxford University Press, London, England.

Restle, F. (1955). A theory of discrimination learning. *Psychol. Rev.* **62,** 11–19.

Restle, F. (1958). Toward a quantitative description of learning set data. *Psychol. Rev.* **65,** 77–91.

Restle, F. (1959). Additivity of cues and transfer in discrimination of consonant clusters. *J. exp. Psychol.* **57,** 9–14.

Reinhold, D. B. and Perkins, C. C., Jr., (1955). Stimulus generalization following different methods of training. *J. exp. Psychol.* **49,** 423–427.

Spence, K. W. (1936). The nature of discrimination learning in animals. *Psychol. Rev.* **43,** 427–449.

Spence, K. W. (1937). The differential response in animals to stimuli varying within a single dimension. *Psychol. Rev.* **44,** 430–444.

Spence, K. W. (1945). An experimental test of the continuity and non-continuity theories of discrimination learning. *J. exp. Psychol.* **35,** 253–266.

Sutherland, N. S. (1964). Visual discrimination in animals. *Brit. Med. Bull.* **20,** 54–59.

Sutherland, N. S. and Holgate, V. (1966). Two-cue discrimination learning in rats. *J. comp. physiol. Psychol.* **61,** 198–207.

Sutherland, N. S. and Mackintosh, J. (1964). Discrimination learning: Non-additivity of cues. *Nature,* **201,** 528–530.

Sutherland, N. S., Mackintosh, N. J. and Mackintosh, J. (1963). Simultaneous discrimination training of octopus and transfer of discrimination along a continuum. *J. comp. physiol. Psychol.* **56,** 150–156.

Sutherland, N. S., Mackintosh, N. J. and Mackintosh, J. (1965). Shape and size discrimination in octopus: the effects of pretraining along different dimensions. *J. genet. Psychol.* **106,** 1–10.

Wagner, A. R., Logan, F. A., Haberlandt, K. and Price, T. (1968). Stimulus selection in animal discrimination learning. *J. exp. Psychol.* **76,** 171–180.

5

Attention Theory and Discrimination Learning

J. M. WARREN AND BRENDAN McGONIGLE

The Pennsylvania State University, University Park,
Pennsylvania, U.S.A.

I. Introduction

Attention theory (Mackintosh, 1965b; Sutherland, 1959, 1964a) provides a simple two-stage model to explain a number of important learning phenomena and to predict patterns of covariation in the occurence of these effects in several species, ranging from octopus to rat (Mackintosh, 1965a; Mackintosh *et al.* 1966).

In this paper we shall review recent research on the acquired distinctiveness of cues, the overtraining reversal effect, cue additivity in discrimination learning, and the effects of partial reinforcement on extinction and reversal learning. Our aim is to assess the adequacy of attention theory as an account of discrimination by animals, with particular emphasis on the results of experiments on mammals other than the rat.

II. The Acquired Distinctiveness of Cues

The basic assumption of attention theory is that discrimination learning involves two distinct processes, learning to attend to the relevant stimulus dimension, and learning to associate appropriate responses with specific stimulus values on the relevant dimension. Lawrence's (1949) demonstration of the acquired distinctiveness of cues is frequently cited as one of the major bases for postulating a two-stage model for discrimination learning. Lawrence observed that rats which were pretrained on a simultaneous discrimination subsequently learned a successive discrimination more rapidly when the same stimulus dimension was relevant in both tasks than when the relevant dimension was shifted between the first and second problem. As far as we know, there has been no published report of a comparable experiment with mammals other than rats. It seems worthwhile, therefore, to summarize two recent experiments with cats on the acquired distinctiveness of cues.

Mumma and Warren (1968) trained two groups of cats on a simultaneous discrimination between rectangles differing in orientation or in brightness, 12 Ss had previously learned a successive discrimination between rectangles differing in both orientation and brightness, and 16 were tested with no prior experience on discrimination learning tasks.

The performance of the pretrained and control groups in learning the simultaneous discrimination is compared in Fig. 1, which shows the

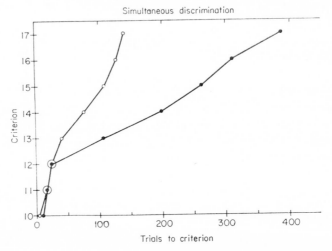

FIG. 1. Mean trials to successive criteria in simultaneous discrimination learning by cats. ○ Pretrained: ● Control.

mean number of trials required to reach successive criteria of learning as measured by increasing numbers of correct responses in daily sessions of 20 trials. The animals pretrained on the successive discrimination learned the simultaneous discrimination in less than half as many trials as their naive controls. The difference between groups in total trials to criterion is significant at the ·025 level of confidence ($U = 51$, $n_1 = 16$, $n_2 = 12$).

A second test of the acquired distinctiveness of cues was carried out with 18 experimentally sophisticated cats. These Ss had all learned to discriminate rectangles differing in brightness and orientation (Mumma and Warren, 1968) and to discriminate geometrical shapes (Derdzinski, 1967), but none had been tested on either a successive discrimination task or on a problem presenting size cues prior to this experiment.

Eight cats, the experimental group, were trained on a simultaneous size discrimination between two inverted T-shaped figures in the Wisconsin General Test Apparatus (WGTA). These animals and a control group, consisting of ten cats with identical testing histories except for training on the simultaneous size discrimination, were then tested on a successive size discrimination with the same stimulus objects in the WGTA.

The results are presented in Fig. 2 which shows the mean number of trials required by each group to satisfy progressively higher criteria in

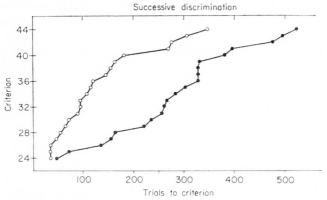

FIG. 2. Mean trials to successive criteria in successive discrimination learning by cats. ○ Pretrained: ● Control.

respect to the number of correct responses per daily session of 48 trials. The pretrained cats learned the successive discrimination more quickly than the controls which were experimentally sophisticated but naive for the dimension of visual size. The difference between groups in total trials to criterion was significant at the 2·5% level of confidence ($U = 16\cdot5$, $n_1 = 10$, $n_2 = 8$).

These experiments demonstrate that cats, like Lawrence's (1949) rats, manifest significant transfer between simultaneous and successive discriminations on the basis of the relevant stimulus dimension, and independent of the response required. To this extent, our findings strengthen the case for attention theory by showing that Lawrence's effect is replicable in cats tested under conditions which differ considerably from his in regard to stimulus, response, apparatus and motivational variables.

III. Overtraining Reversal Effects

Overtraining may facilitate, retard or have no significant effect on reversal learning by animals. According to attention theory, this variation in the effects of overtraining is determined by the salience of the relevant cues (Mackintosh, 1965a, 1965b; Mackintosh *et al*, 1966).

Overtraining facilitates reversal learning when the relevant cues lack salience for *S* and when one or more prominent irrelevant cues, which are initially likely to control *S*'s choice behavior, are present in the training situation (Mackintosh *et al.*, 1966). Under these conditions, the formation of choice responses to specific stimulus values (response attachments) and the development of attention to the relevant stimulus dimension (switching in the correct analyzer) proceed at different rates, with response attachments reaching nearly maximum strength sooner than analyzer strength. Overtraining can add but little to the strength of response attachments since they are close to asymptote, so the major effect of overtraining is to switch in the relevant analyzer more strongly (see Sutherland, 1964a, Figure 3).

Since analyzer strength is greater in overtrained than in nonovertrained animals, they will differ markedly in reversal performance. Nonovertrained *S*s will be likely to switch out the appropriate analyzer at the same time response attachments are extinguished and consequently respond to irrelevant dimensions with chance success for many trials before reinstating attention to the relevant cues. Overtrained *S*s will be more resistant to extinction immediately after reversal, but the relevant analyzer will remain switched in so they will require fewer trials to attain criterion after extinction has proceeded to the point where the two stimuli are chosen with equal (chance) frequencies, since they do not shift to responding to irrelevant cues at this stage as the nonovertrained *S*s do.

These predictions regarding the facilitation of reversal learning by overtraining and the differences in the course of reversal learning between overtrained and non-overtrained groups have generally been confirmed by studies on visual discrimination learning by rats (Mackintosh, 1965b). Overtraining also facilitates reversal learning in octopuses, but only if the discrimination involves irrelevant cues (Mackintosh and Mackintosh, 1963). Chicks reverse difficult discriminations more quickly after overtraining, but overtraining retards the reversal of brightness discriminations by chicks (Mackintosh, 1965a).

Overtraining does not facilitate or retard the reversal of shape discrimination by goldfish (Mackintosh *et al.*, 1966). In order to explain this observation, it is assumed that on a moderately difficult discrimination response learning does not proceed any faster than learning to use the correct analyzer, so that overtraining does not change the *relative* strengths of analyzers and responses which approach asymptote at the same rate. "Overtraining will not, therefore, facilitate reversal learning, since the greater strength of the correct analyzer in the overtrained animals is counterbalanced by the greater strength of the incorrect response attachments (Mackinstosh *et al.*, p. 316)". Presumably, this description of the effects of overtraining also characterizes the situation in spatial discrimination reversal experiments with rats, in most of which overtraining had no effect on reversal performance (Mackintosh, 1965b, Table 2).

Attention theory predicts that overtraining will retard reversal learning when very conspicuous relevant cues are used. Under these circumstances, the strength of the relevant analyzer is near asymptote at the beginning of training and overtraining will retard reversal since it can only strengthen response attachments. Such retardation has been observed in experiments with fish trained with combined visual and spatial cues (Warren, 1960) and with chicks trained with brightness cues (Brookshire *et al.*, 1961; Mackintosh, 1965a).

In summary, attention theory predicts three effects of overtraining on reversal learning: facilitation, when the relevant cues are obscure, and particularly when there are prominent irrelevant cues; no effect, when the relevant cues are moderately salient; and retardation, when the relevant cues are conspicuous cues toward which S automatically attends.

There have recently been several studies of the effects of overtraining on reversal learning by monkeys and cats. Most of the results appear to confirm the predictions of attention theory. When Ss are trained with stimuli that provide multiple relevant cues, like the "junk" objects often used in the WGTA, overtraining retards reversal learning and the amount of retardation is an increasing function of the number of overtraining trials given (Beck *et al.*, 1966; Boyer and Cross, 1965; Cross and Brown, 1965; Cross and Boyer, 1966; Cross, Fickling, Carpenter and Brown, 1964; Warren, 1954b). These findings would be anticipated on the grounds that there were multiple relevant visual cues and position was the sole irrelevant cue. Similarly, D'Amato's (1965) and Tighe's (1965) failures to observe any significant effect in reversal learning by monkeys tested with visual cues differing in a single dimension could be construed as reflecting the fact that both experimenters used discriminanda which were moderately salient to their monkeys.

There is, however, one experiment with cats which can not even superficially be harmonized with the predictions of attention theory.

Hirayoshi and Warren (1967) trained cats on a black-white discrimination with position, shape and size as irrelevant cues. Preference tests before training with differential reinforcement showed that the Ss were initially far more responsive to spatial than to brightness cues. Thus, the relevant cue was not salient and the Ss were required to learn in the presence of multiple irrelevant cues, including one which was much more conspicuous for the animals than the relevant cue. Attention theory predicts that overtrained cats would learn the reversal more quickly than nonovertrained cats. Overtraining did not facilitate reversal learning. In addition, the detailed predictions of attention theory regarding the shapes of the reversal learning curves for the overtrained and nonovertrained groups were also disconfirmed. The overtrained cats were not more resistant to extinction nor less likely to develop position habits than the nonovertrained animals. Failure to obtain facilitation in reversal learning by overtrained Ss under conditions specified by attention theory as most conducive to the effect indicates that the treatment of overtraining reversal effects by attention theory is incomplete or incorrect in some fundamental way.

It is important to note that since attention theory predicts all possible overtraining reversal effects, Hirayoshi and Warren's experiment would have been inconclusive had they not shown that their Ss were initially much less responsive to brightness cues than to spatial cues. In the absence of this essential control, their finding that overtrained and nonovertrained cats learned the reversal task at the same rate could have been rationalized in terms of attention theory on the grounds that the difference between white and black is "moderately salient" for cats. Because any possible outcome of an overtraining reversal experiment can be reconciled with attention theory after the fact by assuming the appropriate level of cue salience, it appears important in future studies of the overtraining reversal effect that the experimenter work with stimuli which have been independently scaled in terms of salience or which have been shown to exert less strong control over the choice behavior of S than one or more of the irrelevant cues present during training. Since salience is the independent variable that determines the effect of overtraining, it must obviously be manipulated or measured directly and must not be inferred from the quality of the effect of overtraining on reversal learning, particularly in experiments with exotic fauna.

IV. The Additivity of Cues

The classical statements of continuity (Spence 1936, 1937) and of non-continuity theory (Lashley, 1942) offer contradictory accounts of how animals learn to discriminate stimuli differing in multiple sensory dimensions. Continuity theory asserts that animals learn simultaneously the significance of all effective relevant cues. Noncontinuity theory maintains that animals attend to and learn about only one cue at a time.

The empirical evidence does not provide unequivocal support for either theory (Terrace, 1966). Cats (Hara and Warren, 1961) and rats (McGonigle, 1967) trained initially to discriminate differences in brightness, form and size separately, subsequently perform more accurately when tested with compound stimuli differing in two or three dimensions, than on stimuli differing in any single dimension. The increases in the accuracy of discrimination performance resulting from the combination of cues in multiple dimensions were sufficiently regular to be described by simple algebraic equations, involving the number and discriminability of the individual cues combined. These findings are rather difficult to reconcile with continuity theory.

However, animals do not always learn to respond equally to all aspects of stimuli differing in multiple dimensions. Pigeons, for example, learn to discriminate stimuli which differ in both color and form solely on the basis of color or form cues (Reynolds, 1961). Monkeys discriminate pattern stimuli differing in color only as efficiently as they do patterns differing in color, form and size (Warren, 1953). Results of this kind are incompatible with continuity theory.

Sutherland and Holgate (1966) have presented a clever explanation of multiple cue learning in terms of attention theory which represents a compromise between continuity and noncontinuity theory and which can be reconciled with many more of the empirical data. Animals are assumed initially to learn discriminations between stimuli that differ in multiple dimensions mainly or wholly in terms of one cue. When only one cue is relevant, some animals may attend to it from the beginning of discrimination training, and learn quickly. Other animals will not initially attend to the single cue, and learn slowly. As the number of relevant cues is increased, the probability that one of the cues provided will have high attention value for each S is enhanced, making it more likely that every individual will learn the discrimination quickly. This assumption makes it possible to explain the fact that animals trained with multiple cues frequently learn faster than those trained on single cues (Eninger, 1952; Warren, 1956; Warren, Grant, Hara and Leary, 1963) in terms of selective attention rather than continuity postulates.

Sutherland and Holgate's reasoning can plausibly be extended to cover studies which fail to demonstrate cue additivity. Additivity would not be anticipated when all Ss are likely to attend to the same highly conspicuous dimension, as in comparisons of color, form and size cues in pattern discrimination learning by monkeys (Warren, 1953, 1954a).

The strongest support for Sutherland and Holgate's argument that rats learn two-cue discriminations predominantly on the basis of a single cue is their observation that the more individual Ss learned about one cue, the less they learned about the other. Rats were trained to discriminate rectangles that differed in orientation and in brightness and were then tested, under conditions of nondifferential reinforcement, with stimulus pairs differing only in brightness and only in orientation. Negative correlations were obtained in several groups between the number of appropriate responses to stimulus values in the two dimensions.

Sutherland and Holgate's experiment poses an important methodological question. Are preference tests with non-differential reinforcement a valid measure of what was learned during training on the two-cue problem?

Two experiments will be described to define the nature of the problem. Cole (1953) trained monkeys to discriminate stimulus objects differing in color and form and then observed the Ss on two preference tests with nondifferential reinforcement. In the first test, the monkeys had to choose between stimuli that combined the positive color and negative form cues and the negative color and positive form; the animals chose the positive color on 39 or 40 out of 40 test trials. Had testing stopped here one might infer that the monkeys had learned the discrimination on color cues only. The stimuli presented in the second test were both positive in color, but one was negative in form and the other positive in form. All of the monkeys preferred the positive object, indicating that they had in fact learned to discriminate forms as well as colors during training on two cues and that the inference suggested by the first test was invalid.

Grice (1952) investigated the same problem that Sutherland and Holgate's experiment was concerned with, namely, specification of what rats learn while solving a two-cue discrimination problem. He trained one group of rats to discriminate circles differing in both size and brightness and a second group to discriminate circles differing only in brightness. The animals were next tested under conditions of differential reinforcement for 20 trials on a new pair of circles differing in brightness but not in size and then trained to criterion on circles which differed in size but not in brightness. Both groups showed immediate and almost errorless transfer to the unfamiliar set of stimuli differing in brightness. On the size discrimination, all Ss trained on both cues learned more quickly than any of those trained on brightness only. The percentage of savings in trials to criterion on the size discrimination for the two-cue group compared to the group trained on brightness only was 92.

Grice quite reasonably interpreted his results as providing very strong support for continuity theory, since his group trained on two cues showed essentially immediate transfer when tested with cues from either of the training dimensions in isolation, and his one-cue group controlled for nonspecific transfer effects in the training and test situations.

It is significant to note in the context of the present discussion that, in designing his investigation, Grice deliberately selected transfer under differential reinforcement rather than equivalence tests with non-differential reinforcement as his dependent variable on the grounds that rats' performances on preference tests with no differential reward are so erratic and variable as to render them unsuitable as indices of what has been learned in prior training.

The papers of Cole and Grice do not inspire confidence in the sensitivity or validity of preference tests as a technique for determining what animals learn during training on a two-cue discrimination. Mumma and Warren (1968) have studied the problem directly. They replicated Sutherland and Holgate's experiment, substituting cats for rats as the Ss, and in addition, determined the correlation between stimulus preferences and trials to criterion in subsequent learning to discriminate differences in only one of the dimensions present in the initial two-cue problem. If preference tests validly measure the attention value of cues for individual animals, a high positive correlation should be found between strength of preference for cues in one dimension and the rate with which a subsequent transfer task on that dimension is learned with differential reinforcement.

The cats averaged 80% correct on training trials given during preference testing, but only 62% appropriate responses to brightness and orientation on the test trials. There was no significant correlation between responses to brightness and to orientation.

The cats' behavior on the preference tests was very different from that of Sutherland and Holgate's rats. The cats' choices were predominantly responses to stimulus novelty. When a novel test figure was paired with the stimulus which had not been rewarded in discrimination training, the novel figure was selected on 79% of the trials; when a novel stimulus was presented with the stimulus that had been rewarded in discrimination training, the novel stimulus was chosen on 55% of the trials, indicating that the attraction to novelty was stronger than the tendency to respond to a familiar stimulus which had been frequently associated with food reinforcement.

Upon completion of the preference tests, groups of cats learned transfer tasks on a single cue, with the cue-reward relation reversed or not reversed relative to initial training on the two-cue discrimination. The animals which were reversed learned the transfer problem significantly more slowly than the group which was not reversed. The correlations between

5*

the strength of preference for the dimension relevant in one-cue learning manifested during the preference tests and trials to criterion in transfer learning were negative and nonsignificant for both the reversed and nonreversed groups.

These findings obviously confirm Grice's argument that preference tests are an unsatisfactory and imprecise means for detecting the effects of reinforced training compared to transfer tests with differential reinforcement. One is clearly not justified in assuming that animals which fail to manifest strong preferences when tested with non-differential reinforcement have failed to learn the significance of the cues in question. These considerations tend rather strongly to render the preference data of Sutherland and Holgate suspect as evidence for their proposition that animals learn two-cue discriminations wholly or mainly on the basis of a single cue.

It is important to note that experiments with monkeys tend to corroborate the findings of our studies with cats, both in respect to the relative insensitivity of preference tests compared to transfer tests with differential reinforcement, and to the influence of novelty on preference responses. Thus, Zimmermann (1962) found that rhesus monkeys consistently performed at a higher level of accuracy on trials with the old negative *versus* a novel stimulus than on trials with the old positive *versus* a novel stimulus, just like the cats trained on the simultaneous discrimination problem, suggesting similar high responsiveness to novelty. Harlow and Poch (1945) also found that monkeys avoid the original negative stimulus more frequently than they approach the original positive when tested on preference trials on which either one or other of the two original stimuli was paired with a novel stimulus.

Zimmermann and Torrey (1965) trained baby monkeys to discriminate a circle and a triangle and then tested two groups for transfer on a series of potentially equivalent shapes. Twenty trials were given on each test pair and the groups were tested with differential or nondifferential reinforcement. The group tested with differential reinforcement performed at levels significantly above chance on several pairs which did not elicit differential responses from *S*s tested with nondifferential reinforcement.

An unpublished experiment by G. Hamilton and D. R. Meyer of the Ohio State University demonstrates the magnitude of the influence of stimulus change upon the behavior of monkeys in experiments dealing with the additivity of cues. Hamilton and Meyer tested 12 naive monkeys on ten 18-trial problems of each of six classes. In the first two types, the stimuli differed in color, form and size (CFS) on trials 1—6, in color (C) only or in form and size (FS) only on trials 7—12, and in all three dimensions again on trials 13—18. These two kinds of problems were designed to determine the effect of removing specific cues from a compound upon the accuracy of performance. The effect of adding a relevant cue was assessed in the second category of problems in which the stimuli differed in FS or C on trials 1—6, in CFS on trials 7 through 12, and FS or C again on trials 13—18. The control conditions involved presentation of constant C or FS cues throughout trials 1—18.

The results obtained by Hamilton and Meyer are shown in Fig. 3 which shows that either addition or subtraction of C or FS cues between

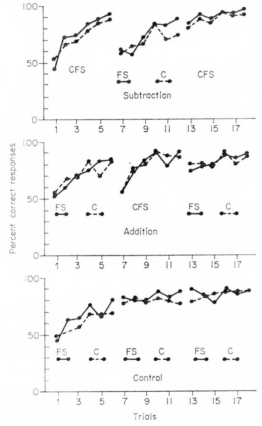

FIG. 3. Mean per cent correct responses in intraproblem learning by monkeys.

trials 6 and 7 results in chance performance on trial 7 and that this effect is equivalent for the two types of cues studied, while similar changes between trials 12 and 13, are ineffective in altering the monkeys' level of performance. The monkeys were clearly attending to both sets of cues since either addition or subtraction of C or FS cues resulted in an immediate and equivalent depression in performance early in learning. This fact poses an additional difficulty for Sutherland and Holgate's explanation of additivity of cues. If the monkeys had learned the CFS problems wholly or mainly in terms of either cue one should expect differential performances on trial 7 depending upon whether the stronger or the weaker cue is subtracted from the compound. Fig. 3 shows that such is not the case, and the fact that analysis of variance failed to yield a significant $Ss \times$ Conditions interaction indicates that the absence of the difference predicted by attention theory in the group learning curves is not an artifact of averaging qualitatively different performances across individuals.

Similarly, if learning response attachments to the outputs of the weaker analyzer lags behind learning differential response attachments to the stronger analyzer one would expect differential responses to stimulus changes between trials 12 and 13. None were obtained under either the addition or subtraction conditions, suggesting that in terms of attention theory, response attachments to the outputs of both analyzers reached relatively high levels, at about the same time.

V. Partial Reinforcement and Resistance to Extinction

Two of the most cogent explanations of the partial reinforcement effect in recent years have been those of Amsel (1958, 1962) and Sutherland et al. (1965). Amsel's theory, based on the notion of a frustration enhanced drive, has received support from drug studies (e.g. Barry et. al. 1962), showing that whereas anxiety-reducing drugs when administered in extinction will prolong extinction, the administration of the same drugs during acquisition of an instrumental response under conditions of partial reinforcement will attenuate the effects of such a schedule on the rate of extinction.

On the other hand, Amsel's theory has some difficulty with the finding (Jenkins, 1962; Theios, 1962) that animals first trained on partial reinforcement and subsequently on continuous reinforcement are more resistant to extinction than are animals trained in the reverse order. It is at this point that the theory proposed by Sutherland et al. (1964) has a decided advantage over all others. In Sutherland's terms, animals who are subject to continuous reinforcement training first are more likely to learn the response required under the control of one analyzer, as this analyzer is consistently confirmed and strengthened; and the more an animal learns in terms of one analyzer, the less it learns in terms of another (Sutherland, 1964b). On being exposed to partial reinforcement conditions subsequently animals who have established a strong analyzer will be likely to maintain that analyzer to the exclusion of others during the partial reinforcement conditions. Hence the speed of extinction will simply depend upon the speed with which such animals 'switch out' this dominant analyzer.

On the other hand, animals given partial reinforcement training first, will tend to switch analyzers often in acquisition as no one analyzer is being consistently confirmed. However, some of the time, individual analyzers will be confirmed—hence the responses of these animals will be controlled by a multiplicity of weak analyzers. During the conditions of continuous reinforcement which follow, all of the analyzers in use will be confirmed, so that there should be no change *in the number of analyzers* controlling the response; a change in the strength of these analyzers should be the only consequence of continuous reinforcement as confirmation of each one occurs now on every trial.

Thus in extinction, animals trained on partial reinforcement followed by continuous reinforcement will have to extinguish responses to a multiplicity of analyzers, and Sutherland makes the assumption that a multiplicity of moderately strong analyzers will take longer to 'switch out' than will a single analyser however strongly it has been established during acquisition. Hence this explanation of the partial reinforcement effect.

Sutherland's theory rests, therefore, on the simple assumptions that the number of cues learned about during acquisition is greater for partially reinforced animals than it is for continuously rewarded Ss; and that the number of cues learned about during acquisition is the major causal factor in determining resistance to extinction.

The authors know of no previous experimental test designed to differentiate between Sutherland's and Amsel's hypotheses. Most partial reinforcement experiments have been carried out in simple run-way apparatus where it would have been extremely difficult (had this been the investigators' intention) to demonstrate significant differences between the population of cues learned about by continuous reinforcement as opposed to partial reinforcement animals. In 1966, however, Sutherland showed that partial reinforcement animals, in a visual discrimination situation, learned about more cues than did the continuous reinforcement controls. Supportive evidence was provided by McGonigle *et al.* (1967) in a study which attempted to reconcile both the Amsel and the Sutherland viewpoints. In neither of these studies just cited, however, was multiple cue learning independent of (frustrative) partial reinforcement schedules. It was thus not possible to claim that the number of cues learned about *per se* during acquisition was the *major causal factor* in determining resistance to extinction. Therefore, it was not possible to differentiate the 'frustration-drive' theory of Amsel from the 'incidental learning' theory of Sutherland.

McFarland and McGonigle (1967) independently varied consistency of reinforcement and the number of cues provided in acquisition training in order to test definitively the hypotheses of Amsel and Sutherland.

The subjects were forty adult hooded male rats, which were 90 days old at the start of the experiment. They were maintained on a schedule in which they were deprived of food for 22 hours per day but allowed *ad libitum* access to water. The animals were first pretrained to make the instrumental response in a Grice box from which the stimuli had been removed. The subjects were then allocated to four groups, matched for performance in pretraining. During training each rat was run for ten trials per day, with a mean intertrial interval of 10 minutes. Rewards consisted of access to food for 10 seconds.

The training procedure for the four groups is summarized in Table I. The subjects were transferred from Part 1 to Part 2 when they reached an individual criterion of eighteeen out of twenty successive correct choices.

TABLE I

Discriminanda used during acquisition and extinction

Reward schedule	Group	Training		Testing
		Part 1	Part 2	Extinction
CR	1a	BW	BW	BW
100 per cent reward on	b	HV	HV	HV
correct choices	2a	BW	HV	BW + HV
	b	HV	BW	BW + HV
PR	3a	BW	BW	BW
50 per cent reward on	b	HV	HV	HV
Correct choices	4a	BW	HV	BW + HV
	b	HV	BW	BW + HV

CR, Consistently rewarded. PR, Partially rewarded. BW, Black versus white "Perspex" squares on a grey background. HV, Horizontal versus vertical 1 cm wide black and white stripes. BW + HV, BW squares on HV background.

Groups 2 and 4 were then run on a second problem until they reached the same criterion. Groups 1 and 3 were overtrained on the original problem until groups 2 and 4 reached their second criterion. Thus all groups had the same number of training trials. The cues which the animals had learned during training were extinguished and the animals run until they reached a criterion of two successive trials on which no choice response was made within 2 minutes.

The critical comparison is between the CR2 and PR1 groups. For if the number of analyzers learned about is the major causal factor in preventing extinction (conceived as the switching out of all the relevant anazlyers) then the 2-cue group should require more trials to meet a criterion of extinction of choice responses. If partial reinforcement schedules cause switching of attention in this situation, then for the PR groups at any rate, the relevant analyzer cannot possibly be as strong as the combination of relevant analyzers in the 2 cue continuous reinforcement condition. It is conceivable, however, that extensive incidental cue learning in the PR condition (to cues which are irrelevant) can lead to heightened resistance to extinction *in terms of a trials measure*. A further comparison between CR1 and CR2, and PR1 and PR2 should also lead to significant differences in resistance to extinction to a choice criterion according to the Sutherland model.

In Amsel's terms on the other hand, the number of cues in any absolute sense is not a variable as it is the drive enhancement produced in relation to goal-stimuli which produces the differences between partial reinforcement and continuous reinforcement groups in terms of resistance to extinction.

The mean number of trials to the extinction criterion is shown in Table II. These results show that there was no significant difference in resistance to extinction between the one and two cue consistently rewarded groups,

TABLE II

Extinction data

Training	Group	Mean no. trials to criterion	Mann-Whitney	Mean percent correct in last 20 ext. trials
CR, 1 cue	1	101.1	n = 19	58.0
CR, 2 cues	2	115.6	U = 25	57.5
			N.S.	
PR, 1 cue	3	205.7	N = 20	64.5
PR, 2 cues	4	207.8	U = 44	62.0
			N.S.	

CR, Consistently rewarded. PR, Partially rewarded.

or between the one and two cue partially rewarded groups, but that there was a very large difference (there was no overlap in the range) between consistently rewarded (CR) and partially rewarded (PR) groups. Moreover, the percentage of correct *choices* made during the last twenty extinction trials (Table II) indicates that there is no significant difference between consistently rewarded and partially rewarded groups.

It is difficult to see how these results can be accounted for on Sutherland's hypothesis because there are no apparent differences in resistance to extinction between groups which learned about one or two cues during training. On Amsel's hypothesis no such difference would be expected, except that the two cue groups might have experienced some extra frustration in learning the second problem. Because training Part 1 took 180 trials and Part 2 took only 80 trials, however, it is evident that few incorrect choices can have been made in learning the second problem. Whatever extra frustration was experienced may be reflected in the nonsignificant difference between the magnitude of the scores for the one and two cue groups (Table II).

The finding that the partially rewarded groups were much more resistant to extinction than the consistently rewarded groups can be accounted for by Amsel's theory, on the basis of the differing degrees of frustration experienced during training. On Sutherland's theory, it can be accounted for on the basis of frustration-induced irrelevant learning. It seems difficult, however, to maintain the latter view in face of the lack of differentiation between the one and two cue groups. If Sutherland's hypothesis were correct, the more cues learned about during acquisition, whether or not frustration is involved, the greater would be the resistance to extinction, on the assumption that all cues learned about have to be extinguished separately, and that this process takes longer even if each cue is learned about to a lesser extent. The most reasonable conclusion is that resistance to extinction is determined primarily by frustration tolerance, and that the correlated incidental learning is a side effect which plays no part in extinction.

VI. Partial Reinforcement and Reversal Learning

Rats trained for 200 trials on a brightness discrimination under a 75 : 25 ratio of reinforcement, subsequently learn the reversal (0 : 100) discrimination significantly more slowly than rats originally trained for 200 trials with a 100 : 0 ratio of reinforcement (Mackintosh and Holgate, 1968). The inconsistently reinforced rats were less resistant to extinction of their initial choice responses following the reversal, but manifested stronger position habits during reversal training than the consistently reinforced Ss. Mackintosh interprets the results as evidence that inconsistent reinforcement militates against the development of attention to the relevant dimension, so that the 75 : 25 rats are at the same sort of disadvantage relative to 100 : 0 rats in reversing as non-overtrained rats are to overtrained rats.

The essential features of Mackintosh and Holgate's experiment have been duplicated in a recent experiment with cats. Three groups of 16 cats each were trained on a brightness discrimination in a Grice box under 100 : 0, 80 : 20 and 60 : 40 ratios of reinforcement. Half the *S*s in each group were aged 45 days at the beginning of training and half were 180 days old at the start of the experiment. All of the cats were given 20 training trials a day for 50 days on the probability learning task with a rerun correction procedure, and then all were required to learn the reversal of the brightness discrimination to a criterion of 10 consecutive correct responses. Conditions were constant for all groups in reversal learning: 20 non-correction trials per day under conditions of consistent reinforcement (0 : 100).

The results obtained in initial training are summarized in Fig. 4 which shows that there was no significant difference in performance on the

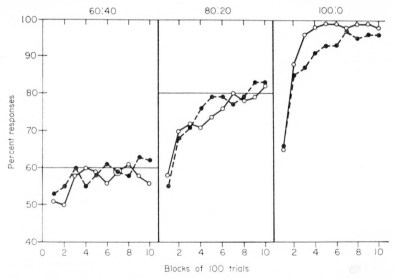

FIG. 4. Brightness discrimination learning as a function of reinforcement ratio.

probability learning task between age groups, and that the partially reinforced groups learned very slowly and imperfectly to select the more frequently reinforced stimulus while the 100 : 0 groups learned to do so in about 100 trials.

Trials and errors to criterion in reversal learning by the three groups are shown in Fig. 5. The consistently reinforced group is inferior to the partially reinforced groups on both measures, and there is no substantial difference in performance between the 80 : 20 and 60 : 40 groups. Analyses of variance indicate that the groups differ significantly in errors ($F = 6.4$, $p < .001$ with 2/36 df), but not in trials to criterion ($F < 1$).

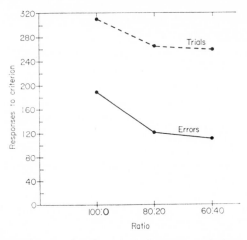

FIG. 5. Reversal learning as a function of reinforcement ratio in acquisition training.

This discrepancy led to a more detailed analysis of the course of reversal learning. Figure 6 shows that the consistently reinforced group was significantly inferior to the partially reinforced groups in respect to the number of consecutive errors made preceding the first correct response ($F = 17$), the number of trials required to attain a criterion of chance performance, 10 correct in 20 trials ($F = 27$), and the proportion of errors to trials preceding the criterion run ($F = 29$). The primary effect of training with consistent rather than partial reinforcement was to enhance greatly the 100:0 group's resistance to extinction of the choice response that was correct in acquisition training. This observation is in good agreement with the findings of Mackintosh and Holgate (1968). The results from cats and rats appear to be diametrically opposed, however, with respect to solution of the reversal problem. Mackintosh and Holgate found the consistently reinforced rats required significantly fewer trials than their 75:25 groups. Our cats did not differ significantly in trials to criterion, but the 100:0 group made significantly more errors than the 80:20 or 60:40 groups. Unfortunately, Mackintosh and Holgate did not report the error scores

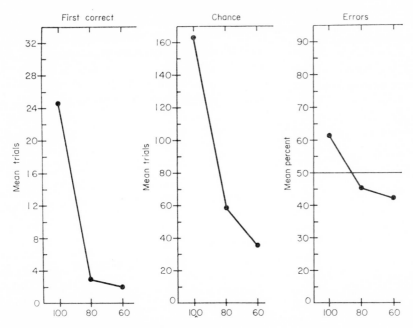

FIG. 6. Trials preceding first correct response, trials to chance, and ratio of errors to trials for groups pretrained with different ratios of reinforcement.

for their rats; it is possible that one exaggerates a little the magnitude of the discrepancy between the two experiments.

Multiple differences in procedure as well as the difference in the species studied preclude elaborate discussion of the possible reasons for our failure to replicate Mackintosh and Holgate's results, but one fact is obvious. The facilitation of reversal learning by prior training with consistent rather than inconsistent reinforcement is apparently, like the facilitative overtraining reversal effect, a phenomenon of limited rather than general occurrence and a great deal of empirical work will probably be required to specify the conditions under which it is likely or unlikely to occur.

It is, nevertheless, difficult to suppress the speculation that the difference in training methods used for training the partially reinforced rats and cats was important. Mackintosh and Holgate used a guidance procedure; after each nonreinforced trial, the rat was forced to the correct alternative by E's occluding the incorrect stimulus. The cats were trained with a rerun correction procedure. Each trial was repeated with stimulus conditions unchanged until S responded to the correct stimulus. There was no limit to the number of incorrect responses a cat could make, as a trial ended only when S finally obtained the reinforcement.

Since the partially reinforced groups were far more frequently exposed to nonreinforcement, they had a much greater opportunity to develop an intratrial "lose-shift" response rule during initial training which could facilitate reversal learning by decreasing resistance to extinction of the original correct response. The 100:0 cats had less opportunity for such learning and Mackintosh and Holgate's rats, none at all.

This interpretation is clearly supported by the data presented in Fig. 5, and by the observation that prior training on position reversals facilitates double alternation learning, as a result of transfer of a "win-stay" response rule (Warren, 1967).

VII Summary and Conclusions

The research described in this paper tested predictions from Sutherland and Mackintosh's duoprocess model of discrimination regarding several experimental phenomena which figure prominently in attention theory. The following conclusions seem justified:

1. Pretraining with the relevant cues in a simultaneous discrimination facilitates solution of a successive discrimination by cats. A similar facilitation of simultaneous discrimination learning results from pretraining on a successive discrimination problem. Thus, the "acquired distinctiveness of cues" obtains for cats as well as rats.

2. Attention theory predicts that overtraining may facilitate, have no effect upon or retard reversal learning, depending on whether the relevant stimulus cues are low, intermediate, or high, respectively, in salience for the subjects. The outcome of any experiment can be reconciled with attention theory by making an appropriate assumption about the conspicuity of the relevant stimulus dimension, unless salience is measured independently. Hirayoshi and Warren (1967) did determine the relative dominance of relevant and irrelevant cues in an experiment on the effect of overtraining on reversal of a brightness discrimination by cats, and obtained results which were directly contradictory of predictions from attention theory.

3. A considerable amount of evidence was summarized to support the argument that preference tests with nondifferential reinforcement provide minimal and equivocal information as to what animals have learned in prior training. Evidence from rats, cats and monkeys raises very serious doubts about the interpretation of Sutherland and Holgate's observation that the more a rat learns about one cue, the less it learns about the other, in the acquisition of a two-cue discrimination, and renders their account of the empirical additivity of cues suspect.

4. Resistance to extinction is determined by the consistency or inconsistency of reinforcement of responses in training, and independent of the number of relevant stimulus dimensions present in the test situation. These

results are more compatible with Amsel's than Sutherland's account of the partial reinforcement effect.

5. Cats trained on a brightness discrimination under conditions of differential partial reinforcement learn the reversed discrimination with significantly fewer errors than cats originally trained with consistent reinforcement. These findings contradict the results obtained by Mackintosh and Holgate in an experiment with rats, and suggest that the effects of training with different ratios of reinforcement on reversal learning may be as variable as the effects of overtraining before reversal.

Only the first conclusion is completely compatible with the version of attention theory (Mackintosh, 1965b; Sutherland, 1964a) tested by the experiments reported here. The inevitable inference must be that contemporary attention theory does not provide an adequate account of discrimination learning by animals, and that it is particularly unsuccessful in predicting the behavior of cats and monkeys.

On the other hand, it must be recognized that predictive accuracy is a criterion of secondary importance for the evaluation of a developing theory. It is far better to ask important questions than answer trivial questions with great precision. Judged from a broader perspective, attention theory must be regarded a success for three reasons. First, it has provoked much research concerned with learning and transfer in a variety of species which have been previously neglected in comparative studies of learning, and more importantly, attention theory has provided a conceptual focus for such comparative studies. Second, there are indications (Warren, 1966) that species differences in transfer are greater and more meaningful than differences in original learning; attention theory provides a necessary theoretical context to encourage further research along these lines. Third, even unsuccessful experimental attempts to verify predictions from attention theory raise important and interesting questions. Our failure to replicate Sutherland and Holgate's observations on two-cue learning by rats, for example, raises two interesting questions. (1) Of what value are data obtained by the classical method of stimulus equivalence for the accurate determination of what an animal has actually learned about the stimuli presented during discrimination training? The absence of any correlation between preference test scores and subsequent transfer learning performance in the experiment with cats described in Section IV suggests that equivalence or preference tests provide a very minimal estimate indeed, compared to transfer tests with differential reinforcement. (2) Do species differ systematically in their responsiveness to visual novelty? The survey of preference test performance by rats, cats and monkeys strongly suggests that rats' choices on preference tests are more strongly affected by past association of stimuli with reinforcement than is the case with monkeys and cats which respond predominantly to stimulus novelty.

Additional questions raised by unsuccesful attempts to verify predictions from attention theory with cats and monkeys have been discussed by Warren, Derdzinski, Hirayoshi and Mumma (1968).

Thus our final verdict is that the 1964–1965 version of attention theory was a predictive failure but an heuristic success. The research which we think has largely discredited the theory has been productive of interesting and potentially important problems for further study.

Acknowledgement

Support for the preparation of this paper was provided by Grant MH 04726 from the National Institute of Mental Health, United States Public Health Service.

References

Amsel, A. (1958). The role of frustrative non-reward in non-continuous reward situations. *Psychol. Bull.* **55,** 102–109.

Amsel, A. (1962). Frustrative reward in partial reinforcement and discrimination learning: some recent history and a theoretical extension. *Psychol. Rev.* **69,** 309–328.

Barry, H., Wagner, A. R. and Miller, N. E. (1962). Effects of alcohol and amobarbital on performance inhibited by experimental extinction. *J. comp. physiol. Psychol.* **55,** 464–468.

Beck, C. H., Warren, J. M. and Sterner, R. (1966). Overtraining and reversal learning by cats and rhesus monkeys. *J. comp. physiol. Psychol.* **62,** 332–335.

Boyer, W. N. and Cross, H. A. (1965). Discrimination reversal learning in naive stump-tailed monkeys as a function of number of acquisition trials. *Psychon. Sci.* **2,** 139–140.

Brookshire, K. H., Warren, J. M. and Ball, G. G. (1961). Reversal and transfer learning following overtraining in rat and chicken. *J. comp. physiol. Psychol.* **54,** 98–102.

Cole, J. (1953). The relative importance of colour and form in discrimination learning in monkeys. *J. comp. physiol. Psychol.* **46,** 16–18.

Cross, H. A. and Boyer, W. N. (1966). Influence of overlearning on single habit reversal in naive rhesus monkeys. *Psychon. Sci.* **4,** 245–246.

Cross, H. A. and Brown, L. T. (1965). Discrimination reversal learning in squirrel monkeys as a function of number of acquisition trials and prereversal experience. *J. comp. physiol. Psychol.* **59,** 429–431.

Cross, H. A., Fickling, R. M., Carpenter, J. B. and Brown, L. T. (1964). Discrimination reversal performance in squirrel monkeys as a function of prereversal experience and overlearning. *Psychon. Sci.* **1,** 353–354.

D'Amato, M. R. (1965). The overlearning reversal effect in monkeys provided a salient irrelevant dimension. *Psychon. Sci.* **3,** 21–22.

Derdzinski, D. (1967). Shape discrimination learning by cats. Unpublished M.S. thesis. Pennsylvania State University, U.S.A.

Eniger, M. W. (1952). Habit selection in a selective learning problem. *J. comp. physiol. Psychol.* **45,** 604–608.

Grice, G. R. (1952). Simultaneous acquisition of differential response strength to two stimulus dimensions. *J. gen. Psychol.* **47,** 65–70.

Hara, K. and Warren, J. M. (1961). Stimulus additivity and dominance in discrimination performance by cats. *J. comp. physiol. Psychol.* **54,** 86–90.

Harlow, H. F. and Poch, S. (1945). Discrimination generalization by macaque monkeys to unidimensional and multidimensional stimuli. *J. comp. Psychol.* **38,** 353–365.

Hirayoshi, I. and Warren, J. M. (1967). Overtraining and reversal learning by experimentally naive kittens. *J. comp. physiol. Psychol.* **64,** 507–509.

Jenkins, H. M. (1962). Resistance to extinction when partial reinforcement is followed by regular reinforcement. *J. exp. Psychol.* **64,** 441–450.

Lashley, K. S. (1942). An examination of the continuity theory as applied to discriminative learning. *J. gen. Psychol.* **26,** 241–265.

Lawrence, D. H. (1949). Acquired distinctiveness of cues: I. Transfer between discriminations on the basis of familiarity with the stimulus. *J. exp. Psychol.* **39,** 770–784.

Mackintosh, N. J. (1965a). Overtraining, extinction and reversal in rats and chicks. *J. comp. physiol. Psychol.* **59,** 31–36.

Mackintosh, N. J. (1965b). Selective attention in animal discrimination learning. *Psychol. Bull.* **64,** 124–150.

Mackintosh, N. J. and Holgate, V. (1968). Effects of inconsistent reinforcement on reversal and non-reversal shifts. *J. exp. Psychol.* **76,** 154–159.

Mackintosh, N. J. and Mackintosh, J. (1963). Reversal learning in *Octopus vulgaris* Lamarck with and without irrelevant cues. *Quart. J. exp. Psychol.* **15,** 236–242.

Mackintosh, N. J., Mackintosh, J., Safriel-Jorne, O. and Sutherland, N. S. (1966). Overtraining, reversal and extinction in the goldfish. *Anim. Behav.* **14,** 314–318.

McFarland, D. J. and McGonigle, B. (1967). Frustration tolerance and incidental learning as determinants of extinction. *Nature,* **215,** 786–787.

McGonigle, B. (1967). Stimulus additivity and dominance in visual discrimination performance by rats. *J. comp. physiol. Psychol.* **64,** 110–113.

McGonigle, B., McFarland, D. J., and Collier, P. (1967). Rapid extinction following drug-inhibited incidental learning. *Nature,* **214,** 531–532.

Mumma, R. and Warren, J. M. (1968). Two-cue discrimination learning by cats. *J. comp. physiol. Psychol.* (in press).

Reynolds, G. S. (1961). Attention in the pigeon. *J. exp. Anal. Behav.* **4,** 203–208.

Spence, K. W. (1936). The nature of discrimination learning in animals. *Psychol. Rev.* **43,** 427–449.

Spence, K. W. (1937). The differential response in animals to stimuli varying within a single dimension. *Psychol. Rev.* **44,** 430–444.

Sutherland, N. S. (1959). Stimulus analyzing mechanisms. *In* "Proceedings of a symposium on the mechanization of thought processes." Vol. 2, pp. 575–609. H.M.S.O., London.

Sutherland, N. S. (1964a). The learning of discriminations by animals. *Endeavour,* **23,** 148–152.

Sutherland, N. S. (1964b). Visual discrimination in animals *Brit. Med. Bull.* **20,** 54–59.

Sutherland, N. S. (1966). Partial reinforcement and breadth of learning. *Quart. J. exp. Psychol.* **18,** 289–301.

Sutherland, N. S. and Holgate, V. (1966). Two-cue discrimination learning in rats. *J. comp. physiol. Psychol.* **61,** 198–207.

Sutherland, N. S., Mackintosh, N. J. and Wolfe, J. B. (1965). Extinction as a function of the order of partial and consistent reinforcement. *J. exp. Psychol.* **69**, 56–59.

Terrace, H. S. (1966). Stimulus control. *In* "Operant behaviour: Areas of research and application." (Honig, W. K. ed.), pp. 271–344. Appleton-Century-Crofts, New York, U.S.A.

Theios, J. (1962). The partial reinforcement effect sustained through blocks of continuous reinforcement. *J. exp. Psychol.* **64**, 1–6.

Tighe, T. J. (1965). The effect of overtraining on reversal and extradimensional shifts. *J. exp. Psychol.* **70**, 13–17.

Warren, J. M. (1953). Additivity of cues in visual pattern discrimination by monkeys. *J. comp. physiol. Psychol.* **46**, 484–486.

Warren, J. M. (1954a). Perceptual dominance in discrimination learning by monkeys. *J. comp. physiol. Psychol.* **47**, 290–292.

Warren, J. M. (1954b). Reversed discrimination as a function of the number of reinforcements during pre-training. *Am. J. Psychol.* **67**, 720–722.

Warren, J. M. (1956). Some stimulus variables affecting the discrimination of objects by monkeys. *J. genet. Psychol.* **88**, 77–80.

Warren, J. M. (1960). Reversal learning by paradise fish (*Macropodus opercularis*). *J. comp. physiol. Psychol.* **53**, 376–378.

Warren, J. M. (1966). Reversal learning and the formation of learning sets by cats and rhesus monkeys. *J. comp. physiol. Psychol.* **61**, 421–428.

Warren, J. M. (1967). Double alternation learning by experimentally naive and sophisticated cats. *J. comp. physiol. Psychol.* **64**, 161–163.

Warren, J. M., Derdzinski, D. A., Hirayoshi, I. and Mumma, R. (1968). Some tests of attention theory with cats. *In* "Attention: A Behavioural Analysis." (Mostofsky, D. I. ed.), Appleton-Century-Crofts, New York, U.S.A.

Warren, J. M., Grant, R., Hara, K. and Leary, R. W. (1963). Impaired learning by monkeys with unilateral lesions in association cortex. *J. comp. physiol. Psychol.* **65**, 241–253.

Zimmerman, R. R. (1962). Form generalization in the infant monkey. *J. comp. physiol. Psychol.* **55**, 918–923.

Zimmerman, R. R. and Torrey, C. C. (1965). Ontogeny of learning. *In* "Behaviour of nonhuman primates: Modern research trends." Vol. 2. (Schrier, A. M., Harlow, H. F. and Stollnitz, F. eds.), pp. 405–447. Academic Press, New York, U.S.A.

6

Comparative Studies of Reversal and Probability Learning : Rats, Birds and Fish.

N. J. MACKINTOSH

Dalhousie University, Halifax, Nova Scotia, Canada

I. Introduction

Comparative studies in biology may be undertaken for a variety of reasons. In much of comparative anatomy, for example, the aim has been to throw light on both the development and historical origin of various characteristics, and also on the interrelationship and phylogenetic status of different animal groups. Clearly such an approach need not be the preserve of the study of morphological characteristics: comparative studies of behaviour and learning capacities can be undertaken with a view to following evolutionary changes in behavioural characteristics, to demonstrating an orderly improvement in learning abilities, or even to placing a given species at its appropriate taxonomic level. While it is not easy to think of examples of this last line of argument (but see Leonard *et al.* 1966), the aim of most earlier essays in comparative psychology has been to trace the "evolution of intelligence", or the orderly progression of learning capacities as one ascends to higher phylogenetic levels.

There is however a second use for comparative studies in biology, namely, as a valuable aid in the biologist's attempt to understand the function of given structures, or the mechanism responsible for given patterns of behaviour. One way of discovering the function of some structure might be to look at the behaviour of an animal lacking it. One way of getting at the neuro-anatomical structures implicated in learning might be to correlate across different animal groups variations in neuro-anatomy with variations in learning processes (Boycott and Young, 1950). Once again such a programme need not be the preserve of the anatomist: it need not be differences in morphology that are correlated with differences in behaviour. Correlation of any set of differences should increase one's undertanding of the causal relationship between them. Even the theoretical psychologist might hope to throw light on the adequacy of a theoretical system by looking at the behaviour of a variety of animal groups. For suppose there exists a theory which purports to explain the behaviour of rats in a given experimental situation, and that when goldfish are trained in this situation their performance differs markedly from that of the rat. The theorist, if sufficiently versatile, ought to be able to account for this difference in the behaviour of rat and fish by postulating, say, some differences between the parameters used to explain the behaviour of rats and those used for the fish; and he ought then, if the model is of any generality, to be able to predict further differences in the behaviour of rat and fish in some different experimental situation. Confirmation of such predictions would provide an interesting and rather powerful line of support for the appropriateness of the model. It is this use to which I wish to put a comparative approach in the present paper.

II. Data

In an important and extensive series of experiments, Bitterman and his collaborators have investigated the behaviour of rats, pigeons and fish (African mouthbreeders and goldfish) in two experimental situations, serial reversal learning and probability learning. These experiments have uncovered a number of apparent differences in the behaviour of these classes of animal, and Bitterman (1965) has summarized the results in the manner shown in Table I. The basic argument of this chapter is that these behavioural differences can be accounted for within the framework of a model of discrimination learning, in other words that changes in the parameters of such a model will predict appropriate differences in behaviour. The argument is not entirely simple, for before it can be developed it is necessary to show that these behavioural differences are real ones (a matter disputed by some), but that Bitterman's analysis is nevertheless misleading. Before doing this, the meaning of Table I must be briefly explained.

In serial reversal experiments, animals are trained to select one of two alternatives that may be either spatially or visually defined (e.g. either left versus right, or black versus white); and after either attaining some

TABLE I

Bitterman's summary of the behaviour of rat, pigeon and fish in serial reversal and probability learning experiments.

Animal	Serial reversal		Probability learning	
	Visual	Spatial	Visual	Spatial
Rat	R	R	R	R
Pigeon	R	R	F	R
Fish	F	F	F	F

arbitrary criterion of learning, or after an arbitrary number of trials, are trained to select the other alternative. Any number of such reversals may be given. The entries in Table I have the following meaning. *R* stands for rat-like behaviour: according to Bitterman, rats improve over a series of reversals, that is to say they learn later reversals faster than earlier ones. *F* stands for fish-like behaviour: fish do not improve over a series of reversals, but learn later reversals at least as slowly as earlier ones.

In probability learning experiments animals are presented with a single problem, and choice of one alternative is rewarded on, say, a random 70% of trials, and choice of the other on the remaining 30% of trials. In the experiments that are of present concern, each trial ends with a reward, since if the unrewarded alternative is chosen on any trial, a further choice is allowed. Rat-like behaviour in probability learning experiments is to "maximise", a term that can either be taken to mean that rats learn to select the 70% (majority) stimulus on 100% of trials, or perhaps more fairly, can be defined by exclusion, namely as not "matching". Fish show matching behaviour: they never learn to select the majority stimulus on appreciably more than 70% of trials.

An important feature of Bitterman's interpretation is his insistence that the difference between rat and fish is not merely a quantitative one. I shall consider in more detail below what this assertion might mean; for the present we need only consider one consequence of this categorization of behaviour into two exclusive and exhaustive classes (improvement versus no improvement in serial reversal; matching versus non-matching in probability learning). If no other categories are allowed, then other animals must behave either like rats or like fish. The results of his pigeon experiments have led Bitterman to fill in the row for pigeons in the manner shown in Table I. On serial reversal tasks, pigeons show improvement and therefore behave in a rat-like manner. In probability learning experiments an important distinction must be made between visual and spatial problems: "the pigeon shows random matching in visual problems; in spatial problems it tends to maximise" (Bitterman, 1965, p. 405). Hence the F and R entries under probability learning.

The fact that pigeons behave like rats in serial reversal experiments, but not consistently like rats in probability learning experiments leads Bitterman to say: "One conclusion which may be drawn from these results is that experiments on habit reversal and experiments on probability learning tap somewhat different processes. If the processes were the same, any animal would behave either like the fish, or like the rat, in both kinds of experiment. We have then been able to separate the processes underlying the two phenomena which differentiate fish and rat by a method which might be called *phylogenetic filtration*." (*loc. cit.*). Given the validity of the initial premisses (that is, given that Bitterman's description of his experimental results is appropriate), the conclusion is an impeccable one, and illustrates the theoretical value of comparative studies.

III. Re-evaluation

If the differences between rat, pigeon and fish observed in probability learning experiments do not coincide with the differences observed in serial reversal experiments, then no single explanation will encompass the data obtained by Bitterman. Equally, a demonstration that the pattern of differences emerging from the two types of experiment was identical, would be consistent with (although it would obviously not entail) the idea that a *single* theoretical difference was responsible for the two sets of behavioural differences. The next step in the argument is to show that Bitterman's analysis is misleading, and that his (and others') data are entirely consistent with the following propositions: first, there are orderly differences in the behaviour of fish (goldfish and mouthbreeders), birds (quail, domestic chick, pigeons, several passerines) and rats in both serial reversal and probability learning experiments. Secondly, that these differences are quantitative: the performance of birds falls about mid-way between that of rat and fish.

In order to establish this conclusion, it is necessary to consider why the argument for a qualitative distinction in performance is in principle unsatisfactory. There are two reasons. First it is questionable whether even at a descriptive level there are valid grounds for drawing a qualitative distinction in both the present instances. It may seem reasonable to argue that when fish fail to improve over a series of reversals while birds and rats do improve, this constitutes a qualitative difference. But it is *prima facie* less easy to see wherein lies the qualitative difference between the probability learning performance of rat and fish. There is nothing intrinsically special about a matching asymptote that makes the behaviour of an animal that selects the majority stimulus of a 70:30 problem on 70% of trials differ in kind from the behaviour of an animal that selects the majority stimulus on 80% of trials. The second is performing somewhat more accurately than the first, that is all: just as it, in turn, would be described as performing somewhat less accurately than an animal that selected the majority stimulus on 90% trials. Bitterman's distinction between matching and non-matching behaviour would imply that the performance of the first animal differs qualitatively from that of the second and third, and that the performance of the second and third animals is essentially similar. It is extremely hard to see why it is not more appropriate to say that the performance of each animal differs quantitatively from that of the others.

Secondly, even where our descriptive categories are such that it seems not unreasonable to talk of qualitative differences in performance, there is no guarantee that these categories correspond to differences in underlying mechanism: apparently qualitative differences in performance need not be due to the operation of qualitatively different processes, but to the quantitatively different operation of one and the same process. For example, were one to accept that matching and non-matching represented qualitatively different behaviour patterns, this would not necessarily imply that they required different theories for their explanation. The two-operator linear model is sufficiently flexible in principle to encompass any level of performance in probability learning experiments. Equally (to choose a behavioural difference more plausibly regarded as qualitative) a single theoretical model is capable of predicting that overtraining will either facilitate, have no effect on, or retard reversal learning. Lovejoy (1966) has shown that a two-stage attentional model will predict either facilitation or retardation depending on the value assigned to the initial probability of attending to the relevant cue; while C. Turner (personal communication) has shown that even when the starting values in Lovejoy's model are fixed, relatively small changes in the values of reward and non-reward operators will alter the direction of the effect of overtraining.

With these considerations in mind, we can turn to a closer examination of the evidence from serial reversal and probability learning experiments. The conclusion that this examination will suggest is that while rats, birds and fish do not behave alike in these situations, the differences between them are no more than quantitative.

A. SERIAL REVERSAL

That rats improve when trained on a series of reversals has been known for more than 30 years: Buytendijk (1930) found improvement in spatial reversals, and Krechevsky (1932) in visual reversals. With the exception of

Fritz (1930) who trained only four rats for a total of only 2, 4, 6, or 13 reversals of a brightness discrimination, all published investigations have obtained large and significant amounts of improvement, and on both spatial problems (Buytendijk, 1930; Dufort *et al.* 1954; Theios, 1965) and easy visual problems (Mackintosh *et al.* 1968), rats have eventually come to reverse with only a single error.

This pattern of results stands in marked contrast to those obtained in experiments with fish. In a total of seven separate studies, Bitterman *et al.* (1958) and Behrend *et al.* (1965) found no evidence of improvement on either visual or spatial problems in either goldfish or African mouth-breeders, while Warren (1960) found no improvement over a series of reversals of a combined visual and spatial problem in paradise fish. This extensive series of failures, occurring under a quite wide variety of conditions, should convince the most hardened sceptic that there is some difference between fish and rats in reversal learning performance. Bitterman, however, has sought to establish more than this, namely, that fish are incapable of improvement over a series of reversals, and therefore differ qualitatively from rats. The statement that fish are not capable of improvement, resting as it does on acceptance of the null hypothesis, is much harder to establish than the altogether weaker statement that they are less efficient than rats. In an early experiment indeed, whose results Bitterman has since questioned, Wodinsky and Bitterman (1957) actually found a significant reduction in errors to criterion made by mouthbreeders over a series of horizontal-vertical reversals; and the results shown in Fig. 1, taken from another visual reversal experiment with mouthbreeders (Behrend *et al.* 1965), suggest that these fish are capable of marginal improvement (the overlap between the median error scores for Reversals 1 to 6 and Reversals 20 to 25 is sufficiently small to be significant at the ·01 level by a nonparametric test). A recent study by Setterington and Bishop (1967) seems to settle the issue: they gave a group of mouthbreeders 20 trials a day on a spatial problem, reversing them every day for 80 days, and found a significant reduction in error scores during the course of the experiment.

Just as the fact that fish occasionally show marginal improvement over a series of reversals hardly implies any equivalence of performance of rat and fish, so the fact that birds nearly always show unequivocal evidence of improvement implies no more than that they are more proficient than fish. It does not imply that they are as proficient as rats. Indeed there is no single answer to questions about the proficiency of birds, since the work of Gossette and his collaborators (Gossette, 1967; Gossette, Gossette and Inman, 1966; Gossette, Gossette, and Riddell, 1966) has established that there are considerable differences in the serial reversal performance of different avian orders, with as one might expect, magpies, mynahs and parrots learning more rapidly than domestic chick or quail. That chicks show significant improvement over a series of reversals was first shown by Warren *et al.* (1960); but the performance of quail over 25 reversals of a visual problem was sufficiently unimpressive to be labelled only "limited or 'marginal' progressive improvement" in a study of Stettner *et al.* (1967, p. 4); and Gonzalez *et al.* (1966) only found improvement when quail were trained for 40 trials per problem, no improvement when they were trained with 20 trials per problem. The first experiments with pigeons (Reid, 1958) failed to obtain significant improvement, possibly, as suggested by Bullock and Bitterman (1962a), because the birds were not very hungry. Subsequent studies (e.g. Bullock and Bitterman, 1962a; Stearns and Bitterman, 1965; Gossette and Cohen, 1966) have established that pigeons are certainly capable of improvement in both visual and spatial reversals, although the pigeons in Bullock and Bitterman's experiment only improved to a limited extent over early reversals of a simultaneous problem, and hardly at all over 55 reversals of a successive visual problem.

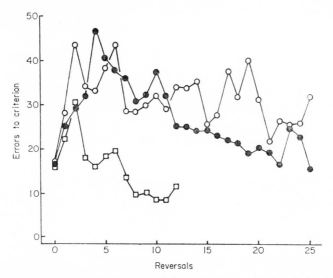

FIG. 1. Performance of rats, pigeons and fish trained on a series of visual reversals. O—O Fish: ●—● Pigeons: □—□ Rats.

The results of all these experiments suggest two points: first, that birds are reliably better at serial reversal learning than are fish; secondly, that with the possible exception of magpies and mynahs, they are not as proficient as rats: rats can achieve one-trial reversals within six reversals; even these two species perform less accurately after twice as many problems. Lending support to this general conclusion, Fig. 1 shows the performance of rats, pigeons and African mouthbreeders trained (to criterion) on a series of visual reversals (brightness for the rats; colour for the birds and fish). The rat data are taken from Gonzalez, Roberts, and Bitterman (1964); the pigeon data from Stearns and Bitterman (1965); and the fish data from Behrend et al. (1965). Since initial learning scores are similar for the three groups, it seems reasonable to compare absolute levels of performance. The results of such a comparison are surely unambiguous. The suggestion that rats and pigeons are alike and both differ from fish seems distinctly less plausible than the alternative proposed here, namely that each class of animal differs quantitatively from the others.

B. PROBABILITY LEARNING

The suggestion that rats maximise in probability learning experiments is misleading if taken to imply that they normally attain 100% selection of the majority stimulus. It is nevertheless closer to the truth than the suggestion once put forward by Estes (1957) that they match. Studies apparently demonstrating matching by rats can be criticized either on the grounds that too few trials were given to ensure that asymptotic performance had been reached (e.g. Brunswik, (1939), gave only 24 trials on a 75:25 schedule, and Hickson, (1961), gave only 90 trials on a schedule gradually changing from 50:50 to 67:33); or on the grounds that a group asymptote approximating to matching is depressed by the inclusion of animals that maintain a preference for the minority stimulus (e.g. Weitzman, 1967: in his Group R70E, one of the five subjects selected the majority stimulus on less than 30% of the final 200 trials); or simultaneously on both grounds (e.g. Estes, (1957), gave 16 rats only 56 trials on a 75:25 schedule, and over the final 16 trials three animals still showed a preference for the minority stimulus). Other studies have shown unequivocally that in both visual and spatial problems rats learn to select the majority stimulus on a proportion of trials significantly greater than its probability of reward (e.g. Bitterman et al. 1958; Gonzalez et al. 1964; Solomon, 1962; Uhl, 1963; Mackintosh, 1968), and in at least one spatial experiment rats have been observed literally to maximize (Roberts, 1966).

There is equally no doubt that fish do not usually significantly exceed matching levels: Bitterman et al. (1958), Behrend and Bitterman (1961, 1966), Marrone and Evans (1966), and Weitzman (1967) have all observed relatively close approximations to matching by both goldfish and mouthbreeders in both visual and spatial problems. The matching is an individual as well as a group phenomenon (see Behrend and Bitterman, (1966), for a detailed exposition of individual scores). The only possible exception to this matching rule is provided by the mouthbreeders trained by Bitterman *et al.* (1958) on a 70:30 spatial problem: over the final 300 trials, the group averaged 75% selection of the majority stimulus, with a range from 71·3% to 79·7%.

Bitterman's suggestion that pigeons behave like rats on spatial probability problems, and like fish on visual problems, seems even less plausible than his analysis of their serial reversal performance. When trained on a 70:30 spatial problem, rats reach an asymptote of at least 95% choice of the majority stimulus (95·33% in Bitterman *et al.* 1958: 99·6% in Roberts, 1966). The only published evidence (Graf *et al.* 1964) shows that a group of 6 pigeons averaged 82% choice of the majority stimulus at asymptote. This falls quite accurately between the matching of fish and near-maximizing of rats.

Just as pigeons perform less accurately than rats on spatial problems, so, the evidence suggests, do they perform more accurately than fish on visual problems. A series of seven sets of results is reported in two papers by Bitterman (Bullock and Bitterman, 1962b; Graf *et al.* 1964). Although no statistics are provided, the results are presented as the group mean (or median) choice of the majority stimulus over blocks of 40 trials, and by counting the proportion of such points falling above and below the matching level, one can perform a reasonably sensitive test of the proposition that pigeons match on visual problems. In the first paper, the first set of results shows matching behaviour (over the final 10 blocks of trials, 5 points lie above, and 4 below the matching level), but the other two show non-matching (18 out of 20 points lie above matching). In the second paper, one out of 4 studies obtained clear matching (only 3 out of 8 points lie above matching), one obtained near maximizing (approximately 90% choice of the majority stimulus), the remaining two obtained performance clearly better than matching (15 out of 16 points better than matching).

In order to provide further evidence on the comparative performance of rats and birds in both visual and spatial probability learning experiments, as well as to obtain data on the pattern of errors made by birds, the following experiment was undertaken. Twenty male hooded rats, four months old, and twenty male chicks, ten days old, were trained for 200 trials on a 75:25 problem. Ten rats and ten chicks learned a brightness discrimination with position irrelevant (half with black, half with white as the majority stimulus); the remaining animals learned a position discrimination with brightness irrelevant (for all subjects the majority stimulus was their non-preferred side). The apparatus was a Grice box with painted black and white goal-boxes; and both apparatus and procedure are described in more detail elsewhere (Mackintosh and Holgate, 1968a). In all essential respects, the procedure for the two classes of animal was identical. The results are shown in Fig. 2. Overall the performance of the rats was superior to that of the chicks ($F = 6·43$, $df = 1,36$, $p < ·025$), but this difference was entirely caused by differences on the spatial problem. The chicks performed hardly less accurately than the rats on the visual problem, and were clearly not matching (only one bird selected the majority stimulus on less than 80% of the final 100 trials—scoring 76%).

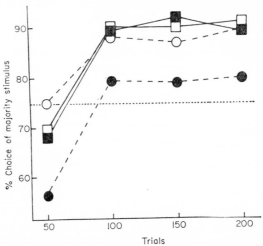

FIG. 2. Performance of rats and chicks trained on either a brightness or a spatial 75:25 problem. Rats: ■—■-Position. □—□ Brightness. Chicks: ●—● position. ○---○ Brightness.

The results can be explained if the following propositions are accepted. First, chicks are less efficient at probability learning than are rats (but do not match on either visual or spatial problems). Secondly, performance in probability learning situations is partly determined by the relative salience of relevant and irrelevant cues. Thirdly, visual cues are more likely to be dominant over spatial cues in birds than in rats. This is not the place to justify the second and third assumptions: for the moment the first is of most importance. This concludes our account of the probability learning performance of various animal groups.

IV. Explanation

The preceding, lengthy analysis of the evidence suggests that in two separate experimental situations, serial reversal and probability learning, the ordering of the performance of three classes of animal—rat, bird and fish, is identical. Rats perform more "efficiently" than birds, and birds perform more efficiently than fish. As noted previously, it is tempting to infer from such a similar patterning that a single theoretical difference underlies both sets of behavioural differences. Furthermore, as Bitterman has pointed out, both kinds of experiment can be regarded as demanding "adjustment to inconsistent reinforcement . . . between sessions in reversal learning and within sessions in probability learning (Bitterman, 1965, p. 402). From these two observations, can we suggest a reasonably precise account of the difference in the processes underlying learning in these animals?

Consideration of the nature of the adjustment to inconsistent reinforcement that is required in the two situations suggests that the task will be none too easy. In serial reversal experiments, an animal is sometimes (over a consecutive series of trials) rewarded for selecting one alternative, sometimes (over the next block of trials) for selecting the other. Efficient performance (as shown by the rat) involves learning to shift choices as soon as reward conditions shift. The development of a "win-stay, lose-shift" strategy will certainly lead to rapid reversal learning, and it might be tempting to argue that the capacity to develop such a strategy is what differentiates rats, birds and fish. There is good evidence that chimpanzees (Schusterman, 1962) and rhesus monkeys (Warren, 1966) do acquire such a strategy during serial reversal training—but equally good evidence from Warren's experiment that cats do not (although their performance on serial reversal as such is just as efficient as that of monkeys). If such a strategy is beyond the intellectual powers of the cat, it seems likely to be beyond those of the rat, and direct tests with rats have yielded entirely negative results (Mackintosh *et al.* 1968). More important for present purposes, the postulation of this sort of difference between rats, birds and fish, while it might in principle explain differences in serial reversal performance, will certainly not explain differences in probability learning. In probability learning experiments, the subject is sometimes rewarded for selecting one alternative, sometimes for selecting the other, but any tendency to choose the last rewarded alternative will lead to matching behaviour. In order to maximize, the subject must precisely not adopt a win-stay, lose-shift strategy, but rather continue to select the majority stimulus even when the minority stimulus has been rewarded.

In both serial reversal and probability learning experiments, reinforcement is shifted from one alternative to the other. Optimal performance in probability learning will be attained by ignoring these changes in reward conditions, and in serial reversal by basing choices on these changes. It is clear that no *single* difference in the response strategies available to rats, birds and fish will explain why the ordering of the three classes of animal is the same in both situations. The only possibility would be to suggest that rats are more flexible than birds or fish, and are capable of adapting the response strategy employed to either the long-term or short-term view. One implication of this idea is that if rats had learned to adopt the strategy appropriate to one type of problem, this would interfere with their performance on the other. To test this possibility, Mackintosh *et al.* (1968) trained rats on a series of reversals of a brightness discrimination. After 8 reversals (by which time performance had stabilized at about 2 errors per reversal), they were trained (in exactly the same apparatus) on a 75:25 brightness probability problem. So far from interfering with brightness probability learning, serial reversal training led to more rapid learning of the probability discrimination and to the attainment of an asymptote (significantly above matching) equal to that of a control group. This result provides no support for the view that serial reversal training develops a strategy inappropriate for probability learning.

It does not look as if further attempts along these lines will be successful. Either the search for a common theoretical difference underlying both sets of behavioural differences must be abandoned or it must be directed toward aspects of discrimination learning other than those of response selection. Several recent formulations (Sutherland, 1964; Zeaman and House, 1963) have suggested that discrimination learning be regarded as comprising two stages: that animals must learn to attend to the relevant dimension as well as learning which value of that dimension is rewarded. The direction of the subject's attention on a given trial is considered to determine both which features will control its choices on that trial, and also what will be learned as a consequence of the outcome of that trial. Attention therefore determines both performance and learning: in a probability learning experiment the accuracy of an animal's performance will depend on the strength of its attention to the relevant cue; in a serial reversal experiment the rate of learning each new reversal will depend on the strength of attention to the relevant cue. Furthermore the problem that confronted any explanation of rat, bird, fish differences in terms of response selection, namely, that serial reversal demands a short-term view of the favourable response, while probability learning demands a long-term view, does not arise for an attentional interpretation. For in both serial reversal and probability learning situations a single cue remains relevant throughout the experiment: the occurrence of reward is predictable on the basis of this stimulus dimension and no other. Both situations, however, involve inconsistent reinforcement of the two values of the relevant dimension; and successful performance on either depends upon the maintenance of attention to this relevant cue in spite of this inconsistency of reinforcement. The simplest explanation, therefore, of the behavioural differences between rat, bird and fish, is to suggest that the three classes of animal differ in the extent to which they can learn to attend to a given cue when it is not consistently correlated with reinforcement. A straightforward difference in the stability of attention in the face of changing reward conditions seems sufficient to explain the data so far presented.

V. Evidence

It only remains to provide some evidence for this interpretation. Two sources of evidence will be discussed: first there are several experiments testing the idea that performance in probability learning situations is determined by the strength of attention to the relevant cue, and that improvement over a series of reversals is due to an increase in the strength of attention from early to late reversals. Secondly, the postulation of differences in attention between rats, birds, and fish leads to the prediction of further behavioural differences between these animals.

A. ATTENTION AND PROBABILITY LEARNING

As has already been mentioned, rats do not normally succeed in literally maximizing when trained on probability problems. Even after several hundred training trials, rats typically continue to select the minority stimulus on between 5% and 20% of trials. The implication of an attentional interpretation is that these "errors" are at least partly due to the subjects having failed to learn consistently to attend to the relevant cue. Three lines of evidence support this interpretation. First, it is possible to influence asymptotic levels of performance by giving pretraining designed to strengthen or weaken attention to the relevant cue (Mackintosh and Holgate, 1967). Rats trained on an absolute brightness discrimination (that is, to select black or white but not grey, or vice-versa) subsequently performed more accurately than controls on a brightness probability problem; while rats trained on a successive orientation discrimination with brightness irrelevant subsequently performed significantly less accurately than controls on a brightness probability problem.

Secondly, the effects of probability learning on subsequent transfer learning are consistent with the idea that probabilistically trained rats have failed to learn consistently to attend to the relevant cue (Mackintosh and Holgate, 1968a). Rats trained for 200 trials on a 75:25 brightness problem learned the 0:100 reversal problem significantly more slowly than rats given equal training on the 100:0 brightness problem. This difference in speed of reversal occurred not because inconsistent reinforcement increased resistance to extinction, but in spite of the fact that it caused more rapid extinction. Rather, inconsistent reinforcement retarded reversal by increasing the occurrence of position habits during reversal, a finding which implies that attention to the relevant brightness cue was weaker. The further finding that inconsistent reinforcement actually facilitated nonreversal shift learning provides very strong evidence for this interpretation: solution of a nonreversal shift precisely demands that subjects stop attending to the originally relevant cue, and learn to attend to a new cue.

Thirdly, the pattern of errors made by rats in probability learning experiments suggests that these errors occur under the control of irrelevant cues: errors are due not so much to a momentary preference for the minority stimulus, as to a momentary failure of attention to the relevant cue (Mackintosh, 1968). When rats were trained on a 75:25 brightness discrimination, no more than a chance proportion of errors occurred on trials following minority stimulus rewards, but an above chance proportion of errors occurred on those trials on which the minority stimulus occupied the position on which reward last occurred. Rats did not reward-follow on brightness (the relevant cue), but on position (an irrelevant cue). When trained on a 75:25 position problem with brightness irrelevant, rats again did not reward-follow on the relevant cue, and although they did not reward-follow on brightness either, errors did not occur at random with respect to brightness, for 87·9% of all errors consisted of responses to the same (preferred) colour, black. These results are shown in Table II along with a similar analysis of the performance of chicks in both visual and spatial problems. Like rats, chicks do not reward-follow on the relevant cue but on an irrelevant cue, and in their case this extends to reward-following on brightness when trained on a position problem.

TABLE II

Analysis of the errors made by rats and chicks on Trials 101–200 of 75:25 probability learning. By chance, 25% of errors would be due to reward-following on the relevant cue, and 55% of errors due to reward-following on the irrelevant cue.

	Rats		Chicks	
	Brightness	Position	Brightness	Position
Percentage of errors due to reward-following on relevant cue	25·7	31·5	29·8	28·0
Percentage of errors due to reward following on irrelevant cue	70·1‡	56·8	70·6†	67·4†

† Different from chance at ·05 level
‡ Different from chance at ·01 level

A probabilistic reinforcement schedule nearly always prevents perfect performance in all animals tested. The above evidence suggests that a major reason for this is that in probability learning situations attention to the relevant cue is not strong enough to control choice behaviour on all trials. If this is true for rats, then other animals, with less ability to maintain attention in the face of inconsistent reinforcement, will be expected to perform even less efficiently.

B. ATTENTION AND SERIAL REVERSAL LEARNING

It is no part of the present thesis to argue that serial reversal improvement depends exclusively on increases in attention to the relevant cue. It is clear that such improvement occurs for a variety of reasons. One reason indeed is the direct antithesis of that suggested here: Sutherland (1966) has shown that in a situation with more than one relevant cue, rats may learn to reverse not by changing preferences within a given stimulus dimension, but by shifting from one dimension to the other. In a situation where such a solution is possible, I should not expect rats to reverse any more rapidly than birds; thus the fact that Bacon *et al.* (1962) found very rapid serial reversal by chicks on a multiple-cue problem is not inconsistent with the present position.

Gonzalez *et al.* (1966) have suggested that a further cause of improvement is the accumulation of proactive interference. This will result in subjects forgetting (between days) which alternative was most recently rewarded, with the consequence that eventually they are not so much learning a reversal each day, as a new problem. Results supporting this suggestion have been obtained by Mackintosh *et al.* (1968). Such an accumulation of proactive interference will obviously cause a decrease in initial errors, and, especially if performance is measured as the total number of errors made over a fixed number of trials on each problem, an improvement in overall performance. Indeed this may well be a major cause of the improvement shown in an experiment by Schade and Bitterman (1966), which they rightly argue cannot be ascribed to increases in the strength of attention.

The present argument only depends on showing that an increase in attention to the relevant cue is *one* cause of serial reversal improvement, and that differences in performance between rat, bird and fish are largely due to differences in this factor. That the development of proactive interference is not the only cause of improvement follows from the results shown in Fig. 3. This gives the within-problem learning curves for early and late reversals in an experiment on brightness serial reversal with rats (Mackintosh *et al.* 1968). It reveals two differences between early and late reversals: first, an increase in the Trial 1 probability of a correct response—

ascribable to an increase in proactive interference; secondly, an increase in the *rate* of learning—which is not so ascribable.

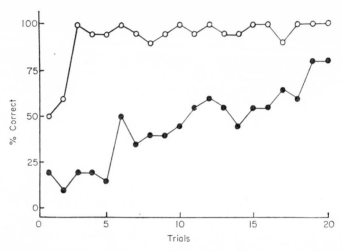

FIG. 3. Within-problem learning curves from early and late reversals of rats learning a series of brightness reversals. ○—○ R7+8. ●—● R1+2.

This increase in the rate at which each new problem is learned is probably not due to the acquisition of any general "reversal learning set", for pretraining on a series of position reversals tends to interfere with rather than to benefit subsequent performance on a series of visual reversals (Bitterman *et al.* 1958; Mackintosh *et al.* 1968). More specifically, the effect of such pretraining is to increase the occurrence of position habits during visual reversal learning, a finding entirely consistent with the idea that serial reversal training establishes a set to respond in terms of a particular cue. One way in which the increasing rapidity of visual reversal learning is usually evidenced is by the reduction of position habits and responses to other irrelevant cues (Lawrence and Mason, 1955; Mackintosh and Mackintosh, 1964; Mackintosh *et al.* 1968), and this again suggests that early reversals are learned slowly because subjects stop attending to the relevant cue, and later reversals are learned rapidly because subjects maintain attention to the relevant cue:

More direct support for this suggestion is provided by some studies of the effects of serial reversal training on nonreversal shift learning (Mackintosh and Holgate, 1968b). In one such experiment, two groups of rats were trained on a black-white problem in a Grice box, one group learning a single problem, the other a series of ten reversals. Both groups then learned a nonreversal shift to position (with brightness irrelevant). If

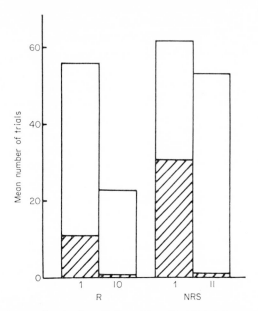

FIG. 4. Learning scores for the first (R 1) and last (R 10) brightness reversal, and for a nonreversal shift to position learned after a single brightness problem (NRS 1) or after 10 brightness reversals (NRS 11). The cross-hatching represents the number of trials during which subjects continued to select their former positive stimulus.

serial reversal training developed any general competence, and even if its only effect were the building up of proactive interference, it should benefit such nonreversal shift learning. The results, shown in Fig. 4, rule out this possibility: in spite of marked serial reversal improvement, the nonreversal shift was learned just about as slowly after 10 brightness reversals as after a single brightness problem ($p > \cdot 10$). Although total trials to criterion were approximately the same for the two groups, the serial reversal subjects spent fewer trials selecting their former positive brightness, and more trials to reach criterion once they had ceased responding to this stumulus. Both differences were significant at the $\cdot 01$ level; the former can be attributed partly to the development of proactive interference; the latter implies some development of attention to brightness in the course of serial brightness reversal.

C. DIFFERENCES IN ATTENTION BETWEEN RAT, BIRD AND FISH

The second line of evidence relevant to the present position concerns the possibility of predicting further differences between rats, birds and fish.

A set of experiments on the effect of extinction trials on an overlearned discrimination habit first revealed behavioural differences between rats, chicks and goldfish ascribable to differences in the stability of attention (Mackintosh, 1965; Mackintosh *et al.* 1966). These experiments revealed differences between these three classes of animal in the extent to which a block of extinction trials succeeded in equalizing response strengths to the two values of the relevant dimension. Since both responses are equally unreinforced during extinction trials, a failure of response equalization indicates failure to learn about the new correlation of the relevant cue with reward, i.e. a failure of attention to the relevant cue early in extinction. The differences obtained—that rats showed greater equalization than chicks, who were in their turn superior to goldfish— thus indicate that attention in the face of a change in reward conditions was maintained longer in rats than in birds, and longer in birds than in fish.

If improvement over a series of reversals is due partly to the development of attention to the relevant cue, and if birds learn reversals more slowly than rats because they never learn to maintain attention to this cue as successfully as rats, then birds should learn a nonreversal shift after a series of reversals at least as rapidly as rats. As a test of this, 16 hooded rats, and 16 ring doves (*Streptopelia risoria*) were trained on a series of reversals in a Grice box with dark grey and light grey goal-boxes. Half of each group learned 10 brightness reversals (with position irrelevant); half learned 10 position reversals (with brightness irrelevant). Ten guidance trials were given each day, and each problem was learned to a criterion of nine correct in any ten successive trials. (Details of the apparatus and procedure for the rats is given in Mackintosh and Holgate, 1968b; procedure for the doves was similar.) After learning their tenth reversal, each subject learned a nonreversal shift under the same conditions: subjects trained on brightness reversals were shifted to position (with their nonpreferred side positive); subjects trained on position reversals were shifted to brightness (half with dark, half with light positive). The results of the experiment are shown in Fig. 5, combined for brightness and position problems. A mixed design analysis of variance performed on the reversal scores showed that later reversals were learned faster than earlier reversals, that position problems were easier than brightness problems, and that rats made fewer errors than doves (all effects significant at the $\cdot 001$ level). Taking the scores on the final reversal only, rats were still superior to doves ($p < \cdot 05$); but from Fig. 5 it is clear that this difference was reversed on the final nonreversal shift problem. Although the nonreversal difference was not significant; an analysis of variance performed on the scores of the final reversal and the nonreversal shift revealed a significant interaction ($p < \cdot 025$) between rats and doves and reversal and nonreversal shift scores. Thus although doves are markedly less proficient at serial reversal learning then are rats, they tend to be somewhat more proficient at a subsequent nonreversal shift problem.

In a second experiment utilizing the same apparatus and procedure, a further 16 rats and 16 doves were trained on a series of brightness and position nonreversal shifts. A typical subject initially learned a brightness problem (dark positive), then a position problem (left positive),

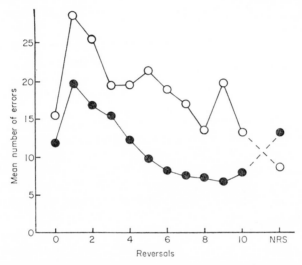

FIG. 5. Performance of rats and doves on a series of reversals (brightness or position), and on a final nonreversal shift. ●—● Rats: ○—○ Doves.

then relearned the original brightness problem, and so on. Each problem was learned (by guidance) to a nine out of ten criterion; and different subjects were trained with all possible combinations of dark, light, left and right positive, while for half the subjects the first problem was a brightness discrimination and for the remainder it was a position discrimination. The doves were trained on four nonreversals, the rats were trained for a total of ten problems in order to check that asymptotic performance had been attained. The results, averaged over brightness and position problems, are shown in Fig. 6. It is obvious that over the four nonreversals the doves learned just as rapidly as the rats. If each subject is assigned a total error score for the four nonreversals in this experiment, and for the first four reversals in the preceding experiment, an analysis of variance reveals a highly significant interaction between rats and doves and reversals and nonreversals ($p < \cdot001$).

Taken together the results of these two experiments show that the superiority of rats to doves in problems where subjects are required to

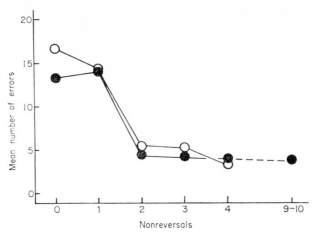

Fig. 6. Performance of rats and doves on a series of nonreversal shifts. ○—○Doves: ●—● Rats.

adapt their behaviour to changing reinforcement conditions is confined to *reversal* learning: doves are if anything better than rats at learning a nonreversal shift following serial reversal training, and are as good as rats at serial nonreversal learning. Indeed it is possible that they are better; since their performance on the original problem was somewhat (although not significantly) inferior to that of the rats, suggesting that the experimental conditions were better suited to the rats. At all events, the interaction between the species difference and the reversal-nonreversal difference provides nice support for the present hypothesis: reversal learning unlike nonreversal shift learning requires the maintenance of attention in the face of changes in reward, and differences in performance that are confined to the former situation are therefore economically explained in terms of differences in the stability of attention.

VI. Conclusions

Comparative studies have been, and still are, regarded with something less than enthusiasm by many psychologists. Two arguments are frequently put forward to justify this reserved attitude: first, that any given difference between two classes of animal may reflect no more than the difference in experimental conditions under which the two animals were studied; secondly, that it is unrealistic to study differences in behaviour across different animal groups without a complete understanding of the behaviour of a single animal.

According to the first argument, if fish fail to improve over a series of reversals while rats improve rapidly, it is only because the fish were not hungry enough or were too hungry, were given too small a reward or too large a reward, or because some combination of these and other variables was inappropriate. There is a little direct evidence against this: for example, Behrend *et al.* (1965) found no serial reversal improvement in goldfish when either a large or a small reward was used; while Gossette and Hood (1967) found that changes in reward size and drive level had no greater effects on reversal than on original learning. The argument, however, is an unlimited one (there is an indefinite number of conditions that might not have been equated in any single comparison of fish and rat), and is not easily disproved by a single demonstration of the ineffectiveness of reward size. Nevertheless, a moment's reflection on the evidence reviewed above should suggest how extraordinarily implausible it is. The argument demands that *by chance* about a dozen experiments with fish should have utilized just that combination of, say, reward size and drive that prevents rapid reversal learning; that an even larger number of experiments with rats should have utilized just that combination that does produce rapid learning; that experiments with birds should have utilized some intermediate combination; and that it just so happened that advanced birds like passerines received a more rat-like combination, and less advanced birds like quails received a more fish-like combination.

A similar interpretation of differences in probability learning has been advanced by Weitzman (1967) and supported by a demonstration that when rats were trained on a 70:30 spatial problem under conditions supposedly analogous to those used for fish, the group did not exceed a matching level. As has already been mentioned, this group matching average was partly produced by the inclusion of one subject that maintained a strong preference for the minority stimulus. A second reason for the poor performance of the rats is most probably that a zero-delay, self-correction procedure was used, which must effectively have minimized the consequences of an error. Fish do not exceed matching even when a delayed guidance procedure is used (Bitterman *et al.* 1958).

It is doubtless true that some combination of conditions can be found under which rats improve but little over a series of reversals, or attain a relatively low asymptote in a probability learning situation. It is always possible to devise inefficient experimental conditions. But to insist that it is solely because they have always been studied under such conditions that fish perform less effectively than rats, is still unconvincing. The only evidence that would support the argument is the demonstration that there are conditions under which fish will achieve a one-trial reversal within half a dozen problems, or learn to select the majority stimulus of a 70:30 problem on more than 90% of trials.

The second argument against comparative psychology, that it is premature, implies that an understanding of the difference in serial reversal performance of rats and fish must await a complete understanding of the performance of rats. The major thesis of this chapter, on the contrary, is that speculations about, and further experimental investigation of the causes of rat-fish differences, may increase our understanding of the behaviour of the rat. As was noted above, the fact that rats, birds and fish appear to be ordered similarly in terms of serial reversal and probability learning proficiency, suggests that these two (apparently diverse) experimental situations share some important features. The fact that rats are not better than doves at serial nonreversal learning severely restricts the range of factors to which the serial reversal difference can be attributed, i.e. demonstrates that there is an important respect in which serial reversal and nonreversal problems differ from one another. (This result also provides compelling evidence against the argument that situational differences are the sole cause of behavioural differences. It is difficult to imagine how differences in reward size or drive level could affect serial reversal learning so markedly without having any effect on nonreversal shift learning.) The present hypothesis, that efficient serial reversal and probability learning demand that subjects maintain attention in spite of imperfect reward conditions, and that differences in the stability of attention underly these behavioural differences, may not be the only feasible explanation. It does, nevertheless, provide a coherent integration of a wide range of data, and surely makes better sense of that data than does the suggestion that all differences are due to differences in reward size.

This is certainly not to say that the phenomena of serial reversal and probability learning experiments are fully or even adequately explained by an attentional analysis, if only because no formal models exist for handling such data in these terms. One particular aspect of the present analysis involves a serious ambiguity which must be mentioned. There are at least two possible ways in which the serial reversal performance of two groups of animals might differ: animals might differ in the rate of improvement over a series of reversals, i.e. in the difference between early and late reversal scores; or they might differ in absolute reversal scores, i.e. in the total number of errors made while learning, say, twenty reversals. Bitterman would seem to be largely interested in the former difference, while the present analysis would seem to be largely concerned with the latter. Although an inspection of published data (see, for example, Fig. 1) suggests that rats and birds differ in both respects, our own study of serial brightness and position reversal in rats and doves revealed only a large difference in the overall number of errors, no difference in the rate of decline in errors from early to late reversals. This ambiguity will not be clarified without much greater theoretical sophistication and understanding.

At present it is not possible to translate the vague hypothesis that serial reversal improvement is partly due to the development of attention, into a formal analysis of serial reversal performance; indeed it is very far from clear just how attention might come to be strengthened by such training. Until the translation is made, however, it will not be possible to see the precise effects of variations in the parameters governing attention, and it will therefore be difficult to predict exactly what behavioural differences are to be expected. Whether this uncertainty is sufficient to condemn the whole of the present enterprise is another matter.

It seems advisable to conclude by entering one final caveat. In the introduction a distinction was drawn between two functions of comparative studies—the tracing of evolutionary developments, and the testing of theories. Although it is obvious that the second has been the major aim in the present chapter, it is not always easy to keep the two apart. For example, the implication of the published evidence on serial reversal learning—that rats perform more efficiently than birds, that passerines perform more efficiently than "lower" birds, and that birds perform more efficiently than fish, was used to argue against an interpretation of all apparent "species-differences" as artifacts of situational differences. It is unlikely that chance alone could have produced results so consistently in line with evolutionary expectations.

Nevertheless the support for the present argument provided by such considerations should be used cautiously. There is no good reason for supposing that the categorization of fish, bird and rat used so glibly here represents a peculiarly appropriate trichotomy; and there is nothing in the present argument that depends upon the validity of this trichotomy. The division is certainly a crude one, for it both ignores differences between members of the same class (mouthbreeders have shown marginal serial reversal improvement, and marginally above-matching performance in spatial probability learning, while goldfish have shown neither; and there are clear, orderly trends in the serial reversal proficiency of various birds). It also assumes, with little justification, that members of different classes must behave differently: given the performance of magpies and mynahs, it would be rash to predict that crows, for example, will be significantly worse at serial reversal than rats. Now given one of the central arguments of this chapter—that the differences being studied here represent no more than quantitative variations in efficiency that can be explained by quantitative changes in the parameters of a model, this gradual change in proficiency is exactly what one would expect. And given that our present interest is less in studying evolutionary changes, and more in the use of comparative studies as a theoretical tool, the fact that crows may reverse as rapidly as rats is by itself no embarrassment. What would constitute damaging evidence is if they did not also perform as efficiently in probability learning experiments.

Acknowledgements

The research reported in this chapter was supported by the Medical Research Council. I am deeply indebted to Valerie Holgate who actually performed most of these published and previously unpublished experiments; and I am grateful to D. M. Vowles for providing us with doves.

References

Bacon, H. R., Warren, J. M. and Schein, M. W. (1962). Non-spatial reversal learning in chickens. *Anim. Behav.* **10**, 239–243.

Behrend, E. R. and Bitterman, M. E. (1961). Probability-matching in the fish. *Am. J. Psychol.* **74**, 542–551.

Behrend, E. R. and Bitterman, M. E. (1966). Probability-matching in the goldfish. *Psychon. Sci.* **6**, 327–328.

Behrend, E. R., Domesick, V. B. and Bitterman, M. E. (1965). Habit reversal in the fish. *J. comp. physiol. Psychol.* **60**, 407–411.

Bitterman, M. E. (1965). Phyletic differences in learning. *Am. Psychol.* **20**, 396–410.

Bitterman, M. E., Wodinsky, J. and Candland, D. K. (1958). Some comparative psychology. *Am. J. Psychol.* **71**, 94–110.

Boycott, B. B. and Young, J. Z. (1950). The comparative study of learning. *Symp. Soc. exp. Biol.* **4**, 432–453.

Brunswik, E. (1939). Probability as a determiner of rat behaviour. *J. exp. Psychol.* **25**, 175–197.

Bullock, D. H. and Bitterman, M. E. (1962a). Habit reversal in the pigeon. *J. comp. physiol. Psychol.* **55**, 958–962.

Bullock, D. H. and Bitterman, M. E. (1962b). Probability-matching in the pigeon. *Am. J. Psychol.* **75**, 634–639.

Buytendijk, F. J. J. (1930). Uber das Umlernen. *Arch. neerl. Physiol.* **15**, 283–310.

Dufort, R. H., Guttman, N. and Kimble, G. A. (1954). One-trial discrimination reversal in the white rat. *J. comp. physiol. Psychol.* **47**, 248–249.

Estes, W. K. (1957). Of models and men. *Am. Psychol.* **12**, 609–617.

Fritz, M. F. (1930). Long-time training of white rats on antagonistic visual habits. *J. comp. Psychol.* **11**, 171–184.

Gonzalez, R. C., Berger, B. D. and Bitterman, M. E. (1966). Improvement in habit-reversal as a function of amount of training per reversal and other variables. *Am. J. Psychol.* **79**, 517–530.

Gonzalez, R. C., Roberts, W. A. and Bitterman, M. E. (1964). Learning in adult rats with extensive cortical lesions made in infancy. *Am. J. Psychol.* **77**, 547–562.

Gossette, R. L. (1967). Successive discrimination reversal (SDR) performance of four avian species on a brightness discrimination task. *Psychon. Sci.* **8**, 17–18.

Gossette, R. L. and Cohen, H. (1966). Error reduction by pigeons on a spatial successive reversal task under conditions of non-correction. *Psychol. Rep.* **18**, 367–370.

Gossette, R. L., Gossette, M. F. and Inman, N. (1966). Successive discrimination reversal performance by the greater hill myna. *Anim. Behav.* **14**, 50–53.

Gossette, R. L., Gossette, M. F. and Riddell, W. (1966). Comparisons of successive discrimination reversal performances among closely and remotely related avian species. *Anim. Behav.* **14**, 560–564.

Gossette, R. L. and Hood, P. (1967). The reversal index (RI) as a joint function of drive and incentive level. *Psychon. Sci.* **8**, 217–218.

Graf, V., Bullock, D. H. and Bitterman, M. E. (1964). Further experiments on probability-matching in the pigeon. *J. exp. Anal. Behav.* **7**, 151–157.

Hickson, R. H. (1961). Response probability in a two-choice learning situation with varying probability of reinforcement. *J. exp. Psychol.* **62**, 138–144.

Krechevsky, I. (1932). Antagonistic visual discrimination habits in the white rat. *J. comp. Psychol.* **14**, 263–277.

Lawrence, D. H. and Mason, W. A. (1955). Systematic behaviour during discrimination reversal and change of dimension. *J. comp. physiol. Psychol.* **48**, 1–7.

Leonard, C., Schneider, G. E. and Gross, C. G. (1966). Performance on learning set and delayed-response tasks by tree shrews (*Tupaia glis*). *J. comp. physiol. Psychol.* **62**, 501–504.

Lovejoy, E. P. (1966). Analysis of the overlearning reversal effect. *Psychol. Rev.* **73**, 87–103.

Mackintosh, N. J. (1965). Overtraining, extinction, and reversal in rats and chicks. *J. comp. physiol. Psychol.* **59**, 31–36.

Mackintosh, N. J. (1968). Attention and probability learning. *In* "Attention: a behavioural analysis." (D. Mostofsky, ed.) Appleton-Century-Crofts, New York, U.S.A. (In press.)

Mackintosh, N. J. and Holgate, V. (1967). Effects of several pre-training procedures on brightness probability learning. *Percept. Mot. Skills*, **25**, 629–637.

Mackintosh, N. J. and Holgate, V. (1968a). Effects of inconsistent reinforcement on reversal and non-reversal shifts. *J. exp. Psychol.* (in press).

Mackintosh, N. J. and Holgate, V. (1968b). Serial reversal and non-reversal shift learning. *J. comp. physiol. Psychol.* (in press).

Mackintosh, N. J. and Mackintosh, J. (1964). Performance of *Octopus* over a series of reversals of a simultaneous visual discrimination. *Anim. Behav.* **12**, 321–324.

Mackintosh, N. J., Mackintosh, J., Safriel-Jorne, O. and Sutherland, N. S. (1966). Overtraining, reversal and extinction in the goldfish. *Anim. Behav.* **14**, 314–318.

Mackintosh, N. J., McGonigle, B., Holgate, V. and Vanderver, V. (1968). Factors underlying improvement in serial reversal learning. *Can. J. Psychol.* **22**, 85–95.

Marrone, R. and Evans, S. (1966). Two-choice and three-choice probability learning in fish. *Psychon. Sci.* **5**, 327–328.

Reid, R. L. (1958). Discrimination-reversal learning in pigeons. *J. comp. physiol. Psychol.* **51**, 716–720.

Roberts, W. A. (1966). Learning and motivation in the immature rat. *Am. J. Psychol.* **79**, 3–23.

Schade, A. F. and Bitterman, M. E. (1966). Improvement in habit reversal as related to dimensional set. *J. comp. physiol. Psychol.* **62**, 43–48.

Schusterman, R. J. (1962). Transfer effects of successive discrimination-reversal training in chimpanzees. *Science N.Y.* **137**, 422–433.

Setterington, R. G. and Bishop, H. E. (1967). Habit reversal improvement in the fish. *Psychon. Sci.* **7**, 41–42.

Solomon, S. (1962). Effects of variations in rearing, drive level, and training procedure on performance in probabililty learning tasks. *Psychol. Rep.* **10**, 679–689.

Stearns, E. M. and Bitterman, M. E. (1965). A comparison of key-pecking with an ingestive technique for the study of discriminative learning in pigeons. *Am. J. Psychol.* **78**, 48–56.

Stettner, L. J., Schulz, W. J. and Levy, A. (1967). Successive reversal learning in the bob-white quail (*Colinus virginianus*). *Anim. Behav.* **15**, 1–5.

Sutherland, N. S. (1964). The learning of discriminations by animals. *Endeavour*, **23**, 148–153.

Sutherland, N. S. (1966). Successive reversals involving two cues. *Quart. J. exp. Psychol.* **18**, 97–102.

Theois, J. (1965). The mathematical structure of reversal learning in a shock escape T-maze; overtraining and successive reversals. *J. math. Psychol.* **2**, 26–52.

Uhl, C. N. (1963). Two-choice probability learning in the rat as a function of incentive, probability of reinforcement, and training procedure. *J. exp. Psychol.* **66**, 443–449.

Warren, J. M. (1960). Reversal learning by paradise fish (*Macropodus opercularis*). *J. comp. physiol. Psychol.* **53**, 376–378.

Warren, J. M. (1966). Reversal learning and the formation of learning sets by cats and rhesus monkeys. *J. comp. physiol. Psychol.* **61**, 421–428.

Warren, J. M., Brookshire, K. H., Ball, G. G. and Reynolds, D. V. (1960). Reversal learning by white leghorn chicks. *J. comp. physiol. Psychol.* **53**, 371–375.

Weitzman, R. A. (1967). Positional matching in rats and fish. *J. comp. physiol. Psychol.* **63**, 54–59.

Wodinsky, J. and Bitterman, M. E., Discrimination-reversal in the fish. *Am. J. Psychol.* **70**, 569–576.

Zeaman, D. and House, B. J. (1963). The role of attention in retardate discrimination learning. *In* "Handbook of mental deficiency: Psychological theory and research" (N. R. Ellis, ed.), pp. 159–223. McGraw-Hill, New York, U.S.A.

7 | Habit-Reversal and Probability Learning : Rats, Birds and Fish

M. E. BITTERMAN, N. J. MACKINTOSH

Bryn Mawr College, Bryn Mawr, Pennsylvania, U.S.A.
Dalhousie University, Halifax, Nova Scotia, Canada.

Part 1 : M. E. BITTERMAN

I. Introduction

In the foregoing paper, Dr. Mackintosh questions my conclusion that experiments on habit-reversal and probability-learning in rat, bird, and fish require us to assume the operation in those animals of learning processes which are, in certain respects at least, qualititavely different (Bitterman, 1965). In his opinion, the experiments have yielded only quantitative differences in performance that may be traced to corresponding differences in a single underlying ability, greater in rat than in bird, and greater in bird than in fish—the ability to attend to cues not consistently correlated with reinforcement. His arguments are unconvincing.

II. Habit-reversal

Mackintosh concludes from the data on habit-reversal that the fish improves in the same way as the bird and the rat, but to a lesser extent, because its ability to attend to inconsistently reinforced cues is much less than that of the higher animals. As evidence of "marginal" improvement in the fish, Mackintosh cites three papers. The first, by Wodinsky and Bitterman (1957) reports out earliest work on habit-reversal. We had very little experience with fish at the time, our technique was a primitive (manual) one, and the improvement we found was of a unique kind which we have been unable to reproduce in subsequent work with a more sophisticated (fully automated) technique. In my opinion, that first effort showed progressive improvement only in Wodinsky and Bitterman. The second paper which Mackintosh cites as evidence of improvement in the fish is by Behrend et al. (1965). It reports some results for eight groups of goldfish and five groups of African mouthbreeders—13 groups in all—trained under a variety of conditions, not one of which yielded a statistically reliable change in performance over reversals. Mackintosh's claim that one of the 13 groups (whose curve he reproduces in his Fig. 1) showed significant improvement is based on two statistical errors. One of his errors is to use only arbitrarily selected portions of the data (the first and last six of 25 reversals). The other is to take no account of individual variance. A proper test (as reported in the original paper) does not permit rejection of the null hypothesis.

The third paper which Mackintosh cites as evidence of improvement in the fish is a recent one by Setterington and Bishop (1967). The improvement there reported is substantial, and its pattern seems quite characteristic of that found in higher animals, but the conditions under which it appears are so restricted as to suggest that it has another explanation. In Fig. 1, the data of the Setterington-Bishop experiment are shown along with those of a replication by Behrend and Bitterman (1967), which gave no indication of improvement. The two experiments were very much alike, with one important exception: the intertrial interval was 2 sec in the original and 10 sec in the replication. Why should improvement occur only in massed trials? Certainly there is nothing in Sutherland's theory to suggest that analyzer-strength is a function of the intertrial interval—nothing in the data for higher animals requires that assumption. It seems more reasonable that the massing contributes, not better attention, but some useful stimuli. I think the improvement found by Setterington and Bishop is due to the development of a simple win-stay discrimination based on carryover from trial to trial of the sensory consequences of response. In higher animals, of course, improvement in reversal is found over so broad a range of intertrial intervals that it must be based on some

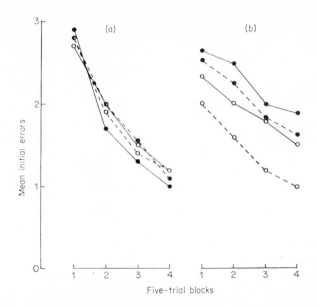

FIG. 1. Spatial habit reversal in the fish as a function of the intertrial interval. Each curve shows the mean within-reversals improvement for a block of 20 reversals. Improvement from one block of reversals to the next appeared with an intertrial interval of 2 sec (b) (Setterington and Bishop, 1967) but not with an intertrial interval of 10 sec (a) (Behrend and Bitterman, 1967). Reversals ●—● 1–20, ●---● 21–40, ○—○ 41–60, ○---○ 61–80.

mechanism other than sensory carryover. There is no evidence yet for even the "marginal" operation of such a mechanism in the fish.

In support of his assertion that birds are less proficient in reversal than rats, Mackintosh reproduces (in his Fig. 1) two curves—one for a group of pigeons in a rather difficult blue-green problem (Stearns and Bitterman, 1965), and the other for a group of rats in a black-white problem (Gonzalez *et al.* 1964). The comparison is justified, Mackintosh believes, by the fact that the two groups made about the same number of errors in original learning (Reversal O). The data on habit reversal make it quite clear, of course, that the levels and slopes of reversal curves may differ widely even for a single species as a function of cue-response-reward contiguity, drive-level, amount of reward, stimulus-similarity, amount of training per reversal, as well as other procedural and contextual variables (Gonzalez *et al.* 1966a, 1966b). Before Mackintosh can conclude that the curves he has selected demonstrate differential proficiency in rat and pigeon, he must establish that the conditions under which they were tested were equated for the effects of all such variables. How does he propose to do that? It should be evident that the number of errors made in Reversal O is not a very good criterion.

Consider, for example, the curves of Fig. 2, which show the performance of two groups of pigeons that were trained to criterion in a series of red-green reversals under conditions identical in all respects except one—the response of the "key" animals on each trial was to peck at one or the other

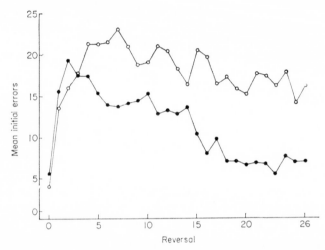

FIG. 2. Habit-reversal in the pigeon as a function of training procedure. The key animals chose between differently colored keys, while the mag animals chose between differently colored food-magazines. The curves are plotted in terms of mean errors to criterion. (From Gonzalez *et al.*, 1966a.) ●—● Mag. ○—○ Key.

of two differentially illuminated keys, while the response of the "mag" animals was to insert the head into one or the other of the differentially illuminated apertures of two grain magazines (Gonzalez *et al.* 1966a). Which, if either, of these rather different curves shall we take as representative of the "proficiency" of the pigeon? Clearly there are important determinants of the difficulty of reversal other than proficiency which are not adequately reflected by the number of errors made in Reversal O. To compare curves obtained from different species of bird (as Mackintosh does with equal assurance) is no more meaningful, of course, than to compare curves of bird and rat. The equation of drive-level or incentive-value or sensory demand is no easier from one species of bird to another than from bird to rat.

I am mystified by Mackintosh's insistence that it is a deficiency of attention which is responsible for species differences in reversal performance, since he admits that a substantial amount of the improvement found in higher animals must be due to factors other than increased attention to relevant cues. He is willing, for example, to attribute *all* the improvement in Schade and Bitterman's (1966) pigeons to proactive interference. Why, then, should he not be willing to attribute the *lack* of improvement in their fish to the *lack* of proactive interference? That the fish's unique performance in reversal experiments is in fact attributable, not to a deficiency of attention, but to what might be called a deficiency of forgetting, is suggested by the results of a recent experiment (Gonzalez *et al.* 1967).

A group of pigeons and a group of goldfish were trained in a series of two-day visual reversals (40 trials per day, using the correction method,

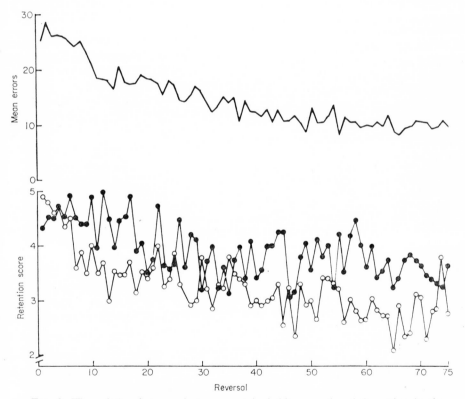

FIG. 3. The relation between improvement in habit-reversal and forgetting in the pigeon. The animals were trained in a series of two-day visual problems. The upper curve shows mean errors per reversal, and mean retention scores are plotted in the two lower curves. The filled circles show retention as measured on the early trials of non-reversal days. The open circles show retention as measured on the early trials of reversal days. (From Gonzalez, *et al.* 1967). ○—○ Day 1. ●—● Day 2.

with red and green stimuli, and with positive and negative colors reversing every two days). The results for the pigeons are presented in
Fig. 3. The course of improvement is given by the upper curve, which is
plotted in terms of mean errors per reversal, while the lower curves show
changes in two independent measures of retention (from the first to the
second day of each reversal, and from the second day of each reversal to
the first day of the next). The implication is clear that forgetting is responsible at least in large part for the improvement. By contrast with the
curves for the pigeons, the curves for the goldfish, which are presented in
FIG. 4, show neither improvement in reversal nor decrement in retention.
It seems reasonable to conclude from these results that fish and pigeon
perform differently in reversal experiments because their learning-
retention mechanisms are different. It is possible, of course, that the
attention of fish and rat also are different, as Mackintosh speculates, and

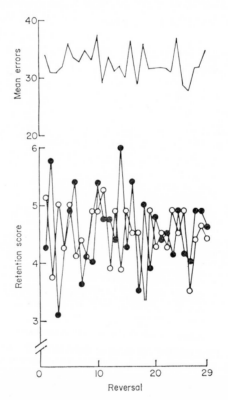

FIG. 4. The relation between improvement in habit reversal and forgetting in the goldfish. These curves are presented for comparison with those of Fig. 2 and are based on the
same measures. (From Gonzalez *et al.* 1967.) ○—○ Day 1. ●—● Day 2.

that the difference in attention does make some contribution to the difference in their reversal performance, but the available data do not require us to take that speculation very seriously.

Sometimes Mackintosh treats the superiority of rat to bird in reversal learning as a fact from which he infers a difference in attention. Clearly, it is not a very substantial fact. At other times, he infers the superiority in reversal from a difference in attention, which in turn is inferred from other facts, hardly more substantial. The hypothesis on which the entire conjectural structure rests—that improvement in reversal is due to the development of attention—is characterized in the end by Mackintosh himself as "vague" and inadequate for predition; "indeed," he writes, "it is very far from clear just how attention might come to be strengthened by such training".

Mackintosh is unfair to his hypothesis. It is vague in many respects, certainly, but not without meaning, and some clear predictions can be made from it—which are just as clearly wrong. Example: If improvement in reversal, like the overlearning-reversal effect, is due to strengthened attention to the relevant stimuli, there should be no improvement for stimuli which are alleged not to give the ORE because attention to them is high to begin with (Schade and Bitterman, 1965, 1966). Example: If improvement in reversal is due to strengthened attention to the relevant stimuli, and if nondifferential reinforcement for response to a pair of stimuli weakens attention to them, then a group of pigeons trained to color (with position irrelevant) on odd days, and to position (with color irrelevant) on even days, should not improve as much in color reversals as a control group which is rested on even days (Gonzalez and Bitterman, 1968). Example: If the different performance of pigeon and fish in habit-reversal experiments is due to a difference in attention to inconsistently reinforced stimuli, and if differences in attention to such stimuli are reflected in the relative difficulty of reversal and dimensional shifting, then the relative difficulty of reversal and shifting should not at the outset be identical in pigeon and fish (Schade and Bitterman, 1966). The only thing unclear to me is how, in the face of the available evidence, Mackintosh can continue to offer his hypothesis as the key to our understanding of the comparative data on habit reversal.

III. Probability Learning

Mackintosh concludes from the data on probability learning that rats are simply more "efficient" than birds (make fewer "errors"—choose the lower-probability alternative less frequently), and that birds are more efficient than fish. In support of his view that the performance of rats and fish lies on the same continuum, he notes that rats usually do not quite maximize, while fish occasionally exceed matching levels (Bitterman *et al.* 1958). It does not seem to me that these facts are critical. If fish occasionally exceed matching levels, so also do they fail occasionally to attain them. Reinforcement-ratios surely are not the only determinants of preference in these experiments—spatial and color biases also affect choice-ratios. For example, there is some preference for red over green in the population of goldfish that we currently sample. On the whole, however, the pooled data of a variety of experiments show remarkably close fits. Why rats often do not quite maximize (that is, why they continue on a small proportion of trials to select the less-frequently-reinforced alternative) certainly remains to be understood, but it is a strikingly inadequate description of their behavior in such problems to say that they simply do more of the same thing that fish do.

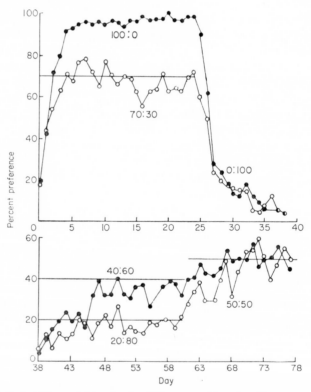

FIG. 5. Probability-matching in the African mouthbreeder. Two groups of animals were trained in a confounded visual-spatial problem with black and white stimuli, one at 100:0 and the other at 70:30. and then subsequent tests at other ratios were made. The preferences plotted are for the majority alternative of the original problem. (From Behrend and Bitterman, 1961.)

The curves of Fig. 5 show the performance of a group of mouthbreeders trained at several different reinforcement-ratios (Behrend and Bitterman, 1961). The relation between choice-ratio and reinforcement-ratio obviously is a close one, and the matching at each ratio is an individual affair, not an artifact of grouping (Behrend and Bitterman, 1966). It is quite easy to produce such curves for pigeons (Bullock and Bitterman, 1962), and even for cockroaches (Longo, 1964). Can Mackintosh produce one for rats? Perhaps the best single indication that something different is happening in rats is provided by the 50:50 visual problem, which Mackintosh does not even mention, and which must be a source of considerable embarrassment. By Sutherland's theory, all the animals should match in such a problem, because all analyzers and all response-attachments should become equal in strength. For the fish and the pigeon, 50:50 is just another ratio, and their individual curves cluster about the 50% levels, both visual and spatial, but properly motivated rats fall into strong position habits.

In Fig. 6, some pooled data for pigeons in visual problems are compared with some pooled data for fish in visual and spatial problems. The close relation there shown is the basis of my conclusion that pigeons behave like fish in visual problems. The basis of my conclusion that pigeons behave like rats in spatial problems is that pigeons have not as yet shown good random matching in such problems (Graf *et al.* 1964). It is interesting to

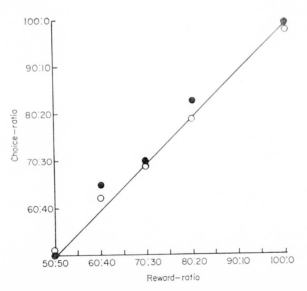

FIG. 6. Probability-matching in fish and pigeon. The data for the pigeon come only from visual problems. (From Bitterman, 1965.) ● Fish. ○ Pigeon.

note that turtles, like pigeons, match randomly in visual problems but not in spatial problems (Kirk and Bitterman, 1965). The performance of a turtle or a pigeon in a visual problem cannot be distinguished from that of a fish, although it clearly is not the performance of a rat. The performance of a turtle or a pigeon in a spatial problem is clearly not that of a fish. Whether or not these differences in behavior are due in part to differences in attention, it seems quite cavalier to describe them simply as differences in amount of maximizing.

In support of his hypothesis that the failure of maximizing is due to a failure of attention to the inconsistently reinforced relevant cues, Mackintosh cites three experimental findings. One is that the asymptotic performance of rats in a 75:25 brightness problem can be increased by pretraining designed to strengthen attention to brightness, but surely this result should cause Mackintosh some discomfort, since it implies the irreversibility of analyzer-strength. If a given probability of reinforcement is not sufficient to produce a given level of attention it should not (by Sutherland's theory) be sufficient to maintain that level. Perhaps Mackintosh does not really mean "asymptotic." A second finding is that rats trained in a 75:25 brightness problem reverse less rapidly when the ratio is shifted to 0:100 than do rats trained originally at 100:0. Mackintosh's explanation is that the 75:25 training produced weaker attention to brightness. If that is true, and if fish match because they are even less able than rats to attend to inconsistently reinforced cues, then an analogous experiment with fish should yield a still greater difference between the two groups, but Behrend and Bitterman (1961) found no difference at all (see Fig. 5). A third finding is that the minority choices ("errors") of rats and chicks trained in 75:25 brightness or position problems were nonrandom with respect to the irrelevant dimensions, from which Mackintosh infers attention to irrelevant cues. Such effects are rather familiar, of course, but so also is the failure of maximizing based on response to relevant cues—for example, spatial reward-following or its opposite (negative recency) in position problems (Wilson *et al.* 1964).

Even if response to irrelevant cues due to failure of attention to relevant cues is responsible in part for the failure of maximizing in rats, it will not account for matching in fish. There are many cases in which fish match without giving any indication of attention to irrelevant cues. It is difficult, in fact, to imagine just what irrelevant dimensions might compete so powerfully for the fish's attention in pure position problems (where the visual characteristics of the stimuli are identical) or in confounded problems (where spatial and visual characteristics are perfectly correlated— e.g. red always on the right and green always on the left). Perhaps the best evidence against Mackintosh's interpretation is that the fish (like all species tested thus far) maximizes sharply when the noncorrection method is used. The species in which matching has been demonstrated match only when they are trained by methods (correction and guidance) which ensure reinforced response to the minority stimulus. If failure of maximizing is due to failure of attention to the relevant cues, and if failure of attention to the relevant cues is due to inconsistent reinforcement, the noncorrection method also should produce poor maximizing. The minority reinforcements ensured by correction and guidance should only be expected to strengthen attention to the relevant dimension and consequently to improve maximizing. A better interpretation (in Sutherland's terms) would be that matching is a product of competing response-attachments. Either this competition is handled differently by animals that match and animals that do not, or their basic mechanisms of response-attachment are different (Lowes and Bitterman, 1967).

IV. Conclusions

The behavior of the pigeon and the rat in experiments on habit-reversal is qualitatively different from that of the fish. The pigeon and the rat show progressive improvement under a wide variety of conditions, but the only indication of improvement in the fish has appeared in highly massed trials and can be explained as a discrimination of the sensory consequences of response carried over from trial to trial. Much of the improvement shown by the pigeon and the rat can be attributed to interference-produced forgetting which has not been found in the fish, a fact that suggests a difference in basic learning-retention mechanisms. If progressive improvement in the pigeon and the rat depends to any extent upon the strengthening of attention to the relevant cues, as Mackintosh proposes, that dependency remains to be demonstrated. Several lines of evidence seem directly to contradict the attentional interpretation.

The behavior of the fish and the pigeon in experiments on probability learning is qualitatively different from that of the rat. A linear relation between choice-ratio and reinforcement-ratio has been found in the fish and the pigeon, but not in the rat. The pigeon shows the relation only in visual problems; in spatial problems, its behavior is like that of the rat. The available evidence contradicts Mackintosh's assumption that matching is simply a failure of maximizing which stems from a failure to attend consistently to inconsistently reinforced cues. It suggests instead that matching animals are responding (to the minority stimulus) in the *relevant* dimensions. Either there are different learning mechanisms in matching and nonmatching species (with conflicting response-tendencies of different relative strength being established as a result by inconsistent reinforcement), or their mechanisms for the resolution of such conflicts are different.

NOTE ADDED IN PROOF

Mackintosh's lengthy rebuttal which follows does not require extended comment from me, since the reader interested enough to examine the arguments carefully will want to evaluate them for himself. Something should, however, be said about the new evidence which Mackintosh introduces.

In his new Fig. 1 (p. 178), Mackintosh purports to show improvement in reversal without correlated decrement in retention. The retention curve, which is plotted in terms of a derived measure for pairs of reversals (with brightness and position data combined?), suggests that the probability of response to the previously rewarded alternative on Trial 1 of each reversal hovers about the 75% level at all stages of training. I do not think that this curve provides an adequate basis for the conclusion that forgetting played no role in the improvement. It leads me only to question the reliability of the measure. If the Trial-1 measure is indeed reliable (representative of the strength of preference at the start of each reversal), we have here a rather atypical instance of improvement. Mackintosh does not, of course, deny that there is improvement which is due to forgetting, nor have I anywhere asserted that forgetting is the only factor in improvement. I have only doubted that Mackintosh knows what the other factors are.

In his new Fig. 2 (p. 181), Mackintosh purports to show a linear relation between choice-ratio and reinforcement-ratio in the rat, but Uhl, who collected the data, notes that the performance of his animals had not yet stabilized at the conclusion of his experiment. The points plotted by Mackintosh reflect the slopes of Uhl's curves rather than their asymptotes. Let is suppose, however, that the four points plotted by Mackintosh are in fact asymptotic values, and let us add two other points predicted from Sutherland's theory—50% choice at 50% reinforcement and 100% choice at 100% reinforcement. The curve which best fits all six points is clearly not a straight line. (Even more important, perhaps, than differences in the shapes of such functions are the vast differences in behavior which like mean values may conceal. The performance of a group of goldfish in a 50:50 visual problem has little in common with the performance of a group of rats. The performance of goldfish is just what we might expect from Sutherland's theory, but the performance of rats is not.)

I am not convinced by Mackintosh's arguments. Differences in attention may be involved in the experiments on habit reversal and probability learning, but they remain to be understood. That there is anything like attention in the fish, we really have no evidence at all. The fish's performance in experiments on probability learning may, in fact, be taken to mean that it does not attend in the usual meaning of the term.

Acknowledgement

The research reviewed here was supported for the most part by Contract Nonr 2829(01) with the United States Office of Naval Research and by Grant MH-02857 from The United States Public Health Service.

References

Bitterman, M. E. (1965). Phyletic differences in learning. *Am. Psychol.* **20**, 396–410.
Bitterman, M. E., Wodinsky, J. and Candland, D. K. (1958). Some comparative psychology. *Am. J. Psychol.* **71**, 94–110.
Behrend, E. R. and Bitterman, M. E. (1961). Probability-matching in the fish. *Am. J. Psychol.* **74**, 542–551.
Behrend, E. R. and Bitterman, M. E. (1966). Probability matching in the goldfish. *Psychon. Sci.* **6**, 327–328.
Behrend, E. R. and Bitterman, M. E. (1967). Further experiments on habit reversal in the fish. *Psychon. Sci.* **8**, 363–364.
Behrend, E. R., Domesick, V. B. and Bitterman, M. E. (1965). Habit reversal in the fish. *J. comp. physiol. Psychol.* **60**, 407–411.

Bullock, D. H. and Bitterman, M. E. (1962). Probability-matching in the pigeon. *Am. J. Psychol.* **75**, 634–639.

Gonzalez, R. C. and Bitterman, M. E. (1968). Two-dimensional discriminative learning in the pigeon. *J. comp. physiol. Psychol.* **65**, 427–432.

Gonzalez, R. C., Behrend, E. R. and Bitterman, M. E. (1967). Reversal learning and forgetting in bird and fish. *Science, N.Y.* **158**, 519–521.

Gonzalez, R. C., Berger, B. D. and Bitterman, M. E. (1966a). A further comparison of key-pecking with an instrumental technique for the study of discriminative learning in pigeons. *Am. J. Psychol.* **79**, 217–225.

Gonzalez, R. C., Berger, B. D. and Bitterman, M. E. (1966b). Improvement in habit-reversal as a function of amount of training per reversal and other variables. *Am. J. Psychol.* **79**, 517–530.

Gonzalez, R. C., Roberts, W. A. and Bitterman, M. E. (1964). Learning in adult rats extensively decorticated in infancy. *Am. J. Psychol.* **77**, 547–562.

Graf, V., Bullock, D. H. and Bitterman, M. E. (1964). Further experiments on probability-matching in the pigeon. *J. exp. Anal. Behav.* **7**, 151–157.

Kirk, K. and Bitterman, M. E. (1965). Probability-learning by the turtle. *Science*, **148**, 1484–1485.

Longo, N. (1964). Probability-learning and habit-reversal in the cockroach. *Am. J. Psychol.* **77**, 29–41.

Lowes, G. and Bitterman, M. E. (1967). Reward and learning in the goldfish. *Science*, **157**, 455–457.

Schade, A. F. and Bitterman, M. E. (1965). The relative difficulty of reversal and dimensional shifting as a function of overlearning. *Psychon. Sci.* **3**, 283–284.

Schade, A. F. and Bitterman, M. E. (1966). Improvement in habit reversal as related to dimensional set. *J. comp. physiol. Psychol.* **62**, 42–48.

Setterington, R. G. and Bishop, H. E. (1967). Habit reversal improvement in the fish. *Psychon. Sci.* **7**, 41–42.

Stearns, E. M. and Bitterman, M. E. (1965). A comparison of key-pecking with an ingestive technique for the study of discriminative learning in pigeons. *Am. J. Psychol.* **78**, 48–56.

Wilson, W. A., Jr., Oscar, M. and Bitterman, M. E. (1964). Probability learning in the monkey. *Quart. J. exp. Psychol.* **16**, 163–165.

Wodinsky, J. and Bitterman, M. E. (1957). Discrimination-reversal in the fish. *Am. J. Psychol.* **70**, 569–576.

Part 2 : N. J. MACKINTOSH

I. Introduction

My argument consisted of the following points: that in serial reversal experiments fish perform (quantitatively) less efficiently than birds, and birds less efficiently than rats; that part of what is involved in serial reversal improvement is the development of attention to the relevant cue; and that part of the difference between rat, bird and fish can be accounted for by postulating differences in the stability of attention. A similar trio of propositions was made about probability learning. To clarify discussion of Bitterman's criticisms I shall deal with them under the six headings suggested by this analysis of my argument.

II. Serial Reversal Learning

A. DIFFERENCES BETWEEN RATS, BIRDS AND FISH

Bitterman maintains that the performance of fish differs qualitatively from that of birds and rats. This was originally because fish did not improve over a series of reversals, now because they improve only under restricted conditions. I pointed out that it is difficult to prove the null hypothesis (that they do not improve), and to support my argument showed that a post hoc analysis of one of Bitterman's experiments could be taken as suggesting possible improvement. We agree anyway that Setterington and Bishop's results demonstrate improvement by fish; but disagree on the conclusions to be drawn from their results. If indeed it was their use of a short intertrial interval that enabled Setterington and Bishop to find significant reversal improvement, it is not clear why Bitterman is so confident that this represents the employment by the fish of a win-stay, lose-shift strategy, when a simpler explanation in terms of proactive interference is available (Clayton, 1966), nor, more importantly is it clear why Bitterman thinks that this result is unique to fish, when it is well known that rats learn serial reversals more rapidly with short rather than long intertrial intervals (North, 1959; Stretch, McGonigle and Morton, 1964), and in two studies have shown no improvement at all when the intertrial interval was 24 hours (Clayton, 1962; Estes and Lauer, 1957). Again it is reasonable to attribute this effect to proactive interference. If the length of the intertrial interval affects serial reversal learning in both fish and rats, this constitutes the best evidence yet obtained for the qualitative similarity of (although quantitative differences in) the processes underlying serial reversal in the two classes of animal.

My second point was that birds, more particularly Columbiformes and other lower birds, are less proficient than rats at serial reversal learning. In support of this, I cited a number of studies: those by Gossette and his collaborators showing that lower birds are less efficient than passerines, and that even passerines do not so rapidly attain the level of performance often reached by rats; two early studies showing either zero or limited improvement by pigeons at visual reversal learning; more recent studies showing equally limited improvement by quail; and an experiment of my own that obtained large differences between rats and doves trained on the same series of reversals in the same apparatus.

Bitterman ignores all this evidence, and concentrates on disputing my interpretation of one further comparison I made between rats and birds— that based on a pair of his own experiments with rats and pigeons. The two sets of data were obtained from a review article (Bitterman, 1965), partly on the assumption that they were reasonably representative, partly because the initial learning scores were reasonably similar. I agree that initial learning scores are not the only determinant of reversal difficulty, but they it is worth noting that when allowance is made for initial rate of learning, *both* groups of pigeons, whose reversal learning curves are given by Bitterman in Fig. 2, (p. 166) show much less rapid improvement than is typically shown by rats.† I did not assume that all conditions were equated for rats and pigeons in the two experiments whose results I showed in Fig. 1. (p. 143). We agree that one can never know this. For this reason, as I argued in my conclusion, it is never possible to base secure conclusion on the results of a single comparison between two species. But if the same difference emerges from a number of studies, it becomes increasingly likely that the difference is a real one. Bitterman's own data seem to me only to confirm what is apparent from other studies—that lower birds are less efficient serial reversal learners than are rats.

B. Attention and Serial Reversal Learning

I suggested that serial reversal improvement may partly depend upon the development of attention to the relevant cue. I characterized the suggestion as vague, and pointed out that no model has been proposed that yields this proposition as a formal deduction. I did not say that it fails to make predictions. It produces a number of predictions, favourable tests of which I reported (e.g. that serial reversal training will not benefit non-reversal shift learning), and which Bitterman ignores. His arguments against this account are as follows:

(1) Serial reversal improvement is more pervasive than the overtraining reversal effect. Since I argued that serial reversal improvement is multiply determined, this would not affect my position, even if Bitterman's analysis of an attentional interpretation were correct. It is not. An attentional model will predict no ORE whenever training beyond criterion fails to strengthen attention more than it strengthens response attachments; serial reversal improvement will occur whenever attention is not so extensively extinguished in later reversals as in earlier reversals, whether this happens because attention is stronger at the end of later than of earlier reversals, or because the rate of extinction of attention changes over the course of a series of reversals.

(2) Serial reversal improvement should be reduced by interposing trials on a different discrimination problem between successive reversals, because such a procedure will interfere with the establishment of attention.

† After less than 10 reversals, rats typically learn each reversal more rapidly than the original problem (see, for example, Fig. 1 and 5, pages 143 and 155). Neither group of pigeons has attained this level of performance after 25 reversals.

It may also plausibly be supposed to increase proactive interference, and to the extent to which developing interference contributes to serial reversal improvement by reducing interfering carry-over from the preceding reversal, this procedure would be expected to improve reversal performance. If two presumed factors are pitted against each other, a null outcome may mean that neither operate, or that both operate in about equal strength.

C. ATTENTIONAL DIFFERENCES AND REVERSAL DIFFERENCES

Bitterman is not really mystified that I ascribe reversal differences between different animals to differences in attention rather than to differences in retention, for it used to be as clear to him as it still is to me that changes in retention cannot possibly be the sole cause of serial reversal improvement (see Gonzalez *et al.* 1966). Proactive interference cannot account for changes in the rate of within-problem learning, and to the extent to which pigeons show such changes in rate (Gonzalez *et al.* 1966)

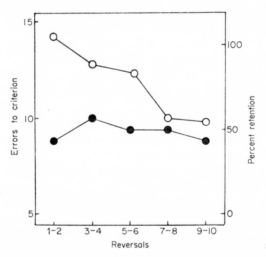

FIG. 1. Serial reversal learning by doves. Error scores consist of the mean number of errors to attain criterion from the first day on each reversal on which S scores at chance. Retention scores are based on the probability of an error on Trial 1 of each reversal: Percentage retention = 2 (Probability of an Error −0·5) × 100. ○—○ Error Scores. ●—● Retention Scores.

and fish do not, the postulation of differences in retention between birds and fish cannot provide a complete explanation of the differences between them in reversal learning.

The point is perhaps important enough to justify calling attention to some features of the reversal performance of the doves we trained on brightness or position reversals (see Fig. 1). Sixteen doves were trained (10 trials per day) to a criterion of 9 out of 10 on each of 10 reversals, showing a substantial reduction in errors over the series. In order to see the basis for this improvement, Fig. 1 gives both retention scores (based on the probability of an error on Trial 1 of each reversal), and a measure of learning rate (based on the number of errors occurring after a chance level of accuracy was attained). It is obvious which factor contributed most to serial reversal improvement in this experiment. Changes in retention simply did not occur: only six animals showed less retention over Reversals 6 to 10 than over Reversals 1 to 5; while 13 of 16 animals showed an increase in learning rate. There is nothing surprising in the failure of these doves to show significant changes in retention, for training on each reversal continued for several days until criterion was reached, and competing responses from the preceding problem should have been quite thoroughly extinguished by the end of each reversal. The important point is that since doves (like rats: see, for example, Theois, 1965) show significant serial reversal improvement not attributable to forgetting, other factors must contribute to the difference between them and fish.

This is not to deny that differences in retention may also contribute to differences in reversal performance. The results of Gonzalez *et al.* (1967) cited by Bitterman suggest that there may be differences in retention between pigeons and fish, although on the basis of the evidence presented, it is arguable that differences in retention are less responsible for differences in reversal than are differences in reversal responsible for differences in retention.† On the other hand, I presented evidence (ignored by Bitterman) to suggest that the reversal differences between rats and doves may be partly attributed to differences in attention, and I was, of course, merely extrapolating such an explanation to the differences between birds and fish. There is nothing, incidentally, in such an explanation that is contradicted by the finding that both pigeons and fish learn non-reversal shifts more rapidly than reversals (the point that appears to be being made by the reference on page 169 to the results of Schade and Bitterman).

---

† Gonzalez *et al.* use a relative retention score (e.g. the difference between the performance at the end of Day 1 and the beginning of Day 2 of each reversal). The amount of retention loss measured depends partly upon the amount of possible loss: a subject performing substantially below 100% at the end of Day 1 could never show the same amount of "forgetting" as a subject that did attain 100% accuracy. Apparently the fish in Gonzalez *et al.*'s experiment continued to average about 20 errors (in 40 trials) over Day 1 of each reversal. They may therefore simply have lacked the opportunity to display increases in forgetting.

III. Probability Learning

A. Differences Between Rats, Birds and Fish

I argued that rats make fewer errors than birds, and that birds make fewer errors than fish, when trained (by correction or guidance) on visual or spatial probability problems. Bitterman reiterates his former position that rats maximise and fish match on both types of problem, while pigeons maximise on spatial and match on visual problems. To a considerable extent we agree about the performance of rats and fish (although not on whether the difference between them is qualitative), but disagree about the performance of pigeons.

(1) I argued that pigeons (and other birds) show performance intermediate between that of rat and fish on visual problems. According to Bitterman, "the performance of a . . . pigeon in a visual problem cannot be distinguished from that of a fish." I analysed the results of all seven of Bitterman's published studies of visual probability learning in pigeons, and showed that in five out of the seven the level of performance attained was significantly above the matching performance of fish. Bitterman does not comment on this analysis; he merely reproduces a figure from his review article which gives the summary results of an unspecified number of birds from an unspecified number of experiments. Nor does Bitterman comment on our own evidence of above matching performance of chicks trained on a visual probability problem. Does this imply to him that the qualitative distinction in mechanisms of probability learning is to be drawn somewhere among the lower birds?

(2) "The performance of a . . . pigeon in a spatial problem is clearly not that of a fish." On this we agree. The question is whether it is the same as that of a rat. Chicks at any rate perform significantly less accurately than rats on spatial problems. The only evidence Bitterman has published indicates that pigeons attained an asymptote of 82% correct on a $70:30$ problem. This compares with an asymptote of 95% attained by rats, and 75% attained by fish (Bitterman *et al.* 1958). The only possible sense in which it is true to say of the pigeon that "in spatial problems, its behaviour is like that of the rat," is that pigeons and rats both exceed matching. But to argue thus is to beg the question of whether a qualitative distinction between matching and nonmatching is valid.

(3) Bitterman appears to challenge me to produce learning curves showing matching behaviour on the part of rats. I do not, of course, believe that rats typically match. He also says that "a linear relation between choice-ratio and reinforcement-ratio has been found in the fish and the pigeon, but not in the rat." This is a different matter: Bitterman is certainly mistaken if he believes that in rats choice-ratio is independent of reinforcement-ratio.

In common with all other animals tested, rats show a monotonic increase in asymptotic performance with increases in reinforcement ratio. The most extensive mapping comes from a study by Uhl (1963) of spatial probability learning in a two-lever Skinner box. Uhl's results are shown in Fig. 2. In this experiment at any rate, the relation between choice- and reinforcement-ratio appears to be essentially linear—although the rats are are at no point merely matching.

(4) Bitterman states that "perhaps the best single indication that something different is happening in rats is provided by the 50:50 visual problem." It is not clear why. Fish and pigeons come to select each visual

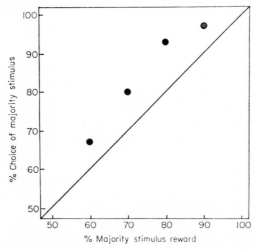

Fig. 2. Spatial probability learning by rats. Percentage choice of the majority stimulus as a function of reinforcement ratio, based on performance over Trials 761–1000 (from Uhl, 1963).

stimulus on about 50% of trials—as, of course, do rats. The question is how their responses are divided between the two positions (a 50:50 visual schedule is equally a 50:50 spatial schedule). Rats perform as one might expect on the basis of their performance on other spatial problems: they tend to select one particular position on a substantial majority of trials. Fish also perform as one would expect from their behaviour on other schedules: they select each position equally. From their behaviour at other schedules, one would expect that pigeons will perform at some intermediate level. The only exact data provided by Bitterman comes from a 50:50 spatial study (two visually identical alternatives): here a group of six birds averaged 65% choice of one alternative (Graf et al. 1964). Bitterman now states that on the 50:50 visually differentiated problem pigeons behave like fish: "their individual curves cluster closely about the 50% level." This is not quite the impression given in the original paper (Bullock and Bitterman, 1962), where it is stated first that they did not select one position on 100% of trials (this is not in question); secondly that "the spatial biases manifested in the 50:50 problem were greater than those which appeared at other ratios"; thirdly that these biases "were rather transient, and not all animals showed them (*loc. cit.*)." Before accepting the conclusions that Bitterman now wishes to base on these results, it would be desirable to know more precisely how transient the position biases were, and just what proportion of animals showed them. As it stands, the evidence available from 50:50 problems only confirms the conclusions I drew from studies of other schedules: rats attain higher asymptotes than birds, and birds attain higher asymptotes than fish.

B. ATTENTION AND PROBABILITY LEARNING

I briefly outlined a number of studies whose results seemed to support the hypothesis that animals never learn consistently to attend to the relevant cue of a probability learning problem. Bitterman's comments on these studies are misleading.

(1) He argues that relevant pretraining ought not to improve asymptotic performance in a probability learning situation, since this would imply "the irreversibility of analyser-strength." This is probably true. In fact, we only found relevant pretraining (on an absolute brightness problem) to enhance asymptotic performance when pretraining trials were given at the outset of each day's brightness probability training.

(2) We found that rats trained on a 75:25 brightness problem learn the 0:100 reversal more slowly than rats originally trained on a 100:0 problem. This in itself does not constitute evidence for an attentional interpretation, since it could equally be ascribed to the effects of partial reinforcement on extinction. What does support the attentional analysis is that probability training does not retard reversal by slowing down extinction but by increasing position habits, and that probability training facilitates nonreversal shift learning. Without more detailed knowledge of the course of reversal learning (and of nonreversal shift learning), it is not particularly profitable to speculate on the reasons for the apparent difference between rats and fish. It is worth noting, however, from Bitterman's Fig. 5, that in fish as in rats probability learning slows down the *rate* of reversal learning. In his experiment, although Group 70:30 and Group 100:0 reached criterion on the reversal problem after the same number of trials, since the starting points for the two groups were markedly different (approximately 30% correct for Group 70:30, and 0% correct for Group 100:0), Group 70:30 showed the slower rate of change in probability of the new correct response.

(3) In all the animals we have trained on probability discriminations with irrelevant cues (rats, chicks, and in some preliminary work, goldfish) we have detected significant nonrandomness of choice behaviour with respect to the irrelevant cue (usually significant reward following on the irrelevant cue). However familiar this result may be to him, Bitterman has not before now commented extensively on it. He argues that responses to irrelevant cues cannot be a cause of errors in all probability learning experiments (especially in fish), since errors still occur when the situation contains no deliberately introduced irrelevant cues. There are three answers to this point. First, if indeed fish make errors because they "are responding (to the minority stimulus) in the *relevant* dimension", it is surprising that one cannot detect this from the pattern of their errors. When rats are trained on a probability discrimination without irrelevant cues, or when they have been successfully pretrained to attend to the relevant cue, it is easy to detect significant relevant cue reward-following—as would be predicted by any reinforcement theory (Cole *et al.* 1965; Mackintosh, 1968). If, as Bitterman has insisted, fish show no such relevant cue reward-following, this suggests precisely that their errors do not occur under the control of the relevant cue, but presumably because they are sometimes controlled by irrelevant cues. Secondly, if errors do occur under irrelevant cue control, then asymptotic performance should depend upon the number and salience of irrelevant cues present. This is true for rats (Mackintosh, 1968), and appears to be true for fish also. Bitterman *et al.* (1958) trained mouth-breeders on 70:30 probability discriminations: either on a visual problem (with position irrelevant) or a spatial problem (with no obvious irrelevant cues). At asymptote, subjects selected the majority stimulus in the visual problem on 69.2% of trials, in the spatial problem on 75% of trials (there is in fact no overlap in the two sets of scores). Behrend and Bitterman (1966) trained goldfish on visual or spatial 70:30 problems, and obtained asymptotes of 66% and 75% (excluding one animal that failed to learn) respectively. Thirdly, it seems to me rash to assume that because the experimenter has not deliberately introduced an irrelevant cue, the experimental situation does not therefore contain any. The absence of deliberately manipulated irrelevant cues does not mean that the situation contains no irrelevant cues at all, only that the experimenter cannot now analyse responses to them.

(4) In common with most other animals (for cats, see Poland and Warren, 1967; for rats, Uhl, 1963), fish attain higher asymptotes on probability discriminations when trained by noncorrection than when trained by correction or guidance. Bitterman argues that an attentional analysis should predict the opposite result, since, he assumes, both correction and noncorrection procedures guarantee an inconsistent reinforcement schedule,

and "the minority reinforcements ensured by correction and guidance should only be expected to strengthen attention to the relevant dimension (p. 10)." It is clear that the actual reinforcement schedule experienced by the subject will not be the same under noncorrection and guidance procedures: guidance ensures continuation of minority stimulus rewards, while under noncorrection, as the subject's choice of the majority stimulus increases, a 70:30 schedule turns into a 70:0 schedule. Models proposed both by Sutherland (1964) and by Lovejoy (1968) assume that the strength of attention to a cue is partly determined by the consistency of the reinforcement schedule in effect on that cue, and on both models consistency is measured in terms of the *differences* in reinforcement schedule experienced on different values of that cue. On both models, therefore, a 70:30 schedule is less consistent than a 70: 0 schedule; and, as is discussed elsewhere at greater length than is here possible (Mackintosh, 1968), both models predict that attention will be stronger under noncorrection than under correction or guidance, and can explain the obtained results.

(5) Bitterman argues that a 50:50 schedule should result in all analyser and response strengths becoming equal. I do not profess to know what should happen to response strengths, but on both the above-mentioned models, analysers would be expected to revert towards their base-levels, and performance would be controlled by innately dominant cues. This is what appears to happen (e.g. rats are more likely to show position habits than visual habits).

C. ATTENTIONAL DIFFERENCES AND PROBABILITY LEARNING DIFFERENCES

I offered no direct evidence to support the suggestion that differences in the stability of attention contribute toward the observed differences in the probability learning of rats, birds and fish. Bitterman does not offer any explanation of the differences.

References

Behrend, E. R. and Bitterman, M. E. (1966). Probability-matching in the goldfish. *Psychon. Sci.* **6**, 327–328.
Bitterman, M. E. (1965). Phyletic differences in learning. *Am. Psychol.* **20**, 396–410.
Bitterman, M. E., Wodinsky, J. and Candland, D. K. (1958). Some comparative psychology. *Am. J. Psychol.* **71**, 94–110.
Bullock, D. H. and Bitterman, M. E. (1962). Probability-matching in the pigeon. *Am. J. Psychol.* **75**, 634–639.
Clayton, K. N. (1962). The relative effects of forced reward and forced nonreward during widely spaced successive discrimination reversal. *J. comp. physiol. Psychol.* **55**, 992–997.
Clayton, K. N. (1966). T-maze acquisition and reversal as a function of intertrial interval. *J. comp. physiol. Psychol.* **62**, 409–414.

Cole, M., Belenky, G. L., Boucher, R. C., Fernandez, R. N. and Myers, D. L. (1965). Probability learning to escape from shock. *Psychon. Sci.* **3**, 127–128.

Estes, W. K. and Lauer, D. W. (1957). Conditions of invariance and modifiability in simple reversal learning. *J. comp. physiol. Psychol.* **50**, 199–206.

Gonzalez, R. C., Berger, B. D. and Bitterman, M. E. (1966). Improvement in habit-reversal as a function of amount of training per reversal and other variables. *Am. J. Psychol.* **79**, 517–530.

Gonzalez, R. C., Behrend, E. R. and Bitterman, M. E. (1967). Reversal learning and forgetting in bird and fish. *Science*, **158**, 519–521.

Graf, V., Bullock, D. H. and Bitterman, M. E. (1964). Further experiments on probability-matching in the pigeon. *J. exp. Anal. Behav.* **7**, 151–157.

Lovejoy, E. P. (1968). *"Attention and discrimination learning."* Holden-Day, San Francisco, U.S.A.

Mackintosh, N. J. (1968). Attention and probability learning. *In* "Attention: a behavioural analysis" (D. Mostofsky, ed.). Appleton-Century-Crofts, New York, U.S.A.

North, A. J. (1959). Discrimination reversal with spaced trials and distinctive cues. *J. comp. physiol. Psychol.* **52**, 426–429.

Poland, S. F. and Warren, J. M. (1967). Spatial probability learning by cats. *Psychon. Sci.* **8**, 487–488.

Stretch, R. G. A., McGonigle, B. and Morton, A. (1964). Serial position reversal learning in the rat: trials/problem and the intertrial interval. *J. comp. physiol. Psychol.* **57**, 461–463.

Sutherland, N. S. (1964). The learning of discriminations by animals. *Endeavour*, **23**, 148–153.

Theios, J. (1965). The mathematical structure of reversal learning in a shock-ecsape T-maze: overtraining and successive reversals. *J. math. Psychol.* **2**, 26–52.

Uhl, C. N. (1963). Two-choice probability learning in the rat as a function of incentive, probability of reinforcement, and training procedure. *J. exp. Psychol.* **66**, 443–449.

8 | Discrimination Overtraining and Shift Behavior

SHEPARD SIEGEL

University of Missouri, Columbia, U.S.A.†

I. Introduction

Ease of reversal learning in a simultaneous, two-choice discrimination situation is known to depend upon the amount of prereversal training. Early experiments concerned with this problem (see Blum and Blum, 1949) generally involved rather small numbers of training trials and typically found that ease of reversal learning was inversely related to amount of prereversal training.

In 1953, however, Reid reported that rats given extensive overtraining on a brightness discrimination learned the reversal faster than rats reversed immediately after reaching an acquisition criterion on the initial problem. A sizeable number of subsequent investigations (summarized by Paul, 1965; Sperling, 1965a, 1965b) have confirmed Reid's observation.

†Present address: McMaster University, Hamilton, Ontario, Canada.

This facilitation of discrimination reversal by extended prereversal training has been termed the "Overtraining Reversal Effect" (ORE).

One category of theoretical explanations of the ORE emphasizes the importance of behavioral tendencies, describable in molar S—R terms, which may positively transfer from the original learning to reversal learning. These behavioral tendencies acquired during training and overtraining are presumably independent of the particular cue values of the discriminanda, and facilitate the subsequent reversal. Reid (1953) has suggested that an effect of overtraining is to strengthen the receptor orienting behavior of "looking at" both discriminanda before responding. This behavior, which would be equally appropriate to original and reversal learning, has also been stressed by Pubols (1956) and Uhl (1964). Harlow (1959) and Spence (quoted in Reid, 1953) have emphasized that overtraining may further eliminate behavioral tendencies, such as position preferences or responses to irrelevant cues, which similarly interfere with original and reversal learning.

A second category of explanations of the ORE utilizes two-stage, mediational models of discrimination learning. During the acquisition of a discrimination habit appropriate choice behavior is presumed to be mediated by a prior reaction of "attending to the relevant stimulus dimension" (Zeaman and House, 1963), "identifying the relevant stimuli" (Goodwin and Lawrence, 1955), or "switching in the relevant stimulus analyser" (Sutherland, 1959). These mediation models of discrimination learning have been characterized as "attentional", or "centralistic", in contrast to the preceding "peripheralistic" interpretations (e.g. Goodrich et al. 1961; Mackintosh, 1965b; Uhl, 1964).

Sutherland (1959, 1964a, 1964b) has been most explicit in relating attentional interpretations of discrimination learning to the ORE.

". . . the effect of overtraining will be to switch the correct analysing mechanism in more firmly so that, when reversal training starts, the analyser remains switched in and the animal has a chance to learn to reverse its responses to the outputs from the analyser. In an animal which has not been overtrained, the correct analyser will not be so firmly switched in: when reversal training starts, it will try out other analysers, and thus will not be able to learn so readily to reverse the responses to the original analyser" (Sutherland, 1964b, p. 57).

The present investigation was designed to evaluate certain implications of such attentional interpretations of the ORE. Groups of rats were trained or overtrained on a simultaneous, two-choice discrimination problem, and then shifted to one of several new problems, including a simple reversal. An attempt was made to arrange conditions in such a way that an attentional mechanism acquired in original learning would still be appropriate following the shift, as well as conditions in which it would be inappropriate.

In general, if reward contingencies are correlated with the same stimulus dimension in the postshift problem as in the original problem, the previously acquired attentional mechanism should continue to be appropriate. In this case, the shift is referred to as an intradimensional shift, and overtraining would be expected to facilitate it. Indeed, the ORE, as commonly reported, is one case of such an effect.

If the postshift discrimination problem involves a relevant stimulus dimension which is different from the relevant dimension in original learning, the previously acquired attentional mechanism should be inappropriate. In this case, referred to as an extradimensional shift, Sutherland's explanation of the ORE has been interpreted (Mackintosh, 1962) as implying that overtraining should hinder acquisition of the postshift problem. The more firmly the original analyzer is switched in, the harder it should be to switch it out before switching in the new relevant analyzer. This tendency should be augmented if the stimulus dimension which is relevant in the post-shift problem is present but irrelevant (uncorrelated with reward) during original learning. Sutherland (1964a) has suggested that organisms specifically learn not to attend to irrelevant stimuli during the acquisition of a discrimination. Thus, it would be expected that overtrained organisms would not only have more difficulty in switching out the original analyzer, but would also have more difficulty in switching in the analyzer appropriate to the previously irrelevant stimulus dimension.

The two experiments in the present investigation each involved intra- and extradimensional shifts, with the expectation being that overtraining would facilitate the intradimensional shifts, but hinder the extradimensional shifts. In the first experiment, the *Simultaneous Shift Experiment*, the post shift problem resembled the original problem in involving a simultaneous discrimination. In the second experiment, the *Successive Shift Experiment*, the postshift problem involved a successive discrimination.

Whereas solution of a simultaneous discrimination involves approaching one of two different simultaneously presented discriminanda, solution of a successive discrimination involves approaching one of two identical discriminanda (the right one or the left one) when they are both one value of the relevant stimulus dimension, and approaching the other when they are both the second value of the relevant stimulus dimension. While the ORE occurs in the simultaneous shift situation, the successive shift may be especially useful for testing attentional interpretations of the ORE. Specific approach and avoidance tendencies to the two discriminanda learned during the preceding simultaneous discrimination have been assumed (e.g., Lawrence, 1949) to be irrelevant to solution of a successive shift problem. Therefore, evidence indicating that simultaneous discrimination experience affects subsequent successive discrimination performance has been interpreted as indicating transfer only of attentional responses (Lawrence, 1949; Mackintosh, 1965b).

Lawrence (1949) trained rats to an acquisition criterion on a simultaneous discrimination and then shifted them to a successive discrimination. He found that a successive intradimensional shift was easier than a successive extradimensional shift. This finding is congruent with attentional theories, i.e. during the initial simultaneous discrimination training, the subjects switched in the analyzer of the relevant stimulus dimension (Sutherland, 1959), or the relevant stimulus dimension became more distinctive (Lawrence, 1949, 1950). According to such interpretations, overtraining on the original simultaneous discrimination should further enhance these transfer effects.

II. Method

A. SUBJECTS AND APPARATUS

The subjects were 96 experimentally naive, male, albino rats. They were 150–170 days old at the start of the experiment. Forty-eight subjects were used in the Simultaneous Shift Experiment, and 48 in the Successive Shift Experiment.

The apparatus used in both experiments, a T-maze, was 3·75 in high. A floor plan of the maze is shown in Fig. 1. On each side of the maze, one

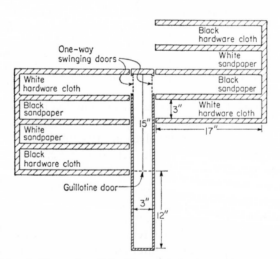

FIG. 1. Floor plan of the T-maze in both experiments.

of four separate arms could be moved into place by sliding a four-com-partmented tray into the appropriate position. These arms differed along two stimulus dimensions (a) brightness (black or white flat enameled walls and floor), and (b) texture of the floor covering (hardware cloth, two strands to the inch, $\frac{1}{8}$in above the floor, or sandpaper "carborundum" grit #60). Each of the arms on each side of the maze contained one of the four possible combinations of these visual and textural stimuli.

The stem of the maze was painted a flat, mid-gray, and was divided by a guillotine door into a 12 in starting section and a 15 in approach to the choice point. Mounted at the choice point, along either wall of the stem, was a one-way swinging door, hinged at the top, opening into an arm of the maze.

In order to expose itself to the visual and textural cues in an arm, a subject was required to push open the swinging door leading to that arm. Since the doors opened in only one direction, the subject could not retrace once it had fully entered an arm.

B. Initial Simultaneous Discrimination Training

Before discrimination training began, subjects were placed on a food deprivation schedule and were habituated to the maze.

Following habituation, subjects were trained on a simultaneous, two-choice discrimination in the T-maze. Half the subjects were trained on a brightness (black versus white) discrimination, and half were trained on a floor texture (hardware cloth versus sandpaper) discrimination. This initial discrimination training defined a subject's *relevant* stimulus dimension (either brightness or texture), one of the two possible values of which was always perfectly correlated with food reward, and the other value of which was never correlated with food reward. Each value of that stimulus dimension which was not relevant was equally as often presented with the positive and negative values of the relevant stimulus dimension, and hence was irrelevant.

Subjects were given eight trials per day, and were run in squads of four in the same order each day. One subject in each squad was trained with one of the four possible stimuli (black, white, hardware cloth, or sandpaper) as the positive stimulus. The inter-trial period was approximately 3–4 minutes.

Over the first two days of training, half the trials were forced in order to equalize runs to the four possible combinations of stimuli and to each side of the maze.

Throughout the remainder of the experiment, all trials were free, and the order of presentation of the discriminanda for each squad was randomly determined, with the constraint that the four possible configurations of the stimuli appear two times in each daily block of eight trials.

Subjects' orientation and choice responses were recorded. An "orientation response" to one side of the maze was scored whenever it was observed that the animal moved with his head one of the one-way swinging doors leading to an arm. If the subject withdrew in such a manner as to allow the swinging door to close again completely, that orientation response was terminated. All orientation responses were sequentially recorded for each subject for each trial. A subject's last orientation response on any trial was to the side to which it finally responded; a choice response was recorded when it entered an arm far enough for the swinging door to close behind it, thereby preventing retracing back to the stem of the T-maze. The trial was terminated by removing the subject from the apparatus immediately after eating on rewarded trials or after 15 sec on nonrewarded trials.

All rats were trained to a criterion of two successive errorless days on the initial simultaneous discrimination. Half the subjects (Criterion), were shifted to a different problem on the day immediately following the attainment of criterion. The remaining subjects (Overtrained) were given 25 additional days of training (200 trials) before being shifted to another problem. Half the subjects trained to each stimulus were assigned to each of these training level groups. This assignment of subjects to Criterion and Overtrained conditions was accomplished by means of a ranking procedure to equate the two groups with respect to the mean and variance of the number of trials required to criterion.

C. SIMULTANEOUS SHIFT EXPERIMENT

After reaching criterion on the initial problem, 12 subjects were assigned to each cell of a 2 × 2 factorial design. The two variables were Level of Training (Criterion versus Overtrained) and Shift Type (Simultaneous Intradimensional Shift versus Simultaneous Extradimensional Shift). The experiment was conducted in two identical replications, with 24 subjects in each replication. Within each of the four experimental groups, for each replication of the experiment, half of the subjects were originally trained with brightness as the relevant stimulus dimension, and half were trained with texture as the relevant stimulus dimension.

Subjects assigned to a simultaneous intradimensional shift (hereafter referred to as Sim-IDS) were required to learn the reverse of their preshift problem. That stimulus dimension which was irrelevant during initial training was still irrelevant. Subjects assigned to a simultaneous extradimensional shift (hereafter referred to as Sim-EDS, were shifted so that the previously irrelevant stimulus dimension was relevant, and the originally relevant dimension became irrelevant.

All subjects were run on the shift problem until they had reached the same criterion of performance that they had attained on the original discrimination problem (two successive errorless days).

D. Successive Shift Experiment

Following the attainment of criterion on the initial problem, independent groups of 12 subjects each were assigned to each cell of a 2 × 2 factorial design in a manner similar to that employed in the Simultaneous Shift Experiment. Level of Training (Criterion versus Overtrained) was varied orthogonally to Shift Type (Successive Intradimensional Shift versus Successive Extradimensional Shift). The experiment was conducted in two identical replications with 24 subjects in each replication.

Subjects assigned to successive intradimensional shift of their initial problem (hereafter referred to as Suc-IDS) were shifted so that the stimulus dimension which was initially relevant was still relevant.

Subjects assigned to successive extradimensional shift of their initial problem (hereafter referred to as Suc-EDS) were shifted so that the initially relevant stimulus dimension was irrelevant.

During the successive problem each value of the irrelevant stimulus dimension was presented equally often with each value of the relevant stimulus dimension, but, on any one trial, the same value was used in both arms of the maze. All animals were run on the successive shift problem until they had reached the criterion of two successive errorless days.

III. Results

A. Days to Criterion

1. *Preshift Performance*

The subjects met criterion on the initial problem in an average of 8·6 days. The matching procedure was effective in yielding similar mean scores for all groups. Subsequent correlational analyses indicated that performance on the initial discrimination was unrelated to the measure of interest in this investigation. Within all groups, correlations (rank order) between days to preshift criterion and days to shift criterion were statistically insignificant. The median correlation was +·29.

2. *Simultaneous Shift Experiment*

Table I presents the mean number of days to reach criterion on the simultaneous shift problems. An analysis of variance revealed a significant

SHEPARD SIEGEL

TABLE I

Mean number of days to criterion on the simultaneous shift problems

Shift type	Level of training	
	Criterion	Overtrained
Sim-IDS	15.5	10.3
Sim-EDS	9.0	9.5

interaction between Level of Training and Shift Type, ($p < \cdot01$). Lower order analyses of variance indicated that, in the case of Sim-IDS, the postshift problem was acquired significantly faster by the Overtrained group than by the Criterion group ($p < \cdot02$), whereas the difference between Overtrained and Criterion Sim-EDS groups did not approach significance. Furthermore, for the Criterion groups, the IDS was significantly harder than the EDS ($p < \cdot005$). No such difference existed for the Overtrained groups.

The obtained facilitation of a Sim-IDS by preshift overtraining is a replication of the ORE. However, contrary to attentional interpretations of the ORE, overtraining had no effect on a Sim-EDS in the same situation. As outlined previously, if the primary effect of overtraining were to teach the subject to pay attention to the relevant stimulus dimension, thereby producing the ORE, it would also be expected that overtraining would hinder the subject's performance on a Sim-EDS, which it does not appear to do.

3. Successive Shift Experiment

Table II presents the mean number of days to reach criterion on the Successive Shift Problems. An analysis of variance indicated a significant effect attributable to Shift Type. The Suc-IDS was learned significantly faster than the Suc-EDS ($p < \cdot001$). No other main effect or interaction approached statistical significance.

That a Suc-IDS was learned faster than a Suc-EDS can readily be interpreted in terms of the subject learning to attend to the relevant stimulus dimension during the initial problem. If, however, overtraining caused the subject to pay greater attention to the relevant stimulus dimension, it would be expected that overtraining would further facilitate a Suc-IDS, and further hinder a Suc-EDS. Neither of these predictions were confirmed.

Therefore, although the ORE was replicated in the Sim-IDS groups of the Simultaneous Shift Experiment, and the phenomenon of a Suc-IDS being learned faster than a Suc-EDS was replicated in the Successive

TABLE II

Mean number of days to criterion on the successive shift problems

Shift type	level of training	
	Criterion	Overtrained
Suc-IDS	13.1	11.7
Suc-EDS	31.2	26.8

Shift Experiment, none of the additional experimental comparisons of days to acquire the shift problem provided evidence supporting attentional interpretations of these phenomena.

B. FURTHER ANALYSES

1. Pre-criterion Performance on Initial Simultaneous Discrimination Problem

Since performance on the initial simultaneous discrimination problem was similar for all subjects, the preshift results of both experiments were combined for purposes of subsequent analyses.

Examination of the protocols of all 96 animals suggested that, at the outset of initial discrimination training, they tended to respond solely on the basis of position. An individual subject, for example, would initially orient towards the right and enter the right arm on almost every trial, regardless of which discriminanda it contained, *without reorienting* towards the other arm. As a result of this behavior, subjects initially received reward 50% of the time. Reorientation behavior did not occur until a few days before each animal reached the criterion of solution of the problem; when it did occur, it exhibited a systematic tendency. Eighty-two of the 96 animals evidenced their *first* reorienting response by turning away from the negative stimulus on the side of their initial orientation and responding to the positive stimulus on the opposite side. The remaining 14 animals reoriented for the first time on a trial when their initial orientation was toward the positive stimulus. This marked tendency for the initial reorientation to involve orienting away from the negative stimulus as compared to the positive stimulus, was highly significant ($p < \cdot 001$).

As noted, solution of the problem quickly followed initial reorientation. To substantiate this observation, homogeneous learning groups were constructed by grouping together all subjects who required the same number of days to reach criterion. This procedure yielded 16 groups, which learned the discrimination in from 1 to 17 days, and which contained from 1 to 18 subjects. For each group, we calculated the mean number of days before which any reorientation responses were noted, and the number of days from the time reorientation responses were first evidenced until the problem was solved. In this analysis, the first two days of discrimination training, which consisted of half forced trials, were ignored. The results are shown in Fig. 2. As may be seen, the different homogeneous

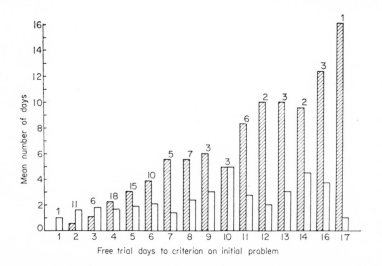

FIG. 2. Mean number of days to criterion on initial simultaneous discrimination problem analyzed into pre-initial reorientation and post-initial reorientation components for homogeneous learning groups. The number above the bars for each homogeneous learning group indicates the number of subjects in that group. Hatched bars—Pre-initial Reorientation. Open bars—Post initial Reorientation.

learning groups varied considerably in the amount of time they took to make the first reorientation response, but there was relatively little variation in the amount of time they required to solve the discrimination once the first orientation response occurred. The rank order correlation between number of days to criterion and number of days until the first reorientation was $+\cdot93$, whereas a similar correlation between number of days to criterion and number of days to solve the problem *after* the first reorientation response was only $+\cdot35$. These correlations indicate that most of the variability in the total number of days to reach criterion was due to differences in the time at which the first reorientation response occurred.

Figure 3 depicts the orderly change from responding solely on a position basis, to reorienting away from the negative stimulus on the side of initial orientation. All animals who took the same number of days to reach criterion on the preshift problem following their last day of total position responding were grouped together. On the last day of position responding, the probability of responding to the positive stimulus on the side of initial orientation was 1.00. The probability of reorienting and responding to the side opposite that of initial orientation when the negative stimulus was on

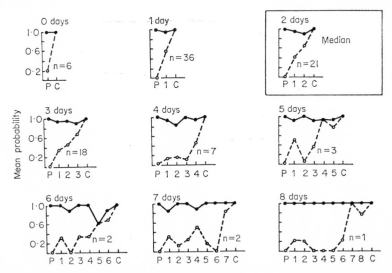

FIG. 3. Response tendencies subsequent to the first reorientation response during the initial simultaneous discrimination training. P indicates the last day of total position responding (all responses made to the side of initial orientation), and C indicates the first criterion day. Subjects were grouped together who required the same number of days to reach criterion following the last day in which all responses were to the side of initial orientation. The median subject required two days. ●——● Response to side of initial orientation when positive stimulus is on side of initial orientation. ○– – –○ response to side opposite that of initial orientation when negative stimulus is on side of initial orientation.

the side of initial orientation was zero. On the criterion days, these probabilities were both 1·00. As may be seen in Fig. 3, subjects solved the initial simultaneous discrimination problem by learning to reorient away from the negative stimulus on the side of initial orientation and respond to the positive stimulus on the nonpreferred side. Throughout training, they rarely failed to respond correctly when the positive stimulus was on the side of initial orientation.

2. *Performance During Overtraining*

Twenty-four subjects in each experiment received 25 days of overtraining on the initial discrimination. In our analysis of behavior during overtraining, all 48 subjects of the Simultaneous Shift and Successive Shift Experiments were combined. Figure 4 shows, for successive blocks of 40 overtraining trials, the mean number of rewarded choice responses per day, and the mean number of trials per day on which subjects initially oriented towards their preferred side, i.e. that side (right or left) to which each

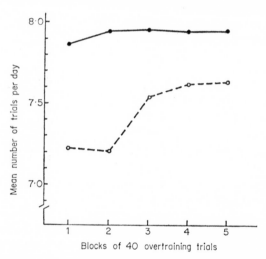

FIG. 4. Initial orientation tendencies and correct choices during overtraining. ●——●
correct choice responses: ○–––○ initial orientation to preferred side.

subject initially oriented most often on its first day of overtraining. On this day, all subjects initially oriented towards one side on more than half of the eight trials. Only four animals (two in each experiment) changed their initial orientation preference during the course of overtraining. For ease of presentation, Fig. 4 shows the initial orientation tendences of only those animals who maintained their original preference.

For the 44 subjects represented in Fig. 4, the tendency initially to orient towards one side of the maze gradually increased until, by the last block of 40 overtraining trials, it was significantly higher than it was on the first block of 40 overtraining trials ($p < .01$).

Throughout the course of overtraining subjects had high tendencies to initially orient to one side of the maze, and they performed almost perfectly in terms of terminal choice behavior. The negative stimulus was on the side of preferred initial orientation on half the trials. In order to respond correctly, subjects had to reorient and respond to the alternative stimulus on these trials. It seems clear that subjects in the Overtrained groups had additional training prior to the shift on the reorientation response with which subjects in the Criterion groups were only minimally trained. Prior to the shift in the discrimination problem, overtrained animals were rewarded for making this response for about two precriterion days plus 25 postcriterion days, or a total of about 27 days. This is to be compared with approximately two days of training on this response for Criterion animals.

3. Successive Shift Experiment

The preceding suggestion concerning the learning of a reorientation response during the initial, simultaneous discrimination problem leads to certain expectations if the subject is shifted to a successive discrimination. That is, at the outset of the successive problem, when both stimuli in the T-maze are the same as the formerly positive stimulus, it would be expected that the subject should respond to the stimulus on the side of its initial orientation, without reorienting on that trial. However, when both stimuli in the T-maze are the same as the formerly negative stimulus, it would be expected that the subjects should reorient and respond to the stimulus on the side opposite that of its initial orientation.

One source of evidence substantiating this analysis of transfer from a simultaneous discrimination problem to a successive problem was obtained by examining each subject's responses on the very first trial following the shift. Combining the Suc-IDS and the Suc-EDS groups, the very first successive discrimination trial involved presentation of the previously positive stimulus in both arms of the T-maze for 20 animals. For the remaining 28 successive shift animals this trial involved presentation of the formerly negative stimulus in both arms of the T-maze. Table III indicates the proportion of trained and overtrained subjects who behaved in the expected manner, i.e. the proportion of subjects who responded to the side of initial orientation, without reorienting, when both arms contained the previously positive stimulus, and the proportion who reoriented at least once and responded to the side opposite that of initial orientation when both arms contained the previously negative stimulus. As may be seen, the proportions were high in each condition for both the Criterion and Overtrained groups. Statistical analyses were performed comparing the obtained proportions with chance expectations. The results of these analyses, also presented in Table IV, indicated that the differences were all highly reliable.

An animal's responses when initially shifted to a successive problem appear to be determined by its previous training with the reward contingencies of the simultaneous problem. It would be expected that the manner in which they continue to behave in the successive discrimination would

TABLE III

The proportion of trained and overtrained subjects who behaved in the expected manner

| Level of training | Stimuli in both arms of maze on first successive discrimination trial | | | | | |
| | Formerly positive | | | Formerly negative | | |
	n	Proportion of subjects	p†	n	Proportion of subjects	p†
Criterion	11	0·82	·03	13	0·85	·01
Overtrained	9	1·00	·001	15	0·73	·06

† The p values are based on the binomial test.

depend, to a great extent, on whether these initial responses are rewarded. Figure 5 illustrates the effects of various reward contingencies in the Suc-IDS situation.

In the top panel of Fig. 5, the preshift simultaneous discrimination performance of a hypothetical subject is schematically represented for two stimulus configurations (A and B) which occur equally often during training (and overtraining). For illustrative purposes, the subject is depicted as having been trained with black as the positive stimulus, and white as the negative stimulus. It is also assumed that the subject has a right orientation preference, i.e. it tends to initially orient right on every trial. If the positive stimulus is on the side of initial orientation, the subject may be expected to respond to it without reorienting (A, top panel of Fig. 5). If the negative stimulus is on the side of initial orientation, the subject should orient and respond to the opposite side (B, top panel of Fig. 5).

When a subject such as that depicted in Fig. 5 is switched to a Suc-IDS problem, the reward contingencies can be arranged in one of two manners. One of these is illustrated in the middle panel of Fig. 5, and the other in the bottom panel of Fig. 5. The middle panel describes the Suc-IDS situation when reward is present (A) in the right arm when both arms are black, and (B) in the left arm when both arms are white. Suppose, in the successive problem, that the subject continues to initially orient and then respond in the same way as at the end of the prior simultaneous problem. On those

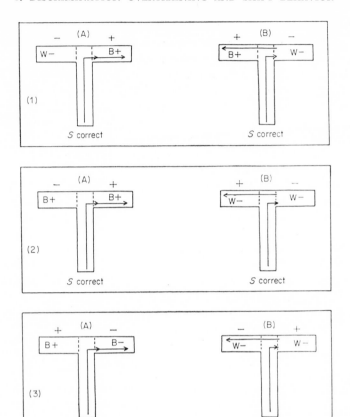

FIG. 5. Schematic representation of manner in which previous simultaneous discrimination experience affects performance on a Suc-IDS. (1) Simultaneous discrimination performance of a subject who tends to initially orient right at the start of every trial. Black (B) is the positive stimulus, and white (W) is the negative stimulus. (2) Subject shifted to a Suc-IDS in which the previous manner of discrimination solution facilitates solution of the new problem. (3) Subject shifted to a Suc-IDS in which previous manner of discrimination solution hinders solution of the new problem. Configuration A occurs on half of each daily block of trials, and configuration B is presented on the remaining trials.

trials when both arms are black (A), the illustrative subject would orient right, respond to the previously positive stimulus which is presented on that side, and get rewarded. On those trials when both arms are white (B), the subject would orient right, present itself with the previously negative stimulus, and reorient and respond to the opposite side. Again, it would be rewarded.

Consider now the second manner of Suc-IDS, as illustrated in the bottom panel of Fig. 5. In this case, when both arms are the same as the previously positive stimulus, reward is placed on the side opposite that of preferred initial orientation (A). When both arms are the same as the previously negative stimulus, reward is placed on the side of preferred initial orientation (B). On those trials (A), when both arms are the same as the previously positive stimulus (black, in this example) the subject would orient right and respond to that side without reorientation. This behavior would not lead to reward. On those trials (B) when both arms are the same as the previously negative stimulus (white, in this example)—the subject would orient right and then reorient and respond to the opposite side. This behavior also would not lead to reward.

The manner of Suc-IDS illustrated in the middle panel of Fig. 5 will hereafter be referred to as Suc-IDS(+). The manner of Suc-IDS illustrated in the bottom panel of Fig. 5 will be referred to as Suc-IDS(−).

If this analysis of transfer effects is correct, it would be expected that Suc-IDS(+) subjects should learn the successive shift considerably faster than Suc-IDS(−) subjects. On the basis of initial orientation behavior at the end of preshift training, subjects were assigned to the Suc-IDS(+) and Suc-IDS(−) conditions in such a way that half the subjects with each level of training were assigned to each condition. Table IV presents the

TABLE IV

Mean number of days to criterion for Suc-IDS subjects shifted in such a way that the previous simultaneous discrimination experience might be expected to facilitate (+) or hinder (−) acquisition of the successive discrimination problem

Manner of Suc-IDS	Training level	
	Criterion	Overtrained
Suc-IDS (+)	5·5†	2·8
Suc-IDS (−)	20·7	20·5

† The score in each cell represents the mean of six subjects.

mean number of days to solve the shift problem for Criterion and Overtrained subjects assigned to each Suc-IDS condition. Our expectation was confirmed: Suc-IDS(+) subjects required significantly fewer days to reach criterion than Suc-IDS(−) subjects ($p < ·01$). The interaction between training level and Suc-IDS's condition was insignificant.

The Suc-IDS(+) subjects apparently solve the successive problem by initially orienting and conditionally reorienting and responding as they did in the prior simultaneous problem. In order to solve the shift problem,

Suc-IDS(−) subjects must abandon this mode of behavior. The changes which occur in the behavior of Suc-IDS(−) subjects as they come to solution are orderly and informative.

Predominant modes of solution of the Suc-IDS(−) problem are schematically represented in Fig. 6. The top panel of Fig. 6 depicts the initial Suc-IDS condition of the same hypothetical subject depicted in the bottom panel of Fig. 5. It is assumed that during the prior simultaneous discrimination training, black was the positive stimulus, and white the negative. Recall that the subject is assumed to initially orient right on each

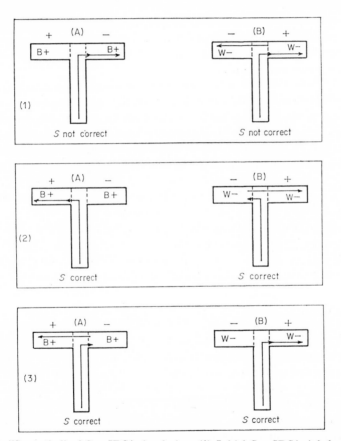

FIG. 6. "Strategies" of Suc-IDS(−) solution. (1) Initial Suc-IDS(−) behavior of a subject who tends to initially orient right on every trial. During preshift training, black (B) was the positive stimulus, and white (W) was the negative stimulus. (2) Solution of Suc-IDS(−) by changing direction of initial orientation and retaining approach and conditional reorientation tendencies learned prior to the shift. (3) Solution of Suc-IDS(−) by retaining initial orientation tendency and changing approach and conditional reorientation tendencies learned prior to the shift.

trial, and that its response tendencies, formerly effective in leading to reward, now do not lead to reward, either when the successive problem involved presentation of (A), the previously positive stimulus, or (B), the previously negative stimulus.

One way of responding correctly on the Suc-IDS(−) problem would simply be for the subject to change the direction of its initial orientation. This possibility is shown in the middle panel of Fig. 6. If the illustrative subject now initially orients left on every trial, instead of right, it will be rewarded for responding as it did during the initial simultaneous discrimination problem. That is, it will be rewarded for approaching the first stimulus it orients towards if it is the previously positive stimulus (A, middle panel of Fig. 6), and reorienting and responding to the opposite side if the first stimulus it orients towards is the previously negative stimulus (B, middle panel of Fig. 6).

If the illustrative subject maintains the same consistent orientation preference (right, in this example), it must learn to make the opposite responses to the discriminanda to those made during the initial simultaneous discrimination. This response pattern is depicted in the bottom panel of Fig. 6. The subject must now reorient and approach the stimulus on the side opposite that of its initial orientation when its initial orientation is towards the formerly positive stimulus (A, bottom panel of Fig. 6), and when its initial orientation is towards the formerly negative stimulus, it must approach that stimulus (B, bottom panel of Fig. 6).

The Suc-IDS(−) subjects can be clearly dichotomized on the basis of the "strategy" they use to solve the successive problem. Twelve animals were shifted to the Suc-IDS(−) condition. Exactly half changed their direction of initial orientation before they reached criterion on the shift problem, i.e. their solution behavior was as depicted in the middle panel of Fig. 6. The remaining six Suc-IDS(−) animals solved the shift problem without changing their direction of initial orientation, i.e. their solution was as depicted in the bottom panel of Fig. 6. It has been shown that Overtrained subjects have significantly higher initial orientation tendencies than Criterion subjects (see Fig. 4). Therefore, it might be expected that Overtrained subjects would tend to solve the Suc-IDS(−) problem in a manner not requiring them to change the direction of their initial orientation. Indeed, of the six subjects who did solve the Suc-IDS(−) problem in this manner, five of them were Overtrained subjects, the other one being a Criterion subject. Five of the six Suc-IDS(−) subjects who solved the problem by changing their direction of initial orientation were Criterion subjects, the sixth being an Overtrained subject. The difference in frequency between the Overtrained and Criterion subjects in the manner of Suc-IDS(−) problem solution was statistically reliable ($p < \cdot05$).

In the Suc-EDS situation any systematic response tendencies to the members of the previously relevant stimulus dimension will lead to reward 50% of the time, since this dimension is now irrelevant. Hence the specific reward contingencies of the successive discrimination problem do not assume roles of such importance in subjects' speed and "strategy" of learning the post shift problem when compared with the specific reward contingencies of the Suc-IDS situation.

It appears then that analysis of the chain of responses that precede the final choice response reveals a wealth of detail about performance in the successive shift problem not apparent in the measure of days to shift criterion. Indeed, the use of this gross measure tends to mask important aspects of the results. This is clearly illustrated in the Suc-IDS versus Suc-EDS comparison. A previous finding, congruent with attentional interpretations of discrimination learning, was replicated in this experiment. The Suc-IDS was learned significantly faster than the Suc-EDS. However, it was subsequently demonstrated that the Suc-IDS group can be divided into two subgroups: Suc-IDS($+$) and Suc-IDS($-$). The apparent superiority of the Suc-IDS group in speed of learning the shift problem was at least partly due to the averaging of the Suc-IDS($+$) and the Suc-IDS($-$) means. A comparison of the performance of the Suc-EDS group with just the Suc-IDS($-$) group indicated that they did not differ significantly in speed of learning the shift problem ($p > \cdot 05$).

The present results cannot be understood simply in terms of approach and avoidance responses to the separate discriminanda, without acknowledging the importance of initial orientation and conditional reorientation tendencies. Nevertheless, it might be expected that response tendencies would be associated with the discriminanda independently of their spatial location. It has been demonstrated that both Criterion and Overtrained subjects tended to approach the stimulus on the side of initial orientation, without reorienting, when both arms were the same as the previously positive stimulus, and they tended to approach the stimulus on the side opposite that of their initial orientation when both arms were the same as the previously negative stimulus. In the latter situation, however, the two training level groups differed in the manner in which they tended finally to approach the stimulus. On those four trials of the first successive shift day when both arms of the maze contained the formerly negative stimulus, Overtrained subjects appeared to be more reluctant in making a final choice response, i.e. they tended to evidence more orientation responses before finally entering one arm of the maze. The Suc-IDS and Suc-EDS data were combined for purposes of analysis of orientation behavior on this first shift day, since the subjects' responses to the discriminanda would presumably not yet be appreciably influenced by their specific shift condition. The mean total number of orientation responses for the Over-trained subjects was 15·88, whereas for the Criterion subjects the mean was 11·96. An analysis of variance indicated that this difference was statistically significant ($p < ·05$).

4. Simultaneous Shift Experiment

In order to solve the simultaneous shift problem, subjects must learn both to approach and to conditionally reorient to stimuli other than those which elicited these responses during the preshift problem. Overtrained subjects have more training than Criterion subjects on both the approach and reorientation responses.

The effects of greater training with the specific reward contingencies of the preshift problem were evidenced by the tendency for Overtrained subjects to respond longer than Criterion subjects in the previously appropriate manner. Table V shows, for all four simultaneous shift groups, the mean number of consecutive postshift days on which all daily choice responses were to the formerly positive stimulus. An analysis of variance

TABLE V

Mean number of consecutive postshift days on which all daily choice responses were to the formerly positive stimulus (simultaneous shift experiment)

Shift type	Level of training	
	Criterion	Overtrained
Sim-IDS	2·8	4·0
Sim-EDS	4·1	5·7

showed that the Overtrained groups persisted significantly longer than the Criterion groups in exclusively approaching the previously positive stimulus ($p < ·05$). Furthermore, the Sim-EDS groups persisted longer than the Sim-IDS groups in responding in this manner ($p < ·05$).

In the case of a Sim-EDS, both values of the previously relevant stimulus dimension were randomly correlated with reward, hence Sim-EDS subject were rewarded 50% of the time for responding in the appropriate preshift manner. They thus continued to be rewarded, albeit partially, for these approach and reorientation responses.

For Sim-IDS subjects, the reward contingencies were reversed on shifting; responses to the previously positive stimulus did not lead to reward, hence approach responses to the previously positive stimulus were extinguished. Reorientation responses learned prior to the shift were also not reinforced, and it might be expected that they also should diminish. It might further be expected that this decrease should be less marked for Overtrained subjects because, prior to the shift, they were more often rewarded for the reorientation response.

A subject's complete abandonment of the reorientation response would be indicated if it responded to all stimuli on the side of initial orientation. Although no Sim-EDS subjects either Criterion or Overtrained, evidenced a single postshift day in which all responses were to the side of initial orientation, 10 of the 24 Sim-IDS subjects did. Seven of the 12 Criterion Sim-IDS subjects responded for at least one day prior to shift solution in this manner, whereas only 3 of the 12 Overtrained Sim-IDS subjects evidenced any days of responding in this manner. The difference in frequency is in the expected direction, but does not reach conventional levels of statistical significance. Considering only those subjects who actually did show at least one day of this manner of responding, the mean for the seven Criterion subjects was 4·4 days, and the mean for the three Overtrained subjects 2·4 days. Assigning to subjects who did not evidence at least one day in which all responses were to the side of initial orientation a score of zero days of responding in this manner, the mean for the Criterion Sim-IDS group was 2·6 days, and the mean for the Overtrained Sim-IDS group was 0·7 days. The difference between these scores is statistically significant (Mann-Whitney $U = 37$, $p = ·05$).

The Criterion Sim-IDS subjects not only tended to respond more often without reorienting, but they also showed this tendency earlier in the shift problem. The Criterion subjects who responded in this manner started to do so with a mean of 5·5 days following the shift, compared with 2·7 days for the Overtrained subjects. This difference is statistically significant ($p < ·02$).

Overtrained Sim-IDS subjects were less likely to abandon the reorientation response when it was not rewarded at the outset of the shift. If they did adopt the response of approaching the stimulus on the side of initial orientation, they did so later in the course of shift solution than the Criterion subjects, and maintained this manner of responding for a shorter period of time. The Sim-EDS subjects, who were all partially rewarded for continuing to reorient, never adopted this manner of responding.

It may be suggested that the relatively high tendency for Criterion Sim-IDS subjects to abandon reorienting behavior accounts for the fact that they take longer than the other simultaneous shift groups to accomplish the shift.

IV. Discussion

The ORE, such as that presently observed in the comparison of the Criterion and Overtrained Sim-IDS groups, has frequently been interpreted (e.g. Mackintosh, 1965b; Sutherland, 1959) as the result of an attentional process. That is, it has been suggested that attentional responses, concerned with identification of the relevant stimulus dimension to the exclusion of other dimensions, are strengthened during preshift overtraining, and serve to facilitate a discrimination shift in which such attentional responses are still appropriate. A simple reversal, i.e. a Sim-IDS, is assumed to represent such a case. This interpretation also implies, however (e.g. Mackintosh, 1965b; Sutherland, 1964a) that extended preshift training should tend to facilitate *any* shift in which the attentional responses remains appropriate, and hinder any shift in which it becomes inappropriate. The results of the present investigation offer little encouragement to this theory.

In both the Simultaneous and Successive Shift Experiments, overtraining did not hinder the extradimensional shifts, in which the previously acquired attentional responses could reasonably be assumed to be inappropriate. Overtraining facilitated the intradimensional shift in the Simultaneous Shift Experiment, replicating the ORE. It did not, however, facilitate the intradimensional shift in the Successive Shift Experiment, in which the previously acquired attentional responses would presumably be just as appropriate as in the Simultaneous Shift Experiment.

The assumption has been made (e.g. Lawrence, 1949; Mackintosh, 1965b) that the successive shift situation is especially useful for evaluating the effects of previously learned attentional responses. While the attentional responses acquired during original simultaneous discrimination training are assumed to be appropriate or inappropriate to solution of the successive problem, molar response tendencies similarly acquired have been seen as irrelevant, rather than appropriate or inappropriate.

In fact, the analysis of the subjects' behavior in the Successive Shift Experiment indicated that there was considerable transfer of molar response tendencies. The specific pattern of initial orientation, conditional reorientation, and approach behavior rewarded during the original simultaneous discrimination continued to be rewarded for Suc-IDS(+) subjects, was non-rewarded for Suc-IDS(−) subjects, and was partially rewarded for Suc-EDS subjects. Furthermore, if the Suc-IDS(−) subjects simply changed their behavior in the first link of the chain, i.e. their direction of initial orientation, the subsequent conditional reorientation and approach behavior was consistently rewarded, and hence provided a basis for positive transfer.

In light of these factors, the finding that a Suc-IDS is learned faster than a Suc-EDS cannot be viewed as demonstrating the role of attentional processes. Each of the molar response tendencies indicated was shown to exert considerable influence on behavior in the Successive Shift problem, and would appear in aggregate to offer a ready interpretation for the overall ease of learning a Suc-IDS relative to a Suc-EDS.

Thus, there is no evidence in either experiment, beyond the replication of the ORE, that necessarily implicates an attentional process in the solution of a shift problem. That the ORE occurs in the absence of such evidence suggests that its interpretation as an attentional phenomenon may be subject to question. It is probable that the several molar response tendencies which were shown to transfer from original training to the successive shift problem were no less important in influencing solution of the simultaneous shift problem.

In order to solve the simultaneous shift problems, subjects must engage in reorienting behavior. That is, in the shift problem, as in the preshift problem, the negative stimulus is on the side of initial orientation on about half the trials. If a subject is to respond correctly, it must reorient on such trials and respond to the stimulus on the opposite side. Although the discriminanda occasioning appropriate reorientation behavior are different for the shift and preshift problems, it is useful to consider the likelihood of reorientation *per se*, independently of the specific discriminanda.

Subjects first evidenced reorienting behavior just prior to reaching criterion on the initial problem, so that this behavior was extensively practiced only by Overtrained subjects. When subjected to an intra-dimensional shift, reorientation responses were initially not rewarded, inasmuch as the reward contingencies were reversed. The effects of prior training were clearly evidenced; Criterion subjects tended to abandon reorienting with a greater frequency, sooner, and for a longer period of time than Overtrained subjects. The finding that Overtrained subjects maintained this manner of responding which was necessary for simultaneous shift solution can account for the relative ease with which they solved the Sim-IDS.

This interpretation of the ORE must be classed with others, such as those of Spence (quoted in Reid, 1953), Harlow (1959), and Reid (1953), which have stressed the positive transfer of molar S-R tendencies. Several recent investigations provide additional evidence that the relevant effect of overtraining is to strengthen molar S-R tendencies, and indicate that detailed analyses of the learning and transfer of overt response "strategies" can parsimoniously account for the ORE without recourse to covert attentional mechanisms (Mandler 1966; Mandler, 1968; Mandler and Hooper, 1967). Furthermore, when situations have been used in which such strategies would not be expected to be significant (e.g. a discrimination box, so constructed that the animal is oriented towards both discriminada from the beginning of training), no ORE has been obtained (Tighe, *et al.* 1967, Hirayoshi and Warren, 1967).

Finally, it should be noted that the Successive Shift Experiment provided an opportunity to test a prediction arising from an alternative explanation of the Ore. A conflict model of the phenomenon has been presented by D'Amato and Jagoda (1961). Briefly, they hypothesized that subjects' experience with the negative discriminanda is virtually terminated during overtraining, thereby decreasing avoidance tendencies towards it and facilitating reversal. If this analysis is correct, it would be expected that when first shifted to the successive discrimination, the orientation behavior would be different for Criterion and Overtrained subjects. The Overtrained animals, who are hypothesized to have less avoidance tendencies towards the negative discriminanda, should show less reluctance in responding to one of the two identical discriminanda on those trials when they are both the same as the previously negative stimulus, i.e. they should show fewer orientation responses before the final choice response. The opposite tendency was found. Overtrained animals showed *more* orientation responses than Criterion animals, on the first postshift day of the successive discrimination, when both stimuli were the same as the previously negative stimulus, indicating that they had a *greater* tendency to avoid the negative stimulus.

V. Summary

Previous investigators have reported that extensive overtraining on a simultaneous, two-choice discrimination facilitates a subsequent discrimination reversal (see Paul, 1965; Sperling, 1965a, 1965b). This phenomenon has been termed the "Overtraining Reversal Effect" (ORE).

One theoretical Explanation of the ORE (e.g. Mackintosh, 1965b; Sutherland, 1959) stresses the importance of the learning of mediating, attentional responses, concerned with the identification of the relevant stimulus dimension, which are appropriate both to the initial discrimination and the subsequent reversal. A second explanation (e.g. Harlow, 1959; Reid, 1953) stresses the importance of molar S-R tendencies which positively transfer from the initial discrimination to the reversal.

The present investigation consisted of two experiments designed to test implications of attentional interpretations of the ORE. The expectation in both experiments was that if overtraining strengthened attentional responses, it should not only facilitate learning a subsequent problem in which they were appropriate, but it should also hinder learning a subsequent problem in which they were inappropriate.

In each experiment, 48 rats were trained on a simultaneous discrimination in a T-maze. This initial problem contained an irrelevant dimension (both values of which were uncorrelated with food reward) as well as a relevant dimension (one value of which was always associated with reward, and the second value of which was never associated with reward). Independent groups of nonovertrained and overtrained subjects were shifted either intradimensionally (i.e. the originally relevant stimulus dimension was still relevant) or extradimensionally (i.e. the originally irrelevant stimulus dimension was made relevant). In the first experiment, the shift problem resembled the preshift problem in that it consisted of a simultaneous discrimination. In the second experiment, the shift problem consisted of a successive discrimination.

In the Simultaneous Shift Experiment, the intradimensional shift was learned faster by overtrained subjects than by nonovertrained subjects, replicating the ORE. However, contrary to expectations arising from attentional interpretations of the ORE, overtraining did not hinder the extradimensional shift.

In the Successive Shift Experiment, it was found that overtraining neither facilitated the intradimensional shift nor hindered the extradimensional shift, contrary to attentional interpretations of ORE.

The fact that the ORE was replicated in the absence of any evidence implicating attentional processes in discrimination shift performance suggests that the ORE is not an attentional phenomenon. In an attempt to find an explanation of the ORE congruent with the results obtained in the other shift conditions, the data were analyzed in more detail. It was found that performance on the shift problem was highly dependent on initial orientation, conditional reorientation, and approach responses rewarded during the preshift simultaneous discrimination. The ORE appeared to be the result of the transfer of these overt responses tendencies. These response tendencies also affected subjects' performance on the successive shift problems, contrary to common expectations (Lawrence, 1949; Mackintosh, 1965b). The manner of transfer of these molar responses appears to explain other results (Lawrence, 1949) usually interpreted as indicating the importance of attentional processes in discrimination learning.

Acknowledgements

The research was supported in part by Grant GB-3523 from the National Science Foundation to Allan R. Wagner. The author is grateful to Allan R. Wagner for his advice. Preparation of this version was aided by grant MH-13479 to the author from the National Institute of Mental Health. This paper is adapted from a doctoral dissertation submitted to Yale University (1966); and is an expanded version of an article appearing in *J. comp. physiol. Psychol.* (1967). The Author is grateful to the American Psychological Association for permission to republish some of the figures and text.

References

Blum, R. A. and Blum, J. S. (1949). Factual issues in the "continuity controversy." *Psychol. Rev.* **56**, 33–50.

D'Amato, M. R. and Jagoda, H. (1961). Analysis of the role of overlearning in discrimination reversal. *J. exp. Psychol.* **61**, 45–50.

Goodrich, K. P., Ross, L. E. and Wagner, A. R. (1961). An examination of selected aspects of the continuity and noncontinuity positions in discrimination learning. *Psychol. Rec.* **11**, 105–117.

Goodwin, W. R. and Lawrence, D. H. (1955). The functional independence of two discrimination habits associated with a constant stimulus situation. *J. comp. physiol. Psychol.* **48**, 437–443.

Harlow, H. F. (1959). Learning set and error factor theory. *In* "Psychology: A Study of a Science" (S. Koch, ed.), Vol. 2, pp. 492–537. McGraw-Hill, New York, U.S.A.

Hirayoshi, I. and Warren, J. M. (1967). Overtraining and reversal learning by experimentally naive kittens. *J. comp. physiol. Psychol.* **64**, 507–509.

Lawrence, D. H. (1949). Acquired distinctiveness of cues: I. Transfer between discriminations on the basis of familiarity with the stimulus. *J. exp. Psychol.* **39**, 770–784.

Lawrence, D. H. (1950). Acquired distinctiveness of cues: II. Selective association in a constant stimulus situation. *J. exp. Psychol.* **40**, 175–188.

Mackintosh, N. J. (1962). The effects of overtraining on a reversal and a nonreversal shift. *J. comp. physiol. Psychol.* **55**, 555–559.

Mackintosh, N. J. (1965b). Selective attention in animal discrimination learning. *Psychol. Bull.* **64**, 124–150.

Mandler, J. M. (1966). Behaviour changes during overtraining and their effects on reversal and transfer. *Psychonom. Monogr. Suppl.* **1**, 187–202.

Mandler, J. M. (1968). Overtraining and the use of positive and negative stimuli in reversal and transfer. *J. comp. physiol. Psychol.* **66**, 110–115.

Mandler, J. M. and Hooper, W. R. (1967). Overtraining and goal approach strategies in discrimination reversal. *Quart. J. exp. Psychol.* **19**, 142–149.

Paul, C. (1965). Effects of overlearning upon single habit reversal in rats. *Psychol. Bull.* **63**, 65–72.

Pubols, B. H., Jr. (1956). The facilitation of visual and spatial discrimination reversal by overlearning. *J. comp. physiol. Psychol.* **49**, 243–248.

Reid, L. S. (1953). The development of noncontinuity behaviour through continuity learning. *J. exp. Psychol.* **46**, 107–112.

Siegel, S. (1967). Overtraining and transfer processes. *J. comp. physiol. Psychol.* **64**, 471–477.

Sperling, S. E. (1965a). Reversal learning and resistance to extinction: A review of the rat literature. *Psychol. Bull.* **63**, 281–297.

Sperling, S. E. (1965b). Reversal learning and resistance to extinction: A supplementary report. *Psychol. Bull.* **64**, 310–312.

Sutherland, N. S. (1959). Stimulus analysing mechanisms. *In* "Proceedings of a Symposium on the Mechanisation of Thought Processes." Vol. 2, pp. 575–609. H.M.S., London.

Sutherland, N. S. (1964a). The learning of discriminations by animals. *Endeavour*, **23**, 148–152.

Sutherland, N. S. (1964b). Visual discrimination in animals. *Brit. med. Bull.* **20,** 54–59.

Tighe, T. J., Brown, P. L. and Youngs, E. A. (1965). The effect of overtraining on the shift behaviour of albino rats. *Psychonom. Sci.* **2,** 141–142.

Uhl, C. N. (1964). Effects of overtraining on reversal and nonreversal discrimination shifts in a free operant situation. *Percept. Mot. Skills,* **19,** 927–934.

Zeaman, D. and House, B. J. (1963). The role of attention in retardate discrimination learning. *In* "Handbook of Mental Deficiency: Psychological Theory and Research" (N. R. Ellis, ed.), pp. 159–223. McGraw-Hill, New York, U.S.A.

9 | Behavioural Contrast and the Peak Shift

T. M. BLOOMFIELD

University of Sussex, Brighton, Sussex, England

I. Introduction

This paper attempts to develop a context in which contrast effects and the peak shift can be understood. It is generally assumed that the mode of explanation in psychology should be modelled on that used in the physical sciences, with the consequence that all phenomena are taken to have equal status. All aspects of an animal's behaviour are, on this view, to be explained by reference to their causal antecedents, or to the independent variable in a functional relationship. Our everyday assumptions about behaviour, however, are quite different. We speak of normal and abnormal behaviour, where the former does not stand in need of explanation. Generally, it is in reference to abnormalities only that we may speak of causes, since a normal piece of behaviour is not "caused" at all, but, in ideal cases, fulfills a person's purposes and advances his plans. It is my intention to argue, in the course of this article, that the asymmetry of explanation enshrined in ordinary language is essential if we are to make sense of animal behaviour. Behaviour which meets the requirements of a particular reinforcement schedule cannot be treated as on the same footing as behaviour which fails to meet those requirements, and in the latter case only may we seek an explanation of the behaviour. Views similar to the above have been elaborated by Peters (1958), Taylor (1964), and Louch (1966).

The notion of normal, or required, behaviour is especially important in connexion with contrast and the peak shift. These phenomena are by now well known by-products of successive discrimination training, where an animal is presented with two discriminable stimuli, one at a time. These stimuli signal different reinforcement contingencies, often variable-interval reward and extinction (mult VI ext). Thus, in the presence of a red light, say, a pigeon will be rewarded intermittently for key-pecking, while during a green light no rewards will be given. The behaviour required by this schedule is simple: respond (by pecking) to red, don't respond to green. Such behaviour is justified by the contingencies, and I do not believe that it is possible to explain it further. The schedule entitles the pigeon to act in this way.

So where a pigeon is first rewarded for pecks to both red and green, and later rewards are witheld during green, we can explain why the pigeon stops pecking to green only by saying that rewards are no longer available in green. Similarly, on these grounds, there is no need to *explain* the continuance of pecking to red, since this behaviour is rewarded. But here the contrast effect comes in. Pecking certainly continues to red, but the rate of pecking *increases* (Reynolds, 1961). This behaviour is not justified by the reinforcement contingencies: it seems to have no point, to achieve nothing. In this way a distinction may be drawn between the contrast effect (increase in pecking to red) and the decrease in pecking to green. The latter is in accordance with the reinforcement schedule, while the former is not. Thus we can seek an explanation of the contrast effect and attempt to put forward a theory of contrast in a way that we cannot have a theory of discrimination learning since the latter is justified by the reinforcement contingencies.

A second case of behaviour in discrimination training that is not called for by the schedule is the peak shift. When a pigeon is trained to peck at one stimulus for reward and later tested with other stimuli similar in one respect to the training stimulus, it is found that the fastest pecking occurs to the original stimulus used in training, the rate decreasing according to the difference between the subsequent test stimuli and the training stimulus (Hanson, 1959). The results of the tests may be plotted as a generalization gradient, which has a peak at the training stimulus. After discrimination training, however, where the pigeon is trained to peck one stimulus from the dimension and not peck another, not only is the rate of responding to the training stimulus increased (the contrast effect), but the peak of the generalization gradient shifts to a new stimulus further away from the non reward-correlated stimulus than the original reward-correlated stimulus. Thus, if pecks at a vertical (0°) line give VI reward while pecks at a slanting (+45°) line go unrewarded, not only does the rate of pecking to 0° increase in training, but the maximum rate of responding in a subsequent generalization test is found at −15° or −30° (Bloomfield, 1967). This effect is termed the peak shift. Both the peak shift and the contrast effect are abnormalities in behaviour: nothing in the experimental procedure either entitles or requires the pigeon to do these things.

I shall attempt to show that the classification of these effects as abnormal has repercussions in defining and explaining them. Something has gone wrong with the animal's interpretation of the experimental situation, so an explanation should be forthcoming. Later, I hope to show that considering these effects in the normal/abnormal framework can lead to an improved analysis of what behaviour is necessary before we can decide whether a pigeon has really learned a discrimination. Two of the hypotheses I shall consider are mentioned briefly in Bower's (1966) discussion of contrast and the peak shift. The first treats these phenomena as products of frustration–a hypothesis that has an ambiguous status. The second claims that rewards in a context of non reward are judged better than in a context of other rewards. Thus the faster responding occurs, since for the pigeon, it is for a larger reward.

But before I can turn to the problems of interpretation the experimental evidence needs some clarification. There has been disagreement in the literature about the definition of contrast and the generality of the peak shift. These conflicts need to be considered, and, where it is possible, resolved. This is the object of the next few sections.

II. Experiments

A. THE DEFINITION OF CONTRAST

Reynolds (1961b) defines contrast as follows:

". . . an interaction is termed a *contrast* if it is a change in rate in a direction away from the rate prevailing in the other component . . .";

or, in another paper (Reynolds 1961a):

"If the rate of responding with a red key increases when the rate with a green key decreases (or decreases when the other increases), the change in rate during the presence of red is called a *contrast*."

This definition is open to question. First, it is not clear which time interval is in mind when a rate change is specified. Figure 1 shows two graphs, 1a. adapted from Reynolds (1961a), and 1b. from one of my experiments (Bloomfield, 1966). Reynolds' procedure involved a transition from mult

VI VI to mult VI ext, while the procedure I used was a shift from VI to mult VI ext. In my experiment, no preliminary training was given with the stimulus subsequently correlated with the extinction component of the multiple schedule. So when extinction was introduced, the stimulus accompanying this contingency was a novel one. In Reynolds' experiment, this stimulus had been correlated previously with VI reward. It should be clear from a comparison of the two figures that there is little difference between the main effects.

Two alternative decisions could be taken about the time interval over which rate changes are to be measured. In Fig. 1 the interval could be measured from (a) to (c) or from (b) to (c). In Fig. 1a, where a transition occurs from mult VI VI to mult VI ext, both interpretations of a rate change agree in classifying the result as a case of contrast. The rate changes between (a) and (c) in the VI and ext components are in opposite directions, as are the changes between (b) and (c). Thus, on this interpretation of Reynolds' definition we have a case of contrast. However, the formulation depending upon a change between (a) and (c) has no application to

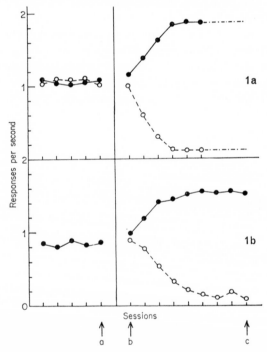

FIG. 1. Both figures show a contrast effect developing in a mult VI ext schedule (1a. adapted from Reynolds 1961a). Response rate is plotted against days of training.

Fig. 1b, since the stimulus subsequently correlated with extinction does not appear at (a). Therefore, if the results in both figures are to be incorporated into an account of contrast, the rate change must be specified between (b) and (c), that is, within a particular multiple schedule.

But is it necessary to mention divergent rates, as Reynolds does, in the definition of contrast? Certainly, contrast is a rate change in one component of a multiple schedule, but it is not clear that the definition should include reference to a rate change in the opposite direction in the other component. Rather, citing a rate change in the other component may be to propose an *explanation* of contrast by pointing to its causal antecedents. I shall consider this explanation among others later. As to the definition of contrast, I think a start can be made as follows. To begin with, all cases of contrast are cases of an increase (or decrease) in response rate, but not all increases or decreases in response rate are cases of contrast. Response rate often changes for obvious reasons—e.g. change in size of reward, change in frequency of reward, rewards given following long or short IRTs, etc. Under these circumstances, a rate increase does not need further explanation since it is justified by the contingencies. What is interesting about the contrast effect is that it occurs when there is no apparent justification for it: there is no contingency which requires an increase in response rate.

Thus contrast effects are to be understood against a context of normal changes in responding. As a start, contrast could be defined simply as an *uncalled for* change in responding in a component of a multiple schedule. We could go further and add: where a required change in responding in the other component goes in the opposite direction. This, however, is open to the criticism set out above, that definition has become entangled with explanation, although reference to a required change in responding in the other component, and by implication to a change in the contingencies in that component, *may* be an essential part of what is meant by contrast effects. Discussion of this point is best left to a later section, where I shall argue that, whether as definition or explanation, this is only part of the story. It seems that all cases of contrast are cases where there is some worsening of the conditions which require the change in responding in the second component. It may be that contrast is best defined by spelling out the general things known about it: only then can we really decide whether analogous effects occur in circumstances other than the multiple schedule in operant conditioning situations. Thus it may well be premature to attempt a definition of contrast before it can be explained. We can begin simply by examining changes in responding in multiple schedules that are not called for by the contingencies, in the attempt to understand why these occur.

B. THE CAUSES OF CONTRAST—TERRACE'S VIEWS

To the extent that Reynold's account of contrast includes the suggestion that an important determiner of the effect is a reduction in response rate in one component of the schedule, it is open to question. Reynolds himself (Reynolds, 1961b) puts forward an opposing account in a later paper in terms of a reduction in reinforcement frequency. This conflict has received discussion in an article by Terrace (1966a), where the author comes to the conclusion that the account in terms of rate changes is the more correct one. Terrace's arguments are mostly aimed at clarifying the determinants of contrast and the peak shift together, on the assumption that these phenomena have a common source. He argues that, in most experiments, changes in rate of response and rate of reinforcement are confounded, and cites three experiments as cases where such confounding is avoided.

The first of these is a study by Brethower and Reynolds (1962) in which the reinforcement frequencies in both components of multiple VI 3' VI 3' schedule were held nearly constant, while each response in one component of the schedule was punished by electric shock for a brief period. Since Brethower and Reynolds found that the rate of responding in the un-punished component rose proportionately to the intensity of the shock, Terrace argues that this experiment demonstrates a contrast effect depen-dant upon changes in response rate only, and not upon changes in re-inforcement frequency. I would suggest that the approach embodied in this analysis is a narrow one, which misses important parallels in the data. Reduction in reinforcement frequency could be considered one case of conditions getting worse in that component of the schedule. The introduc-tion of a response-contingent shock would be another case. The notion of one component of a schedule getting worse than another can be elucidated, if necessary, in terms of preference in a choice situation. So an alternative account of contrast could be stated: response rate in one component of a multiple schedule tends to increase when conditions in the other compo-nent change for the worse. To take account of the objection raised to Reynolds' definition of contrast on the basis of Fig. 1, it will be necessary to add: or when a second component is introduced where conditions *are* worse than in the first component.

Terrace's second case is an unpublished experiment in which pigeons were trained on a mult VI 5' drl 7" schedule. Although more reinforce-ments per unit time were obtained in drl 7", a peak shift from the VI 5' stimulus away from the drl stimulus was obtained for some birds in generalization testing. Terrace interprets this as a case of a low response rate becoming aversive, in line with his claim that reduction in response is the main determiner of contrast. Given that there is an aversive aspect to a drl schedule, it is not obvious that a reduced response rate is to blame;

perhaps the required pause is a more likely culprit. The length of pause required before the next peck can be rewarded in drl is probably difficult to estimate, and it seems reasonable to suppose that other things being equal, a pigeon will prefer a schedule which does not make demands on its timing capacities. The question could be settled by testing with a schedule similar to drl except for a signal for the end of the required pause. On the above grounds, it is quite possible that a preference test between VI 5' and drl 7" would show preference for the VI schedule, even though more reinforcements per hour were obtained in drl. If this were the case, the contrast effect/peak shift could be related to a change for the worse in the other component of the schedule. Further difficulties arise in any situation where a generalization gradient is plotted after training on schedules where a reward is given for certain response *rates* (e.g. drl, drh, limited hold, etc.). It is not clear what such a gradient can be said to represent.

This sort of objection can be made to a later study that might be thought to support Terrace's claims. Yarczower *et al.* (1966) used a variety of multiple schedules in training prior to generalization testing. The authors repeated Terrace's observation that a peak shift away from a reduced rate of responding would appear in generalization testing. A number of mult (tand VI drl) (tand VI drl) schedules were employed to manipulate rate of pecking and rate of reinforcement more or less independently. The findings showed that the characteristics of the generalization gradient during testing were a function of the rate of pecking to the stimuli at the end of training. To quote: ". . . if responding in the presence of a stimulus (570 nm) associated with less frequent reinforcement is maintained at a relatively high level compared with responding in the presence of a stimulus (550 nm) associated with more frequent reinforcement, then the peak shift does not occur".

Before appraising these findings, it will be as well to make clear that they do not go against the sort of hypothesis I have been putting forward. I have argued that contrast effects in the first component of a multiple schedule can be related to conditions getting worse in the second component, or to conditions being worse in the second component than in the first. The peak shift, I believe, can be treated in the same way. Honig (1962) has shown that the peak shift is not only a shift in the point of maximum responding on the generalization gradient, it is also a shift in preference for the new point. Given a choice between the $S+$ used in training and the new peak on the gradient, pigeons choose the new peak. It seems reasonable, therefore, to attempt to subsume the peak shift under the same hypothesis as the contrast effect, and to relate both to conditions changing for the worse in the presence of a different stimulus. In this case, any procedures which reinforce certain *rates* of pecking remove the conditions where it is possible for a change in preference to appear in rate measures.

The use of a rate measure is itself suspect in drl schedules and the like. It is usually assumed that the rate of pecking, for instance, can be taken as an indicator of underlying response strength or tendency to make the response. Clearly, it does not follow from the fact that rate of pecking is lower in a drl schedule than in an FR schedule that there is less tendency to meet the schedule requirements in drl than in FR. Once contingencies have been applied to the rate of pecking itself, then the response that is being made may change. Compare VI, FR and drl. Where rate of pecking produces little change in the rate of reinforcement, as in VI schedules, it seems reasonable to take this rate as an indicator of the tendency to respond. Even in FR schedules, where reinforcement rate varies *continuously* with pecking rate, it is possible that rate of pecking within a particular FR schedule may indicate willingness to respond. But, in drl, all IRTs of greater than or equal to t sec are rewarded, while all IRTs less than t sec go unrewarded. Thus response rate is constrained by the reinforcement contingencies according to a step function, and we are no longer able to use rate of pecking as an index of tendency to respond. Further, in drl schedules, the response which is rewarded is not the response which is recorded. The rewarded response is not pecking or lever-pressing, but rather pecking or pressing after a pause of t sec in drl t. Thus, by recording only the operations of the key or lever in the form of a rate measure, genuine "drl-responses" are confused with non-drl pecks or lever presses.

Hence there is an ambiguity about what counts as an increase in response rate in drl. This can be made clearer with a diagram.

1. $(R_{drl}, \text{not-}R_{drl})$ pausing and pecking;
2. $(R_{peck}, \text{not-}R_{peck})$ pecking;
3. $(M_{key}, \text{not-}M_{key})$ a break in the contact behind the key.

1, 2 and 3 are three possible partitions of events during a drl schedule. The only one recorded by the apparatus is $3-M_{key}$. That this latter event occurred does not imply that an R_{peck} was made; the key could have moved because the pigeon flapped its wings, or could even have occurred by an accidental movement of the pigeon's head. Nor does the occurrence of an R_{peck} imply the occurrence of an R_{drl}. I do not want to develop further the intricacies of the situation here, although I do want to stress that it is a matter of experiment to sort out which events do occur in any given situation. Such analyses are important in assessing the effects of drugs on behaviour, for instance, and Sidman (1955) has made an interesting start in considering relative effects upon timing (R_{drl}) and pecking (R_{peck}) of amphetamine and alcohol. Unfortunately, Sidman's interpretations have passed unheeded in a later review (Dews and Morse, 1961). In our present context, such experimental work is an essential prerequisite to answering the question: given that a drl schedule changes for the better, how can we expect performance to change? Will there be an increase in R_{peck} or in R_{drl}?

Thus, there is little point in describing the results of the experiment by Yarczower *et al.* (1966) as showing that the peak shift is dependent upon a difference in rates to the stimuli used at the end of training. The authors showed that no peak shift was obtained if the rates were the same to both stimuli. But it does not follow from this that a difference in response rates is what is responsible for the shift in subsequent generalization testing. A rate-difference after training is a necessary, not a sufficient condition for the occurrence of the peak shift. Further, the use of generalization gradients following training after mult VI drl (e.g. Terrace, 1966a), at least where IRT distributions are not analyzed, can be criticized as comparing incomparables. After such training, and without further experimental work, we can have little idea what key-pecks mean in generalization testing. If the peak shift effect is a shift in preference along the generalization gradient, as I have suggested, it should be possible to measure the pigeon's preference between the particular schedules used. But, whatever the results of such an investigation, it should be clear that there is little to gain from a superficial use of pacing procedures. Certainly, the rate of pecking may be manipulated freely by appropriate scheduling, but only at the cost of making pecks harder to interpret. The mere fact that the apparatus records only key-pecks or lever-presses by no means implies that these are the responses made by the animal, or indeed, the responses required by the schedule.

Terrace cites a third set of experiments to support his case that contrast is sufficiently explained by pointing to a reduction in response rate in the other component of a multiple schedule. These are his own earlier experiments on errorless discrimination learning (Terrace, 1963a; 1963b). He states:

"in errorless discrimination learning there is no reduction in response rate in the presence of S2 since responding to S2 never occurred. The opposite, of course, is true in discrimination learning with errors".

But the relevance of Terrace's errorless training methods in this context can be disputed, and in the next section I hope to show that by a comparison of different methods of discrimination training we can arrive at a better understanding of the sort of context in which contrast effects occur together with a clearer specification of what is involved in learning a discrimination. None of this, I shall argue, is possible without the use of concepts which closely approximate those current in ordinary language.

C. Two Aspects of Discrimination Learning

There is one clear result of discrimination training: an animal comes to behave differently in the presence of two stimuli. It follows logically from this fact that the animal must have seen the difference between the stimuli, and must have classified them separately. So one aspect of discrimination learning concerns the animal's *classification* of the stimuli; another concerns what the animal *does* in the presence of each stimulus. In the presence of the stimulus which signals nonreward ($S-$), for instance, the animal could refrain from doing what was rewarded during $S+$; or, alternatively, it could do something quite specific that happened to conflict with making the $S+$ response. I stress that by $S-$ I mean the class of stimuli in the presence of which the animal either refrains from responding or makes a specific response incompatible with the $S+$ response. Thus I am referring to the *animal's $S-$*, not the experimenter's. The particular stimulus that the experimenter correlates with nonreward is only one member of this class, and the question of interest is how the animal draws the limits of its own $S-$ class after different types of discrimination training.

The distinction between classification of $S-$ and behaviour during $S-$ throws light on a recent controversy between Deutsch (1967) and Terrace (1967) on the interpretation of some earlier results of Terrace's (1966c). Terrace showed that the generalization gradients around $S-$ (the experimenter's) on a dimension orthogonal to the $S+$ dimension depended upon the type of discrimination training given. After discrimination training with errors, where $S+$ and $S-$ were presented successively, he found that responding began to increase when test stimuli were shifted away from $S-$, although these stimuli were no nearer to $S+$. Thus the $S-$ gradients were curved. After errorless discrimination learning, however, the gradients found after an identical testing procedure were flat: varying $S-$ othogonally to $S+$ did not change the rate of responding, which was zero throughout. Deutsch argued that since responding to $S-$ was *zero* after errorless discrimination training we should infer relatively more inhibition than after successive discrimination, training with errors, where low responding persisted throughout training in the presence of $S-$. Terrace replied as he had argued in the earlier paper, that the curved gradients around $S-$ after training with errors demonstrate "stimulus control over not-responding", which is how we define inhibition. Thus he claimed that inhibition could be said to be present only after discrimination training with errors, and so came to the opposite conclusion from that reached by Deutsch.

However, both authors seem to have missed the point that two aspects of discrimination training were being confused in their discussion: the two aspects separated above. When a flat generalization gradient is obtained, the correct inference is that the dimension being varied is not a significant one for the animal. Thus the curvature, or otherwise, of the $S-$ gradients in Terrace's experiment shows only that the animal's $S-$ class does not centre on the experiment's $S-$. Quite possibly, $S-$ for the animal is absence of the experimenter's $S+$. This is an important result for the understanding of errorless discrimination learning, but it has nothing to do with the question of whether inhibition is present or not.

How do we decide, then, whether an animal inhibits the $S+$ response during $S-$? First, I do not believe that it is any help to define inhibition in terms of what Terrace calls "not-responding". This only raises the original question again in the form: how do we distinguish between different types of "not-responding"? Essential to the notion of inhibition is the idea of restraint of a response that would otherwise tend to occur: the animal *refrains* from making the $S+$ response. This gives us two clues to help decide whether inhibition is involved. An animal will not refrain from doing anything it would otherwise tend to do unless it is somehow advantageous to refrain. Second, any behaviour which is the result of inhibiting what the animal would otherwise tend to do is likely to be disrupted by stress or drugs, or even a disturbance. Extinction, for instance, could well be a case of an animal coming to inhibit a previously learned response, and Pavlov (1927) coined the term "disinhibition" to apply to the recovery of an extinguished response when a novel stimulus was introduced. Two pieces of evidence suggest, on these lines, that successive discrimination learning with errors sets up inhibition in the presence of $S-$, at least initially. Hearst (1965) showed that the introduction of a third stimulus which signalled shock into a multiple schedule increased the amount of $S-$ responding considerably. He also showed that non-signalled shock had the same effect. This can be interpreted as a case of stress causing a breakdown in inhibition. Terrace (1963c) showed that chlorpromazine, a tranquillizing drug, had the effect of disrupting completely a discrimination learned with errors, while having no effect on an errorless discrimination. This result is readily understandable on the assumption that the animal is inhibiting the $S+$ response during $S-$ after learning a successive discrimination with errors, but not after errorless discrimination learning.

Thus on the basis of the $S-$ gradients (Terrace, 1966c) and the evidence on inhibition (Terrace, 1963c; Hearst, 1965) we can analyse successive discrimination learning with and without errors differently. I have argued that successive discrimination performance with errors, to the extent that it involves inhibition of the $S+$ response during $S-$, should be susceptible to breakdown by stress or disturbance. A different sort of weakness should be evident in errorless discriminations however. The animal appears not to be sensitive to $S-$ as a stimulus in its own right, but to regard as $S-$ all stimuli other than $S+$. This lack of responsiveness to the experimenter's $S-$ is demonstrated by the flat gradients around $S-$ obtained by Terrace. Such a situation may be rather unstable, especially if it is natural for the pigeon to see the experimenter's $S+$ and $S-$ stimuli as similar. For instance, Terrace has reported (1963b) that it was not possible to train a horizontal/vertical discrimination without errors from the start: this was achieved only by transfer from red/green discrimination previously learned without errors. Terrace has also reported (1966a) that extinction of a discrete-trial discrimination learned with errors causes a full extinction curve to $S-$. The animal begins to respond to $S-$ again. We can make sense of these results on the assumption that errorless training is a method of preventing the animal from classifying $S-$ as a stimulus in its own right. Thus, there is no tendency through generalization to make initial respones to $S-$ in discrimination training, and hence no necessity for any responses to be inhibited. Near perfect discrimination performance will result, but any breakdown in the performance will be complete: once the animal has seen $S-$ as similar to $S+$, the process of inhibiting responses to it must go through, and with this process the large number of responses during $S-$ typical of successive discrimination learning will be made.

D. Necessary and Sufficient Conditions for Contrast and the Peak Shift

Contrast does not occur in errorless discrimination learning, as Terrace has demonstrated. It seems to occur only when errors have occurred in training, and thus can be related to the presence of inhibition. I have already suggested that one of the main determiners of contrast is a change for the worse in one component of a multiple schedule. It is time now to spell out in more detail the sorts of things that could constitute changes for the worse, and to relate these to the above discussion of discrimination learning. Clearly, a drop in rate of reinforcement frequency is a change for the worse, and Reynolds' suggestion that contrast relates to relative reinforcement frequency seems correct as far as it goes. Electric shock, or punishment of other kinds, usually constitutes a worsening of the situation, and Brethower and Reynolds' use of shock in a multiple schedule showed a clear contrast effect, as would be expected. Inhibition can now be added to the list. In both errorless and nonerrorless discrimination learning of the kinds studied by Terrace there is a disparity in rates of reinforcement between the two components of the schedule. But only where errors have occurred, and thus only where inhibition has been developed, is there a contrast effect. I have suggested that inhibition is a positive restraint on responding, and thus something which requires effort. It is also not easy, as the fluctuations in $S-$ responding in successive discrimination learning suggest (Bloomfield, 1966). Thus we may expect that where an animal is required to inhibit a response, we will find a contrast effect in the other component of the schedule. Similar considerations apply to a mult VI drl schedule, for instance, where the animal must refrain from rapid pecks in drl if reinforcements are to be obtained. In this case, however, the restraint necessary can be counterbalanced by a higher rate of reinforcement.

One of my experiments (Bloomfield, 1967a) ran pigeons on a number of such mult VI drl schedules. The results are shown in Fig. 2, plotting rate of response in VI against rate of reinforcement in drl. This, incidentally, is evidence against Terrace's claim that contrast is sufficiently explained by a rate reduction hypothesis. In my study, rate of pecking in drl was inversely correlated with rate of reinforcement: yet contrast was negatively related to rate of reinforcement, not to rate of pecking.

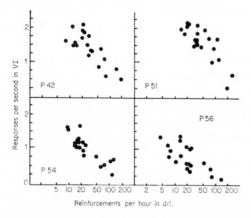

FIG. 2. Response rate in VI is plotted against reinforcement rate in drl from a series of mult VI drl schedules (from Bloomfield, 1967a).

A further experiment was carried out by Reynolds (1961a) to show that reduction in response rate is not sufficient to produce contrast. He showed that where a pigeon was rewarded on a VI schedule in one component of a multiple schedule, while in the other component rewards were delivered only if no pecks had occurred for time t, then no contrast effect appeared. Thus, although response rate was reduced in this second component, there was no contrast in the first component. Clearly, the present account would not require contrast to appear, since there is no reason to suppose that the change in the second component was a change for the worse, since rewards were still given. Thus Reynolds' experiment demonstrates that reduction in response rate is not a sufficient condition for contrast, and my mult VI drl study shows that it is not a necessary condition: thus we may conclude that rate reduction is neither necessary nor sufficient for contrast to appear.

On the evidence currently available, a change for the worse seems to be both a necessary and sufficient condition for contrast. The need for stating the condition in terms of a "change for the worse" is that we do not have a complete list of events that constitute changes for the worse. I have suggested three in the course of the discussion: reduction in frequency of reinforcement; introduction of shock; and development of inhibition. There may well, however, be others, and I would suggest that the best policy for flexible research is to think intuitively about what sorts of things could be construed as a worsening in the situation, then see if they fit in with what we already know about the occurrence of contrast.

Now we turn to evidence specific to the peak shift. Before I can consider this in the context developed so far, one point needs clarification. Guttman (1965) has suggested recently that this phenomenon may occur only on a dimension of colour. His reasons for holding this view appear to derive from two experiments, one of his own (unpublished) on pitch generalization in cats, and one by Jenkins and Harrison (1960) on pitch generalization in the pigeon. Neither of these experiments showed a peak shift, although contrast effects were still reported. Thus this might appear to cast doubt on the idea that contrast and the peak shift stem from the same source. However, Jenkins and Harrison used only presence/absence of a tone as their two discriminative stimuli. Under these conditions, it is difficult to see how a peak shift could occur, since no shift could be characterized as a shift *away* from the negative stimulus. In this case, it seems a reasonable assumption that all points on a pitch continuum are equidistant from

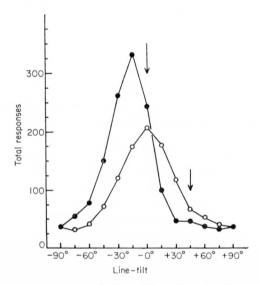

FIG. 3. Percentage responses to a selection of line orientations in generalization testing. Arrows show the $S+$ and $S-$ points (from Bloomfield, 1967d).

absence of pitch, at least over the range used in these experiments. Such an assumption is made by Honig *et al.* (1963) in their study of "inhibition" gradients, as it was by Terrace (1966c) and Jenkins and Harrison themselves. Figure 3 shows data from one of my experiments (Bloomfield, 1967d) in which I showed an absence of peak shift with presence/absence training, while a peak shift developed when the discriminative stimuli were taken from the same dimension. Both results used orientation of a line as the continuum, thus establishing that colour plays no special role in peak shift effects.

A number of experimental results support the attempt to relate the peak shift to the same main determinant as contrast—a change for the worse in the presence of one stimulus. Terrace (1964) has shown that a peak shift occurs only after discrimination learning with errors. An earlier experiment by Honig (1962) demonstrated that it was necessary for the pigeon to have had *successive* discrimination training before a peak shift would appear in generalization testing. Honig trained two groups in either a simultaneous or a successive situation, then split the groups between either simultaneous or successive testing. He found that if training had been given with single stimuli presented successively, then, whether testing was carried out with single stimuli or with pairs of stimuli, a peak shift occurred. Thus it seems that the pigeon will choose the new peak over the previous $S+$ when confronted with the pair of stimuli, after successive, single-stimulus training. After simultaneous training, neither testing procedure gave a peak shift. Terrace's result, however, showed that successive training is not *sufficient* to produce the effect, since no peak shift was obtained after successive errorless discrimination learning. However, what simultaneous and errorless discrimination situations have in common, and what differentiates them both from ordinary successive discrimination training, is the absence of inhibition. In errorless discrimination learning inhibition fails to develop probably because there is no initial tendency to make the $S+$ response during $S-$, and therefore no need to inhibit it: in simultaneous discrimination learning, all that is required is that the pigeon choose $S+$ above $S-$, since both are present at the same time, and this need involve only the development of a preference for $S+$. Thus it seems that where we have reason to believe that responses are being inhibited, we can expect a peak shift to appear in generalization testing. It seems as though the peak shift is related to at least one of the possible ways in which a situation can change for the worse. Guttman (1959) has shown a similar effect in a mult VI 1' VI 5' schedule. There is an important piece of evidence in this context which makes it seem that other changes for the worse can produce a peak shift. Grusec (1968) carried out an experiment on pigeons that had been trained to discriminate an $S+$ from an $S-$ without errors. After showing lack of a peak shift on generalization testing, he introduced electric shock during the negative stimulus. Subsequent generalization testing indicated that a peak shift now occurred. Thus, once conditions during $S-$ change for the worse, a peak shift appears.

To summarize the conclusions about the evidence. Two experiments at least suggest that reduction of response rate in one component of a multiple schedule is neither a necessary nor a sufficient condition for the occurrence of contrast. The evidence seems largely in support of the idea that both contrast and the peak shift are related to a worsening of the conditions in one component of a multiple schedule. This worsening seems to include drop in reward frequency, introduction of punishment, and restraint involved in the development of inhibition. Thus we have arrived at the conclusion that when conditions in one component of a multiple schedule change for the worse, or are worse than expected, an increase in rate of responding occurs in the other component. Now we must turn to the further question that arises: why should a worsening of conditions in one part of the schedule produce an increase in responding in the other part? What *is* contrast?

III. Interpretations

A. Emotions and Emotionality

Bower (1966) suggested that an interpretation of contrast could be made in terms of Amsel's (1958) frustration theory. Terrace (1966c) also refers to Amsel on more or less the same lines, although neither author elaborates in any detail how Amsel's theory could accomplish the required explanation. This type of explanation, I suggest, is really one of *emotionality*, to which the term "frustration" is not appropriately applied. The idea behind this account is that absence of reward in $S-$, where reward is at first expected, sets off an increase in the animal's emotionality. Amsel would probably go on to claim (cf. Amsel and Ward, 1965) that the repeated experience of nonreward heightens emotionality to such an extent that responding ceases in $S-$. During $S+$, however, lesser emotionality is induced through its similarity to $S-$, and this is sufficient only to increase activity. As I have argued in the introduction, I believe this account to contain a logical error. We do not need to, nor can we explain the cessation of pecking in $S-$ other than by pointing to the absence of reward where reward was previously available, or was initially expected. But the increased pecking characteristic of contrast that occurs during $S+$ does need an explanation because we cannot see the point of it. We must either find out what its point is, or discover that it has none, in which case we need some account of what has gone wrong with the animal's behaviour.

But, for the present, it is possible to ignore the fact that this theory contains the error of putting forward the same type of explanation for behaviour which is required by the schedule and behaviour which occurs without apparent justification. I propose to consider the account suggested by Bower, based on Amsel's theory, in its application to contrast alone. There seems to be a crucial objection to an emotionality account as the principal interpretation of contrast. It would seem to imply that the vigour of a whole range of activities in $S+$ should be increased, but, when a pigeon is pecking at three responses per second, a rate not uncommon in contrast effects, there is little time for other activities to *occur*, still less occur more vigorously. Why should pecking be the one activity heightened by increased emotionality? This question raises a central problem in the whole r_g-r_f structure in contemporary theorizing: the selection of responses. In view of the criticisms of r_g explanations of maze running (Deutsch, 1960, ch. 8) and discrimination learning (Taylor, 1964, ch. 6) it seems unlikely that r_g theory can explain the selection of responses within its *avowed* framework. As both Deutsch and Taylor show, the "explanation" is often accomplished by trading on the ordinary meanings of "frustration" or "anticipation". These points do not, of course, exclude the possibility that there is increased emotionality in the discrimination situation. But they do, I think, preclude the use of emotionality as a primary explanation of contrast. It could still be the case that heightened emotionality raised further a response rate that had increased for other reasons.

I have been arguing that contrast effects and the peak shift can both be related to a change for the worse in one component of a multiple schedule, or to the introduction of a component schedule where conditions are worse than in the current one. Both of these antecedents involve changes in the situation which cannot initially have been anticipated by the animal. Thus contrast occurs (if I am correct) if and only if there is an unexpected change for the worse (or better), and this lends prima facie plausibility to the suggestion that it is an emotional effect. I use the word "emotion" as it is normally used: to refer to things like fear, anger, elation, joy, frustration, and so on. Emotions tend to come midway between motives on the one hand and "pure" feelings on the other, although there are clearly no hard and fast dividing lines to be drawn. It is characteristic behaviourist's mistake to suppose that the function of emotion-words is to *denote* inner feelings, the existence of which (the behaviourist claims) can be assessed directly by the subject alone, only inferred by others. The behaviourist's confusions on these points have been elaborated in a monograph by Kenny (1963), and I do not propose to argue the case in any detail. Suffice it to say that if a person is afraid, for example, at least two things follow. First, in any normal case, and certainly in paradigm cases, he must be afraid *of* something. Fear is in its nature directed, and must have an *object*. Second a person who is afraid of something will, unless he has good reason for doing the contrary, try to avoid the object of his fear. A persistant failure to attempt avoidance action on the part of one who claims to be afraid eventually disqualifies his avowal. Thus, as Kenny points out, fear is logically linked to avoidance as well as to a threatening situation. So we do not depend upon inference to discover another's fear: we read it in his actions and their context. To assert this is not to deny, of course, that both the actions and the context in which they occur may need interpretation.

So I propose to consider whether contrast is an emotional effect, and what kind of emotional effect it is. I shall not "define" any of the emotional terms I use, since the attempt would presuppose the probably incorrect view that neat boundaries can be drawn around our everyday concepts, or that it is possible to talk about behaviour in the simple-minded terms current in psychology. Ordinary language does not work in terms of nice logical delineations, but neither is our ordinary system of concepts impossibly vague or subjective for scientific investigation (cf. Waismann, 1965). Instead, ordinary discourse seems to work through a system of paradigms, of standard cases. Individual examples are assessed through their similarity in certain respects to these typical situations. The concept of fear, for instance, depends upon a threatening situation, feeling afraid, and avoidance action. The notion of a threatening situation is naturally elastic: patients for the psychiatrist may consist of a number of people who see threats where the ordinary man sees none. But our application of the concept of fear becomes very uneasy if we just cannot see how a man's situation can be seen as threatening, nor can we see any actions of his that are interpretable as avoidance action. Thus there are limits beyond which we just cannot say a man is afraid; and there are cases where we are certain that he is. In between these lies a region of conduct and situation in which we are often not sure what to say about another's emotions: and this does not mean that *he* is sure himself. The elasticity lies in what people feel, not just in how they describe their feelings.

Thus I propose to proceed by drawing on the clear paradigms that exist for the application of emotion-words to our actions. Naturally, I am not suggesting that pigeons experience emotions with the subtlety of which men are capable: but I am arguing for the view that the most rudimentary distinctions we commonly make in our emotional language probably have their counterparts in animal behaviour. Through their transgression of basic paradigms, many cases of contrast can be shown not to be examples of some emotions, whereas I hope to show that in other cases, situational and behavioural paradigms can be fulfilled to an extent that it seems most probable that the human emotion-word under consideration has application.

B. Accidents and Achievements

One rudimentary distinction can be drawn between the emotional consequences that arise from a failure to achieve, or an unexpected success in achieving what has been strived for: and those that stem more from happenings that do not involve individual effort. This I term the difference between accidents and achievements, or alternatively, the difference between accidents and failures. Failure to get a reward, or the blocking of the path to the goal will make a hungry animal frustrated. Note that frustration (in spite of Amsel) is an *emotion*, so that a frustrated animal is frustrated *with* the block or the absence of food. The concept of frustration itself implies a certain amount of activity. An extremely frustrated man just cannot be sitting quietly in an armchair. On the other hand, disappointment typically arises when something hoped for (but not worked for) fails to materialize. It is usually a more passive emotion than frustration since, however the two may shade into each other in borderline cases, one cannot imagine putting forward an explanation of, or excuse for violent behaviour in terms of recent disappointment in a way that it would be quite appropriate to make reference to extreme frustration. The counterparts of these two negative emotions could be construed as relief and elation: elation more naturally occurring after sudden achievement, and relief following sudden alleviation of the circumstances.

The relevance of this talk about the distinction between accidents and achievements is that both occur in the course of a multiple schedule. The cycling of $S+$ and $S-$ periods usually occurs regardless of what the pigeon is doing (cases where it does not will be considered later) so that any emotional effects of these changes should be of the relief/disappointment type. The onset of $S+$ might be the occasion for relief since the frustrating conditions of $S-$ are terminated: similarly, the termination of $S+$ and consequent onset of $S-$ could be disappointing. As far as the pigeon is concerned, these schedule changes are accidents. Achievement enters the scene with the reward contingency itself. Continued pecking in $S-$ is likely to be frustrating, and we might expect the pigeon to show analogues of the human symptoms of frustration in violent, erratic activity. This, in fact, has been reported by Terrace (1966a), and has been the object of many other informal observations. On the same grounds, working for and obtaining reward in $S+$ could have elating effects. A further characteristic of elation and frustration is relevant in this context: they can lead to enthusiasm and discouragement, respectively. If an animal is elated about getting a reward, then it can easily become enthusiastic about activity that was rewarded. Note that the object of the emotions is the crucial difference here. Elation is elation *about the reward*: enthusiasm is enthusiasm *for the activity* that was rewarded. Similarly, if an activity consistently fails to pay off, and results in prolonged frustration, then discouragement with the activity tends to set in. These latter effects can be seen in the course of extinction in the Skinner box (Skinner, 1938, Thompson, 1962). First, response rate increases (through frustration with absence of reward), then later falls (as discouragement with responding sets in).

There is another side to the story that needs filling out before we can turn to the experimental evidence. This concerns what the animal believes. Relief and elation often involve, and the normal concepts may imply, an overestimate of the extent to which conditions have improved. Thus the pigeon may exaggerate either the value of being in $S+$ (as opposed to $S-$) or the value of the reward received in $S+$. Alternatively, the pigeon may be optimistic about pecking $S+$. These possibilities are summarized in Table I. It must be stressed that this table is *not* a collection of intervening variables, hypothetical constructs, or whatever. An animal's (or person's) beliefs or emotions are not things that are causally intermediate between

TABLE I

Possible interpretations of the contrast effect

Event	Onset of $S+$	Reinforcement in $S+$	
Emotion	RELIEF	ELATION	ENTHUSIASM
Belief	EXAGGERATION		OPTIMISM
Object of emotion/belief	$S+$	Reward	Pecking for reward

"stimuli" and "responses". They are not "intermediate" in this sense at all. Because there are paradigms for the application of emotional concepts —paradigms that draw on both situations and actions in these situations— it is possible to assess directly the content of emotions or beliefs from interpretation of the person's situation and behaviour. Thus, emotions and beliefs cannot be *causes* of behaviour since they are logically linked to the behaviour in the paradigm cases. By Humean criteria for causality, it is not possible for the cause of an event to be linked *logically* with that event. Although the content of emotional concepts is not defined in the manner of the physical sciences, there are equivalents of "definitions" in the system of paradigmatic or typical cases. Thus, application of the concept of fear, say, in a given example can be precluded if nearly all paradigms seem remote from the case under examination. Thus we *characterize* behaviour by talking about emotions and beliefs rather than list its "inner causes".

Now how can the possibilities in Table I be tested? As a start, the available evidence can be sifted to see whether any of the cells of the table are already excluded. If the pigeon were enthusiastic about key-pecking in $S+$ for reward, we should expect that this $S+$ be preferred to a stimulus which was not cycling in a multiple schedule with $S-$, although signalling the same reinforcement conditions. Similarly, if the pigeon were over-optimistic about the efficacy of its responses in bringing reward, the same consequences would follow. An earlier experiment of mine (Bloomfield, 1967c) constitutes a test of this hypothesis, with negative results. Pigeons were trained to peck two keys on a concurrent VI 2' VI 2' schedule. When performance had stabilized, one key was covered, and the other changed its stimulus light from red to green. Extinction was in force in the one-key sessions. The concurrent VI schedule and extinction alternated with each other on separate days. In effect, the left-hand key of the box was scheduled with mult VI 2' ext, with red and green as $S+$ and $S-$; the other key was present during $S+$ phases of the multiple schedule only, and showed slanting stripes. The keys remained in the same positions throughout. The effect of the extinction procedure was to shift preference dramatically *away* from the experiment $S+$ in the multiple schedule (Fig. 4). Since a

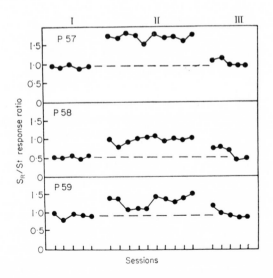

FIG. 4. Preference ratios for three birds against days of training. In the discrimination sessions, responses to the single key, previously VI 1', were extinguished (adapted from Bloomfield, 1967c).

previous experiment had demonstrated contrast effects in the same situation without the second key (Bloomfield, 1967b), the result seems to rule out the possibility that contrast is due to enthusiasm for, or optimism in, pecking during $S+$.

A hypothesis similar to the one about optimism, but not at variance with the experiment cited above, would be that the pigeon was trying harder at $S+$. The incorrectness of this view is brought out in an experiment by Reynolds and Catania (1961). These authors trained pigeons to peck on a mult drl 21″ drl 21″ schedule, then shifted them to mult drl 21″ ext. The effect of this change was to increase the rate of pecking in drl. Analysis of IRT distributions showed that the greatest change occurred in IRTs in the 0–3 sec interval. Thus it appears that the pigeons were simply *pecking faster* in drl, not trying harder to make drl responses. It is understandable that trying harder at drl might not actually produce more *successful* drl responses with the required pause; but at least the greatest effect on the IRT distribution should be in the 15–25 sec region, say, not in the region from 0–3 sec.

So the most likely account seems to be that the pigeon is elated by the reward in $S+$. Together with such elation, we might expect that the pigeon exaggerates the value of the reward. This effect would not have appeared easily in the experiment described (Bloomfield, 1967c) since the reward given was actually the same in both schedules. In the next section, I shall describe an experiment which gave results in support of the present analysis, but first I should like to mention a pilot study carried out to check the validity of the general distinction between the effects of accidents and achievements. I have argued that accidents typically give rise to more passive emotions than achievements, and the experiment (unpublished) tested this assumption. Pigeons were trained to respond on a mult VI 1 VI 1 schedule, with red and green as the discriminative stimuli. When performance had stabilized, the second component (green) was changed to extinction, and the usual contrast effect appeared. This is shown for two birds in the first two parts of Fig. 5. The change from $S-$ to $S+$ here comes into the category of an accident: it was independent of the bird's activity. According to the above analysis, the most likely emotion in these circumstances would be relief at the onset of $S+$, and this should have little effect on responding. The third stage of the experiment changed the schedule into chain FI 1′ VI 1′. Green, previously extinction, now signalled FI 1′. As in the mult VI ext schedule, no rewards were available in green, but now the first peck after one minute after the onset of green would change the stimulus to red and the schedule to VI 1′. At first, there was little effect, as responding during green had almost ceased, but later the rate of responding in red increased again over and above the previous level. Thus

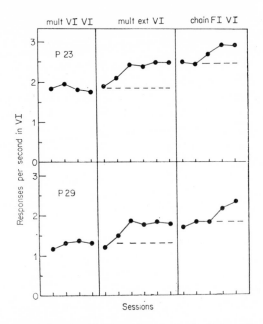

FIG. 5. Rates of responding for 2 birds against days of training. The schedule in force is shown above the appropriate panel.

it seems that the results of working to produce $S+$ as against merely waiting for it are consistent with the elation/relief scheme introduced above.

C. AN EXPERIMENTAL TEST

It seems that the remaining possibility for the explanation of contrast as an emotional effect involves either elation at being rewarded in $S+$ and/or exaggeration of the value of the reward. I have shown already that the pigeon does not prefer $S+$ itself above another stimulus similar in all respects except that it does not alternate with an $S-$. Thus the possibility of contrast as enthusiasm was excluded. But this leaves open the possibility that although $S+$ may not be exaggerated or associated with elation, the reward obtained in $S+$ might be treated in these ways. The disadvantage with the earlier experiment was that the reward was the same in both discrimination and nondiscrimination schedules, so that it was not possible to test whether any preference had developed during discrimination training. The present experiment (submitted for publication) used as a substitute for a direct reward the last component in two chained schedules. These were distinctively signalled, which allowed for testing of preference between them. The procedure is simpler to explain if for the moment these last components are treated as two different primary rewards.

Six pigeons were trained to peck on a mult (mult VI VI) VI schedule. Two separate keys were used for the two components of the outer multiple schedule, instead of the usual one. The multiple schedule cycled every 20 minutes. So one key would be illuminated with either a vertical or horizontal line (mult VI VI) for 10 min or the other would be illuminated with a white light (VI) for 10 min. The inner multiple schedule cycled each 2 min on a single key correlated with the vertical/horizontal lines. When performances on this schedule had stabilized, the pigeons were tested in their preferences for the two rewards—associated with the response keys. Then the mult VI VI schedule (vertical/horizontal) was changed to mult VI ext with the same stimuli. The cycling between keys, and the VI schedule on the other key continued as before. This provided a situation in which one reward had been obtained for pecking during an $S+$ (vertical) in a mult VI ext schedule, while the other reward was obtained only for pecking on VI (white). After the discrimination had been learned, the pigeons' preferences between the two rewards were measured. It was found that the change in preference correlated highly (·96, Spearman's rho) with the contrast effects found in the mult VI ext schedule. Thus, the more contrast shown on VI in mult VI ext relative to VI on its own, the more the reward obtained for pecking on VI in mult VI ext was preferred over the reward obtained for pecking on VI alone.

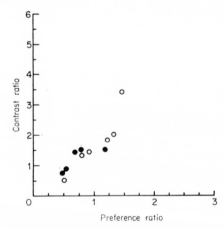

FIG. 6. Shift in preference for reward as a function of extent of the contrast effect. Averaged results for 6 birds are shown. The preference change was obtained by dividing the preference ratio *after* discrimination training by the ratio *prior to* discrimination training. The contrast ratio was calculated by a similar procedure, using the ratio of the rates of responding to VI in the multiple schedule and to VI in isolation.

I mentioned earlier that the rewards used were not primary ones. In fact, instead of operating directly the grain magazine, rewarded pecks on either key lit a different (red- or green-illuminated) key which could be pecked on VI 1 to produce reward. Measures of preference consisted of time spent pecking each key when a green choice was allowed (with continued reward) for 20 minutes each on two successive days. The graphs of the correlations are shown in Fig. 6.

IV. Conclusions

It appears that the most tenable hypothesis about contrast is that it is the result of elation at, or exaggeration of the value of reward in a discrimination situation which is caused by worse conditions (absence of reward) in $S-$. This exaggeration is a misinterpretation of the situation by the pigeon, which, although it has parallels in human behaviour, is not justified by the reward contingencies. Thus, it seems that contrast can be regarded as a case of over-compensation, though not, as was once thought (Smith and Hoy, 1954), in response during $S+$, but in the assessment of the value of reward.

The approach implicit in the discussion has been an intuitive one: an attempt to show that thinking about operant conditioning phenomena can be carried out in ordinary language with the object of generating testable hypotheses about those phenomena. I hope it has been made clear that, while the use of ordinary language with its ensuing asymmetry of explanation precludes modelling psychology on the physical sciences, it does not therefore render it "subjective" or unscientific. I have implied throughout that important distinctions may be missed if the current language of operant conditioning is used. I have argued in various places that this language perpetuates logical mistakes about behaviour and mentality which, although exposed in detail in the current philosophical literature, have passed largely ignored by psychologists, especially in the field of animal behaviour. The fact that experimental hypotheses can be generated in ordinary language is surely sufficient indication that nothing is lost in terms of objectivity by doing psychology in this way. On the contrary, we stand to lose a great deal if the conceptual framework currently fashionable is not radically revised.

Acknowledgements

This chapter was written during tenure of a Research Fellowship from the Science Research Council. I am indebted to Dr. D. A. Booth for discussions of the material in the text.

240   T. M. BLOOMFIELD

References

Amsel, A. (1958). The role of frustrative nonreward in noncontinuous reward situations. *Psychol. Bull.* **55**, 102–119.

Amsel, A. and Ward, J. (1965). Frustration and persistence: resistance to discrimination following prior experience with the discriminanda. *Psychol. Monogr.*

Bloomfield, T. M. (1966). Two types of behavioral contrast in discrimination learning. *J. exp. Anal. Behav.* **9**, 155–161.

Bloomfield, T. M. (1967a). Behavioral contrast and relative reinforcement frequency in two multiple schedules. *J. exp. Anal. Behav.* **10**, 151–158.

Bloomfield, T. M. (1967b). Some temporal properties of behavioral contrast. *J. exp. Anal. Behav.* **10**, 159–164.

Bloomfield, T. M. (1967c). Frustration, preference, and behavioural contrast. *Quart. J. exp. Psychol.* **19**, 166–169.

Bloomfield, T. M. (1967d). A peak shift on a line tilt continuum. *J. exp. Anal. Behav.* **10**, 361–366.

Bower, G. H. (1966). Recent developments II: Discrimination learning and attention. *In* "Theories of Learning" E. R. Hilgard and G. H. Bower, Appleton Century-Crofts, New York, U.S.A.

Brethower, D. M. and Reynolds, G. S. (1962). A facilitative effect of punishment on unpunished behavior. *J. exp. Anal. Behav.* **5**, 191–199.

Deutsch, J. A. (1960). "The Structural Basis of Behaviour." Cambridge University Press, London.

Deutsch, J. A. (1967). Discrimination learning and inhibition. *Science* **156**, 988.

Dews, P. B. and Morse, W. H. (1961). Behavioral Pharmacology. *Ann. Rev. Pharmacol.* **1**. 145–174.

Grusec, T. (1968). The peak shift in stimulus generalization: equivalent effects of errors and non-contingent shock. *J. exp. Anal. Behav.*, **11**, 239–249.

Guttman, N. (1959). Generalization gradients around stimuli associated with different reinforcement schedules. *J. exp. Psychol.* **58**, 335–340.

Guttman, N. (1965). Effects of discrimination formation on generalization measured from a positive-rate baseline. *In* "Stimulus Generalization" (D. I. Mostofsky, ed.), pp. 210–217. Stanford University Press, Stanford, U.S.A.

Hanson, H. M. (1959). Effects of discrimination training on stimulus generalization. *J. exp. Psychol.* **58**, 321–334.

Hearst, E. (1965). Stress-induced breakdown of an appetitive discrimination. *J. exp. Anal. Behav.* **8**, 135–146.

Honig, W. K. (1962). Prediction of preference, transposition, and transposition-reversal from the generalization gradient. *J. exp. Psychol.* **64**, 239–248.

Honig, W. K., Boneau, C. A., Burstein, K. R. and Pennypacker, H. S. (1963). Positive and negative generalization gradients obtained after equivalent training conditions. *J. comp. physiol Psychol.* **56**, 111–116.

Jenkins, H. M. and Harrison, R. H. (1960). Effect of discrimination training on auditory generalization. *J. exp. Psychol.* **59**, 246–253.

Kenny, A. (1963). "Action, Emotion, and Will". Routledge and Kegan Paul, London.

Louch, A. R. (1966). "Explanation and Human Action". University of California Press, Berkeley, U.S.A.

Pavlov, I. P. (1927). "Conditioned Reflexes" (tr. G. V. Anrep). Oxford University Press, London.

Peters, R. S. (1958). "The Concept of Motivation". Routledge and Kegan Paul, London.

Reynolds, G. S. (1961a). Behavioral contrast. *J. exp. Anal. Behav.* **4,** 57–71.

Reynolds, G. S. (1961b). An analysis of interactions in a multiple schedule. *J. exp. Anal. Behav.* **4,** 107–117.

Reynolds, G. S. and Catania, A. C. (1961). Behavioral contrast with fixed-interval and low-rate reinforcement. *J. exp. Anal. Behav.* **4,** 387–391.

Sidman, M. (1955). Technique for assessing the effects of drugs on timing behavior. *Science,* **122,** 925.

Skinner, B. F. (1938). "The Behavior of Organisms". Appleton-Century-Crofts, New York, U.S.A.

Smith, M. H. and Hoy, W. J. (1954). Rate of response during operant discrimination. *J. exp. Psychol.* **48,** 259–264.

Taylor, C. (1964). "The Explanation of Behaviour". Routledge and Kegan Paul, London.

Terrace, H. S. (1963a). Discrimination learning with and without errors. *J. exp. Anal. Behav.* **6,** 1–27.

Terrace, H. S. (1963b). Errorless transfer of a discrimination across two continua. *J. exp. Anal. Behav.* **6,** 223–232.

Terrace, H. S. (1963c). Errorless discrimination learning in the pigeon: Effects of chlorpromazine and imipramine. *Science* **140,** 318–319.

Terrace, H. S. (1964). Wavelength generalization after discrimination learning with and without errors. *Science* **144,** 78–80.

Terrace, H. S. (1966a). Stimulus control. *In* "Operant Behavior: Areas of Research and Application" (W. K. Honig, ed.), pp. 271–344. Appleton-Century-Crofts, New York, U.S.A.

Terrace, H. S. (1966b). Behavioral contrast and the peak shift: Effects of extended discrimination training. *J. exp. Anal. Behav.* **9,** 613–617.

Terrace, H. S. (1966c). Discrimination learning and inhibition. *Science* **154,** 1677–1680.

Terrace, H. S. (1967). Discrimination learning and inhibition. *Science* **156,** 988–989.

Thompson, T. (1962). The effect of two phenothiazines and a barbiturate on extinction-induced rate of a free operant. *J. comp. physiol. Psychol.* **55,** 714–718.

Waismann, F. (1965). "The Principles of Linguistic Philosophy". Macmillan, London.

Yarczower, M., Dickson, J. F. and Gollub, L. R. (1966). Some effects on generalization gradients of tandem schedules. *J. exp. Anal. Behav.* **9,** 631–639.

10

An Arousal-decision Model for Partial Reinforcement and Discrimination Learning

JEFFREY A. GRAY AND PHILIP T. SMITH

Institute of Experimental Psychology, Oxford, England

I. A Difficulty in Frustration Theory

Amsel's (1958, 1962) theory of frustration is able to predict with some degree of success a number of phenomena in learning experiments. However, it also encounters certain difficulties. It was in attempting to cope with these difficulties that the impetus for the model outlined in this paper arose. At the same time, the model is intended to have wider application than to the runway experiments with which Amsel's own theory has largely been concerned. In particular, it also applies to a number of phenomena which have been observed in operant conditioning experiments and which bear an obvious resemblance to frustration effects observed in runways—notably, "behavioural contrast" (Reynolds, 1961) and "peak shift" (Hanson, 1959; Friedman and Guttman, 1965). We shall follow the logic of the actual development of the model and start with partial reinforcement experiments in runways. We shall then deal with the application of the model to the operant conditioning experiments.

The need for a modification of Amsel's frustration theory springs in the first instance from the way in which the partial reinforcement acquisition effect in a straight alley depends on distance from the goal. Compared to continuously reinforced animals, animals on a random partial reinforcement schedule run slower early on in training, then catch up, and finally, late in training, run faster (Goodrich, 1959; Haggard, 1959). According to Amsel's theory both the initial decrement in speed and the final increment in speed shown by the partial reinforcement group relative to continuously reinforced (CRF) controls are due to conditioned frustration (r_f). This occurs in the following manner.

After a number of rewards have been received the partially reinforced animal develops an expectation of reward (defined in Hullian terms as an "anticipatory goal response", r_g). If reward is now not received after the instrumental response is made, there is an unconditioned response† termed "frustration"; the operation which leads to frustration is termed "frustrative nonreward". Frustration is deemed to be subject to classical Pavlovian conditioning, so stimuli in the stem and startbox of the runway (which regularly precede the occurrence of the primary frustration response) are able to become conditioned stimuli eliciting conditioned frustration. Frustration (whether of the conditioned or unconditioned form) is said to be an aversive state, so that the animal's initial reaction will be to attempt to escape from the stimuli which elicit it. It is this aversive property of conditioned frustration which is said to lead to the initial decrement in speed shown by the partially reinforced animal. In effect, the animal is in an approach-avoidance conflict of the kind analysed by Miller (1959) in experiments in which the aversive state is set up by a noxious stimulus, such as an electric shock.

The final superiority in running speed displayed by the partially reinforced animals is accounted for in the following manner. The conditioned frustration response is said to set up stimulation (s_f) which is able to act for the animal like a cue. Since this cue is followed on a proportion of trials by the instrumental behaviour of running down the alley and the receipt of primary rewards, it becomes a discriminative stimulus (S^D) for running. In this way, the initially disruptive effects of anticipatory frustration are overcome and the animal continues to run to the goalbox in spite of the aversive aspects of the situation. However, more than this is needed if we are to account for the actual *superiority* in speed of running shown by the partially rewarded animals. This something else is provided by the joint assumptions that frustration has drive properties (i.e. increases the vigour of ongoing behaviour) and that summation can take place between the frustration drive and the approach drive. Empirical support for these assumptions can be found in the double-runway "frustration effect" demonstrated by Amsel and his co-workers (Amsel, 1958; Amsel and Roussel, 1952). Other evidence in favour of these assumptions is reviewed by Gray (1967); while McFarland's (1966) review of work relevant to drive-summation leads to

† i.e. an unconditioned change in a state of the "conceptual nervous system".

the conclusion that, though the evidence for drive-summation in general may be weak, there is ample evidence that an *aversive* drive may add to the vigour with which an appetitive response is performed.† It follows, then, that, once the disruptive effects of conditioned frustration in a partial reinforcement experiment are overcome by the associative process described above, partially rewarded animals will actually run faster than their continuously reinforced controls.

This, then, is the account given by Amsel's frustration theory of the effects of partial reinforcement on performance during acquisition. Without considering the adequacy of this theory in more general terms, we wish to focus attention on one particular difficulty which it encounters. This difficulty arises from the fact that the initial slowing down shown by the partially reinforced animals is strongest the *closer* the animal is to the goal; whereas their final superiority in speed is greatest the further away the animal is from the goal (Wagner, 1961; Goodrich, 1959). The same thing is found when distance from the goal is measured, not in spatial terms, but by setting up an operant response chain (Becker and Bruning, 1966). Thus, in terms of frustration theory, the early aversive effects of conditioned frustration are greatest nearer the goal, but its later drive-inducing effects are greater further away from the goal. There is nothing in the theory as it stands which would lead one to expect this difference. Since r_f is set up by the normal processes of classical conditioning, it should be strongest nearest the point of reinforcement, so the spatial gradient shown by the early aversive effects is as expected; the difficulty arises rather with the late drive-inducing effects. Why should these too not be stongest nearest to the goal?

II. The Model

In an attempt to answer this question, we have called upon the distinction between *intensity* and *direction* of behaviour which is emphasized by the so-called "energetics" group (Freeman, 1948; Duffy, 1962). Briefly, it is supposed that animals on a partial reinforcement schedule in a runway are in an approach-avoidance conflict, in which the approach and avoidance functions‡) may be depicted in the type of diagram used by Miller (1959) and shown in Fig. 1. (The significance of the symbols in this figure is

---

† It is clear that the addition of an aversive drive may also reduce the performance of an appetitive response, as in the case of conditioned suppression. The analysis proposed in this paper is an attempt to predict *when* these incremental and decremental effects will each be observed.

‡ To avoid the ambiguity of the word "gradient" (in learning theory it often refers to a generalization curve, in mathematics it would be taken to mean the *slope* of this curve) we use the terms *function* to denote a complete generalization curve and *level* to denote its value at any particular point.

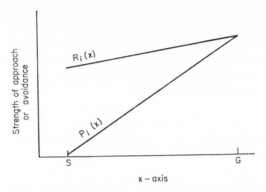

FIG. 1. Approach $R_i(x)$ and avoidance $P_i(x)$ functions. The x-axis represents distance along an ideal runway stretching from the point S, where the avoidance level is zero, to the point G, where the two functions meet.

explained later.) This diagram calls for two comments. We have not allowed the avoidance function to rise higher than the approach function, since we are only concerned (in partial reinforcement experiments) with the case in which the animal *does* reach the goal, and we have assumed that the greater steepness of the avoidance than the approach function which has been shown in the runway in experiments using electric shock to set up the avoidance drive (Miller, 1959) also holds for the partial reinforcement situation.†

The distinction between intensity and direction of behaviour is then made in the following way. It is supposed that, at any instant, the animal may be engaging in one of two kinds of behaviour: he may be moving toward the goal or avoiding it, by which we mean suppressing approach behaviour. It is then postulated that the proportion of time for which S engages in the one kind of behaviour or the other depends on the relative heights of the two functions at that point in the runway. In symbolic terms $p_R(x) = f\ [R_i(x),\ P_i(x)]$, where $p_R(x)$ is the probability of engaging in approach behaviour at the point x and $R_i(x)$ and $P_i(x)$ are the approach and avoidance levels at the point x. For fixed R, f decreases as P_i increases; for fixed P_i, f increases as R_i increases. The variable x could be a measure of the physical distance along a runway or (in the case of other experimental

† It is clear from Hearst's (1965) experiments that the avoidance function is not always steeper than the approach function. A comparison between Miller's results and Hearst's suggests that the steepness of the two functions depends on the extent to which each of them is controlled by exteroceptive or interoceptive stimuli: the greater the contribution of interoceptive (including drive) stimuli, the flatter the function. In the case which we are considering, there is every reason to suppose that a "frustration" function would behave in the same way as a "fear" function, since both are largely controlled by exteroceptive stimuli in the type of runway experiment concerned.

situations which we shall be considering later) of the position of a stimulus along a stimulus similarity continuum. So much for the direction of behaviour. The postulate concerning the intensity of behaviour is that, *whichever* direction the behaviour takes, its intensity is the result of a combination of the contributions of the approach and avoidance functions: $I_R(x) = g[R_i(x), P_i(x)]$, where $I_R(x)$ is the intensity of approach behaviour occurring at x, and g is a monotonic increasing function of both $R_i(x)$ and $P_i(x)$.

Before proceeding further, we wish to recast these basic ideas in a slightly different form, giving them at the same time a degree of physiological underpinning. Let us suppose that there are two basic drive-and-reinforcement mechanisms of the kind described by Olds and other workers (Olds and Olds, 1965; Stein, 1964) on the basis of self-stimulation studies with implanted electrodes: a reward mechanism and a punishment mechanism. It is assumed that these mechanisms are set into operation by the usual positive and negative reinforcers and also that activity in them is subject to the laws of classical conditioning. It is further assumed that the operation of frustrative nonreward causes an increment in the activity of the punishment system. [Data supporting the view that frustrative nonreward and noxious stimuli act on the same physiological system are reviewed by Wagner (1966) and Gray (1967).] Level of activity in the reward and punishment systems, then, would, underlie the approach and avoidance functions, respectively. We now suppose that both these mechanisms feed into a general arousal mechanism such as the "ascending reticular activating system" (Samuels, 1959). This is to adopt Hebb's (1955) suggestion that this system is the basis of Hull's construct of general drive. Next, we suppose that the reward and punishment mechanisms are in competition for control of the motor apparatus, and that there is a decision mechanism whose job it is to choose between them. Whichever behaviour occurs, it is then facilitated by the output it receives from the arousal mechanism. These ideas, which are essentially identical with those developed in the preceding paragraph in less concrete terms, are depicted in Fig. 2, in a block diagram of the kind described by McFarland (1966) in his model for frustration and attention. In terms of this diagram, the problem is to specify (1) how the inputs to the "behaviour command" for "approach" depends on the inputs to the reward and punishment mechanisms and (2) how the decision mechanism arrives at its decision.

Before leaving Fig. 2, a few further comments are necessary. (1) The negative feedback loop, linking the reward mechanism to the consequences of approach behaviour is to allow the animal to compare the *actual* reward or punishment received with the *expected* reward. It is the outcome of this comparison which determines whether there is now an

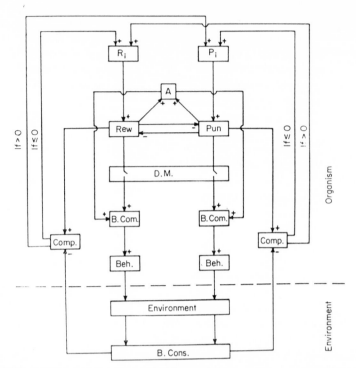

FIG. 2. Block diagram of the arousal-decision model. R_i and P_i: inputs to the reward and punishment mechanisms, Rew and Pun. D.M.: the decision mechanism. A: the arousal mechanism. B.Com.: behaviour command to "approach" (on the reward side) or to "avoid" (on the punishment side). Beh.: the observed motor behaviour. B.Cons.: the consequences (rewarding or punishing) of the behaviour that occurs. Comp.: comparator mechanisms which compare the actual consequences of behaviour with the expected consequences and make appropriate reward or punishment inputs. See text for further explanation.

input to the reward mechanism or to the punishment mechanism. For the sake of greater generality, it is supposed that there will be an input to the punishment mechanism not only if the consequence of approach behaviour is *zero* reward, but also if it is some non-zero reward which is *less* than the expected reward.†

† A recent experiment by Peckham and Amsel (1967) has succeeded in showing that the magnitude of the double-runway frustration effect is positively correlated with the degree of reward reduction in spite of earlier failures (McHose and Ludvigson, 1965) to obtain this result. The design of this experiment, however, involved a reduction to zero reward from two different non-zero values. It still remains to be shown that a reduction of reward to a non-zero value has frustrating effects, and the available data (McHose and Ludvigson, 1965; McHose, 1966) do not support our assumption. However, it is a necessary assumption if the model is to deal with the phenomenon of behavioural contrast when the negative stimulus ($S^\triangle$) is associated with a non-zero reward.

If the consequence of approach behaviour is the receipt of a reward which is equal to or greater than the expected reward, there is an input to the reward mechanism. (2) It should be noted that the reward and punishment mechanisms have been given reciprocal inhibitory links with each other. This has been done partly because of the evidence from the central stimulation studies that such links do in fact exist (Olds and Olds, 1965; Stein, 1964) and partly because changing the values of the transmittances[†] along these links is one way (though not the only one) of providing for trial-by-trial changes in the output of the system (see below). (3) Finally, we should note that the system depicted in Fig. 2 is symmetrical for approach and avoidance behaviour. We shall confine our analysis, however, to the approach behaviour predicted by the model.

Our analysis has taken us to the point where, if we symbolize the predicted approach behaviour by E_R, we have:

$$E_R = p_R(x) \times I_R(x) \qquad (1)$$
$$= f[R_i(x), P_i(x)] \times g[R_i(x), P_i(x)]$$

The problem, then, is to specify the functions f and g. Let us deal with the intensity component, $I_R(x) = g[R_i(x), P_i(x)]$, first.

We may approach a specification of the function, g, by use of the method of flow-graph simplification described by McFarland (1965). Figure 3 shows a translation of the relevant parts of the block diagram of Fig. 2 into an equivalent flow-graph. We are interested for the moment in analysing only for the output along the reward or approach path, R, so we can ignore the branches connecting P_M to P (the output of the punishment pathway) and A (the arousal mechanism) to P. The transmittances (small letters written along the branches) are assumed to be constants. As a result of flow-graph simplification (McFarland, 1965), the following result is obtained:

$$I_R = R = R_i \times \left(\frac{r + v - tw}{l - tu}\right) + P_i w - P_i u \left(\frac{r + v - tw}{i - tu}\right)$$

Putting $m = \dfrac{r + v - tw}{l - tu}$

and $n = w - um$, we obtain:

$$I_R = R = mR_i + nP_i \qquad (2)$$

It may also be noted that, if we make use of a simpler model and omit the

---

†The transmittance is the function that must be applied to the input (i.e. the upstream node in a flow graph) to obtain the value at the output (downstream node).

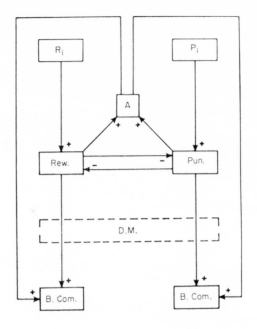

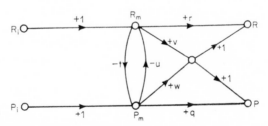

FIG. 3. Block diagram and equivalent flow graph of parts of the arousal-decision model required to specify the function

$$I_R(x) = g[R_i(x), P_i(x)]$$

R_m is the same as Rew and P_m is the same as Pun. R is the Behaviour Command for approach. P is the Behaviour Command for avoidance. For general method, see McFarland (1965).

assumption of reciprocal inhibitory links between the reward and punishment systems, we obtain (by setting $t = u = 0$)

$$I_R = R = (r + v)R_i + wP_i \qquad (2a)$$

It is clear, then, that the value obtained for the intensity of the approach behaviour is a linear combination of the values for the inputs to the reward and punishment systems.† If we consider the behaviour of this function, as we move to the right along the abscissa of Fig. 1 (from startbox to goalbox in a straightway), taking the ordinate in this figure to represent the values of the inputs to reward (approach function) and punishment (avoidance function) mechanisms, we see that it increases linearly with a slope that will depend on the values of the constants in equation (2).

We have so far dealt with the function $I_R(x) = g[R_i(x), P_i(x)]$; that is, in terms of Fig. 2, we have supposed that the action of the decision mechanism has been to favour approach behaviour. We now turn to the problem of specifying $p_R(x) = f[R_i(x), P_i(x)]$. In other words, we must specify the decision rule followed by the decision mechanism. Let us suppose that R_d and P_d (the inputs along the reward and punishment pathways, respectively, to the decision mechanism) vary randomly and independently in time about some mean values, $R'(x)$ and $P'(x)$. The simplest initial assumptions are that they are normally distributed with the same standard deviation, σ. The simplest decision rule in such circumstances is that the animal responds with approach behaviour if $R_d > P_d$ and with avoidance behaviour if $R_d < P_d$. This gives us $p_R(x)$ as a simple function of $\dfrac{R'(x) - P'(x)}{\sigma}$, i.e. the number of standard deviations separating the means

of R_d and P_d. Such a function can be calculated with the use of normal probability tables. The variation of $p_R(x)$ with $\dfrac{R'(x) - P'(x)}{\sigma}$ is indicated by Table I.

TABLE I

The variation of $p_R(x)$ with $R'(x) - P'(x)$

$\dfrac{R'(x) - P'(x)}{\sigma}$	0	1	2	3	4	5
$P_R(x)$	0·500	0·692	0·841	0·933	0·977	0·994

The relation of $R'(x)$ and $P'(x)$ to the other parameters in our model can be achieved if we return to our flow-graph analysis. Figure 4 shows the truncated part of Fig. 3 which it is necessary to submit to analysis in order

† The linearity is, of course, a simple consequence of the assumption of linear transmittances; the value of the derivation is that it specifies the contribution of the various components in the model to the coefficients in the equations.

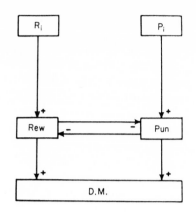

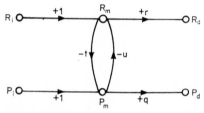

Fig. 4. Block diagram and equivalent flow graph of parts of the arousal-decision model required to specify the inputs, R_d and P_d, from the reward and punishment mechanisms to the decision mechanism.

to obtain the inputs R_d and P_d into the decision mechanism. The results of this analysis are that

$$R_d = R_i \frac{r}{l-tu} - P \frac{ur}{l-tu}$$

(3)

$$P_d = P_i \frac{q}{l-tu} - R_t \frac{tq}{l-tu}$$

(4)

and if we consider mean values in this system we can replace R_d and P_d by R′ and P′, respectively, in (3) and (4), on the understanding that R_i and P_i represent the means of the initial inputs to the system. We can eliminate R_i and P_i between equations (2), (3) and (4) to obtain:

$$I_R = \alpha R_d + \beta P_d$$

(5)

where $\alpha = \dfrac{r+v}{r}$ and $\beta = \dfrac{w}{q}$; that is, α and β are constants determined by

the flow-graph analysis. Our assumptions about the variability of R_d and P_d

and the constancy on any given trial of the transmittances in our flow-graph imply (because of equation (5)) that I_R is also subject to random variation, but since the point of view of equation (1) we are only interested in the mean value of I_R, we can take means in equation (5), and adopting the convention that from now on $I_R(x)$ refers only to the *mean* intensity at the point x, we obtain:

$$I_R(x) = \alpha R'(x) + \beta P'(x) \tag{6}$$

This, together with our equation for the decision mechanism,

$$p_R(x) = f\left(\frac{R'(x) - P'(x)}{\sigma}\right)$$

forms the basis of our further analysis. Fig. 5 shows the way in which

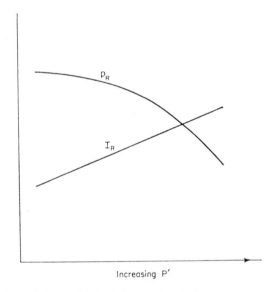

Increasing P'

FIG. 5. Probability of approach behaviour (p_R) and intensity of behaviour (I_R) as the mean punishment input (P') to the decision mechanism approaches the mean level of reward input.

probability of approach behaviour (p_R) and the intensity of approach behaviour (I_R) each varies as the input to the punishment mechanism approaches the level of the input to the reward mechanism. It is the multiplication of these two functions upon which Fig. 6 is based.

The question also arises of how the values of α, β influence the behaviour of the function $E(x) = I_R(x) \cdot p_R(x)$. The relation between E and P', for α and R' fixed and for various values of β is shown in Fig. 6. For $\beta = 0$,

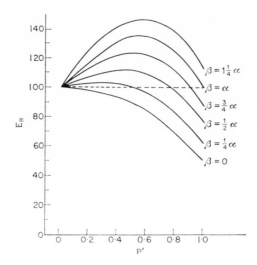

FIG. 6. E_R plotted against P' for different values of β. R' is held constant. E_R is expressed as a fraction of R'.

P' has no effect on I_R and reduces $f\left(\dfrac{R'-P'}{\sigma}\right)$ as P' increases, thus E must decrease as P' increases. For $\beta \geqslant \alpha$, increases in I_R due to the presence of P' more than compensate for the decreases in $p_R(x)$, and thus E is never less than its level when P' was absent. For intermediate values of β, low P' produces an increase in E, high P' a decrease in E. For our analysis, the natural assumption is that β is intermediate between 0 and α. The assumption that there is a general arousal mechanism means that we are taking β as significantly different from zero. We also note that if all the transmittances in Fig. 3 are equal (remembering that, in analyzing for I_R, the pathways to P make no contribution), then $\beta = \frac{1}{2}\alpha$. This is the value we tentatively adopt in our analysis: a different value of β within the general restriction $0 < \beta < \alpha$ will give qualitatively the same results.

III. The Partial Reinforcement Acquisition Effect

We return now to the partial reinforcement acquisition effect. Because of the linear equations (3) and (4), $R'(x)$ and $P'(x)$ will have the same general form as $R_i(x)$ and $P_i(x)$ respectively, and the latter, according to Miller's (1959) data and theoretical analysis, take the form shown in Fig. 1. The argument x is the distance along the runway. It is not critical to the model that $R'(x)$ and $P'(x)$ be *linear* functions of x: almost any continuous monotonic functions with the same end points will produce the same qualitative results. For convenience, measure $R'(x)$ and $P'(x)$ in standard deviation units (i.e. take $\sigma = 1$). The points S and G on the abscissa of the figure are to be taken, in any real situation, as lying beyond the real start and goal boxes, and they mark, respectively, the point at which the avoidance function falls to zero and the point at which the approach and avoidance functions meet (i.e. the probability of approach behaviour $= 0.5$). $P'(S)$, then, $= 0$ and $R'(G) = P'(G)$. Now, in a runway situation, it is experimentally difficult to separate intensity from direction of behaviour, so what we are interested in is $E_R = p_R(x) \cdot I_R(x)$. We are now in a position to show how E_R depends on x and on the slope of the intensity function, $I_R(x)$. Figure 7 shows the general form of this dependence. The abscissa of

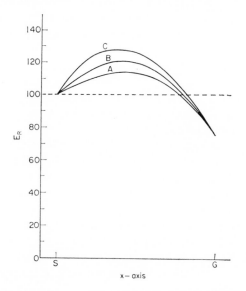

FIG. 7. E_R plotted against distance along runway for various slopes of the approach and avoidance functions. All the curves are plotted with $R'(S) = 5$, $P'(S) = 0$, and $R'(G) = P'(G)$. They differ only in the value of $R'(G)$; $R'(G) = 6$ in Curve A, 10 in Curve B and 20 in Curve C. E_R is expressed as a percentage of the value it would take if P' were absent.

this figure is distance along an ideal runway stretching from $x = S$ to $x = G$. The ordinate shows E_R as a percentage of the net approach behaviour in the absence of any input to the punishment system (i.e. for a CRF control group).

The curves differ only in the slope of the approach and avoidance functions from which they are derived. We see that choice of a suitable set of parameters (e.g. $R'(S) = 5$, $R'(G) = 6$) results in a curve which, over its middle range (which is where the real runway would lie) depicts what is in fact obtained for a partial reinforcement group relative to CRF controls early in training: a decrement in performance which is greater, the nearer the animal is to the goalbox.

The next thing to consider is what happens during continued training. In this connection, Amsel talks of the stimulus feedback from conditioned frustration (r_f–s_f) becoming a cue for approach behaviour. Here we intend to part company with him. Instead, we shall make use of the inhibitory loops connecting the reward and punishment mechanisms. (This could be viewed as giving content to the expression "counter-conditioning", which is sometimes used to describe the tolerance for frustration which the animal appears to develop in a partial reinforcement situation.) We suppose that, whenever an animal is exposed to both rewards and punishments in the same situation over and over again, the transmittances along the reciprocal inhibitory links, t and u, are gradually adjusted so as to increase the more powerful input at the expense of the less powerful.† (The reader is referred in this connection to equations (3) and (4), from which it is clear that increasing t and decreasing u increases R_d and decreases P_d. Decreasing t and increasing u would have the reverse effects.) In the case of a partial reinforcement experiment, it is clear that reward is more powerful than punishment.

With continued training, then, the approach and avoidance functions (Fig. 1) will rise and fall, respectively, thus increasing the separation between them. (It should be noted that essentially the same results are obtained if the approach function only rises, as it perhaps might on the hypothesis that s_f becomes a cue for running; or if the avoidance function only falls. Furthermore, very similar effects are obtained if the mean inputs to the decision mechanism, $R'(x)$ and $P'(x)$, are left unaltered, but their variability is reduced—see below, in connection with behavioural contrast.) It is clear that increasing the separation between $R'(x)$ and $P'(x)$ is going to have rather similar effects to moving the "real" runway along the abscissa of Fig. 6 to the left. Figure 8 shows the curves that result from altering the heights of the approach and avoidance functions in this way. We see that continued training results in a reduction in the speed decrement shown by the partial reinforcement group near the goal, and an increase in their superiority early on in the runway. Thus our model appears to be able to accommodate the results obtained by such workers as Wagner (1961) and Goodrich (1959). However, it is clear that it also predicts

† When a reward is *followed* regularly by a punishment, or vice versa, some adjustment appears to be made to enhance the event which comes later in this sequence at the expense of the earlier one (perhaps by classical conditioning); for an animal will accept a more intense punishment to get to a subsequent reward than he will accept when it is contingent upon taking a preceding reward (Solomon, 1964). On a random partial reinforcement schedule, this consideration does not apply, as reward and punishment follow each other equally often and, in any case, the intervals between them are ordinarily too large.

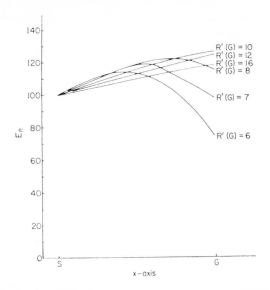

FIG. 8. E_R plotted against distance along runway for different separations between the approach and avoidance functions. In this particular set of curves $P'(x)$ is kept constant $[P'(S) = 0, P'(G) = 6]$ and $R'(x)$ is varied so that its slope is constant $[R'(G) - R'(S) = 1]$. The same type of result is obtained if $R'(x)$ is held constant and $P'(x)$ reduced, or $R'(x)$ increased and $P'(x)$ reduced simultaneously. E_R is expressed as a percentage of the value it would take if P' were absent; i.e. for the partial reinforcement case, we plot the performance of partial reinforcement animals relative to constant reinforcement controls.

further changes with continued training. Thus, the maximum locus of superiority for the partial reinforcement group should move towards and eventually reach the goal; while, with still further training the superiority of the partial reinforcement group should become smaller and eventually disappear.

The model, then, makes predictions about the effects of continued training which could be tested in the partial reinforcement situation for which it was initially developed. (Ordinarily, experiments on partial reinforcement effects in runways are not continued beyond about 100 trials, so there do not appear to be any data in the literature which we could use for this purpose at present. It also makes predictions about the effects of increasing the lengths of the runway. Although it does not seem possible to extend a real runway to approach any closer to the ideal point "G" in Fig. 1, increasing its length should take one closer to the point "S". Thus the model predicts (Fig. 7) that, for a given number of training trials, the locus of maximum superiority of the partial reinforcement group should move forward from the startbox as the runway is lengthened. Finally, it is clear that the model predicts the greater variability of running times observed in the partial reinforcement group, relative to CRF controls, during the phase of acquisition at which the decrement effects of partial reinforcement are greatest (Amsel, 1958). For, according to the model, these decremental effects occur when $p_R(x)$ tends to $0 \cdot 5$; and the variability of a sampling distribution of two alternatives is greatest when they are equally likely.

IV. Extensions of the Model to Induction, Transposition and Peak Shift

An adequate test of our model would obviously be much easier to carry out if it were possible to obtain separate measures of $p_R(x)$ and $I_R(x)$. It is impossible to do this using running speed in the typical runway experiments which we have so far considered. Operant conditioning techniques are more promising, since it should not be difficult to obtain measures of both proportion of time spent responding (p_R) and rate of response while responding (I_R). Fortunately, there are a number of phenomena observed in operant conditioning experiments which bear considerable similarities to runway frustration effects. The most important of these are "behavioural contrast" (Reynolds, 1961, 1963; Terrace, 1966a) and "peak shift" (Hanson, 1959; Friedman and Guttman, 1965).

Since the terminology in this area is a little confusing, it will help if we first define a number of terms used in the following discussion. It has been found in a number of experiments (see Terrace, 1966a, for review) that response rate in the presence of a stimulus correlated with a given frequency and magnitude of reward (which we shall call "reward value") can be altered by exposing the animal, in the same experimental environment, to a different stimulus correlated with a different reward value. We shall use the usual Skinnerian terminology and indicate the stimulus associated with the higher reward value by S^D and the stimulus associated with the lower reward value by S^Δ. The alterations in response rate which have been observed take four forms: an *increase* in response rate as a result of exposure to S^Δ; a *decrease* in response rate in S^D as a result of exposure to S^Δ; an *increase* in rate in S^Δ as a result of exposure to S^D; and a *decrease* in rate in S^Δ as a result of exposure to S^D; in each case relative to the rate obtaining when S^D or S^Δ is the only stimulus to which the animal is exposed and its associated reward value is the same. Very similar phenomena were observed by Pavlov (1927, p. 188), using classical conditioning techniques. The four kinds of alterations in response are indicated in Table II, together with the terms used to describe them by Reynolds (1963) and by Pavlov (1927). The confusion of terminology evident in this Table requires no further comment.

Our own practice will be to use the term "induction" to refer to the general phenomenon whereby response vigour in the presence of one

TABLE II

Four kinds of alteration in response

Inducing stimulus	Stimulus in which changed response observed	Direction of change in response vigour	Pavlovian term	Reynolds' term	Suggested term	
1 S^Δ or $CS-$	S^D or $CS+$	Increment	Positive induction	Behavioural contrast	Positive induction	Incremental
2 S^Δ or $CS-$	S^D or $CS+$	Decrement	Irradiation of inhibition	Induction		Decremental
3 S^D or $CS+$	S^Δ or $CS-$	Decrement	Negative induction	Behavioural contrast	Negative induction	Decremental
4 S^D or $CS+$	S^Δ or $CS-$	Increment	Irradiation of excitation	Induction		Incremental

stimulus correlated with a certain reward value is altered by the presence of another stimulus correlated with a different reward value—i.e. to cover all four rows of Table II. We shall follow Pavlov in describing the case in which the inducing stimulus is $S^\triangle$ and the change is observed in S^D as "positive induction", though including by this term his "irradiation of inhibition" as well. Similarly, the case in which the inducing stimulus is S^D and the change is observed in $S^\triangle$ will be called "negative induction", which includes Pavlov's "irradiation of excitation". Where the change in S^D or in $S^\triangle$ is an increment in response vigour, we shall describe it simply as an "increment"; and similarly a fall in response vigour, whether in S^D or $S^\triangle$, is a "decrement". Reynolds' "behavioural contrast" includes, therefore, incremental positive induction and decremental negative induction.

In showing how our model may be applied to induction, we shall for the present limit ourselves to the case of positive induction in which the $S^\triangle$ is correlated with zero reward. Later in the paper, we shall extend the analysis to cover both negative induction and non-zero reward values associated with $S^\triangle$.

A limitation on our analysis in the present paper is that we shall consider only "sustained" induction effects, as distinct from "transient" ones (Bloomfield, 1966a; Nevin and Shettleworth, 1966). A transient effect is one whose duration is measured in terms of minutes or seconds after termination of exposure to the inducing stimulus; a sustained effect is one whose duration is measured in hours or days after exposure to the inducing stimulus.

The other phenomena to which we intend to apply our model are the "peak shifts" (Hanson, 1959; Friedman and Guttman, 1965) and "transposition" and "transposition reversal" (Hebert and Krantz, 1965). Although the latter have not usually been studied in operant experiments, they are most easily discussed alongside the peak shifts. If we use "positive" and "negative" in the same way as above, we may distinguish both a "positive peak shift" and a "negative peak shift". Both kinds of shift are concerned with changes in generalization gradients (or, better, generalization functions) produced by discrimination training between two values along a stimulus continuum. In the positive peak shift (Hanson, 1959) maximum overall response rate is shifted along the stimulus continuum from S^D in the direction away from $S^\triangle$; in the negative peak shift (Guttman, 1965), minimum overall response rate is shifted along the stimulus continuum from $S^\triangle$ in the direction away from S^D. In these definitions, we have used the words "*overall* response rate" in the same sense of $E_R = I_R \cdot p_R$, to distinguish the peak shifts from transposition. Transposition refers to the fact that an animal trained to discriminate S^D from $S^\triangle$ chooses a stimulus removed along the stimulus continuum from S^D in the direction away from $S^\triangle$ in preference to the S^D itself; here, then, we are concerned only with *probability* of approaching one or the other stimulus. If pairs of stimuli both removed from S^D in the direction away from $S^\triangle$ are offered to the animal, at some distance from S^D the animal will choose the stimulus *closer* to S^D; this is termed "transposition reversal" (Hebert and Krantz, 1965).

A. INDUCTION

With these definitions in hand, we turn first to positive induction with the $S^\triangle$ reward value set at zero. Terrace (1966a) in his review of the relevant data, concludes that this phenomenon is probably a type of frustration effect, and we shall not repeat his arguments here. In terms of our model, the experimental situation may be pictured as in Fig. 9. The animal is trained with a stimulus correlated with reward, S^D, whose position on a stimulus continuum is x^D and a stimulus correlated with zero reward, $S^\triangle$ (whose position is $x^\triangle$). An approach function, $R'(x)$, has its peak at x^D and an avoidance function, $P'(x)$—set up by the frustrative nonreward experienced during exposure to $S^\triangle$—has its peak at $x^\triangle$. $R'(x)$ and $P'(x)$ are assumed to be smooth curves (their differential coefficients are continuous) and asymptotically zero for extreme values of x. For convenience, we define the stimulus scale such that $x^D > x^\triangle$.

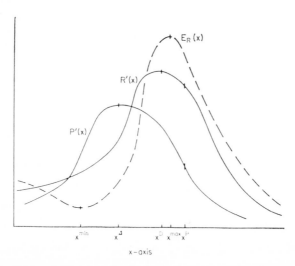

Fig. 9. $E_R(x)$, $R'(x)$ and $P'(x)$ in a discrimination learning task. $R'(x)$ has a peak at x^D and $P'(x)$ one at $x^\triangle$. $E_R(x)$ has a peak at x^{max} and a minimum at x^{min}. x^P is where $R'(x) - P'(x)$ is maximutm.

In Fig. 9, we sketch $E(x) = I_R(x).p_R(x)$. It can be seen that, according as $E(x)^D$ is greater than or less than the level of the approach function at x^D, so incremental or decremental positive induction will occur. To establish the conditions under which the one or the other type of induction will be observed we may refer to Fig. 6. From this we see that the effect of introducing a small value of $P'(x)$ at x^D is to increase E, but a large value of $P'(x^D)$ will decrease $E(x^D)$. It follows that incremental induction (Reynolds' "behavioural contrast") will be observed if $P'(x^D)$ is small and decremental induction (Reynolds' "induction") if $P'(x^D)$ is large. The size of $P'(x^D)$ can be manipulated by changing the separation between the two stimuli or by altering the overall height of the avoidance function. (The latter effect may be obtained by, for example, increasing the reward value associated with $S^\triangle$ to some non-zero value which is still less than the S^D reward value.) Increasing stimulus separation for fixed overall level of $P'(x)$ will reduce $P'(x^D)$ and increasing the overall level of $P'(x)$ for fixed stimulus separation will raise $P'(x^D)$. Thus the relation between the size and direction of the positive induction effects, stimulus separation and overall frustration level will be that shown in Fig. 10.

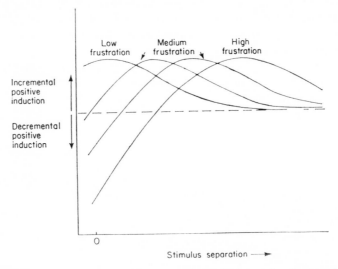

Fig. 10. Positive induction as a function of overall frustration level and stimulus separation.

The predictions of the model are thus in general agreement with the experimental finding (Hanson, 1959; Bloomfield, 1966b) that, if S^D and $S^\triangle$ are separated by a small amount, decremental induction occurs, but if they are separated by a large amount, incremental induction (behavioural contrast) is observed. Note, however, that our model predicts that only incremental induction, no matter what the stimulus separation, would occur in a situation in which the overall frustration is small.

Another way in which the predictions of the model agree with existing data concerns the effects of continued training on induction. It has been shown that positive incremental induction (behavioural contrast) disappears after lengthy periods of testing. (Terrace, 1966b) As we have discussed earlier in connection with runway partial reinforcement effects, there are several ways of representing the effects of continued training in our model, but they all lead to similar conclusions, as shown in Fig. 8. The most natural assumption for continued discrimination training is that $R'(x)-P'(x)$ gets larger at x^D. Fig. 8 shows that, on this assumption, continued training should lead to the disappearance of an incremental induction effect as observed.

Note further that the curves shown in Fig. 10 plot $E(x)=I_R(x).p_R(x)$. That is, in terms of operant measures, they show relative change in overall number of responses in a unit testing period, which is in fact the way in which most of the data in this field are presented. However, the model makes quite detailed predictions concerning the separate changes in $I_R(x)$ and $p_R(x)$ which may easily be translated into observational terms for an operant experiment. If a distribution of inter-response times (IRT) for a single S^D is obtained, this may be used as a base-line for estimating changes in both I_R and p_R as a result of introducing S^Δ. Increases in I_R should appear as a shortening of IRTs *when the animal is responding*. Decreases in p_R should appear as unusually long pauses. Thus the model predicts that, when incremental induction occurs, the overall increase in number of responses should be accompanied by an increased variability of IRTs, both shorter and longer times being observed. When decremental induction occurs, the overall fall in number of responses should be accompanied by the same kind of change in the IRT distribution, though, of course, the lengthened IRTs should be longer or more in number, and the shortened IRTs shorter or fewer in number than for incremental induction.

B. Transposition

We turn now to consider transposition and transposition reversal. Our analysis here is essentially the same as Spence's (1937).† We assume that an animal faced with a choice between two stimuli S', S'' will more often choose the stimulus for which $p_R(x)$ is larger.

---

† Spence's model can handle transposition with no difficulty, but, because he treats an S^Δ as setting up purely *inhibitory* tendencies, he cannot cope with incremental induction.

Now at x^D, $R'(x) - P'(x)$ is an increasing function of x (since $\dfrac{dR'}{dx} = 0$ and $\dfrac{dP'}{dx}$ is negative), but $p_R(x)$ is continuous and tends to zero as x becomes large. Therefore $p_R(x)$ reaches a peak† at a point x^P (see Fig. 9), $x^P > x^D$. Thus for any x', x'' such that $x^P \geqslant x' > x'' \geqslant x^D$, transposition will occur (since $p_R(x^P) \geqslant p_R(x') > p_R(x'') \geqslant p_R(x^D)$). Similarly, for $x' > x'' > x^P$, transposition reversal will occur. The conclusion is that if S', S'' are both sufficiently close to S^D transposition will always occur, and if S', S'' are both sufficiently far from S^D transposition reversal will always occur (this latter conclusion assumes $R'(x) > P'(x)$ for all large x, a not unreasonable assumption).

If we consider the relations between transposition and peak shift, we see that the model predicts that x^P (the critical point for transposition/transposition reversal) is greater than $x^{\max}$ (see Fig. 9), the point where the overall number of responses is maximum. This can be seen as follows:

$$E = I_R(x)p_R(x),$$
$$= [aR'(x) + \beta P'(x)] f(R'(x) - P'(x)) \tag{7}$$

Taking logarithms and differentiating with respect to x gives:

$$\frac{1}{E}\frac{dE}{dx} = \frac{1}{aR' + \beta P'}\left[a\frac{dR'}{dx} + \beta\frac{dP'}{dx}\right] + \frac{1}{f(R' - P',}\frac{df}{dx} \tag{8}$$

At $x = x^P$, $\dfrac{df}{dx} = 0$ (x^P is at the peak of $p_R(x)$) and $\dfrac{dR'}{dx}$ and $\dfrac{dP'}{dx}$ are both negative (since $x^P > x^D$ and x^Δ),

$\therefore$ since all other terms in (8) are positive, $\dfrac{dE}{dx}$ is negative;

i.e. E (the overall response measure) has already passed its peak, therefore $x^P > x^{\max}$.

This result offers another test of our analysis of E into p_R and I_R components: as far as we know, no published data looks at transposition‡ (based on $p_R(x)$) and response rate (based on E) at the same time.

A similar analysis around S^Δ will yield a similar set of predictions (which, however, are different in detail) for preferences between stimuli in this

---

† This is assuming that $R'(x) - P'(x)$ is sufficiently well behaved to have only one peak: if $R'(x) - P'(x)$ has more than one peak, the argument is more complicated but leads to essentially the same results.

‡ Honig's (1962) experiment measures what he calls "transposition" in terms, not of choice responses, but overall number of responses directed to each member of his pairs of stimuli.

region. As far as we know "negative transposition" of this kind has not been observed.

C. PEAK SHIFT

The requirement for positive peak shift is that $x^{max} > x^D$, i.e. when $\frac{dR'}{dx} = 0, \frac{dE}{dx}$ is positive.

Developing equation (8):

$$\frac{1}{E}\frac{dE}{dx} = \frac{1}{\alpha R' + \beta R'}\left[\alpha\frac{dR'}{dx} + \beta\frac{dP'}{dx}\right]$$

$$+ \frac{1}{f(R' - P')}\left[\frac{df(y)}{dy}\right]_{y\,=\,R'\,-\,P'}\left[\frac{dR'}{dx} - \frac{dP'}{dx}\right]$$

when

$$\frac{dR'}{dx} = 0 \quad \frac{dE}{dx} > 0 \quad \text{if}$$

$$\frac{1}{I_R}\beta\frac{dP'}{dx} - \frac{1}{p_R}\left[\frac{df(y)}{dy}\right]_{y\,=\,R'\,-\,P'} \times \frac{dP'}{dx} > 0$$

Dividing by $\frac{dP'}{dx}(< 0)$ and rearranging we obtain

$$\frac{1}{\beta}\left[\frac{df(y)}{dy}\right]_{y\,=\,R'(x^D)\,-\,P'(x^D)} > \frac{p_R(x^D)}{I_R(x^D)} \tag{9}$$

Now $\frac{df(y)}{dy}$ is a function entirely dependent on the properties of the normal distribution (it is the probability density function), and it is bounded: moreover, as

$$p_R(x) \to 1{\cdot}0 \quad \left[\frac{df(y)}{dy}\right]_{y\,=\,R'\,-\,P'} \to 0,$$

∴ by suitable selection of large $p_R(x)$ or small $I_R(x)$ it would be possible to violate equation (9). Thus positive peak shift will *not* occur—and there may be a shift in the opposite direction—if $R'(x^D) - P'(x^D)$ is too large (implying that the separation between S^D and S^Δ is too large) or if $I_R(x)$ is too small, i.e. there is a low level of arousal.

Hanson's (1959) paper affords some evidence relating to these last derivations from the model. If we consider the expectations for peak shift together with those for positive induction (see below), it is clear that there should be a greater positive peak shift, the greater the decremental positive induction at S^D, for both these phenomena should increase with decreasing

separation between S^D and S^Δ. As positive induction at S^D changes from
decremental to incremental (with increasing stimulus separation), peak
shift should be reduced and eventually the peak might even move away from
S^D in the direction of S^Δ Hanson's data suggest that this is exactly what
occurs: in his curve (Fig. 11) for the smallest stimulus separation there

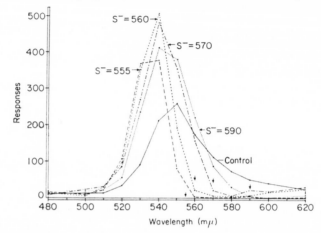

FIG. 11. Stimulus generalization curves for different distances along the wavelength
continuum between S^D ("CS" at 550 mμ) and S^Δ ("$S-$" at 555, 560, 570 and 590 mμ)
compared to a control condition without S^Δ.
    (Data from Hanson (1959). *J. exp. Psychol.* **58**, 321-324 copyright by the American Psychological Associ-
ation, and reproduced by permission.)

appears, together with decremental induction, a swing of the peak still
further away from S^D; and in the curve for the greatest stimulus separation,
together with incremental induction, there is a swing of the peak back
towards S^D.

    The same type of condition applies to negative peak shift: the condition
for negative peak shift will in fact be that

$$\frac{1}{a}\left[\frac{df(y)}{dy}\right]_{y\ =\ R'(x^\Delta)\ -\ P'(x^\Delta)} > \frac{p_R(x^\Delta)}{I_R(x^\Delta)} \tag{10}$$

Although it is possible to construct pathological cases when (9) is satisfied but (10) is not, and vice versa, generally speaking presence or absence
of positive peak shift should be coupled with presence or absence of negative peak shift.

V. Non-zero Frustrative Reward

    Now behavioural contrast (incremental positive induction) has been
observed with nonzero reward correlated with S^Δ (Reynolds, 1961, 1963;

Terrace, 1966). Furthermore, the magnitude of the contrast which is observed is a function of the disparity between the reward values associated with S^D and S^Δ (Reynolds, 1963). It is clear, then, that if our theoretical framework is to be of any value it must also deal with this case. In considering the case in which S^Δ is correlated with zero reward we had to take into account only an approach function centred on S^D, and an avoidance function centred on S^Δ. When reward is also received during S^Δ it becomes necessary to take explicit account of the effects of this reward as well.

We do not propose to present a detailed solution to the problem of non-zero S^Δ reward, though detailed solutions involving a few additional assumptions and a little more mathematics could easily be developed; these solutions would take the form of specifying the amount of unconditioned frustration at S^Δ associated with the difference between expected and actual reward. All we need assume for our present purposes is that a steadily increasing reward value at S^Δ, with reward at S^D fixed, will produce a steadily decreasing frustration input to the punishment mechanism at S^Δ and thus a steadily decreasing generalized frustration input at S^D. As far as the effects of S^Δ reward on the approach function at S^D are concerned, there are several sorts of assumptions one can make. For example, we could assume that the input to the reward mechanism at S^D is entirely dependent on the larger reward which is actually obtained during S^D. In that case, with reward at S^Δ steadily decreasing from a value the same as or close to the S^D reward value, one of the family of curves for E_R presented in Fig. 6 is obtained. Similar curves would be obtained by the alternative assumption that the reward actually experienced at S^Δ adds by generalization to

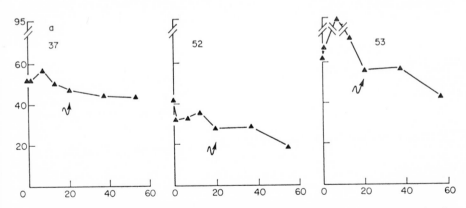

FIG. 12. Response rate per minute (ordinate) in the presence of a stimulus associated with 20 reinforcements per hour as a function of number of reinforcement per hour (abscissa) in the second component of a multiple schedule.

(Data for three separate pigeons from Reynolds (1963). *J. exp. Anal. Behav.*, **6**, 131-139 copyright (1959) by the Society for the Experimental Analysis of Behavior, Inc., and reproduced by permission.)

the approach function at S^D. The predicted joint effects of varying S^Δ reward value and stimulus separation, with S^D reward value fixed, have already been presented in Fig. 10.

The available empirical data fit these predictions reasonably well. Reynolds' (1963) data (Fig. 12) show that with fixed stimulus separation, the greatest degree of incremental positive induction (behavioural contrast) occurred at an intermediate value of S^Δ reward, though Bird 52 shows a particularly high S^D response rate with zero S^Δ reward. Furthermore, it is of some interest (since our analysis began with runway data) to note that Mackinnon (1967) has observed very similar phenomena in an experiment in which rats ran in two runways for different reward values. His data are

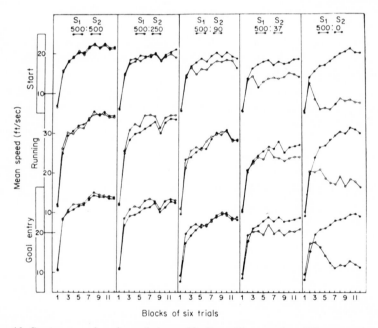

FIG. 13. Start, run and goal speeds in an S^D alley with reward $= 500$ mg as a function of the magnitude of the reward given for running in a second, S^Δ, alley. $S_1 = S^D$, $S_2 = S^\Delta$ and numbers indicate magnitude of reward in mg.

(Data from Mackinnon (1967). *J. exp. Psychol.* **75**, 329-338. Copyright (1967) by the American Psychological Association, and reproduced by permission.)

shown in Fig. 13, from which it can be seen that, for fixed stimulus separation and fixed S^D reward value (500 mg), running speeds in the S^D alley varied systematically with the reward given for running in the S^Δ alley. For S^Δ reward $= 250$ mg, there is an increment in speed of running the S^D alley; for S^Δ reward value decreasing below 250 mg, there is a steadily greater decrement in S^D alley running speed. Moreover, it is clear from our earlier discussion that, in terms of the model, movement towards the goalbox in a runway experiment is the equivalent of reducing stimulus separation in an operant experiment. We would therefore predict, in line with Fig. 10, that the incremental positive induction observed in Mackinnon's experiment will be transformed into decremental-positive induction by a joint decrease in $S^\triangle$ reward value and closer approach to the goal. It is clear from Fig. 13 that these predictions are a reasonably accurate description of his results.

We turn finally to consider the predictions of the model for negative induction with nonzero $S^\triangle$ reward, inductive effects being measured against the response rate maintained when $S^\triangle$ and its correlated reward value are the only conditions to which the animal is exposed. It is clear that, as $S^\triangle$ reward value decreases, the frustration input at $S^\triangle$ increases. Thus we would again make the predictions shown in Fig. 6: for $S^\triangle$ reward value close to S^D reward value, there should be an increment in $S^\triangle$ responding; as $S^\triangle$ reward value approaches zero there should be a reduction in this increment which turns into a decrement for very low reward values. From Fig. 14 it can be seen that Reynolds' (1963) data again fit these predictions well in the case of two of his three pigeons.

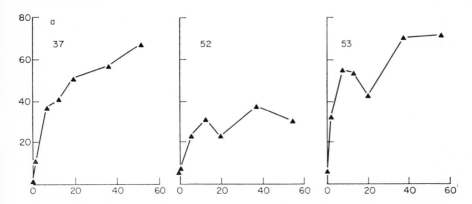

FIG. 14. Response rate per minute (ordinate) in the presence of a stimulus associated with the number of reinforcements per hour shown on the abscissa. Reinforcement frequency in the second component of the multiple schedule was always 20 per hour
(Data for three separate pigeons from Reynolds (1963), *J. exp. Anal. Behav.* **6**, 131-139. Copyright (1963) by the Society for the Experimental Analysis of Behavior, Inc., and reproduced by permission.)

This completes our extension of the model to situations other than the runway partial reinforcement experiments with which we began. The model has still wider generality than we have been able to indicate here. It can obviously be applied to experiments involving interactions between rewards and punishments (e.g. food in one stimulus, shock in another), for it is a key assumption in the model that frustrative nonreward acts on a punishment system.

VI. Summary

Arising from a critique of Amsel's theory of frustration a mathematical model is developed for application to situations involving conflict either between reward and punishment or between reward and frustrative nonreward. The model consists essentially of a translation of Amsel's theory into a "black box" with various interacting components. By specifying the mathematics of the interactions between the components, the model is able to achieve a higher degree of precision and to overcome certain difficulties and ambiguities contained in Amsel's theory. Behaviour is analyzed into separate "direction" and "intensity" components which multiply together to produce the final observed performance. The direction of behaviour (approach or avoidance) is determined by a "decision mechanism" whose activity is analyzed according to statistical decision theory. The intensity of behaviour is determined by a weighted function of the inputs to "reward" and "punishment" mechanisms. The model is couched in terms which should facilitate attempts to match its components with elements in the central nervous system. Its application to existing data on the effects of partial reinforcement in runway studies and on behavioural contrast, peak shift and other inductive phenomena in operant conditioning situations is illustrated and new predictions are deduced.

Acknowledgements

We would like to acknowledge the help of David McFarland; many of the ideas contained in this paper first became clear in discussion with him. Our thanks are also due to David Newstead, who first suggested that we apply statistical decision theory to the operation of our decision mechanism.

References

Amsel, A. (1958). The role of frustrative nonreward in noncontinuous reward situations. *Psychol. Bull.* **55**, 102–119.

Amsel, A. (1962). Frustrative nonreward in partial reinforcement and discrimination learning: some recent history and a theoretical extension. *Psychol. Rev.* **69**, 306–328.

Amsel, A. and Roussel, J. (1952). Motivational properties of frustration: I. Effect on a running response of the addition of frustration to the motivational complex *J. exp. Psychol.* **43**, 363–368.

Becker, P. W. and Bruning, J. L. (1966). Goal gradient during acquisition, partial reinforcement, and extinction of a five part response chain. *Psychon. Sci.* **4**, 11–12.

Bloomfield, T. M. (1966a). Two types of behavioral contrast in discrimination learning. *J. exp. Anal. Behav.* **9**, 155–161.

Bloomfield, T. M. (1966b). Behavioural induction in multiple reinforcement schedules. Unpublished Ph.D. thesis, University of Exeter, England.

Duffy, E. (1962). "Activation and Behaviour." London: Wiley.

Freeman, G. L. (1948). "The Energetics of Human Behavior." Ithaca, Cornell Univ. Press, U.S.A.

Friedman, H. and Guttman, N. (1965). Further analysis of the various effects of discrimination training on stimulus generalization gradients. In "Stimulus Generalization". (Mostofsky, D. I., ed.), pp. 255–267. Stanford University Press, U.S.A.

Goodrich, K. P. (1959). Performance in different segments of an instrumental response chain as a function of reinforcement schedule. J. exp. Psychol. 57, 57–63.

Gray, J. A. (1967). Disappointment and drugs in the rat. The Advancement of Science, 23, 595–605.

Guttman, N. (1965). Effects of discrimination formation on generalization measured from a positive-rate baseline. In "Stimulus Generalization". (Mostofsky, D. I., ed.), pp. 210–217. Stanford: Stanford University Press, U.S.A.

Haggard, D. F. (1959). Acquisition of a simple running response as a function of partial and continuous schedules of reinforcement. Psychol. Rec. 9, 11–18.

Hanson, H. M. (1959). The effects of discrimination training on stimulus generalization. J. exp. Psychol. 58, 321–334.

Hearst, E. (1965). Approach, avoidance, and stimulus generalization. In "Stimulus Generalization". (Mostofsky, D. I., ed.), pp. 331–355. Stanford: Stanford University Press, U.S.A.

Hebb, D. O. (1955). Drives and the c.n.s. (conceptual nervous system). Psychol. Rev. 62, 243–254.

Hebert, J. A. and Krantz, D. L. (1965). Transposition: a revaluation. Psychol. Bull. 63, 244–257.

Honig, W. K. (1962). Prediction of preference, transposition, and transposition-reversal from the generalization gradient. J. exp. Psychol. 64, 239–248.

Mackinnon, J. R. (1967). Interactive effects of the two rewards in a differential magnitude of reward discrimination. J. exp. Psychol. 75, 329–338.

McFarland, D. J. (1965). Flow graph representation of motivational systems. Brit. J. math. stat. Psychol. 18, 25–43.

McFarland, D. J. (1966). On the causal and functional significance of displacement activities. Z. Tierpsychol. 23, 217–235.

McHose, J. H. (1966). Incentive reduction: simultaneous delay increase and magnitude reduction and subsequent responding. Psychon. Sci. 5, 215–216.

McHose, J. H. and Ludvigson, H. W. (1965). Role of reward magnitude and incomplete reduction of reward magnitude in the frustration effect. J. exp. Psychol. 70, 490–495.

Miller, N. E. (1959). Liberalization of basic S-R concepts: extensions to conflict behavior, motivation, and social learning. In "Psychology: A Study of a Science". Study 1: Conceptual and Systematic. Vol. 2. (Koch, S., ed.), pp. 196–292. McGraw-Hill, New York, U.S.A.

Nevin, J. A. and Shettleworth, Sara J. (1966). An analysis of contrast effects in multiple schedules. J. exp. Anal. Behav. 9, 305–315.

Olds, J. and Olds, M. (1965). Drives, rewards and the brain. In "New Directions in Psychology". Vol. II. (Barron, F. et al., eds.), pp. 329–410. Holt, Rinehart and Winston, New York, U.S.A.

Pavlov, I. P. (1927). "Conditioned Reflexes." Transl. G. V. Anrep. Oxford University Press, England.

Peckham, R. H. and Amsel, A. (1967). The within-S demonstration of a relationship between frustration and magnitude of reward in a differential magnitude of reward discrimination. *J. exp. Psychol.* **73,** 187–195.

Reynolds, G. S. (1961). Behavioral contrast. *J. exp. Anal. Behav.* **4,** 57–71.

Reynolds, G. S. (1963). Some limitations on behavioral contrast and induction during successive discrimination. *J. exp. Anal. Behav.* **6,** 131–139.

Samuels, Ina (1959). Reticular mechanisms and behavior. *Psychol. Bull.* **56,** 1–25.

Solomon, R. L. (1964). Punishment. *Am. Psychol.* **19,** 239–253.

Spence, K. W. (1937). The differential response in animals to stimuli varying within a single dimension. *Psychol. Rev.* **44,** 430–444.

Stein, L. (1964). Reciprocal notion of reward and punishment mechanisms. *In* "The Role of Pleasure in Behaviour". (Heath, R. G., ed.), pp. 113–139. Harper and Row, New York, U.S.A.

Terrace, H. S. (1966a). Stimulus Control. *In* "Operant Behavior: Areas of Research and Application". (Honig, W. K., ed.), pp. 271–344. Appleton-Century-Crofts, New York, U.S.A.

Terrace, H. S. (1966b). Behavioral contrast and the peak shift: effects of extended discrimination training. *J. exp. Anal. Behav.* **9,** 613–617.

Wagner, A. R. (1961). Effects of amount and percentage of reinforcement and number of acquisition trials on conditioning and extinction. *J. exp. Psychol.* **62,** 234–242.

Wagner, A. R. (1966). Frustration and punishment. *In* "Current Research on Motivation". (Haber, R. N., ed.). Holt, Rinehart and Winston, New York, U.S.A.

Consciousness, Discrimination and the Stimulus Control of Behaviour

J. D. KEEHN

Alcoholism and Drug Addiction Research Foundation, Toronto, Ontario, Canada

I. Intention

When Watson launched Behaviourism he set the goal of psychologica-
research to be the discovery of laws such that "given the stimulus, psychol
logy can predict what the response will be; or, given the response, it can
specify the nature of the effective stimulus" (Watson, 1924, p. 10). This
goal has been interpreted to mean that "the subject becomes nothing more
than a stimulus-response machine: you put a stimulus in one of the slots,
and out comes a packet of reactions" (Burt, 1962). This interpretation
accuses Watson of denigrating the status of a subject, and implies that his
meta-psychology does not accord with fact. Behaviourists have long known
that given *only* the designation of a contemporary stimulus it is not possible
to predict an organism's responses, and given *only* a description of the
response it is not possible to specify the stimulus to which it was made

(Goss, 1961). What must be decided is the kind of additional information necessary for Watson's goal to be achieved.

Specification of the stimuli which control an organism's responses falls within the compass of discrimination learning, and on the assumption that a simple single-stage S-R formulation does not account for the facts of discrimination learning various multi-stage models have been proposed (Goss, 1961). Two kinds of such models have been identified—additive and subtractive (Tighe and Tighe, 1966). Recent examples of these are the mediation theory of Kendler and Kendler (1962) and the theory of selective attention proposed by Sutherland (1959) and by Mackintosh (1965). The former is additive in the sense that "the subject is assumed to make a hypothetical implicit response (r) which in some way modifies the external source of stimulation to produce a transformed stimulus (s) that elicits behaviour" (Kendler and Kendler, 1966). The latter is subtractive in the sense that "animals do not classify the stimulus input in all ways at once but react selectively . . ." (Mackintosh, 1965).

Mackintosh (1965) has charged that the Kendlers' mediation theory is vague, and they have not disagreed (Kendler and Kendler, 1966). Instead they have questioned whether Mackintosh's selective attention theory is any more precise than their own; they have concluded that it is not, and that "both the mediational S-R and selective attention formulations are in need of further conceptual articulation".

The exercise which follows is addressed to this question of conceptual clarification. It is not set specifically in the context of the dilemma facing discrimination learning theorists as described above but is concerned more with the general problem of scientific revolution as elucidated by Kuhn (1962). According to Kuhn, major progress in science is exemplified not by expanding catalogues of information but by shifts in over-riding conceptual frameworks, which he calls "shared paradigms". These shared paradigms are the concensus of facts and opinions important to a group of scientists which guide their theoretical activities and research. Within a shared paradigm there may be local pockets of disagreement, like that over additive and subtractive models of discrimination learning, and it is these differences of opinion that research is supposed to resolve. Unfortunately, research sometimes serves less to eradicate theoretical difficulties than it does to occasion pleas for further research (Gardner, 1966). Such pleas are usually for further research within the established paradigm, just as the Kendlers' appeal for conceptual articulation is for articulation within the paradigm they espouse. An alternative is to appeal for paradigm clarification, and possibly change.

The remainder of this chapter displays two alternative paradigms extant in contemporary psychology, each of which encourages different kinds of theorizing and research. Choice between them principally rests on the status accorded to the empirical Law of Effect (Thorndike, 1898).

II. Consciousness, Discrimination and Behaviour

A. THE EXISTENCE OF PSYCHOLOGY

There is a palpable difference between a live man and a dead one: the live one can move in a way that a dead one cannot. The fact of their mobility, or more generally of their behaviour, is the peculiarity of living organisms that justifies the science of psychology. Justification of the name of the science, however, is less direct for the name refers not to the property of living organisms studied by the science but to a presumptive psyche, spirit or mind that only living men are supposed to possess. Psychology, the name of the science, is therefore not derived from direct observations of differences between the living and the dead, but from the assumption that living bodies contain a psychical facet co-existent with the physical characteristics they share with the dead.

A more compelling reason for accepting the dualistic nature of man is the fact of man's conscious experience. Men may be divided in their opinions about the conscious experience of the dead, but no man can deny the existence of consciousness in himself. Psychology exists, then, because man is conscious and because he behaves, but it is the fact of his consciousness rather than that of his behaviour which justifies psychology in name. For much of the history of psychology behaviour has been regarded as subservient to experience, and psychologists have concentrated more on elaborating the properties of consciousness than they have on examining the lawfulness of behaviour. In this context mind has been taken both as the respository of experience and as the initiator of action, a viewpoint expressed by the familiar linear symbolization S-O-R (Woodworth, 1929), which summarizes the traditional conception that behaviour (R) is indicative of mental contents and processes (O) and that mental content is provided through stimuli (S) describable in physical terms. Although the symbol O is meant to emphasize *organismic* rather than *mentalistic* variables the linear arrangement of the symbols serves to delineate a duality between organisms and their responses and to ossify behaviour in its traditional role of a mere exemplar of events occurring inside an organism.

B. THE DATA OF PSYCHOLOGY

Behaviour is now a more acceptable psychological datum than mental content and psychologists accordingly define their subject as the scientific study of behaviour and not as the systematic study of the mind. The classical concept of conscious experience as a structure composed of associated mental elements detectable by sophisticated analytical introspection is replaced by the conception of consciousness as discriminations revealed by differential responses. As Boring said:

"A very simple way to think of the nature of consciousness is to realize that introspection is discriminative and that a discrimination can be reduced to a differential response, e.g. the right forefinger can be flexed for event A and extended for event not-A." (1933, p. 212).

This very simple way of thinking of the nature of consciousness may dispose of the problem of mental content as a subject for psychological consideration but it does not dispose of the problem of mental initiative. In Boring's example, the forefinger response is presumably made to the instruction, "Kindly flex your right forefinger when you experience event A and extend it when you do not". The appropriate responses then indicate not only that events A and not-A are discriminated but also that the instructions have been properly understood. Evidence that events A and not-A are discriminated is therefore also evidence that the sound *flex* and *extend* are discriminated, and that the appropriate responses to each have been learned. It is also evidence that the instructions are obeyed, but obedience to instructions is left unexplained. A psychology devoted to the scientific study of behaviour cannot afford to leave the occurrence of this important behaviour unexplained. It must account for the fact that the right forefinger is flexed in the presence of stimulus A, but this account will be incomplete if it includes only reference to the mere presence or absence of A.

By stressing differential responding rather than introspected mental contents as the subject matter of psychology, Boring contributed to the transition of psychology from a mentalistic to a behaviouristic science, but had he chosen the differential responses "I see A" and "I do not see A" instead of forefinger flexion and contraction as his indicants of discrimination, his failure to advance substantive psychological knowledge over that of the introspectionists would have been apparent. His choice of simple forefinger movements over verbal responses conceals the fact that differential responses must be learned. The introspectionists used differential responses—words—as indicants of discriminated mental contents but they did not account for the acquisition and emission of the appropriate words. Boring's rendition suffers from the same limitation.

A scientific psychology committed to the functional analysis of *behaviour* cannot be content with a mere translation of its subject matter from mental contents to differential responses, verbal or otherwise, but must attempt to account for how these responses are acquired and maintained. An alternative paradigm for behaviouristic psychology to that of verbal conversion is available and will be described below. For the moment the point may be illustrated by reference to the well known psycho-physical experiments with pigeons performed by Blough (1961). Using an experimental arrangement inspired by one devised by von 'Békésy (1947) to study human auditory thresholds, Blough investigated the course of dark adaptation in the pigeon just as it has been traditionally investigated in the case of man. The form of the curves produced by the pigeons and those typically produced with human subjects are the same. We do not talk of the bird's conscious experience in experiments of this kind, but of the way it was trained to respond. Yet if the subject is a man the data are taken as records of his visual experience. Without denying this experience we can note that the man, like the pigeon, emits a learned response. Each organism makes the response it has learned according to the different stimulus conditions. The only difference is that the bird learns its response in the course of the experiment whereas the human may have learned its response years before.

The problem which, in the man, derives from curiosity about the nature of conscious content, stems in the bird from curiosity about the nature of initiative. The question to answer in the case of the bird is not "What is the nature of consciousness?" but "Why does the pigeon peck the key?". The same kind of question can be asked about the man.

III. Learning and the Stimulus Control of Behaviour

A. LEARNING AND *S-O-R* PSYCHOLOGY

Contemporary answers to the above question take the form, "Because that is what the animal learned to do", and the nature of learning has superseded the nature of consciousness as the principal interest of psychological theory.

When an organism's behaviour changes through experience in life or in an experiment, the change is normally attributed to learning. While it is permissible to *label* some kinds of behaviour change as learning it is incorrect to call learning the *cause* of the change unless some independent evidence of learning is available, otherwise the event to be explained as learning is itself the evidence that learning has occurred. Most theories of learning are guesses about the locus of this independent evidence. In this sense theories of learning are theories about events that accompany behaviour change, and insofar as these events are located within the organism these theories fall within the traditional *S-O-R* framework described above.

Although it is now more fashionable to attribute neurological rather than mentalistic properties to *O*, traditional dualistic conceptions still prevail. This is evident in the following passage by Mackintosh (1965):

"Animals (particularly lower animals) have nervous systems of limited size and therefore of limited capacity for *processing* and *storing* information. Thus they are confronted with the problem of selection. At some stage they must *discard* irrelevant or redundant information so as not to interfere with the *storage* of important information." (p. 124, italics added).

Lovejoy (1966) says much the same. Here and there throughout their papers Mackintosh and Lovejoy refer to animals solving discrimination problems, establishing appropriate choice reactions, revealing preferences, classifying inputs, ignoring particular cue dimensions, making "decisions", and remembering choices. What, one wonders, does the selecting, discarding, solving, choosing, deciding, preferring, classifying, storing and ignoring? What is it that has access to processed and stored information in the nervous system?; and what does the storing and processing?

The kinds of situations to which Mackintosh and Lovejoy refer are those in which animals respond differentially in the presence of different stimuli. Describing such behaviour as establishing a choice, solving a problem or revealing a preference reveals a commitment to S-O-R psychology because whatever the animal does is taken merely to indicate the outcome of the mental acts of choosing, solving or preferring, and because a dualism between the nervous system and another part of the animal that processes, selects and discards from information stored within it is implied.

A different kind of "theory of learning" has been envisaged, a theory which does not begin by attributing changes in behaviour to an underlying process of learning, but which sets out to organize the facts of behaviour and to relate them systematically to the kinds of environmental events that occasion behaviour modification (Skinner 1950). In such a theory the concept of discrimination learning can be replaced by the concept of the stimulus control of behaviour.

B. STIMULUS CONTROL AND S-R-S^R PSYCHOLOGY

"Natural" reflexes are elementary examples of behaviour under stimulus control. Examples are a knee-jerk to a tap on the patellar tendon, an eye-blink to a puff of air on the cornea, and salivation to the presence of food in the mouth. Such reflexes are characterized by stimulus-response specificity; that is, a tap on the patellar tendon evokes a knee-jerk but it does not evoke an eye-blink or a flow of saliva, air-puffs evoke eye-blinks but not knee-jerks, and so on. The responses are specific to the evoking stimuli, but they are not inevitable. Not all taps produce knee-jerks, not all air-puffs evoke eye-blinks, and salivation does not always follow food in the mouth. However, although reflex action is not inevitable it does occur according to a number of known laws (Sherrington, 1906). Some of these laws, e.g. the

Law of Threshold, the Law of Reflex Fatigue and the Law of Temporal Summation of Subliminals (Millenson, 1967) expressly specify relationships such that predictions can be made as to when stimuli are likely to evoke responses and when they are not. Other laws, e.g. the Law of Intensity-Magnitude (Millenson, 1967) summarize relationships between intensities of evoking stimuli and magnitudes of evoked responses. These laws describe functional relationships and may be expressed in the form $R = f(S)$ without reference to intervening mentality.

The specific reflex stimulus-response correlations are described as involuntary, mechanical and automatic, and descriptions of the sequence of events from stimulus input to response output include only the terms of neurophysiology. The functional laws, however, are purely psychological, behavioural, laws. They systematize elementary facts about behaviour and the environmental events by which it is controlled.

More extensive stimulus control of behaviour can be achieved by means of respondent and operant conditioning (Skinner, 1938). Respondent conditioning (Pavlov, 1927) extends the range of stimuli capable of evoking available reflexes but it does not *by itself* seem to generate new classes of behaviour or modify old ones in predictable ways. That is, Pavlovian conditioning destroys the specificity of natural reflexes by arranging for new stimuli to evoke natural responses. Insofar as Pavlovian conditioning pertains only to elicited behaviour no expansion of the above-mentioned functional laws to incorporate mental activity appears to be required. All that is necessary is to formulate *additional* laws specifying the manner of transfer or extension of stimulus control.

Operant conditioning is not restricted to evoked, reflexive, responses, but is applicable to all the behaviour that an organism may emit. The principal function of a stimulus in this form of conditioning is not to evoke responses but rather to reinforce responses whose initial causes may be unknown. Stimulus control of a response once it is emitted is attained by differential reinforcement: the response is reinforced when a particular stimulus is present, otherwise it is not (Skinner, 1938). If proper care is taken, eventually the response is emitted with high probability in the presence of the stimulus (S^D) and low probability in its absence (S^Δ). In this case there is still no need to invoke mentalistic concepts like "establishing a preference" or "exhibiting a choice", or to admit the usual dualistic overtones of S-O-R psychology. It is enough to observe the history by which the stimulus came to control the response, and to specify functional relationships between stimuli and responses with the same logical status as the laws of natural reflexes described above.

This paradigm may be symbolized S-R-S^R, which summarized the fact that behaviour (R) is emitted when a stimulus (S) is presented if it has been followed by reinforcement (S^R) in the presence of the stimulus. This abbreviation expresses an empirical discovery, in contrast to the traditional S-O-R conception, which expresses only a reasonable point of view. Both paradigms apply to behaviour that is called "voluntary", although neither of them concedes that such behaviour is controlled by a freely acting will. However, whereas the older paradigm eliminates consciousness by an act of translation—conscious content equals discrimination, will equals motivation—the newer one recognizes consciousness as irrelevant to an analysis of the stimulus control of behaviour (Keehn, 1964; Skinner, 1963) and will as a redundant explanation of the outcome of procedures that result in bringing behaviour under stimulus control. These tactics are, respectively, those of analytic behaviourism (Mace, 1957) and functional behaviourism (Keehn, 1964), tactics which differentiate a kind of behaviourism which merely translates the concepts and concerns of traditional S-O-R psychology from mentalistic into behaviouristic terms, from another kind which casts the whole of psychology into an entirely different paradigm.

IV. *S-O-R* versus *S-R-S^R* Psychology

A. THE STATUS OF *O*

Defined as the science of behaviour, psychology is committed to the study of differential responses to discriminative stimuli, and *nothing else* (Mace, 1957); S-O-R psychology is reduced to S-R psychology. This reduction has not gone uncontested, even by psychologists who might regard themselves as "behaviourists". As Eysenck and Rachman (1965) remark:

". . . it is becoming (sic) more and more widely recognized that between stimulus and response interposes an organism, and the formula S-O-R has pretty well superseded the old S-R paradigm. The recognition of the existence of an organism intervening between stimulus and response is made necessary by the very simple fact that identical stimuli applied to different organisms frequently lead to different responses, and even identical stimuli applied to the same organism do not always lead to similar responses" (p. 14).

These observations reduce to the one that a response cannot be predicted from knowledge of the presenting stimulus or stimuli alone. It is this observation that appears to cause theorists to conclude that animals process, select, discard, classify and store, and to abandon Watson's goal for psychology as unattainable in principle. But is it necessary to adopt an S-O-R paradigm for psychology, in which research is directed to analyzing the psychological or physiological properties of *O*? Or can an S-R-S^R

paradigm, in which research is committed to discovering lawful relationships between stimulus events and response events, be made to suffice? If
so, and only if so, can psychology justifiably be called the scientific study
of *behaviour*.

In fact it is not necessary to adopt *S-O-R* psychology on account of the
elementary facts that Eysenck and Rachman (1965) describe. The passage
previously reproduced continues:

"There are two possible reasons for this [the fact that responses cannot
be predicted through knowledge of external stimuli alone], both involving
the concept of an *intervening organism*. In the first place, individuals may
differ with respect to their past reinforcement schedules; on this hypothesis,
we are simply saying that past learning determines *in part* the reactions
which we now make to different types of stimuli. There is nothing very
novel in this, of course, and even commonsense recognizes the importance
of past learning in present activities. However, the fact that this is so is
incompatible with a *simple-minded* application of the principles of stimulus-
response psychology" (pp. 14, 15, italics added).

There is nothing very novel in that, of course, and even commonsense
recognizes that a simple-minded application of a theory is simple-minded.
But it is not necessary to be simple-minded and it is not necessary to
recognize the existence of an organism *intervening between* a stimulus and a
response. Stimuli and responses do not exist independently of an organism,
one on one side and one on another; they exist *in the context* of an organism.
It is an organism that is stimulated and it is an organism that responds.
Likewise its past history does not determine *in part* the responses of an
organism, it determines *in toto* the responses of *that* organism. This is not
to deny that organisms differ but to assert that they exist as particulars. The
simple fact that identical stimuli applied to different organisms frequently
lead to different responses, or the equally simple fact that the same stimulus
applied to the same organism does not always produce the same
response is not incompatible with a *sophisticated* application of the
principles of stimulus-response psychology. A Frenchman and an Arab
do not make identical verbal responses when naming a table or a baby,
and similar stimuli applied to a bilingual Canadian may result in
different responses according to whether he is in Ontario or in Quebec.
The differences are determined entirely by the reinforcement histories
of the individuals in question (Skinner, 1957) and if these reinforcement
histories are known then the predictions that Watson envisaged can be
made.

These predictions are not based just on the physical characteristics of
the here-and-now contemporary stimulus, but take account of the whole

10*

reinforcement history of an organism's behaviour in relation to the stimulus in question (Keehn, 1964, 1967b).

Eysenck and Rachman's implication that different organisms *should* respond identically to physically identical stimuli is only reasonable in the case of evoked behaviour featurized by stimulus-response specificity, and even then differences in responding would be expected according to the laws described above. In the case of operant behaviour, identical responding in the presence of identical stimuli would be predicted only if different organisms had been exposed to congruent reinforcement histories *vis-à-vis* the stimuli. Such congruence is necessary only for definitional responses; it need not occur for any other. Thus, when two organisms agree that two stimuli are identical they are each emitting behaviours that identify the stimuli, e.g. red, square, 3·9 in and even these responses must display only functional equivalence, (cf. Skinner, 1957); topographical equivalence is not essential, for the same stimulus may be identified in French, as rouge, carré, 10 cm or in many other ways. Beyond this there is no limit to the topographical range of responses that a stimulus might control. Likewise a single organism need not behave identically when confronted with the same stimulus on different occasions, for its functional history may prepare the organism to respond differentially according to when the stimulus appears (Keehn, 1965).

B. The Equivalence of Responses

Elevation of S-R-S^R psychology to the status of a paradigm depends on the generality of the Law of Effect. The empirical validity of the law is known well beyond the boundaries of academic psychology, as any pet merchant or animal trainer will vouchsafe, but for the law to occasion a revolutionary paradigm change from S-O-R to S-R-S^R psychology, rather than to remain merely a piece of incremental information within the S-O-R paradigm, more is demanded of the law than just its empirical validity. One such demand is that the effect of reinforcement need not depend on the conscious state of the organism; that reinforcement can modify behaviour even though the organism is unaware that its behaviour has changed. Without this requirement it is possible that reinforcement only operates *through* psychological O-processes, i.e. the organism *understands* the response reinforcement contingency and *decides* whether or not to behave in accordance with it.

A second, related, requirement of the law is that the effect of reinforcement is felt not only on the response that produces it but also on all other responses occurring at the same time, otherwise some O-variable process of selection among responses may have to be admitted. If responses $R_1 R_2 R_3 \ldots R_N$ simultaneously occur at the time of reinforcement then the reinforcing event must affect them all alike; all responses must be equivalent in the face of the law, at least as a first approximation. In view of these requirements the Law of Effect is better announced as the Law of Reinforcement, a formulation which refers only to a temporal contingency, not to one of effect (Skinner, 1963). In this form the law encompasses all response-reinforcement incidents whether or not the response actually produces the reinforcement and whether or not the response is emitted under conscious control (Hefferline and Keenan, 1963; Keehn, 1967a; Keehn *et al.* 1965; Skinner, 1948).

It is well to note from the outset that for any animal, or animal species, it is not reasonable to expect all responses or all stimuli to be equivalent within the context of a restricted set of experimental operations. As Breland and Breland (1966) observe, every animal carries with it its evolutionary as well as its personal history, and the evolutionary history of a species predisposes its members to condition more easily in the case of some responses than in the case of others. Thus, it is a simple matter to condition a pigeon to displace a key placed at eye level by pecking with its beak, but it is difficult to train a pig to push a similarly located panel with its snout. Likewise, a goat may learn to jump under conditions which will not cause it to bleat (Breland and Breland, 1966). Additionally, different reinforcers need not have equivalent effects. It is easy to train laboratory rats to press a bar when the reinforcement is water or food, but difficult when the reinforcement is avoidance of electric shock (D'Amato and Schiff, 1964; Hurwitz, 1964; Meyer, Cho and Wesemann, 1960), although with this reinforcement they quickly learn to jump out of a box (Denny and Weisman, 1964) jump on a shelf (Baum, 1965; Maatsch, 1959) hold down a bar (Keehn, 1967c) or run in a wheel (Mowrer and Keehn, 1958).

Nevertheless, some evidence of equality of responses before the law is necessary if only to give us comfort to proceed. Some such evidence is presented in Fig. 1. The data were generated in an experiment in which college students were given monetary reinforcements on various schedules first for pressing a key and later, unbeknowingly, for blinking. Records A and B are cumulative records of a subject's eye-blinks when blinking was not reinforced. Record D, collected concurrently with records A and B, is a sample of the subject's key-pressing behaviour when reinforcements were delivered once every 200 presses on the average (VR200). At a point during the session reinforcement of key-pressing was discontinued and a reinforcement was delivered after every 8th (FR8) eye-blink instead. Unreinforced key-pressing continued unabated, as shown by record E, while the subject's rate of blinking, shown in record C, rose from about 13 to 30 blinks per min. Although key-pressing did not produce reinforcements the coincidental occurrence of reinforcements while the subject was pressing the key

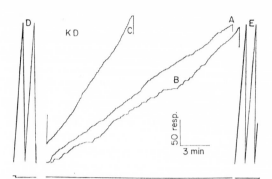

FIG. 1. Cumulative records of a human subject's rate of eye-blinking, and rate of key-pressing, when the subject was instructed that reinforcements were contingent on key-pressing but were sometimes contingent upon blinking instead. Records A and B are continuous and show the eye-blink rate when reinforcements were delivered for key-pressing on reinforcement schedule VR200. Record D shows a typical portion of the key-pressing record at this time. Record C shows the rate of eye-blinking when this response was reinforced on FR8, and record E shows a typical part of the accompanying key-pressing performance, which did not then produce reinforcements.

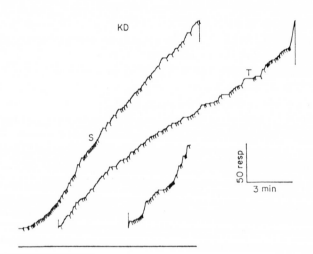

FIG. 2. From left to right the figure shows a continuous cumulative record of a human subject's eyeblinking in a session in which blinks were reinforced on schedule DRL 2 sec (up to S), DRL 4 sec (from S to T) and DRL 2 sec (after T). The subject believed that reinforcements were dependent on key-pressing, which continued at a high rate throughout the session.

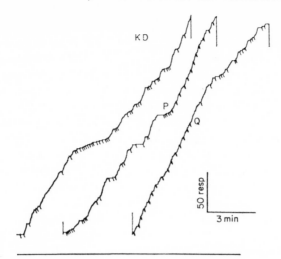

FIG. 3. From left to right the figure shows a continuous cumulative record of a human subject's eyeblinking in a session in which blinks were reinforced on schedule DRL 4 sec (up to P), FR 10 (from P to Q) and DRL 4 sec (after Q). The subject believed that reinforcements were dependent on key-pressing, which continued at a high rate throughout the session.

served to maintain this behaviour at full strength. The subject believed that key-pressing produced reinforcement at all times yet her eye-blink rate rose in accordance with the response-reinforcement contingency actually employed.

Other examples of the same subject's unconscious responsiveness to environmental control are shown in Fig. 2 and Fig. 3. Both figures are cumulative records of eye-blinks alone during sessions in which only eye-blinks were reinforced. In Fig. 2, up to point S a blink was reinforced only if it occurred at least 2 sec after the preceding blink (reinforcement schedule DRL 2 sec). From S to T an interval of at least 4 sec between blinks was required before a blink was reinforced, and from point T to the end of the session the original 2 sec interval was restored. The subject's blink rate rose and fell according to the prevailing reinforcement schedule. The same effect is also clear in Fig. 3, which shows the subject's blink rates under reinforcement schedules DRL 4 sec (up to P), FR10 (from P to Q) and DRL 4 sec (after Q). In both sessions adventitiously reinforced key-pressing continued unabated. Similar effects with other subjects and reinforcement schedules have also been observed (Keehn, 1967b; Keehn et al. 1965; Lloyd, 1966).

C. THE EQUIVALENCE OF STIMULI

The Law of Reinforcement operates regardless of whether the reinforced response actually produces reinforcement or whether the subject is aware of the response that is reinforced. All that is necessary is that reinforcement immediately follows a response. Reinforcement, as far as the evidence goes, can be shown not to act selectively on the response that actually produces a reinforcer but on all the responses that the reinforcer happens to follow. Consequently, if and when selection does occur the reason can be sought within the S-R-S^R paradigm without resort to O-variables necessary for accounting for the selection process. The next question to consider is whether the same applies in the case of the stimuli that come to control a response. That is, if reinforcement follows a response made in the presence of a stimulus complex $S_1 \, S_2 \, S_3 \ldots S_N$, will all of these stimuli equally come to control the further emission of the response or does some selection among stimuli, or stimulus dimensions, occur?

Non-equivalence of stimuli at some levels of analysis has been well documented by Gestalt psychologists and by ethologists, the former by providing many examples in human visual perception of stimulus organization into dominant and subservient aspects (cf. Hochberg, 1964) and the latter by demonstrating response-releasing properties of specific parts of stimulus arrays in the case of "instinctive" behaviour in animals (Tinbergen, 1951). Likewise, human adults react selectively to the colour of a stimulus or to its shape (Keehn, 1954, 1955), so much so that personality typologies have been constructed on the basis of individuals' reactivity to colour or to form (Eysenck, 1947, 1950; Lindberg, 1938; Rorschach, 1942). However, these are examples of "end effects" and bear only indirectly on the present issue. More direct evidence that all stimuli present at the time a response is reinforced need not acquire equal capacity to control a response is provided by an experiment conducted by Reynolds (1961).

In this experiment Reynolds trained two pigeons to peck a key in the presence of a white triangle on a red background but not in the presence of a white circle imposed on green. He then tested the separate capacities of triangle, red, circle and green to control the response. Appropriately, neither bird responded to the circle or to green, but one bird responded only to the triangle and the other only to red. Both birds had been reinforced in the presence of red and a white triangle together, but for one bird redness did not become a controlling stimulus, and for the other the white triangle did not acquire the power of controlling the response. Similar findings have been reported by Eckerman (1967) from an experiment in which different components of a complex stimulus compound correlated with non-reinforcement exhibited differential inhibiting control over a response.

A comparable result to that of Reynolds appeared in a study in which rats were trained to press and release a bar to avoid electric shocks. The animals were required to press and hold the bar while a tone and a white light were on, and to release the bar when the stimuli went off. Normally the stimuli changed in alternating on-off sequence every 30 sec, and 5 sec after each change the animals were shocked at 5 sec intervals unless or until they made the appropriate response. The stable behaviour of one animal during part of a session in which stimulus on-off times were varied is shown in Fig. 4. The figure shows the cumulative bar holding of the animal (upper record) according to whether the stimuli were on or off (lower record). The cumulative holding record was obtained by arranging for the recorder to step

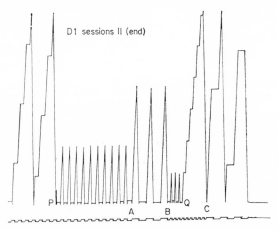

FIG. 4. Cumulative bar-holding record of a rat trained to avoid electric shocks by holding a bar depressed in the presence of a signal and releasing it in the signal's absence. The lower trace shows onsets and offsets of the signal (light-tone combination) which was ON for 30 sec and OFF for 30 sec up to A, ON and OFF for 60 sec each from A to B and after C, and ON and OFF for 15 sec each from B to C. Between P and Q the pen reset with each onset and offset of the signal, otherwise it made a full excursion of the paper, which represents about 100 sec bar-holding time.

once for about every ·2 sec that the bar was held depressed, so the step-wise character of the records shows times when the animal was on (rising portions) and off (horizontal portions) the bar. The different appearance of the record between the points marked P and Q represents only a change in recording technique; the pen was reset whenever the stimuli changed. Between A and B, and after C, the stimuli were on for 60 sec and off for 60 sec, from B to C on-off times were each 15 sec, and before A they were 30 sec each. During the period covered by the record the animal received only 1 shock, shown by the oblique blip near the start. The light-tone combination, therefore, efficiently controlled the animal's behaviour of pressing and releasing the bar.

The relative effects of the light and the tone in controlling bar holding and bar releasing can be seen in Fig. 5. Up to point *A* on the cumulative record the normal procedure prevailed, and after a typical period of "warm-up" the animal's usual behaviour in the presence and absence of the combined light-tone signal is evident. At A the tone was disconnected. There was a brief period of disruption, after which the animal's behaviour returned to normal up to B, at which point the tone was reinstated. At point C the light was no longer used. Again the behaviour was disrupted but this

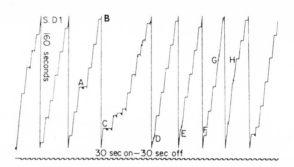

Fig. 5. Cumulative bar-holding record of a rat trained to avoid electric shocks by bar-holding in the presence of a light-tone signal and bar-releasing in its absence when the light and tone components were fractionated. A to B, light stimulus only, tone OFF continuously; C to D, tone stimulus only, light OFF continuously; E to F, light stimulus only, tone ON continuously; G to H, tone stimulus only, light ON continuously. At all other times the stimulus was the normal light-tone combination.

time normal behaviour did not re-appear until point D, when light and tone were again used in combination. The animal's behaviour is clearly controlled more by the light than by the tone. At *E* the tone was left on continuously, but again only a brief disruption of responding occurred; the animal showed no more tendency to continue responding during light-off periods than it did after point F, when normal conditions were restored. From G to H, however, when the light was left on continuously, the animal remained almost entirely on the bar regardless of the on-off status of the tone. From H to the end of the record the normal light-tone combination was used. The tone and the light, although equally likely to come to control bar holding and releasing according to the contingencies of the experiment, did not in fact attain equal control of responding. Another rat, trained with a more conventional discriminated avoidance procedure in which bar-presses avoided signalled electric shocks was also tested for the separate response-controlling properties of the separate components of the light-noise combination stimulus used in original training. In this case it was the auditory component of the signal that controlled responding; the light did not. In successive groups of 25 trials the animal avoided 25, 2, 20 and 19 shocks when the warning signal was, respectively, light and noise, light alone, noise alone, and light and noise.

Webster, in another experiment, trained guinea pigs to avoid shock with a hold and release procedure almost identical to that used with the rats described above, and also found that the separate components of the light-tone combination warning stimulus with which the subjects were trained did not obtain equal control of avoidance responses. A summary of his data, showing the number of shocks received by each of three guinea pigs in half-hour periods when the light and the tone were used separately as warning signals in comparison with the number of shocks received when the stimuli were used in combination, is contained in Table I. Removal

TABLE I

Number of shocks received by each of 3 guinea pigs in a 30 min period after extensive avoidance training with a light-tone stimulus combination, and in similar periods when the light and tone were each used as "warning" signals alone.

Subject	Light plus tone	Light alone	Tone alone
M1	1	2	101
M3	10	15	47
M4	3	4	8

of the tone hardly affected the avoidance performance of the animals, but all three of the subjects exhibited poorer performance when the tone alone was used as the signal, two of them markedly so. Like the pigeons, the rats and the guinea pigs apparently were responding to the presence of only one aspect of the total stimulus complex. The tone and light stimuli were not equivalent from the standpoint of stimulus control, even though they were simultaneously present at the time of reinforcement.

Baron (1965) reports other investigations leading to the same conclusion. In one, pigeons were reinforced for pecking in the presence of a white vertical line on a green circular surround but not when the surround was red and there was no line. Both line and colour were correlated with reinforcement and so had equal opportunities of coming to control responding. But no differential control was exhibited by the vertical line in comparison to other lines tilted up to 45° left or right of the vertical. The gradient of generalization was flat. Another group demonstrated response control by the surround colour difference alone. Using monkeys, D'Amato and Fazzaro (1966) have also shown that responses are controlled by only the colour component of a compound colour-line stimulus.

Control of a response by only one aspect of a stimulus compound, or by only one of the dimensions of a simple stimulus, is not an inevitable result (Butter, 1963; Fink and Patton, 1953), but the fact of its occurrence must be explained. Such explanations, in either psychological paradigm, have appealed, among other things, to the concept of "selective attention".

V. Rival Accounts of Selective Attention

A. THEORETICAL

An account of selective attention has been proposed by Baron (1965):

"In conflict with the simple assumption that all stimuli are equally capable of controlling behaviour, psychological literature . . . includes statements to the effect that various organisms respond more readily or with greater sensitivity to some modalities than others. Rats are considered to be highly proprioceptive, pigeons especially visual, and humans . . . more visual than auditory . . . What is being suggested is that for any organism presented a complex of stimuli there may be an attending hierarchy, i.e. an ordering of the degree to which each element of dimension of the complex will come to control behaviour" (pp. 62–63).

This statement does not *explain* selective attention but provides a label— "attending hierarchy"—for describing a set of observations. From this description Baron proceeds to examine how stimuli may be re-ordered within the hierarchy, or how position within the hierarchy affects the ability of a stimulus to acquire control of responding. He concludes that differential reinforcement with respect to one stimulus dimension affects the specificity of response control by a second dimension only if the second dimension is at the same or a higher level in the attending hierarchy than the first (see also Lovejoy, 1966). This conclusion, if correct, would give Baron's proposal the status of a psychological law, or rule for determining the likelihood of responding coming under stimulus dimension control. Specification of such a rule in the form $R = f(Sp)$—responding is a function of stimulus hierarchical position—is a natural target for research in the S-R-S^R paradigm.

A more theoretical employment of the concept of selective attention is exemplified in Sutherland's (1959, 1964) theory of discrimination learning. He assumes that,

"In learning a discrimination animals have to learn two things: first they must learn which analyser to switch in, namely the one which yields different outputs for the two stimuli to be discriminated. Secondly, they must learn to attach the correct responses to the two outputs" (1964, p. 57).

Lovejoy (1966) has made the same assumption. The assumption may be stripped of its dualistic overtones and restated as the belief that organisms must tact stimuli (Skinner, 1957) before these stimuli can control other responses. This is not inconceivable, and the different controlling contingencies of tacts and mands can serve as examples.

A tact is a naming response, and a mand is a request or demand (Skinner, 1957). In the S-R-S^R paradigm the tact *apple*, in the context "That is an apple", is acquired according to the following contingency:

S	R	S^R
physical presence of an apple	apple	confirmation by agreement

whereas the mand *apple*, in the sentence "I want an apple", is emitted in the circumstance:

S	R	S^R
deprivation of an apple	apple	production of apple removes deprivation

Plainly, in this case, the tact must be acquired before the mand—a child must learn the name "apple" before he can ask for one by name—and although the two responses are topographically identical they are controlled by two different discriminative stimuli and reinforced by two different reinforcing stimuli.

When an animal jumps towards a triangle, say, behind which it finds food, and away from a circle behind which it does not, a similar multiple contingency might apply. The tact analogue would be:

S	R	S^R
physical presence of a triangle	jump to triangle	food as confirming information

and the mand analogue would be:

S	R	S^R
deprivation of food	jump to triangle	production of food removes deprivation

In this example, as in Blough's psycho-physical experiment, the response of the animal is controlled entirely within the bounds of the experiment, in contrast to comparable human performances where the different controlling contingencies may be in effect on occasions far apart in time. Sutherland's assumption, presumably, derives from introspection about the human condition, and projection of the conclusion into the experimental condition of the rat. But the rat experiment cannot support such an approach unless the tacting and manding processes in the rat experiment are unconfounded. But in the traditional discrimination learning type of experiment they are not. And there is no point in unconfounding them, or in conducting animal experiments at all, if they are only to be interpreted in accordance with human introspection.

The dual process which Sutherland assumes does not in fact require such a fanciful analysis but may be examined in the light of properties acquired by stimuli differentially paired with reinforcement. Two such properties have been identified, one discriminative and the other reinforcing (Keller and Schoenfeld, 1950; Skinner, 1938; Zimmerman, 1959). The reinforcing property of a discriminative stimulus is not apparent in the abbreviation S-R-S^R, but this abbreviation is only a convenient representation in which a whole sequence of behaviour emitted by an organism is condensed into the single symbol R (Millenson, 1967; Skinner, 1938). A slight expansion of the formula is necessary to expose the (conditioned) reinforcing role of a stimulus. This expansion may be written S-R_1-S^D . S^r-R_2-S^R, where the discriminative and conditioned reinforcing properties of the original S are designated, respectively, S^D and S^r.

If R_1 and R_2 represent the behaviours of attending and approaching then the stimulus that sets the occasion for approaching serves also as the conditioned reinforcer for attending. However, it is well known that response chains are most efficiently established backwards, which is the exact opposite of the theory that Sutherland, Mackintosh and Lovejoy propose. It may not be necessary, though, for them to commit their theories to an assumption of order, (although the order they suggest—attending then responding—is the natural one to adopt from the S-O-R point of view) but only to one that the stimulus control of behaviour is complex. And on this there is no dispute.

B. METHODOLOGICAL

The data a scientist collects, the kinds of experiments he performs, are determined by the paradigm in which he is working, and the utility of these data is circumscribed by the methods used for their collection. A paradigm, then, is defined not only by its theoretical preconceptions but also by its methodology, each reinforcing the other. Because of its uncompromising commitment to behaviour as the subject matter of psychology, S-R-S^R theory adopts a different experimental methodology from the one that is conventionally employed. Traditional S-O-R experimental psychology claims behaviour as its datum, but it is not the behaviour of *an organism* that it attempts to bring to order. Instead it studies the averaged behaviour of groups. It uses this tactic ostensibly to control for variable experimental errors, but the tactic also reveals an implicit acceptance of "Aristotelian" in contrast to "Galileian" science in the sense described by Lewin (1931).

Another way to control for variability in data is by way of experimental, instead of by statistical, refinement (Sidman, 1960). According to this methodology, variability is not a matter for disguise but a matter for analysis: when similar experimental arrangements do not produce acceptably congruent results, the tactic is to search for uncontrolled aspects of the experiment, not to accept uncontrollable errors in the results. Thus, confronted by findings like those of Reynolds (1961) and Eckerman (1967), the psychologist using S-R-S^R methodology employs additional experimental subjects not to arrive at a democratically acceptable result but to discover the reasons why every subject behaves the way it does. A good example of the power of this approach is some research reported by Skinner (1965). He reinforced a group of eight pigeons on a fixed-interval 1 min schedule for responding to any part of a green field containing a small white triangle. When the triangle was removed seven of the birds ceased to respond, showing the response to be entirely under control of the triangle. However, all these birds were, apparently, pecking *at* the triangle, in contrast to the eighth bird which pecked at other parts of the field. This bird did not stop responding when the triangle was removed, although its response rate did decrease. In this case attention is exemplified in the actual topography of the response "attached" to the stimulus.

This kind of consideration for detail, both for the form of the emitted response and for the conditions under which it occurs, contrasts with the objectives of S-O-R methodology. In this case, because the only requirement is the generation of data pertinent to a problem posed in the context of S-O-R psychology, attention is devoted entirely to gross aspects of correctness or incorrectness of a response regardless of how the response is obtained or what detailed differences between responses may occur. Thus, for example, if the problem is to discover to which of a pair of stimuli a rat on a Lashley apparatus will jump after prior training with another pair of stimuli, the only datum of interest is the stimulus the rat actually jumps towards. The facts that it is sometimes necessary to prod, push, shock or otherwise induce the rat to jump, and that some jumps are energetic and others abortive (Feldman, 1953; Maier, 1940; Wilcoxon, 1952; Yates, 1962) are not entered into statistical analyses of the relative frequencies of contacts with one stimulus or the other. Such a methodology, in contrast to the investigation of rate of response emission of individual organisms in components of multiple schedules of reinforcement correlated with different exteroceptive stimuli (Ferster and Skinner, 1957; Jenkins, 1965), resembles that of the chemist who examines the effects of adding one chemical to another by averaging the results of several additions of impure elements instead of purifying his chemicals and verifying his results by several repetitions of the experiment.

Statistical control of error entered psychology as a convenience during the transition from classical mentalistic to contemporary behaviouristic psychology, before modern methods of individual organism control were conceived and developed. Now that these methods are available reliance on comparisons of group rather than of individual performances may hinder rather than help the experimental analysis of the stimuli by which behaviour in an experiment is controlled. Such a hindrance is exemplified by research on the over-training reversal effect first reported by Reid (1953). This is one of the phenomena that the selective attention theory of discrimination learning is supposed to explain (Mackintosh, 1965; Sutherland, 1964), but which, in spite of an enormous volume of research, has still not been shown incontrovertibly to exist (Gardner, 1966).

Another aspect of S-R-S^R methodology is its attention to function instead of to aspect (Skinner, 1953) or to means rather than to "end-effects". The S-O-R paradigm that psychologists have shared for ages takes as its datum the behaviour of organisms exposed to static experimental arrangements that are more or less tightly controlled. The kinds of questions asked are, "How well do organisms perform in such and such a situation after different amounts of training?" "Which kinds of problems are organisms able to solve?" "Can organisms discriminate this stimulus from that one?" and the like. Such questions encourage answers pointing on the one hand to psychological aptitudes and abilities, and on the other hand to the shape of hypothetical curves of learning or conditioning. In either case what is demanded is an answer that is once-and-for-all; a statement of *the* capacity of an organism or a function expressing *the* form of a conditioning curve (Spence, 1956).

S-R-S^R methodology recognizes no such "*thes*". It aims instead to shape a particular mode of performance, and adjusts experimental contingencies to serve this end. By such means numerous animals have been trained to emit behaviours quite atypical of their species (Breland and Breland, 1966; Morgan, 1961, p. 202; Pierrel and Sherman, 1963), and "errorless learning" of discriminations that would ordinarily be erratically exhibited has been experimentally achieved (Terrace, 1963). These achievements were possible because S-R-S^R methodologists have recognized the power of the Law of Reinforcement and have attended to response-reinforcement contingencies at all stages of their work, in contrast to S-O-R methodologists who have not accepted reinforcement as the ground-rule for putting the behavioursitic programme envisaged by Watson into effect, but have used it merely as a convenient way of collecting data demanded by the S-O-R paradigm.

VI. Conclusion

The above analysis of the problem of discrimination learning has proceeded not through a direct and detailed examination of data but by elucidation of alternative paradigms that different groups of contemporary experimental psychologists seem to share. These paradigms, S-O-R and S-R-S^R psychologies, differ fundamentally in the status they accord to the Law of Reinforcement. On the one hand the law is accepted merely as an increment of psychological information, on the other as a datum requiring the psychologist's paradigm to change. As a fact, the Law of Reinforcement finds general recognition in the catalogue of psychological data; as a theory, its revolutionary aspect has hardly been perceived. Witness that in only Ferster and Perrot, 1968; Millenson, 1967, of a dozen major contemporary textbooks is the law accorded revolutionary rather than incremental status in the sense that these terms are used by Kuhn (1962). Witness also Mace's (1957) contention that we are all behaviourists now but that Behaviour*ism* is dead, and the variety of authoritative statements reproduced above.

The relative utilities of S-R-S^R and S-O-R theories as general paradigms for psychology cannot be settled by argument, only by demonstration, and a body of data specific to the problem of the stimulus control of behaviour has been summarized and evaluated in S-R-S^R fashion by Terrace (1966). As Kuhn (1962) observes: "To be accepted as a paradigm, a theory must seem better than its competitors, but it need not, and in fact never does, explain all the facts with which it can be confronted". Even before that there must be agreement on what are to count as facts.

Acknowledgements

I wish to express my gratitude to Dr. C. D. Webster for supplying data and constructive criticisms. Dr. J. R. Millenson also made valuable suggestions that have been incorporated in this chapter.

References

Baron, M. R. (1965). The stimulus, stimulus control, and stimulus generalization. *In* "Stimulus Generalization". (D. Mostofsky, ed.), pp. 62–71. Stanford University Press, Stanford, U.S.A.

Baum, M. (1965). An automated apparatus for the avoidance training of rats. *Psychol. Rep.* **16**, 1205–1211.

Békésky, G. von (1947). A new audiometer. *Acta oto-lar.* **35**, 411–422.

Blough, D. S. (1961). Animal psychophysics. *Scient. Am.* **205**, 113–122.

Boring, E. G. (1933). "The Physical Dimensions of Consciousness". Appleton-Century, New York, U.S.A.

Breland, K. and Breland, M. (1966). "Animal Behaviour." Macmillan, ew York, U.S.A.

Burt, C. (1962). The concept of consciousness. *Br. J. Psychol.* **53**, 229–242.

Butter, C. M. (1963). Stimulus generalization along one and two dimensions in pigeons. *J. exp. Psychol.* **65**, 339–346.

D'Amato, M. R. and Fazzaro, J. (1966). Attention and cue-producing behavior in the monkey. *J. exp. Anal. Behav.* **9,** 469–473.

D'Amato, M. R. and Schiff, D. (1964). Long-term discriminated avoidance performance in the rat. *J. comp. physiol. Psychol.* **57,** 123–126.

Denny, M. R. and Weisman, R. G. (1964). Avoidance behavior as a function of length of nonshock confinement. *J. comp. physiol. Psychol.* **58,** 252–257.

Eckerman, D. A. (1967). Stimulus control by part of a complex S^Δ. *Psychon. Sci.* **7,** 299–300.

Eysenck, H. J. (1947). "Dimensions of Personality". Kegan Paul, London, England.

Eysenck, H. J. (1950). Cyclothymia and schizothymia as a dimension of personality. I. Historical review. *J. Personality,* **19,** 123–152.

Eysenck, H. J. and Rachman, S. (1965). "The Causes and Cures of Neurosis". Knapp, San Diego, U.S.A.

Feldman, R. S. (1953). The specificity of the fixated response in the rat. *J. comp. physiol. Psychol.* **46,** 487–492.

Ferster, C. B. and Perrott, M. C. (1968). "Behavior principles," New York, Appleton-Century-Crofts.

Ferster, C. B. and Skinner, B. F. (1957). "Schedules of Reinforcement". Appleton-Century-Crofts, New York, U.S.A.

Fink, J. B. and Patton, R. M. (1953). Decrement of a learned drinking response accompanying changes in several stimuli characteristics. *J. comp. physiol. Psychol.* **46,** 23–27.

Gardner, R. A. (1966). On box score methodology as illustrated by three reviews of overtraining reversal effects. *Psychol. Bull.* **66,** 416–418.

Goss, A. E. (1961). Early behaviorism and verbal mediating responses. *Am. Psychol.* **16,** 285–298.

Hefferline, R. F. and Keenan, B. (1963). Amplitude-induction gradient of a small-scale (covert) operant. *J. exp. Anal. Behav.* **6,** 307–315.

Hochberg, J. E. (1964). "Perception". Prentice Hall, Englewood Cliffs.

Hurwitz, H. M. B. (1964). Method for discriminated avoidance learning. *Science,* **145,** 1070–1071.

Jenkins, H. M. (1965). Measurement of stimulus control during discriminative operant conditioning. *Psychol. Bull.* **64,** 365–376.

Keehn, J. D. (1954). The color-form responses of normal, psychotic, and neurotic subjects. *J. abnorm. soc. Psychol.* **49,** 533–537.

Keehn, J. D. (1955). A factorial study of tests of color-form attitudes. *J. Personality,* **23,** 295–307.

Keehn, J. D. (1964). Consciousness and behaviourism. *Br. J. Psychol.* **55,** 89–91.

Keehn, J. D. (1965). Temporal alteration in the white rat? *J. exp. Anal. Behav.* **8,** 161–168.

Keehn, J. D. (1967a). Behaviourism and the unconscious. *Acta Psychol.* **26,** 75–78.

Keehn, J. D. (1967b). Experimental studies of "the unconscious": Operant conditioning of unconscious eyeblinking. *Behav. Res. Therap.* **5,** 95–102.

Keehn, J. D. (1967c). Running and bar pressing as avoidance responses. *Psychol. Rep.* **20,** 591–602.

Keehn, J. D., Lloyd, K. E., Hibbs, M. and Johnson, D. (1965). Operant conditioning without awareness: a preliminary report. *Psychon. Sci.* **2,** 357–358.

Keller, F. S. and Schoenfeld, W. N. (1950). "Principles of Psychology". Appleton-Century-Crofts, New York, U.S.A.

Kendler, H. H. and Kendler, T. S. (1962). Vertical and horizontal processes in problem-solving. *Psychol. Rev.* **69,** 1–16.

Kendler, H. H. and Kendler, T. S. (1966). Selective attention versus mediation: Some comments on Mackintosh's analysis of two-stage models of discrimination learning. *Psychol. Bull.* **66,** 282–288.

Kuhn, T. S. (1962). "The Structure of Scientific Revolutions". University of Chicago Press, Chicago, U.S.A.

Lewin, K. (1931). The conflict between Aristotelian and Galileian modes of thought in contemporary psychology. *J. gen. Psychol.* **5,** 141–177.

Lindberg, B. J. (1938). Experimental studies of color and non-color attitude in children and adults. *Acta psychiat. neurol. Scand. Suppl.* XVI.

Lloyd, K. E. (1966). Paper presented to Psi Chi Chapter, Eastern Washington State College, U.S.A.

Lovejoy, E. P. (1966). An analysis of the overlearning reversal effect. *Psychol. Rev.* **73,** 87–103.

Maatsch, J. L. (1959). Learning and fixation after a single shock trial. *J. comp. physiol. Psychol.* **52,** 408–410.

Mace, C. A. (1957). Behaviourism. *In* "Education and the Philosophic Mind". (A. V. Judges, ed.). Harrap, London, England.

Mackintosh, N. J. (1965). Selective attention in animal discrimination learning. *Psychol. Bull.* **64,** 124–150.

Maier, N. R. F. (1940). An electric grill as a substitute for the starting platform in the Lashley discrimination apparatus. *J. gen. Psychol.* **22,** 223–224.

Meyer, D. R., Cho, C. and Wesemann, A. S. (1960). On problems of conditioning discriminated lever-press avoidance responses. *Psychol. Rev.* **67,** 224–228.

Millenson, J. R. (1967). "Principles of Behavioral Analysis". Macmillan, New York, U.S.A.

Morgan, C. R. (1961). "Introduction to Psychology". McGraw-Hill, New York, U.S.A.

Mowrer, O. H. and Keehn, J. D. (1958). How are intertrial "avoidance" responses reinforced? *Psychol. Rev.* **65,** 209–221.

Pavlov, I. P. (1927). "Conditioned Reflexes". Oxford University Press, London, England.

Pierrel, R. and Sherman, J. G. (1963). Barnabus, a rat with college training. *Brown Alumni Monthly.*

Reid, L. S. (1953). The development of noncontinuity behavior through continuity learning. *J. exp. Psychol.* **46,** 107–112.

Reynolds, G. S. (1961). Attention in the pigeon. *J. exp. Anal. Behav.* **4,** 203–208.

Rorschach, H. (1942). "Psychodiagnostics". Grune and Stratton, New York, U.S.A.

Sherrington, C. S. (1906). "The Integrative Action of the Nervous System". Yale University Press, New Haven, U.S.A.

Sidman, M. (1960). "Tactics of Scientific Research". Basic Books, New York, U.S.A.

Skinner, B. F. (1938). "The Behavior of Organisms". Appleton-Century-Crofts, New York, U.S.A.

Skinner, B. F. (1948). "Superstition" in the pigeon. *J. exp. Psychol.* **38,** 168–172.

Skinner, B. F. (1950). Are theories of learning necessary? *Psychol. Rev.* **57,** 193–216.

Skinner, B. F. (1953). "Science and Human Behavior". Macmillan, New York, U.S.A.

Skinner, B. F. (1957). "Verbal Behavior". Appleton-Century-Crofts, New York, U.S.A.

Skinner, B. F. (1963). Operant behavior. *Am. Psychol.* **18,** 503–515.

Skinner, B. F. (1965). Stimulus generalization in an operant: a historical note. *In* "Stimulus Generalization". (D. Mostofsky, ed.), pp. 193–209. Stanford University Press, Stanford, U.S.A.

Spence, K. W. (1956). "Behavior Theory and Conditioning". Yale University Press, New Haven, U.S.A.

Sutherland, N. S. (1959). Stimulus analysing mechanisms. *In* "Proceedings of a Symposium on the mechanization of thought processes". Vol. 2, pp. 575–609. H.M.S.O., London, England.

Sutherland, N. S. (1964). Visual discrimination in animals. *Br. Med. Bull.* **20,** 54–59.

Terrace, H. S. (1963). Discrimination learning with and without "errors". *J. exp. Anal. Behav.* **6,** 1–27.

Terrace, H. S. (1966). Stimulus control. *In* "Operant Behavior: Areas of Application and Research". (W. K. Honig, ed.). Appleton-Century-Crofts, New York, U.S.A.

Thorndike, E. L. (1898). Animal intelligence. *Psychol. Rev. Monogr. Suppl.* **2,** No. 8.

Tighe, L. S. and Tighe, T. J. (1966). Discrimination learning: Two views in historical perspective. *Psychol. Bull.* **66,** 353–373.

Tinbergen, N. (1951). "The Study of Instinct". Oxford University Press, London, England.

Watson, J. B. (1924). "Psychology from the Standpoint of a Behaviorist". Lippincott, New York, U.S.A.

Wilcoxon, H. C. (1952). "Abnormal fixation" and learning. *J. exp. Psychol.* **44,** 324–333.

Woodworth, R. S. (1929). "Psychology". Holt, New York, U.S.A.

Yates, A. J. (1962). "Frustration and Conflict". Wiley, New York, U.S.A.

Zimmerman, D. W. (1959). Sustained performance in rats based on secondary reinforcement. *J. comp. physiol. Psychol.* **52,** 353–359.

Temporal Discrimination

12

PETER HARZEM

University College of North Wales, Bangor, Wales

I. Introduction

A basic difference exists between temporal discrimination and the other types of discrimination considered in this book. The latter refers to a relationship between a stimulus and a response such that the stimulus "sets the occasion" for responding (Skinner, 1938). In the simplest case, for example, a response may be reinforced only in the presence of a stimulus and never in the presence of a different stimulus. An organism discriminates the two conditions by responding appropriately when the stimulus which signals the availability of reinforcement is presented. In temporal discrimination a similar pattern of behaviour occurs in the *absence* of discriminative stimuli: although the stimulus situation remains unaltered, responding correlates with the temporal restrictions imposed upon reinforcement.

An important consideration is that such correlations do not necessarily indicate the existence of temporal discrimination. An observed relationship between the pattern of responding and the temporal contingencies in operation may be due to other factors. In his discussion of temporal discrimination, Skinner (1938) illustrated this by pointing out that the emission of different response rates on fixed-interval 5 min and fixed-interval 6 min is the result of the relationship between the rate of responding and the frequency of reinforcement. Similarly, if two different responses are reinforced, one after a delay of two seconds and the other after eight seconds, the former would be emitted in preference. However this is attributable to the differential strengthening of the responses rather than temporal discrimination.

On the other hand, a temporal point in the course of a continuous stimulus may be distinguished by an organism if that point is reliably associated with some other event, in particular reinforcement. This, according to Skinner, is temporal discrimination. The formulation emphasizes that in no way "does 'time' or 'an interval of time' enter with the status of a stimulus. Time appears as the single property of duration, comparable with intensity, wavelength, and so on" (1938, p. 269).

Of course, discrimination of intensity is discrimination of a stimulus in terms of its intensity. But what of temporal discrimination which occurs in the absence of stimulus change? There is no difficulty when the duration of an explicit stimulus is discriminated (e.g. Reynolds and Catania, 1962) because this fits exactly the above formulation. However, a different (and more commonly studied) type of temporal discrimination is one in which the onset of the interval to be discriminated is signalled by a brief event. Usually this event is a response or a reinforcement, so that the onset of the interval is controlled by the subject (Skinner, 1938). This need not always be the case since a brief signal could be presented independently of behaviour and the next response reinforced only if it occurred after a given interval (e.g. Zimmerman, 1961). One basic characteristic of this type of arrangement is that the prevailing stimulus situation is identical before and after the signal. Assuming that temporal discrimination of the required interval after the signal does develop, what is being discriminated in terms of its duration? It is this kind of consideration which has led some writers to appeal, by analogy, to internal stimuli (Anger, 1963). The suggestion is that the event signalling the onset of the interval to be discriminated also initiates some change within the organism, and this change serves as a stimulus which is then discriminated in terms of its duration.

Recently Morse (1966) strongly argued that "our understanding of schedule performances is fettered by the tendency of many authors . . . to explain schedule performances . . . as discriminations of subtle differences in inferred stimulus conditions" (p. 86). The point is taken. It is well documented that time correlated cyclical processes do take place within organisms (e.g. Cold Spring Harbor Symposia on Quantitative Biology: Biological Clocks, 1960; Rohles, 1966, pp. 694–695) and it seems reasonable to assume that temporal discrimination is in some way related to such internal processes (cf. Brady and Conrad, 1960). However, references to such processes do not serve as explanations in the experimental analysis of behaviour. Some relevant questions which need to be answered are of the following sort: (i) can organisms discriminate time intervals? (ii) if so, under what conditions is this type of discrimination acquired and maintained? (iii) what are its limits?

This chapter is a selective review of recent research directed at answering these and related questions. Experiments which deal with the behavioural effects of three types of schedules of positive reinforcement are discussed: differential reinforcement of low rates (DRL); fixed-interval (FI); and progressive-interval (PI). A major area of operant research in which temporal discrimination plays a part, free-operant avoidance (Sidman avoidance), has not been included. Other contributors to this volume deal with the topic, and it has also been discussed in detail by Anger (1963) and Sidman (1966).

II. Differential Reinforcement of Low Rates

Under differential reinforcement of low rates (DRL) a response is reinforced only if a specified minimum interval has elapsed since the preceding response. If a response is preceded by an interresponse time (IRT) shorter than the specified interval no reinforcement occurs and timing starts again from that response. In DRL all IRTs which exceed the required minimum are reinforced. However, a further restriction may be imposed by the addition of a limited hold (LH) specification which sets an upper limit to the IRTs which will be followed by reinforcement. Thus in DRL 20 sec, for example, all responses which occur after IRTs longer than 20 sec are reinforced; in DRL 20 sec LH 5 sec, on the other hand, reinforcement occurs only if an IRT is longer than 20 sec and shorter than 25 sec.

A. Pattern of Behaviour

Organisms are in fact able to distribute their responses in time so that a correlation emerges between the rate and temporal patterning of responding and the requirements of a DRL schedule. In this section the evidence relating to the basic characteristics of DRL performance are discussed.

1. Rate of Responding

Skinner (1938, pp. 306–307) briefly described an experiment in which rats were trained to respond at a high rate, first on a fixed-ratio (FR) and then on a fixed-interval (FI) schedule of reinforcement. A DRL 15 sec schedule was then superimposed upon the FI so that a response was reinforced only if it met the criteria of both the FI and the DRL. The rates of responding gradually declined and became stable at a low level. Reinstatement of the FR schedule resulted in abrupt recovery of the previously observed high rates.

Subsequent research has shown that the rate of responding on a DRL schedule is inversely related to the duration of the minimum IRT required for reinforcement in that schedule (Wilson and Keller, 1953). Further, the specific control of rate by a given DRL can be demonstrated in the following way: if two different DRL schedules are alternated, each in the presence of a discriminative stimulus, a different response rate occurs under each schedule. Zimmerman and Schuster (1962) employed such a multiple (mult) schedule with two DRL components and a time-out period (TO) during which no reinforcement was available (mult DRL 36 sec DRL 18 sec TO 3 min). TO intervened between the two DRLs at every alternation and a continuous tone was present during DRL 36 sec. In each complete cycle of the multiple schedule DRL 36 sec was in effect for 16 min and DRL 18 sec for 8 min. The rats developed two different, stable rates of responding under the two DRL schedules. Approximately equal numbers of reinforcements were obtained in the two components, and this matched the equal reinforcement opportunity provided by the experimental conditions.

The control of rate by DRL is also seen when this schedule alternates with one which generates a high response rate. In an investigation by Ross et al. (1962) monkeys responded under a multiple schedule with free-operant avoidance (Sidman avoidance) and DRL components, TO separating the alternations as in the above experiment. Efficient stable behaviour developed so that a very high rate of responding occurred in avoidance and the animals rarely received a shock. In DRL the rate was low and steady; the efficiency of temporal discrimination was such that in every 15 minute period of DRL 25–30 reinforcements were obtained, and "during the several months of this study the animals received no food other than that which they acquired during DRL periods" (p. 469). Long (1962) has demonstrated that responding of pre-school children could be similarly controlled by a mult DRL FR schedule.

When a DRL contingency is superimposed upon another schedule as in Skinner's original experiment, the rate of responding declines. Ferster and Skinner (1957) found that with FI schedules the decline is roughly proportional to the minimum IRT requirement of the DRL. In a detailed study of this phenomenon Farmer and Schoenfeld (1964) superimposed 1, 2, 4, 8, 16, and 24 sec, in successive blocks of 20 daily sessions (40 for DRL 24 sec) and in that order, upon baseline performance on FI 30 sec. Reinforcement occurred only if a response met the criteria of both FI and DRL. The response rates of rats declined as an inverse function of the minimum IRT specified by the DRL schedule in operation. However the characteristic pattern of responding under the FI schedule was preserved. Even the shorter DRL values of 1, 2, and 4 sec were effectively related to the rate of responding, even though these represented only a small proportion of the FI 30 sec which limits the frequency of reinforcements.

2. *Inter-response Times*

The rate measure is, of course, a statement of the average number of responses which occur per unit time, and it is therefore perfectly correlated with the *average* IRT. Since studies of temporal discrimination are concerned with the distribution of responses in time, such averaging may over-

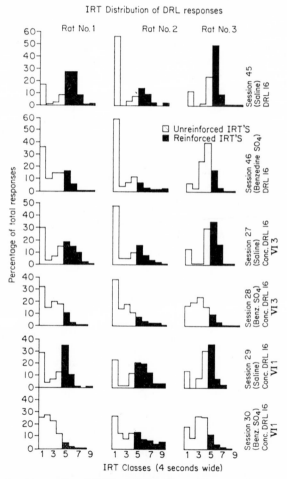

FIG. 1. Relative frequencies of IRTs on DRL 16 sec. Top row shows typical bi-modal distributions obtained from 3 animals, and the other rows the persistence of this type of distribution under treatment with benzedrine sulphate.

(Reproduced with permission from Segal (1963). *J. expl. Anal. Behav.* 5, 108. Copyright 1963 by the Society for the Experimental Analysis of Behaviour Inc).

look details which, from the present point of view are of particular importance. The difficulty may be overcome by recording individual IRTs and summarizing the results in relative frequency distributions (Sidman, 1956) or in distributions of conditional probabilities. Anger (1956) has argued in favour of the latter type of analysis and has introduced the "IRTs per opportunity" measure which is based on the consideration that in a given interval the opportunity for the occurrence of short IRTs is greater than for long IRTs.

In fact analysis of IRTs, in addition to providing more detail, may reveal temporal discrimination which is not always reflected in measures of response rate. For example, in a study of the effect of conditional fear on timing behaviour, Migler and Brady (1964) found that the presentation of a warning stimulus which is terminated by an unavoidable shock suppresses the response rate but it does not alter the temporal distribution of the responses which are emitted.

Typically, the frequency distributions of IRTs are bimodal (Fig. 1). One mode occurs at the shortest recorded interval (approximately 0–2 sec) and the second mode at or just below the minimum reinforced IRT class (e.g. Conrad et al. 1958; Sidman, 1955; Holz et al. 1963). The latter mode signifies that the temporal distribution of a large proportion of responses matches the requirements of the DRL schedule in operation. IRT classes on either side of this mode gradually decline in relative frequency, so that the distribution resembles a generalization gradient. Sidman (1956) has pointed out that the gradient of the frequencies below the minimum reinforced IRT class may reflect a generalization effect. However, the large IRTs are under different control since they are always reinforced. The decline in the frequency of these may be due to the fact that they reduce the overall frequency of reinforcement (cf. Ferraro et al. 1965).

The relatively high frequency of very short IRTs reflects the occurrence of response bursts. The reasons for the persistence of these response bursts is poorly understood; they occur not at random but with a high probability after an IRT which is just short of the minimum required for reinforcement (Sidman, 1956). This has led some writers to suggest that the response bursts are in some way related to the "timing process" (Conrad et al. 1958). Recently Ferraro et al. (1965) presented evidence, one part of which has a bearing on this suggestion. They found that the probability of an IRT which meets the DRL criterion is higher after very short IRTs than after longer but still unreinforced IRTs. It seems that an interval initiated by a burst of responses may be better discriminated; and this may explain the maintenance of response bursts in DRL performance.

Although most of the published studies report relatively high frequency of the shortest recorded IRT class, this finding is not uniform. In a detailed study Kelleher *et al.* (1959) investigated the behaviour of rats under several DRL schedules with LH. They found no bursts of responding; in general the probability of a response remained very low during the first ¾ of the minimum interval required for reinforcement and then increased sharply to a peak in the region of the reinforced IRT. The LH contingency tends in general to sharpen the IRT distribution; also, Kelleher *et al.* used a loud "click" which occurred at each response. However, to check whether this accounts for the difference of their results from most others, they ran a further experiment with different rats and without the LH or the click. Again no bursts were observed. The writers suggest that other differences in their experiment such as deprivation conditions, reinforcers, or apparatus† may have contributed to the difference of their results. It seems that while bursts of responses do commonly occur in DRL performance, accurate temporal distribution of responses can also be observed in the absence of such bursts. Evidence relating to the possible function of these bursts in temporally spaced responding was mentioned above. Related to this are the findings that certain operations such as punishment (Holz *et al.* 1963) and extended exposure to different DRLs (Staddon, 1965) selectively reduce the frequency of these bursts.

3. *Sequential Characteristics*

Several investigators have noted that in performance under a DRL schedule reinforcements tend to occur in relatively long sequences (Kelleher *et al.* 1959; Mallott and Cumming, 1964); and that the probability of a sequence of two reinforced responses is greater than the probability of a sequence of two responses of which only the second is reinforced (Farmer and Schoenfeld, 1964). Two studies in the literature report detailed analyses of these apparent serial dependencies. In one, Ferraro *et al.* (1965) investigated the sequential properties of behaviour under DRL 60 sec. With rats as subjects, about 140 consecutive daily conditioning sessions were run, followed by five extinction and one reconditioning sessions. Overall results of the final two conditioning days showed a high level of accuracy in the temporal distribution of responses: slightly better than 2 out of every 3 responses were reinforced; long runs of successive reinforcements occurred, interrupted by either a long pause or a burst of responses. A trend

---

†In this writers' laboratory it has been possible to produce response bursts at will, with the same animals under the same schedule. When a lever which operates a microswitch is attached to the experimental box, "response bursts" are recorded; when a lever with solid state circuitry is used, few bursts occur. Although a very short pulse length (5 msec) is produced by the second lever, the arrangement is such that two pulses cannot occur in succession unless the lever is briefly returned to resting position after each press. If the first lever is held approximately midway in its travel, at a point coinciding with the trip-over of the microswitch, small movements produce several pulses. Whether these are recorded as responses or not depends on the sensitivity of the related units.

was observed toward longer IRTs as a session progressed. First order sequential analysis of IRTs revealed a positive correlation; i.e. there was a high probability that an IRT would be followed by an IRT of similar duration. The difference between two successive IRTs was very small when the duration of the preceding IRT was in the region of 60 sec (the minimum reinforced IRT), and somewhat larger when the preceding IRT was farther from that region. This kind of relationship involves a relatively high frequency of reinforcement, especially if IRTs longer than 60 sec are followed by shorter IRTs, and the IRTs shorter than 60 sec by longer IRTs. Inspection of the sequential dependency functions show that this was the case for two of the three subjects. For all subjects the effect was most marked in the case of very short IRTs (0–6 sec) which tended to be followed by IRTs around 60 sec.

An even more detailed analysis (carried out by the use of a digital computer) of serial interactions in DRL performance was reported by Weiss *et al.* (1966). These investigators used monkeys as subjects, responding on DRL 20 sec. No preliminary training was given, yet the subjects began to respond almost immediately and sequential interactions were observable as early as the first session. Efficient responding developed rapidly, and by about the 8th session 50% of responses were reinforced. At that time more marked sequential effects were evident: "the IRTs drifted up and down in extended trains of reinforced and unreinforced responses" (p. 621). In further sessions remarkably stable responding occurred; in one session, for example, 233 of the first 256 responses of one subject were reinforced. The records of this performance were subjected to detailed analyses by two techniques: *autocorrelation analysis* and *spectral analysis*. The techniques are described in detail by the authors (pp. 622–624); the results indicated the existence of subtle sequential interactions. First order dependencies were predominant but other dependencies were also evident in diminished amplitude. The pattern of responding was in the form of a slow wave-like drift in which IRTs, some just short of the DRL criterion and some above it, alternated in sequences. The authors suggest that the subtle effects revealed in this experiment may be based on overt chains of behaviour which are thought to mediate temporally spaced responses: these chains would drift since they are adventitiously reinforced.

The evidence relating to the role of collateral behaviour in temporal discrimination will be discussed later. As Weiss *et al.* point out, the important point here is that detailed analysis of sequential interactions reveal subtle characteristics of temporal discrimination.

B. EXPERIMENTAL MANIPULATIONS

In this section we shall be considering what happens to DRL performance when certain independent variables are systematically manipulated. In general the rate of responding and the temporal distribution of responses are differently affected by experimental changes. It appears that once established temporal discrimination is less susceptible to these changes. When IRT distributions are affected, longer IRTs within the distribution still occur with a relatively high frequency; when responding recovers after complete cessation, it recovers rapidly with little or no change in its temporal characteristics.

1. *Deprivation and Satiation*

The positive correlation between deprivation level and the rate of responding is also observed in DRL performance. Conrad *et al.* (1958) found that the response rate of a rat on DRL 20 sec increased sharply at lower levels of water deprivation between 9 and 21·5 hours. Beyond this, between 21·5 and 65·5 hours of deprivation, the increase in rate was very gradual. They tested the subject once a week at different durations of deprivation in mixed order and maintained the stable responding of the rat in the remaining daily sessions on 21·5 hours of deprivation. A monkey was similarly trained but without access to food or water during deprivation and was tested at different periods. The results were essentially similar; the rate of responding rose sharply at 0–7 hours of deprivation and more gradually beyond this, up to 72 hours. There was little change, however, in the IRT distributions of both animals. The most noticeable effect was observed on long IRTs exceeding 30 seconds. The percentage of these durations of deprivation and slightly at longer deprivations. The percentage of IRTs shorter than 10 seconds showed very little change.

Similar results were obtained by Mechner and Guevrekian (1962) with water-deprived rats. These investigators used a modified DRL procedure which enabled a distinction to be made between the post-reinforcement pause and the temporal discrimination pause. The procedure required a chain of two different lever responses for reinforcement, with a DRL 5 sec contingency between the two responses. A response on the second lever was reinforced if the DRL criterion was met; if not, a response on the first lever re-started the cycle. The mean duration of the pauses between the two responses was around 5 seconds and remained unaffected by deprivation periods of 8, 16, 24, 32, 40 and 56 hours. There was no change in the variability of these pauses. The inverse relation observed by Conrad *et al.* between the long IRTs and the deprivation period at low levels was also observed in this experiment, but the effect was on the durations of post-reinforcement pauses and not on timing. With increases in the duration of deprivation up to the middle ranges the animals paused less after reinforcement; beyond the middle ranges there was little difference. The accuracy of timing the minimum required interval between the two responses, however, remained remarkably stable.

In the same study, Conrad *et al.* (1958) also investigated the effects of satiation with four different rats. The schedule was DRL 20 sec LH 2 sec for one rat and DRL 20 sec LH 4 sec for another. A satiation session lasted 10 hours. The results were similar to those obtained with different levels of deprivation: the rates of responding declined in the latter part of a session. There was little change in IRT distributions except at extreme satiation when long IRTs became more frequent.

An inverse relationship between the rate of responding and the deprivation weight is also observed in the pigeon, whether the weight is manipulated by deprivation or deprivation and satiation (Holz and Azrin 1963; Reynolds, 1964b). However, the selective effect is not observed in this bird and IRT distributions change as well as the rate. Reynolds found (1964b) that a decline in the response rate was related to a selective decline in the relative frequencies of short IRTs. There appeared to be an improvement in the temporal distribution of responses with satiation and low levels of deprivation. However, the pigeon performs poorly under DRL schedules (Reynolds and Catania, 1961; Holz and Azrin, 1963) and it is doubtful whether the change can be attributed to improved temporal discrimination.

2. *Aversive Stimulation*

When a punishment contingency is added to all responses maintained under a schedule of positive reinforcement the rate of responding declines as a function of the intensity of the punishing stimulus (Azrin and Holz, 1966). This effect is also seen in DRL performance with accompanying changes in relative frequencies of IRTs. Holz *et al.* (1963) superimposed a shock contingency on each response, upon stable performance of pigeons on DRL 30 sec. An ascending series of shock intensities from 30 V to 120 V were used in successive blocks of daily sessions. As the shock intensity increased, the rate of responding declined, with concomitant increases in the number of reinforcements obtained in a session. The increase in the overall rate of reinforcement reflected the change which occurred in the IRT distribution. Punishment produced a marked reduction in the relative frequency of very short IRTs, and the median IRT successively shifted to longer durations with increases in punishment intensity. These findings were confirmed in a further study by Holz and Azrin (1963).

Other aversive events also result in suppression of DRL performance. Leaf and Muller (1964) found that a conditioned emotional response (CER) procedure completely suppressed the responding of rats during the conditioned stimulus. Migler and Brady (1964) studied the effects of a similar procedure specifically on timing behaviour. They trained rats on a modified DRL schedule, similar to that used by Mechner and Guevrekian (1962). Two successive nose-presses, one on each of two keys were followed by reinforcement provided that the interval between the two responses exceeded a specified minimum. In the final phase of the experiment the following conditions were in effect: the minimum required interval between the two responses was 5 seconds and reinforcement occurred according to a variable-ratio (VR) 2 schedule. A clicking sound which lasted 5 minutes alternated with 5 minutes of no sound throughout a session. Each presentation of the sound was terminated by a brief electric shock. Daily sessions lasted 7·5 hours and no additional food, apart from pellet reinforcers, was provided in the course of the entire experiment. The rate of responding declined each time the sound was presented: the number of responses emitted during the sound was $\frac{1}{4}$ of the number of responses during no sound. However good temporal discrimination was maintained under both conditions; the mean of the intervals between the two different responses was slightly above 5 seconds. There was little variability around the mean for two animals and slightly greater variability for one animal.

3. *Extinction and Reconditioning*

The change in behaviour which occurs in extinction resembles the effects of manipulating the motivational variables, discussed above. In their study Kelleher *et al.* (1959) also reported the results obtained in single 2-hour extinction sessions with the rats which had been trained on DRL 20 sec LH 5 sec. They found that responding continued throughout the session at a declining rate with little change in the IRT distributions apart from a slight increase in the frequency of IRTs between 9 and 15 seconds and a slight decrease in longer IRTs. The IRTs which met the criterion continued to occur in sequences.

The final phase of the study by Ferraro *et al.* (1965) consisted of five extinction sessions followed by one reconditioning session. Responding declined sharply in extinction, as few as a total of 50–60 responses being emitted in the five extinction sessions. When the responses did occur, however, they occurred in sequences with IRTs appropriate to the DRL 60 sec schedule under which the rats had been trained (cf. Hurwitz, 1957).

The difference of the pigeon's DRL performance is also seen in extinction. Reynolds (1964) found that extinction, after training on DRL 20 sec, changed both the overall rate and the IRT distribution. The conditional probability of short IRTs declined more rapidly than that of long IRTs, resulting in a more appropriate spacing of responses with respect to the

DRL schedule. However the results obtained by Holz and Azrin (1963) are not in complete agreement. In their study, the frequency of short IRTs remained unchanged for two pigeons and increased for one pigeon. However the IRT distribution became more uniform in the latter stages of extinction, due to a gradual increase in the frequency of long IRTs. The rate of responding declined slowly in the first two sessions, then more sharply in the next two, and again slowly after that.

After extinction reinstatement of the DRL schedule results in very rapid recovery of performance. Ferraro *et al.* (1965) found that, although reconditioning of rats was rapid, temporal discrimination was not as accurate as in the final conditioning session. Reynolds (1964a) reported that the response rate and the IRT distributions of pigeons recovered after as few as two reinforcements in reconditioning. He suggested "that the process in this instance is related to performance rather than to relearning. From the two reinforcements, the bird does not relearn the temporal spacing of successive pecks that prevailed before extinction any more than it relearns to peck" (pp. 274–275). However, the behaviour which recovered was one of high rate and very few reinforcements; the distribution of responses in the final extinction session was such that 10 reinforcements would have occurred in about 15 minutes. This behaviour continued in the first 3 minutes of the reconditioning session and the two reinforcements were obtained. This was followed by a sharp return of the rate of responding to its pre-extinction level with the consequence that no reinforcement occurred in the next hour.

4. *Rate of Reinforcement*

Performance under a variety of schedules of reinforcement is related to the overall frequency of reinforcement as well as the effect of reinforcement at the time it occurs. For example a proportional relationship exists between the rate of reinforcement and the rate of responding on interval schedules (Skinner, 1938; Herrnstein, 1961). In DRL performance the gradual decline in the relative frequency of IRTs above the minimum reinforced IRT has been thought to be due to the fact that long IRTs reduce the overall frequency of reinforcement (Anger, 1956; Conrad *et al.* 1958). For this reason analysis of the effect of reinforcement frequency on DRL performance is of particular interest. The rate of reinforcement is, of course, commonly controlled by the behaviour of the subject; a schedule imposes limits on that rate. However, Zimmerman (1961) has reported a study in which the rate of reinforcement was controlled as an independent variable. This study used a modified discrete trial DRL procedure. Each interval to be timed was signalled by a discriminative stimulus (S^D); if a specified interval elapsed before the next response reinforcement occurred and S^D was terminated. A response after a shorter interval resulted only in the termination of S^D. If S^D was not present (S^A) responses were ineffective. An LH contingency was also in operation so that if a response was not emitted within a given interval after reinforcement became available S^A occurred. Three schedules were used: DRL 18 sec. LH 12 sec, DRL 6 sec LH 24 sec, and DRL 6 sec LH 2 sec, each under two different conditions. In the recycling schedule a fixed 6 second period of S^A followed the termination of the LH period, as well as all of the responses which occurred in the presence of S^D whether reinforced or not. Thus, the overall rate of reinforcement was controlled by the subject within the limits of the schedule in operation. In the fixed-trial S^A occurred as described above but its duration depended on the duration of the interval between the onset of S^D and the next responses. The time between S^D onsets and therefore the number of occasions in which reinforcement could occur was held constant.

Analysis of S^D-R intervals showed very low relative frequencies below the minimum reinforced interval and a sharp mode just above it. The distributions of recycling and fixed-trial schedules differed under DRL 18 sec LH 12 sec and DRL 6 sec LH 24 sec but a more marked difference was observed under the latter schedule. In fixed-trial schedules the distributions were less peaked and the frequencies above the minimum reinforced interval declined more gradually, reaching zero in the final part of the LH period. DRL 6 sec LH2 minimized the difference in reinforcement rate between the two schedules since LH was very short. As a result no difference was observed between the relative frequency distributions.

The evidence indicates that the overall rate of reinforcement is an important variable in the control of temporally spaced responding. However, relatively sharp peaks just above the minimum reinforced interval were also observed in the fixed-trial schedule. As Zimmerman points out "some factor or factors besides the rate of reinforcement must account for the subjects' great tendency to respond shortly after a reinforcement is set up" (1961, p. 224).

5. *Drugs*

A great deal of evidence has shown the importance of the application of operant conditioning techniques in the analysis of the effect of drugs on behaviour (Boren, 1966). DRL schedules are particularly useful in the study of the effects of some drugs such as the amphetamines since their effects are best revealed on responses which occur at a low rate (Sidman, 1955). Some of these studies provide further evidence related to the distribution of responses in time and will therefore be considered here.

Dews and Morse (1958) studied the effect of dextro amphetamine on human performance on two DRL schedules with FR requirement. On one schedule every 10th response which met the criterion of DRL 25 sec was reinforced; on the second, FR 100 and DRL 2·5 sec were in effect. The IRT distributions were similar under the two schedules, with a peak just above the minimum reinforced IRT and declining frequencies of IRTs above that. Administration of dextro amphetamine (5 mgm) resulted in a shift of the IRT distributions in the direction of the shorter IRTs. Schuster and Zimmerman (1961) found a similar but considerably more marked effect on the performance of rats under DRL 17·5 sec. They prolonged the administration of *dl*-amphetamine (0·75 or 1·5 mgm/Kg) in alternate daily sessions and on other days recorded the activity level of the animals. The chronic treatment with the drug resulted in gradual return to longer IRTs but the activity which was initially increased by the drug showed no decline. In a later study Zimmerman and Schuster (1962) found that chronic administration of *dl*-amphetamine (1·0 mgm/Kg) differentially disrupted performance on a multiple DRL schedule. The frequency of short IRTs increased in both components and then gradually declined. The initial effect was more pronounced on DRL 38 sec than it was on DRL 18 sec. This initial difference was maintained throughout the subsequent shifts observed in the IRT distributions of the two DRL schedules. Segal (1962a) also reported similar results. He administered *dl*-amphetamine (0·5 to 2.5 mgm/Kg) to rats under DRL and concurrent VI DRL schedules of reinforcement. The effect was a shift of the IRT distributions towards the shorter IRTs but the temporal distribution of responses was not lost. Segal concluded: "the main effect of the drug was apparently a motor-excitatory one, and not a specific disruption of some *internal* timing mechanism" (p. 111).

C. COLLATERAL BEHAVIOUR

Segal's reference to an internal timing mechanism again raises the question of what enables organisms to space their responses in time with considerable accuracy. One suggestion is as follows. Any behaviour which precedes a response is also reinforced when that response is reinforced. In DRL schedules a response is reinforced only if a given interval has elapsed since the previous response and thus the behaviour preceding the reinforced response occupies an interval which meets the criterion. This collateral (or mediating: cf. Ferster and Skinner, 1957) behaviour is gradually, and "superstitiously", strengthened so that it regularly intervenes between responses. As a result responses are spaced in time with considerable accuracy.

The occurrence of fairly stereotyped collateral behaviour in DRL performance was first observed by Wilson and Keller (1953). Since then the phenomenon has been well documented. Bruner and Revusky (1961) reported a study in which collateral responses were recorded and analyzed. They reinforced the key pressing responses of schoolboys on DRL 8·2 sec. Three irrelevant keys were also provided; responses on these were without consequence but they were recorded. Each subject developed a characteristic pattern of responses on these keys, terminated by a single response on the DRL key, and followed by reinforcement. In contrast, responding was erratic during the first (operant level) and the final (extinction) phases of the experiment. Kapostins (1963) reinforced the verbal responses of college students according to one of five DRL schedules: 7, 17, 27, 37, or 47 seconds. The subjects were required to say words and a selected word was reinforced if it was emitted at intervals which met the criterion of the DRL in operation. Systematic patterns of behaviour occurred between the reinforced responses. Some subjects repeated the same chain of words, some changed the pitch of voice in a cyclical fashion, and some stopped emitting words apart from the reinforced ones but reported counting between the verbal responses.

Several other investigators have also noted the development of collateral behaviour in the course of DRL training. In their study concerned with the effect of punishment Holz et al. (1963) observed that the behaviour of one pigeon differed from the others. This bird paced to the back of the box between responses and consequently obtained a sharply increased number of reinforcements. Two studies in the literature report extensive analyses of collateral behaviour taking advantage of its occurrence in the course of other experiments.† During an investigation of E.E.G. changes related to performance under DRL and free-operant avoidance schedules, Hodos et al. (1962) observed that movements of the monkeys caused artefacts, with apparent regularity, on the E.E.G. records. The schedule consisted of 15 min each of DRL 21 sec, TO, avoidance ($R - S = S - S = 20$ sec), and TO which cycled in that order in daily 6-hour sessions. One monkey made head movements during all the components. IRT distributions of these movements were rectangular during avoidance and TO but had a peak at 1–2 sec interval during DRL. After administration of pentobarbital (12 mgm/Kg) the head movements almost disappeared and DRL performance deteriorated. Administration of dl-amphetamine (3 mgm/Kg) altered the IRT distributions of head movements during avoidance and TO so that these resembled the distribution previously seen only in DRL. The IRT distribution of the lever responses on DRL shifted towards the shorter IRTs. In the second monkey the collateral behaviour consisted of licking the holder of the water bottle. The temporal distribution of trains

---

†". . . a first principle not formally recognized by scientific methodologists: when you run onto something interesting, drop everything else and study it" (Skinner, 1959, p. 263).

of licks and their temporal relations to the lever responses were distinguishable under the three components of the schedule. IRT distribution of licking was similar to IRT distribution of lever presses on DRL; longer trains of licks occurred during avoidance responding and licking appeared to be random during TO. Pentobarbital and *dl*-amphetamine had similar effects: both the collateral behaviour and the responses were suppressed in DRL and TO. During avoidance the response rate declined but all shocks were successfully avoided.

In the second of these studies Laties *et al.* (1965) observed an example of collateral behaviour in a rat. The animal had been responding on a mult DRL 30 sec FR30 with TO 2 min separating the components at every change. Collateral behaviour emerged after about 35 experimental hours and consisted of the rat "biting its tail and moving its mouth over the surface from one end to the other while holding the tail in its front paws" (p. 108). This behaviour occurred only when DRL was in effect. Duration of mouth-tail contacts and IRTs were positively correlated; the longer the mouth-tail contact the higher the probability that the next response would be reinforced. The effects of the following experimental manipulations were studied: (i) extinction and reconditioning; (ii) removal of the lever; (iii) suppression of mouth-tail contacts; and (iv) administration of amphetamine sulphate. The mouth-tail contacts were suppressed by painting the tail with cycloheximide. In extinction the mouth-tail contacts as well as the responses became erratic and the former ceased after about 10·5 minutes; both types of behaviour recovered almost immediately after the first reinforcement in reconditioning. Removal and presentation of the lever gained discriminative control over the collateral behaviour so that it only occurred in the presence of the lever. DRL performance became disrupted, with the result that fewer reinforcements were obtained. The mouth-tail contacts disappeared 10 minutes after the administration of amphetamine sulphate (0·5 mgm/Kg), and then occurred rarely; in parallel with this the frequency of short IRTs increased.

Nevin and Barryman (1963) reported a study in which pigeons were reinforced on a two-key DRL procedure. A response on the first key turned off the light on that key and simultaneously illuminated the second key. A response on the second key was reinforced if a minimum of 2 sec had elapsed since the first response on the first key. When the second key was illuminated a response on that key, whether reinforced or not, turned off the light on that key, illuminated the first key, and thus recycled the procedure. Responding on an unlit key had no programmed consequence. The relative frequency distributions of the intervals between a first response on the first key and the next response on the second key showed a sharp peak just above 2 sec; 80% of these intervals were followed by reinforcement.

All birds continued to respond on the first key although the first response in such a run illuminated the second key. Durations of these response runs often met the DRL criterion for reinforcement on the second key. Further, the probability of shifting to the second key was an increasing function of the length of the response run on the first key. The persistence of these response runs was remarkable in view of the fact that they were never directly reinforced and never formed a part of the contingencies imposed by the experiment. Clearly, they mediated the temporal spacing of the responses required for reinforcement, but these responses, in turn, occurred with remarkable regularity. Analysis of their IRTs showed that the relative proportion of IRTs, in the 0·15–0·3 sec class was 0·75 and only two other classes of IRTs occurred, one on either side of this mode. As Nevin and Barryman point out, "temporal discrimination of one response may be based on the length of a chain of other responses, (but) the finding that the latter responses may themselves be regularly spaced in time leads to an infinite regression" (1963, p. 113).

The evidence is clear that regular, somewhat stereotyped, collateral behaviour or chains of responses can be observed to intervene between temporally spaced responses. But there is evidence that temporal discrimination may also occur in the absence of such behaviour. Anger (1956) and Kelleher *et al.* (1959) were unable to observe collateral behaviour in their experiments. Belleville *et al.* (1963) described the behaviour on a four component, three lever multiple schedule, of chimpanzees two of which were later used in space flights. They reported that superstitious responding involving the irrelevant levers did occur, but on the FR component. During the DRL component some responses were made on the levers other than the one related to the schedule but such responses initiated a further pause before a correct response. There were no chains of responses between the DRL responses although the DRL performance was highly efficient.

Some of the studies of collateral behaviour have taken advantage of the fact that this type of behaviour occurred in some, but not all of the subjects exposed to the same experimental conditions (e.g. Laties *et al.* 1965). It seems that overt, stereotype behaviour does often develop in the course of DRL performance and when it does it contributes to the efficiency with which responses are spaced in time. But it is not a necessary condition of temporal discrimination. Of course, as Hodos *et al.* have pointed out, "there is . . . no reason to suppose that the collateral responses observed . . . represent (ed) anything more than a fraction of some more complex pattern. Such a pattern might be further composed of respiratory responses and small movements of skeletal musculature" (1962, p. 479). This is to raise once again the question of time correlated internal events.

III. Fixed-interval Schedule of Reinforcement

In FI schedules a response is reinforced only if a specified interval has elapsed since the previous reinforced response but unlike the DRL contingency, responses which occur between reinforcements do not re-cycle the interval. The start of an interval may be timed in either of two ways: (i) from the previous reinforcement, or (ii) "by the clock", i.e. from the end of the preceding interval irrespective of the occurrence of reinforcement.

As Ferster and Skinner (1957) have pointed out, in effect there is little difference between the two procedures. If the interval is timed from the preceding reinforcement none of the inter-reinforcement intervals will be smaller than the schedule specification but some will be greater. Consequently the mean inter-reinforcement interval will be somewhat greater than the interval specified by the schedule. If the FI is timed by the clock the mean inter-reinforcement interval will coincide closely with the schedule specification since some of these intervals will be smaller and some greater than the interval designed by the schedule.

FI schedules generate a characteristic pattern of responding, typically consisting of a relatively long post-reinforcement pause followed by a gradually accelerating rate of responding. The response rate reaches a stable high level which is terminated at the next reinforcement (Fig. 2). This pattern is called the FI *scallop*.

The characteristic pattern of FI performance is observed under a variety of experimental conditions. Scallops occur when the reinforced response is, for example, aggressive behaviour (Azrin and Hutchinson, 1967); when reinforcement consists of TO from a noxious stimulus (Morse and Kelleher, 1966); with conditioned reinforcement (De Lorge, 1967); and when a punishment contingency is imposed on every response (Azrin and Holz, 1961). If time-correlated stimuli are introduced into the experimental situation the behaviour comes under the control of these stimuli. Scallops occur but with prolonged post-reinforcement pauses and the overall rate of responding is lower (Ferster and Skinner, 1957; Segal, 1962b; Ferster and Zimmerman, 1963). No attempt is made here to review the extensive literature concerned with behaviour under FI schedule of reinforcement. Discussion will be limited to studies which have been specifically directed at analysis of temporal control in FI performance.

Although the gradual increase in response frequency in the course of an interval is generally taken to be evidence of temporal discrimination the pattern can also be explained in a similar way to the explanation based on collateral behaviour in the case of DRL performance. Since in FI regular responding occurs between the reinforced responses the suggestion is that in each interval the responses constitute a chain. A chain is a sequence of

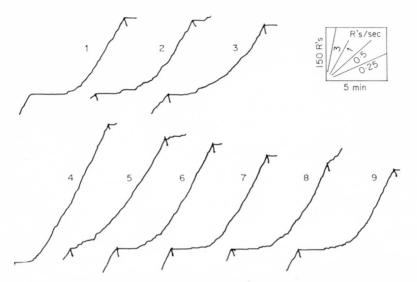

FIG. 2. Examples of smooth acceleration in responding under FI 8 min. Occasionally, as in curve 3, the transition is fairly rapid and the high rate is maintained with little further change until reinforcement.

(Reproduced with permission, from Ferster and Skinner (1957). Copyright 1957 by Appleton-Century-Crofts, Inc.)

responses in which every response serves as a discriminative stimulus for the next response; it is maintained since the final component in the chain is reinforced.

Although this explanation appears to deal parsimoniously with FI responding, it leaves one important aspect of the scallop to be accounted for: the relatively long post-reinforcement pause. These pauses can in part be attributed to the discriminative function of reinforcement. Responses which closely follow reinforcement are never reinforced and thus the probability of such responses is very low. The discriminative effect of reinforcement may be further extended in time since the residual stimuli such as food in the mouth and chewing are likely to acquire a similar function (Ferster and Skinner, 1957). However, the duration of post-reinforcement pauses are positively correlated with the duration of the intervals specified by FI. Some point in the course of the interval seems to be discriminated so that the post-reinforcement pause gives way to responding. Even if the responses constitute a chain, the temporal relation between the onset of this chain and the preceding reinforcement is regular.

Further, Kelleher (1966) has pointed out that "when it is assumed that a response sequence is a response chain, the stimuli in the chain are hypothetical. Hypothetical response-produced stimuli have enabled theor-

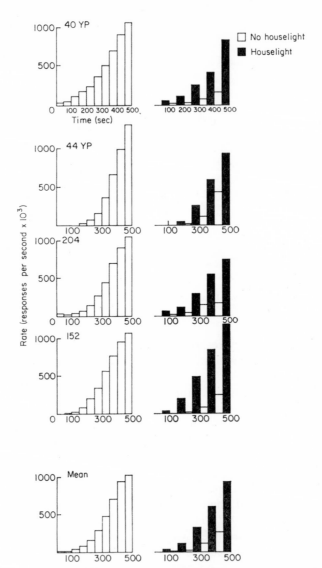

Fig. 3. The mean rates of responding in successive 50-sec segments of FI 500 sec, without S^Δ presentations (left column) and with alternate S^Δ presentations (right column). The top four rows show the results obtained from individual pigeons; the bottom row gives the means of these results.

(Reproduced with permission from Dews (1962). *J. expl. Anal. Behav.* **5,** 371. Copyright 1962 by the Society for the Experimental Analysis of Behaviour, Inc.)

ists to provide plausible accounts of many characteristics of response sequences, but there is no *a priori* reason for assuming that response sequences are response chains" (p. 163). One important question which needs to be answered is whether the apparent temporal discrimination in FI performance is dependent on the supposed response chain of the scallop: does disruption of the response sequence disrupt the characteristic FI behaviour?

In their studies of the FI performance Ferster and Skinner (1957) occasionally interrupted the responding of pigeons by introducing $S^\triangle$ periods. Lights in the experimental box were switched off during $S^\triangle$. In one experiment 30-second $S^\triangle$ periods interrupted responding on FI 60 sec; in another up to 5 minutes of $S^\triangle$ interrupted FI 10 min. Although no responses occurred during $S^\triangle$, the scalloped pattern of responding survived during the remainder of the interval.

In an extensive series of experiments Dews (1962–1966b) investigated the effect of multiple $S^\triangle$ periods on FI performance. In the first of these studies (1962) pigeons were first trained on FI 500 sec TO 250 sec; a house-light (HL) was then introduced in alternative 50-second periods during every interval of the schedule. Each 500-second interval of the FI started with a 50-second period of no-HL so that the 5th HL presentation coincided with the final part of the interval. On that occasion HL continued until reinforcement was obtained. The results are shown in Fig. 3; the periods without HL disrupted responding in that rate of responding was low on these occasions. However, a gradual increase in the frequency of responses continued to occur in successive HL periods. A similar tendency, at a much lower level, was also seen in the successive no-HL periods. Further, a "miniature" scalloped pattern of responding was evident in individual HL periods. In his second study Dews (1965a) replicated this experiment with a squirrel monkey and obtained similar results.

The third study (1965b) is of added interest because unusually long FI values, up to 27 hours were used. This study investigated the effects of less regular and prolonged interruptions in FI performance. In the first experiment TO 50 sec FI 500 sec was interrupted by a single period of HL for 50 seconds; TO 540 sec FI 900 sec by two 180-second presentations of HL; and TO 300 sec FI 3000 sec by one HL period which lasted 600 sec. Again, the scallops survived under all the conditions and the rate of responding was very low during $S^\triangle$. Similar results were also obtained in the second experiment with FI intervals of 10,000, 30,000, and 100,000 seconds and alternating $S^\triangle$ periods of 1000, 3000, and 10,000 seconds; with these very long intervals reinforcement consisted of 10 successive magazine presentations on *crf* and HL was $S^\triangle$. Figure 4 shows cumulative records of individual FI segments under FI 30,000 sec and FI 100,000 sec.

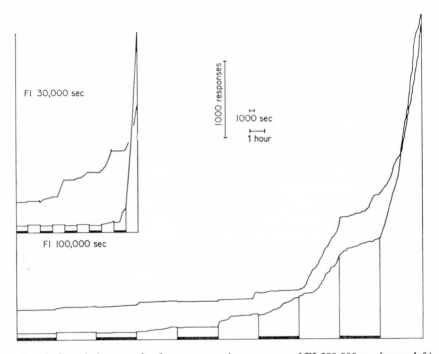

Fɪɢ. 4. Cumulative records of two consecutive segments of FI 300,000 sec (upper left) and FI 100,000 sec (lower right). The thickened black portions of the abscissa show the intervals in which $S^\triangle$ was presented.

(Reproduced with permission, from Dews (1965b). *J. expl. Anal. Behav.* **8**, 431.   Copyright 1965 by the Society for the Experimental Analysis of Behaviour, Inc.

It is clear that over these very long intervals the gradually increasing tendency to respond was retained; although the effect of the $S^\triangle$ periods was less obvious under FI 100,000 sec the related change in behaviour is nevertheless unmistakable.

The next in this series of studies by Dews (1966a) investigated the effect of presenting long $S^\triangle$ periods and brief S^D's. Pigeons were reinforced under FI 500 sec; $S^\triangle$ (HL) was presented throughout the interval except in two 50-second periods when no HL was on. One of these S^D periods of 50 seconds always occurred at the end of the interval and continued until reinforcement; the position of the other was at one of consecutive 50-second segments of the interval. These "probe" sessions were separated by sessions in which S^D and $S^\triangle$ periods alternated. In the probe sessions few responses occurred during $S^\triangle$; the rates of responding in S^D was low in the early parts of the interval and a clear tendency was observed to respond at progressively higher rates when S^D was presented in latter parts of the interval.

Finally, Dews (1966b) investigated whether the results so far obtained were dependent on (i) extensive previous training on FI, and (ii) on continued presence of the keylight which remained on during the $S^\triangle$ periods. He reported that pigeons placed directly on the $S^\triangle$ procedure also showed a gradually increasing tendency to respond in the course of an interval of FI schedule. Further, the tendency survived when $S^\triangle$ was complete darkness.

The results of these studies are clear: the scalloped pattern of FI behaviour cannot be accounted for by reference to response chains. Dews has suggested that the appropriate explanation is in terms of the retroactive enhancing effect of reinforcement. For example, reinforcement which follows a response with a delay of some 100 seconds may nevertheless result in an increase in the future probability of that response (Dews, 1960). Such an effect would also operate in the FI situation so that those responses which precede the reinforced response would be strengthened. The extent of this effect would depend on the temporal distance between any one response in the scallop and reinforcements. However, Dews (1965b) adds that "the constancy of the FI pattern over large ranges of parameter value, with similar proportions of total responding occurring in successive segments of the intervals, shows that it cannot be the absolute delay of reinforcement of responding that determines the rate, but may be rather the delay as a fraction of the consistently imposed schedule cycle" (p. 435).

The absence of a direct relationship between delay of reinforcement and the probability of response suggests that this relationship may not be the only factor contributing to the FI pattern. Of course, responses can be strengthened by subsequent reinforcement only if they occur in the course of an FI interval. One pertinent question is whether the increase in response probability would still be observed even when responses, other than the immediately reinforced response, are never followed by reinforcement in the history of the subjects. A study by Wall (1965) provides an answer to this question.

In this experiment rats were trained on a discrete-trial FI 60 sec procedure. During initial training a retracting lever was presented once every 60 seconds and a single response was followed by reinforcement and removal of the lever. The lever was available at first for 30 seconds and later for 5 seconds, at each presentation. In subsequent test sessions, the lever was introduced once in the course of each 60-second interval as well as at the end of the interval. A response was reinforced only on latter occasions. The additional presentations of the lever occurred at 15, 30, or 45 seconds after the reinforced presentation for different groups of rats. A further group was presented the lever at all of these intervals once in every 60-second period, in random order. It was found that the shortest response latencies, i.e. the intervals between the introduction of the lever and response, occurred on reinforced occasions. The duration of the latencies on non-reinforced occasions was an inverse function of time since previous reinforcement: as the availability of the next reinforcement approached latencies became shorter.

This relationship was observed in the first part of the first of three test sessions so that the results cannot be attributed to the effect of reinforcement on nonreinforced responses during these sessions. However inspection of the results reveals that there was some evidence of such an effect in the later test sessions. The shortest latencies remained unchanged but the longer latencies, at 15 and 30 seconds after reinforcement, gradually decreased. The decline in latencies was sharper in the last test session.

Finally all groups were placed in extinction. For the group presented with the lever at 30 seconds from the previous reinforcement as well as every 60 seconds, extinction consisted of regular lever presentations. No differential responding was observed under these conditions. However, the other groups continued to respond with shorter latencies on those occasions when a response would have been reinforced in training, e.g. at intervals of 60 seconds.

Unfortunately the results of this experiment have been presented in terms of group averages averaged over trials or sessions. No data have been provided about the behaviour of individual subjects and this seriously detracts from the value of the findings. However, the implication is clear: the probability of responding increases in the course of an interval of FI even though such responses have never been reinforced remotely. Delayed reinforcement, although a factor in the development of FI scallops, does not fully account for this behaviour. This evidence, if confirmed, would strongly support the view that discrimination of the intervals plays a part in FI performance.

IV. Progressive-interval Schedules of Reinforcement

One fact which emerges from the studies discussed above is that in general organisms show a remarkable ability to adjust to the temporal contingencies imposed upon them. The finding by Dews (1965b), for example, that the FI scallop occurs in intervals of more than 27 hours is quite astonishing. One pertinent question is whether organisms can also adjust to temporally based *changes* in contingencies. For evidence on this question let us turn to PI schedules.

The current literature on temporal discrimination is concerned with the discrimination of a single, repeatedly presented interval. The studies which have used more complex schedules of reinforcement such as multiple DRL and concurrent FI DRL differ only to the extent that the same organism is exposed to two repetitive intervals, the two presentations alternating singly or in sequences, or superimposed one upon the other. Of course, more than two intervals can be used in this way by increasing the number of schedule components.

In all of these cases, it is the repeated occurrence of equal intervals which renders explanations in terms of mediating behaviour tenable. When the schedules involve two or more such intervals, a corresponding number of mediating behaviours has to be postulated. However, collateral behaviour or response chains could not account for behavioural adjustment to the successively changing temporal conditions of the PI schedules.

In PI schedules, as in FI, a response is reinforced only if a specified interval has elapsed since previous reinforcement; other responses have no effect. Unlike FI however, durations of the successive intervals of PI are increased according to some rule.

Studies by the present author of performance on PI schedules are reported in this section.† In all of these studies rats responded in standard operant conditioning boxes. The experiments were programmed by solid state logic elements, the results were recorded on cumulative recorders and

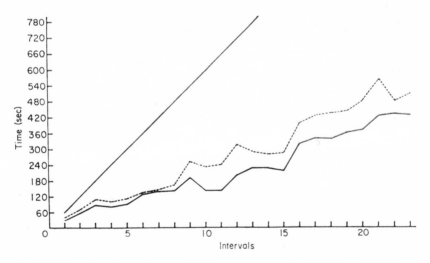

FIG. 5. Mean durations of post-reinforcement pauses obtained from Rat 73 under arithmetic PI 60 sec. The solid line indicates the pauses timed to the first response; the dotted line, to the second response after reinforcement. The straight line shows the progression of the intervals in this schedule. Closure of the experimental box started the first interval.

†Part of these data was presented in papers read to the Experimental Analysis of Behaviour Group, April 5–6, 1967, Sussex; and to the Annual Convention of the American Psychological Association, Sept. 1–5, 1967, Washington, D.C.

324   PETER HARZEM

punched tape, and were analysed by an Elliott 803 computer. The
reinforcer was 0·05 ml or 0·5 ml diluted condensed milk.

A. Arithmetic Progressive-interval Schedule

In this schedule the durations of successive intervals increase arithmetically, so that each interval is extended by a constant amount of time.
For example, in arithmetic PI 60 sec the intervals are 60 sec, 120 sec,
180 sec, and so on. This type of schedule was first used by Findley (1958)
in a study of switching under concurrent schedules.

One experiment by the present writer was concerned with performance
on arithmetic PI 60 sec. The animals were first trained on FI 60 sec in
five, daily, 1-hour sessions and then switched to the PI schedule and the
sessions were extended to include 23 intervals. By the second session,
scallops similar to those seen under FI were evident. Figure 5 shows the
mean durations of post-reinforcement pauses for one animal, in the last
five of thirty sessions. As the intervals progressed so did the post-reinforcement pauses, but more gradually; the difference between the duration of an
interval and the duration of the post-reinforcement pause in that interval
was greater in the latter part of a session.

On the other hand, the number of responses emitted in each interval
remained relatively stable. Figure 6 shows the mean number of responses

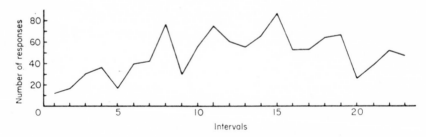

Fig. 6. Mean number of responses emitted by Rat 73 in each interval of arithmetic PI
60 sec.

emitted by the same animal in successive intervals of the same sessions.
The variability in the number of responses from interval to interval was
similar to the variability observed under FI schedules (Ferster and Skinner,
1957). The sequential characteristics of responding demonstrated a
further aspect of behavioural adjustment to the schedule. In every interval
most responses occurred with IRTs between 1 and 2 seconds; however,
as the schedule progressed longer IRTs emerged and the relative frequency of these IRTs increased (Fig. 7).

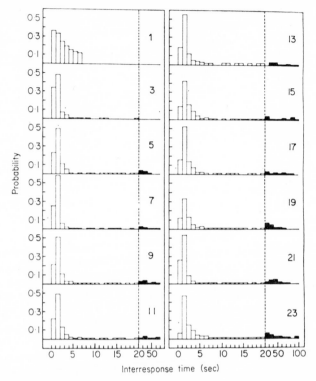

Fig. 7. Relative frequency distributions of IRTs in every other interval of arithmetic PI 60 sec. The IRTs obtained from Rat 73 in five sessions were pooled, interval by interval, to compute the data. 1-second categories are shown up to 20 seconds and thereafter 10 second categories (filled in blocks).

In further experiments with different rats, similar results were obtained under arithmetic PI schedules of 15, 30, 45, and 90 seconds.

A characteristic of arithmetic progression is that successive increments are proportionally smaller; for example, the first increment is 100% of the preceding interval but the next increment is 50% of the interval which preceded it, and so on. Thus, in the later intervals the proportional increments are small and in a sense the schedule gradually approximates to a FI schedule. There was some indication that this characteristic of the arithmetic PI schedules was reflected in the pattern of responding. The post-reinforcement pauses tended to be of similar duration in blocks of 3–5 intervals of the schedule and increased between one such block and another. Thus, the number of responses emitted in each interval within such a block gradually increased, then declined sharply in the first interval of the next block. This pattern is seen in the cumulative records shown in

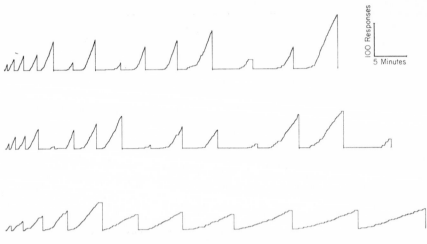

F<small>IG</small>. 8. Selected cumulative record segments to illustrate the block by block adjustment of responding under arithmetic PI 30 sec (upper two segments), and arithmetic PI 60 sec (lower segment). The pen reset to baseline at reinforcement. The occasional pauses which intervened between a run of responses and the response which was reinforced are also seen. The lower segment was obtained in the second session under arithmetic PI 60 sec, before post-reinforcement pauses developed. Even at this stage the regularity of the number of responses per interval is seen in the latter part of the segment.

Fig. 8; these records were selected for the purpose of illustration and they are not representative of PI performance in general. The pattern was observed fairly often but not consistently in any one animal. In some animals only a slight tendency of this type was discernible.

Another unusual feature observed in the performance of some animals was the interruption of steady responding shortly before the reinforced response. Figure 8 also shows instances of this phenomenon. Remarkably, when they occurred these pauses were within the interval soon to be terminated. Often the next response was emitted almost immediately at the onset of the next interval and it was reinforced. No systematic explanation could be found for these pauses.†

The overall results indicated that behaviour adjusts to the changing temporal contingencies of the arithmetic PI schedules. However, the gradual increase in the post-reinforcement pauses was slower than the increase in the durations of the intervals. Further, although the number of

†The possibility of an auditory cue from the programming equipment can be ruled out. Each experimental box was in a sound insulated cabinet and the programming equipment was in a separate room. In any case there was no sound to be heard: apart from cumulative recorders and tape punch, all units were solid-state.

responses per interval showed relative stability, there appeared to be increase in the early intervals, i.e. when the increments by which the intervals increased were larger. Thus it was possible to attribute the subsequent stability of responding to the fact that the increments of the later intervals were relatively small. It might then be said that stable performance occurs because arithmetic PI differs only to a limited extent from FI, after the first few intervals.

The relative proportion of the increments was held constant in the next series of studies.

B. Geometric Progressive-interval Schedule

Each increment of this schedule was a constant proportion of the preceding interval so that the absolute duration of the increments increased successively. In geometric PI 20 60 sec, for example, the duration of the first interval was 60 seconds; the next interval was increased by 20% of 60 seconds, i.e. it was 82 seconds; the next interval, by 20% of 82 seconds, making a total duration of 98·4 seconds and so on.

In one experiment four rats were first trained on FI 60 sec and then placed under the geometric PI which has just been described as an example. Each daily session included 23 intervals. Data obtained in the last five of

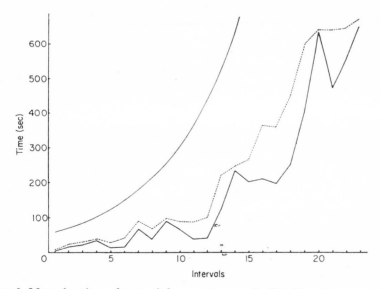

Fig. 9. Mean durations of post-reinforcement pauses for Rat 91 under geometric PI 60 sec, timed to the first response after reinforcement (solid line) and the second response after reinforcement (dotted line). Smooth line shows the durations of the intervals of this schedule. The timing of the first interval started when the experimental box was closed.

thirty sessions from one subject are presented here; similar results were obtained from the other animals. Post-reinforcement pauses increased at first slowly and then more sharply (Fig. 9). This increase was more marked than in arithmetic PI; in the latter it was linear whereas the present results show a positive acceleration. However, the temporal distance between the end of the post-reinforcement pause and the onset of the next interval also increased gradually. The number of responses per interval remained stable (Fig. 10), with less variability than in arithmetic PI. There was no

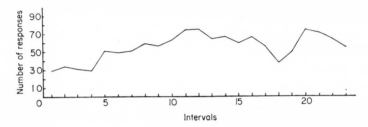

Fig. 10. Mean number of responses emitted by Rat 91 in successive intervals of geometric PI 60 sec.

indication of the pattern of change in blocks of intervals which had been observed in arithmetic PI performance. The IRT distributions revealed a further difference in the effects of geometric and arithmetic progressions. Figure 11 shows the relative frequencies of IRTs; although the distributions have high peaks at 1–2 second class in the early intervals of the schedule the frequencies of these IRTs gradually declined.

Other studies with geometric PI increments of 10 and 20% produced similar results.

An important finding in all of the experiments with both schedules was that although pauses occurred in the course of responding, reinforcement was obtained almost immediately after it was set up. There was seldom a delay between the beginning of a new interval and the next response; when such delays occurred they were brief. The longest delay of this kind which occurred in geometric PI 20 60 sec, for example, was 60 seconds and this occurred in the interval the total duration of which was 2748·2 seconds (the 23rd interval).

It appears that under both types of PI schedules behaviour adjusts to the temporal requirements of the schedules. This adjustment shows greater regularity under geometric PI although under arithmetic PI the difference between the intervals become smaller. This would suggest that the relative magnitude of temporal change is more important in the control of behaviour than the absolute values of the intervals involved in such a change.

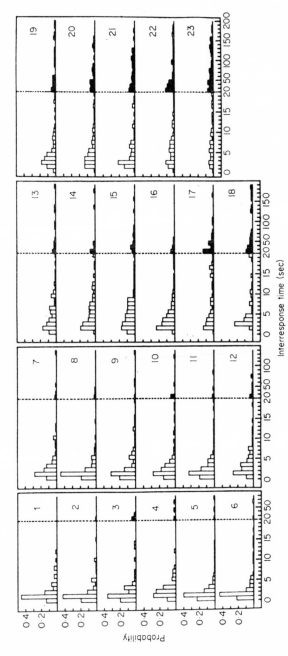

FIG. 11. Relative frequency distributions of IRT's in successive intervals under geometric PI 60 sec. The data obtained from Rat 91 were pooled over 5 sessions to compute the distributions. 1-second bins are shown up to 20 seconds and thereafter, 10 second bins (filled in blocks).

The control of responding by the temporal contingencies of the PI schedules demonstrates that a repeated pattern of behaviour between reinforced responses, whether collateral behaviour or a chain of responses, can not satisfactorily explain temporal discrimination. These behaviours may and do occur under some conditions, and when they do they may contribute to the accuracy of discrimination. But their occurrence is not a necessary condition of temporal discrimination. Further, behavioural adjustment to temporal contingencies can be more complex than the discrimination of a single duration.

V. Conclusion

The evidence reviewed in this chapter strongly supports the following statements: (i) organisms can discriminate time intervals in the absence of external cues; (ii) they can discriminate very long intervals; and (iii) they can discriminate complex temporal relations. Much of the emphasis has been on DRL performance because this schedule imposes a stringent temporal requirement, especially when a LH contingency is in effect. In DRL, reinforcement occurs only if the temporal requirement is met whereas in FI and PI some responses would be reinforced given that the organism responds. As Ferster and Skinner (1957) point out, FI schedules favour responding at a relatively low rate since the probability of reinforcement is greater after a long pause than after a short pause. The frequency of reinforcement is clearly an important variable in the control of behaviour. In the case of PI, this frequency gradually declines so that a corresponding decline in the frequency of responding would be expected. This is what in fact happens since the number of responses in successively longer intervals remains more or less the same. However these responses are distributed in time in a characteristic pattern indicating the effect of the temporal relations which obtain in the PI schedules. Significantly, reinforcement occurs almost immediately it becomes available.

That behaviour adjusts to temporal relations even more complex than the discrimination of uniform durations is shown in PI performance. The complexity of temporal discrimination is also indicated by the results of Weiss *et al.* (1966) who found subtle serial interactions in DRL performance. Further evidence is provided by Dews (1965b) that it must be the *proportional* temporal relations which contribute to the regularity of change in performance, in his experiments. As Dews has suggested and as it is demonstrated in the experiments on PI performance, proportional constancy effectively determines behavioural adjustment to the temporal conditions affecting an organism.

It is clear that adventitiously reinforced and repetitive overt (or covert) behaviour can not account for all of temporal discrimination. This has an important relevance for some of the other biological sciences: time orientation can not be based on any number of recycling clocks unless a different clock is postulated for every different interval in a PI schedule. Other complex mechanisms which relate to such clocks must exist.

Finally, apart from the intrinsic interest in temporal discrimination, there is also a general implication for the experimental analysis of behaviour. As Skinner (1938) pointed out, whenever regular temporal relations exist between events, whether explicitly programmed or not, sooner or later temporal discrimination will develop. The present evidence indicates that temporal discrimination may enter into the determination of the pattern of behaviour in an experiment not only when the regularity is absolute but also when it is proportional.

Acknowledgements

I am indebted to Professor T. R. Miles for a critical reading of the manuscript and to Professor H. M. B. Hurwitz for many hours of helpful discussions.

References

Anger, D. (1956). The dependence of interresponse times upon the relative reinforcement of different interresponse times. *J. exp. Psychol.* **52,** 145–161.

Anger, D. (1963). The role of temporal discriminations in the reinforcement of Sidman avoidance behavior. *J. exp. Anal. Behav.* **6,** 477–506.

Azrin, N. H. and Holz, W. C. (1961). Punishment during fixed-interval reinforcement. *J. exp. Anal. Behav.* **4,** 343–347.

Azrin, N. H. and Holz, W. C. (1966). Punishment. *In* "Operant Behaviour: Areas of Research and Application". (W. K. Honig, ed.), pp. 380–447. Appleton-Century-Crofts, New York, U.S.A.

Azrin, N. H. and Hutchinson, R. R. (1967). Conditioning of the aggressive behavior of pigeons by a fixed-interval schedule of reinforcement. *J. exp. Anal. Behav.* **10,** 395–402.

Belleville, R. E., Rohles, F. H., Grunzke, M. E. and Clark, F. C. (1963). Development of a complex multiple schedule in the chimpanzee. *J. exp. Anal. Behav.* **6,** 549–556.

Boren, J. J. (1966). The study of drugs with operant techniques. *In* "Operant Behaviour: Areas of Research and Application". (W. K. Honig, ed.), pp. 531–564. Appleton-Century-Crofts, New York, U.S.A.

Brady, J. V. and Conrad, D. V. (1960). Some effects of brain stimulation on timing behavior. *J. exp. Anal. Behav.* **3,** 349–350.

Bruner, A. and Revusky, S. H. (1961). Collateral behavior in humans. *J. exp. Anal. Behav.* **4,** 349–350.

Cold Stream Symposia on Quantitative Biology (1960). "Biological Clocks". The Biological Laboratory, Cold Spring Harbor.

Conrad, D. G., Sidman, M. and Herrnstein, R. J. (1958). The effects of deprivation upon temporally spaced responding. *J. exp. Anal. Behav.* **1,** 59–65.

De Lorge, J. (1967). Fixed-interval behavior maintained by conditioned reinforcement. *J. exp. Anal. Behav.* **10,** 271–276.

Dews, P. B. (1960). Free-operant behavior under conditions of delayed reinforcement: I. CRF-type schedules. *J. exp. Anal. Behav.* **3,** 221–234.

Dews, P. B. (1962). The effects of multiple S^Δ periods on responding on a fixed-interval schedule. *J. exp. Anal. Behav.* **5,** 369–374.

Dews, P. B. (1965a). The effects of multiple S^Δ periods on responding on a fixed-interval schedule: II. In a primate. *J. exp. Anal. Behav.* **8,** 53–54.

Dews, P. B. (1965b). The effects of multiple S^Δ periods on responding on a fixed-interval schedule: III. Effects of changes in pattern of interruptions, parameters and stimuli. *J. exp. Anal. Behav.* **8,** 427–433.

Dews, P. B. (1966a). The effects of multiple S^Δ periods on responding on a fixed-interval schedule: IV. Effect of continuous S^D with only short S^Δ probes. *J. exp. Anal. Behav.* **9,** 147–151.

Dews, P. B. (1966b). The effect of multiple S^Δ periods on responding on a fixed-interval schedule: V. Effect of periods of complete darkness and of occasional omissions of food presentation. *J. exp. Anal. Behav.* **9,** 147–151.

Dews, P. B. and Morse, W. H. (1958). Some observations on an operant in human subjects and its modification by dextro amphetamine. *J. exp. Anal. Behav.* **1,** 359–364.

Farmer, J. and Schoenfeld, W. N. (1964). Effects of a DRL contingency added to a fixed-interval reinforcement schedule. *J. exp. Anal. Behav.* **7,** 391–399.

Ferraro, D. P., Schoenfeld, W. N. and Snapper, A. G. (1965). Sequential response effects in the white rat during conditioning and extinction on a DRL schedule. *J. exp. Anal. Behav.* **8,** 255–260.

Ferster, C. B. and Skinner, B. F. (1957). "Schedules of Reinforcement". Appleton-Century-Crofts, New York, U.S.A.

Ferster, C. B. and Zimmerman, J. (1963). Fixed-interval performances with added stimuli in monkeys. *J. exp. Anal. Behav.* **6,** 317–322.

Findley, J. D. (1958). Preference and switching under concurrent scheduling. *J. exp. Anal. Behav.* **1,** 123–148.

Harzem, P. (1967). Temporal adjustments of behavior under arithmetic and geometric progressive interval schedules. *Am. Psychol.* **22,** 476 (abstract).

Herrnstein, R. J. (1961). Relative and absolute strength of response as a function of frequency of reinforcement. *J. exp. Anal. Behav.* **4,** 267–272.

Hodos, W., Ross, G. S. and Brady, J. V. (1962). Complex response patterns during temporally spaced responding. *J. exp. Anal. Behav.* **5,** 473–479.

Holz, W. C. and Azrin, N. H. (1963). A comparison of several procedures for eliminating behavior. *J. exp. Anal. Behav.* **6,** 399–406.

Holz, W. C., Azrin, N. H. and Ulrich, R. E. (1963). Punishment of temporally spaced responding. *J. exp. Anal. Behav.* **6,** 115–122.

Hurwitz, H. M. B. (1957). Periodicity of responses in operant extinction. *Quart. J. exp. Psychol.* **9,** 177–184.

Kapostins, E. E. (1963). The effects of DRL schedules on some characteristics of word utterance. *J. exp. Anal. Behav.* **6,** 281–290.

Kelleher, R. T. (1966). Chaining and conditioned reinforcement. *In* "Operant Behaviour: Areas of Research and Application". (W. K. Honig, ed.), pp. 160–212. Appleton-Century-Crofts, New York, U.S.A.

Kelleher, R. T., Fry, W. and Cook, L. (1959). Interresponse time distribution as a function of differential reinforcement of temporally spaced responses. *J. exp. Anal. Behav.* **2,** 91–106.

Laties, V. G., Weiss, B., Clark, R. L. and Reynolds, M. D. (1965). Overt " mediating" behavior during temporally spaced responding. *J. exp. Anal. Behav.* **8**, 107–115.

Leaf, R. C. and Muller, S. A. (1964). Effect of CER on DRL responding. *J. exp. Anal. Behav.* **7**, 405–407.

Long, E. R. (1962). Additional techniques for producing multiple-schedule control in children. *J. exp. Anal. Behav.* **5**, 443–455.

Malott, R. W. and Cumming, W. W. (1964). Schedules of interresponse time reinforcement. *Psychol. Rec.* **14**, 211–252.

Mechner, F. and Guevrekian, L. (1962). Effects of deprivation upon counting and timing in rats. *J. exp. Anal. Behav.* **5**, 463–466.

Migler, B. and Brady, J. V. (1964). Timing behavior and conditioned fear. *J. exp. Anal. Behav.* **7**, 247–251.

Morse, W. H. (1966). Intermittent reinforcement. *In* "Operant Behaviour: Areas of Research and Application". (W. K. Honig, ed.), pp. 52–108. Appleton-Century-Crofts, New York, U.S.A.

Morse, W. H. and Kelleher, R. T. (1966). Schedules using noxious stimuli: I. Multiple fixed-ratio and fixed-interval termination of schedule complexes. *J. exp. Anal. Behav.* **9**, 267–290.

Nevin, J. A. and Barryman, R. (1963). A note on chaining and temporal discrimination. *J. exp. Anal.* **6**, 109–113.

Reynolds, G. S. (1964a). Accurate and rapid reconditioning of spaced responding. *J. exp. Anal. Behav.* **7**, 273–275.

Reynolds, G. S. (1964b). Temporally spaced responding by pigeons: development and effects of deprivation and extinction. *J. exp. Anal. Behav.* **7**, 415–421.

Reynolds, G. S. and Catania, A. C. (1961). Temporal discrimination in pigeons. *Science*, **135**, 314–315.

Rohles, F. H. (1966). Operant methods in space technology. *In* "Operant Behaviour: Areas of Research and Application". (W. K. Honig, ed.), pp. 677–717. Appleton-Century-Crofts, New York, U.S.A.

Ross, G. S., Hodos, W. and Brady, J. V. (1962). Electroencephalographic correlates of temporally spaced responding and avoidance behavior. *J. exp. Anal. Behav.* **5**, 467–472.

Schuster, C. R. and Zimmerman, J. (1961). Timing behavior during prolonged treatment with *dl*-amphetamine. *J. exp. Anal. Behav.* **4**, 327–330.

Segal, E. F. (1962a). Exteroceptive control of fixed-interval responding. *J. exp. Anal. Behav.* **5**, 49–57.

Segal, E. F. (1962b). Effects of *dl*-amphetamine under concurrent VI DRL reinforcement. *J. exp. Anal. Behav.* **5**, 105–112.

Sidman, M. (1955). Technique for assessing the effects of drugs on timing behavior. *Science*, **122**, 925.

Sidman, M. (1956). Time discrimination and behavioral interaction in a free operant situation. *J. comp. physiol. Psychol.* **49**, 469–473.

Sidman, M. (1966). Avoidance behavior. *In* "Operant Behavior: Areas of Research and Application". (W. K. Honig, ed.), pp. 448–498. Appleton-Century-Crofts, New York, U.S.A.

Skinner, B. F. (1938). "The Behaviour of Organisms". Appleton-Century-Crofts, New York, U.S.A.

Skinner, B. F. (1950). Are theories of learning necessary? *Psychol. Rev.* **57**, 193–216.

Skinner, B. F. (1959). A case history in scientific method. *In* "Psychology: A Study of Science". (S. Koch, ed.). Vol. 2, pp. 359–379. McGraw-Hill, New York, U.S.A.

Staddon, J. E. R. (1965). Some properties of spaced responding in pigeons. *J. exp. Anal. Behav.* **8,** 19–27.

Wall, M. (1965). Discrete-trials analysis of fixed-interval discrimination. *J. comp. physiol. Psychol.* **60,** 70–75.

Weiss, B., Laties, V. G., Siegel, L. and Goldstein, D. (1966). A computer analysis of serial interactions in spaced responding. *J. exp. Anal. Behav.* **9,** 619–626.

Wilson, M. P. and Keller, F. S. (1953). On the selective reinforcement of spaced responses. *J. comp. physiol. Psychol.* **46,** 190–193.

Zimmerman, J. (1961). Spaced responding in rats as a function of some temporal variables. *J. exp. Anal. Behav.* **4,** 219–224.

Zimmerman, J. and Schuster, C. R. (1962). Spaced responding in multiple DRL schedules. *J. exp. Anal. Behav.* **5,** 497–504.

Cortical Mechanisms and Learning

13

I. STEELE RUSSELL

Medical Research Council, Unit for Research on Neural Mechanisms of Behaviour, University College, London, England

I. Introduction

Within the last decade two main methods of creating a split-brain preparation have been established. The *surgical split-brain*, developed by Myers (1955, 1956), Sperry *et al.* (1956) and Downer (1958), entails mid-line division of the brain by section of the corpus callosum, the optic chiasma and in some cases the anterior and posterior commissures. With this preparation it is possible to localize learning to one cortical hemisphere by restricting visual inputs to that hemisphere due to occlusion of one eye during training. After acquisition, when the visual inputs are presented to the untrained hemisphere via the other eye, no signs of retention of learning are found. The *functional split-brain*, pioneered by Bureš (1959) and Russell and Ochs (1960), utilizes spreading depression to abolish cortical function in one hemisphere, and thus restrict inputs to the remaining hemisphere during conditioning. The animals are then tested for retention of learning with the originally trained hemisphere depressed and the other functional. In both split-brain procedures such lateralized information when once established does not spontaneously transfer to the untrained hemisphere even over long periods of time (Myers, 1961; Russell and Ochs, 1963).

II. Split-brain Learning

Using either of the two preparations it is possible to produce two functionally independent hemispheres capable of learning different and opposite problems either sequentially (Bureš and Burešová, 1966) or even simultaneously (Trevarthen, 1966). Thus from this point of view the split-brain animal is a creature possessed of two separate brains each with its complete set of cerebral integrating centres and all their interrelations. Further they are not only identical genetically but they are also identical in terms of any organization derived from the effects of previous experience. Such a preparation provides virtually unique experimental advantages. By making unilateral lesions and comparing the learning of the lesioned hemisphere with that of the intact hemisphere it is possible to get perfectly matched control and experimental observations from the same animal. This possibility of using unilateral lesions has a further advantage in reducing the error due to sparing of tissue around the lesion. With the usual practice of making bilateral lesions the majority of the sparing stems from a failure to make ablations symmetrical. Finally perhaps the most striking advantage is that it becomes possible to investigate the effect of lesions which if made bilaterally would be incapacitating. In the split-brain animal such secondary undesirable effects would be avoided. Large or multiple removals can be made unilaterally because the functions involved can be handled by the remaining integrating centres on the opposite side. For example Sperry (1961) successively extended cortical lesions on one side until only the isolated region of the primary visual cortex remained. It was found that the striate area alone was insufficient to support visual discrimination learning.

The present line of enquiry developed from a consideration of certain general problems that arose in the use of the functional split-brain preparation to analyse cortical function in learning. It was found that to a considerable extent the validity of this experimental strategy rested on two underlying assumptions. The first assumption is that the learning of a split-brain animal with only one hemisphere functional is the same as that of a normal animal with two hemispheres. The second assumption is that learning can be considered as a unitary process and that therefore as far as the brain is concerned different learning procedures are equivalent. With continued experimentation it became clear in fact that neither assumption was tenable.

Concerning the unitary nature of learning a recent review of the literature on neural mechanisms of learning indicates that different conditioning paradigms have differential representation in the brain (Russell, 1966a). Learning that is encoded as classical conditioning would appear to have no cortical involvement in either its storage or retrieval mechanisms, whereas learning that is instrumentally encoded is highly dependent on cortical factors for its storage and retrieval (Russell, 1966b). Hence one must consider learning to consist of several possible types of data encoding rather than assuming a single unitary process. The importance of recognizing that different types of encoding underlie learning is that it is possible that they may involve different cerebral structures. Furthermore it is also feasible that separate mechanisms exist for the storage and retrieval phases of learning.

Considering the nature of learning in the split-brain animal Russell (1966b) has shown that under certain conditions it may be very different than in the normal animal. With regard to the acquisition of classical conditioning no differences were found between split-brain or normals.

Instrumental learning on the other hand was markedly impaired in the functionally hemidecorticate split-brain rat. Whilst the learning of either hemisphere in the split-brain appeared to be identical, such hemidecorticate acquisition was clearly impaired by comparison with that of a normal brain. In contrast to classical conditioning it would appear that the efficiency of encoding for instrumental conditioning was significantly reduced by hemidecortication. It was considered appropriate therefore to examine the nature of this hemidecorticate defect further in order to clarify our appreciation of split-brain learning.

III. Mass Action

The effect of hemidecortication was examined using a variety of instrumental discrimination tasks and the results were found consistently to dramatically confirm Lashley's notions of cortical mass action (Lashley, 1929). Before presenting the experimental evidence it would seem appropriate to first briefly describe Lashley's position and also the main difficulties his formulation encountered. Central to the notion of mass action was the concept of equipotentiality. Lashley took the view that various parts of the cortex are interchangeable in their function. Any area of the cortex in addition to its specialized functions, such as can be seen in the visual projection areas, also possesses a general computing capacity common to all cortical elements. The efficiency of the brain in learning operations was related to the number of such equipotential elements, or to the mass of participating cortex. In other words equipotential function provides the necessary conditions for mass action. The scheme that Lashley proposed in many respects has obvious analogies to the present day usage of redundant circuits in computer design. From this point of view we would see mass action not as a function as did Lashley, but as an operating characteristic of a network of equipotential elements.

Lashley in essence supported his position from two clearly distinguishable types of experimental procedure. Firstly there were studies showing that maze learning impairments in rats were proportionately related to the amount of bilateral removals of cortex. A second group of experiments showed that the striate cortex possessed additional functions to those of visual projection. Lashley (1943) showed that rats which had sustained both straite cortex ablation and peripheral blinding were more severely impaired in maze learning than animals that had merely been peripherally blinded.

The objections to these sources of evidence for mass action are well known and have been extensively considered elsewhere (Zangwill, 1963). It will suffice therefore to make only brief mention of what are considered to be the most critical difficulties. Hunter (1930) criticized Lashley's maze learning experiments on the grounds that such learning involves the operation of many different channels as well as motor activities. As cortical lesions are progressively extended, there must be a progressive reduction in the number of sensory channels remaining available for use in maze learning. Further it is possible that in maze acquisition some animals use one sensory channel and other animals another. Some animals may also learn by utilizing several sensory channels, without the experimenter being necessarily able to identify them. For individual rats, whether or not a lesion would involve the particular projection area of the sensory channel mediating acquisition is purely a matter of chance. The more extensive the lesion, however, the greater the probability of removing tissue involved in learning in the majority of cases. This summation of a chance sampling factor could well create the impression that learning depends on the amount of cortex available.

The experiments by Tsang (1934, 1936) and Lashley (1943) purporting to show non-visual functions for the striate areas were criticized on the grounds that the lesions extended beyond the purely visual areas and therefore probably involved the loss of additional sensory channels. By and large these criticisms though to some extent blunted by Lashley and his collaborators were never effectively refuted. What is surprising is that Lashley in defending his principle of mass action chose to do so under conditions that inherently favoured the opposition. In utilizing preparations involving bilateral lesions of variable extensity it is virtually impossible to construct a complete defence against criticisms of this kind.

The obvious test of mass action would seem to lie in the use of unilateral lesions of varying extensiveness which would not be open to the objections of sensory channel reduction. In the rat complete hemidecortication produces no motor deficits other than a loss of Magnus reflexes. With regard to visual impairment a minimal homonymous hemianopsia will be present in the rat, where the main defect would be in terms of an almost complete loss of vision in the contralateral eye. Due to the repeated decussations across the midline in the auditory pathways no impairment in audition would be expected. With regard to cutaneous sensitivity it is difficult to assess to what extent there would be any loss due to hemidecortication. In rat the representation in somatic sensory area I is mainly contralateral, and bilateral in area II (Woolsey, 1958). Further it should be noted that the rat can learn tactile discriminations even after bilateral ablation of both somatic I and II, (Zubek, 1951). It is doubtful if there would be any effect on kinaesthesis, but it is certain that pain reception would be unaffected.

In using spreading depression to obtain a functional split-brain preparation in the rat it has been assumed that solely neocortical function in one hemisphere is abolished. The early reports of Van Harreveld and Bogen (1956) and Bureš (1959) supported this view by indicating that cortical spreading depression (CSD) did not propagate from neocortex to the cingulate or entorhinal regions. More recent observations in rat, however, indicate that CSD not only enters cingulate cortex dorsomedially, but at the same time continues ventrally to invade entorhinal as well as pyriform juxtallocortex (Fifková, 1964). Fifková and Syka (1964) further demonstrated that propagation continues into the amygdala, via the claustrum, involving most major nuclei. Fifková and Bureš (1964) finally completed the picture on extracortical spread of CSD by observing entry into the striatum. Striatal SD was found to spread throughout the caudate reaching the nucleus accumbens septi where it terminated. It is thus clear that CSD as a functional ablation procedure is not without its drawbacks.

Nonetheless in the writer's opinion CSD as a technique of hemidecortication possesses several clear advantages over the more traditional methods of tissue removal. Firstly its effects are immediate and involve no vascular damage. Without any need for post-operative recovery, problems of compensation are excluded. In addition the difficulties due to secondary damage that so frequently accompany surgical lesions are avoided. Secondly decortication or hemidecortication is complete with no tissue sparing, whereas the opposite would be the case with ablation. A third advantage of CSD is that due to its reversible nature it permits extremely flexible experimental designs which would not be feasible with irreversible lesions. Finally because of the simplicity of the technique it enables large numbers of animals to be run in a relatively short period of time. The involvement of subcortical regions with CSD need not be an insuperable difficulty, and in any event subcortical damage frequently is associated with some cortical lesions. Where appropriate these effects can be controlled by a comparison with either surgical hemidecortication or unilateral amygdala lesions.

In the present series of experiments over 100 rats, either functionally or surgically hemidecorticated, were tested on a variety of instrumental learning tasks. Invariably such animals were found to be impaired in their learning by comparison to normal rats with two hemispheres functional. As there seems to be no sound anatomical reason why hemidecorticates should show such a defect, these findings provide a basis from which one can investigate mechanisms of mass action.

IV. The Effect of Hemidecortication on Simple GO Learning

With one exception (Russell and Ochs, 1960) most split-brain experiments involving instrumental learning have used relatively complex tasks ranging from avoidance conditioning to pattern discriminations. It is possible therefore that task difficulty is a major contributing factor to the hemidecorticate deficit. The present study was designed to investigate hemidecorticate acquisition in an instrumental situation that placed minimal encoding difficulties on the animal. If a defect could be found under very simple conditions then task complexity could be excluded as a major cause. In addition with very simple learning it should be possible to thereby characterize the nature of the defect with maximum clarity. It was for these reasons that escape learning was selected as an instrumental task of minimal complexity.

Rats were trained to escape from shock in a runway. The apparatus consisted of an opaque white perspex runway, 72 inches long, 4 inches high and 54 inches wide. At one end of the runway was a 6 inch long start box and at the other end a similar goal box. Both the start box and the alley were electrifiable through a grid floor, whereas the goal box floor was made of perspex. The entire runway was covered by a transparent perspex ceiling.

The training procedure involved placing the rat in the start box in a position facing away from the door. After 30 sec the door was raised and shock (0·65 mA) was simultaneously delivered to the entire grid. Latencies to leave the start box and running times in the alley were automatically recorded on each trial. After each escape response the rats were allowed 30 sec reinforcement time in the goal box before being placed in the home cage for an intertrial interval of 1 min. The learning of one group of normal rats was compared to that of two groups of hemidecorticates. There were 7 animals in each group. All animals were trained to a criterion of 9 consecutive perfect escape responses. A perfect escape response was scored in terms of three requirements. First the exit from the start box had to occur without any competing behaviour, i.e. circling, entry into corners, etc. Secondly the run in the alley had to be similarly devoid of competing responses such as retracing or stopping. Finally the entry into the goal box was to occur without any hesitation.

The results of a comparison of the acquisition of normals and hemidecorticates are given in Fig. 1. It can be seen that on each of the three days of training the hemidecorticates required approximately twice as many trials to reach criterion as did normals. An examination of the running times revealed no significant differences between groups. This indicated that

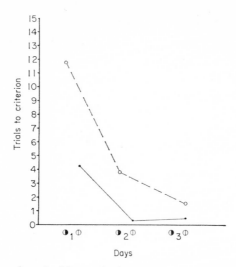

FIG. 1. Average number of trials to criterion are given for both normals and hemidecorticates. The solid lines indicate the scores for the normals, the dashed lines those for the hemidecorticates.

hemidecortication did not produce any possible locomotor impairment that could be responsible for the differences in acquisition. It would appear that the depression of one hemisphere during training produces a learning defect.

This point is further substantiated from a consideration of a breakdown of the escape learning into its component parts. The trials required to reach criterion on each of these components is given in Fig. 2 for all three groups. Considering the learning of the normal animals it can be seen that the main source of difficulty presented by escape learning is the acquisition of the exit response in the start box. The entry response to the goal box is the first to be learned and the running response in the alley is also rapidly acquired. The learning of hemidecorticates shows that their impairment is solely restricted to the start box component. The acquisition of the alley and goal box components is identical to that of normals. The fact that twice as many trials were needed to acquire the initial component of the escape behaviour was due to a failure to eliminate competing GO responses as efficiently as normal rats.

The second group of hemidecorticates in the split-brain group is of particular interest in this regard. This group of rats was trained for the first two days with the right hemisphere functional. On the third day this hemisphere was depressed and the animals exposed to the escape situation with a naive or untrained hemisphere functional. As can be seen in Fig. 2

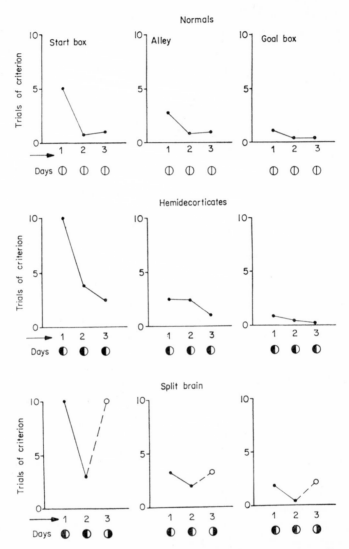

FIG. 2. Average number of trials to criterion are given for the start box, alley and goal box components of the escape response. The acquisition of each is given over three days of training for normals, hemidecorticates and a split-brain group. For this last group the scores on the third day represent performance with the new hemisphere. The hemisphere depressed is indicated by the shading in circles below each daily score.

a clear lateralization of learning to the originally trained hemisphere was found. The rats had to relearn every instrumental component of the escape task when confronting the situation with a new hemisphere. This is despite the fact that when they were placed in the apparatus with this untrained hemisphere they displayed a marked CER in the start box. This differed markedly from their behaviour on the initial trial of the first day. Then no difficulty was encountered in placing them in the start box. Further after they were placed into the apparatus a characteristic pattern of exploratory behaviour was observed in the period before the first escape trial was initiated. In sharp contrast to this, great difficulty was encountered when putting the rats into the start box on the first trial with the new hemisphere functional. Once in the start box no exploratory activities were seen, instead the rats manifested clear signs of fear by crouching, squeaking and defaecating in the preshock period. Despite this clear indication of emotional "anticipatory" behaviour, when the door was raised and the shock delivered no escape responses occurred. It was as if the animals *recognized* the situation with the new hemisphere, but did not *know what to do* about it.

This experiment like the majority of split-brain experiments suggests the importance of the cortex for storage or retrieval of instrumental learning. It further indicates the interesting possibility of using the split-brain preparation as a *behavioural fractionation* technique for separating the different types of encoding or conditioning that are inherent in any learning situation.

This conjecture is not, however, the main point of interest at present. The learning defect shown by the hemidecorticate would appear to be clear evidence for mass action, as the present results cannot be attributable to any sensory deficit. Further, these results provide support for the previous suggestion that mass action was a characteristic of instrumental learning but not of classical conditioning. Two separate sources of evidence support this conjecture. Firstly in the present experiment the classically conditioned CER did not lateralize suggesting an involvement of subcortical mechanisms. Secondly a comparison of acquisition of classical conditioning in normal and hemidecorticate rats found no signs of a mass action deficit (Russell, 1966b).

Speculating on the nature of mass action, Lashley (1929) attributed the manifestation of such learning defects to be produced by task complexity or difficulty. In utilizing an extremely simple situation the present findings would indicate task complexity is not a necessary condition for mass action by any means. Considering the escape response in the runway as a three member chain, it is clear that it is the initial member of the sequence that is the "source" of the impairment for hemidecorticates. These animals do not seem to have any cue discrimination impairment, it is rather a decreased efficiency in the utilization of such cues. It would appear that in part this difficulty results from a failure to exclude such GO responses as circling, entry into corners of the start box, etc.—all of which compete with the required correct GO response of leaving the start box. Hence there is a lack of precision in starting the sequence of behaviour.

V. The Effect of Hemidecortication on GO NO-GO Learning

The suggestion from the previous experiment that the hemidecorticate learning deficit could be attributed to a difficulty in elimination of competing responses implies that the deficit is a quantitative one. Further it is well known that this issue is of central importance in theorizing about the nature of the learning (Harlow, 1959). To examine the generality of this point however, hemidecorticate learning must be examined under different conditions which permit quantitative measurement of competing responses. To meet this requirement a series of experiments was undertaken to investigate the effects of hemidecortication on acquisition of a GO NO-GO discrimination. The presence of a NO-GO component in the learning should present difficulties for hemidecorticates as they must eliminate the GO responses from NO-GO periods if they are to make a discrimination. By using surgical removal of cortex a second objective was to control for the possibility that spread of CSD to the subcortex had been responsible for the results of the previous experiment.

The ablations were made 4 to 6 weeks before any training to allow optimal post-operative recovery time. All operations were performed under aseptic conditions and with the aid of a Zeiss surgical microscope to facilitate aspiration of cortex. An extensive craniotomy was made on either the right or left side of the skull and the dura was opened longitudinally to provide access to the brain. The central sinus, cerebellum, olfactory bulb and the rhinal fissure served as demarcation lines for the extent of the ablation. After removal of tissue was complete and all bleeding staunched, the area was packed with sterile gelfoam and the incision closed. Preliminary histological examination has so far indicated that the extent of ablation ranged from 80% to 95% of complete hemidecortication in all cases. The majority of the sparing appeared to lie on the upper margins of the rhinal fissure and in the frontal pole.

All animals were given identical pretraining in the Skinner box before being presented with the discrimination. After 10 days of bar training under CRF food reinforcement conditions they were transferred to FR 15 via the following stages: 2 days FR 5, 2 days FR 10 and then 5 days of FR 15. At this juncture the GO NO-GO discrimination was introduced. One normal and one hemidecorticate group was given an auditory discrimination consisting of the presence of white noise as the $S+$, and its absence as the $S-$. The other normal and hemidecorticate groups received the same procedure only the presence and absence of light was used instead of white noise. The presentation of the $S+$ and $S-$ periods was alternated at 2 min intervals, with FR 15 reinforcement during $S+$ and no reinforcement available during $S-$ periods. In each daily session 17 such alternations of each stimulus were given. Each group of 5 rats had at least 30 days of training on this Mult FR 15 Ext schedule.

The results showed a clear learning deficit for both hemidecorticate groups on either the sound or brightness discrimination. Acquisition curves for normals and hemidecorticates are given for both discrimination problems in Figs. 3 and 4. For both, the percentage of correct responding out of the daily session total is given for each group over the 30 days of training. It can be seen that for the visual and auditory problems the normals asymptote at about 80% and 90% discrimination levels respectively. The hemidecorticates never attain the same degree of success on either task. They asymptote at about 70% for the visual discrimination and just below 80% for the auditory task.

These differences between hemidecorticates and normals in GO NO-GO learning would appear to involve a similar encoding difficulty to that seen

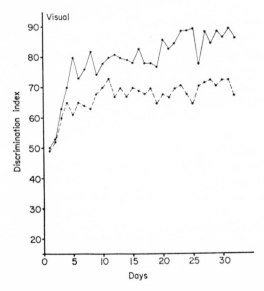

FIG. 3. The average daily discrimination index, GO/(GO + NO − GO), throughout the 30 days of acquisition for normals and hemidecorticates. The normal animals are represented by the solid line, and the hemidecorticates by the dashed line.

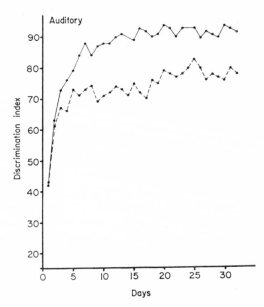

FIG. 4. The average daily discrimination index, GO/(GO + NO − GO), throughout the 30 days of acquisition for normals and hemidecorticates.

in the escape situation. An examination of the response rates for the GO and NO-GO periods for both discrimination tasks reveals that the source of the hemidecorticate impairment lies again in an inefficient control of competing responses. As can be seen in Figs. 5 and 6, there are no significant differences in GO rates. For the visual problem GO rates are overlapping for both groups, whereas for the auditory task the hemidecorticates in fact have a higher response rate than normals for the last 15 days of training. The main difference emerges from the fact that hemidecorticates have approximately three times the amount of NO-GO responding as that of normals. What is not apparent from these rate curves is that this high level of error responding by the hemidecorticates does not represent any difficulty in cue discrimination. The hemidecorticates stopped responding to the bar with the change from $S+$ to $S-$ just as efficiently as normals. However unlike normals they appeared unable to withold responding until the onset of the next $S+$ period. This responding in $S-$ periods was "anticipatory" in form, in that a pronounced FI scallop developed as the end of the $S-$ period approached. In contrast such FI behaviour whilst present in normals was considerably less. With continued training it would become minimal or even absent (see Fig. 7).

A striking feature of the present results is that hemidecortication

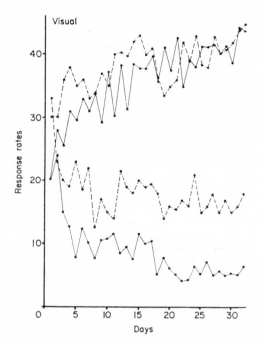

FIG. 5. Average daily rates for GO and NO-GO responding in acquisition for normals and hemidecorticates. The normal response rates are represented by solid lines, those of the hemidecorticates by dashed lines. The two upper curves are GO rates and the two lower curves are NO-GO rates.

produced the same impairment for tasks involving either the visual or the auditory sensory system. It is therefore unlikely that any sensory deficit could be responsible for these results. Hemianopsia following hemidecortication can be discounted as a contributing factor in the rat because there is almost complete cross-over of the optic fibres in the chiasma. In any event no discrimination loss has been found where one eye has been occluded either during acquisition or on retention tests. In fact these control observations on rabbits were somewhat redundant in nature as the choice of ambient illumination to provide the brightness cue avoids such difficulties. Striate loss would be only likely to alter discriminability of pattern vision. Finally the fact that the same defect was found for the auditory discrimination provides the most decisive evidence on this point as the auditory cortical projections are bilaterally symmetrical unlike those for the visual system.

In Lashley's maze learning experiments on mass action a relationship between task difficulty or maze complexity was only found for brain lesioned animals. It will be recalled that the normal rats learned the three

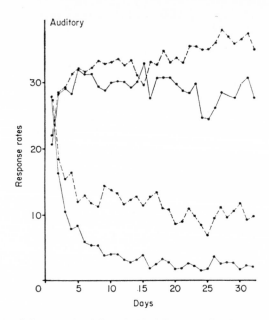

FIG. 6. Average daily rates for GO and NO-GO responding in acquisition for normals and hemidecorticates. The normal responses rates are given by the solid lines, those of the hemidecorticates by dashed lines. The two upper curves are GO rates and the two lower curves are NO-GO rates.

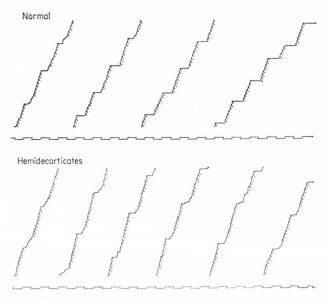

FIG. 7. Cumulative response for individual normal and hemidecorticate performance in a brightness GO NO-GO discrimination. The sequence of $S+$ and $S-$ periods in the session is indicated by the event marker.

different levels of maze complexity in approximately the same number of trials. In the present series of experiments a quantitative defect such as mass action is suggested from the results of the discrimination learning. There is an indication that the normals attained a higher level of performance on the auditory discrimination than that on the visual task. Whilst the hemidecorticates showed a deficit on both discriminations, their performance on the auditory task was significantly superior to that on the visual problem. Further the "errors" made by hemidecorticates in both escape and discrimination learning were different only in quantitative terms from those made by normal rats.

There is in many respects a striking similarity between hemidecorticate errors in the GO NO-GO learning and those observed in the escape situation. In both situations efficient acquisition was impaired by the presence of "inappropriate" GO responses competing with the required response. In escape learning the presence of competing GO responses in the start box component of the task prevented or delayed the initiation of the required behaviour sequence. With regard to the discrimination problems the learning was retarded due to GO responses in the NO-GO periods. This difficulty in elimination of competing responses which seems to be quantitatively enhanced in the hemidecorticate is not easy to account for. It is possible that the animal with a reduction in cortical mass has difficulty in learning due to a loss of inhibitory mechanisms that are involved in the "gating" out of responses. From this point of view it would be expected that the hemidecorticate would show general similarities with the frontal lobe syndrome, where animals have difficulty in GO NO-GO learning due to response perseveration. This similarity breaks down on closer scrutiny. Pribram *et al.* (1961) has shown that frontal perseverative responding in the FI component of a Mult FR FI schedule is characterized by the animal ignoring the $S-$ cue and working though the period. As has been seen hemidecorticate behaviour in a comparable situation is quite different. The fact that frontal animals do not always show perseverative responding has lead Pribram (1964) to suggest that the effect depends on prior reinforcement conditions. He showed that perseveration occurred in all situations in which a perseverative response had been repeatedly reinforced. Response switching occurred in a situation that never reinforced perseverative responses. As competing responses were never reinforced in the escape situation it seems clear that the hemidecorticate impairment cannot be attributed to perseveration.

An alternative explanation is that hemidecortication results in a switching defect, i.e. the animal has difficulty in changing from one response strategy to another. These speculations whilst they may have some descriptive merit, suffer from the quite obvious limitation that they have little explanatory validity. It would seem that perhaps the most profitable line of attack on the problem would be to investigate hemidecorticate learning under parametrically varied conditions. Only by these means is it possible to see whether or not there are any differences in the way this animal processes the information in the learning situation.

VI. Quantitative Nature of the Mass Action Deficit

From the experiments considered so far the salient feature of the learning deficit following unilateral ablation has been an impairment in the rat's ability to cope with errors. It has been seen that from this point of view there are indications that the defect appears to be essentially quantitative in nature rather than qualitative. If this is true it suggests that fundamentally quantitative cortical mechanisms are responsible. Assuming that the high degree of redundancy of connections in the cortex is analogous to the use of redundant circuits in computers, then the principle function of such connections would be to safeguard against errors of information flow. A basic theorem of redundancy theory is that the probability of failure in a redundant network can decrease exponentially as the degree of redundancy is increased arithmetically. Hence it follows that as hemidecortication approximates a 50% reduction in redundant circuits the rat would be left with a potentially error sensitive brain.

Continuing this line of conjecture a little further, a useful property of such a mass action system would be that a loss of network redundancies could be compensated for by appropriate quantitative adjustment of the environmental input to the brain. By isolating the necessary and sufficient inputs that are required to "rebalance" the system some insight into the general computing operations might be gained. The following experiments were performed by Dr. Plotkin, as part of his doctoral thesis, to test this notion in the hope that some clarity in this direction might be gained.

The first experiment was derived from a consideration of certain broad principles of stimulus sampling theory. In analysing learning mechanisms it is important to recognize that the final acquisition of information is achieved via two different sources. Firstly there is what might be termed the *pick-up* of information due to stimulus sampling during the animal's exposure to the situation. This is what has been referred to as acquisition or encoding. Secondly there is a process of *equilibration* of this information gain when the animal is in fact outside the learning situation. Here reference is made to the apparent gain or loss of information as is exemplified by the phenomena of spontaneous recovery or forgetting. These apparently spontaneous changes in learning are highly lawful and related to the effects of distribution of practice. In a closely related series of papers Estes (1953, 1955a, 1955b) was the first to point to the intimate relationship of these phenomena while at the same time providing a coherent theory to explain them. Estes accounts for spontaneous recovery and regression in terms of random changes in the stimulating environment from one time to another. At any time it is assumed that only a fraction of the total population of stimulus elements is available for sampling, the remainder being unavailable to the animal. Over a period of time different stimulus elements may become available for sampling and previously available elements can become unavailable. Hence during such stimulus fluctuation if previously available conditioned elements are replaced during a rest interval by unconditioned elements (formerly unavailable) then forgetting or regression of information occurs. Spontaneous recovery will take place in those elements which have been involved in extinction are replaced by conditioned elements that were formerly unavailable to the animal during extinction. Finally, this notion of constant random stimulus fluctuation has direct relevance to the factor of spacing effects on learning. With long intertrial intervals a substantial turnover of stimulus elements will occur and thus the probability that a broader spectrum of the relevant stimulus complex will be gained over a given number of trials. With short intertrial intervals and little turnover of stimulus elements less information will be gained from the same number of trials.

This time-dependent notion of stimulus fluctuation has a direct relevance for the principle of mass action. A possible hypothesis concerning its nature would be to assume that the mass of cortex in some way determines the rate of change in the proportion of stimulus elements available for sampling. The hemidecorticate impairment was thereby considered to result from a reduction in amount of random turnover of stimulus elements. If this assumption is correct it follows that progressively increasing the spacing between trials would eventually compensate for this defect and result in normal performance.

Eight groups, each of 10 rats, were given two days of avoidance training on the runway. A group of normal and functionally hemidecorticate (CSD) rats were compared at each of the four different intertrial intervals (ITI) involved. The same general training routine and apparatus was used as has been described for the escape learning study. The only difference was that for avoidance training the raising of the start box door presented a buzzer (CS) for 5 sec at the end of which time shock was delivered to the grid floor of the runway. Each days training consisted of a single block of 20 avoidance trials. The latencies and running times were recorded on each trial. An avoidance response was defined in terms of the rat reaching the goal box before the onset of shock.

The results are given in Fig. 7, where the mean number of avoidance responses made out of the first block of 20 trials is given for each group.

The curves for both normals and hemidecorticates are completely parallel, with normals making significantly more avoidances at each ITI. The effect of different time intervals between trials would thus appear to be exactly the same for normals as well as hemidecorticates. Severe impairment of learning was found for both at an ITI of 15 sec. With longer intervals, however, learning approached asymptotes appropriate to the amount of cortex and independent of further time increases between trials.

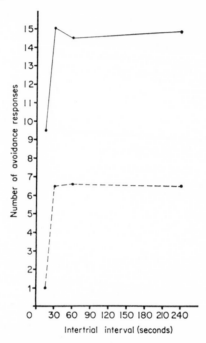

FIG. 8. Average number of avoidance responses made out of the first 20 training trials for normals and hemidecorticates at differing ITIs. The solid line represents the normal performance, the dashed line that of the hemidecorticates.

This flat asymptote is exactly what would be expected from the literature on the effect of distributing acquisition inputs for normal animals. The expectation that there would be a progressive improvement with longer ITIs for hemidecorticates was not fulfilled. Their encoding or acquisition impairment cannot therefore be attributed to equilibration defect due to a reduction in random stimulus fluctuation of stimulus elements. However the model in suggesting a quantitative mechanism on a general level was decisively confirmed by the present results. Both groups responded to changes in ITI in the same qualitative fashion. Only quantitative differences were found between groups.

The hypothesis of alteration in stimulus fluctuation between learning trials as a basis of mass action was abandoned. An alternative hypothesis was made in terms of relating mass of cortex to the duration of sampling on each trial. A second series of experiments was designed where the ITI was held constant and the duration of the CS systematically varied in an attempt to manipulate the nett sampling time of the rat on each trial. In this last study some 14 groups, each of 10 rats, were examined in the same avoidance situation. Normals were compared to hemidecorticates for learning under 7 different durations of the CS warning cue. The ITI used

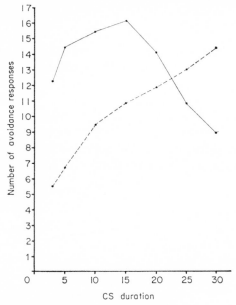

FIG. 9. Average number of avoidance responses made out of the first 20 training trials for normals and hemidecorticates at differing CS durations. Solid line represents normal performance and the dashed line that of hemidecorticates.

throughout was 60 sec which from the previous study was found to be well within the optimal range for both groups.

As can be seen in Fig. 9, entirely different results were found than had been obtained in the previous study. Increasing the CS duration from 3 to 15 sec produced a steady gain in encoding efficiency for normals. It is interesting to note that the 5 sec group here is a replication of the 60 sec ITI normal group of the previous experiment. The scores are in very close agreement. With further increases in CS duration a progressive deterioration of learning was found. This could be expected on the grounds that the CS warning characteristics were becoming progressively more remote from shock onset. In sharp contrast the results for the hemidecorticates show that increase in CS duration was effective in improving learning throughout the entire range. Starting from 3 sec where the encoding was vastly inferior to that of normals, continued gains were made until from 15 to 25 sec the performance neared that of normals and thereafter the hemidecorticate learning was as efficient as that of normals under optimal conditions. At this point it can be seen that the mass action deficit has completely disappeared. The reliability of these results can again be seen by comparing the score of the 5 sec hemidecorticate group in this study with that of the 60 sec hemidecorticate group in the ITI experiment. Both groups had identical treatment and this is reflected by their virtually identical scores. It is clear from these results that a major characteristic of the deficit involves temporal determinants of stimulus sampling. The animal with a reduction in redundant cortical circuits is error sensitive given a brief sampling time. With longer durations this proneness to errors disappears. Clearly what is crucial to know before speculating further, is in what way does the rat utilize the sampling time provided in these experiments by the CS duration. It is felt that this would then given some understanding of why mass action appears to utilize time dependent processes. Current experiments are attempting to clarify this issue.

VII. Conclusions

In considering the experiments as a whole it has been seen that a 50% reduction in cortical mass has produced a marked impairment in learning. By using a hemidecorticate preparation this deficit could not be attributed to any sensory impairment and must therefore provide strong evidence for mass action. The differences found between normal and hemidecorticate animals were seen to be of a quantitative nature. Variables such as task difficulty and changes in ITI that influence normal acquisition also affected hemidecorticates in the same way. Finally quantitative manipulation of stimulus sampling time was found to determine the extent to which the hemidecorticate was able to learn. As this evidence was lacking in Lashley's original observations, the present findings would indicate that the principle of mass action can no longer be disregarded.

A recognition that the cortex has mass action characteristics has important implications for considerations about brain-behaviour mechanisms. The most important consequence could be a drastic devaluation in the currency of localization theories of memory. Perhaps, however, in making that statement one is guilty of considerable naïvety.

A striking and curious feature of localization theories of memory is that they persist in the face of an almost total lack of evidence in their support. probably the main reason for approaching memory in these terms is that it is difficult to conceive of any other approach to the problem. However with the advent of optical holograms (Gabor, 1949; Leith and Upatnieks, 1964) we now have an example of information storage which is not localized but distributed. Leith and Upatnieks (1964) have shown in fact the most remarkable mass action characteristics are possessed by holograms. For example any small portion of the hologram, whose area is above a certain minimum is capable of producing a reconstruction of the entire image of object recorded. Further, the smaller the area of the hologram that is used to reconstruct the image, the more its reconstruction is degraded. In terms of the past tendency of neurophysiology to be influenced in its thinking by the technology of the times, it is to be hoped that the hologram will perhaps remove the necessity for thinking of the brain in terms of localization theory.

Perhaps one further but less polemical point may be made before concluding. At the onset of this chapter the rationale given for beginning was a concern with evaluating the learning characteristics of the split-brain animal. An answer may now be given. In the rat at least while the exclusion of one hemisphere will produce a quantitative impairment on some learning tasks, it will not be in any way qualitatively different from a normal animal.

References

Bureš, J. and Burešová, O. (1966). The effect of independent storage of left and right turn discrimination in both hemispheres on subsequent reversal and alternation learning. *Act. neuroveg. Sup.* **8**, 198.

Bureš, J. (1959). Reversible decortication and behavior. *In* "Central Nervous System and Behavior". (M. A. B. Brazier, ed.). Jos. Macy Found., New York, U.S.A.

Downer, J. C. L. (1958). Role of corpus callosum in transfer of training in Macaca mulatta. *Fedn. Proc. Fedn. Am. Socs exp. Biol.* **17**, 37.

Estes, W. K. and Burke, C. J. (1953). A theory of stimulus variability in learning. *Psychol. Rev.* **60**, 276.

Estes, W. K. (1955a). Statistical theory of spontaneous recovery and regression. *Psychol. Rev.* **62**, 145.

Estes, W. K. (1955b). Statistical theory of distributional phenomena in learning. *Psychol. Rev.* **62**, 369.

Fifková, E. (1964). Spreading EEG depression in neo, paleo, archicortical structures of the brain of the rat. *Physiologia bohemoslov.* **13**, 1.

Fifková, E. and Bureš, J. (1964). Spreading depression in mammalian striatum. *Archs. int. Physiol. Biochem.* **72**, 171.

Fifková, E. and Syka, J. (1964). Relationships between cortical and striatal spreading depression in the rat. *Expl. Neurol.* **9**, 355.

Gabor, D. (1949). *Proc. R. Soc. Lond.* **A197**, 454.

Harlow, H. F. (1959). Learning set and error factor theory. *In* "Psychology: A Study of a Science". (S. Koch, ed.), Vol. 2. McGraw-Hill, New York, U.S.A.

Lashley, K. S. (1929). "Brain Mechanisms and Intelligence". University Press, Chicago, U.S.A.

Lashley, K. S. (1943). Studies of cerebral function in learning. XII. Loss of the maze habit after occipital lesion in the blind rat. *J. comp. Neurol.* **79,** 431.

Hunter, W. S. (1930). A consideration of Lashley's theory of the equipotentiality of cerebral action. *J. gen. Psychol.* **3,** 455.

Leith, E. and Upatnieks, J. (1964). *J. opt. Soc. Am.* **54,** 1295.

Myers, R. E. (1955). Interocular transfer of pattern discrimination in cats following section of crossed optic fibers. *J. comp. physiol. Psychol.* **48,** 470.

Myers, R. E. (1956). Function of the corpus callosum in interocular transfer. *Brain,* **79,** 358.

Myers, R. E. (1961). Corpus callosum and visual gnosis. *In* "Brain Mechanisms and Learning". (J. Delafresnaye *et al.,* eds.). Blackwell, Oxford, England.

Pribram, K. H. (1961). A further experimental analysis of the behavioral deficit that follows injury to the primate frontal cortex. *Exp. Neurol.* **3,** 432.

Pribam, K. H., Ahumada, A., Hartog, J. and Ross, L. (1964). A progress report on the neurological processes disturbed by frontal lesions in primates. *In* "The Frontal Granular Cortex and Behavior". (J. M. Warren and K. Akert, eds.). McGraw-Hill, New York, U.S.A.

Russell, I. S. (1966a). Animal learning and memory. *In* "Aspects of learning and Memory". (D. Richter, ed.). Heineman, London, England.

Russell, I. S. (1966b). Differential role of the cerebral cortex in classical and instrumental conditioning. *In* "Biological and Physiological Problems of Psychology" XVIII Intern. Cong. Psychol. Symposium on Classical and Instrumental conditioning. Moscow.

Russell, I. S. and Ochs, S. (1960). Localization of behavioral control in one cortical hemisphere. *Physiologist,* **3,** 3.

Russell, I. S. and Ochs, S. (1963). Localization of a memory trace in one cortical hemisphere and transfer to the other hemisphere. *Brain,* **86,** 37.

Sperry, R. W. (1961). Cerebral organization and behavior. *Science,* **133,** 1749.

Sperry, R. W., Stamm, J. S. and Miner, N. (1956). Relearning tests for interocular transfer following division of optic chiasma and corpus callosum in cats. *J. comp. physiol. Psychol.* **49,** 529.

Trevarthen, C. (1956). Functional interactions between the cerebral hemispheres of the split-brain monkey. *In* "Functions of the Copus Callosum". (E. G. Ettlinger, ed.). Ciba Study Group, **20,** J. & A. Churchill, London, England.

Tsang, Y. S. (1934). The functions of the visual area of the cerebral cortex of the rat in the learning and retention of the maze. I. *Comp. Psychol. Monog.* **10,** 4.

Tsang, Y. S. (1936). The functions of the visual areas of the cerebral cortex of the rat in the learning and retention of the maze. II. *Comp. Psychol. Monog.* **12,** 57.

Van Harreveld, A. and Bogen, J. E. (1956). Regional differences in the propagation of spreading cortical depression in the rabbit. *Proc. Soc. exp. Biol. Med.* **91,** 297.

Woolsey, C. N. (1958). Organization of the somatic sensory and motor areas of the cerebral cortex. *In* "Biological and Biochemical Bases of Behavior. (H. F. Harlow and C. N. Woolsey, eds.). University of Wisconsin Press, Madison, U.S.A.

Zubek, J. P. (1951). Studies in somesthesis. I. Role of the somesthetic cortex in roughness discrimination in the rat. *J. comp. physiol. Psychol.* **44,** 339.

14

Response Continuity and Timing Behaviour

R. A. BOAKES

University of Sussex, Brighton, Sussex, England

I. Introduction

In most studies of discrimination learning the situation is defined by the experimenter in terms of discrete response alternatives: the subject can approach or avoid, go left or go right, peck a key or not peck a key. This paper is concerned with the question of what is learned in a discrimination in which the response alternatives are only quantitatively different. More specifically the experiments described here are relevant to the following question: if an animal is trained to delay a certain time in the presence of a light of one intensity, and to delay a different time to some other intensity, how does it respond to lights of intermediate intensity?

One possible answer is that there is effectively no difference between this kind of situation and one in which the discreteness of the responses is made explicit. If timing behaviour is based on some mediating chain of responses, it seems likely that an animal might learn two distinct response patterns to the two training stimuli. The evidence for this kind of learning would be a tendency to alternate between these patterns in the presence of intermediate stimuli.

However, there are reasons for believing that under some conditions there must be a difference between these two kinds of discrimination. For example, suppose that the training procedure was extended so that the animal was exposed to more than just two pairings between an intensity level and an imposed delay in such a way that an orderly relationship between intensity and delay was maintained. It is possible that at a certain stage the behaviour of the animal could no longer be described as a set of independent stimulus-response units, but would take the form of a continuous relationship between a stimulus dimension and a response dimension.

II. Response Continuity

The subject of response continuity is of particular interest in animal psychophysics for the problem of devising methods for obtaining sensory scales. Consider an analogous experiment with human subjects: an observer is instructed that a certain bright light has the value "100" and a dim light has the value "10"; subsequently a series of lights of intermediate intensity are presented to which he is asked to assign numbers that seem appropriate with respect to the two original values. If the numbers he assigns change continuously and monotonically as a function of luminous intensity, the results of such an experiment may be interpreted as giving information about the visual system of the observer. If, further, certain features of the obtained function are found to be invariant under a range of different conditions, it becomes possible to construct a scale for perceived brightness.

It is not at all clear whether animals can behave in such a way and even less clear is the kind of training procedure that might be equivalent to the brief verbal instructions given to the human observer. The latter's competence may depend on a long history of various kinds of training and getting an animal to display a similar type of behaviour may require a similarly extended training procedure.

The research reported here does no more than scratch the surface of the general problem of how the above kind of behaviour is acquired. The training procedure was limited to the case of just two alternatives, partly because this is the obvious place to start and partly because one of the reasons for performing the experiments was to explore the use of the method as a way of scaling sensory continua; for the latter purpose it is desirable to minimize the constraints imposed by the procedure. The findings are tentative in that they are obtained from small groups of subjects. This limitation arose because it was found that to produce precise timing behaviour that is sufficiently resistant to extinction to allow adequate testing, demands an extremely careful and lengthy training procedure.

There has been little research on this type of problem. Two studies have obtained results which suggest that when training is limited to two stimulus-response pairings the situation is effectively identical to one in which only discrete alternatives are possible. In an experiment by Migler (1964) rats were trained to press two levers in succession. With one click frequency reinforcement was contingent upon a correct sequence of responses; with a second and higher frequency reinforcement was in addition contingent upon the occurrence of a certain delay between the two responses. Once the subjects were responding appropriately occasional probe trials were introduced in which clicks of intermediate frequencies were presented. It was found that the intervals between responses, the response-response times, were distributed bimodally in these probe trials: the subjects responded to a test stimulus with delays appropriate to one of the two training stimuli and no intermediate values were obtained. A similar result was obtained by Cumming and Eckerman (1965) from an experiment in which pigeons were used as subjects, spatial position as the response dimension and light intensity as the stimulus dimension. Both studies suggest that such a discrimination is learnt in terms of discrete response alternatives.

The possibility that the response can vary in a continuous fashion is implied in a paper by Herrnstein and van Sommers (1962), which describes a study in which luminous intensity is used as the stimulus dimension and rate of responding as the dependent variable. During training a multiple DRL schedule with five components was used, such that short DRL values were associated with high intensity stimuli. When test stimuli of intermediate intensities were presented, rates of responding were obtained that were intermediate to the response rate to the two adjacent training stimuli. The procedure used in this study was proposed as a method for scaling sensory magnitudes with animals, apparently on the assumption that what the subjects had learned could be described as "the brighter the light, the faster I go". However, these intermediate rates could well have been the result of averaging over mixed patterns of responding in the manner described by Migler. To discover whether such a mixing process is responsible for changes in rates of responding one needs to obtain information about the distribution of inter-response times in this kind of situation.

When this was done, by using the oscilloscope technique described by Blough (1963) to analyse inter-response times, it became clear that there was no simple basis underlying changes in response rates (Boakes, 1966). Differences in rates of responding to stimuli of different intensities resulted from a number of factors; for example, the relative frequency of bursts, the occurrence of long pauses, and changes in the position and variability of the primary modes. The results suggested the interesting possibility that continuous changes in responding could occur only if higher response rates were correlated with the brighter stimuli during training. When the training conditions were reversed so that high response rates were correlated with dim stimuli, mixing behaviour occurred. However, the principle result of the experiment was to indicate that some other approach should be taken to explore this kind of possibility.

The procedure used in the following experiments is very similar to the one described by Migler. This was adopted because the response variable— that of the time elapsing between a response on one manipulandum and a response on a second manipulandum—appears from his data and that from similar studies (e.g. Mechner and Guevrekian, 1962) to give a very clean measure of timing behaviour, in that the distributions of intervals are unimodal, regular and relatively compact. One important change was introduced. This was to remove what appeared to be a lack of symmetry in Migler's procedure, which may well have been a critical factor causing mixing behaviour. This asymmetry arises because, whereas in the presence of one frequency reinforcement is contingent upon a pause of a certain duration between the two responses, in the presence of the second frequency no pause is required. Though the measure used by the experimenter varies along a single dimension, it seems possible that the units of behaviour acquired by the animal are qualitatively different. Essentially the point is that with this procedure the animal learns to pause t seconds to one frequency and not to pause to another frequency; to investigate response continuity what is required is that the animal learns to pause t_1 seconds to frequency f_1, and to pause t_2 seconds to frequency f_2.

Experiment 1 was performed to find out what happens when this asymmetry is removed by imposing temporal constraints on both components of the training schedule.

III. Experiment 1

In the initial stage of this experiment two groups of subjects were used (Groups A and B) for which the only difference in conditions was the size of the shorter delay interval. An unexpected discovery was that the size of this interval appeared to be an important factor in determining the manner in which the subjects responded to intermediate stimuli. In order to ascertain that this was the critical variable a third group (Group C) was subsequently added. In the intervening period slight changes occurred in the intensity values of the stimuli. Since the procedure and apparatus were otherwise identical for all three groups, the study is reported as a single experiment and the differences for Group C are noted where necessary.

A. METHOD

Subjects

Six adult male White Carneau pigeons with a prior experimental history limited to CRF and extinction. These were arbitrarily assigned to three groups. All six birds were maintained at 80% of their free feeding weight throughout the experiment.

Apparatus

A standard experimental chamber, measuring $12'' \times 12'' \times 12''$, was used, in which one wall contained a grain magazine and two response keys. Key 1 was mounted at a height of $9\frac{1}{2}''$ above the floor. Key 2 was displaced $3\frac{1}{2}''$ to the left at a height of $7\frac{1}{2}''$ above the floor. Key 1 was transilluminated by two 6W AC bulbs, whose intensity could be maintained at any one of nine levels by means of a resistor network. An amber filter was placed between the bulbs and the key to minimize spectral changes. The luminance of the key was measured at intervals throughout the experiment using a Macbeth illuminometer. These values are shown in Table I, in dB. re 10^{-7} lamberts, where "Stimulus 1" indicates the least intense and "Stimulus 9" the most intense of the levels. Key 2 was transilluminated by a dim red bulb. Reinforcement consisted of the presentation of mixed grain for a 3 sec period.

TABLE I

Luminous intensity of Key 1 in dB. re 10^{-7} lamberts for Groups A, B and C

Stimulus	1	2	3	4	5	6	7	8	9
Groups A and B	57·8	60·4	65·7	67·8	73·0	75·1	79·9	81·6	85·7
Group C	56·3	59·2	64·4	67·4	72·0	74·5	79·1	81·6	85·5

Daily sessions consisted of 400 trials. At the beginning of a trial Key 1 was illuminated. A single response (R_1) on this key switched on the red light behind Key 2 and each trial lasted 8 seconds from this first response. Reinforcement was contingent upon a single response (R_2) on Key 2 that occurred at a time greater than T, but less than $T + h$, after R_1. The values of T and h are specified below. If R_2 occurred outside this "correct" interval, both key lights were extinguished for the remainder of the trial. A feed-back relay sounded for the first response on Key 1 and the first response on Key 2 and only these responses were at all effective. During an inter-trial period of 3 sec the test chamber was completely dark and no response had any effect.

The interval between the beginning of a trial and R_1 is termed the "latency" and the interval between R_1 and R_2 the "response-response time" (RRT). During probe trials both latency and RRT were measured in units of $\frac{1}{3}$ sec.

The length of a daily session depended only on the latency period before R_1 and was of the order of 100 minutes. The values of the imposed delay interval (T) and the limited hold (h) were varied in the following manner.

B. PRELIMINARY TRAINING

With the illumination of Key 1 at its lowest value (Stimulus 1) the subjects were first shaped to peck Key 1 and then Key 2. Very few reinforcements were needed to establish this behaviour before introducing the pause conditions. Initially the value of T was small, with a large limited hold value. T was progressively increased until it reached a value of $5\frac{1}{3}$ sec and the value of h was then reduced to $1\frac{1}{3}$ sec. Thus at this stage reinforcement was contingent on a pause of between $5\frac{1}{3}$ sec and $6\frac{2}{3}$ sec.

When the RRT distribution had become stable, with a single mode at or around $5\frac{1}{3}$ sec, Stimulus 9 was introduced and from then on the two training stimuli were presented with equal frequency in a semi-random sequence. For Group A the value of T in the presence of this second stimulus was $1\frac{1}{3}$ sec for Group B, $\frac{2}{3}$ sec and for Group C, $\frac{1}{3}$ sec. For all groups the value of h for this second component was initially 2 sec. When the birds had received from ten to fifteen reinforcements in the presence of Stimulus 9, the size of the hold was progressively decreased to a value of $h = \frac{1}{3}$ sec. Thus at the end of the preliminary training in the presence of Stimulus 9 reinforcement was contingent on the following delay times:

$$\text{Group A: } 1\tfrac{1}{3}\text{--}1\tfrac{2}{3} \text{ sec}$$
$$\text{Group B: } \tfrac{2}{3}\text{--}1 \quad \text{ sec}$$
$$\text{Group C: } \tfrac{1}{3}\text{--}\tfrac{2}{3} \quad \text{ sec}$$

C. FINAL TRAINING

The final stage of the preliminary training was maintained until the RRT distributions were consistently appropriate to the conditions correlated with the two stimulus values. This was achieved from two to three weeks after the beginning of training. The probability of reinforcement following a correct response chain was then reduced from 1·0 to 0·4. In order to reduce the variability at the beginning of a session this reduction did not take effect until the bird had received ten reinforcements in any daily session.

The reduction in probability had little or no effect on the RRT distributions. This schedule was maintained for fifteen sessions to ensure stability prior to beginning the testing procedure.

D. TESTING PROCEDURE

During test sessions probe trials were introduced on average every nine trials, after the bird had obtained the first ten reinforcements. The minimum separation between probe trials was five trials. During a probe trial a test stimulus was introduced on Key 1 and the latency and RRT were recorded on print-out counters. No reinforcement was available, but otherwise conditions were identical to those of a training trial. In Migler's study only one test stimulus was used per session; in the present experiment all nine stimuli were each presented four times in a session. This made it possible to study changes during the testing period, which lasted for fifteen successive sessions. Stimuli 1 and 9 were included among the probe trials as a check against possible artefacts in the test procedure. Sequences of stimuli were programmed on punched tape and order was randomized within the constraint that each stimulus occurred once per block of nine stimuli.

E. RESULTS

The performance of each bird on the final day of training is shown in Fig. 1. The RRT distributions for Stimuli 1 and 9 are in terms of the relative frequency of the R_2 response for successive intervals of $\frac{2}{3}$ sec and are obtained over the entire session. The clear separation between the distributions indicates that the two behaviour patterns were fully differentiated and under the control of the stimulus conditions.

The fifteen test sessions were divided into three successive groups of five in order to analyse overall changes during the testing period. Since an R_2 response in the presence of any stimulus other than 1 or 9 was never allowed by reinforcement, the test procedure is also a form of discrimination training. This was reflected in an increase in the frequency of probe trials in which no R_2 response occurred as testing was continued. In calculating the median response-response times, shown in Fig. 2, only those trials in which R_2 did occur were included. Counting failures to respond on the second key as extra long RRTs would have distorted the results for the later test sessions. This statistical decision appeared to be justified by the form of the distributions. The median values in Fig. 2 were obtained from twenty readings, except when failures to respond occurred. When less than five readings were available, no median is shown.

It can be seen from Fig. 2 that the functions for Group A are very different to those obtained for the other groups. For Group A the median

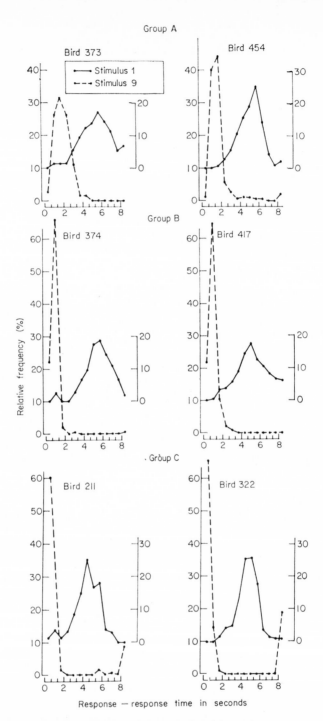

FIG. 1. RRT distributions for Groups A, B and C from the session immediately prior to testing. The distributions are obtained over all 400 trials of the session and thus the relative frequencies are calculated from about 200 trials for each stimulus.

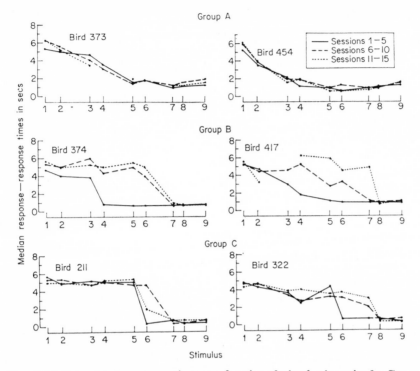

FIG. 2. Median response-response times as a function of stimulus intensity for Groups A, B and C.

Each median is calculated from a possible twenty probe trials, omitting those in which no response was made on Key 2. Where, for a given stimulus, there were less than five RRTs in a group of five sessions, no median is shown.

RRT changes continuously with intensity and the function remains stable throughout the testing period. For Group C and Bird 374 of Group B the change of RRT with intensity is more in the nature of a step function. No clear pattern emerges from the results for Bird 417 of Group B: for the first five sessions the function is similar to that obtained for Group A, whereas that for the final five sessions possibly resembles a step function.

The origin of these differences can be seen by examining the distributions from which the medians are obtained. These are shown in Fig. 3 where the unit of analysis is again $\frac{2}{3}$ sec as in Fig. 1. The distributions shown were obtained over the first five test sessions; with further testing the only change was an increase in overall variability for stimuli in the middle of the range which was most marked for Group B. The frequencies are relative to the total number of probe trials. The distributions for Group A show that the median functions are based on continuous changes

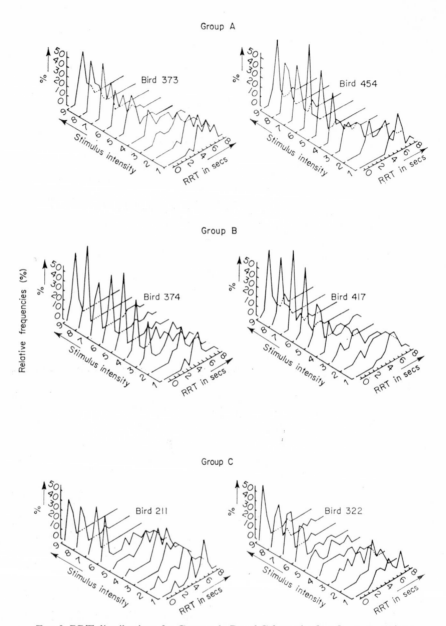

FIG. 3. RRT distributions for Groups A, B and C from the first five test sessions.

in the underlying behaviour. This appears to apply also to Bird 417 of Group B. On the other hand the origin of the step functions for the remaining birds is shown to be the result of averaging over bimodal distributions. If instead of using the median in Fig. 2 we had used some kind of mean, then the result of averaging would have been to produce a continuous function for these birds also.

The latencies for the six birds are shown in Fig. 4. Each point represents the median of twenty readings and since the range of latencies varies widely between subjects, the values are shown on a logarithmic scale. The general pattern is that latency is least at the extremes of the range, with the latency for Stimulus 1 greater than that for Stimulus 9. For group A continued testing results in an increase in the latencies to all stimuli, but particularly in the middle of the range, while the overall form of the function is not greatly changed. No general pattern can be detected in the latency functions for the remaining birds.

It seems worth pointing out that the relationship between latency and stimulus intensity indicates a dependency between the two components of the response chain. If they were independent, one would expect no change in the latency since an R_1 response is always followed by the same conditioned reinforcement, the onset of the red light behind Key 2, irrespective of the luminance of Key 1.

F. Discussion

The results show that both mixing behaviour, which is equivalent to a discrimination involving discrete alternatives, and a continuous change in the response variable can occur in this kind of situation. Thus, removing the asymmetry present in Migler's design is not a sufficient condition for obtaining the continuous case. The fact that the latter becomes more likely as the shorter delay interval is increased suggests that an additional condition is that both imposed delay intervals exceed a certain threshold value. It seems reasonable to suppose that, if the delay interval set by the experimenter is made sufficiently short, the result is equivalent to imposing no pause conditions whatsoever. Furthermore if this is accompanied by a short "hold" value so that a bird fails to receive reinforcement unless it responds on the second key very quickly after its response on the first (as for Group C), it does not seem surprising that the resultant behaviour might be qualitatively different from that produced by a longer pause interval when "delaying" is reinforced. In other words, the apparent symmetry of the conditions defined by the experimenter might mask what is a distinct difference for the subject.

In the present situation this threshold value appears to be of the order of 1 sec; it seems plausible to believe that this would depend very much on

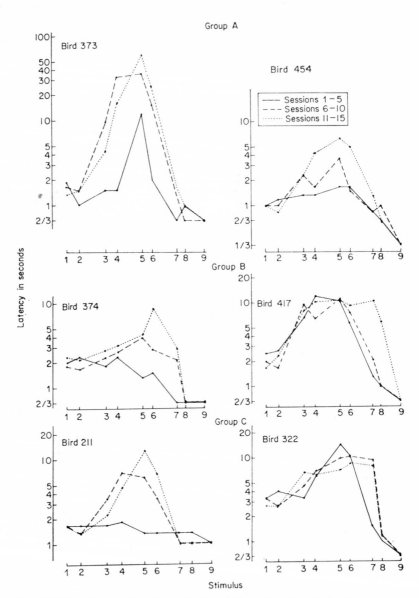

FIG. 4. Median latencies for Groups A, B and C as a function of stimulus intensity.

the spacing of the response keys and would be minimal in the case where temporal constraints are imposed on successive responses on the same manipulandum—as with the DRL schedules used by Herrnstein and van Sommers. From this point of view the instability of Group B during testing may reflect the fact that the imposed delay interval for Group B was approximately the same as the threshold value for this situation.

IV. Experiment 2

The functions relating response-response time to stimulus intensity for the birds in Group A are continuous, but not monotonic, as would be the case if they had learned something of the kind: "the dimmer the light, the longer the delay". In order to determine whether this finding was limited to the particular combination of stimulus range and temporal parameters used in Experiment 1 a second experiment was undertaken, which was designed also to provide evidence on two further points.

The first of these was whether the way in which the response and stimulus dimensions are related is a purely arbitrary matter. The evidence from the earlier study referred to above suggested a directional effect for luminous intensity, in that there appeared to be a greater likelihood of mixing behaviour when increases in brightness were correlated with decreases in response rate. Therefore two groups were used in the present experiment: for Group F the conditions were identical to those for Group A in Experiment 1, except that the stimulus range was reduced, while for Group G an additional change was to associate the dimmer training stimulus with the shorter imposed delay interval.

The second point concerned the significance of behaviour occurring between the first response on Key 1 and the response on Key 2. It had been noted that this frequently took the form of continued responding on the first key, even though only the first response was accompanied by the sound of the feed-back relay and was required to switch on the red light behind Key 2. It was decided to record these responses in order to determine whether they could be regarded as mediating the observed timing behaviour.

A. METHOD

Subjects

Seven adult male White Carneau pigeons which were arbitrarily assigned to two groups. Group F consisted of Birds 202, 368, 289 and 250. Group G consisted of Birds 246, 287 and 346. All birds were maintained at 80% of their free feeding weight throughout the experiment.

Apparatus

The apparatus differed from that used in the previous experiment in two ways. The two keys were in this case both at the same level, $9\frac{1}{2}''$ above the floor. Key 1 was mounted in the mid-line of the panel and Key 2 was displaced $3\frac{1}{2}''$ to the left. To illuminate Key 1 a projection bulb (Sylvania Type DFC) was operated at a maximum of 90V AC using a step-down transformer and variety of intensity levels could be obtained by tapping the transformer at a number of points. The beam passed through a narrow band green filter (Kodak Wratten 73) before projecting on to the back of Key 1. Nine different intensity levels were again used. The luminance values of Key 1 are shown in Table II. It should be noted that the total luminance range is only 16 dB. as compared with the 18 dB. range in Experiment 1.

TABLE II

Luminous intensity of Key 1 in dB. re 10^{-7} lamberts for Groups F and G

Stimulus	1	2	3	4	5	6	7	8	9
Intensity	71·8	74·2	76·8	78·0	79·6	81·9	83·8	85·9	88·1

B. PROCEDURE

The training schedule for both groups was identical to that used in Experiment 1 and illustrated in Fig. 1, with temporal parameters the same as those for Group A. For Group F the longer delay was imposed in the presence of Stimulus 1 and the shorter delay in the presence of Stimulus 9. The stimulus conditions were reversed for Group G.

Preliminary training differed only in some details from the previous account. Both groups were initially trained on the long delay component, which mean that Group G was first trained in the presence of Stimulus 9. One change consisted of making the progressive reduction in the size of the hold (h) for the short component slower than before. For the session in which the second stimulus was first introduced, the value was 2 sec; for each successive session this was made $\frac{1}{3}$ sec less, until the terminal value of $\frac{1}{3}$ sec was reached. Similarly the transition to a lower probability of reinforcement was made less abrupt than before. This was effected by first waiting until the first fifty reinforcements had been obtained before reducing the probability to 0·4; in the next session until forty reinforcements had been obtained, and so on. If after ten sessions at the final training stage, where the reduction in probability took place after ten reinforcements, behaviour remained stable and appropriate to the conditions, test sessions commenced. As before these consisted of the introduction of probe trials on average every nine trials. Latency, response-response time and the number of responses occurring on Key 1 were recorded for each probe trial.

No interruption occurred in the development of the behaviour of the birds under the inverse stimulus conditions (Group G). In contrast some difficulty arose in the training of each member of Group F. With one of the subjects no response occurred on the second key in up to 50% of the short component trials and this behaviour persisted even after the training procedure had been repeated (Bird 202, see Figs. 6 and 7). With the other three birds of the group disturbances occurred in the long component. In the final stage of training there was a tendency for the RRT distributions in the long component to drift towards shorter values, thus leading to lower rates of reinforcement. With Birds 368 and 289 this tendency was halted by reverting to a probability of reinforcement of $P = 1$ for one session. This proved sufficient for Bird 368, but with Bird 289 a similar deterioration in performance occurred again under the test conditions. The performance of Bird 250 collapsed completely in the final stage and the training procedure was twice repeated. On the final attempt it was decided to omit the reduction in reinforcement probability and so under the test conditions the probability of reinforcement for this bird was $P = 1$.

C. Results and Discussion

1. Response-response Times and Continuity

The RRT distributions for the session immediately prior to testing are shown in Fig. 5. For Group G these are seen to be appropriate to the conditions, with modes around the lower bounds of the correct intervals and little variability between subjects. For Group F the distributions are far less regular. Inappropriate features of the behaviour include the high frequency of failures to respond on Key 2 in the case of Bird 202 and the relative preponderance of short RRTs in the case of Bird 250. For the latter this meant that, though the probability of reinforcement following a correct response sequence was $P = 1$, the actual rate of reinforcement was not very different from that of the other birds.

As in Experiment 1 median response-response times for each stimulus during probe trials were calculated over successive groups of five test sessions. Those are shown in Fig. 6. Trials in which no R_2 response occurred were again omitted and where less than five readings remained no median is given. After a few sessions Bird 368 seldom responded on the second key to stimuli in the middle of the range, so that for this subject a median function could be obtained only for Sessions 1—5. Since the median functions in Fig. 6 do not provide a very clear picture on their own, they are better considered in conjunction with the distributions from which they are obtained. Those for the first five sessions are shown in Fig. 7.

The only major difference between Group F in the present experiment

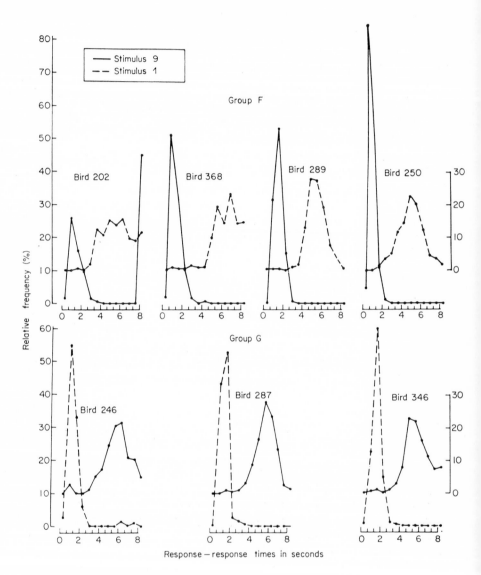

FIG. 5. RRT distributions for Groups F and G from the session immediately prior to testing.

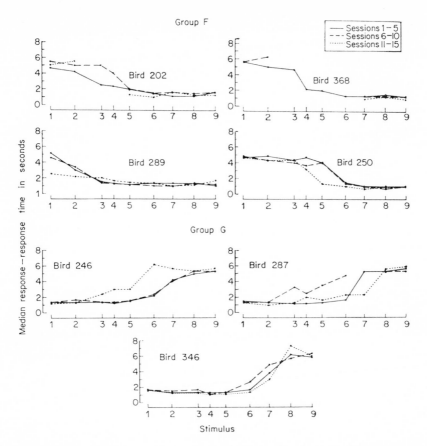

FIG. 6. Median response-response times as a function of intensity for Groups F and G.

and Group A in Experiment 1 is the reduction in the stimulus range. The major effect of this is to increase the difficulty of the learning situation and to decrease the stability of the final performance. Examination of Figs. 6 and 7 shows that for all subjects in Group F, except for Bird 250, the same kind of test performance is obtained, namely a continuous change in response-response times. At low intensities the distributions for Bird 289 in Fig. 7 are bimodal but this is misleading in that it represents the collapse of performance in the long component in Session 5. This collapse took the form of consistently short RRTs in the presence of Stimulus 1 and thus almost no reinforcement, extremely long latencies and an absence of continued responding on Key 1. This collapse also occurred in Sessions 6, 7, 11, 12 and 13 and had a major effect on the median function for the final

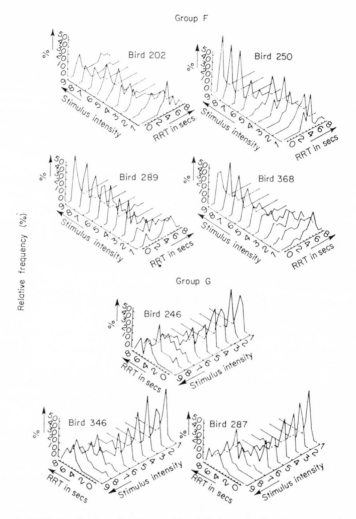

FIG. 7. RRT distributions for Groups F and G from the first five test sessions.

five sessions, as is shown in Fig. 6. However, within a single session the RRTs were distributed unimodally.

In contrast Bird 250 quite clearly exhibits mixing behaviour in Fig. 7. The explanation for this discrepancy is suggested by the RRT distributions for Stimulus 9 in both Figs. 5 and 7. These delay times are abnormally short as compared both to those of the remaining members of the group and to those of Group A. Thus it seems that, like Group C in Experiment 1, this subject learned to delay to one stimulus but not to the second. Bird 250 was exceptional in two other respects: its behaviour was the least stable of all seven birds and it was the only bird which did not continue to peck the first key during the long component. This last feature was present from the very beginning of training, while continued responding in the first key in the short component occurred soon after the second training stimulus was introduced. This again suggests that this subject had acquired two distinct response patterns.

On the other hand the presence of continued responding on Key 1 during both components indicates (for reasons that are discussed in more detail below) that the remaining subjects in Group F and also Group G had not acquired distinct response patterns. Thus the appearance of mixing behaviour during testing for all members of Group G, as shown in Fig. 7, must be due to something more fundamental. This result confirms the suggestion of the single-key experiment (Boakes, 1966) discussed earlier of a directional effect along the dimension of luminous intensity. A similar finding occurs in human psychophysics where subjects can scale "brightness" or "loudness" more easily than they can "dimness" or "softness".

Other indications of this directional effect are the differences between Groups F and G in the speed of acquisition and the stability of the final performance. The only previous reference to this kind of effect is by Green (1953) who reported that response differentiation developed much more quickly when a schedule reinforcing high rates of responding was paired with a large stimulus and one leading to low rates was paired with a small stimulus, than when the conditions were reversed.

The results of these two experiments that are relevant to response continuity can be summarized as follows. When a pigeon has been trained to delay a certain time to one luminance level and to delay some other time to a second luminance level, its delay times will vary continuously as the value of the stimulus intensity is changed within this range, unless (a) the acquired behaviour consists of two distinct response patterns, as is particularly likely to happen if the shorter imposed delay interval is brief, or (b) the relationship between stimulus and response dimensions is such that the longer delay time is associated with the brighter stimulus. These results may be peculiar both to pigeons and to time as a response dimension. The experiment by Cumming and Eckerman (1965) suggests that it does not hold when spatial position is the response dimension. Also when two Rhesus monkeys were used as subjects, under conditions very similar to those for Groups A and F, clear mixing behaviour was obtained during testing. A full description of this experiment and a more detailed presentation of the experiments discussed here are found in Boakes (1966).

2. *Latencies*

It was noted in Experiment 1 that latencies were larger for Stimulus 1 than for Stimulus 9 and that this difference could not be attributed to any systematic difference in the rates of reinforcement in the two components of the schedule. However, the experimental conditions leave open the question of whether the latency difference is due to the temporal contingencies or to the stimulus intensities. Do the subjects pause longer before pecking Key 1 because it is dimmer or because, following the response, there is a longer delay before reinforcement becomes available? The present experiment allows an answer to this question. The latencies for all subjects are plotted in Fig. 8 and it can be seen that for Group G latencies are greater for Stimulus 9 than for Stimulus 1, while for all birds in Group F the opposite holds. This provides strong evidence that the temporal contingencies are the major determinants of latency. No residual effect due to intensity differences could be detected.

3. *Timing and Behaviour During the Delay Interval*

A problem of analysis arises whenever an animal's behaviour exhibits some form of temporal patterning. Given that it does not arise because of a periodic external change, it is of interest to discover whether this pattern is controlled by an internal clock and thus represents "timing" behaviour, or whether it results from the accurate repetition of some overt chain of responses. When the situation is one in which the animal is required to make a single temporal discrimination this question is quite difficult to answer. One has first to identify regular behaviour patterns occurring during the timing interval and then, in order to discover whether this is primary and the "timing" secondary, manipulate this behaviour in various ways which on the whole give only indirect evidence on the question of mediation. An example of this approach is the experiment by Laties *et al.* (1965) and the whole topic is reviewed elsewhere in this volume by Harzem.

The situation described in this chapter, in which each subject is required to make two temporal discriminations, is a powerful method for approaching this question. In the first place if the delay between responses on the two keys were mediated by response chaining, the subjects would have to learn a different chain to each of the two training stimuli. If the interpolated activity were incidental to the timing behaviour (and there is no reason to expect birds to be patiently immobile) it could quite well take the same form in both components. As reported above and shown in Fig. 9, the behaviour of Bird 250 took a different form in the two components, but this was not true of any other subject in either Groups F or G. With the latter the interpolated activity took the very convenient form for recording

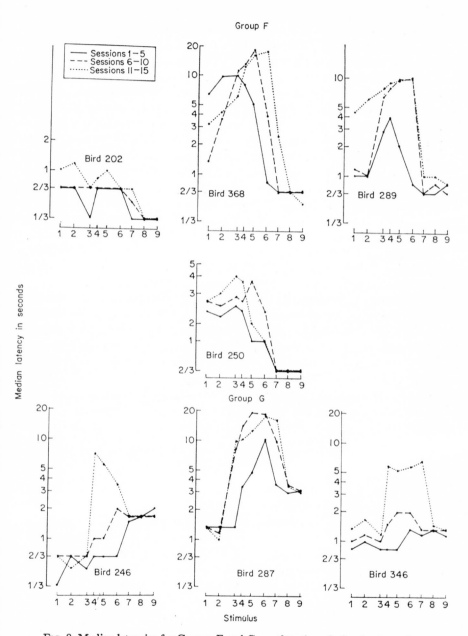

FIG. 8. Median latencies for Groups F and G as a function of stimulus intensity.

purposes of continued responding on Key 1 and this occurred during both long and short delays. The second point is that mediation by response chaining becomes an implausible description when the response chains consist of repetitions of the same response, as is true here.

The possibility remains that the subjects were not timing the interval between the two responses, but were counting off a certain number of responses on the first key before transferring to the second key. Since Mechner and Guevrekian (1962) have shown that animals can learn to perform such a task this possibility was examined by comparing the variability of the number of interpolated responses with that of the delay time. The rationale for this comparison is that if the basis of the behaviour is a counting process with the timing secondary, then the delay times must be at least as variable as the number of responses. The best estimate of the variances is obtained from performance in the long component and the critical ratio, i.e. the standard deviation divided by the mean, was calculated for both response-response times and number of responses on Key 1 for all subjects in Experiment 2 except Bird 250. These values, which are shown in Table III together with the means and standard deviations, were calculated over all fifteen test sessions, but omit trials in which no response occurred on the second key and also, for Bird 289, those sessions in which performance in the long component collapsed. The comparable values for performance in the short component are not given, since the small numbers

TABLE III

Mean, standard deviation and critical ratio for response-response times and number of responses on Key 1 from performance in the long component

Subject	Response-response times			Number of responses on Key 1		
	Mean	Standard deviation	Critical ratio	Mean	Standard deviation	Critical ratio
Group F (Stimulus 1)						
Bird 202	5·19	1·03	0·20	18·89	4·50	0·24
Bird 368	5·32	1·01	0·19	8·70	3·61	0·42
Bird 289	5·19	1·41	0·27	9·79	3·83	0·39
Group G (Stimulus 9)						
Bird 246	5·70	1·09	0·18	13·11	4·11	0·31
Bird 287	5·71	1·05	0·18	2·88	1·46	0·51
Bird 346	6·04	0·92	0·15	11·46	4·52	0·39

of both responses and units of $\frac{1}{3}$ sec for the time intervals make estimates of variance unreliable. Table III indicates that for each bird the critical ratio for RRTs is appreciably less than that for number of responses. Thus the process underlying the observed timing behaviour cannot have been that of counting responses on the first key.

In the presence of intermediate stimuli the likelihood of continued responding on Key 1 decreases. This is shown in Fig. 9 where the relative frequency of cycles in which only a single response occurred is plotted as a function of stimulus intensity. Also shown in this figure is the rate of responding on Key 1, given that more than one response occurred. It can be seen that both the probability of such intervening behaviour occurring and the rate of responding decline to some minimum value in the middle of the stimulus range. A further feature of Fig. 9 is that for both Group F and Group G the rates of responding are higher for Stimulus 1 than for Stimulus 9 (excluding Bird 250 which consistently made only a single R_1 response in the presence of Stimulus 1). Thus stimulus intensity appears to be an important factor in determining rate of responding, but not in the direction predicted by the principle of "stimulus intensity dynamism". However this result is compatible with the only study on this topic using pigeons as subjects and rate of responding as the response variable, where a similar inverse "dynamism" was found over the stimulus range used here (Blough, 1959).

4. *Psychophysical Scaling*

One of the purposes of Experiment 2 was to discover whether the fact that the median functions for Group A were not monotonic (see Fig. 2) was due to the particular stimulus range used during training. When the range is reduced to that used in Experiment 2 these functions become more nearly monotonic (see Fig. 6) but there is some evidence from the distributions in Fig. 7 that the shortest delays occur to Stimulus 7 and not to Stimulus 9. This is most marked in the case of Bird 202. The basic conditions for a method of direct scaling are that stimulus and response dimensions are both continuously and monotonically related. This study shows that the continuity condition is satisfied only if a careful choice of experimental parameters is made and suggests that the monotonicity condition can be satisfied only by changing the stimulus range in a trial-and-error fashion. Thus the prospects for direct scaling in animals do not seem very encouraging and appear to require a lengthy experimental programme.

An indirect approach to the problem of scaling is to treat the test results for the subjects that exhibited mixing behaviour as bisection data. This is done by finding the point of indifference along the stimulus range, that is, the stimulus intensity for which half the responses are appropriate to one

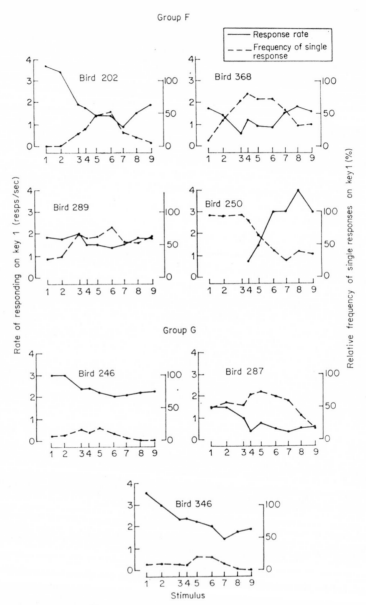

FIG. 9. Rates of responding on Key 1 and relative frequencies of single responses on Key 1 as a function of stimulus intensity.

The rates of responding are calculated by dividing the number of responses, if this exceeds one, by the response-response time for a given trial. The median of these values over all fifteen test sessions is plotted.

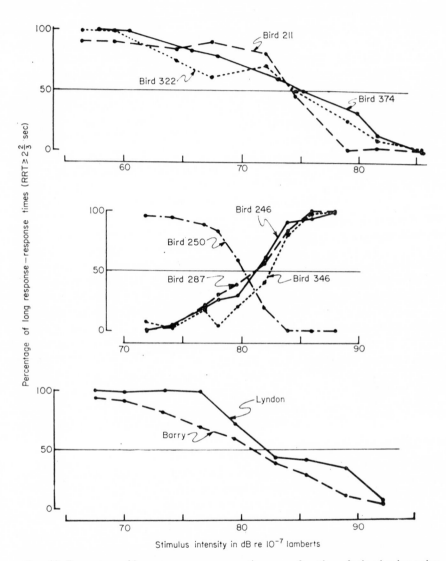

FIG. 10. Percentage of long response-response times as a function of stimulus intensity for subjects that exhibited mixing behaviour.

For each stimulus the percentage of long response-response times is determined by calculating the proportion of all RRTs greater than $2\frac{2}{3}$ sec over all fifteen test sessions. Failures to respond on Key 2 are not included in this percentage.

training stimulus and half to the other stimulus. RRT values were divided into two classes, using $2\frac{2}{3}$ sec as the criterion. This value was chosen partly because it is the geometric mean of the pair of lower bounds most commonly used during training ($1\frac{1}{3}$ sec and $5\frac{1}{3}$ sec) and is therefore most appropriate when variability is a linear function of the mean. Also, when the individual distributions were examined, this value most cleanly divided the obtained distributions for Stimuli 1 and 9 (see Figs. 1 and 5). The percentage of RRTs which exceeded this value is plotted as a function of stimulus intensity in Fig. 10. These points represent percentages obtained over all fifteen test sessions from Bird 374 of Group B, Birds 211 and 322 of Group C, Bird 250 of Group F, all three members of Group G and the two monkeys, Lyndon and Barry, referred to above.

The important point of Fig. 10 is that, although the shape of the functions vary widely, the points of intersection with 50% line for a given range are fairly uniform. To explore this consistency use was made of the general mean theorem, which can be expressed as:

$$I_{\frac{1}{2}} = \tfrac{1}{2} (I_0^r + I_1^r)^{\frac{1}{r}}$$

where I_0 and I_1, represent the upper and lower limits of the interval and $I_{\frac{1}{2}}$ the bisection point. An exponent of $r = 0$ would indicate that bisection occurs at the geometric mean and thus a logarithmic function for perceived brightness. An exponent of $r = 1$ would indicate that bisection occurs at the arithmetic mean. The intersections with the 50% line in Fig. 10 were used to estimate the value of the exponent for each subject and these are shown in Table IV. All values are above zero, which means that bisection occurs at a point greater than the geometric mean. The median value of the exponent for pigeons is 0·15. The values for three birds deviate appreciably from this figure, but in two of these cases this difference could be traced to a considerable drift in the final five test sessions.

The bisection results were an incidental product of this research and their consistency indicates that this might be a very fruitful approach to scaling in animals. A more direct technique for obtaining bisection points that is being employed in current research by the author makes the differences between the responses much more distinct by training animals in a successive discrimination situation, in which one stimulus indicates a response to the left and the other a response to the right. This task is considerably easier than that of the present study and also reduces the possible effect of response biases. It seemed quite probable that a strong preference for short RRTs would affect the present results, but the only evidence for a bias of this kind is the fact that in Fig. 10 the bisection point for Bird 250 is slightly below those for Group G.

TABLE IV

Bisection points and exponents obtained from the general mean theorem

Subjects	$\log.I_0$	$\log.I_1$	$\log.I_{\frac{1}{2}}$	r
Bird 374	5·78	8·57	7·51	0·20
Bird 211	5·63	8·55	7·42	0·14
Bird 322	5·63	8·55	7·45	0·15
Bird 250	7·18	8·81	8·02	0+
Bird 246	7·18	8·81	8·12	0·15
Bird 287	7·18	8·81	8·11	0·14
Bird 346	7·18	8·81	8·24	0·30
Lyndon	6·75	9·23	8·21	0·31
Barry	6·75	9·23	8·10	0·16

V. Summary

This chapter is concerned with the problem of what kind of learning takes place in a discrimination situation in which the response alternatives vary along a single dimension. The experimental procedure used was one in which the subject is first trained to delay its response a certain time in the presence of a light of one intensity and to delay some other time to a second intensity. Subsequently, its response to lights of intermediate intensity is determined.

The imposed delays are between a response on one key and a response on a second key; the interval elapsing between responses on the two keys is termed the response-response time.

It was found that behaviour in the presence of intermediate levels of intensity can take two basic forms. One form consists of an alternation between the response-response times appropriate to the two training stimuli; this is referred to as "mixing behaviour" and is taken to indicate that the situation is equivalent to one consisting of discrete response alternatives. The other is one in which response-response times change continuously as a function of stimulus intensity.

Factors determining which form occurred include the duration of the imposed delay intervals used during training and the way in which the intensities of the training stimuli are related to the two components of the training schedule. When, in the component with the shorter delay, the interval is less than about one second, mixing behaviour is likely to occur. It is suggested that under such conditions the procedure is asymmetrical for the subject, in that a "delay" is in effect only for the component requiring the longer delay. The response-response times are most likely to change continuously when both imposed delay intervals exceed the above value and when the brighter stimulus is correlated with the shorter interval. When the stimulus conditions are reversed, mixing behaviour again occurs.

During the delay interval subjects frequently continue to respond on the first key, although this behaviour is ineffective. Since the number of such responses is more variable than the response-response times, it is concluded that this activity does not mediate the observed timing behaviour.

This research offered little encouragement to the prospect of developing direct sensory scaling methods for animals, but the result from the subjects that exhibited mixing behaviour suggested that an indirect approach to this problem might be very promising. It was found that these subjects bisected the various stimulus ranges in a consistent manner and that, using the general mean theorem, an exponent of 0·15 accurately predicts the bisection point, at which responses are evenly divided between those appropriate to one extreme of the range and those appropriate to the other.

Acknowledgement

This work was supported by grants from the National Science Foundation to Harvard University.

References

Blough, D. S. (1959). Generalization and preference on a stimulus intensity continuum. *J. exp. Anal. Behav.* **2**, 307–317.

Blough, D. S. (1963). Interresponse times as a function of continuous variables: A new method and some data. *J. exp. Anal. Behav.* **6**, 237–246.

Boakes, R. A. (1966). "Brightness scaling in the pigeon and monkey." Unpublished doctoral dissertation. Harvard University, U.S.A.

Cumming, W. W. and Eckerman, D. A. (1965). Stimulus control of a differentiated operant. *Psychon. Sci.* **3**, 313–314.

Green, E. J. (1953). Stimulus control of operant responding in the pigeon. *Am. J. Psychol.* **66**, 311–312.

Herrnstein, R. J. and van Sommers, P. (1962). A method for sensory scaling with animals. *Science*, **135**, 40–41.

Laties, V. G., Weiss, B., Clark, R. L. and Reynolds, M. D. (1965). Overt "mediating" behavior during temporally spaced responding. *J. exp. Anal. Behav.* **8**, 107–116.

Mechner, F. and Guevrekian, L. (1962). Effects of deprivation upon counting and timing in rats. *J. exp. Anal. Behav.* **5**, 463–466.

Migler, B. (1964). Effects of averaging data during stimulus generalization. *J. exp. Anal. Behav.* **7**, 303–307.

15 Outlines of a Theory of Visual Pattern Recognition in Animals and Man

N. S. SUTHERLAND

University of Sussex, Brighton, Sussex, England

I. Introduction

The bulk of this paper is being published elsewhere (Sutherland, 1968). It is reproduced here with some changes of emphasis and some second thoughts to make it more readily accessible to psychologists. It has been argued elsewhere (Sutherland, 1959) that we shall never fully understand discrimination learning without taking perceptual processes into account: the same view is implicit in Hebb (1949). With the exception of Mackintosh's chapter and the second half of that by Thomas, the chapters in this book deal with discrimination learning without any consideration of perceptual processes. This may be legitimate where the controlling stimulus is varied along a single dimension such as wavelength or sound frequency, but in more complex discriminations the question of what perceptual information is stored and how it is stored is surely crucial to an understanding of discrimination learning. Mackintosh and I have argued that in all discrimination learning two distinct processes are involved— learning what incoming information to use and learning how it is to be used to control responses. The first process we have called "learning to switch in an analyser". Provided we are dealing with simple sensory dimensions, the term "analyser" is perhaps adequate but it is totally inadequate as an account of discrimination between patterns. This chapter deals with the problem of visual pattern recognition and considers how our theory of selective attention must be modified to incorporate animals' capacities to store information about patterns and utilize this information to control discriminative responses.

The question of how visually presented patterns are recognized is one of the most intriguing and important problems in psychology. It is intriguing because we can at the moment hardly begin to specify the logic of the complex information processing that underlies this ability. Whereas it is relatively easy to make machines that at least exhibit some analogy to trial and error learning, to classical conditioning or to muscular control involving error correcting loops, there is no machine or computer programme in existence that comes near to mimicking the capacity of a pigeon or an octopus to recognize patterns in a two dimensional array. The problem is important because until we know more about how the input to the animal is processed and stored, we shall be severely handicapped in specifying the subsequent processes that occur in the brain and that lead to the emission of responses.

Although we are still groping towards an adequate theory of pattern recognition, recent developments in experimental psychology, neurophysiology and computing science do enable us to do two things. First, we can specify many of the conditions that an adequate theory must meet and secondly, we are for the first time in a position to sketch the outlines of the information processing that occurs in pattern recognition, though it must be confessed that the task of filling in the details is Herculean. This paper states some of the major conditions that an adequate theory must fulfil, sketches the outlines of a theory and attempts to show that the theory satisfies the conditions.

II. Facts to be Explained

We begin then by stating twelve conditions that a good theory of pattern recognition must fulfil. These conditions are certainly not exhaustive but they are a reasonable starting point. In what follows, we shall take techniques and technical terms for granted. A discussion of techniques and a general review of the evidence will be found in Sutherland (1961).

A. SIZE INVARIANCE

It has been found over and over again that when animals have been trained to discriminate between a pair of shapes they transfer the discrimination when the sizes of the shapes are altered (Sutherland, 1961). Sutherland and Carr (1963) showed that in the octopus such transfer occurs when the area of the transfer shapes differs from that of the training shapes by a factor of 16. Unfortunately the full range over which such transfer occurs has not been adequately established since the use of transfer tests is an insensitive method for measuring transfer of training and no experiments have been undertaken using the more sensitive savings method. It has been suggested (Parriss and Young, 1962) that size transfer occurs because during training the animal is often exposed to a range of retinal sizes: the animal usually sees the training shapes from different distances and hence it may actually learn to make the correct responses to shapes of different sizes. However, good size transfer occurs in experimental situations such as the Lashley jumping stand where the distance from which the training shapes are viewed is well controlled and where one can be sure that the retinal size of the transfer shapes lies outside the range of retinal sizes of the training shapes. Hebb (1940) suggested that the capacity to transfer to different sized shapes is partly learned and partly mediated by eye movements. Both suggestions have been largely refuted by more recent evidence. It will be sufficient to quote here the results of one experiment. Ganz and Wilson (1967) trained young monkeys with no previous experience of pattern vision to discriminate between a vertical and horizontal bar. The animals were trained with stabilized images so that the training shapes always occupied the same part of the retina and could not be displaced by eye-movements. Significant transfer was obtained when tests were given with shapes one quarter the area of the originals. We conclude that many species have the capacity to classify a shape as the same shape regardless of changes in size at least over a considerable range and that this capacity is innate.

B. RETINAL POSITION

It is easy to demonstrate that if a man learns to identify a shape using one part of his retina, he is able to identify the same shape when presented to many other parts of the retina: this ability is of course limited by acuity differences in different parts of the retina. It is well known that many animals exhibit interocular transfer—that is having learned to discriminate between two shapes with one eye, they continue to discriminate without the need for relearning when the shapes are shown to the other eye. Cronly-Dillon, Sutherland and Wolfe (1966) have demonstrated that goldfish exhibit intra-retinal transfer—having learned to discriminate with one part of the retina, they transfer the discrimination when another part of the retina is used. In the experiment outlined above, Ganz and Wilson showed that in the monkey this capacity is also innate over a displacement range of 5° of visual angle.

C. BRIGHTNESS INVARIANCE

Although there is some tendency to transfer when the brightness of a shape and its background is inverted, such transfer does not always occur (Sutherland, 1961). An early experiment by Fields (1932) suggests that if transfer were to be measured by relearning rather than by transfer tests considerable savings would be found. In general, the more simple the shape, the more likely it is that brightness transfer will occur. Failure of equivalence when brightness relationships are changed can be illustrated by the difficulty of recognizing the negative of a face. How far such transfer is mediated by innate mechanisms and how far it is a learned capacity we do not know: Ganz and Wilson found no brightness transfer in monkeys lacking previous experience of pattern vision but since under the conditions of their experiment experienced animals also showed no transfer, this result does not prove that there is no innate mechanism for achieving brightness transfer at least with simple shapes.

D. EQUIVALENCE OF OUTLINE AND FILLED-IN SHAPES

Many species exhibit transfer of a discrimination learned with filled-in shapes to outline shapes and *vice versa* (Sutherland, 1961). There is evidence that different species have this ability to a greater or lesser extent, for example rats transfer more readily from filled-in to outline shapes than do octopuses (Sutherland, 1969). Our own ability to recognize cartoon line drawings demonstrates the existence of this capacity in man. It is not known how far innate mechanisms are involved.

E. NON-EQUIVALENCE OF ROTATED SHAPES

One of the major mistakes made by theorists in the field of pattern recognition has been to assume that any rotation of a shape will be treated as equivalent to the original shape. This is not true either for man or for other animals. For example, Sutherland (1960a) and Sutherland and Carr

(1964) have shown that when rats or octopuses are trained to discriminate between a horizontal rectangle and a square and are then presented with a vertical rectangle they treat the rotated rectangle as equivalent to the square. Again after being trained with a square and a triangle, octopuses respond to a diamond (a 45° rotation of the square) in the way they have been trained to respond to the original triangle (Sutherland, 1958). Our own ability to respond to a rectangle as a rectangle in any orientation is almost certainly mediated by learning and possibly by the use of language. Men have great difficulty in recognizing faces presented upside down. The fact that there is often no equivalence between a shape and its rotation does not mean that such equivalence never exists. Many species including men show some equivalence between mirror-image shapes. Moreover, Bowman and Sutherland have recently shown that while goldfish show no transfer to a 45° rotated square after being trained to discriminate between a square and a circle, they show almost perfect transfer if they are trained to discriminate between a circle and a square with a knob on it, and are then presented with a 45° rotation of the square with the knob.

F. Confusions Between Shapes

There is a growing body of evidence on the sorts of confusions animals tend to make between visually presented shapes or patterns. Any adequate theory of shape recognition must be capable of explaining the confusions that are made and also why some pairs of shapes are much more readily discriminated than others. Some examples of confusions have already been given—mirror-image shapes are readily confused, and a diamond tends to be confused with a triangle after animals have been trained to discriminate between a square and a triangle. It is not possible to review the literature on this problem here, but some further instances of shapes and patterns that are readily confused will be given below.

It is worth noting that there is a remarkable similarity between the types of confusion made by different species with simple eyes. Sutherland has conducted a series of behavioural experiments on shape recognition in the octopus in the expectation that very different results would be obtained from those found with mammals. Despite the enormous difference in the way in which the visual systems of octopus and rat have evolved, the confusions made by the octopus are very similar to those made by rats and other vertebrates. The anatomical similarities between the visual pathways of rat and octopus are also striking although they have evolved from very different structures. This suggests that there has been strong convergent evolutionary pressure towards the production of similar mechanisms of pattern processing in the visual system of widely different species. Although the similarities in the way in which visual discrimination operates are much more striking than the differences, detailed investigation has revealed some differences (Sutherland, 1969). The nature of the differences suggests that we are dealing with small variations in a common basic mechanism.

G. Jitter

A shape can be recognized as the same shape when subjected to varying amounts of local distortion. For example a square can still be recognized as a square or as very like a square when some or all of the lines are not quite straight, when they are tilted relative to one another so that the angles are no longer right angles and under a variety of other local perturbations.

H. Segmentation

Man has the ability to segment an input picture in different ways. This can be seen at a very simple level if we consider a simple "H" shape made up from three straight lines. As well as being able to see this as a capital letter "H" we can see it as two vertical lines joined by a horizontal bar about midway up, as a "T" on its side joined by a common horizontal bar to a "T" turned through 90° the other way, as a rectilinear "U" shape joined at its base to an inverted rectilinear "U" shape and so on. Our ability to segment in different ways explains our capacity to identify say the figure "4" in a scrambled array of lines (Gottschaldt, 1926). It is moreover probably connected, as we shall show, with our capacity to see ambiguous figures—such as the wife and mother-in-law—Boring (1930) in different ways. Very little work has been done on this problem with animals. We shall show, however, that the capacity to segment a picture in different ways is so fundamental for pattern recognition that it is almost certain that higher animals possess it.

I. Recognition of Complex Scenes

Although no systematic work has been done on this issue, there appears to be an interesting paradox in the human ability to categorize a complex scene presented for a brief time such as 100 milliseconds. Men are quite capable of seeing that a picture exposed for this duration is a beach, or a forest, a horse race or a wedding. Although they may fail to detect small inconsistencies in the picture, they will notice any large systematic inconsistency. For example if a checkerboard pattern is exposed in one quadrant of the picture or if one part of the picture is simply left blank the presence of these anomalies will be reported. The paradox is as follows: the same person who can identify this type of error when it appears in the picture may be completely incapable of reporting what appears in the place of the error when the picture is errorless and complete. Now clearly that part of the picture must be processed or the error could not be detected. If it is processed when a normal picture is shown, why cannot the details of each part of the picture be reported? Putting the paradox another way, it is clear that in order to identify a picture much processing of the parts must have occurred but if the picture is presented for a very short time very few of the results of this processing will be available to control the response.

J. Perceptual Learning

Although picture processing is almost certainly dependent on highly specific innate mechanisms (Sutherland, 1959), it is clear that man has a capacity for perceptual learning. It is not merely that we learn to identify now one object and now another, we can also learn something about a general class of pictures which facilitates recognition of the relevant differences between new members of that class and previously experienced members. Slides of neural tissue look very different to the experienced neuroanatomist from the way they appear to the novice. A more everyday example is the difficulty that Europeans experience on going to China in remembering a new Chinese face well enough to identify the owner when they meet him for a second time. With sufficient exposure to Chinese faces, it becomes as easy to remember new Chinese faces as Western ones. Some account of the capacity for this rather general kind of perceptual learning must be included in any adequate theory of pattern recognition.

K. Redundancy

It is certain that the mechanism of pattern recognition takes advantage of the redundancy of our visual environment. Some instances of the ways in which it does so will be given below but in the meantime it is sufficient to consider the following argument.

Suppose that visual acuity is 1' of arc or better within a radius of 5° of the fovea centralis (Polyak, 1941—acuity is in fact considerably better than this over most of the area). This means that within this area there are approximately 1,000,000 different points that could be illuminated by light and that can be resolved from one another. If light is quantized into only two levels (black and white), $2^{1,000,000}$ different patterns could be projected onto this area of the retina. Pattern recognition, however, is concerned not merely with individual patterns but with classes of pattern and there are $2^{2(1,000,000)}$ such classes of pattern. Given the (comparatively) very small number of neurons in the human brain, it would clearly be impossible to make provision genetically for the formation of all possible classes of patterns. Provision could only be made for forming a tiny fraction of the number of possible classes and our own remarkable powers of pattern recognition indicate that the classes of pattern that can be formed have been selected by a genetic mechanism to be those that are going to be most useful to us, i.e. those which take advantage of the redundancy of our visual environment.

Using our visual system alone it is clearly impossible to recognize the difference between the two patterns shown in Fig. 1, yet a large number of picture points are different in the two patterns. We could of course learn to tell the difference between the two patterns by a trick—we could count down 50 lines from the top and count in 40 lines and discover that that picture element was black in one picture and white in the other. However, provided we are not allowed to use counting or some learned symbolism (such as a natural language) there is clearly no possibility of our being able to recognize the difference between these two pictures let alone form arbitrary classes made up of such pictures. An adequate theory of pattern recognition must then explain why we cannot see the difference between certain pictures where the limitation is not one of acuity and how it is that we take advantage of the redundancy of our visual environment in forming the classes of picture that we do form.

FIG. 1. Julesz random patterns. (Published by permission of Bell Telephone Laboratories; Copyright 1960, the American Telephone and Telegraph Company).

L. PHYSIOLOGICAL EVIDENCE

Any satisfactory theory must clearly not merely explain facts about pattern perception derived from behavioural experiments, it must also be consistent with what is known of the neuroanatomy and physiological functioning of the visual pathways.

DISCUSSION

It should be noted again that this list of conditions is not exhaustive. In particular no mention has been made of the capacity of animals and man to take account of and process information about depth. Apart from the invariances mentioned above, simple shapes remain invariant under perspective transformations provided the appropriate depth information is present. It is hoped that a theory of the type given below could be extended to take into account three dimensional pattern recognition, but in order to simplify the problem, this paper deals only with the recognition of two dimensional patterns.

III. The Outlines of a Theory

In this section we shall state rather baldly the outlines of a theory of visual pattern recognition. The final section will be concerned with the theory's plausibility.

It will be obvious that the theory suggested has been influenced by the physiological findings of Hubel and Wiesel. Indeed one point of the theory is to suggest what is the function of the detailed neurophysiological arrangements found in the early stages of visual processing: it is not enough to know the detailed wiring of parts of the brain—we must also try to understand the function of such wiring in the overall role of the brain in controlling behaviour. A second major influence on the theory outlined below is the theoretical research and ideas of Max Clowes (1967): he has been working on the problem of inventing a formal language to facilitate the processing and identification of pictorial structures by computer. Although the way in which computers can best be made to carry out a given type of information processing may often differ from the way in which the brain carries out that type of information processing, it seems likely that in the case of picture processing there is considerable similarity between the mechanisms used by the brain and some of the mechanisms at present being explored by computer scientists. Some of the ramifications of the theory to be put forward differ from Clowes's theoretical ideas, but the basis of the theory derives very largely from his work.

In recent years the work of Hubel and Wiesel (1962, 1965, 1968) and others has shown that in the early stages of the visual system of mammals, the input picture is decomposed into parts and these parts are labelled. The retina is projected onto successive layers of cells and at each level there are units that fire when a particular feature is present in a particular part of the retina. Some of the features detected by such units in the cat and monkey brain are as follows: a vertical dark bar against a bright ground, a bright bar at a particular angle against a dark background, a horizontal edge bright above and dark below. Some units appear to perform simple generalizations: for example, there are units that respond to a horizontal bar on a particular part of the retina whether it is brighter or darker than the background and others that respond to a horizontal bar appearing in any position within a rectangular area of the retina elongated along the vertical axis: Hubel and Wiesel have termed such units "complex units". Further into the system, there are yet other units (hypercomplex cells) that respond to a bar or edge in a particular orientation provided it ends at a certain point. It is most important to note that the single units map the retina: when two or more units at a given level are firing, the spatial relationships of the features analysed are preserved by this mapping. Although there are probably many more different types of units still to be discovered, it is clear that one of the functions of the early stages of the visual system (including cortical areas 17, 18 and 19) is to label the parts of an input picture. The arrangement of the cells is columnar and there appears to be little opportunity for wide lateral interaction. Lashley *et al.* (1951) and Sperry *et al.* (1955) have in fact found that making criss-cross lesions at right angles to the surface of the cortex has little effect on vision, and this again suggests that lateral interaction may not be very important.

We shall refer to this stage of the system as a "Processor" and we shall assume that memorizing and recognizing an input shape take place in a different part of the brain that we term a "Store". The lack of opportunity for wide lateral interaction makes it difficult to see how invariance of retinal position and size invariance could be achieved within the processor. We assume that in the store information about an input shape is preserved in a form that is free from retinal position and size. In particular we assume that the information is preserved in a highly abstract symbolism so that many different outputs from the processor can be matched to a single stored description of an input pattern. The reasons for making this assumption will be set out below.

The theory assumes that when a shape is input it is analysed into component parts (lines, edges and ends) by a pre-set processor. Recognition corresponds to a successful process of matching the output from the processor to a stored abstract description. Memorizing a new shape corresponds to writing a new description into store. The two processes are not of course mutually exclusive. That is to say, when a novel shape is input a description may be retrieved that partly matches the output from the processor but the description may have to be modified to apply to the new shape. What we see depends upon the rule selected to describe the input pattern. It is the rule selected that determines both which aspects of the shape we are conscious of and which aspects we can respond to. The same input pattern can be matched to different descriptive rules and hence may be seen in different ways. Moreover, if two patterns are presented side by side, seeing a difference between them will depend upon our being able to form different descriptions of them. Patterns cannot be compared in the processor (except in the special case of binocular vision—see below), they can only be compared at the level of the store where they are represented by abstract descriptive rules. We shall attempt in what follows to do three things. Firstly, we try to show that the theory is plausible and is consistent with the twelve conditions with which we started. Secondly, we shall elaborate the theory and in particular try to show what is meant by "descriptive rule". Thirdly, we shall consider some of the implications of the theory for the problem of selective attention in discrimination learning.

IV. Plausibility of Theory

A. Size, Brightness and Position Invariance

It is of course extremely difficult to get at the form of the descriptions used by the brain when a shape is "memorized" but to make it clear what we mean by an abstract description, let us consider a symbolism which provides a description of simple shapes free from size and retinal position. One expression describing an outline square is as follows:

$$_wH(x)_e = {}_nV(x)_s = {}_eH(x)_w = {}_sV(x)_n =$$

The notation used can be grasped by referring to Fig. 2 (i). In brief, the letters "H" and "V" refer to horizontal and vertical lines or to the output from horizontal and vertical bar detectors. The lower case subscripts refer to the retinal co-ordinates of the west and east ends of the horizontal lines ("e" and "w") and to the south and north ends of the vertical lines ("s" and "n"). The equals sign joining the subscripts means that the retinal co-ordinates of one end of one line are to be the same as the retinal co-ordinates of the specified end of the next line. The variable "x" refers to the length of the lines and can take any value though it must be the same value for all lines. The expression is to be read cyclicly—that is the final "n" has the same retinal co-ordinates as the initial "w". In every day language the expression reads—"A horizontal line of length x joined at its east end to the north end of a vertical line of length x joined at its south end to the east end of a horizontal line etc." Such an expression could be regarded as a rule for generating an outline square of any size at any position on the retina and correspondingly this description of a square could be matched by an input square falling on any retinal position. It should be noted that all the information necessary to test whether this description fits is preserved in the processor. In particular the hypercomplex cells preserve information about where bars end and this must be used to check that the junctions between lines occur in the way specified.

Now since it is known that animals do not immediately generalize over the whole size range we have thrown away too much information in writing this description of a square. Moreover, a cat can be trained to select a triangle when a small triangle and square are presented and to select the square when a large triangle and square are presented (Warren, 1961).

It is clear that animals can store information about size along with information about shape. We can take this into account by adding to our description an expression specifying the approximate size of the shape, for example by writing

$$[_wH(x)_e = {}_nV(x)_s = {}_eH(x)_w = {}_sV(x)_n =] [1° < x < 5°]$$

In practice of course real size calculated by constancy scaling would be stored, not retinal size.

Before considering the implications of storing information about size, we will deal with the problem of brightness equivalance. Although this is more complicated we assume that it is done in the same way—that is a further bracketed expression is added that contains information about brightness. More specifically, it would need to contain symbols with the following meanings: dark outline, bright outline, outline, dark filled-in, bright filled-in, or filled-in. When "dark outline" or "bright outline" occur, the symbols in the expression describing shape are to be interpreted in terms of outputs from bright or dark bar detectors in the processor. Hubel and Wiesel have found that in cat and monkey striate cortex there are both units detecting *either* bright *or* dark bars, and also individual units that respond to bars of *both* brightnesses and these units would be referred to by "outline".

Filled-in shapes are more complicated since if it is specified in a description that the interior is black, this means in the case of a square that the north horizontal contour will be detected by an edge unit bright above and dark below, the east contour by an edge unit bright to the right and dark to the left and so on. This means that in interpreting a description there must be a mechanism for determining the inside of a closed shape and for assigning in accordance with this the correct one of the two types of complementary edge detectors at each point of the periphery of the shape. Such a mechanism certainly exists in man (cf. the well known figure-ground phenomenon investigated by Rubin, 1921). It is practically certain to exist in animals since the language used to describe shapes must contain symbols for "inside" and "outside". Although no previous experiments have been undertaken on this issue with animals, we are at present investigating the capacity of pigeons to respond differentially to a square presented with a dot depending on whether the dot is inside or outside the square.

We now have an explanation for the facts of brightness transfer. If an animal has been trained to discriminate a pair of shapes of a particular brightness it will not necessarily show immediate transfer when the brightness of shape and background is inverted. However, if an animal is trained to discriminate between two shapes with changing brightness values, it will

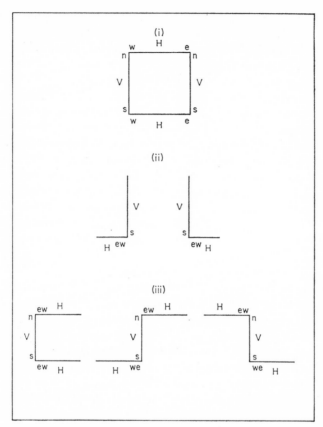

FIG. 2. Descriptions of simple figures.

learn not to store information about brightness: if it is next trained on a new pair presented with only one brightness value, it will show immediate generalization when the brightness value of that pair is changed (Fields, 1932). Moreover, the theory gives us some understanding of why men generalize immediately when the brightness of a simple shape is changed but not when the brightness values of a complex shape (such as a human face) are inverted. In the latter case brightness values must be sorted along with the description of each part of the face and the problem of inverting them all simultaneously will be much more complicated. Moreover, since we do not normally see faces with inverted brightness values we will have learned to store specific brightness values since they will assist us in identification.

The above account of how size and brightness transfer are achieved is clearly compatible with Sutherland's (1964b) theory of selective attention.

Experiments such as those of Lawrence (1949) and Sutherland and Holgate (1966) suggest that animals can learn in a given situation to store and utilize information about only the brightness or only the size of a shape. On the present theory, this process is facilitated by storing such information separately from the information about pattern. The same object can be described in many different ways and the process of selective attention corresponds to selecting a particular description for storage and to control further responses. As we shall see below the description chosen is affected by two factors. It will be affected by reward contingencies and it will also tend to be in some sense the simplest description available.

Although the theory being advanced here envisages innate mechanisms for achieving size and brightness transfer it allows for great flexibility in the specificity with which a description of an object is written into store; depending on an animal's previous experience in a given situation, it will store information at different levels of specificity about different aspects of its environment.

B. CONFUSIONS AND DESCRIPTORS

It is clear that the present theory accounts well for the lack of rotational equivalence. Both the output from the processor and the descriptive rules placed in the store are cast in terms of specific contour orientations. Unless a complex mechanism is provided for transforming a descriptive rule into an expression that fits a rotation of the shape originally described, rotational equivalence will normally not occur.

We have already seen that there are special instances in which there is considerable equivalence between rotated shapes—in particular mirror-image shapes are frequently treated as equivalent (though not all mirror-image shapes are rotations of one another). Consider the description that might be written for an "L" shape:

$$V(2x)_{s\ =\ w}(Hx)$$

In ordinary language this says that there is a vertical line joined at its south end to the west end of a horizontal line and that the vertical line is about twice the length of the horizontal line. Now supposing that in the vocabulary for describing shapes, the separate symbols "e" and "w" do not occur but there is only one symbol "ew" which is interpreted to mean either the east or the west end. We now obtain the description

$$V(2x)_{s\ =\ ew}H(x)$$

and this description clearly fits both an "L" shape and its mirror-image (see Fig. 2, ii). If we assume that in many animals all three symbols are available but that "ew" tends to be used much more readily than "e" or "w" then we have an explanation for the tendency of animals to confuse mirror-image shapes and for why, with special training, they can be taught to discriminate between such shapes.

The explanation unfortunately contains a flaw. Consider the description of the "U" on its side shown in Fig. 2 (iii):

$$H(x)_{ew} = {}_nV(x)_s = {}_{ew}H(x)$$

This description again of course fits equally well the mirror-image of the "U" shape. Unfortunately, it also fits the other two shapes shown in Fig. 2 (iii) and it seems unlikely that animals would confuse the "U" with these two shapes (though the relevant experiments have not been undertaken).

There are two possible ways round this. (1) The symbols "ew" and "we" might be used to describe a shape where "ew" is interpreted as either the east or west end but always the same one at any given time and "we" means either east or west but at any one time always the opposite end to that referred to by "ew". (2) Another possibility is that the description of a shape is redundant and contains some information about its global properties For example, the two shapes in Fig. 2 (iii) would be given a different description using only "ew" and not "we" if we add an expression describing the ratio of their maximum horizontal extent to their maximum vertical extent. Thus the "U" shape might have as part of its description

$$[vert/hor = 1\,]$$

while the description of the shapes on the right hand side of Fig. 2 (iii) might contain the expression

$$[vert/hor = \tfrac{1}{2}]$$

In verbal terms these descriptions would mean that the vertical and horizontal extents of the shape are approximately equal in one instance and that the shape was elongated along the horizontal axis in the other. Although adding global descriptors of this sort to a more detailed descriptive rule is redundant and increases storage space, it might well be necessary to do so in order to cut down the search time for retrieving a matching rule when a shape is input. If an input shape generates a global description of itself then fewer stored rules would need to be searched to find the matching rule since only those rules would be entered that had the same global descriptors as the input shape: if only detailed rules from which the whole shape can be generated are preserved, it is extremely difficult to see how it would be possible to cut down search time.

We have already spelled out how one type of confusion may be accounted for in a simple way by the theory proposed. It is impossible here to review the extensive data on confusions made between shapes or to show how these data can be accounted for within the framework of the theory. Within the descriptive language we have proposed, a triangle will be more readily confused with a diamond than with a square since the description of the triangle will have more elements in common with the diamond than with the square. In particular the description of both triangle and diamond will contain expressions referring to the two oblique lines joined at the apex in the top half of the shape and it is precisely this feature which discriminates the triangle from the square since square and triangle have the same base line. It should be noticed that in terms of the proposed theory, the differences in the confusions made by different species could result from three rather different causes.

(1) If there are different features detectors present in different species this may lead to different confusions being made. Sutherland (1969) has obtained behavioural evidence that suggests that bar detectors may be relatively more common than edge detectors in the octopus and *vice versa* in the rat. When these two species are trained to discriminate between a square and a parallelogram, transfer results in the octopus are largely determined by the presence versus absence of thin segments of shapes occurring in the positions of the acute angles of the parallelogram whereas the presence vs. absence of oblique contours is more important for the rat. This interpretation can be tested by existing physiological techniques.

(2) The language used to give a detailed description of the structure of a shape may vary from species to species and will be to some extent determined by the types of receptive field present in that species. We have integrated mirror-image equivalance as resulting from the symbolism available in the brain to provide a detailed description of a shape. Once again, different species differ markedly in the extent to which they are prone to confuse mirror-images (Sutherland, 1969).

(3) If different descriptors of global characteristics are used by different species this would also produce differences in the confusions made between shapes. The instance of a descriptor given above (the ratio of vertical to horizontal extent) in fact explains many results obtained by Sutherland on octopuses and rats. It clearly accounts for the equivalence between horizontal rectangle and square after training on vertical rectangle and square since the ratios for these three shapes can be regarded as lying on a continuum with the horizontal and vertical rectangle at either end and the square in the middle. Sutherland (1960b) has obtained evidence that a further global descriptor that may be employed by both rats and octopuses is the ratio $P/\sqrt{A}$ where P is total periphery of a shape and A is its area. Both of these ratios are invariant with changes in size.

It is perhaps worth pausing for breath at this point and taking stock. The mechanism we have outlined so far is extremely complex and the task of attributing a given confusion to one or other part of the mechanism with any certainty is very difficult. On the other hand I believe that earlier theories of visual pattern recognition including my own were wholly inadequate and did not begin to explain the fantastic capacity that men and animals have for processing pictorial data, including the great flexibility in such processing. We must, unfortunately, take Nature as we find her and both behavioural and physiological investigations suggest that the mechanism of pattern recognition is at least as complex as that advanced here. When such a complex mechanism is proposed, it can of course be argued against it that it is very difficult to draw hard and fast predictions from it.

This paper states only the outlines of a theory of how pictorial information is processed by the nervous system. There is an enormous amount of detail to be filled in before we can begin to give an adequate account of the behaviour of one species. To develop and test the theory it will be necessary to resort to detailed computer simulation, to derive and test predictions, to alter the model in the light of the experimental results and by repeating this process many times gradually to obtain an approximation nearer and nearer to the detailed truth. It could be said that for any set of data there will be many possible models to account for them. The problem in pattern recognition at the moment, however, is less to think up ways of testing different models than to think of one model which comes anywhere near to giving us an understanding of the enormous range of data both physiological and behavioural. In the present theory, predictive power has been sacrificed for generality but it could be argued that it is useful at this stage to have a model that gives us a broad understanding of a wide range of data and which can be refined by carrying out experiments that are at least suggested by the model but whose detailed results are not actually predicted by it. In a moment we shall proceed to complicate the model still further, but first we deal with the problem of jitter.

C. Jitter

The problem of jitter can to some extent be explained by the operation of the receptive field units themselves. According to Hubel and Wiesel many of these units are relatively insensitive to small amounts of local distortion such as small angular rotations of a bar and small amounts of distortion induced by bending or by adding random noise. Other types of jitter may be dealt with at the level of the store. For example, we do not discriminate very accurately small differences in line length and in size and this suggests that the information held in store about size is not very precise. This would account for our insensitivity to small variations in the relative lengths of the component contours making up a shape. Again, a

square can be recognized as a square even when two lines forming an angle
do not quite meet. Although we may recognize the shape as a square we also
have no difficulty in recognizing that it is deformed in this respect. An
output from the processor may be accepted as matching a rule even when
the rule is not quite satisfied—in this instance when the retinal co-
ordinates of two ends set equal in the store are not quite equal in the output
from the processor.

D. HIERARCHICAL DESCRIPTIONS AND SEGMENTATION

Of more interest is the problem of segmentation. Consider a complex
shape like a face: it would clearly be uneconomical to hold in one part of the
storage system a description of an eye, elsewhere a description of an ear and
to repeat these descriptions and others in a location holding a description
of a face. It would be much more economical when describing a face to use
in the description terms like "eye" and "ear" and in order to obtain their
descriptions to refer to other locations where descriptive rules for these
items are held. It seems likely, then, that the storage system will be
hierarchically arranged so that descriptive rules can occur at many different
levels and a high level rule will contain elements which refer to lower level
rules. If this is true it immediately opens the possibility of providing
different descriptions of the same input pattern. To go back to our example
of an "H" shape formed by three straight lines, such a shape could be
described in many different ways. For example we could write the description as

$$V(2x)_{m\,=\,w\,=\,w}H(x)_{e\,=\,m}V(2x)$$

where "m" refers to the midpoint of the feature immediately to its left
or right. We could however write the following description:

$$[\phi_{\,e\,=\,m}V]\,[\text{vert/hor} = 2]$$

where the symbol ϕ is the name for the rule

$$V(2x)_{m\,=\,w}H(x)$$

and where "e" refers to the easternmost point of the structure named ϕ.
This new rule for the input "H" corresponds to someone seeing the "H"
as a rotated "T" joined to a vertical line.

In this way different descriptions can be formed of the same input
pattern. What we see corresponds to the description selected to match the
input. The same type of process allows us to understand how it is that a
picture can be ambiguous. The whole appearance of the wife-grandmother
figure (Boring, 1930) changes when we switch from seeing it in one way to

seeing it in the other. When we are seeing the figure as a young girl we are matching the input to a rule describing a young girl seen in profile. When we switch to seeing an old lady we are matching to a rule describing an old lady seen full face. The part of the input that was matched to a rule for an ear is now matched to a rule for an eye and so on. This reversible figure dramatically illustrates our concention that what we see is not the pattern on our retina but the rule or series of hierarchical rules to which we match an input pattern: by this we mean that all that is available to determine our responses is the rule formed (or matched) to describe the input picture—the details of the picture are not available to govern responses (or to consciousness) except to the extent that they are represented in a rule selected. Halle and Chomsky have called attention to very similar phenomena in listening to speech. We hear gaps between words although such gaps often do not exist in the input sound wave: the reason we hear such gaps is because of the hierarchical structure of the rules to which the auditory signal has been matched. As in vision, so in hearing, what we hear is not the actual waveform received by the ear but the descriptive rules to which that waveform is matched.

The same type of considerations explain the paradox about human recognition of complex scenes. When a scene such as a forest is recognized as a forest, the general rule to which it has been matched is available to determine our responses but the details of how the matching process was achieved are not available. If, however, there is a big mismatch somewhere in the picture, then, because the matching process has failed, a separate rule will need to be written to describe the mismatch ("a black square towards the upper right" etc.). Although all parts of a picture are processed, the extent to which the parts can determine responses depends on the generality of the descriptive rules to which the output from the processor is matched.

The simultaneous processing of many picture points is demonstrated by Julesz's (1960) experiments. If the two pictures in Fig. 1 are viewed in a stereoscope, a central square array of black and white elements will be seen standing out in front of the remainder of the pattern. The two patterns are in fact identical except that a central square array of elements of one pattern has been displaced laterally with respect to the other. When the patterns are fused stereoscopically this displacement is detected by the nervous system and results in a depth effect: the displacement could only be detected if individual picture points were being simultaneously processed. The reason why when both patterns are viewed with both eyes we cannot see any difference between them is that we cannot form different descriptive rules for each pattern—the rule selected for such random arrays must be of a very general form and specifies merely that there is a large square containing a random array of small black and white squares having a certain overall level of brightness.

E. THE RULE FORMING MECHANISM AND REDUNDANCY

We have repeatedly emphasized that different descriptions of the same visual input may be formed and stored and this must be the key to perceptual learning. When we learn the capacity to individuate the members of a class of pictorial structures (such as individual Chinese faces), we presumably learn to modify our description forming mechanism so that just that information is stored that readily differentiates one member from another. We do not in fact know what features are used in discriminating between Western faces nor what features are used in discriminating Chinese faces but the lack of immediate transfer of one capacity to the other suggests that rather different features are involved: when we learn to identify individual Chinese faces readily, we are learning to modify the type of descriptive rule we form when a new face is presented in such a way that information that differentiates different Chinese faces is preserved in the rule.

The same type of process has been investigated at a much more simple level in experiments showing that rats can learn to store information about brightness but not orientation and can learn to store information about orientation but not brightness, depending upon which cue is most useful in solving a problem set to them (Sutherland, 1964b). Although it may be reasonable to describe this type of process as learning to switch in an analyser, such a description is not appropriate to the process whereby an organism learns selectively to store a particular kind of structural description for new members of a given class. In the latter instance, an organism has learned not merely to store information from one analyser and not another but has learned a complicated programme which when brought into play will result in a particular type of structural description being written for a particular kind of pictorial input. Reverting to our previous language it is as though the brain can construct for itself new high level analysers appropriate for the recognition of different Chinese faces or aeroplanes or styles of Gothic architecture or whatever. The present treatment resolves an issue previously skirted round (see for example Sutherland 1959), namely, the question of whether all analysers are innate While the way in which the processor works yielding a set of local features and information about brightness values is almost certainly innate, the rule forming mechanism despite innate biases must be subject to considerable learned modifications and these modifications could be thought of as resulting in animals having at their disposal new and very complicated analysers appropriate for the discrimination of particular types of pattern.

As the reader may have noticed, there is a marked similarity between what we are trying to say here and Bartlett's (1932) concept of a "schema".

We now turn to the question of how the brain takes advantage of the redundancy of the visual world. If a picture of a natural scene is revealed to a subject element by element and he is using what he can see of the parts already exposed to guess the brightness or colour of the next element to be exposed, he will be remarkably accurate except where contours occur. What we know about the physiology of the visual cortex of mammals suggests that the processor itself is adapted to the redundancy of the visual environment since most of the single units found are for the detection of contours. Those parts of the input that carry the maximum amount of information are processed in most detail.

However, it seems certain that the mechanism that derives a descriptive rule from the output of the processor also has biases that allow it to take advantage of the redundancy of the environment and to form in some sense the simplest rule to describe a particular pattern. If we consider regular and irregular checkerboard patterns of the type shown in Fig. 3, it seems likely that men would find it easier to discriminate between the regular checkerboard than between many pairs of irregular ones. This is despite the fact that irregular patterns (2) and (4) differ from one another by changes in the brightness of four of the small squares whereas they each differ from the regular checkerboard by changes in only two squares. Now if the rule formed to describe each of these patterns listed all sixteen small squares and the spatial relationships between them, it should actually be easier to discriminate patterns (2) and (4) from one another than to discriminate either from the regular pattern. The rule inducing mechanism must be capable of forming a simple rule to describe the regular pattern that takes advantage of the regularity in it. Once such a rule is formed, any pattern deviating from it will fail to match and will be readily identified as different whereas more complex rules are required to give an exact description of the irregularities contained in each irregular pattern.

That this capacity is not limited to man is demonstrated by an experiment performed by Sutherland and Williams (1969) on rats. The animals were trained to discriminate between two patterns of the type shown at the top of Fig. 3 and were then given transfer tests with further patterns of which a few examples are shown. All the patterns on the left hand side of Fig. 3 were treated by the animals as (more or less) equivalent to the original regular pattern while those on the right hand side were treated as equivalent to the original irregular pattern. For such generalization to occur, it is clear that the stored descriptions of the original two patterns must have been highly abstract. It would be possible to multiply instances, but it is perhaps worth quoting here one other example of the very

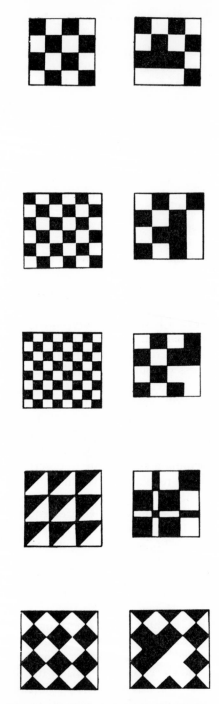

FIG. 3. Rats were trained to discriminate between the top two patterns. Below each of these patterns are shown examples of other shapes treated as similar to it.

abstract form in which descriptive rules of shapes must be stored. Bowman and Sutherland (unpublished) trained goldfish to discriminate between the first two shapes of Fig. 4. Animals were then given transfers tests including tests with the three shapes shown on the next row of Fig. 4. Although, in terms of overlapping area, shapes (4) and (5) correspond more closely to the square than to the square with a knob on it, they were classified in the transfer tests as resembling the square with the knob. This implies that the descriptive rule for the original square with a knob must again have been of a highly abstract form specifying not merely the presence of a knob but the presence of some break in the line at the top of the shape.

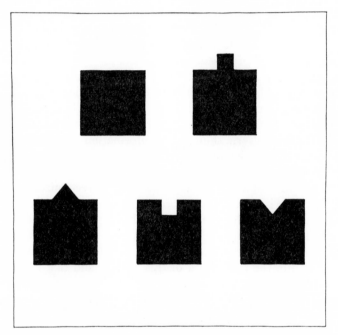

Fig. 4. Goldfish were trained to discriminate between the top two shapes. The other three shapes were treated as similar to the right hand training shape.

F. Physiology of Pattern Recognition

Since in our description of the processor we have relied heavily on neurophysiological data, the theory we are proposing is certainly consistent with physiological findings. There is no physiological evidence either in favour of or against our postulated description of the store. It is, however, known that at least in monkeys one output from the visual cortex goes to the inferotemporal lobe and it is further known that lesions in this area tend

N. S. SUTHERLAND

selectively to impair pattern discrimination (Mishkin, 1966). Moreover, whereas electrical stimulation of the visual cortex in waking human subjects produces only very confused visual images, stimulation of the temporal lobe may under some conditions produce highly organized sequences of images that appear very real to the subjects (Penfield, 1959). The infereotemporal lobe is therefore a likely candidate for the locus of the store. Gross (unpublished) has shown that there are units responsive to a visual input in this area but there is no sign of any topographical representation of the retina there and this fits with our idea that the rules written into the store do not contain information about retinal position.

V. Conclusions

We began by stating some of the conditions that a theory of visual pattern perception must satisfy. The following theory was put forward. The visual input is analysed by a processor that extracts local features (mainly bars, edges and ends) simultaneously at all points on the input picture. When a picture is memorized, a rule is written into a store describing the output from the processor in a highly abstract language. The rules make no reference to retinal position but they can record information about the size and brightness of a pattern, though this information is recorded separately from the stored description of a shape. The language used for the descriptive rules contains hierarchical elements and this allows for pictures to be segmented in different ways. When a picture is "recognized" the output from the processor is matched to a stored description. What we see depends upon the rule to which the picture is matched so that many details of the input picture are not available to determine our response. We have tried to show that some of the main phenomena of pattern perception can be understood within the framework of this theory, and that it is consistent with the facts of selective attention.

Two reservations should be made. Firstly, we have not discussed all the phenomena of visual pattern perception. In particular we have not discussed depth perception nor such problems as how an object can be recognized when it is partially obscured by another object in front of it.

Secondly, the theory is only the outlines of a theory. It is vague in many respects, some of which may be worth listing. (1) We have not specified the mechanism which operates on the output from the processor and induces a rule to describe it. This is a very difficult problem since little is known about mechanisms for performing even very simple inductions. (2) There must be a similar mechanism for retrieving a matching description when a familiar pattern is input. Since a very large number of descriptive rules must be stored in the human brain, the problem of how the appropriate rule is retrieved within a fraction of a second is a formidable one. We have suggested that some global descriptors may be stored along with the detailed rules, and by using such descriptors to address rules the search space could to some extent be cut down. The detailed heuristics used in retrieval are, however, completely unknown. (3) Although we have made some suggestions about the language in which descriptions are cast, our suggestions are very crude and it is difficult to know whether they are along the right lines. The language suggested leaves many unsolved problems—for example how is a circle or regular curve described in a language whose basic elements refer to straight edges?

The question remains of where we go from here. The theory has the advantage of generality over previous theories put forward but it remains extremely vague. How do we put flesh on its bones? The theory suggests a wealth of behavioural experiments aimed at discovering the generality and nature of the descriptions stored by different species. The results of such experiments, some of which have been briefly referred to here, should help us to be more specific about the type of descriptions formed. One useful technique is to compare across species variations in the behaviour associated with pattern perception with variations in the physiological workings of the visual system (processor). Such comparisons should help us to understand the actual use made by the individual species of the outputs from the processor. It is possible that we shall find a way of tackling the workings of the store from a neurophysiological standpoint, though at the moment it is difficult to see any way into this problem. The logic of the whole system appears to be so complex that to test and refine our own theories we shall be driven to computer simulation. It may be that we shall have to put up with having only a general understanding of the system. If we can programme a computer to recognize and operate upon visually presented patterns in the same way that we ourselves do from the standpoint of input-output relations, this would still not prove that our brains used the same logic as the computer programme. It would, however, be an outstanding scientific achievement in its own right and it could hardly fail to suggest further testable hypotheses about the workings of the human brain.

Acknowledgements

The research described was supported by the American Office of Naval Research (Contract N62558–4791) and the Scientific Research Council. This ch. is a modified version of an article to appear in *Proc. R. Soc.* (B) (1968). The author is grateful to the Royal Society for permission to publish much of the text and some of the figs.

References

Bartlett, F. C. (1932). "Remembering: an experimental and social study." Cambridge University Press, London.

Boring, E. G. (1930). A new ambiguous figure. *Am. J. Psychol.* **42**, 444–445.

Clowes, M. B. (1967). Perception, picture processing and computers. *In* "Machine

Intelligence, 1" (N. L. Collins and D. Michie, eds.), pp. 181–97. Oliver & Boyd, Edinburgh.

Cronly-Dillon, J. R., Sutherland, N. S. and Wolfe, J. B. (1966). Intraretinal transfer of a learned visual shape discrimination in goldfish after section and regeneration of the optic nerve brachia. *Exp. Neurol.* 15, 455–462.

Fields, P. E. (1932). Studies in concept formation: The development of the concept of triangularity by the white rat. *Comp. Psychol. Monogr.* 9, (No. 2), 1–70.

Ganz, L. and Wilson, P. D. (1967). Innate generalization of a form discrimination without contouring eye movements. *J. comp. physiol. Psychol.* 63, 258–269.

Gottschaldt, K. (1926). Uber den Einfluss der Erfahrung auf die Wahrnehmung von Figuren. *Psychol. Forsch.* 8, 261–317.

Hebb, D. O. (1940). "The Organization of Behaviour". Wiley, New York, U.S.A.

Hubel, D. H. and Wiesel, T. N. (1962). Receptive Fields, Binocular Interaction and functional architecture in the Cat's visual cortex. *J. Physiol.* 160, 106–154.

Hubel, D. H. and Wiesel, T. N. (1965). Receptive Fields and Functional Architecture in two non-striate visual areas (18 and 19) of the Cat. *J. Neurophysiol.* 28, 229–289.

Hubel, D. H. and Wiesel, T. N. (1968). Receptive Fields and Functional Architecture of Monkey striate cortex. *J. Physiol.* 195, 215–243.

Julesz, B. (1960). Binocular depth perception of computer-generated pattern. *Bell System Technical J.* 39, 1125–1162.

Lashley, K. S., Chow, H. L., and Semmes, T. (1951). An examination of the electrical field theory of cerebral integration. *Psychol. Rev.* 58, 123–136.

Lawrence, D. H. (1949). Acquired distinctiveness of cues: 1. Transfer between discriminations on the basis of familiarity with the stimuli. *J. expl Psychol.* 39, 770–784.

Mackintosh, N. J. (1965). Selective attention in animal discrimination learning. *Psychol. Bull.* 64, 124–150.

Mishkin, M. (1966). Visual Mechanisms Beyond the Striate Cortex. *In* "Frontiers of Physiological Psychology." (R. W. Russell, ed.), pp. 93–119. Academic Press, New York.

Parriss, J. R. and Young, T. (1962). The limits of transfer of a learned discrimination to figures of larger and smaller sizes. *Z. verg. Physiol.* 45, 618–635.

Penfield, W. (1959). The interpretive cortex. *Science.* 129, 1719–1725.

Polyak, S. L. (1941). "The Retina." Univ. of Chicago Press, Chicago, U.S.A.

Rubin, E. (1921). Visuell wahrgenommene Figuren, Kobenhavn.

Sperry, R. W., Miner, N. and Myers, R. E. (1955). Visual perception following subpial slicing and tantalum wire insertion in the visual cortex. *J. comp. physiol. Psychol.* 48, 50–58.

Sutherland, N. S. (1959). Stimulus analysing mechanisms. *In* "Proc. Symp. Mechanization of Thought Processes.

Sutherland, N. S. (1960a). Visual discrimination of shape by Octopus: squares and rectangles. *J. comp. Physiol. Psychol.* 53, 95–103.

Sutherland, N. S. (1960b). Theories of shape discrimination in Octopus. *Nature.* 186, 840–844.

Sutherland, N. S. (1961). The methods and findings of experiments on the visual discrimination of shape by animals. *Quart. J. exp. Psychol. Monogr.* No. 1, 1–68.

Sutherland, N. S. (1963). Shape discrimination and receptive fields. *Nature.* 197, 118–122.

Sutherland, N. S. (1964a). Visual discrimination in animals. *Brit. Med. Bull.* **20**, 54–59.

Sutherland, N. S. (1964b). The learning of discrimination by animals. *Endeavour.* **23**, 148–152.

Sutherland, N. S. (1968). Outlines of a theory of visual pattern recognition in animals and man. *Proc. R. Soc.* (In press.)

Sutherland, N. S. (1969). Shape discrimination in rats, octopus and goldfish: a comparative study. *J. comp. physiol. Psychol.* (in press).

Sutherland, N. S. and Carr, A. E. (1963). The visual discrimination of shape by Octopus: the effects of stimulus size. *Quart. J. exp. Psychol.* **13**, 225–235.

Sutherland, N. S. and Carr, A. E. (1964). The discrimination of shape by rats: squares and rectangles. *Brit. J. Psychol.* **55**, 39–48.

Sutherland, N. S. and Holgate, V. (1966). Two-cue discrimination learning in rats. *J. comp. physiol. Psychol.* **61**, 198–207.

Sutherland, N. S. and Williams, C. F. (1969). Discrimination of Checkerboard Pattern by rats. *Quart. J. exp. Psychol.* (in press).

Warren, J. M. (1961). Individual differences in discrimination learning by cats. *J. genet. Psychol.* **98**, 89–93.

16

Discrimination Learning Under Avoidance Schedules

HARRY M. B. HURWITZ AND
PAUL V. DILLOW

University of Tennessee, Knoxville, Tennessee, U.S.A.

I. Introduction

For many investigators the phenomenon of avoidance has been an example, par excellence, of higher order activity or, to use the historical label, of higher mental processes. The similarity of avoidance to *anticipation of consequences* or to *expectations,* terms commonly used to describe large segments of human behavior, is so striking that the ability of an animal to cope with a harmful but avoidable situation has seemed to be an acceptable index of a species' standing in the evolutionary scale of intellectual abilities. In taking avoidance learning as a diagnostic tool for testing higher mental processes, however, psychologists committed themselves to a theoretical position which runs counter to much current thinking. If avoidance is a case of prescience, or is linked to the development of *sign-gestalten,* as Tolman (1951) suggested, or acts as a model of cognitive functioning, then an analysis in terms of the behavioristic paradigms elaborated by Pavlov (1927), Guthrie (1951), Hull (1952) and Skinner (1938) seems to be excluded. For instance, critics of the Pavlovian position were quick to point out that the avoidance response was strengthened without any identifiable reinforcing event. Some theorists have sought to

413

support the behavioristic position by admitting a class of variables which intervene between stimulus and response but which do not conform to the requirements of a cognitive type theory. They argued that in learning to avoid, the subject learns to respond to non-environmental events, namely, internal stimulus conditions or states. Such internal states have been named *fear* or *anxiety* because of their apparent similarity to human subjective experiences. At the present time this line of reasoning stunts the growth of behavioral analysis by quietly but effectively opening the gates to old entelechies in modern dress. Our understanding of avoidance phenomena would be better advanced by working within the framework of a rigorous analysis in terms of stimuli and responses.

II. Some Analyses of Avoidance

An avoidance situation may be defined most generally as one where an organism can prevent the occurrence of an aversive stimulus. *Aversiveness* can be operationally defined. A stimulus is aversive if behavior which reduces its intensity is strengthened. In many experiments the selected response is effective within a relatively short period preceding the aversive stimulus. This time period may be associated with a distinctive event termed the warning stimulus. The behavior which develops under these conditions does not appear to conform to the rules of classical or instrumental conditioning. For example, Bekhterev's (1932) studies created an explanatory problem for Pavlovian (1927) conditioning theory because the conditioned (avoidance) response was being strengthened in the absence of an unconditioned or primary aversive stimulus.

A classical procedure employing an aversive unconditioned stimulus differs fundamentally from an instrumental or operant discriminated avoidance procedure (Hunter, 1935; Schlosberg, 1937). In the former case the conditioned response has no programmed effect on shock presentation, whereas in the discriminated avoidance procedure the response, by definition, prevents the occurrence of shock. According to the instrumental learning paradigm the probability of the future occurrence of a response may be changed by closely following the response by a stimulus change. Such stimulus changes which are effective in producing an increase in the probability of occurrence of the referent response are termed reinforcers. Both escape and reward training are subsumed in this category. Stimulus changes which produce decreases in the probability of occurrence of the referent response are involved in both punishment and omission training.

Hilgard and Marquis (1940) in their pioneering attempt to create order for the then already confused field of Learning Research indicated that the referent response in an instrumental avoidance situation is not typically followed by an immediate stimulus change, like food or cessation of shock, but that the response is strengthened in the apparent absence of any such stimulus change. Thus, neither the classical nor the instrumental learning paradigm alone seemed capable of explaining avoidance learning. Hilgard and Marquis' (1940) solution to the analytical dilemma they had discovered sounds somewhat mentalistic to modern ears. "Absence of stimulation", they wrote, "can obviously have an influence on behavior only if there exists some *expectation* of the stimulation" (italics ours). This statement removes the avoidance phenomenon from the sphere of conditioning theory. However, a compromise solution, which viewed avoidance as a joint product of classical conditioning and instrumental learning was cogently stated by Mowrer as early as in 1939. According to this theory the warning stimulus, through its frequent pairing with the aversive stimulus, comes to control a fractional component of the unconditioned response. This fractional component, the conditioned response, was termed *fear* by Mowrer. Its development follows exactly the procedure of classical conditioning. Since the warning stimulus has the properties of a conditioned aversive stimulus, behaviors which terminate this fear-eliciting stimulus will be selectively reinforced (Law of Effect Learning). He therefore concluded that avoidance did not differ from escape behavior; the escape in this case was from an internal state elicited by the warning stimulus. Mowrer's analysis inspired a great deal of research. Amongst the most recent studies which support this theory are those of Rescorla and Lolordo (1965) and Rescorla and Solomon (1967) who demonstrated that classically conditioned stimuli can increase or decrease the probability of an instrumental response when they are superimposed upon a non-discriminated avoidance procedure.

Mowrer's theory implied that a warning stimulus was necessary for the occurrence of the avoidance response. However, Mowrer and Lamoreaux (1942) noted in an early paper on the functional role of the warning stimulus, that the response which was being conditioned occurred frequently during the intertrial interval when the warning stimulus was absent. This tendency to respond between successive trials only gradually subsided. By way of explanation one could assume that at first fear is conditioned to general apparatus or situational cues and that only later do these responses become specific to the warning stimulus. Comparisons have been made of the discriminative control exerted by the warning stimulus over the instrumental response, with the control exerted by the intertrial stimuli. In addition, comparisons have been made with behaviors other than those programmed to effect termination of the warning signal: autonomic responses, grooming frequency in the rat, suppression of ongoing behavior, and so on (McAllister and McAllister, 1962a, 1962b;

Kamin *et al.* 1963; Hoffman and Fleshler, 1962; Brown *et al.* 1951; Azrin *et al.* 1967). The findings of all these studies indicate an increasing control over such collateral behavior by the warning stimulus.

Another problem was raised when Sidman (1953) demonstrated that avoidance behavior could be acquired and maintained in a situation where no exteroceptive warning stimulus was used. In that study, shock was delivered whenever a certain time elapsed without a lever press. This procedure, known as the free-operant avoidance schedule, differed from the discrete trial discriminated procedure in at least two respects: there was no exteroceptive stimulus to which one could attribute the intermittent arousal of fear; and secondly, there was no stimulus change following the instrumental response which would serve as a reinforcer.

A number of attempts have been made to analyse Sidman's findings within Mowrer's dual process theory, the most recent of which we owe to Anger (1963). A principal feature of the results reported by Sidman and others (e.g. Verhave, 1959) is that rats (and other species) *will* avoid shock in non-discriminated avoidance learning situations. However, subjects often need an extraordinarily long time to learn the task (Weissman, 1962; Hurwitz and Bounds, 1968). Moreover, eventually the rate of response becomes increasingly related to the period by which each response is programmed to postpone shock; when the delay of shock is long, the response rate is low; when the delay is short, the response rate is high. According to Anger's analysis, the appropriate pacing of the response is due to the existence of a timing mechanism whose anchoring point is the stimulus consequences of a response. Since such response-produced stimuli are entirely inferred from overt behavior, however, the argument contains an unacceptable and discomforting element of circularity.

A different explanation for the acquisition and maintenance of free operant avoidance behavior was given by Dinsmoor (1954), who made no explicit recourse to the notion of fear reduction (See also Schoenfeld, 1950). Dinsmoor's analysis assumed that all incorrect instrumental responses are at one time or another coincidental with shock. As a result all behaviors with the exception of the correct instrumental response undergo differential suppression, the rate of suppression presumably being related to the initial strength of the response. Note that this interpretation bypasses the problem of the nature of the event which *reinforces* the avoidance response. Sole emphasis is placed on the idea that punishment is an agent for suppression of behavior.

Finally, we would like to draw attention to an analysis of avoidance formulated by Sidman (1962) who suggested that the reinforcement for the avoidance response is due to the subject's ability to discriminate the density of shocks before and after the occurrence of the referent response.

The theory is certainly appealing in the light of available evidence, but it is too early to judge whether Sidman's interpretation will be able to handle the results of experiments outside the free operant avoidance situation.

In none of the above theoretical analyses has distinction been made between the necessary factors contributing to the *acquisition,* as opposed to the *maintenance* of an avoidance response. According to early formulations of Mowrer, it was necessary that the termination of the warning stimulus occurred in close temporal contiguity with the performance of the response. Later experiments (e.g. Kamin, 1956, 1957), however, showed that this is not critical. Similarly, many writers assume *fear arousal* and *fear reduction* to be necessary factors. Whilst there is some support from studies of collateral behavior, such as autonomic response levels and defecation frequency, that fear may be involved in the acquisition of the avoidance response (Overmier, 1966), there is no evidence that it is involved in the maintenance of the behavior. Freud (1936) stated long ago that avoidance behavior was maintained as a defense against anxiety arousal rather than as a response to it. The positions of Mowrer and Freud may not be as opposed as would appear at first. Mowrer's theory handles simple avoidance involving only a first-order classical pairing, whereas it may be assumed that Freud's statement applies to a higher-order classical pairing situation. Thus, fear or anxiety for Freud is the aversive event to be avoided, comparable to the shock in the conventional animal learning situation.

The concept of fear has been used in at least two distinct, but not necessarily incompatible ways; as a conditioned response to the warning stimulus, or as an acquired drive stimulus whose reduction acts as a reinforcer for ongoing responses (Hull, 1943; Mowrer, 1939; Miller, 1948 and Solomon and Turner, 1962). There is an urgent need to objectify these usages. In an attempt to objectify *fear* as a *response,* investigators have made extensive use of measures of autonomic activity, including peripheral, neural and hormonal changes. More recently indices of functioning within the central nervous system have been used (John and Killiam, 1960). When fear is used as a drive stimulus its strength may be assessed in several ways.

One way is to relate the strength of the avoidance response to the number of pairings of warning stimulus and shock, on the assumption that the level of the acquired drive stimulus controls the strength of the avoidance response. Another way is to compare measures of autonomic activity preceding and following the execution of the avoidance response, on the assumption that such changes reflect the reduction of the hypothetical drive stimulus, fear.

Since the concept of *fear* seemingly refers on the one hand to measureable responses and on the other to a hypothetical stimulus condition it has been difficult to avoid ambiguity and confusion. Even if these difficulties in terminology were resolved, the very nature of such concepts as *internal responses* and *internal stimuli* would continue to guide research toward investigation of presumptive mechanisms which accompany or which mediate the avoidance response. What we need is to direct research towards increasing the control and predictability of the observed phenomena. This can be accomplished through a better knowledge of response repertoires and the environmental conditions which are found to control these behaviors.

III. An Operational Approach

Often explanatory concepts like fear are introduced into specialized scientific vocabulary as stop gaps. They are designed to serve until a more satisfactory analysis of the phenomenon can be arrived at. An alternative strategy is to avoid using concepts which refer to hypothetical intermediary events and to provide an operational analysis of all terms used to describe the events under investigation. The first requirement of such an operational analysis for behavioral phenomena is a precise delineation of the procedure or schedule to which the animal is exposed in terms of the stimuli to be presented, their sequential flow, and the programmed consequences of the different responses the animal makes. In addition one should note that an organism brings to a situation a repertoire of behaviors, some of which may be the result of previous exposure to similar or dissimilar procedures (under arranged or natural conditions), and also behaviors for which origins cannot be given, including species specific behavior. Ideally, a full account of the consequences of a procedure must include response profiles pertinent to the situation, obtained prior, during and after the procedure has been imposed. In practice this is rarely done (*c.f.* Bindra, 1961). It should be noted, for example, that the frequency of a response will not necessarily change just because it has a programmed consequence. The experimental task is to discover the range of parametric values which *de facto* produce distinctive outcomes for subjects of a given species under a basic procedure, for which the nature of the stimuli, response topographies, and time values are stated only in general terms. Whether a subject will acquire the referent response under a discriminated avoidance procedure will depend upon the type (Myers, 1964) and duration (Pearl and Edwards, 1962) of the warning and intertrial stimuli; upon the nature of the aversive stimulus (Hurwitz and Dillow, 1966a, 1966b); upon the required response topography (Bolles, 1967); the species of animal (Krieckhaus and Wagman, 1967) and its previous history (Seligman and Maier, 1967).

Care should be taken in making categories judgement concerning the effectiveness of a given basic procedure. For example, Meyer *et al.* (1960) after many unsuccessful attempts to train rats to lever press under a discriminated avoidance procedure, incorrectly concluded that the difficulty was inherent in the species and in the response topography required in the situation. Subsequent work (D'Amato *et al.* 1964; Hurwitz, 1964) showed that a change in the temporal characteristics of the shock stimulus, namely the use of a pulsed shock series instead of a continuously presented shock, resulted in rapid acquisition of the lever response. Later it was found that the procedures used by these investigators led to more stable and more effective avoidance than had been obtained by the traditional shuttle box technique. Much of avoidance behavior appears explicable in terms of interactions between the nature of the warning and aversive stimuli, the topography of the learned escape response, and the topography of the to-be-conditioned avoidance response. Consequently, theoretical intervening variables are rendered unimportant.

IV. Interaction of Escape and Avoidance Topographies

Any movement of an animal may be designated as a response, and that response may be given environmental consequences. Among the response requirements which have been extensively used in escape and avoidance experiments where rats have served as subjects are the lever press (Hurwitz, 1964); alley running (Santos, 1960); hurdle jumping and shuttling (Theios and Dunaway, 1964); wheel turning (Fitzgerald and Brown, 1965; Mathers, 1957; Thompson, 1950); immobility, as in passive avoidance experiments (Bindra and Anchel, 1963); and many others. Bolles (1967) recently proposed that the ease with which an avoidance response is acquired is related to the similarity of the response to the innate defensive reaction already available to that species of animal. He cites as evidence for this broad assumption the relative ease with which a rat learns to run the length of an alley as opposed to the difficulty encountered in training it to lever press in avoidance situations (Meyer *et al.* 1960). The former response is regarded as an innate defensive response to aversive situations. However, Greene and Peacock (1965) have reported considerable difficulty in training rats to perform *any* active movement in order to avoid shock. Perhaps under some conditions running is the innate defensive (escape and avoidance) response of the rat whereas under others immobility or freezing is more readily available.

The first experiment to systematically investigate the possibility that the development of an avoidance response might in some manner be determined by similarities of the escape and avoidance response was reported by Mowrer and Lamoreaux (1946). Four groups of rats were trained in a shuttle box. The avoidance and escape response requirements were either the same within each group or they differed. One of the responses was shuttling, that is running from side to side in a box, and the other was jumping in the air. The results revealed that a running avoidance response was readily acquired irrespective of the topography of the required escape response but that a jump was only acquired as an avoidance response if the escape response requirement was also jumping. With running as the escape response and jumping as the avoidance response, acquisition of the avoidance response was very poor. Perhaps for the rat exposed to this kind of aversive situation, running comes more easily† than jumping. If this is true, running will tend to occur even if jumping is reinforced as an escape response; however, if running is reinforced as an escape response the probability of jumping occurring is very low.

Bixenstine and Barker (1964) report an interesting study in which rats could escape shock by performing a lever press. However, in order to avoid they had to run from one side of the box to the other. Acquisition of the running avoidance response was slow but when shock termination following escape was delayed, shuttle-avoidance performance improved. A more thorough analysis of the behaviors arising in this situation might have shown that the rats had developed extensive lever holding as an escape from shock response, and that this behaviour necessarily limited their active shuttling behavior. We suggest that the reasons for the differences in the rate of acquisition of avoidance and escape responses are not necessarily found in schedule of reinforcement factors, but reflect something about the response topographies involved. This point is illustrated by considering more carefully what happens in the lever press situation. It is well documented that rats engage in extensive lever holding behavior when exposed to a shock escape schedule (e.g. Dinsmoor et al. 1957; Migler, 1963a). Similar behavior has been observed during early exposure to lever press avoidance procedures which included an escape procedure (Hurwitz and Dillow, 1967). How does such lever holding come about? Typically, upon first exposure to the shock the rat runs around the experimental chamber and in the course of this activity bumps into and depresses the lever, so terminating the shock. The rat will probably probably remain in the position it was in at the time of shock termination so that it will continue to hold the lever down. Now if shock occurs when the rat is holding the lever, the onset shock will induce a reflexive response of the rat's musculature thereby throwing it momentarily off the lever. The return to the lever constitutes an escape response. Moreover, extended

---

† We shall later take up this argument again. It is not sufficient just to assume that one response is more probable in an aversive situation than another. We can go further: for example, much depends on the nature of the aversive and warning stimuli involved.

lever holding behavior may also serve a preparatory function in that it enables the rat to perform very short latency escape responses (Dinsmoor and Hughes, 1956; Campbell, 1962). The strength of this type of escape response is seen when attempts are made to reduce or eliminate it. For example, Migler (1963b) reported that even punishment of lever holding produced only minor changes in this behavior. The high probability that a rat will freeze on the lever in a shock-escape situation is also reflected in the ease with which a rat can be trained to continuously hold down the lever to avoid shock compared with the far slower acquisition of a lever press-escape response which initiates a shock free period. In fact Keehn (1967) found the acquisition of the escape response of continuous holding to be almost as fast as that of escape in a running wheel.

Although many investigators have speculated that the extended lever holding which typically develops during early exposure to an escape-avoidance procedure interferes with the aquisition of the avoidance response (e.g. Hoffman, 1966), the present writers came to a different conclusion (Hurwitz and Dillow, 1967). They trained rats in a discriminated avoidance situation where the warning period was signalled by the absence of a buzz and the intertrial interval was signalled by the presence of that buzz.† The experiment showed that as the percent avoidance increased, lever holding behavior deteriorated. The deterioration in lever holding and the probability of an avoidance response were related to the duration of the warning stimulus. For as long as lever holding was a part of a generalized freezing pattern which lasted throughout a complete cycle from one shock until the next, the probability of the rat performing an *avoidance* response increased only as the holding behavior lessened during the warning period. If the total cycle time from warning period to warning period is increased, the rat is less likely to hold for the full length of the cycle, and such an arrangement may favour acquisition of avoidance, especially if the warning period, rather than the intertrial interval, is increased (Hurwitz, 1965; Pearl and Edwards, 1962).

V. Stimulus—Characteristics

The evidence surveyed so far emphasizes that the characteristics of the response learned in relation to escape from shock interact with the behavior which has been defined as the avoidance response. We have concentrated on the *durations* of the warning and intertrial intervals as factors which often effect the topographies of the relevent responses. We must now consider the importance of the nature of the stimuli presented

---

† It is known from research by Myers (1960) that such an arrangement of stimuli in a discriminated avoidance situation results in a slow rate of acquisition of the avoidance response.

during (or associated with) the warning and intertrial periods, since many experiments have demonstrated that these factors act as determinants of the rate of acquisition of an avoidance response.

Biederman *et al.* (1964) for example showed that the acquisition of a discriminated lever press avoidance response was facilitated by spatially separating the source of the warning stimulus from the manipulandum: that is, by placing the warning light on the wall opposite the lever rather than on the same wall. Presumably the warning stimulus, through its association with shock, had acquired a conditioned aversive property, so that the animal tended to withdraw from this stimulus. Placing the light on the rear wall of the chamber would increase the probability that the animal came into contact with the lever as it fled from the area of the warning stimulus.

In a study designed to investigate Hull's (1952) concept of stimulus dynamism Kessen (1953) demonstrated that the rate of acquisition of a wheel turning avoidance response was related to the absolute intensity of the warning stimulus light. More recently Bower, *et al.* (1965) extended Kessen's results by showing that the rate at which a shuttle response was learned was a function of the difference between the physical energies of the stimuli associated with the warning and intertrial periods. Another approach has been to study the relative effectiveness of the presence or absence of an event, e.g. a tone, as warning stimulus. Kish (1955) obtained more rapid avoidance response acquisition when an auditory stimulus was used as a warning signal than when it was used to identify the intertrial period. A study by Schwartz (1958) focussed on the terminal performance of subjects exposed to the above type conditions. He found that a large number of subjects exposed to energy-absence during the warning period failed to reach the terminal avoidance level obtained under energy-present conditions even when the subjects were given much extra training. Additional work by Myers (1959, 1960, 1962, 1964) confirmed and extended these earlier findings, specifically that a buzz is more effective than a pure tone as a warning stimulus for rats. Other research (Dewson, 1965) has shown that high frequency pure tones are more effective than low frequency tones when used as the warning stimulus; whilst Levis (1966) reported that the presence of physical energy during the warning period results in faster runway avoidance than the use of this stimulus to indicate the intertrial interval.

The effects we have briefly considered could have been the result of an interaction between the characteristics of the required avoidance response and the responses typically evoked by the warning stimulus. This possibility was not taken into account either in Hull's stimulus dynamism concept or in the suggestion by Perkins (1953) and by Logan (1954) that

differences in the rate of learning reflect differences in the discriminability
of the warning signals. We have recently investigated possible interaction
(Hurwitz and Dillow, 1968).

Rats were trained in a lever press avoidance situation. Three conditions
were studied. In the WARN BUZZ condition a buzz was used to indicate
the 15 second warning period during which a lever response was effective
in terminating the signal and preventing the onset of shock. In the ITI
BUZZ condition the warning signal was silence and the intertrial interval

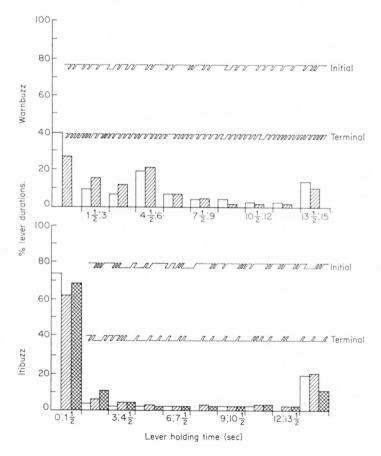

FIG. 1. The histogram distributions present the lever holding times expressed as a
percentage of the total number of responses. The data are averaged over all sessions and
each subject is represented by a distinctive bar-column. Representative sample records
of lever holding behavior at initial and terminal sessions are presented above the histograms. The pen moved upwards when the lever was depressed.

period was indicated by a five second buzz. In the third condition only the beginning of the warning period was indicated by a buzz (TRACE BUZZ). Our first concern was whether the use of a buzz as a warning signal was more effective in training the animal to lever press than when the buzz was used to indicate the intertrial interval. The faster learning rate for the WARN BUZZ subjects confirmed earlier studies by Myers (1960) and others. These results could be accounted for in terms of the disruption of lever holding by the buzz at the onset of the warning period. Under the WARN BUZZ condition approximately 75 percent of the latencies of the avoidance response fell within the first three seconds of the warning period, whereas only 30 percent of the latencies under the ITI BUZZ condition fell into this category. An analysis of lever holding behavior (See Fig. 1) showed that the WARN BUZZ condition resulted in frequent lever holds of 4·5 to 6 seconds duration whereas in the ITI BUZZ condition the holds

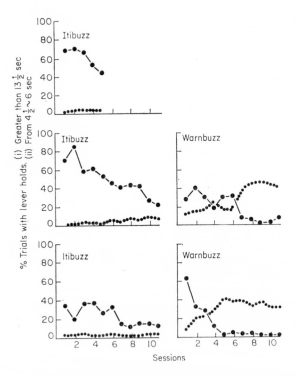

FIG. 2. The solid lines show for each session the number of trials during which the lever was held for longer than 13·5 sec as a percentage of total trials. Similarly, dotted lines show percentages of trials during which the lever was held for between 4·5 and 6·0 sec. The data from two WARN BUZZ and from three ITI BUZZ subjects are presented.

were very short (0 to 1·5 sec) or very long (13·5 to 15 sec). A session by session analysis of lever holding (See Fig. 2) showed that extensive lever holding was typical of both WARN BUZZ and ITI BUZZ subjects during initial sessions, but that on terminal sessions the ITI BUZZ subjects rarely held the lever for long, whereas the WARN BUZZ subjects held for a period which corresponded to the length of the intertrial interval, namely five seconds. In other words the WARN BUZZ animals apparently held the lever almost continuously except at the onset of the buzz when they briefly released the lever. These data strongly suggest the following interpretation. All subjects first learned to lever hold because this response was reinforced by shock termination (as outlined in our earlier discussion). In order to shift from escape to avoidance persistent holding must necessarily be discontinued; the lever must be released and pressed shortly before shock. This requirement was facilitated by the use of a buzz as the warning stimulus. When the buzz occurred the subject momentarily released but immediately fell back onto or returned to the lever. In this way the animal exposed himself to the avoidance contingencies.

To what extent did the rate of learning under the WARN BUZZ condition depend on the disruptive effect of the buzz on lever holding, as against the reinforcing effect of terminating the warning signal. Our question was partially answered by comparing the results of the TRACE BUZZ and WARN BUZZ procedures. The results showed that the TRACE BUZZ procedure, where a brief buzz was presented at the beginning of each warning period, facilitated the momentary release of the lever which, as we have already seen, exposed the subject to the avoidance contingency. At first this resulted in high avoidance but the conditions were ineffective in maintaining such behavior for long. Our conclusion was that the availability of the buzz until the response was executed, and its occasional coincidence with shock, appear to be critical factors in explaining the rapid learning by the animal trained under the WARN BUZZ condition. More experiments on these lines clearly need to be done. In general our experiment encouraged us in the notion that the characteristics of the stimuli used as warning signals may influence the rate of acquisition of an avoidance response by changing the probabilities of occurrence of other responses which may interact with the response to be conditioned.

VI. Separation of Acquisition of Avoidance and Acquisition of Control by the Warning Stimulus

In our discussions so far we have referred only to conventional discriminated avoidance procedures in which the subject had to learn the avoidance response at the same time as he had to learn to discriminate between the warning and intertrial stimuli. The conventional avoidance procedure confounds the development of stimulus control, that is, of performing the response in the presence of the warning stimulus, with the actual acquisition or differentation of the referent response. These two aspects of the learning task may be separated by first training a subject to avoid under a non-discriminated or temporally defined avoidance schedule and introducing a warning stimulus only when the response has been fully developed. Such studies have been reported by Sidman (1955) and Sidman and Boren (1957). In these experiments rats were trained to avoid shock under a free operant avoidance schedule (Sidman, 1953) in which each lever response postponed the presentation of a series of shocks: shock was administered when the subject paused beyond a given time. After the resulting behavior had stabilized, a warning stimulus was introduced for a short period before the next shock and terminated whenever a response occurred in the presence of the warning stimulus. It should be noted that responses performed in the presence or in the absence of the warning stimulus also avoided shock. Under these conditions subjects tended to restrict most of their responses to the warning stimulus period. Ulrich et al. (1964) performed a similar experiment but included in their design a number of different warning signal durations. They report that the latencies of response to stimulus onset were typically very short. An experiment by Stretch and Skinner (1967a) failed to confirm the finding: on the contrary, short latencies of response to the warning signal were rare. An explanation of this contrary finding may lie in the shock intensities and warning stimuli used. Ulrich et al. used a 5 mA shock intensity and a buzz; Stretch and Skinner used a 2·5 mA shock intensity and a white noise. Thus the short latencies of response to the warning signal may in part be attributable to the high shock level and the disruptive nature of the warning stimulus.

The procedures used in the above studies did not conform strictly to the usual method of studying discriminated avoidance since *all* lever responses, whether in the presence of the warning signal or not, functioned to avoid shock. Hurwitz, DeNise and Dillow (1968) employed a discriminated avoidance procedure in which emission of the specified response did not always postpone shock.† The schedule is defined by two successive time intervals, t^Δ and t^D. Responses occurring in t^Δ have no programmed effect. Response in t^D prevent the shock which would otherwise occur at the end of the t^Δ—t^D cycle. If a stimulus difference is correlated with the t^Δ and t^D periods, the typical discriminated avoidance schedule is produced. In the experiment under discussion, a warning stimulus, light, was introduced in the t^D period only after the behavior under the t^Δ—t^D schedule had stabilized. A lever response in t^D terminated this light and

† In this experiment the t^Δ–t^D avoidance schedule described by Hurwitz and Millenson (1961) was used.

prevented the shock. Subjects who had achieved at least 80 percent avoidance during non-discriminated training sessions drastically reduced their response rates and typically made only one response in each t^D period and almost none during $t^\triangle$ periods. When the signal was not terminable during t^D, the subjects tended to respond throughout the t^D period but not during the $t^\triangle$ period. It was notable that these manipulations with the warning stimulus significantly effected only rats who had achieved a high percentage of avoidance under the non-discriminated procedure. This finding suggests that the avoidance response itself must be acquired before it becomes controlled by the warning stimulus. If this conclusion is generalized to apply to the traditional discriminated training procedures, it becomes clear to what degree the primary variables of selective response strengthening and stimulus discrimination have been confounded in the majority of past experiments.

VII. Interaction of Stimuli and Responses

We shall consider now how the nature of the aversive stimulus interacts with the responses to-be-conditioned in determining the rate of learning of the avoidance response. A variety of aversive stimuli have been employed in escape and avoidance situations including: electric shock (Mowrer and Lamoreaux, 1946); noise (Myers, 1965; Harrison and Abelson, 1959); light (Keller, 1941); air blast (Ray, 1966) and high carbon dioxide concentration (Van Sommers, 1963). The effectiveness of the aversive stimulus may be due to several factors; for example, in the case of electric shock, to the potential difference, the current flow, the wave form, and so on. Moyer and Korn (1964), Johnson and Church (1965). D'Amato and Fazzaro (1966), and Levine (1966), amongst others, have reported a $\cap$-shaped function relating-shock intensity and the rate of acquisition of the *avoidance response*. With weak shock the subjects persist in escape behavior, but as shock is intensified the rate of learning to avoid increases for a while, reaches a maximum, and then once again declines. The poor avoidance acquisition at high shock levels may be due to the disabling effects of the shock. Investigators have often ignored the nature of the unconditioned responses evoked by shock and their compatibility or incompatibility with the behaviour experimentally designated to function as the avoidance or escape response. In addition to stating the physical parameters of the shock, one should specify the characteristics of the responses evoked by the shock. These behaviors, some of which may have a learning history, may depend, in the case of shock, not only on the physical parameters but also on where the stimulus is applied. Thus Fowler and Miller (1963) compared the use of hind- and fore-paw shock in the avoidance training of rats in a runway situation. The hind-paw shock elicited a response of lurching forward which was compatible with running and therefore facilitated acquisition of the avoidance response. Fore-paw shock elicited a backward recoil which was incompatible with the avoidance response of running the length of the runway and, therefore, retarded learning. Warren and Bolles (1967) conducted a similar experiment in a running wheel situation. Their results appear to contradict those of the above experiment in that fore-paw shock produced faster acquisition than hind-paw shock. The discrepancy may be explainable in terms of the nature of the apparatus and the type of movements elicited by shock and their relationship to the response selected as the avoidance response.

A study by Fitzpatrick (1967) investigated these problems more intensively. Shock was delivered to rats through implanted electrodes which were placed at different locations; across the chest, on the right rear leg, over the upper leg muscles, or on the side in the skin of the right gonad. Four levels of constant current shock were employed; 0·5 mA, 0·9 mA, 1·5 mA and 2·3 mA. The rat was observed both whilst the shock was applied, as well as between shock presentations. The observations were time-sampled into five behavioral categories: immobility, grooming, chewing, jerking and generalized activity including sniffing and rearing. Behavior in response to shock was found to vary with the location of the implant, the intensity of shock and with the time spent under shock. When the subjects were exposed to an escape training situation, the rate of learning was found to vary with location of the implant and the intensity of the shock used. It appears that the major impediment to learning to escape from shock by depressing a large lever placed into the rat's relatively small environment, was the degree of immobility induced by shock. The subject's learning of the escape response was related to the character and intensity of the unconditioned response to shock. The results of Fitzpatrick's study on escape learning clearly underscore our thesis that in order to evaluate the effects of different strategies for training subjects in a discriminated avoidance learning task account must be taken of the relationship between the avoidance response requirements and the responses produced by the aversive stimuli.

VIII. An Application of the Analysis: Fixed Ratio Avoidance

We have now explained several phenomena reported in the avoidance literature in terms of interactions between the responses the subject brings to the situation (that is, the characteristic modes of response to critical stimuli like shock and warning signals), the topography of the response the subject learns to aversive stimuli (that is, the learned escape response), and the topography of the avoidance response. In the final section of this chapter we discuss some experiments which owe their origin to a detailed analysis of the interaction of responses and stimuli, and which were aimed at producing behaviors in the rat which have hitherto been very difficult to obtain, namely lever pressing under a fixed ratio discriminated avoidance schedule. We regard these experiments as a test of the pragmatic value of our methodological approach.

A discrete trial, fixed ratio, discriminated avoidance schedule may be defined as one where the completion of a fixed number of lever press responses in the presence of a warning stimulus prevents the occurrence of shock which would otherwise occur at the end of this warning period. Relatively few studies (Stretch *et al*. 1966; Badia, 1965) have been reported in which such a procedure has been strictly followed although there are a number of studies which use procedures which conform partially to the above definition. We shall first review the literature pertaining to the latter.

High rates of lever pressing involving response requirements as high as 350 have been conditioned in monkeys using a schedule in which the reinforcement was a period of time-out from a stimulus complex consisting of a neutral stimulus (light or tone) and a series of brief shocks, and in which no restriction was placed on the number of shocks that a subject could receive while performing the fixed ratio requirement (Azrin *et al*. 1962; Azrin *et al*. 1963; Morse and Kelleher, 1966; Stretch and Skinner, 1967b). By definition such a procedure is not strictly a fixed ratio avoidance schedule since "shocks could and often did occur during the rapid run of responding that characterized ratio performance" (Azrin, *et al*. 1963). However, once the behavior was established in the presence of the shocks the shock frequency could be gradually reduced to as low as one shock every two hours before responding broke down. It is possible that the development of such fixed-ratio like behavior came about as a by-product of extended post-shock response activity, known as *bursting* (Sidman, 1958). Specifically, on receiving a shock, the subject would be likely to respond at a high rate on the lever. Because the experimental conditions were arranged so that the warning signal remained available until the fixed ratio response requirement was met, the chances that a post-shock response burst would be responsible for terminating the warning signal and preventing additional shocks would be considerable at first. As a result, the warning signal would become a conditioned stimulus and gain control over response bursting. Our analysis, which at this stage is speculative, emphasizes that in the studies cited so far, success in conditioning fixed-ratio-like behavior to a signal may be due to the use of a training schedule which did not enforce avoidance of shock as its primary requirement.

In contrast to the above procedures, in a discrete trial fixed ratio discriminated avoidance procedure as defined by the authors, the subject has necessarily a limited time in which to perform the required response(s). Indeed, as Pearl and Edwards (1962) demonstrated, the duration of the warning period, and consequently the time available for the response, is related to success in training a rat to perform a *single* lever press under a discriminated avoidance schedule. With a warning period of 60 seconds duration only 50 percent avoidance was achieved and with a five second warning period only 4 percent. It is possible that the relatively low avoidance percentages reported by Pearl and Edwards may have been partially due to the use of a continuous rather than an intermittent shock. Hurwitz (1964) using a warning period of 7·5 sec showed that the avoidance percentage obtained by rats in a lever pressing situation increased from approximately 15 to 85 percent when the continuous shock was replaced by intermittent shock.

When the avoidance response requirement involves a number rather than a single lever press, difficulties of training the rats are magnified, and to date maximum ratio reported is only eight. (Badia, 1965; Stretch *et al.* 1966). The avoidance percentages obtained under these ratio schedules was generally low: for example, only three of the five rats trained by Badia reached the fixed ratio of eight, and then on only 40 percent of the trials. Badia suggested that the difficulties encountered in training a rat to emit a number of responses could be overcome by extending the warning period. He reasoned that the extra time available would increase the probability that the required number of responses occur even though the interresponse times might be long. It should be pointed out, however, that such an extension of the warning period is not guaranteed to produce or to maintain the required behavior, for unless the responses occur in close temporal order reinforcement would be effective only on those responses and interresponse times which immediately precede the terminal response rather than on the entire series. Furthermore, as the duration of the warning period is increased the temporal association between onset of the warning stimulus and the presentation of shock necessarily becomes weaker. Kaplan (1956) who trained rats to press a lever under a fixed ratio schedule to escape an aversive light, and Badia and Levine (1964) who trained rats to perform fixed ratio shuttle responses in the presence of a warning stimulus to avoid shock, found that the latencies of the first response to stimulus onset tended to increase as the fixed ratio requirement was increased. Given that the latency of the first response to warning stimulus onset is long in comparison to the duration of the warning period, so that the time remaining for completing the response run is short, then the probability that the subject will complete

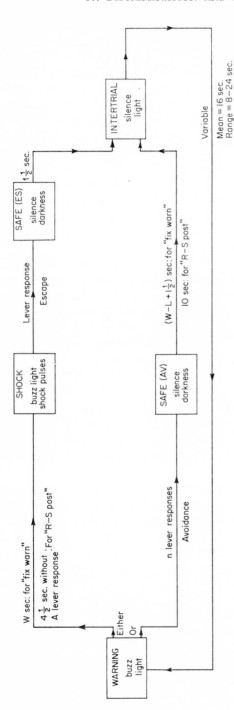

Fig. 3. Each square represents a stage within the procedure. Only one stage was enforced at a given time. The name of the stage and the stimulus events presented while the stage was in effect are described within each square. The arrowed lines represent the possible transitions between the stages, and the descriptions adjacent to these arrows refer to either the duration of the preceding stage or to the termination of that stage by a response(s). Note that the requirements for transition from the warning to shock stage and from the safe (av) to the intertrial stage differ under the FIX WARN and R–S POST procedures. The duration of the safe (av) stage following a given successful avoidance under the procedure FIX WARN was given by the expression (W–L + 1·5) sec, where W represents the programmed duration of the warning stage, and L the latency of the nth and final ratio response to the onset of the warning stage on that particular trial. In procedure FIX WARN values were assigned to both W and n, and in procedure R–S POST a value was assigned to n.

the ratio requirement would be low. This implies that the chances are high that a shock will occur before the responses of the fixed ratio requirement have been completed. The result of this chain of events, signal, incomplete response requirement, shock—can readily be predicted from experiments on the effects of punishment; after repeated punishment of incomplete response runs, these responses will be suppressed and the subject is likely to adopt a pattern of behavior known as *freezing*.

In the experiments reported here (Dillow and Hurwitz, 1968) an attempt was made to arrange conditions which on the one hand would reduce the punishment of response runs and on the other hand increase the effectiveness of the warning signal in promoting repetitive lever pressing. The first objective we sought to accomplish was to reduce the effectiveness of shock in suppressing response runs. For this reason we allowed a short period to elapse after each shock. Our approach to the second objective, that of promoting the required behavior by using special signal conditions, was dictated by our earlier observation that the lever holding behavior which develops during early escape-avoidance training may be disrupted by the onset of a novel though not necessarily aversive stimulus. We therefore reasoned that the use of an intermittent rather than a continuous stimulus during the warning period would promote the emission of a series of responses which would satisfy the fixed ratio response requirement.

The flow diagram, Fig. 3, shows the sequence of stages which will be referred to as procedure FIX WARN. Each session began with the presentation of the warning stage. During the shock-stage brief shocks were presented at 0·33 sec intervals. Different stimuli were presented during the safe-stages and the intertrial-stage, since the acquisition by rats of a discrete trial discriminated avoidance response in a lever pressing apparatus is enhanced by the use of safety signals following avoidance and escape responses (Dillow, 1968). An intertrial-stage of variable duration was used to eliminate the possibility of a temporal discrimination; the mean intertrial interval was 16 sec and the range was from 8 to 24 sec.

The preliminary training of our two female rats (No. 14 and 15) consisted of daily sessions of 400 trials under the procedure FIX WARN. The duration of the warning period, W, was set at 4·5 sec, and the avoidance response requirement, n, was one. An intermittent buzz, $\frac{1}{3}$ sec on, $\frac{2}{3}$ sec off, was presented during the warning and shock stages. In the shock stage, buzz and shock pulses always coincided. The preliminary training was terminated as soon as 75 percent avoidance was achieved on three consecutive sessions.

Following this preliminary training both subjects were exposed to the FIX WARN procedure with the addition of an adjusting fixed ratio response requirement. Each session began with a fixed ratio avoidance

TABLE I

Parameter values during two avoidance procedures

Fixed ratio avoidance response requirement, n (Procedures "Fix Warn" and "R–S Post")	Duration of warning period W sec (procedure "Fix Warn" only)
1 minimum	4·5
2	
3	
4	
5	9
6	
7	
8	13·5
9	
10	
11	10
12	
13	
14	22·5
15	
16	
18	27
20	
22	
24	31·5
26	
28	
30	36
32 maximum	

response requirement, n, set at one. Following every five consecutive avoidances, n was increased to the next programmed value, as shown in Table I. If five consecutive escapes occurred the value of n was decreased to its immediately preceding value. Also shown in Table I are the durations of the warning period, W, which were in effect at each value of n. Throughout all sessions only one response was required to terminate the train of shocks. The experiment consisted of three phases of ten sessions each under the adjusting fixed ratio, FIX WARN procedure. In phase one an

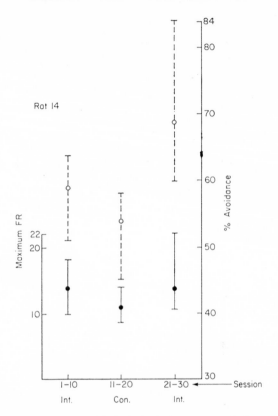

FIG. 4. The solid lines and the filled circles indicate respectively the ranges and the means of the maximum fixed ratios attained in three successive phases by one rat (INT—intermittent warning stimulus; CON—continuous warning stimulus). The broken lines and the open circles likewise indicate percentage avoidance data.

intermittent buzz, as used in preliminary training, was presented during the warning and shock stages. In phase two a continuous buzz was employed, and in phase three the intermittent buzz was reinstated.

The results for Rat 14 only will be presented and discussed.† Figure 4 shows the mean avoidance percentage and maximum fixed ratio attained during each phase of the experiment. There was a slight increase in the maximal fixed ratios attained when an intermittent warning stimulus was used. The fact that the transition from an intermittent buzz in phase one to continuous buzz in phase two resulted in a decrement in maximum fixed ratio as well as a decrement in avoidance percentage, may be taken as evidence for the superiority of the intermittent over the continuous

† The results for Rat 15 were similar but not identical to those of Rat 14.

warning stimulus. The avoidance percentage was highly correlated with the maximum fixed ratio; when the maximum fixed ratio was high, avoidance was also high, though it should be noted that the avoidance percentage had dropped from the level observed during the final sessions under the

TABLE II

Distributions of the mean interresponse times during the warning period averaged across each phase and expressed as percentages. (*The data are from Rat* 14.)

PHASE:	1	2	3
Warning Stimulus: Interresponse Times (sec)	Intermittent	Continuous	Intermittent
0·0–0·2	6	30	5
0·2–0·4	35	22	42
0·4–0·6	10	12	7
0·6–0·8	6	7	7
0·8–1·0	5	5	5
1·0–1·2	3	2	2
1·2–1·4	3	2	2
1·4–1·6	2	1	1
1·6–1·8	2	1	2
1·8–2·0	28	18	27

preliminary training procedure. A high correlation between maximum fixed ratio and avoidance percentage is not of course a necessary consequence of the procedure, since the schedule made it possible for a subject to maintain avoidance at the 80 percent level without an increase in the response requirement, as when four consecutive avoidances are achieved and the fifth trial ends in shock.

As shown in Table II, measures of interresponse times, IRT's, in the warning period for Rat 14 show a substantial difference between the continuous and intermittent warning stimuli. The use of a continuous warning stimulus resulted in shorter IRT's, namely, 30 per cent of the interresponse times in the warning period fell in the 0·0 to 0·2 sec category, whereas with the intermittent stimulus only five percent of the IRT's fell into this category. Although shorter IRT's occurred in the presence of the continuous warning stimulus, this behavior was not consistent as evidenced by the lower maximum fixed ratios obtained with this warning stimulus. The intermittent stimulus produced slightly longer but more consistently maintained IRT's which resulted in higher maximum fixed ratios. The latter may have been the result of a direct driving of the

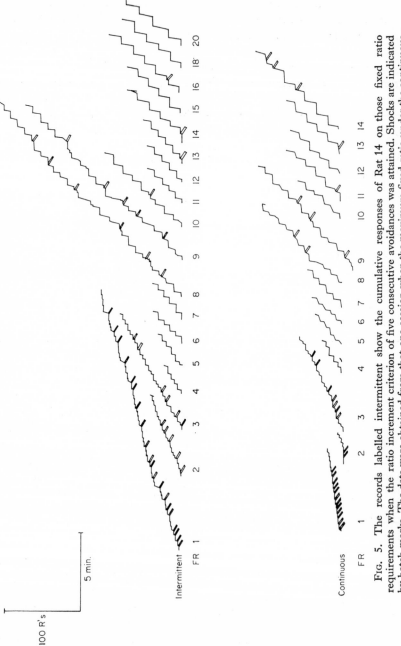

Fig. 5. The records labelled intermittent show the cumulative responses of Rat 14 on those fixed ratio requirements when the ratio increment criterion of five consecutive avoidances was attained. Shocks are indicated by hatch marks. The data were obtained from that one session when the maximum fixed ratio under the continuous warning signal was attained, and the series is presented in order of sequence of time. Similar records from the same rat under the continuous warning signal are also presented. The recorder ran throughout the session.

responses by the intermittent stimulus pulses. Figure 5 shows a representative sample of the cumulative response record of Rat 14. The marked stepwise character of these records suggests that the behavior was under the control of the warning stimulus in each condition.

Thus, our first experiment provided evidence for a slight advantage in the use of an intermittent as opposed to a continuous warning stimulus for establishing fixed ratio avoidance behavior, for this method not only resulted in fixed ratio runs considerably higher than those previously reported, but also maintained a higher avoidance percentage. As already noted the results were anticipated in the light of earlier evidence that stimulus onsets interrupt the rat's lever holding behavior.

Nevertheless, under the procedure of the above experiment, an animal was given shock not only for failing to respond on the lever but also for making incomplete runs on the lever. The latter could have happened because the latency of the first response to the onset of the warning stimulus was too long, so that little time remained for the required number of responses to occur, because the interresponse times were too long, or for both reasons. A method for directly operating upon latencies and interresponse times would be to make the onset of the shock (stage) contingent on both long latencies and long interresponse times. The next experiment combined such a procedure with the adjusting fixed ratio avoidance procedure employed in the previous experiment.

Again, in order to explain the operations performed, we refer to the flow diagram in Fig. 3. This shows the sequences of events which will henceforth be referred to as the R–S POST procedure. The basic difference between procedure FIX WARN and the procedure R–S POST is that whereas in the former case the warning period was terminated either by the completion of the ratio response requirement, or failing this, by the elapse of the fixed warning period, in the R–S POST procedure the termination of the warning period was contingent on completion of the response requirement, or alternatively by the elapse of 4·5 sec without a response. Note that in procedure FIX WARN the duration of the safe (av) stage following an avoidance was given by the expression $(W–L + 1·5)$ sec, where W represents the programmed fixed warning period duration, and L represents the latency of the nth, and final, response of the ratio requirement to the onset of the warning stimulus. This expression is not applicable to procedure R–S POST since in this case the time from the warning stimulus onset to presentation of the shock stage was not fixed; rather it varied from 4·5 sec for the case when no response occurred, to a maximum of 4·5 sec times the fixed ratio avoidance requirement when each interresponse time was just less than 4·5 sec. For this reason the duration of the safe (av) stage was held constant at ten seconds in procedure R–S POST. Apart from the above mentioned differences, procedures R–S POST and FIX WARN were identical.

The preliminary training of two rats (No. 17 and 18) consisted of daily sessions of 200 trials under the R–S POST procedure, with the avoidance response requirement, n, set at one. A continuous buzz was presented during the warning and shock stages. Preliminary training was terminated when a criterion of 75% avoidance was achieved on three consecutive sessions.

Following preliminary training, both subjects were exposed to the R–S POST procedure to which was added an adjusting fixed ratio response

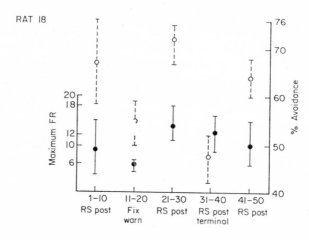

FIG. 6. The solid lines and the filled circles indicate respectively the ranges and the means of the maximum fixed ratios attained in five successive phases by one rat. Details of the procedure at each of the phases, RS POST etc., are given in the text. The broken lines and the open circles likewise indicate percentage avoidance data.

requirement. Each session began with the fixed ratio avoidance response requirement, n, set at one. Following every five consecutive avoidances, n was increased to the next programmed value, as shown in Table I. Furthermore, whenever five consecutive escapes occurred, the value of n was decreased to its immediately preceding value. The warning period durations, W, shown in Table I, do not apply to procedure R–S POST. The escape response requirement was maintained at one throughout.

The experiment consisted of five phases of ten sessions each. The procedures employed during each of these phases were as follows: in phase one, the R–S POST procedure; in phase two, the FIX WARN procedure; in phase three, the R–S POST procedure; in phase four, the R–S POST procedure was modified so that the rat started each session with the value of n, the fixed ratio avoidance response requirement, set at the terminal value obtained on the preceding session (we refer to this procedure as the R–S POST TERMINAL procedure); in phase five, the basic R–S POST procedure; in phase six, Rat 17 only was exposed to the procedure used in phase two, namely, FIX WARN. A continuous buzz was employed as the warning stimulus in all phases of the experiment. (We apologize to the reader for the awkward nomenclature.)

The results of Rat 18 only will be discussed.† Figure 6 shows the means for each phase of the experiment of the avoidance percentage and maximum fixed ratios attained. A higher maximum fixed ratio and higher avoidance

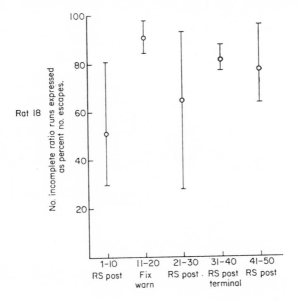

FIG. 7. The solid lines and the open circles indicate respectively the ranges and the means of the numbers of incomplete ratio runs emitted by one rat in five successive phases. Details of the phases are given in the text.

† The results for Rat 17 were similar but not identical to those of Rat 18.

percentage was attained under the R–S POST than under the FIX WARN procedure. A comparison between R–S POST and R–S POST TER-MINAL showed that the latter condition resulted in a decrease in avoidance percentage and that a subsequent return to the R–S POST condition resulted in an increase in avoidance percentage. However, the maximum fixed ratio attained was unaffected by the latter manipulations.

Figure 7 represents the means for each phase of the experiment of the number of trials with incompleted ratio runs expressed as a percentage of the number of trials on which the subject escaped. This measure serves as an index of the proportion of escape trials on which lever response(s) were made during the warning period. Under the FIX WARN condition, the percentage of incompleted runs was greater than under either R–S POST or R–S POST TERMINAL, a result which was in line with our predictions, for by definition there was a 4·5 delay between the last response of an incompleted run and the presentation of shock under the R–S POST schedule whereas under FIX WARN the last response of an incompleted run could be, and often was, immediately followed by shock.

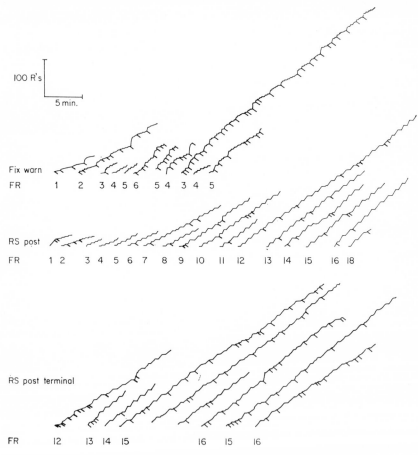

FIG. 8. The records labelled FIX WARN show the cumulative responses of Rat 19. The data constitute a complete record of that session when the maximum fixed ratio under the FIX WARN procedure was attained. Shocks are indicated by hatch marks. Similar records from the same rat under the R–S POST and R–S POST TERMINAL procedures are also presented. The recorder ran throughout the session.

The data showed that under the FIX WARN procedure, 90% of the incompleted ratio runs were followed by shock within two seconds. The nature of the R–S POST procedure also precluded latencies of first response to warning stimulus onset greater than 4·5 sec, whereas under the FIX WARN procedure 40% of the latencies exceeded 4·5 sec. The data used for this comparison was taken from that FIX WARN session when the respective subject had achieved its maximum overall fixed ratio and corresponding maximum warning period duration, W.

In order to assess the degree of discriminative control exerted over responding, the number of extra responses following an avoidance was expressed as a ratio of the number of trials on which the subject successfully avoided; that is, mean number of responses occurring in the safe (av) and intertrial periods following an avoidance response. Such a measure is not contaminated by post shock response bursts and indicates the degree to which responding ceased following completion of the fixed ratio requirement and termination of the warning stimulus. The mean number of extra responses following an avoidance computed over all sessions was 0·4, a value which reflects effective stimulus control. Representative samples of cumulative response records are presented in Fig. 8 and demonstrate in their stepwise nature the degree of discriminative control which the warning stimulus exerted over responding; under procedures FIX WARN and R–S POST stimulus control was good; under R–S POST TERMINAL a slight loss of discriminative control is suggested by the response record.

In the final experiment the use of a continuous versus an intermittent buzz was combined with the use of the FIX WARN versus the R–S POST procedures. The object was to establish which of the different combinations favored the development of high fixed ratios when these conditions were imposed on a single subject.

Two naive female rats (No. 16 and 19) were used. The preliminary training consisted of daily sessions of 400 trials under the FIX WARN procedure as described earlier. The response requirement for avoidance, n, was set at one. A continuous buzz was presented during the warning and shock stages. Preliminary training was terminated as soon as at least 75% avoidance was achieved on three consecutive sessions.

Following preliminary training the subjects were exposed to the following combinations of procedures; in phase one, FIX WARN and continuous buzz; in phase two, FIX WARN and intermittent buzz; in phase three, FIX WARN and continuous buzz; in phase four, R–S POST and continuous buzz. Since during phase four, Rat 19 attained the maximum fixed ratio which was then programmed by the apparatus (that is fixed ratio 32), the following modification was made; the fixed ratio response

15*

requirement n, described in Table I were doubled by the addition of a binary counter into the circuit so that the smallest value of n was now two and the largest 64. Each session commenced with fixed ratio two. Under the R–S POST procedures the response shock postponement interval remained at 4·5 sec, but under the procedure FIX WARN the durations of the warning period as presented in Table I were doubled. Thus the following combinations of procedures and warning stimulus buzz types were employed in phase five: R–S POST and continuous buzz; in phase six, R–S POST and intermittent buzz; in phase seven, R–S POST and continuous buzz, and in phase eight, FIX WARN and continuous buzz.

The results (for Rat 19) in terms of the means across each phase of avoidance percentage and the maximum fixed ratio attained are shown in Fig. 9. During the first and second FIX WARN and continuous buzz phases the maximum fixed ratio showed a difference which suggests that this subject's performance was still relatively unstable during phases one and two, that is the experimental conditions were changed before the

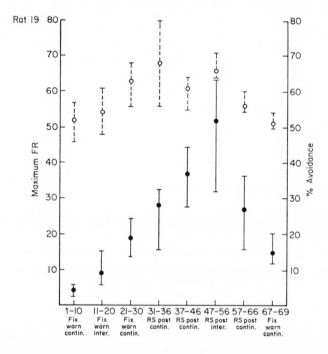

FIG. 9. The solid lines and the filled circles indicate respectively the ranges and the means of the maximum fixed ratios attained by one rat during eight successive phases. Details of the phases are given in the text. The broken lines and the open circles likewise indicate percentage avoidance data.

behavior had stabilized. Note that the R–S POST procedure yielded higher fixed ratios and higher percentage avoidance that the FIX WARN procedure. When Rat 19 was presented with an intermittent warning stimulus in combination with the R–S POST procedure even higher fixed ratios were attained; a maximum fixed ratio of 64 was reached while the subject maintained 70 % avoidance. Since on the average only 1·9 extra responses were made during the safe (av) and intertrial periods following an avoidance the possibility that the subject was merely a high overall responder must

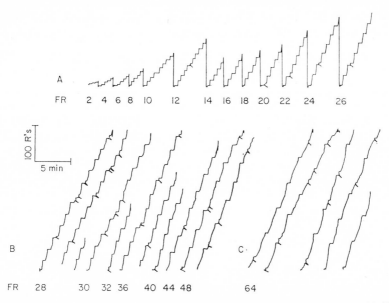

FIG. 10. The records labelled A and B show the cumulative responses of Rat 19. The data constitute a continuous record of that session when the maximum fixed ratio under the R–S POST procedure with an intermittent warning signal was attained. The records labelled C are from the same rat and session and show performance under the maximum fixed ratio of 64. Shocks are indicated by hatch marks. The recorder ran throughout the session.

by excluded. Rather an explanation in terms of stimulus control by the warning stimulus over lever responding seems in order. The mean number of extra responses computed over all sessions again demonstrated a high degree of discriminative control. The stimulus control over ratio responding can be clearly seen in Fig. 10 which presents representative samples of the cumulative response records for rat 19.

Figure 11 shows the means across phases of the number of trials with incompleted ratio runs expressed as a percentage of the number of trials on which the subject escaped, that is the percentage of escape trials on which the subject made at least one lever response during the warning period. Under the FIX WARN conditions, the percentage of such incompleted runs was greater than under the R–S POST conditions. The percentage of incompleted ratio runs which were followed by shock within two seconds under the FIX WARN procedure was 67% for Rat 19. By definition under the R–S POST procedure, shock followed the last response of an incompleted run by 4·5 sec, furthermore, the nature of the R–S POST procedure precluded latencies of first response to warning stimulus onset greater than 4·5 sec. Table III presents a distribution of the latencies of the first response for both subjects on that FIX WARN session on which the maximum overall fixed ratio and corresponding

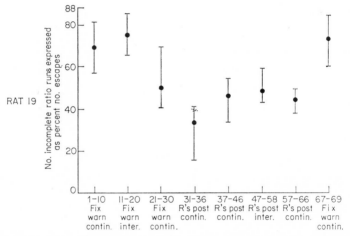

FIG. 11. The solid lines and the open circles indicate respectively the ranges and the means of the numbers of incomplete ratio runs emitted by one rat in eight successive phases. Details of the phases are given in the text.

maximum warning period duration, W, had been attained. Note that the data is averaged over all values of W for that particular session, and that this operation necessarily biases the computed distribution towards short latencies. In view of this fact, the frequences of longer latencies strongly suggest that the subject had a tendency to withhold its first response to warning stimulus onset, often until most of the programmed warning period had elapsed.

The results of this experiment lend support to the findings of the earlier experiment that an intermittent warning stimulus buzz was more effective than a continuous buzz. The results are also consonant with the finding that the R–S POST procedure was superior to the FIX WARN procedure for generating and maintaining fixed ratio avoidance behavior. In general,

TABLE III

Distribution of latencies of first response for Rats 16 and 19.

RAT 16	
Response latency	Percentage frequency
in Sec	
0–4·5	48
4·3–9	27
9–13·5	25

RAT 19	
Response latency in Sec	Percentage frequency
0–9	55
9–18	28
18–27	13
27–36	2
36–45	1
45–54	1

The data are obtained from the last block of "Fix Warn" sessions and are from that session when the maximum overall fixed ratio and corresponding maximum warning period duration, W, was attained. The maximum value of W was 13·5 sec for Rat 16 and 54 sec for Rat 19.

the results show that the combination of an intermittent warning stimulus with a procedure in which each response during the warning stimulus postponed shock by 4·5 sec, the R–S POST procedure, produced the highest fixed ratios, that is of 64. When Rat 19 was given a continuous rather then an intermittent warning stimulus in conjunction with the R–S POST procedure it achieved a fixed ratio of 48. By contrast a change in the programming of the warning period duration so that this period was fixed and not related to the rate of response, the FIX WARN procedure, resulted in relatively lower fixed ratios of approximately 20. All of these values far exceed the ratios previously reported in the literature for the rat, and suggest that the gradual incrementation of the response requirement in accordance with the subject's performance was a critical, though not an experimentally varied, factor.

This problem was studied in a separate experiment by Hurwitz and Dunn (1968). In this experiment the main experimental variable was the size of the criterion for increasing the response requirement which was set at either 1, 5, 10, 15, or infinity. For example, at criterion 15, whenever fifteen successive avoidances occurred the response requirement was increased by one response. The increasing criterion was designed to give the subject more pratice at a specific response requirement. It was hoped

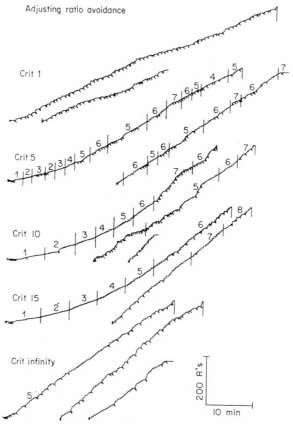

Fig. 12. Cumulative response records are presented for a single subject under each of the avoidance increment criterions. The hatch marks indicate shocks, and the numbers above the records indicate the avoidance response requirements.

that this procedure would result in less punishment of incomplete response runs. Criterion *infinity* represents a non-adjusting procedure, that is the response requirement remained constant throughout the entire session. Each session consisted of 200 trials. Figure 12 shows cumulative response records for one subject; the other 11 subjects exhibited similar behaviors. With a criterion of one avoidance for incrementation of the response requirement, the overall avoidance percentage was 30 and the maximum fixed ratio attained was four. The subject received little practice at avoiding shocks in making only one bar press before the response requirement was increased. As a result, many responses were punished and little advancement of the response requirement occurred. At criterion five a larger number of successive avoidances occurred, which led to a higher avoidance percentage and a higher maximum fixed ratio. At criteria 10 and 15 there was little or no increase in the maximum fixed ratio obtained but a higher avoidance percentage was achieved. The fact that the subjects did not attain *lower* fixed ratios with these two criteria is surprising, since at criterion 15, for example, the subject had to complete 15 successive avoidances in order to increase the response requirement. At criterion infinity each session was run throughout at fixed ratio five. A slight decrement in the avoidances percentage occurred, but not enough to convince us that the within session adjustment procedure was completely necessary.

The results of the experiment suggest that an increase in the number of trials given at each fixed ratio results in a higher avoidance percentage being reached, although the maximum fixed ratio attained would not necessarily increase. A problem in the use of the above procedure is that with an increase in the adjustment criterion, the number of trials per session would have to be increased to allow a higher maximum response requirement to be reached. Furthermore, the procedure permitted many incompleted ratios runs to be punished since there was no explicit control of the response-shock interval.

When compared to either the FIX WARN conditions or when compared to the results of the study by Hurwitz and Dunn, the greater effectiveness of the R–S POST procedure for developing high fixed ratio runs may be explained in two ways. Firstly, the R–S POST procedure allowed the subject a maximum of 4·5 sec for *each* interresponse time, whereas the FIX WARN procedure allowed an *average* interresponse time equal to the programmed warning period, W, divided by the fixed ratio response requirement, n, which ranged from 4·5 sec per response at fixed ratio one, to 1·10 sec per response at fixed ratio 36. For the modified schedule employed with Rat 19 this average ranged from 4·5 sec per response at fixed ratio two, to 2·5 sec per response at fixed ratio 64. Thus, it might be argued that the R–S POST procedure favoured the acquisition of high ratios because more time was potentially available for the emission of the response series. A comparison, of either of the actual warning period durations, or of response rates during the warning periods could be used to decide this issue. No consistent differences were found between the interresponse time distributions obtained from any single subject under these two schedules. In fact the model interresponse times for all subjects fell well within the zero to one second category under both the R–S POST and FIX WARN procedures. This indicates that the subjects had sufficient time in which to execute the response series and did not in fact make use of the additional time provided by the R–S POST procedure.

An alternative explanation may be given in terms of punishing effects of the shock on incompleted ratio runs. Under the FIX WARN procedure it was possible for an incomplete ratio run to be followed immediately by shock, and it was found that on average 78% of such incompleted ratio runs were followed by shock within two seconds. This figure is derived from the means of the measure across all FIX WARN sessions for Rats 16, 16, 18 and 19. By contrast, all incompleted response runs under procedure R–S POST were by definition separated from shock by 4·5 sec. Furthermore the, subjects made substantially fewer incomplete runs under the R–S POST procedure than under FIX WARN. Thus, the delay of punishment of incompleted response runs appears to be the critical factor which accounts for the demonstrated superiority of the R–S POST procedure. The authors favor this interpretation.

Finally, we would like to draw attention to the fact that the R–S POST procedure contains an additional element which has not yet been fully discussed. The specification of the R–S POST procedure not only sets a value to the interval between the last response of an incompleted run and shock, but also specifies the interval between the onset of the warning stimulus and the presentation of shock in the absence of a response. The experiments yielded evidence that the latencies of the first response to the onset of the warning stimulus tended to increase as the duration of the warning period increased in the FIX WARN procedure. Since in the absence of a response the R–S POST procedure fixed the temporal association between onset of warning stimulus and presentation of shock, more constant response latencies were obtained. Additional experiments would be required if one wished to differentiate between the contribution made to the conditioning and maintenance of high ratio avoidance by the delay of punishment of incompleted ratio runs, and the fixed temporal relationship between the onset of the warning stimulus and presentation of shock.

IX. Summary

In this chapter we have prepared a case for applying an operational analysis to a set of problems which the lore of psychology, as transmitted by introductory and graduate textbooks, groups under the heading of Avoidance Learning. We have argued that our understanding of the phenomena under this heading is aided by an operational analysis of the procedure employed. Such an analysis reveals in what way if any, the procedures used in an avoidance experiment differ from those used in the study of other behavioral phenomena and in what ways the results of these different procedures are comparable. We have specially emphasized the nature of the stimuli used and how these stimuli (e.g. pure tones as against a buzz) may influence the experimental outcome. Furthermore, we discussed the nature of the behavior defined as escape and avoidance and how topographies of such responses interact with the warning and aversive stimuli. In our experience this approach reduces the temptation to use higher order intervening or mediating variables, like fear; the explanation of what happens is sought within the overt behaviour of the organism. Lastly, we have related how our analytical framework was instrumental in solving, for us, a recurrent problem in the study of avoidance learning, namely the persistent failure to condition high fixed ratio responding under an avoidance learning paradigm.

Acknowledgements

This chapter was written and some of the research supported in the chapter was completed under a grant from NSF #GB–5379, and by a USPHS pre-Doctoral Grant, 5–F1–MH–31, 493–02 to Paul V. Dillow.

References

Anger, D. (1963). The role of temporal discrimination in the reinforcement of Sidman avoidance behavior. *J. exp. Anal. Behav.* **6,** 477–506.

Azrin, N. H., Holz, W. C. and Hake, D. F. (1962). Intermittent reinforcement by removal of a conditioned aversive stimulus. *Science.* **136,** 781–782.

Azrin, N. H., Holz, W. C., Hake, D. F. and Allyon, T. (1963). Fixed-ratio escape reinforcement. *J. exp. Anal. Behav.* **6** (3), 449–456.

Azrin, N. H., Hutchinson, R. R. and Hake, D. F. (1967). Attack, avoidance and escape reactions to aversive shock. *J. exp. Anal. Behav.* **10,** 131–148.

Badia, P. (1965). Fixed ratio discriminated avoidance responding. *Psychol. Rec.* **15** (3), 445–448.

Badia, P. and Levine, S. (1964). Stable long term avoidance responding and fixed ratio avoidance training. *Psychol. Sci.* **1** (5), 91–92.

Bekhterev, V. M. (1932). "General Principles of Human Reflexology." International, New York.

Biederman, G. B., D'Amato, M. R., and Keller, D. M. (1964). Facilitation of discriminated avoidance learning by dissociation of CS and manipulandum. *Psychon. Sci.* **1,** 203–230.

Bindra, D. (1961). Components of general activity and the analysis of behavior. *Psychol. Rev.* **68,** 205–215.

Bindra, D. and Anchel, H. (1963). Immobility as an avoidance response and its disruption by drugs. *J. exp. Anal. Behav.* **6,** 213–218.

Bixenstine, V. E. and Barker, E. (1964). Further analysis of the determinants of avoidance behavior. *J. comp. physiol. Psychol.* **58,** 339–343.

Bolles, R. C. (1967). "Theory of Motivation." Harper and Row, New York.

Bower, G., Starr, R. and Lazarowitz, L. (1965). Amount of response—produced change in the CS and avoidance learning. *J. comp. physiol. Psychol.* **59,** 13–17.

Brown, J. S., Kalish, H. I. and Farber, I. E. (1951). Conditioned fear as revealed by magnitude of startle response to an auditory stimulus. *J. exp. Psychol.* **41**, 317–328.

Campbell, S. L. (1962). Lever holding and behavior sequences in shock escape. *J. comp. physiol. Psychol.* **55**, 1047–1053.

D'Amato, M. R. and Fazzaro, J. (1966). Discriminated lever-press avoidance learning as a function of type and intensity of shock. *J. comp. physiol. Psychol.* **61**, 313–315.

D'Amato, M. R., Keller, D. and DiCara, L. (1964). Facilitation of discriminated avoidance learning by discontinuous shock. *J. comp. physiol. Psychol.* **58**, 344–349.

Dewson, J. H. III. (1965). Avoidance responses to pure tones in the rat. *Psychon. Sci.* **2**, 113–114.

Dillow, P. V. (1968). The function of safety signals in the acquisition of a discriminated lever press avoidance response by rats. Doctoral dissertation, University of Tennessee.

Dillow, P. V. and Hurwitz, H. M. B. (1968). Some determinants of fixed ratio discriminated avoidance behavior. In preparation for press.

Dinsmoor, J. A. (1954). Punishment: I, the avoidance hypothesis. *Psychol. Rev.* **61**, 34–46.

Dinsmoor, J. A. and Hughes, L. H. (1956). Training rats to press a bar to turn off shock. *J. comp. physiol. Psychol.* **49**, 235–238.

Dinsmoor, J. A., Matsvoka, Y. and Winograd, E. (1958). Bar holding as a preparatory response in escape from shock training. *J. comp. physiol. Psychol.* **51**, 637–639.

Fitzgerald, R. D. and Brown, J. S. (1965). Variables affecting avoidance conditioning in free-responding and discrete-trial situations. *Psychol. Rep.* **17**, 835–843.

Fitzpatrick, L. J. (1967). Behavior under shock and escape training in rats. Master of Arts Thesis, University of Tennessee.

Fowler, H. and Miller, N. E. (1963). Facilitation and inhibition of running performance by hind- and fore-paw shock of various intensities. *J. comp. physiol. Psychol.* **56**, 801–805.

Freud, S. (1936). "The Problem of Anxiety." Norton, New York.

Greene, J. T. and Peacock, L. J. (1965). Response competition in conditioned avoidance. *Psychon. Sci.* **3**, 125–126.

Guthrie, E. R. (1951). "The Psychology of Learning." Harper and Brothers, New York.

Harrison, J. M. and Abelson, R. M. (1959). The maintenance of behavior by the termination and onset of intense noise. *J. exp. Anal. Behav.* **2** (1), 23–42.

Hilgard, E. R. and Marquis, D. G. (1940). "Conditioning and Learning." Appleton-Century-Crofts, New York.

Hoffman, H. S. (1966). The analysis of discriminated avoidance. *In* "Operant Behavior." (W. K. Honig, ed.), Appleton Century Crofts, New York.

Hoffman, H. S. and Fleshler, M. (1962). The course of emotionality in the development of avoidance. *J. exp. Psychol.* **64**, 288–294.

Hull, C. L. (1943). "Principles of Behavior." Appleton-Century-Crofts, New York.

Hull, C. L. (1952). "A Behavior System." Yale University Press, New Haven.

Hunter, W. S. (1935). Conditioning and extinction in the rat. *Br. J. Psychol.* **26,** 135–148.

Hurwitz, H. M. B. (1964). Method for discriminative avoidance training. *Science.* **145,** 1070–1071.

Hurwitz, H. M. B. (1965). Effect of preliminary training and signal duration on the maintenance of an avoidance response. *Psychon. Sci.* **3,** 529–530.

Hurwitz, H. M. B. and Bounds, W. (1968). Response topography and the acquisition of free operant avoidance. Psychological Reports. (In press.)

Hurwitz, H. M. B., DeNise, H. and Dillow, P. V. (1968). Signal utilization in discriminated avoidance. (In preparation for publication.)

Hurwitz, H. M. B. and Dillow, P. V. (1966a). The effect of constant current shock intensities on the acquisition of a discriminated avoidance response. *Psychon. Sci.* **5,** 109–110.

Hurwitz, H. M. B. and Dillow, P. V. (1966b). The effect of constant power shock on the acquisition of a discriminated avoidance response. *Psychon. Sci.* **5,** 111–112.

Hurwitz, H. M. B. and Dillow, P. V. (1967). Avoidance and response duration as a function of the length of the warning period. *Psychol. Rec.* **17,** 517–524.

Hurwitz, H. M. B. and Dillow, P. V. (1968). The effects of the warning signal on response characteristics in avoidancing learning. *Psychol. Rec.* (In press.)

Hurwitz, H. M. B. and Dunn, M. (1968). Multiple response avoidance under progressive and adjusting schedules. (In preparation for press.)

Hurwitz, H. M. B. and Millenson, J. R. (1961). Maintenance of avoidance under temporally defined schedules. *Science.* **133,** 284–285.

John, E. R. and Killam, K. F. (1960). Electrophysiological correlates of differential approach-avoidance conditioning in the cat. *J. Nerv. Ment. Dis.* **131,** 183–201.

Johnson, J. L. and Church, R. M. (1965). Effects of shock intensity on non-discriminative avoidance learning of rats in a shuttle box. *Psychon. Sci.* **3,** 497–498.

Kamin, L. J. (1956). The effects of termination of the CS and avoidance of the US on avoidance learning. *J. comp. physiol. Psychol.* **49,** 420–424.

Kamin, L. J. (1957). The effects of termination of the CS and avoidance of the US on avoidance learning: an extension. *Can. J. Psychol.* **11,** 48–56.

Kamin, L. J., Brimer, C. J. and Black, A. H. (1963). Conditioned suppression as a monitor of fear of the CS in the course of avoidance training. *J. comp. physiol. Psychol.* **56,** 497–501.

Kaplan, M. (1956). The maintenance of escape behavior under fixed-ratio reinforcement. *J. comp. physiol. Psychol.* **49,** 153–157.

Keehn, J. D. (1967). Running and bar pressing as avoidance responses. *Psychol. Rep.* **20,** 591–592.

Keller, F. S. (1941). Light-aversion in the white rat. *Psychol. Rec.* **4,** 235–250.

Kessen, W. (1953). Response strength and conditioned stimulus intensity. *J. exp. Psychol.* **45,** 82–86.

Kish, G. B. (1955). Avoidance learning to the onset and cessation of the conditioned stimulus energy. *J. exp. Psychol.* **50,** 31–38.

Krieckhaus, E. E. and Wagman, W. J. (1967). Acquisition of the two-way avoidance response in chicken compared to rat and cat. *Psychon. Sci.* **8,** 273–274.

Levine, S. (1966). UCS intensity and avoidance learning. *J. exp. Psychol.* **71,** 163–164.

Levis, D. J. (1966). Effects of serial CS presentation and other characteristics of the CS on the conditioned avoidance response. *Psychol. Rep.* **18**, 755–766.

Logan, F. A. (1954). A note on stimulus intensity dynamism (V). *Psychol. Rev.* **61**, 77–80.

Mathers, B. L. (1957). The effect of certain parameters on the acquisition of fear. *J. comp. physiol. Psychol.* **50**, 329–333.

McAllister, W. R. and McAllister, D. E. (1962a). Role of the CS and of apparatus cues in measurement of acquired fear. *Psychol. Rep.* **11**, 749–756.

McAllister, W. R. and McAllister, D. E. (1962b). Post conditioning delay and intensity of shock as factors in the measurement of acquired fear. *J. exp. Psychol.* **64**, 110–116.

Meyer, D. R., Cho, C. and Wesemann, A. S. (1960). On problems of conditioning discriminated lever-press avoidance responses. *Psychol. Rev.* **67**, 224–228.

Migler, B. (1963a). Bar holding during escape conditioning. *J. exp. Anal. Behav.* **6**, 65–72.

Migler, B. (1963b). Experimental self-punishment and superstitious escape behavior. *J. exp. Anal. Behav.* **6**, 371–385.

Miller, N. E. (1948). Studies on fear as an acquirable drive: I, fear as motivation and fear reduction as reinforcement in the learning of new responses. *J. exp. Psychol.* **38**, 89–101.

Morse, W. H. and Kelleher, R. T. (1966). Schedules using noxious stimuli: I. multiple fixed-ratio and fixed-interval termination of schedule complexes. *J. exp. Anal. Behav.* **9** (3), 267–290.

Mowrer, O. H. (1939). A stimulus-response analysis of anxiety and its role as a reinforcing agent. *Psychol. Rev.* **46**, 553–565.

Mowrer, O. H. and Lamoreaux, R. R. (1942). Avoidance conditioning and signal duration: a study of secondary motivation and reward. *Psychol. Monogr.* **54** (247).

Mowrer, O. H. and Lamoreaux, R. R. (1946). Fear as an intervening variable in avoidance conditioning. *J. comp. physiol. Psychol.* **39**, 29–50.

Moyer, K. E. and Korn, J. H. (1964). Effects of UCS intensity on the acquisition and extinction of an avoidance response. *J. exp. Psychol.* 352–359.

Myers, A. K. (1959). Avoidance learning as a function of several training conditions and strain differences in rats. *J. comp. physiol. Psychol.* **52**, 381–386.

Myers, A. K. (1960). Onset versus termination of stimulus energy as the CS in avoidance conditioning and pseudoconditioning. *J. comp. physiol. Psychol.* **53**, 72–78.

Myers, A. K. (1962). Effects of CS intensity and quality in avoidance conditioning. *J. comp. physiol. Psychol.* **55**, 57–61.

Myers, A. K. (1964). Discriminated operant avoidance learning in Wistar and G–4 rats as a function of type of warning stimulus. *J. comp. physiol. Psychol.* **58**, 454–455.

Myers, A. K. (1965). Instrumental escape conditioning to a low-intensity noise by rats. *J. comp. physiol. Psychol.* **60**, 82–87.

Overmier, J. R. (1966). UCS duration as a determiner of the efficacy of Pavlovian fear conditioning. *J. comp. physiol. Psychol.* **62**, 15–20.

Pavlov, I. P. (1927). "Conditioned Reflexes." Translated by G. V. Anrep. London, Oxford.

Pearl, J. and Edwards, R. E. (1962). Delayed avoidance conditioning: warning stimulus (CS) duration. *Psychol. Rep.* **11**, 375–380.

Perkins, C. C. Jr. (1953). The relation between conditioned stimulus intensity and response strength. *J. exp. Psychol.* **46**, 225–231.

Ray, A. J. (1966). Shuttle avoidance rapid: acquisition by rats to a pressurized air unconditioned stimulus. *Psychon. Sci.* **5**, 29–30.

Rescorla, R. A. and Lolordo, V. M. (1965). Inhibition of avoidance behavior. *J. comp. physiol. Psychol.* **59**, 406–412.

Rescorla, R. A. and Soloman, R. L. (1967). Two-process learning theory: relationships between Pavlovian conditioning and instrumental learning. *Psychol. Rev.* **74**, 151–182.

Santos, J. R. (1960). The influence of amount and kind of training on the acquisition and extinction of avoidance responses. *J. comp. physiol. Psychol.* **53**, 284–289.

Schlosberg, H. (1937). The relationship between success and the laws of conditioning. *Psychol. Rev.* **44**, 379–394.

Schoenfeld, W. N. (1950). An experimental approach to anxiety, escape and avoidance behavior. (P. H. Hoch and J. Zubin, eds.) *In* "Anxiety." Grune and Stratton, New York.

Schwartz, M. (1958). Conditioned—stimulus variables in avoidance learning. *J. exp. Psychol.* **55**, 297–299.

Seligman, M. E. P. and Maier, S. F. (1967). Failure to escape traumatic shock. *J. exp. Psychol.* **74** (1), 1–9.

Sidman, M. (1953). Two temporal parameters of the maintenance of avoidance behavior by the white rat. *J. comp. physiol. Psychol.* **46**, 253–261.

Sidman, M. (1955). Some properties of the warning stimulus in avoidance behavior. *J. comp. physiol. Psychol.* **48**, 444–450.

Sidman, M. (1958). Some notes on *bursts* in free-operant avoidance experiments. *J. exp. Anal. Behav.* **1**, 167–172.

Sidman, M. and Boren, J. J. (1957). A comparison of two types of warning stimulus in an avoidance situation. *J. comp. physiol. Psychol.* **50**, 282–287.

Sidman, M. (1962). Reduction of shock frequency as reinforcement for avoidance behavior. *J. exp. Anal. Behav.* **5**, 247–257.

Skinner, B. F. (1938). "The Behavior of Organisms." Appleton-Century-Crofts, New York.

Solomon, R. L. and Turner, L. H. (1962). Discriminative classical conditioning in dogs paralyzed by curare can later control discriminative avoidance responses in the normal state. *Psychol. Rev.* **69**, 202–219.

Stretch, R., Blackman, D. and Alexander, D. (1966). Some effects of methylphenidate on stimulus control of ratio avoidance behavior in the rat. *J. exp. Anal. Behav.* **9** (4), 389–398.

Stretch, R. and Skinner, N. (1967a). Methylphenidate and stimulus control of avoidance behavior. *J. exp. Anal. Behav.* **10**, 485–493.

Stretch, R. and Skinner, N. (1967b). Schedule—control of behavior in squirrel monkeys: effects of methylphenidate. *Psychon. Sci.* **8** (9), 385–386.

Theios, J. and Dunaway, J. E. (1964). One-way versus shuttle avoidance conditioning. *Psychon. Sci.* **1**, 251–252.

Thompson, R. F. (1950). Primary stimulus generalization as a function of acquisition level in the cat. *J. comp. physiol. Psychol.* **51**, 601–606.

Tolman, E. C. (1951). "Collected Papers in Psychology." University of California Press, Berkeley, California.

454 HARRY M. B. HURWITZ AND PAUL V. DILLOW

Ulrich, R. E., Holz, W. C. and Azrin, N. H. (1964). Stimulus control of avoidance behavior. *J. exp. Anal. Behav.* **7** (2), 129–133.
Van Sommers, P. (1963). Carbon dioxide escape and avoidance behavior in the brown rat. *J. comp. physiol. Psychol.* **56**, 584–589.
Verhave, T. (1959). Avoidance responding as a function of simultaneous and equal changes in two temporal parameters. *J. exp. Anal. Behav.* **2** (3), 185–190.
Warren, J. A. Jr. and Bolles, R. C. (1967). A re-evaluation of a simple contiguity interpretation of avoidance learning. *J. comp. physiol. Psychol.* **64** (1), 179–182.
Weissman, A. (1962). Non-discriminated avoidance behavior in a large sample of rats. *Psychol. Rep.* **10**, 591–600.

17 Discrimination Learning?

R. M. GILBERT

*Alcoholism and Drug Addiction Research Foundation,
Toronto, Ontario, Canada*

I. Introduction

Although this chapter comes at the end of the book and in places attempts to relate and comment upon other contributions, it may also serve for some readers as an introduction, albeit idiosyncratic, to some of the issues covered in the previous pages. Reference to certain verbal difficulties precedes the main section and the chapter concludes with a brief attempt to place the phenomena of discrimination learning in a wider biological context.

II. Learning to Discriminate

Among other things, this collection of articles illustrates a division between experimental psychologists in terms of experimental technique, use of explanatory models, and use of language. Some features of this division are discussed by Keehn (Chapter 11) who presents the difference in terms of a paradigm clash (Kuhn, 1962; Katahn and Koplin, 1968) of the order of Copernican as opposed to pre-Copernican astronomy and Newtonian as opposed to pre-Newtonian dynamics. The term "discrimination learning", in something very close to the lay sense of the term, finds favour within one paradigm and not within the other. I shall begin by considering objections to each of the component words of the term.

A. LEARNING

Experimental psychologists might be loosely described as scientists who study situations in which the behaviour of organisms is the dependent variable. Two kinds of qualification are needed. One concerns the definition of the "behaviour of organisms", and in this respect riders emphasizing individual organisms on the one hand, and intact whole organisms on the other, would provide a better approximation. The other necessary kind of qualification concerns the provenance of the behaviour, and thus concerns independent variables. In this respect psychologists may be distinguished from other scientists who study the behaviour of organisms by their relative emphasis upon independent variables which have their impact during the lifetime of the organisms being investigated, and which may be related to the behaviour of the same organisms. Learning, if it is anything, is something to do with changes in the behaviour of organisms, and occupies a central place in the psychologist's conceptual fortification to the extent that psychological accounts of behaviour change are often expected by non-psychologists to be accounts in terms of learning. "The Psychology of Learning" must be among the most popular of book titles (e.g. Borger and Seaborne, 1966; Bugelski, 1956; Deese, 1952; Guthrie, 1935; Hall, 1966) and yet not one of four recent texts (Honig, 1966; Millenson, 1967; Nurnberger *et al.* 1963; Reynolds, 1968), all of which would seem from their titles and contents to be about the behaviour of organisms and the ways in which this behaviour changes, has space in its index for the entry "learning" or some variant. (Millenson, it must be allowed, uses "learning set" in the special, technical sense of H. F. Harlow.) Eschewers of the term "learning" among experimental psychologists are likely to consider themselves adherents to the new paradigm, designated S-R-S^R by Keehn.

1. *Occasions for the Use of "Learning"*

There are at least four ways in which "learning" is used in everyday discourse and by scientists who favour the term:

(a) As a description of a change in behaviour. Miller (1962) has defined learning in this way. He and others who make this use of the term would be unlikely to apply it to all changes in behaviour, probably only those which are seen or merely believed to have followed certain kinds of contingency

between the behaviour and the environment of an organism. When the term "learning" is used to describe such changes it falls unhappily between being a synonym for behaviour change and being a loose term for a certain kind of change, the defining features of which are the main interest.

(b) As a description of a change in behavioural potentiality. Kimble and many others have defined learning in this way "because it is obvious that learning may occur when there is no change in behaviour" (Kimble, 1967, p. 86). Such use of the term necessitates a distinction between "learning" and "performance", giving "learning" the status of an intervening variable, i.e. an inference from performance, or behaviour. Making such an inference may be a way of making a prediction about future behaviour, in which case it might be more appropriate to talk about the probability of occurrence of behaviour (Skinner, 1953). In a similar vein, "learning" might be considered to be just a name for the relationship between the source of a change in behaviour and the behaviour change itself, which avoids the dignification imposed by the term "inference". In view of the large and uncertain number of kinds of relationship, calling all such relationships "learning" might impede the analysis of behaviour by presuming similarity where none may exist.

(c) As behaviour. No self-respecting experimental psychologist would confess that he can observe "learning" in the same way as he can observe a lever press or a galvanic skin response. "Learning" is not supposed to be behaviour in this sense. Everyday discourse, however, includes the verb "to learn" used much as the verb "to kick" is used: "Eustace was in there learning that poem" and "Sybil learnt some typing today" might be retorts to questions asking what Eustace of Sybil were *doing*. This "doing" cannot actually be observed, whereas most kinds of "doing" can be observed, which might lead the layman, and occasionally the experimental psychologist, to believe that something inside the "doer" is doing the "doing".

(d) As an explanation of behaviour. Keehn, in Chapter 11, notes the need for independent evidence if learning is to be inferred only from the behaviour to be accounted for in terms of learning. He notes also that "most theories of learning are guesses about the locus of this independent evidence". Breaking this tautology would be facilitated by an alternative use of terminology.

Writers on "learning", both lay and technical, tend to use the term in all of these four ways, and more. Authors of textbooks on "learning" are usually chary about defining their subject matter. Most definitions of "learning" are in the spirit of *(b)* but authors who arrive at or begin with this kind of definition rarely employ it consistently. Such is the confusion surrounding the term "learning" that authors who abstain from its use gain my sympathy. Scientists operating within the S–R–S^R paradigm avoid the term not only because of the confusion concerning the control of this tact (Skinner, 1957) but also because its use tends to deny the pre-eminence of the contribution of reinforcement contingencies to behaviour change. They are content to notice changes in the probability of emission of particular forms of behaviour and to relate these changes to other events, both those which are immediately available and those which are associated with the ontogenetic and phylogenetic histories of the organism.

2. Respondent and Operant Conditioning

Confusion about the referents of "learning" has long been recognized, and may have been partly responsible for the popularity of the adoption of the term "conditioning" from the Russian literature. Behaviour is said to be conditioned by the environment rather than learnt by the behaver, and an account of behaviour change in terms of conditioning rather than learning points to extra-organismal rather than to intra-organismal determinants.

Current analyses of conditioning procedures usually settle for two basic types, respondent and operant conditioning, although attempts to include one as a special case of the other should be noted (e.g. Sheffield, 1965; Perkins, 1968). Respondent conditioning consists typically of the presentation of an environmental event just prior to the elicitor of a reflex. After a number of such pairings, the environmental event, now known as the conditioned stimulus, is seen to be followed regularly by a particular form of behaviour which did not follow it regularly before the series of pairings. Often the particular form of behaviour evoked by the conditioned stimulus is similar to the behaviour component of the original reflex, and comes to bear a similar temporal relationship to the conditioned stimulus as it does to the elicitor when presented alone. The frequent similarity of the behaviour evoked by the conditioned stimulus and the behavioural component of the original reflex has led to the suggestion that *stimulus substitution* results from respondent conditioning: by pairing, the conditioned stimulus has acquired the properties of the elicitor with respect to the elicited behaviour. Evidence against the stimulus substitution account is reviewed by Millenson (1967). Whatever the fate of the substitution account, it is certain that this stimulus pairing procedure produces consistent changes in the relation of behaviour to its environment. Some kind of analogy to respondent conditioning may be found in the procedure for making a neutral stimulus a conditioned reinforcer by pairing it with an unconditioned reinforcer (Egger and Miller, 1963; Thomas et al. 1968). It is possible that a pairing procedure might result in the transfer of stimulus control over an operant (see below).

Operant conditioning is chiefly concerned with the consequences of behaviour. In a typical operant conditioning procedure the rate of emission

of a particular form of behaviour (called an operant, in view of its suscepti-
bility to operant conditioning) is seen to increase when it is followed by an
environmental event and subsequently to decrease when the contingency
is discontinued. Environmental events which increase the probability of
occurrence of behaviour which they follow are known as reinforcers. In
general, reinforcers may be seen as occasions for responding at higher
rates, the rate differences pertaining to the proportions of time spent
behaving in non-contingent preference situations (Premack, 1965);
presentation of a food pellet to a food-deprived animal after a lever press
may increase the probability of lever pressing because a food pellet provides an occasion for eating and because, when eating is not dependent
upon prior lever pressing, a food-deprived animal spends more time eating
than it does lever pressing. As well as increasing the probability of emission
of an operant, the effect of reinforcement may be to maintain the rate of
emission at a stable value (or at a stable pattern of values) which is higher
on the average than the rate of emission without reinforcement. The effects
of an operant conditioning procedure may usually be noticed only to the
extent that the environment of the organism under observation is similar
to the environment of the organism during the original conditioning. In
this book, "learning" refers mainly to the effects of various operant conditioning procedures, with emphasis being placed upon the relation between
the effects of the procedures and the environments of the organisms whose
behaviours are the objects of the procedures.

B. Discrimination

As a technical term "discrimination" has all the faults of "learning",
attenuated by less frequent usage: it is used variously to describe behaviour,
changes in behaviour, and behavioural potentiality, and it is used in explanations of behaviour. "Discrimination" shares with "learning" eschewal
by adherents to the S–R–S^R paradigm on the grounds that its use tends to
emphasize internal events and distracts an analysis of the relevant behaviour
in terms of environmental contingencies. Like "learning", the term "discrimination" is something to do with the differences between the behaviour
of an organism on one occasion and its behaviour on another occasion and,
as with "learning", what is important is not so much the change in behaviour itself as the relation of the change to certain environmental events.
In the case of "learning", the events usually of prime interest are those
which both follow the behaviour under observation and affect its rate of
emission. In the case of "discrimination", the important events are usually
considered to be those which precede and occasion different behaviour, or
different rates of emission of the same behaviour.

An organism is said to discriminate between two environmental states†
to the extent that, other things being equal, its behaviour in one state is
different from its behaviour in another: a pigeon may be said to discriminate red from blue if it consistently pecks a panel at a low rate when the
panel is blue and at a high rate when the panel is red, and a rat may be said
to discriminate a high tone from a low tone if it reliably pulls a trapeze
during the high tone and presses a lever during the low tone. ("Discrimination learning" is concerned with the dynamics of such rate and
topography changes, with how the pigeon came to peck more often at the
red panel, etc.) The states usually differ objectively in terms of energy
distribution at the organism's receptors, but this kind of difference does
not include the observed differentiation of behaviour with respect to
temporal variables, as discussed by Harzem (Chapter 12) and by Boakes
(Chapter 14).

1. *Stimulus Control*

As dissatisfaction with "learning" may have promoted the use of "conditioning", so may dissatisfaction with "discrimination" have allowed
increased popularity of a term which gives greater emphasis to environmental events. Adherents to the $S–R–S^R$ paradigm have come to use the
term "stimulus control" (Skinner, 1953; Terrace, 1966) to describe the
relation between antecedent environmental states and behaviour. Stimulus
control by a continuum over some behaviour is greater to the extent that the
probability of emission of the behaviour covaries with changes along the
continuum. If a pigeon is trained to peck at a key which may have projected
upon it either a white triangle on a red background $(S+)$ or a white circle
on a green background $(S-)$, and only pecking to $S+$ is ever reinforced,
then control over pecking either by shape or by colour may be found
(Reynolds, 1961). In the case of control by colour and not by shape, the
rate of pecking can be shown to vary with changes in colour but not with
changes in shape, whereas in the case of control by shape and not by colour,

---

† I am aware of considerable vagueness in my use of "environmental event" and
"environmental state"—obvious circumlocutions around the term "stimulus". "State"
here refers to something which is more persistent than "event" but the two are essentially
interchangeable. It might seem silly to try and avoid the use of "stimulus". I have avoided
its use for four reasons: (1) As commonly used, "stimulus" is no less vague than "environmental state" or "environmental event". (2) An "event" is neutral with respect to the
behaviour which follows it, whereas a "stimulus" might be believed to provoke the behaviour in some kind of causal sense. (3) I prefer to reserve its use for referring to certain
aspects of an experimental manipulation, following Schoenfeld and Cumming (1963).
(4) As used by Schoenfeld and Cumming, a clear distinction can be made between stimuli
that control behaviour and stimuli that do not. By "environmental state" or "environmental
event" I suppose I mean something which is potentially detectable at the receptors of the
organism concerned.

the rate of pecking can be shown to vary with changes in shape and not with changes in colour. Although the assumption of one continuum along which both red and green lie is reasonable, and has some empirically based validity as far as the pigeon is concerned (Guttman and Kalish, 1956), such an assumption may not be justified in the case of a triangle and a circle. Triangles and circles may differ in many respects and further tests of stimulus control must be made, involving values of each of the continua along which the points of difference between the triangle and the circle may be believed to lie, before it could be said which continua are controlling behaviour.

2. *Attention*

Scientists who would prefer to talk of the pigeon discriminating between red and green, or between the triangle and the circle, might also invoke the notion of "attention" in this instance, to describe or account for the different degrees of variation of rate of pecking when colour and shape are varied independently. "Attending only to colour" and "control only by colour" are synonymous as descriptions of the relations between behaviour and certain environmental events (Terrace, 1966). "Attending", however, might appear to be some kind of behaviour of the organism which is responsible for the observed differences in behaviour—"the pigeon pecked more to red than to green because he was attending to colour, and his rate of pecking was unaffected by the change in shape because he was not attending to shape"—in which case some independent evidence of the "attending" is required to avoid a tautologous account. If there is no independent evidence of "attending" then "attention" as used by Mackintosh (1965; Chapter 6) and Warren and McGonigle (Chapter 5) remains either a synonym for stimulus control or a hypothetical suceptibility to being controlled by a particular continuum following appropriate differential reinforcement but prior to manifestation of that control. A different use of "attention", "attentional state", and "attentional process" is proposed by Honig (Chapter 2). He suggests that these terms may have use in describing the effects of certain training procedures upon the control by dimensions not available during the original training procedure. The role of "attention" is also discussed by Thomas in Chapter 1.

3. *Stimulus Control in Respondent Conditioning*

In most cases, the experiments and discussion in this book are concerned with the stimulus control over operant behaviour following differential reinforcement of an operant. There is a sense in which the term "discrimination learning" may apply to some respondent conditioning phenomena. Pairing one value of a continuum with food presentation, and presenting another value in isolation, may produce control over the conditioned salivary response when there was no control before, and may increase control by the continuum when there was some control (Pavlov, 1927). Such pairing may also affect the subsequent acqusition of control over a food-reinforced operant by the same dimension (Bower and Grusec, 1964).

C. FURTHER COMMENTS ON LANGUAGE

I have presented objections to the words in the title in an attempt to account for their relative unpopularity among workers who share the $S–R–S^R$ paradigm. Bloomfield, who shares the paradigm as far as experimental techniques and selection of phenomena are concerned, offers views in Chapter 9 about the use of language which appear contrary to those which might be inferred from what I have just written. Bloomfield argues, among other things, that using lay terms in the analysis of behaviour can be helpful in generating testable hypotheses about the relevant phenomena. To use lay terms, such as "frustration" and "disappointment" is to draw upon the product of many successful descriptions and accounts of behaviour which gave rise to the terms, and in this way the benefit of many thousand years' behaviour analysis can be reaped. However, the non-experimental nature of any lay analysis precludes the shearing of superfluous referents from such terms. Formal incorporation of lay language into a post-experimental account of behaviour often allows for confusion of the order illustrated above for "learning". If Bloomfield advocates the use of lay terms only in pre-experimental speculation then there may be no conflict between us.

Another of Bloomfield's opinions, expressed in Chapter 9, and which can be commented upon here, is that "we cannot have a theory of discrimination learning since [discrimination learning] is justified by reinforcement contingencies", a view which is in accordance with the writings of Louch (1966) and others. Louch begins his book by saying that he is satisfied by commonplace descriptions of human behaviour and ends by suggesting that to require more is to lack respect for human dignity and integrity. His intervening arguments concern chiefly the lack of progress of experimental psychology, the undesirability of greater knowledge of the controlling features of behaviour, and the sufficiency of describing human behaviour as "action"—this term being undefined. Bloomfield extends these views, particularly the last, to non-humans, and hence seems to deny the possibility of an account of any behaviour which can be accurately predicted from knowledge of the relevant reinforcement contingencies. It seems to me that (a) whether or not a particular experimenter can make a prediction about the incidence of some behaviour has no bearing upon the lawfulness of the behaviour, and (b) even if behaviour can be predicted from knowledge of contingencies, it might still be useful to investigate how it is that the contingencies are effective.

Whilst commenting on the component terms of the title of this book I should both account for its use and explain the restriction to animals. The last follows simply from an enumeration of the species employed in the experiments which are described and discussed in the book; nearly all of the experimental subjects were non-human. A further consideration is the applicability to human behaviour of functional relationships involving non-human behaviour. There is little doubt that most of the phenomena discussed here could be demonstrated in human behaviour. There is some question, however, as to whether some of the phenomena of stimulus control over human behaviour depend upon processes which humans do not share with non-humans. Most important of these would be the relation between verbal behaviour and stimulus control. It is possible to affect stimulus control by verbal behaviour: "turn left at the green light; no, I mean turn right at the green light" may change the probability of certain forms of the listener's behaviour at the green light. That it may do would depend upon the existence of a certain kind of reinforcement history. Nevertheless, fine stimulus control over human behaviour can be engendered by verbal events without the obvious, immediate implication of processes such as differential reinforcement and stimulus generalization. There is also some question of the generality of stimulus control phenomena throughout non-human species. Issues relevant to this problem are discussed by Warren and McGonigle (Chapter 5), Mackintosh (Chapters 6 and 7), and Bitterman (Chapter 7).

Any justification for the use of the terms "discrimination" and "learning" must, in view of the above, be couched in terms of an appeal to the community. Scientists who favour "conditioning" and "stimulus control" are presently fewer than scientists who favour "learning" and "discrimination". In any case, members of the first group generally understand, and even use, the second pair of terms, whereas many members of the second group of scientists are not familiar with the first pair of terms.

III. Changes in Stimulus Control

Terrace (1966), in his much-cited account of the stimulus control of behaviour, draws a distinction between the acqustion and the sharpening of stimulus control. For Terrace, stimulus control by a continuum over behaviour is evidenced when a measure of the behaviour varies with changes in the value of the continuum; stimulus control is acquired when such variability develops out of invariability and stimulus control is sharpened when the variability of the behavioural measure with changes in the continuum is further increased. Changes in variability alone are insufficient definition of changes in stimulus control; the detailed features of the relationships between the two measures must be capable of replication. A procedure which changed the relationship from I to II in Fig. 1 would not be said to have produced control by the continuum over the behaviour. A procedure which produces relationship III has produced variability when compared with I, but not necessarily stimulus control by the continuum. If relationship III were demonstrated repeatedly, then it might be said that the procedure had promoted the acquisition of stimulus control. If relationship III were transient, and a subsequent test revealed another pattern with similar variability, then the variability might be attributed to features of the procedure which were not related to the continuum. The degree of stimulus control is usually considered to be shown by the steep-

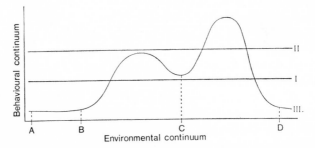

FIG. 1. Three hypothetical relationships between values along a behavioural continuum and values along an environmental continuum.

ness of the curve depicting the relationship. In the hypothetical case III given in Fig. 1, the mean gradient between B and C is greater than the mean gradient between A and B, and the mean gradient between C and D is greater than the mean gradient between B and C (ignoring the signs of gradients in all cases). The degree of control might be considered to be different in different parts of the continuum along which A, B, C and D lie. If differences in degree of control along the continuum are allowed, then it might be difficult to reconcile a statement that the curve between A and B demonstrates a lack of control by the continuum between its values A and B with a statement that the curve between A and D indicates control by the continuum. A way around this problem of definition would be to assume that "continuum" in the phrase "stimulus control by a continuum" refers only to that part of a continuum over which replicable variation of behaviour with respect to changes in the continuum has been demonstrated.†

† Of course, the gradient at any point can be arbitrarily varied, within limits, by making transformations of the abscissal scale (Shepherd, 1965), which further complicates the making of statements about control by different parts of a continuum.

A. Acquisition of Stimulus Control

Terrace concludes that differential reinforcement with respect to two values of a dimension is both a necessary condition (*op. cit.*, pp. 297 and 339) and a sufficient condition (*op. cit.*, p. 296) for the acquisition of stimulus control by that dimension over behaviour. Certainly differential reinforcement cannot be a sufficient condition for stimulus control to occur. Trivial conditions, like possession by the organism of the appropriate receptors, are necessary, as may be less obvious conditions like the absence of certain other sources of control (Lovejoy and Russell, 1967; Miles, 1965).

The question of the necessity of differential reinforcement for stimulus control is discussed in some detail by Terrace. He cites evidence from (1) studies in which control was evidenced after differential reinforcement but not before; (2) a study which demonstrates the possibility of unsuspected differential reinforcement during non-differential training; (3) a study in which prior differential reinforcement of some behaviour with respect to one dimension facilitated the gaining of control over the same behaviour by another dimension, compared with the gaining of control by the second dimension when the behaviour had been non-differentially reinforced with respect to the first dimension (see also Chapter 2 by Honig); (4) studies in which differential reinforcement with respect to a dimension facilitated control by that dimension in another experimental situation (see also Chapter 5 by Warren and McGonigle); (5) studies in which one value of a dimension was paired with food, and another value was not so paired, giving rise to subsequent control by the dimension over food-reinforced behaviour. Although Terrace concludes that differential reinforcement is a necessary condition for the acquisition of stimulus control, only the data referred to in (5) above bear directly on this requirement. These findings lead to the suggestion that stimulus control by a dimension over some behaviour may be engendered by pairing values of a stimulus dimension in a consistent manner with appropriate values of another dimension which is known to have stimulus control over behaviour. Rescorla and Solomon (1967) came to a similar conclusion about such cross-dimensional pairing after reviewing many studies of the effect of respondent conditioning procedures on the stimulus control of operant behaviour. It is an empirical question as to whether or not this procedure for producing stimulus control has generality beyond situations in which control over behaviour is gained by pairing with the reinforcer which is maintaining the behaviour. The evidence as presented by Terrace is inconsistent with a statement that differential reinforcement of an operant with respect to values of a dimension is a necessary condition for control to be acquired by the dimension over the operant. The data referred to in (1)–(4) above indicate that differential reinforcement may produce or facilitate the production of stimulus control, but they do not bear directly on the question of necessity. Hoffman presents data in Chapter 3 which may be further evidence against the necessity of differential reinforcement for the acquisition of stimulus control.

Differential reinforcement and cross-dimensional pairing provide two sources of stimulus control. A third source results mainly from phylogenetic contingencies: an elicitor has stimulus control over its reflex behaviour, according to the definition of stimulus control given above. Furthermore, in as much as respondent conditioning may produce stimulus control over the conditioned response by a continuum along which the conditioned stimulus can be located, then we have a further case of cross-dimensional pairing producing stimulus control. Brown and Jenkins (1968) have implicated both phylogenetic history and pairing procedures in their account of the effectiveness of their auto-shaping procedure.

B. Sharpening Stimulus Control

The results of Terrace's work on the effects of errorless discrimination training (reviewed in Terrace, 1966) suggest that there are four features of training procedures which are especially likely to sharpen stimulus control: (1) initially correlating non-reinforcement with a value of one of the dimensions of $S+$ (the state correlated with reinforcement) which is sufficiently different from $S+$ to produce non-emission of the reinforced operant as a result of ontogenetic or phylogenetic histories; (2) arranging for a gradual reduction of the differences between $S+$ and $S-$ (the set of states not correlated with reinforcement), particularly in respect of the dimension by which control is sought; (3) making the relative duration of $S-$ initially short, perhaps such as to reinforce non-emission of the operant by the reintroduction of $S+$, and only gradually lengthening the period for which $S-$ is available; (4) introducing $S-$ shortly after the operant has been established. Features (1)—(3) each have an obvious relation to the object of avoiding situations in which the organism might emit the operant during $S-$. Terrace notes that if emission during $S-$ occurs then it is usually persistent, possibly because $S-$ becomes an occasion for emission once it has been paired with the sources of proprioceptive control which themselves have been paired with $S+$: if the operant is not emitted during $S-$, then $S-$ does not become an occasion for the emission of the operant. Introducing $S-$ shortly after the operant has been established (the fourth feature given above), when compared with later introduction, may tend to avert control by a dimension along which $S-$ can be located, both by providing for a lower rate of emission, and by providing for fewer occasions on which the relevant proprioceptive events and $S+$ could have been paired. If, before the experimental situation, the operant already has a high probability of occurrence in other situations, then proprioceptive control over the operant might be considerable: whether or not $S-$ is introduced early or late in training might be expected to make less difference in this case than in the case of a newly trained operant. In Terrace's studies, the operant under examination has been the peck at a wall-key by a pigeon. Untrained pigeons rarely peck with the head at this angle, and, shortly after shaping, proprioceptive control over key-pecking might be expected to be minimal. Thus there might have been little opportunity for $S-$ to gain control by being paired with proprioceptive events which control behaviour and which have been paired with $S+$. Detailed discussion of some of these points, and of some of the phenomena which may distinguish organisms which emitted the defined operant during $S-$ in training from those which did not, are offered by Bloomfield in Chapter 9, and a theoretical treatment is given by Gray and Smith (Chapter 10).

C. Which Continua Gain Control?

A book on discrimination learning might be expected to include substantial reference to the conditions for the acquisition of stimulus control. Although these conditions are considered in almost every chapter of this book, greater prominence is given to a set of assumptions about the way in which stimulus control is acquired, known as attention theory or stimulus-selection theory, and to the experimental testing of hypotheses based on these assumptions. Outlines of versions of the theory are given in the chapters by Wagner, (4) Warren and McGonigle, (5) and Siegel, (8).

1. *Attention Theories*

A characteristic feature of attention theories is the assumption of a set of analysers within each organism, one for each of the dimensions which can have control over the organism's behaviour. Organisms, at least those organisms for which the theory is deemed to apply, are assumed to be so constructed that (1) at any particular instant only some of the analysers are working, or switched in, i.e. only some continua control behaviour; 2) the more one analyser is switched in, the less other analysers are switched in; (3) an analyser is switched in, or more switched in, by *pairing* one value of the appropriate dimension with reinforcement and another with non-reinforcement; (4) to the extent that an analyser is switched in then the reinforced behaviour is more likely to occur in the presence of the value of the dimension paired with reinforcement than in the presence of the other value. Of these, (4) concerns a well-established empirical finding, if reference to the analyser is omitted: the reference may be redundant, since (4) provides for the pairing procedure described in (3) which switches analysers in. If an organism's contact with a dimension of its environment is mediated only through its appropriate analyser, and if (3) is the only way in which analysers can get switched in, then it is difficult to see how an analyser, once switched out, could ever be switched back in again. Obviously further assumptions are needed. Usually attention theories make more assumptions than the few common ones indicated here.

Three implications of attention theories stand out. One is the implication of amenability to control of an organism's behaviour by a continuum without any particular behaviour being specified. Such an amenability might be attributed to "conditioned looking" and other behaviours or quasi-behaviours. With or without evidence of orientating behaviours amenability can only be inferred from differences in the effects of various training procedures. Another implication is that of some kind of dynamic balancing of amenabilities: a change in control by one dimension may affect the control by, or amenability to control by, another dimension. This possibility is given extensive treatment in this book by Thomas (Chapter 1), Honig (Chapter 2), Wagner (Chapter 4) and Warren and McGonigle (Chapter 5). The third implication is that of a hierarchy of controlling or potentially controlling continua, which follows from (1) above and to a lesser extent from (2). The hierarchy implied here would be temporary, determined for an individual by former and ongoing reinforcement contingencies. Baron (1965), Baron and Vacek (1967), and Sutherland and Andelman (1967) have raised the possibility of phylogenetically determined hierarchies.

2. *Attending Hierarchies*

There is evidence to suggest that a phylogenetically determined predisposition on the part of an organism to come under the control of some dimensions rather than others, called an "attending hierarchy" by Baron (1965), could be specific to the operation of a certain kind of reinforcement contingency. Sidman (1955) found that a temporal discrimination was more likely to develop under a discriminated avoidance procedure when a visual warning signal was used with rats than when an auditory signal was used with cats. Field and Boren (1963) compared the control by the auditory and visual components of a correlated compound display over rat behaviour under an adjusting avoidance schedule and found that the behaviour was mainly under auditory control. Biederman (1967) found that white noise could be used more effectively to shape and maintain discriminated avoidance in rats than could light onset, which he accounted for in terms of more bar-holding when light was used. Keehn (Chapter 11) has found that auditory control is more likely than visual control over the discriminated avoidance behaviour of rats when both are possible and seem equally likely to occur. I have made a similar finding. Four adult, male, hooded rats were trained to work under a schedule in which a 100 sec, 4.2 Hz. click, safety signal was followed by a compound light and white noise warning signal after 32 sec of which 0.24 ma. shocks of 0.5 sec duration were delivered at 1.0 sec intervals. Lever pressing was ineffective during the safety signal but in the warning signal, which continued during the shock train when it occurred, a lever press reinstated the safety signal and initiated a new cycle. Thus a rat could avoid shock by pressing the lever within 32 sec after the onset of the warning signal, and could escape shock

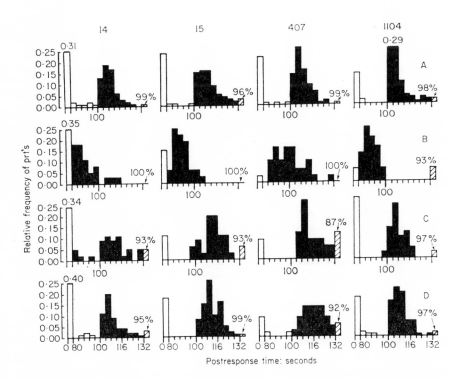

FIG. 2. Each histogram shows the distribution of the lever presses of one rat during certain cycles when working under a discriminated avoidance schedule. Histograms in row A each refer to 200 normal cycles, those in rows B and C each refer to 30 cycles in which either the auditory component of the warning signal (row B) or the visual component (row C) was brought on 20 sec early, and histograms in row D each refer to 90 normal cycles. See text for further explication. Open bars show the proportions of lever presses which occurred during the safety period. Filled and hatched bars show the relative frequencies of lever presses which avoided and escaped shock respectively, removing the warning signal and reinstating the safety signal. At the right of each histogram is shown the percentage avoided of shocks which were possible during the cycles for which the histogram applies.

by pressing during the shock train. Row A of Fig. 2 indicates the performance of each rat separately during four sessions shortly after initial training; all sessions were of 60 cycles, the first 10 cycles being disregarded for the analysis. For one-fifth of the cycles of three subsequent sessions, interspersed by normal sessions, the click was removed after 80 sec and the white noise component of the warning signal was brought on 20 sec early; likewise the light component of the warning signal was brought on early for the same number of cycles of these sessions. During these probe cycles the warning signal began effectively only 80 sec after the beginning of the safety signal and it could last for 52 sec before the onset of the shock train. During a probe cycle the component of the warning signal which was not brought on early was brought on 100 sec after the onset of the safety signal, unless the cycle had already been terminated. Rows B and C of Fig. 2 indicate the performance of the rats during probe cycles in which auditory and visual components respectively were brought on early. Row D shows performance during the normal cycles of these three sessions. Each rat tracked the onset of the auditory component but not the onset of the visual component. In the five studies just mentioned the defined operant was lever depression, release of the lever being required before another operant could be emitted. The findings of these studies lead to the suggestion that for rats, and possibly for cats, there is an "attending hierarchy" such that auditory control is more likely than visual control, other things being equal.

However, Keehn has shown with rats, and Webster with guinea pigs (both reported in Chapter 11), using a discriminated avoidance procedure in which the operant was defined alternately as one of depression and release of a lever, depending on whether a compound auditory and visual signal has just been presented or removed, that the behaviours were less likely to be under auditory control than under visual control. Gilbert (1966) and Gilbert and Moore (1967) have shown that visual control over the components of simple operant chains tends to persist whereas auditory control tends to decline. In a recent study in this series eight food-deprived, adult, male, hooded rats were divided into two groups matched according to (non-experimental) history and the rapidity with which lever-pressing was shaped using food reinforcement. With the lever removed one group (A) was trained to pull a trapeze, also using food. Food delivery was then made contingent upon emission of the sequence "trapeze pull then lever press". When emission of the sequence was stable, a compound white noise and light signal was correlated with the availability of reinforcement for lever pressing; after food delivery a pull on the trapeze produced the signal in the presence of which a lever press produced food. The white noise was of greater intensity and the light of lesser intensity than the respective components of the compound warning signal used in my avoidance study which was described in the previous paragraph. These rats were then run for more than 1000 trials, with occasional probes during which only one or neither component of the compound was given. The lever pressing of the other group (B) was brought under exteroceptive control by reinforcing lever pressing only in the presence of the compound signal; probes for control by each of the components were given occasionally at the end of this training. Then the trapeze was introduced and onset of the signal was used to shape trapeze pulling. When the sequence "trapeze pull then lever press' was well-established, group B, like Group A, was given more than 1000 trials with occasional probes to test for stimulus control. Preliminary analysis of the data from this study suggests that, for both groups, lever pressing comes to be predominantly under visual control. For one group (B) lever pressing was formerly under both auditory and visual control and these sources remained available. For the other group the original source of control over lever-pressing in the sequence was unidentified (and presumably proprioceptive) and this source probably remained available. The findings of the studies mentioned in this paragraph lead to the suggestion that for rats, and possibly for guinea pigs, there is an "attending hierarchy" such that visual control is more likely than auditory control, other things being equal.

Under discriminated avoidance procedures, an efficient mode of behaviour, in terms of effort per shock avoided, is to wait until the onset of the signal before emitting the required operant. Use of a visual signal might promote orientation towards the lever, especially if the lamp is near the lever (Biederman *et al.* 1964), which may lead to lever pressing and holding when the signal is absent. With an auditory signal a rat may engage more readily in suitable competing behaviour and yet remain under control of an auditory dimension. In the simple chaining situation, both auditory and visual components of a signal are redundant in that rats may be trained to emit the sequence without any correlated exteroceptive events. However, a visual signal might promote orientation towards the lever more than either an auditory signal or the (presumed) proprioceptive sources, and such orientation might facilitate behaviour in a situation such as this in which temporal restriction upon the availability of reinforcement is minimal. In Keehn's and Webster's procedure, which gave rise to greater visual control, it is possible that the characteristics of this kind of control which lead to lever holding in the single-operant discriminated avoidance situation may have facilitated appropriate differentiation of the two required forms of behaviour. Whatever kind of account is given of the differences which have just been described, the data remain inconsistent with a simple notion of "attending hierarchy".

D. IRRELEVANT CONTINUA

Wagner, in Chapter 4, emphasises the importance of an analysis of the properties of environmental states which are available during training but which are uncorrelated with reinforcement delivery, a sentiment shared by Thomas in Chapter 1. Wagner describes a study by himself, Logan, Haberlandt and Price in which the lever-pressing of rats was less likely to come under the control of an irrelevant visual dimension following training in which one auditory signal had been paired with reinforcement and another had been paired with non-reinforcement (correlated or true-discrimination training), than following training in which both auditory signals were equally often associated with reinforcement and non-reinforcement (uncorrelated or pseudo-discrimination training). Thomas, on the other hand, reports studies by Klipec and by Lyons in which control by an irrelevant visual dimension over a pigeon's key-pecking was *greater* following true-discrimination training than following pseudo-discrimination training. Wagner concludes that discrimination training reduces the control over the behaviour by incidental continua: Thomas concludes that an effect of discrimination training may be to increase generally the attribution of significance to environmental differences. According to Wagner, the data he presents are such as to provide support for stimulus-selection theory. According to Thomas, his own data are such as to provide little comfort for a stimulus-selection theory. Thomas adds ". . . it seems clear that attention can be specific or general, and that rather than arguing about which condition is typical, it would be more fruitful to attempt to determine the circumstances under which the two types or levels of attention attain."

In all the studies referred to by Thomas a free operant procedure was used in which one or the other of the signals correlated with reinforcement availability during true-discrimination training was always present. Wagner reports studies in which a fixed trial procedure was used: a period of no signal alternated with a period in which a signal was presented. In the studies referred to by Thomas the irrelevant state was continuously available. In Wagner's studies the irrelevant state appeared only with one or the other of the signals.

Melching (1954) has shown that an event which is inconsistently paired with a reinforcer, such that reinforcement occurs as often as 50 per cent of the time without the event, is unlikely to become a conditioned reinforcer. Thus the two auditory signals might not have been expected to become conditioned reinforcers during Wagner's uncorrelated condition. On the other hand, the so-called irrelevant stimulus was intermittently paired with reinforcement in this condition and might, according to Zimmerman (1957), have been expected to become a durable conditioned reinforcer.

Thomas (1965) has emphasised the parallel nature of discriminative and reinforcing functions. From all these considerations it might be predicted that the "irrelevant stimulus" in a fixed trial situation would exert greater control than a signal which fails to appear on about half of the occasions when reinforcement is available. That such an "irrelevant stimulus" may exert greater control is suggested by a preliminary analysis of a study of mine which was very similar to that of Wagner *et al.* except that the onset of the compound event was produced by the rat's pulling a trapeze rather than by an automatic timer. In the studies by Lyons and by Klipec, the continual availability of an irrelevant state might not have been so conducive to the development of control by a dimension of the state as was the temporal correlation of the onset of the "irrelevant stimulus" with reinforcement availability in the study reported by Wagner. It seems that the discrepancy between the effects of pseudo-discrimination training in the two studies may be accounted for in terms of the differences in environmental contingencies.

In the free operant studies true-discrimination training sharpened control by an irrelevant continuum: in the fixed trial studies true-discrimination training had an opposite effect. The evidence for generality of the effect of true-discrimination training in free operant situations is considerable and unequivocal (see also Honig, Chapter 2) and it may be advantageous to look again at the differences between the two situations in order to suggest how a fixed trial procedure might produce a contrary effect.

In the fixed trial situation the "irrelevant stimulus" and the pair of signals were both correlated with reinforcement availability during true-discrimination training, the latter more precisely so. Other things being equal, the more precise correlation might have been expected to provide for the greater control, especially as differential training with respect to a continuum was given in the case of the auditory signals. In the study of mine just mentioned the application of a true-discrimination procedure to the component of the chain nearer reinforcement seems to have had a similar effect to that found by Wagner in his fixed trial situation: control by a dimension of an "irrelevant stimulus" was relatively depressed when compared with control following pseudo-discrimination training, although there are indications that a more detailed analysis of the data tapes will reveal a more complex picture. Although the *ad hoc* interpretation in terms of the precision of correlation with reinforcement might be a sufficient account of the reversal of the order of predominance of control by the "irrelevant stimulus" and the pair of signals, it has no obvious bearing on the absolute changes in degree of control by a dimension of the "irrelevant stimulus" found between conditions in both the fixed trial and the chaining studies. The data at present suggest that the gaining of control by one dimension in a fixed trial situation interferes with the control by another dimension, whereas control by one dimension in a free operant situation promotes control by another dimension. I expect that visual control in Wagner's true-discrimination procedure would have been facilitated rather than depressed had the light been left on continuously or otherwise un-correlated with reinforcement availability. The limiting conditions of the different effects of true-discrimination training procedures remain to be explored.

E. STIMULUS CONTROL OVER STIMULUS CONTROL

Control by a dimension may be made to be explicitly conditional upon the values of another dimension. This has been demonstrated in pigeons by Heinemann et al. (1968). Following a certain training procedure these experimenters were able to obtain flat generalization functions relating the distribution of key-pecks between two simultaneously available keys and tone frequency when the keys were one colour, and somewhat peaked functions from the same birds during the same sessions when the keys were another colour. A more complicated interpretation of this finding may be made. The procedure used by Heinemann et al. was symmetrical in important respects as far as both tone frequency and wavelength of light were concerned. Had generalization functions with respect to wavelength been obtained then it would probably have been found that control by wave-length was conditional upon tone frequency. Goldiamond and Dyrud (1968) have made a distinction between dimensional stimulus control and instructional stimulus control, the former referring to control by a dimen-sion over behaviour and the latter referring to environmental control over which dimension controls behaviour. The conclusion of Heinemann et al. may be rephrased as saying that, in their experimental situation, wave-length exerted instructional control over whether or not tone frequency had dimensional control. Because of the symmetry of their procedure with respect to wavelength and tone frequency it may be presumed that each dimension exerted both instructional and dimensional control during the generalization tests, the instructional control being continuously available and the dimensional control being evident only when appropriate. Studies of the environmental control of a dimension by another dimension which involve only two dimensions are essentially symmetrical and cannot be used to provide a demonstration of exclusively instructional control. It might seem possible, however, to arrange that the control of a pigeon's pecking by one or another of two dimensions is under the control of a third dimension which has only instructional control.

A dimension exerting instructional control has control over behaviour in the sense that, under some sets of constant environmental conditions, changes in the value of the dimension in question give rise reliably to changes in behaviour. In this sense exclusively instructional control cannot be demonstrated. Suppose, for example, that a pigeon has been trained so that its rate of key-pecking varies according to the typical generalization function with respect to wavelength and not with respect to orientation when a tone of 1000 Hz is sounding, and varies with orientation and not with wavelength when a tone of 3000 Hz is sounding, the highest rate of pecking being associated with 560 mμ at 1000 Hz and with a vertical line at 3000 Hz. With the wavelength set at 560 mμ and the line vertical, variations in the tone between 500 Hz and 5000 Hz might produce a bimodal distribution of rates of pecking at the key, with peaks at 1000 Hz and 3000 Hz, which would indicate dimensional control by the tone frequency. In the same, hypothetical situation, dimensional control by tone frequency might not be demonstrated if the wavelength were 620 mμ and the line were horizontal, in which case it might be said that wavelength and orientation were jointly exercising instructional control over the dimensional control by tone frequency. Thus it appears that, given empirical substance to the above suppositions, any dimension which appears to be exercising instructional control is also exercising dimensional control, and that a dimension whose control appears to be subject to the instructional control of another dimension is also exercising instructional control over the other dimension. It seems that it might be possible for a dimension to exercise purely dimensional control but not purely instructional control. However, a continuum exerting only dimensional control would have to do so without the instructional control of any other continuum, since it has been demonstrated above that a continuum which is subject to instructional control by another continuum also has instructional control over that other continuum. This means that a continuum which exerted only dimensional control would do so under all possible environmental conditions. Some of these conditions might be trivial with respect to the argument being developed, such as the occurrence of extreme events which produce startle reactions. However, even excluding such cases, the likelihood of observing control by a dimension which is not also dependent upon the values of other dimensions is probably low. The independence of other environmental conditions required by the notion of exclusively dimensional control may be approached only in the control found over respondent behaviour by some dimensions of the appropriate elicitor.

It is thus useful to question the nature and value of a distinction between dimensional and instructional control. It seems that one cannot be observed without the other, and that which kind of control appears to be exercised by a particular dimension might depend only upon the role of that dimension in the observer's definition of his experimental situation. The main difference between continua which are said to exercise dimensional control and continua which are said to exercise instructional control might be merely the degree of complexity of the generalization functions of the latter when compared with those of the former. Another difference may lie in the nature of the signals involved: dimensional control may refer most obviously to signals which can be readily arranged along a continuum whereas instructional control may be associated with discrete and complex events, most often tacts in the case of instructional control over human behaviour. Ignorance about precisely which dimensions along which to arrange signals does not invalidate or render useless the notion of stimulus control, and the addition of the label "instructional" to particular features of an experimental situation should not affect the status of the concept. A third difference between a continuum which is noted as exerting instructional control over the first continuum might be that, although each continuum may be seen as instructional with respect to the other, the second continuum may have complete control over the dimensional control by the first continuum whereas the dimensional control of the second continuum may be subject also to the instructional control of other continua. This difference can be illustrated by reference to the hypothetical situation described above. Tone frequency has instructional control over both wavelength and orientation. Within the limits of the situation, whether or not the pigeons rate of pecking varies with orientation is completely determined by tone frequency, but whether or not the rate of pecking varies with tone frequency is dependent upon wavelength as well as orientation.

Much of the above discussion of stimulus control over stimulus control depends upon guesses about the outcome of an experimental procedure which has not yet been implemented. The results from the second part of a study by Reynolds (1961) indicate that the guesses may be accurate: he demonstrated that which of two continua (shape of pattern or wavelength of light) controlled behaviour could be made conditional upon the state of a third continuum (intensity of light). An analysis of the interactions between different sources of environmental control over behaviour, within the context of the $S–R–S^R$ paradigm, would constitute a valuable experimental programme.

A superficial resemblance may be noticed between the two stages of attention theories and the two kinds of stimulus control discussed here. Attention theorists argue that in learning a discrimination, organisms first learn to attend to the relevant dimension and then learn to vary their behaviour appropriately with respect to the dimension. Coming under the instructional control of continuum might be an exteroceptive analogue of "learning to attend to the relevant dimension", in as much as "attention" can be distinguished from stimulus control. Attention theorists might also argue that instructional control must occur before dimensional control. The necessary interrelatedness of instructional and dimensional control, both of which can be empirically defined, does not augur well for the eventual separation of the two stages of attention theories, both of which remain hypothetical.

F. Shifting and Blunting Stimulus Control

Once stimulus control has been gained it usually persists until there has been a departure from the contingencies which maintain control. A particularly impressive demonstration of the lack of effect of mere passage of time upon stimulus control is mentioned by Hoffman in Chapter 3. There are three ways in which the shape of a generalization function may change. The case of sharpening has already been considered in this part of the chapter. *Shifting,* whereby the function changes in the number or location of its peaks, without necessarily changing in mean gradient, and *blunting,* whereby a function assumes a lower mean gradient, without necessarily changing in the number or location of its peaks, will be considered in this section.

1. *Shifting*

There are at least two ways of shifting generalization functions. One is to give differential reinforcement with respect to two values of a continuum in a free-operant successive discrimination situation such as to allow emission of the operant in the presence of $S-$ (errors). A generalization function gained following such training is usually found to peak on the side of $S+$ away from $S-$, whereas after non-differential training in the presence of $S+$ the function usually peaks at $S+$. By following non-differential training with differential training a *peak shift* can be procured. This phenomenon is given considerable discussion by Bloomfield (Chapter 9) and by Gray and Smith (Chapter 10).

Another procedure for procuring shifting is to designate another value of the continuum as $S+$ and to revise the correlation with reinforcement availability accordingly. A special case of this may be where $S-$ is unaltered and $S+$ approaches $S-$ along the continuum. This is similar to a method for "errorless training", investigated by Terrace (1966), in which $S+$ is held constant and the interval between $S+$ and $S-$ is reduced. Procedures in which the interval between $S+$ and $S-$ is merely reduced usually produce sharpening and, even though shifting might also occur, the former feature is probably of greater significance.

The shifting investigated most often is provided by reversing the values of $S+$ and $S-$ following simultaneous differential training using a fixed trial procedure. Generalization functions are not usually established in such studies and have to be inferred from the reported behavioural measures in the presence of $S+$ and of $S-$. Reversal has the predictable effect of giving rise to what is probably a complementary generalization function, although the details of this change might be more interesting than the assumption of complementarity. The use of the effects of reversal training to make inferences about the phylogenetic status of different species is discussed by Mackintosh (Chapters 6 and 7) and by Bitterman (Chapter 7). Warren and McGonigle provide data on the relation between the effects of reversal training and the reinforcement schedules which maintain the examined behaviour. Researchers have frequently employed reversal training procedures in connection with the investigation of a somewhat capricious set of phenomena known as "overtraining reversal effects", whereby the facility with which a complementary generalization function is achieved is found to be related to the extent of training involving the two values of the continuum. Warren and McGonigle provide a review of the salient literature in Chapter 5. Siegel, in Chapter 8, provides an account of an overtraining reversal effect which is based on his own work on orientating behaviour in a T-maze, and argues that his results are inconsistent with the kind of attentional interpretation which has usually been the preoccupation of workers employing reversal procedures.

Functions which relate a behavioural continuum to an environmental continuum, and which have more than one peak, usually refer to a different kind of behavioural continuum from that of the rate of emission of a discrete operant. Examples of this kind of function may be found within Chapter 14 by Boakes and within a book by Notterman and Mintz (1965). In both these cases a continuous behavioural measure is shown to vary with an environmental continuum such that a kind of generalization function with two peaks could be drawn which has the proportion of the most frequently occurring interval along the behavioural continuum as ordinate, although in each case the data are presented in another way. It is an empirical question as to whether double peaking could be produced using a discrete operant. One procedure might be to train with respect to a continuum which has two values correlated with the availability of reinforcement and a third value, which lies between the two, correlated with non-reinforcement. Another possible procedure is discussed in the previous section. There is also slight evidence for "octave generalization" in the rat following training with a single $S+$ value (Blackwell and Schlosberg, 1943).

2. Blunting

The ways in which stimulus control may be lost by a continuum have been investigated less often than have other control dynamics. One source of blunting has been indicated in the discussion of the studies employing true- and pseudo-discrimination training procedures: in a fixed trial situation a true-discrimination procedure interferes with control by continua other than the one which is correlated most precisely with reinforcement availability. Another source is described by Thomas in Chapter 1: non-differential reinforcement of behaviour in the presence of one of two signals, whose apparently significant features may not be located along a single dimension (inter-dimensional training), reduces control by a dimension along which the other of the signals may be located.

These two procedures for blunting stimulus control by a continuum seem to be relatively subtle when compared with the obvious procedure which is to discontinue reinforcement and to continue to allow emission of the operant in the presence of one or more values of the continuum. This is, of course, a standard procedure for testing for stimulus control. Friedman and Guttman (1965) found sharpening of control during successive generalization tests following various free-operant discrimination training procedures and concluded that an effect of extinction is to sharpen stimulus control. They noted, however, that much of the effect could be attributed to an initial blunting of control, which was especially obvious when extinction sessions did not begin with a "warm-up" period in which reinforcement was available. Thus it might be condluded that an initial effect of withdrawing reinforcement availability is to blunt stimulus control, and a subsequent effect is to sharpen control. Continued extinction usually produces non-emission of the designated operant for all values of the environmental continuum, which must provide a special case of lack of control. The two phases of extinction suggested just now may be followed, when they occur, by a third phase of blunting, prior to the manifestation of lack of control.

Terrace (1968) has systematically investigated the key-pecking of pigeons to $S-$ during extinction following various training procedures. His data are presented graphically in the form of cumulated key-pecks to $S+$ and to $S-$ as extinction progressed. Control by a continuum along which both $S+$ and $S-$ lay can only be inferred from the extent of the differences between amounts to key-pecking to $S+$ and to $S-$: parallel or convergent cumulative records indicate blunting, although divergent records, which show when the rate of pecking remained higher in the presence of $S+$ than in the presence of $S-$, cannot be assumed to indicate that sharpening occurred. Substantial blunting during the early part of extinction was evidenced by birds which had been previously trained without errors (pecking in the presence of $S-$) using a fixed trial procedure in which all pecks to $S+$ were reinforced, and not by birds trained in a similar manner but with errors. Birds which had had intermittent reinforcement in a trial procedure, and which did not make errors during training, did not peck to $S-$ during extinction and did not show early blunting. Birds previously trained using a free operant procedure in which reinforcement was intermittently available showed initial blunting during extinction if they had made errors during training and no blunting if no errors had been made—the reverse of the relationship between the making of errors during training and the occurrence of early blunting during extinction that had been found for birds trained under a fixed trial procedure with continuous reinforcement. Blunting during extinction was eventually demonstrated by all birds as rates of pecking approached zero. These results suggest an effect of prior training on what happens to stimulus control during extinction. They also point to another difference between the effects of free operant and fixed trial procedures. Because of the absence of some relevant information, Terrace's data cannot be readily compared with those of Friedman and Guttman. Cumming *et al.* (1967) have reported that the extinction of well-established matching-to-sample behaviour of pigeons has little or no effect upon the accuracy of matching. These authors concluded, on the basis of their own and other studies, that changing the over-all level of performance does not greatly affect the stimulus control of behaviour. This conclusion may be rephrased as saying that stimulus control is not necessarily affected by changes in variables related to performance. Although the data mentioned here are not inconsistent with Kimble's (1961) conclusion that ". . . the generalization gradient steepens with extinction, unless training was under conditions of intermittent reinforcement." (p. 359), it seems clear that a more specific statement will be required.

G. Other Matters

A number of topics presented in this book have been ignored or given relatively little consideration in the foregoing discussion. Two of these, the stimulus control of behaviour maintained by negative reinforcement and the control of behaviour by temporal relationships, have obvious relevance to the main theme but do not fit comfortably within the framework of the discussion. They stand outside because of a number of interrelated features: partly because of methodological peculiarities in their investigation, partly because of the uniqueness of some of their phenomena, and partly because historically they have been subject to a relatively independent analysis (but see Hearst, 1965). These factors have enabled the comparatively self-contained discussions of temporal discrimination (Harzem Ch. 12) and discriminated avoidances (Hurwitz and Dillow Ch. 16).

Other topics given little or no mention here but which are discussed within this book are probability learning, frustrative effects, intermittent reinforcement, behavioural contrast, and perceptual processes. I shall not attempt to discuss them within the present framework but merely add that, as operant behaviour is relatively specific to some features of the environment available at its inception, and as therefore the subsequent emission of operant behaviour can be powerfully influenced by variations in this environment, it follows that any investigation of operant behaviour has implications for the analysis of the phenomena of stimulus control, and *vice versa*. Authors who, in this book, have considered problems which are not immediately and obviously related to an analysis of stimulus control, or discrimination learning, have done so usually because the analysis of these problems has highlighted the implication of the phenomena of stimulus control.

IV. Evolution, Revolution and Reinforcement

The behaviour of organisms is biological in the sense that it is a manifestation of living matter, and in the more important sense that it is ultimately circumscribed by processes which have given rise to the development and differentiation of organic complexity. The relation of behavioural phenomena to other biological considerations has usually taken one or more of four paths. In the first place there have been the attempts to consider the development and maintenance of behaviour solely in terms of an appreciation of the relevant phylogenetic contingencies. A recent good example of this is the analysis of the behaviour known as "fighting" by Lorenz (1966). Somewhat related to the first path of enquiry are the comparisons of the emergence of different behavioural forms at different phylogenetic levels with the other characteristics of these levels, as illustrated by Lenneberg (1967) and in the contributions of Mackintosh and Bitterman to this book. A third type of enquiry concerns the relation between behavioural phenomena and what goes on inside the skins, and especially the skulls, of organisms, represented in this book in rather different ways by Russell (Chapter 13) and Sutherland (Chapter 15). Fourthly, there have been attempts to emphasize both the interrelatedness and the separateness of the effects of ontogenetic and phylogenetic contingencies on the development and maintenance of behaviour, notably by Skinner (1966). In this part of the chapter, I want to consider briefly a parallel between ontogeny and phylogeny and to note a place for the phenomena of stimulus control within this parallel.

A. EVOLUTION

It is almost a truism to say now that the composition and the behaviour of an organism have arisen as a consequence of two fundamental and inextricably interwoven types of history of relevant events. One history concerns events prior to conception: the other concerns subsequent events. The first of these, initially emphasized in the later half of the last century, is an accepted part of scientific discourse. The "Theory of Evolution" is a cornerstone upon which rest most accounts of biological phenomena. Indeed, a biologist may be defined as someone who accepts and makes use of the following four precepts of phylogeny, or evolutionary development (adapted from Bolles, 1967):

(1) The survival of a particular structure is related to the relative fertility of an organism having the structure, fertility being given the restricted sense of "having fertile offspring".

(2) The existence of any structure in an organism is the result of a history of selection for fertility involving that organism's forbears.

(3) The only mechanisms which need be invoked to account for any particular phylogeny are mechanisms relating to variation in structure and mechanisms relating to the selection of structures by the environment.

(4) Phylogeny is continuous. The apparent stability of phenotypes reflects only the stability of the relevant phylogenetic contingencies or, as one might say, the stability of the relevant ecological niches.

Phylogeny is based upon mechanisms for variation, the most important of which happens to be genetic mutation, and upon mechanisms for selection, which are summarized in the phrase "viability to the extent of producing fertile offspring". These apparently simple processes of variation and selection are all that is needed to account for the richness and variety of living matter, at least at one level of description. Of course there is a lot more than fills in the gaps. Investigation of respiratory function, and the decoding of DNA, to give two of countless examples, may be pursued independently of phylogenetic considerations, but the basic evolutionary precepts underwrite all biological endeavour.

These precepts of phylogeny have been offered cursorily; a chapter on each would be required for their qualification. In particular, it is not clear what is being operated upon by the phylogenetic contingencies, what features of the environment are involved in the selection, and what constitutes an effective contingency between the significant features of the environment and what is being operated upon. One kind of answer is to say that some genes rather than others are being selected out by participation in successful reproduction. But it may be more useful to talk of the inheritance of characteristics than of the change in composition of a gene population even though a characteristic implies an ontogeny which is merely limited by the phylogenetic contingencies.

B. Reinforcement

The behavioural plasticity of organisms is particularly unamenable to straightforward analysis in terms of phylogenetic contingencies. The on-going selection of phenotypes by the environment implicates a particular organism only slightly. Individual organisms do not change as a result of natural selection, and change only trivially as a result of genetic mutation. Yet the behaviour of an organism changes markedly in ways which can be accounted for only in terms of other kinds of environmental contingency. Underwriting these changes may be a set of precepts concerning behavioural variability and selection, or reinforcement, which is parallel to the phylogenetic precepts. These precepts of ontogeny could be listed in the same way as the precepts of phylogeny were listed:

(1) The survival of a particular form of behaviour within an organism's repertoire is related to the relative frequency of reinforcement of that behaviour. This is a general restatement of the Law of Effect, or Law of Reinforcement, with reinforcement being given the extended meaning of "the affecting of probability of emission by consequential environmental events".

(2) The existence of a particular form of behaviour in an organism's repertoire is the result of the reinforcement history of that organism with respect to the particular form of behaviour.

(3) The only mechanisms which need be invoked to account for any particular ontogeny are mechanisms relating to variability and mechanisms relating to the selection of variations by the environment.

(4) Ontogeny is continuous. Behaviour is continually sensitive to onto-genetic contingencies and the apparent stability of particular forms of behaviour reflects only the stability of the appropriate reinforcement contingencies.

The development and differentiation of behaviour could be based upon mechanisms for variation and mechanisms for selection. These apparently simple processes may be all that is required to account for the richness and variety of behaviour, whether fish, rat or human, at least at one level of description. The analysis of behaviour is obviously more complex than the recognition of selection of varieties of behaviour but, in the same way as the phylogenetic precepts underwrite biological endeavour, the ontogenetic precepts may underwrite psychological endeavour, to the extent that the two kinds of endeavour are distinguishable. Phylogenetic contingencies necessarily circumscribe ontogenetic contingencies, although the effectiveness of the latter may be essential for the effectiveness of the former, at least as far as the more complex organisms are concerned.

This drawing of a parallel between the ontogeny of the behaviour and the phylogeny of the composition of organisms is a far from novel enterprise.

Darwin (1859 and 1872) was more concerned with the inheritance of behavioural forms than with either ontogenetic processes or the phylogeny
of such processes. His contemporary, Spencer (1870), postulated a parallel
set of ontogenetic contingencies to the phylogenetic contingencies spelt out
by Darwin (1859) and noted a possible phylogenetic basis for the ontogenetic
processes; but he did not make the parallel explicit, preferring instead to
enunciate his Doctrine of Mental Evolution. More recently, Osgood (1953)
has noted a parallel in that ". . . a replica of selective 'survival of the
fittest' begins to appear with the behaviour of individual members of
species." (p. 299). A more extensive tracing of a parallel was carried out
by Broadbent (1961) who observed that "The attraction both of natural
selection and of the Law of Effect, to certain types of mind, is that they
do not call on explanatory principles of a quite separate order from those
needed in the physical sciences." (p. 56), concluding both that ". . . with
these [i.e. some forementioned] cautions it is still possible to think of
behaviour as being adapted to the environment in the same way as
anatomy is: it varies, and the successful variations are selected." (p. 75),
and that "The study of behaviour has forced us to realize that even for
animals a simple rule like the Law of Effect will not wholly serve." (p. 120.)
Skinner (1966), in a recent discussion of the provenance of behaviour, has
outlined the similarities and the differences between ontogenetic and
phylogenetic contingencies, and between their products, and has commented on their inter-relations.

C. Revolution

Whereas the hegemony of phylogenetic contingencies in the creation of
organisms is now considered uncontroversial in most places, the revolutionary nature of the Law of Reinforcement is still far from general
acceptance. This is in spite of the considerable experimental evidence
from which the Law of Reinforcement has been derived, and the relative
lack of empirical support for the Theory of Evolution. The Law of Reinforcement is certainly no more a "pompous rendering of a platitude"
(Louch, 1966, p. 30) than is the Law of Natural Selection. Various accounts
of behaviour have been given priority, notably those based on "inner
states", whether private or physiological, or quasi-physiological, and those
which hold that behaviour is merely a product, or a by-product, of phylogeny. Some details of the clash between a paradigm which gives revolutionary status to the Law of Reinforcement and other paradigms within
psychology are presented by Keehn in Chapter 11. Terms such as "paradigm" and "revolutionary" belong more happily to the vocabularies of the
historians of science, and their use in the present context is little more than
a prediction about the way in which some parts of future histories will be

prepared. This is said not to deny the reality and the importance of the differences between the various accounts, but merely by way of apology for overt enthusiasm.

D. THE ADAPTIVENESS OF BEING UNDER EXTEROCEPTIVE STIMULUS CONTROL

Industrial melanism (Kettlewell, 1961) is one of the few well-established instances of currently operating natural selection. Southern Lancashire, one of England's industrial regions, has many trees whose barks have been darkened by the belching chimneys of the last two hundred years. Darker varieties of the Peppered Moth, *Biston betularia*, are more likely to survive to reproduction on the barks of these trees, and in other places in industrial regions, than are the speckled varieties, who survive more readily in nearby, rural North Wales. The phylogenetic contingencies in these cases need a three-term description, including the environment, whether sooty or not, the phenotype, and the agency of natural selection, usually robins or hedge-sparrows. It has happened, as a result of these contingencies, that dark moths are more probable in industrial places and that light moths are more probable in rural places.

I have already pointed out that a similar three-term description is necessary for ontogenetic contingencies: the effects of reinforcement are relatively specific to some features of the environment in which it occurred. It might be said that such a mechanism of specificity is almost a necessary counterpart to a reinforcement mechanism: non-specifically operating reinforcement contingencies would require tedious processes of extinction, or satiation, or punishment, and then reconditioning before topographical change could be effected, and the chaining of behaviour into complex sequences might be impossible, unless alternative mechanisms were available. One consequence at least of the processes of stimulus control is that the sensitivity of the behaviour of organisms to changes in reinforcement contingencies is enhanced. Many authors have noted the increase in this kind of adaptiveness during phylogenetic development (e.g. Hebb, 1958). Certain anomalous findings have been made. Kelleher (1966), has reviewed work on the phenomenon whereby pausing in the early components of extended chained schedules is very much greater than pausing in the comparable components of equivalent tandem schedules under which reinforcement could be available with equal frequency. He observed that "Attending to environmental stimuli is usually considered an important adaptive characteristic of an organism's behaviour. Under some extended chained schedules, however, attention to environmental stimuli works to the severe detriment of the organism." (p. 192). Gilbert (1968) has obtained data which suggest that parts of a simple operant chain which are predominantly under exteroceptive control are less sensitive to withdrawal of reinforcement availability than are parts which are not known to be predominantly under exteroceptive control. An analysis of the latter phenomenon in terms of proprioceptive or some other sources of control might show that a principle of facilitation of sensitivity to reinforcement contingencies by stimulus control is not violated. However, the anomalous nature of the data discussed by Kelleher would not be resolved by such an analysis.

Acknowledgements

Some of the data mentioned in this chapter were collected at the University of Aberdeen, Scotland, with the assistance of Gordon A. Young and with support by grant G967/154/B from the Medical Research Council.

References

Baron, M. R. (1965). The stimulus, stimulus control, and stimulus generalization. *In* "Stimulus Generalization". (D. I. Mostofsky, ed.) Stanford University Press, Stanford, U.S.A.

Baron, M. R. and Vacek, C. T. (1967). Generalization gradients along wavelength and angularity dimensions in pigeons. *Psychon. Sci.* **9**, 423–424.

Biederman, G. B. (1967). Discriminated avoidance conditioning: Stimulus functions in shaping and training. *Psychon. Sci.* **9**, 263–264.

Biederman, G. B., D'Amato, M. R. and Keller, D. M. (1964). Facilitation of discriminated avoidance by dissociation of CS and manipulandum. *Psychon. Sci.* **1**, 229–230.

Blackwell, H. R. and Schlosberg, H. (1943). Octave generalization, pitch discrimination, and loudness thresholds in the white rat. *J. exp. Psychol.* **33**, 407–419.

Bolles, R. C. (1967). "Theory of Motivation." Harper and Row, New York.

Borger, R. and Seaborne, A. E. M. (1966). "The Psychology of Learning." Penguin Books, London.

Bower, G. and Grusec, T. (1964). Effect of prior Pavlovian discrimination training upon learning an operant discrimination. *J. exp. Anal. Behav.* **7**, 401–404.

Broadbent, D. E. (1961). "Behaviour." Eyre and Spottiswood, London.

Brown, P. L. and Jenkins, H. M. (1968). Auto-shaping of the pigeon's key-peck. *J. exp. Anal. Behav.* **11**, 1–8.

Bulgelski, B. R. (1956). "The Psychology of Learning." Henry Holt, New York.

Cumming, W. W., Barryman, G., Cohen, L. R. and Lanson, R. N. (1967). Some observations on extinction of a complex discriminated operant. *Psychol. Rep.* **20**, 1328–1330.

Darwin, C. A. (1859). "On the Origin of Species." Reprint of the first edition, 1950. Watts and Co., London.

Darwin, C. A. (1872). "The Expression of the Emotions in Animals and Men." J. Murray, London.

Deese, J. (1952). "The Psychology of Learning." McGraw-Hill, New York.

Egger, M. D. and Miller, N. E. (1963). When is a reward reinforcing? An experimental study of the information hypothesis. *J. comp. physiol. Psychol.* **56**, 132–137.

Field, G. E. and Boren, J. J. (1963). An adjusting avoidance procedure with multiple auditory and visual warning stimuli. *J. exp. Anal. Behav.* **6**, 537–543.

Friedman, H. and Guttman, N. (1965). Further analysis of the various effects of discrimination training on stimulus generalization gradients. In "Stimulus Generalization." (D. I. Mostofsky, ed.) Stanford University Press, Stanford, U.S.A.

Gilbert, R. M. (1966). Some studies of chained operants. Unpublished doctoral dissertation, Queen's University, Belfast.

Gilbert, R. M. (1968). Effects of manipulation of auditory and visual controlling stimuli, extinction and satiation on the emission of simple operant chains. Submitted to *J. exp. Anal. Behav.*

Gilbert, R. M. and Moore, M. (1967). Auditory and visual control over chained operants. *Psychon. Sci.* **8**, 267–268.

Goldiamond, I. and Dyrud, J. E. (1968). Some applications and implications of behavioral analysis for psychotherapy. In "Research in Psychotherapy." Vol. III. (J. M. Shlien, ed.) American Psychological Association, Washington, D.C., U.S.A.

Guthrie, E. R. (1935). "The Psychology of Learning." Harper and Row, New York.

Guttman, N. and Kalish, H. I. (1956). Discriminability and stimulus generalization. *J. exp. Psychol.* **51**, 79–88.

Hall, J. F. (1966). "The Psychology of Learning." Lippincott, Philadelphia.

Hearst, E. (1965). Approach, avoidance, and stimulus generalization. In "Stimulus Generalization." (D. I. Mostofsky, ed.) Stanford University Press, Stanford, U.S.A.

Hebb, D. O. (1958). "A Textbook of Psychology." W. B. Saunders Co., Philadelphia.

Heinemann, E. G., Chase, S. and Mandell, C. (1968). Discriminative control of "attention". *Science,* **160**, 533–534.

Honig, W. K. (Ed.) (1966). "Operant Behavior: Areas of Research and Application." Appleton-Century-Crofts, New York.

Katahn, M. and Koplin, J. H. (1968). Paradigm clash: Comment on "Some recent criticisms of behaviorism and learning theory with special reference to Breger and McGaugh and to Chomsky". *Psychol. Bull.* **69**, 147–148.

Kelleher, R. T. (1966). Chaining and conditioned reinforcement. In "Operant Behavior: Areas of Research and Application." (W. K. Honig, ed.) Appleton-Century-Crofts, New York.

Kettlewell, H. B. D. (1961). The phenomenon of industrial melanism in Lepidoptera. *Ann. Rev. Ent.* **6**, 245–262.

Kimble, G. A. (1961). "Hilgard and Marquis' Conditioning and Learning." Methuen, London.

Kimble, G. A. (1967). The definition of learning and some useful distinctions. In "Foundations of Conditioning and Learning." (G. A. Kimble, ed.) Appleton-Century-Crofts, New York.

Kuhn, T. S. (1962). "The Structure of Scientific Revolutions." University of Chicago Press, Chicago.

Lenneberg, E. H. (1967). "Biological Foundations of Language." Wiley, New York.

Lorenz, K. (1966). "On Aggression." Methuen, London.

Louch, A. R. (1966). "Explanation and Human Action." University of California Press, Berkeley, U.S.A.

Lovejoy, E. P. and Russell, D. G. (1967). Suppression of learning about a hard cue by the presence of an easy cue. *Psychon. Sci.* **8**, 365–366.

Mackintosh, N. (1965). Selective attention in animal discrimination learning. *Psychol. Bull.* **64**, 124–150.

Melching, W. H. (1954). The acquired reward value of an intermittently presented neutral stimulus. *J. comp. physiol. Psychol.* **47**, 370–374.

Miles, C. G. (1965). Acquisition of control by the features of a compound stimulus during discriminative operant conditioning. Unpublished doctoral dissertation, McMaster University.

Millenson, J. R. (1967). "Principles of Behavioral Analysis." Macmillan, New York.

Miller, G. A. (1962). "Psychology: The Science of Mental Life." Harper and Row, New York.

Notterman, J. M. and Mintz, D. E. (1965). "Dynamics of Response." Wiley, New York.

Nurnberger, J. I., Ferster, C. B. and Brady, J. V. (1963). "An Introduction to the Science of Human Behavior." Appleton-Century-Crofts, New York.

Osgood, C. E. (1953). "Method and Theory in Experimental Psychology." Oxford University Press, New York.

Pavlov, I. P. (1927). "Conditioned Reflexes." Oxford University Press, London.

Perkins, C. C., Jr. (1968). An analysis of the concept of reinforcement. *Psychol. Rev.* **75**, 155–172.

Premack, D. (1965). Reinforcement today. *Nebraska Symposium on Motivation.* Vol. XIII. University of Nebraska Press, Lincoln.

Rescorla, R. A. and Solomon, R. L. (1967). Two-process learning theory: relationships between Pavlovian conditioning and instrumental learning. *Psychol. Rev.* **74**, 151–182.

Reynolds, G. S. (1961). Attention in the pigeon. *J. exp. Anal. Behav.* **4**, 203–208.

Reynolds, G. S. (1968). "A Primer of Operant Conditioning." Scott, Foresman and Co., Glenview, Illinois, U.S.A.

Schoenfeld, W. N. and Cumming, W. W. (1963). Behavior and perception. *In* "Psychology: A Study of a Science." Vol. V. (S. Koch, ed.), McGraw-Hill, New York.

Sheffield, F. D. (1965). Relation between classical conditioning and instrumental conditioning. *In* "Classical Conditioning." (W. K. Prokasy, ed.) Appleton-Century-Crofts, New York.

Shepherd, R. N. (1965). Approximation to uniform gradients of generalization by monotone transformations of scale. *In* "Stimulus Generalization." (D. I. Mostofsky, ed.) Stanford University Press, Stanford, U.S.A.

Sidman, M. (1955). Some properties of the warning stimulus in avoidance behavior. *J. comp. physiol. Psychol.* **48**, 444–450.

Skinner, B. F. (1953). "The Science of Human Behavior." Macmillan, New York.

Skinner, B. F. (1957). "Verbal Behavior." Appleton-Century-Crofts, New York.

Skinner, B. F. (1966). The phylogeny and ontogeny of behavior. *Science*, **153**, 1205–1213.

Spencer, H. (1870). "The Principles of Psychology." Second edition, Vol. I. Williams and Nordgate, London.

Sutherland, N. S. and Andelman, L. (1967). Learning with one and two cues. *Psychon. Sci.* **7**, 107–108.

Terrace, H. S. (1966). Stimulus control. *In* "Operant Behavior: Areas of Research and Application." (W. K. Honig, ed.) Appleton-Century-Crofts, New York.

Terrace, H. S. (1968). Extinction of a discriminative operant following discrimination learning with and without errors. *J. exp. Anal. Behav.* (in press).

Thomas, D. R. (1965). Stimulus generalization of a positive conditioned reinforcer. *In* "Stimulus Generalization." (D. I. Mostofsky, ed.) Stanford University Press, Stanford.

Thomas, D. R., Berman, D. L., Serednesky, G. E. and Lyons, J. (1968). Information value and stimulus configuring as factors in conditioned reinforcement. *J. exp. Psychol.* **76,** 181–189.

Zimmerman, D. W. (1957). Durable secondary reinforcement: method and theory. *Psychol. Rev.* **64,** 373–383.

Author Index

Numbers in italics are the pages on which the References are listed

A

Abelson, R. M., 427, *450*
Ahumada, A., 349, *356*
Alexander, D., 429, 430, *453*
Allyon, T., 429, *449*
Amsel, A., 124, *134*, 230, *240*, 243, 244, 248, 258, *270*, *272*
Anchel, H., 419, *449*
Andelman, L., 27, 30, *33*, 61, *62*, 468, *488*
Anger, D., 300, 301, 301, 310, 315, *331*, 416, *449*
Asch, S. E., 4, 13, *33*
Azrin, N. H., 304, 305, 308, 309, 313, 316, 317, *331*, *332*, 416, 426, 429, *449*, *454*

B

Bacon, H. R., 151, *160*
Badia, P., 429, 430, *449*
Ball, G. G., 117, *134*, 143, *162*
Barker, E., 420, *449*
Baron, M. R., 2, *32*, 37, 60, *62*, 239, 290, *295*, 468, *486*
Barry, H., 124, *134*
Barryman, G., 480, *486*
Barryman, R., 314, 315, *333*
Bartlett, F. C., 405, *409*
Baum, M., 283, *295*
Beck, C. H., 117, *134*
Becker, P. W., 245, *270*
Behrend, E. R., 142, 144, 157, *160*, 164, 165, 167, 168, 170, 171, 172, *174*, *175*, 179, 183, *184*, *185*
Békésky, G., von, 277, *295*
Bekhterev, V. M., 414, *449*
Belenky, G. L., 183, *185*
Belleville, R. E., 315, *331*

Berger, B. D., 143, 151, *160*, 165, 166, *175*, 178, *185*
Berman, D. L., 458, *489*
Biederman, G. B., 422, *449*, 468, 471, *486*
Bindra, D., 418, 419, *449*
Bishop, H. E., 142, *161*, 164, 165, *175*
Bitterman, M. E., 138, 140, 142, 143, 144, 145, 147, 151, 152, 157, *160*, *161*, *162*, 163, 164, 165, 166, 167, 168, 169, 170, 171, 172, 173, *174*, *175*, 176, 178, 179, 180, 181, 182, 183, *184*, *185*
Bixenstine, V. E., 420, *449*
Black, A. H., 416, *451*
Blackman, D., 429, 430, *453*
Blackwell, H. R., 478, *486*
Bloomfield, T. M., 16, *31*, 217, 226, 227, 228, 229, 235, 236, *240*, 260, 262, *270*, *271*
Blough, D. S., 2, 15, *31*, 277, *295*, 359, 379, *384*
Blum, J. S., 187, *212*
Blum, R. A., 187, *212*
Boakes, R. A., 359, 375, *384*
Bogen, J. E., 339, *356*
Bolles, R. C., 418, 419, 428, *449*, *454*, 482, *486*
Boneau, C. A., 57, *61*, 229, *240*
Boren, J. J., 311, *331*, 426, *453*, 468, *487*
Borger, R., 456, *486*
Boring, E. G., 276, *295*, 390, 402, *409*
Boucher, R. C., 183, *185*
Bounds, W., 416, *451*
Bower, G. J., 217, 230, *240*, 422, *449*, 462, *486*
Boycott, B. B., 138, *160*
Boyer, W. N., 117, *134*
Brady, J. V., 68, *82*, 300, 302, 304, 308, 313, 315, *331*, *332*, *333*, 456, *488*
Breland, K., 283, 294, *295*

Subject Index

A

Acquired distinctiveness of cues, 113–116, 391, 403

Adaptation, *see* Neutralization of cues

Additivity of cues, 118–124

Amphetamine, *see* Drugs

Approach-avoidance tendencies, 245–270

Arousal, 247

Attention, selective and otherwise, 16, 21, 24–31, 35–61, 86, 95, 98, 100–102, 105–110, 113–134, 141, 148–160, 166, 168, 169, 171–174, 175–184, 188, 208–211, 274, 290–295, 386, 397–398, 404–405, 461, 467–472

Avoidance learning, 286–290, 351–354, 413–449, 468–470

B

Brightness invariance, 388, 395–398

C

Classical conditioning, 336–337, 414–415, *see* Conditioned emotional response, and Eyelid conditioning.
virtues of, *see* Instrumental conditioning defects in

Conditioned emotional response (CER), 63–82, 91–92, 308, 343

Consciousness, 275–277

Conspicuousness of cues, *see* Salience of cues

Corrective vs. non-corrective training, 173

Cortex
Auditory, 72
Lesions to, 335–355
Visual, 338, 393–394

Cues, *see* Incidental cues, Irrelevant cues, and Saliency of cues

D

Delay of reinforcement, 16

Discrimination, types of, *see* Stimuli, types of, and Time, discrimination of

Drive level, 78–79, 125, 165, 307–308

Drugs, effects of, 124, 311–312, 313, 314

E

Emotion, 230–232, *see* Conditioned emotional response

Errorless learning, 16, 23–24, 223–226, 229

Escape learning, 340–344, 419–421

Evolution, 159, 481–486

Experience, deprivation of, 14–20, 387–388

Extinction, 73–74, 84, 124–128, 149, 153–156, 309–310, 314, 322, 479–480

Extradimensional shifts, 60, 150–153, 154–156, 159, 189–210

Extradimensional training, 15, 24–31, 37–61

Eyelid conditioning, 93–95, 97–100, 102–105

F

Fear, 415–418, *see* Punishment

Forgetting, 168, 179, 230–231

Frustration, 124–128, 230–231, 233–234, 243–270

G

Generalization gradients, 15–31, 35–61, 69–82, 95–105, 477–480

H

Habit strength, 71–72, 85–86

Spreading depression, 339, 342–343
Split-brain preparation, 334–355
Stimuli, types of
  Auditory, 36, 57, 65–82, 88–95, 97–105, 338, 344–349, 423–425, 468–471
  Body-tilt, 27
  Position, 141–146, 151–152, 154, 172
  Tactile, 57, 339
  Vibratory, 77–105
  Visual, 141–146, 172, 338, 468–471
    Brightness, 114–115, 118, 154, 359–382
    Light onset/offset, 88–95, 97–105, 344–349
    Orientation, 2–14, 37–61, 114, 388–389
    Pattern, 385–405
  Wave length of light, 27, 36–61
Stimulus compounds, see Multiple cue learning

Stimulus control, 278–280, 463–481, see Generalization gradients
Stimulus intensity dynamism, 422
Stimulus sampling theory, 351–354
Stimulus selection, see Attention
Strategies, 147–149, 164, 176, 187–211, 215–240, 243, 260
Superstitious behaviour, 312–315

T

Time, discrimination of, 299–331, 357–384
Transfer along a continuum, 87, 102
Transposition, 260–261, 263–265
Two process learning theory, see Attention

V

Visual field dependence, 9–14